CASES AND MATERIALS ON THE CARRIAGE OF GOODS BY SEA

Second Edition

Cavendish
Publishing
Limited

London • Sydney

026000199

CASES AND MATERIALS ON THE CARRIAGE OF GOODS BY SEA
Second Edition

Martin Dockray, LLB, PhD, Solicitor
Professor of Law and
Head of the Department of Law
City University

with the assistance of
Katherine Reece-Thomas, BA, LLM, Solicitor
Member of the New York State Bar
Lecturer in Law, City University

Cavendish
Publishing
Limited

London • Sydney

First published in Great Britain 1987 by Professional Books Limited.

Second edition published 1998 by Cavendish Publishing Limited, The Glass House, Wharton Street, London WC1X 9PX.

Telephone: 0171-278 8000 Facsimile: 0171-278 8080

E-mail: info@cavendishpublishing.com

Visit our Home Page on http://www.cavendishpublishing.com

KD 1818
(DOC)

ESSEX UNIVERSITY LIBRARY

0260 0019 9

© Dockray, M 1987, 1998

All rights reserved. No part of this publication may be reproduced, stored in a retrieval system, or transmitted, in any form or by any means, electronic, mechanical, photocopying, recording, scanning or otherwise, except under the terms of the Copyright Designs and Patents Act 1988 or under the terms of a licence issued by the Copyright Licensing Agency, 90 Tottenham Court Road, London W1P 9HE, UK, without the permission in writing of the publisher.

Dockray, Martin
Cases and materials on the carriage of goods by sea – 2nd ed
1. Shipping – Law and legislation – England 2. Shipping – Law and legislation – Wales 3. Maritime law – England 4. Maritime law – Wales 5. Maritime law– Cases
I. Title
343.4'2'096
ISBN 1 85941 346 3

Printed and bound in Great Britain

PREFACE

The aim of this book is to provide a convenient selection of cases and standard form documents for law students. It tries to provide a supplement rather than a substitute for lectures and textbooks.

The second edition sees a number of changes. About a quarter of the text has been rewritten. The selection of cases has also inevitably changed. The 20 or so volumes of law reports dealing with maritime cases published in England since the first edition appeared have resulted in around 60 new extracts. Other new material includes two important statutes and a new version of the York-Antwerp Rules. To make space, all the longer extracts in the first edition have been edited; a few have been excised, as have the questions which appeared in notes to some chapters.

Another alteration is in the order in which topics are covered. When I first taught this subject, it seemed to me to be helpful to follow the order of events of a carrying voyage. The disadvantage of this approach is that it postpones for far too long the consideration of the basis of a sea carrier's liability for goods which are lost or damaged. In a book such as this it now seems to me to be better to follow the logic of the law rather than the chronology of commerce. So this edition commences with cargo claims, before carrying on with other issues which arise under charterparties.

A third pleasant change to be recorded is that I have been joined for this edition by Katherine Reece-Thomas, who has rewritten Chapter 17 which deals with general average.

As in the first edition, judgments which consider the reason for a rule or which analyse previous case law have been preferred to those which do not. With regard to style, place names and the names and offices of judges are generally reproduced as originally reported and without note of subsequent changes. Matter omitted is generally indicated by three points, whatever the length of the omission. In reproducing cases and other materials, the following are not generally specifically noted: (a) omission of original footnotes; (b) original typographical errors, whether corrected or not; (c) the length and nature of omissions; (d) alterations or substitutions in the form of citations. A short glossary is again included to explain some of the trade, technical or obsolete terms which appear in the materials.

Martin Dockray
July 1997

ACKNOWLEDGMENTS

The publishers and author wish to acknowledge with thanks the permissions given by the following to reprint material from the copyright sources listed below:

The Baltic and International Maritime Council: *BALTIME 1939; BARECON 89; ERLOAD; GENCON 1994; MULTIDOC 95; MULTIWAYBILL 95; WORLDFOOD*

Butterworth & Co: *All England Law Reports; Law Times Reports; Commercial Cases*

Comité Maritime International: *The York-Antwerp Rules 1994*

Cornell Maritime Press: *The Business of Shipping*, by Lane C Kendall and James J Buckley, 6th edn, 1994

The Incorporated Council of Law Reporting: *The Law Reports; The Weekly Law Reports*

Lloyd's of London Press: *Lloyd's Law Reports*

P&O Nedlloyd Limited: *Bill of Lading; Waybill*

Shell International Trading and Shipping Company Limited: *SHELLVOY 5 with December 1996 Standard Amendments and Additional Clauses; SHELLTIME 4 with Standard Amendments; Shell Tanker Bill of Lading*

The Simpler Trade Procedures Board: *Standard Shipping Note; SITPRO Dangerous Goods Note; Common Short Form Bill of Lading; Sea Waybill*

Times Newspapers Limited: *The Times Law Reports*

United Nations: *Bills of Lading*, a report by the Secretariat of UNCTAD; *Charter Parties*, a report by the Secretariat of UNCTAD; *The Hamburg Rules*

Every effort has been made to trace all the copyright holders but if any have been inadvertently overlooked the publishers will be pleased to make the necessary arrangement at the first opportunity.

CONTENTS

TABLE OF CASES

TABLE OF STATUTES

INTRODUCTION

The law of carriage by sea is a distinct part of English law. But this is not because the field is regulated by a separate maritime code. It is true that the subject does include some special rules which have no direct counterpart in other areas of domestic law. Nevertheless, for the most part, English law relating to the carriage of goods by sea consists only of the application of general common law ideas, together with a small number of important statutes. The basis of the subject is the law of contract. It also draws on the laws of tort, bailment, agency, property and equity.

But if only familiar principles of general law are involved, how can the law of carriage be said to be distinct? One answer can be found in the way in which general legal ideas have been adapted to meet the special features of the sea trade. One feature of this business is its international nature; this produces a great desire for international uniformity in maritime law. This desire has been satisfied in a few areas of the law of carriage of goods, although not always by the same means: inter-governmental agreements resulted in the Hague and the Hague-Visby Rules (see Chapter 9); international agreement amongst interest groups produced the York-Antwerp Rules (Chapter 17). The widespread use of standard form documents as the basis of most carriage contracts (see the examples reproduced in Appendix I) also has something of a unifying effect.

A second obvious feature of the shipping industry is that contracts for the carriage of goods by sea fall to be performed in special and often hazardous conditions in which it is practically impossible for one party to supervise the work of the other from day to day. This factor was clearly instrumental in the development of the sea carrier's general duties, including the duty to provide a seaworthy ship (Chapter 4) and the duty not to deviate from route (Chapter 5), as well as in relation to general average (Chapter 17). It also influenced those parts of the law dealing with the shipper's duty to disclose the dangerous nature of goods shipped, the master's powers of jettison and other extraordinary powers conferred on the master in the event of an emergency.

A third notable feature is that shipping is directly dependent on other commercial activities. Contracts for the carriage of goods by sea are not made in commercial isolation. They are typically entered into in order to sell goods or to give effect to a previous sale. This means that contracts for sea carriage are often of direct interest to persons such as buyers or lenders as well as to the original parties to the contract. Third parties may become involved in the carriage of goods in other ways. Even when a cargo remains in the ownership of a single shipper throughout an ocean voyage it is quite possible that the whole or part of the contract (loading or discharging the cargo, for example) may actually be performed by someone other than the party who originally contracted to carry and deliver. This leads to complex questions about who can sue and who can be sued. In the absence of a statute dealing with the particular problem, in English law satisfactory answers to these questions often involve the creative application of ideas drawn from contract (eg implication of a contract or of a term), tort (eg recognition or denial of a duty of care), bailment (terms of bailment), or the law of evidence or of damages.

The endemic use of standard forms has already been mentioned. This use amounts in itself to an important feature of the sea trade. It means that much of the law in this area consists either of settled interpretations of common clauses or of decisions as to the terms which can be implied into contracts of carriage in the absence of express agreement. One consequence of the addiction to the use of standard forms is that judicial decisions on the interpretation of standard terms are of wide interest in the shipping industry, which pays marked attention to the law reports. But the wide use of certain forms also means that a judicial decision which disturbs an accepted construction of a document may retrospectively affect many transactions entered into on the basis of that previously accepted meaning. This may influence the willingness of the courts to reverse a settled interpretation. But so too does the knowledge that shipping circles show no reluctance to make amendments to standard forms in order to avoid anything seen as an unsatisfactory precedent.

So much for some of the special features of the trade. Can these special features be proved to have influenced the form of what is mostly judge-made law? It would not be easy to show this in some branches of the common law, but the difficulty is not so great in the case of the law of carriage by sea. For there is a tradition of looking at this subject as much more than a closed set of technical rules. Long before contextualism became fashionable amongst law teachers, and at times when, in general, it was rare for policy issues to be discussed in judgments or in textbooks, it was common for sea carriage disputes to be determined by judges in accordance with their express views of what policy made the most sense in the special context in which maritime contracts are made and performed. The well known decision in *Behn v Burness* in 1863 (Chapter 10) is a clear example. Other examples from the same chapter include *McAndrew v Adams* (1834) and *Bentsen v Taylor* (1893). These are not isolated instances. Other examples could be found in every chapter.

As background to the key judgments, the remainder of this chapter sketches the outlines of some of the more common varieties of contract for the carriage of goods by sea and compares the basic features of two major types of shipping service: liner shipping and chartered or tramp operations. The chapter concludes with a review of the ways in which both contracts for carriage by liner and charterparties are made.

1 CHARTERED SHIPPING

CHARTER PARTIES

Report by the secretariat of UNCTAD

(United Nations Conference on Trade and Development, Geneva)

Published by the United Nations, New York, 1974

A. Contracts of affreightment

20 Cargo vessels are usually under contracts by which the shipowner, in return for a sum of money – the freight – agrees to carry goods by sea, or to furnish the services of a vessel for the purpose of such carriage. Such contracts, commonly called contracts of affreightment, encompass a heterogeneous mass of maritime agreements, comprising such differing types as contracts for the lease of a vessel (bare boat or demise charters), voyage and time charterparties, and bills of lading ...

21 A brief review of the various types of contract is made below.

(1) Bare boat (demise) Charters

22 A special type of contract of affreightment consists of an agreement by which a person for a period of time takes over the possession and control of the vessel in return for a certain hire payable to the shipowner. Such a contract, which is in the nature of lease (locatio rei), is commonly known as a bare boat or demise charter, and the person to whom the vessel is leased is named the bare boat or demise charterer. Under this type of contract, the charterer mans and equips the vessel and assumes all responsibility for its navigation, management and operation; he thus acts as the owner of the vessel in all important respects during the duration of the charter.

23 Bare boat chartering has been used in connection with government shipping activities, particularly in time of war or other emergency, or during pilgrimage seasons. In the private sector, bare boat chartering is less common than other types of contract of affreightment. It is sometimes used, however, where a shipowner or ship operator wishes to operate ships or supplement his fleet for a period of time without incurring the financial commitments of actual ownership, but at the same time requires to have full control of the chartered vessel, including control of its navigation and management. Further, bare boat chartering is sometimes employed in connection with the financial arrangements for purchase of the vessel on instalment terms; the bare boat charter then serves as a 'hire/purchase' contract, by which the owner/seller retains formal ownership and thereby security in the vessel until the full purchase price is paid.

(2) Contracts of Carriage

24 As distinct from the bare boat charter, there is a category of contracts of affreightment which may be classified as contracts of carriage. These are contracts under which the owner, broadly speaking, undertakes to perform a carrying service with a vessel that is equipped and manned by him, and for the navigation and management of which he remains

responsible throughout the performance of the contract. This category includes contracts for voyage and time chartering.

25 Voyage and time chartering consists in the employment of tramp vessels (ie vessels not employed on scheduled routes) and involves, generally, the engagement of the entire vessel for one or several voyages, or for a period of time. Voyage chartering is adaptable in any commercial situation where the movement of a shipload of cargo from one point to another is required. Typically, the need for chartering a vessel on voyage terms emanates from a contract of sale of goods under which the charterer – either in his capacity as seller if the contract is on cif terms or as buyer if on fob terms – undertakes to arrange and pay for the transport of the goods. Time chartering, on the other hand, is used where the charterer desires to operate a vessel for a period of time without undertaking either the financial commitments of ownership or the responsibilities of navigation and management of the vessel; it is common, for example, for an operator who finds himself temporarily short of tonnage to supplement his fleet by taking a vessel on time charter. The relevant contracts are called respectively voyage charterparties and time charterparties, or merely voyage charters and time charters.

B. Voyage and time charterparties

(1) Distinctive Features

26 Under a voyage charterparty the owner undertakes to provide a vessel for the carriage of specified goods on one or several voyages between named ports (or within certain ranges of loading and discharging places), while under a time charterparty the owner undertakes to place the use of the vessel at the charterer's disposal for a period of time during which it is agreed that the charterer may freely employ the vessel for his own account.

27 Apart from the divergent manner in which the duration of the contract is determined – for one or several voyages, or for a period of time – voyage and time charterparties are distinguishable in several other respects.

28 As regards the charterer's partaking in the operating of the vessel, each provides fundamentally different regulations.

29 Under the voyage charterparty, it is true that the charterer's task is not confined to delivering and receiving the cargo: he is also in various ways directly involved in the marine adventure. For example, under the rules of laytime and demurrage, he assumes responsibility for delays in the loading and discharging ports; furthermore, he sometimes undertakes the performance of the loading and discharging operations; in certain respects, also, the charterer assumes the risks for hindrances and obstacles preventing the vessel from performing the contract voyage. However, the actual operation of the vessel is no concern of his – this is in all important respects left to the owner.

30 The situation is quite different under a time charterparty, when the contract entitles the charterer during the stipulated period to direct the vessel on such voyages and to load it with such cargoes as he may wish, subject to such limits or restrictions as are set out in the contract. This right of direction is laid down in the so-called 'employment clause' which

usually prescribes: 'the master to be under the orders of the charterer as regards employment agency or other arrangements'. The time charterer thus takes a substantial part in the operation of the vessel ...

31 One result of the time charterer's partaking in the operation of the vessel is that he assumes the costs which are directly incidental to the various voyages on which he directs the vessel. He has, as a rule, to bear the costs for bunkers, port charges, towage, etc, which, under a voyage charterparty, are borne by the owner.

32 The fact that the time charterer is in charge of important operational functions is, moreover, reflected in the system often found in time charterparties of allocating on the charterer liability for damages ensuing (eg) 'from the Master, Officers or Agents signing Bills of Lading or other documents or otherwise complying with such orders [of the charterer], as well as from any irregularity in the Vessel's papers or for overcarrying goods'.

33 Another point of difference is the basis for calculating the freight. As a rule, the freight, under a voyage charterparty, is fixed in proportion to cargo size or in the form of a lump sum for the voyage, while under a time charterparty it is fixed in proportion to the time occupied.

34 There is a close connection between the basis for the freight calculation and the allocation of the loss-of-time risk. Under a voyage charterparty, the freight calculation takes no account of the time to be consumed by the performance of the voyage, and the risk of loss of time at sea is therefore in principle borne by the owner. Under a time charterparty, on the other hand, where the freight is directly related to the time during which the vessel is used by the charterer, loss of time is normally for the charterer's account. There are however, important exceptions to this main rule, entailing a certain redistribution of this risk as between the parties. Under a voyage charterparty, part of the risk of delay in loading and discharging ports is transferred to the charterer through the provisions on laytime and demurrage. And the time charter reallocates on the owner some of the loss-of-time risk by means of the so-called 'off-hire' clause (sometimes called 'suspension of hire', 'breakdown' or 'cesser of hire' clause), which, briefly stated, provides that the charterer shall not be required to pay freight (hire) for such time as is lost to him in consequence of circumstances attributable to the owner or the vessel.

35 From the above discussion it may be seen that the type of charter, whether voyage or time charter, bears no direct relationship to the duration of the charterparty, although by common usage in the past the term 'long-term charter' generally implied a time charter. However, it is not uncommon to fix a vessel on a time charter basis for one specific voyage only and for the carriage of a specific cargo. In such a fixture, called a trip charter, the important feature of the time charter is still there: the charterer has to pay hire according to the time spent in performance of the voyage, although the period is determined by the duration of the contract voyage(s). Conversely, some charters on a voyage basis resemble time charters in that their duration is related to periods of time. Such charters may be of two types: consecutive voyage or long-term freighting contracts. Consecutive

voyage contracts are concerned with as many voyages as a specified vessel can perform during a certain period, which may be stated as, say, three consecutive voyages (between ports A and B) or three months in consecutive voyages.

36   In long-term freighting contracts, the ship operator undertakes to carry quantities, generally large, of a specified product on a particular route or routes, over a given period of time, using ships of his own choice which are not specified in the contract. The use of this type of carriage contract has increased rapidly in recent years.

37   Consecutive voyage contracts are classed as voyage charters; long-term freighting contracts also resemble voyage charters in certain respects. Certain special problems may result from the use of those types of contract, as, for example, the question of the divisibility of a consecutive voyage contract so as to permit the cancellation of one or more voyages.

(2)   Subchartering

38   It is customary to stipulate in both voyage and time charterparties that the charterer has the right of subletting the whole or part of the vessel, subject to the charterer remaining responsible to the owner for the due fulfilment of the original charterparty. This right is of considerable importance to the charterer since it gives him a certain freedom to utilise the vessel in the way that is most economical to him. Subletting frequently occurs in practice; the charterer may have chartered the vessel for the sole purpose of making a profit by rechartering or otherwise subletting it; or he may find that the cargo which he intended to ship is not available or, alternatively, that he is not in a position to utilise the vessel for the original intended purpose, in which case he will seek other employment for it in order to be covered for the freight which he is due to pay to the owner. He may also find, because of a rise in freight market rates, that it is more profitable for him to recharter the vessel than to utilise it in the way originally intended.

39   Where the contract for subletting is embodied in a charterparty, two independent charterparties will be running concurrently, placing the original charterer in a dual position: as against the owner of the vessel his position remains that of a charterer, whilst as against the subcharterer it is in effect that of an owner.

40   Thus, the voyage or time charterer may not only be the user of the services provided by the shipowner; he may also and often does himself act, simultaneously, as the supplier of the same services by means of the chartered vessel.

2 LINER SHIPPING

As the above extract suggests, a charterparty may be the type of contract which is most appropriate where shiploads of cargo are involved. But where smaller quantities such as a container load are concerned, a shipper is more likely to contract with the operators of a shipping service (a line) which regularly visits the ports in which the shipper is interested. In liner shipping the terms of the contract are traditionally printed on the bill of lading, which is a receipt for the goods issued by the carrier. At the end of the voyage the carrier will demand that this receipt be produced and surrendered. In this way, the bill of lading operates like a cloakroom ticket. However, this is a ticket which can be transferred by the shipper to someone else. Often it will be a buyer or subbuyer of the goods from the shipper who will eventually produce the bill of lading and claim delivery from the carrier.

Although a bill of lading may itself be a contract (or evidence of a contract) of affreightment, there is in practice no rigid distinction between operations governed by charterparties and those in which a bill of lading makes an appearance. Where a vessel is under charter it very often happens that bills of lading are issued. If a vessel is voyage chartered to carry the charterer's own goods, the charterer may want a bill of lading in order to be able to prove, if a dispute arises, that goods were delivered to the carrier. And if the charterer wishes to be able to sell the goods before retaking possession from the carrier, he will want the receipt to be in the transferable form of a bill of lading. Moreover, if a vessel is being operated by a charterer who wishes to trade with it and make a profit by carrying goods belonging to other shippers, it is almost inevitable that bills of lading will be issued to those shippers. The following extract summarises the basic features of the bill of lading.

CHARTER PARTIES
Report by the secretariat of UNCTAD
(United Nations Conference on Trade and Development, Geneva)
Published by the United Nations, New York, 1974

324 The bill of lading is, as a rule, issued to the shipper when the goods have been loaded on board, either by the master as the owner's (the carrier's) representative, or on the master's behalf by the vessel's agents. If the vessel is chartered, the shipper may be, but is not necessarily, identical with the charterer.

325 The issuing of a bill of lading is generally preceded by a contract of affreightment made at an earlier stage, as, for instance, a charterparty or, in liner trades, an agreement concluded in connection with the booking of space in the vessel.

326 The bill of lading describes the goods and confirms that they have been received on board; it states further to whom the goods are to be delivered at the destination, and it contains a reference to the freight (which may be pre-paid or payable on delivery of the goods); it also contains the other conditions attaching to the carriage either by reproducing them in full, as is the practice in liner trades, or, in some cases, by referring to the terms of the charterparty, where the bill of lading is issued under it.

327 As to the specific functions of the bill of lading, it follows from the above description that the document serves as a receipt for the goods. As regards shipments on liner vessels, it furthermore evidences the contract of affreightment concluded prior to its issuing. When it is issued in respect of a shipment made under a charterparty, the bill of lading will, in general, only acquire the function of evidencing the contract of affreightment if it is held by a third party; in the hands of the charterer it is merely a receipt for the goods.

328 Besides being a receipt for the goods and – depending on the circumstances – evidence of the contract of affreightment, the bill of lading constitutes a document of title to the goods. This quality is of great importance since it not only enables the consignee armed with possession of the document to take delivery of the goods at the destination, but also makes it possible while the goods are in transit to pass ownership in them by endorsement and transfer of the document to a buyer. As a document of title, the bill of lading moreover serves as a basis for documentary credits in international trade ... For the charterer, whether he is the seller or the buyer of goods or the shipper of goods not yet sold, the bill of lading will therefore often serve as the necessary instrument for carrying through the commercial purpose of the transport.

3 COMPARISON OF LINER AND CHARTERED SHIPPING

THE BUSINESS OF SHIPPING
Sixth Edition, 1994
Lane C Kendall and James J Buckley
Cornell Maritime Press
Centreville, Maryland
Copyright 1973, 1994 by Cornell Maritime Press. Inc
Reprinted by permission

LINER SERVICE AND TRAMP SHIPPING

Merchant shipping, considered from the standpoint of types of service provided, may be divided into two major categories: *Liner Service* and *Tramp Shipping*. While there are some similarities, the differences in the theory and techniques of management of these two types of marine transportation are notable. The service rendered, the geographic area covered, the operating problems, the relationship between vessel owner and vessel user, and the actual employment of the ship vary markedly between the two categories. It is important, therefore, to be aware of those areas where the management procedures are congruent; it is equally significant that the differences be comprehended.

Liner Service

1 Sailings are regular and repeated from and to designated ports on a trade route, at intervals established in response to the quantity of cargo generated along that route. True liner service is distinguished by the repetition of voyages and the consistent advertising of such voyages. Once the service is established, the operator must conform, within narrow time limits, to the published schedule. Although the frequency of sailings is related directly to the amount of business available, it is general practice to dispatch at least one ship each month. Vessels engaged in liner service may be owned or chartered; it is the regularity and repetitious nature of the operation, rather than the proprietorship, which is crucial.

Tramp Shipping

1 Sailings under voyage charters are based on cargo commitments that vary with the vessel's employment, and are usually different for every voyage. There is no expected repetition of voyages as a normal part of tramp operation. Each trip is scheduled individually, subject to the requirements of the cargo to be carried and the particular route to be followed. In certain trades, such as oil and coal, owners often agree to make a number of repetitive voyages carrying the same commodity. These 'consecutive voyages' are arranged expressly to fit the charterer's convenience, and do not establish a 'liner service'.

Sailings under time charters may be for a single voyage between major geographical areas, or may be repetitive, transporting the same commodity such as coal or grain or lumber; or may take the form of a long trading voyage consisting of a series of legs on which different cargoes are lifted; or may be placed in the liner service operated by the charterer. The time chartered vessel may be subchartered to other persons for voyages to be accomplished within the time limits imposed by the charter.

2 Liners are common (public) carriers,[1] required by law to accept without discrimination between offerors any legal cargo which the ship is able to transport. Some liner operators

2 Tramps are contract (private) carriers, and normally carry full shiploads of a single commodity, usually in bulk. In most cases there is only one shipper, but two or more shippers of the same

---

1 Under English law, few if any shipping lines are common carriers today: see Chapter 2.

stipulate the minimum quantity of cargo which must be presented by a single shipper; so long as the limitation is reasonable, this is permissible. In the break-bulk trades, cargo usually is varied, and is called either 'general' or 'package'. In the container trades, the shipper fills and seals the container before it is delivered to the carrier. This sealed container is placed aboard the ship as a single unit. Small shipments are consolidated by the carrier or a third party, who loads these 'less than container lots' (LCL) into containers which are sealed by the party loading for the voyage, and opened by the carrier or a third party at the port of discharge, where the lots of cargo are distributed to the consignees.

kind of cargo occasionally may use a single ship.

3   Goods carried in liner service ships usually are of higher value than the cargo hauled in tramps, and are charged higher freight rates. All shippers of a given item moving in a specified ship pay the same freight rate, which always includes handling (stevedoring) costs. In break-bulk operation, the variety of cargo and the number of shippers require procedures to assure that what is accepted for transportation is delivered in like good order to the consignee at the port of discharge. Containers, except refrigerator units, do not require individual attention beyond being secured aboard ship. In both break-bulk and container services, cargo requiring special care (such as refrigerated meats and fruits) is accepted but is assessed a higher freight rate than less sensitive items.

3   Cargoes carried in tramps generally are those which can be transported in bulk ('homogeneous cargoes') and have low intrinsic value. Typical cargoes are coal, ores, grain, lumber, sugar, and phosphate rock. The cost of loading and unloading the ship in most cases is paid by the charterer, but this is subject to negotiation between shipowner and charterer. Freight rates for tramps reflect the fact that movements frequently are from a single port of loading to a single port of discharge, with minimum expense involved in the care of the cargo while it is in transit.

4   Freight rates in the liner services are stabilised by setting identical charges for all shippers of the same item aboard a certain ship. Rates may vary, however, from one sailing to another, but increases are announced in advance. Rates are compiled into detailed listings ('freight tariffs') which are made available to shippers on demand.

On many trade routes, two or more carriers serving the same range of ports will form an association (known either as a 'conference' or a 'rate agreement') for the purpose of stabilising rates and regulating competition between these carriers. The rates established by the association are binding uniformly on all the members, although independent action is permitted. In the United States, these agreements and rate structures are subject to review by the Federal Maritime Commission ...

4   Freight rates ... for tramps vary according to the supply of and demand for ships. The charterers' position is always strong, and rates are low, when there are few cargoes being offered and many ships are competing for the business. The shipowners' position is always strong, and rates are high, when there are plentiful cargoes and a scarcity of ships. In either case, competition among owners is always keen ...

Abrupt changes in the level of charter rates are evident whenever there is a major event of international significance, as, for instance, the outbreak of a war, a major crop failure, or widespread strikes in a particular country.

Freight tariffs are not compiled by the owners of vessels engaged in tramping, and no associations exist for the purpose of setting rates and stabilising competition. Summaries showing the trends in charter hire are published frequently and include specific quotations of the rates at which ships have been chartered.

5   A liner-service company issues a standard (or uniform) contract of carriage or bill of lading. Regardless of the size of the shipment, or the number of different commodities or items comprising a given lot of cargo, the provisions of the contract apply equally to all shippers who use any one vessel. These provisions are not subject to negotiation, but are unilaterally imposed by the carrier. Only in very exceptional cases will a senior executive of the common

5   The owner of a tramp ship must negotiate a separate contract (charterparty) for every employment of its vessel. The terms of the charterparty vary from ship to ship, depending upon the bargaining abilities of owner and charterer, and the general trend of the market. The terms of the agreement are applicable only to the ship named in the charterparty. Although the basic charterparties are printed and follow a set form, they may be changed in any manner

carrier alter the terms of the bill of lading to accommodate an individual shipper.

desired by the contracting parties. Since the changes apply to a particular ship for a particular voyage or a period of time, the alterations are not publicised widely.

6   Services – frequency of sailings and ports of call, as well as the capabilities of the ships themselves – are adjusted to meet the demands of shippers. Many liner operators arrange their schedules to meet minimum needs during the year, and then augment sailings when seasonal increases occur. Changes in liner service often are influenced as much by political and technological considerations as they are by economic factors. Drastic changes in established liner operations are infrequent; carriers' intentions, especially relating to withdrawals from the route, usually are well publicised in advance. This is essential to the dependability of the liner trade.

6   Services, as well as rates, are determined by negotiation between shipowner and charterer, and reflect the specific requirements of the contracting parties. Regular and repeated voyages on the same route are not part of tramp operation, and therefore no conferences exist. Supervision in the public interest by a regulatory authority is unnecessary; the natural working of the laws of supply and demand assure adequate control.

7   Liner-service vessels often reflect in their design the special requirements encountered in their employment. Refrigerated fruit and meat carriers, roll-on/roll-off vessels, break-bulk general carriers and container ships are operated on most sea routes, depending upon the demand for these specialised capabilities. Because very nearly identical cargoes move in all the dry-cargo break-bulk liners on a given route, the capabilities of these ships are similar, regardless of ownership ...
Container ships began transoceanic service in 1966, and today are found on all trade routes. They range in size from less than one thousand 20-foot containers to over

7   Most tramp ships are intended for worldwide service, and are of moderate size and draft. Although used primarily to transport cargoes in bulk, many of these tramps have one or more 'tween decks and sufficient booms or cranes to permit them to carry assorted general cargo on a self-sustaining basis. Very large bulk carriers, designed to carry iron ore or coal, are now tramping on many trade routes. Compared to container ships, some of which are available for charter to liner-service companies, the conventional tramp is still simpler in design and less expensive to build.

four thousand containers and are among the fastest ships in the world. Owing to their regular schedules and established berths in fixed ports, many liner-service vessels are not self-sustaining.

8 Liner-service companies may have a large and somewhat complex organisation in the shore establishment, especially in the home office. Normally there are several divisions defined by function: traffic, operations, financial, and managerial, each with appropriate staff. Outport offices may duplicate this organisation on a smaller scale. Liner service operations entail personal contact with shippers, maintenance of an active cargo-handling terminal, and processing a great amount of detail work inherent in general cargo service on a repetitive schedule.

8 Tramp owners usually have small staffs in the home office, with little division of functions. No traffic department is needed; charters are negotiated by telephone, cable, or fax ... Face-to-face contact with charterers is unusual. Because agents are employed to service the ships in ports of call and are paid on a fee basis for each task performed, there is no need for an operating department. Instead the home office may send supervisory personnel to oversee the functions of the agents. Some owners contract with firms specialising in ship management to do everything except negotiate contracts. Stevedoring is very rarely the responsibility of the shipowner, and therefore no terminal department is included in organisation of the home office.

9 Procurement of cargo is the responsibility of the traffic department, which includes salesmen ('solicitors') to call on regular as well as prospective shippers. Advertising is extensive and continuous, and major efforts are made to disseminate information concerning the capabilities of the line. Arrival and departure times of ships are widely publicised. Shippers are assisted in the development of markets for their goods as a means of increasing cargo offerings.

9 Procurement of cargo is handled through brokers who represent the tramp shipowner in negotiations with other brokers representing cargo interests. There is no advertising and no promotional activity. Ship movements normally appear only in the newspaper listings of vessels which have arrived or sailed.

10 Passengers sometimes are carried in cargo liners. By international agreement the number is limited to 12.

10 Passengers are not carried aboard tramp ships, and no provision for their accommodation is made in the vessels' design.

4 SHIPPING WITH A LINE

The last extract referred to the way in which contracts to carry goods by sea are made in break-bulk liner shipping. Until the last quarter of this century, contracts were often made informally and indirectly. The judgment in *Heskell v Continental Express* (1950) 83 Ll L Rep 438 contains a description of how this was done: at that time, no contract would normally be concluded until the goods were loaded or accepted for loading. Having learned from an advertisement or otherwise of a date and place of sailing, a shipper would forward his goods to the dock or berth. At the docks, a dock receipt or a mate's receipt would be given in exchange for the goods. The shipper or his agent would then prepare a draft bill of lading in the form used by the particular line and deliver it to the shipowner or his agent. Meanwhile the various consignments of what might be a very mixed cargo would be loaded and stowed on board, the location of a particular parcel depending on its size, shape and other properties, including density and packing as well as on the order in which its port of discharge would be reached in the course of the voyage. A good deal of manual labour was needed to stow break-bulk cargo on a liner. After loading, the draft bill of lading would be checked against the earlier receipt, signed by the master or more often an agent employed by the shipping line and issued to the shipper or his agent in exchange for the freight. In these circumstances, the contract between shipper and carrier depended on the contents of advertisements, and on any public and private statements, trade practice and prior dealings, as well as on the terms printed on the bill of lading.

Containers and computers have changed all this. Probably the most noticeable physical change in UK liner shipping since *Heskell* has been that conventional break-bulk services to many destinations have been replaced by container shipping. A typical general purpose container is manufactured to the International Standards Organisation's agreed dimensions of 8ft in width x 8ft 6in high by 20ft in length; it is made of steel and capable of carrying up to 24 tonnes weight. Other lengths (eg 40ft), heights and materials are also used. Refrigerated and other non-standard containers are available, including open top, half-height, ventilated containers and tank containers for liquids.

The vessel on which such a container is loaded is also likely to be very different from the type of general purpose liner in use when *Heskell* was decided. Today's liner is likely to be specially designed for carrying containers; a fully or partly cellular container ship uses a cell guide system to enable quick mechanical stowage of containers either by shore-based cranes or possibly by the ship's own gear.

From the point of view of a shipper who wants to move either a full container load (FCL) or less than full container load (LCL), it has been said that containers have a number of advantages. Goods shipped move faster and are better protected from damage and theft; a container can be sealed before the start of a journey. It may not then be necessary for the contents to be touched until the seal is broken when the box is opened at its destination.

Containerisation has also resulted in the development of integrated transport services in which carriers are willing to contract to carry from door-to-door or from terminal-to-terminal, and not simply from port-to-port. When a shipper reserves space with a carrier for door-to-door transport of his goods, a container can be delivered to the shipper's own premises where it can be packed ('stuffed') and later collected for delivery by road to a container terminal where it will be stored until loaded on board ship. Carriers who offer this multimodal type of transport service are often referred to as Combined Transport or Through Transport Operators. As a matter of terminology, some parts of the UK shipping industry use 'combined transport' to refer to a contract under which the carrier contracts as a principal to carry out the performance of the whole of a transport by two or more modes of transport, while in 'through transport' the carrier contracts as principal in respect of one stage of a journey but only as the agent of the owner of the goods to arrange all other stages. It is, however, important to appreciate that many bills of lading do not recognise this distinction and use the terms through/combined transport indiscriminately.

Containers also have advantages from the point of view of the sea carrier. Mechanical handling is quicker and cheaper than traditional methods of loading and stowing. And quicker handling means that container vessels need to spend less time in port and can spend more time at sea so that their productivity is improved. However, a fully containerised liner operation is not cheap. Container ships are faster, more sophisticated and more expensive than their break-bulk counterparts. High costs are involved in building the necessary shore facilities and in providing enough ships of the right size to take advantage of economies of scale and yet at the same time provide the frequent and regular service needed by shippers. This is one reason why some shipowners have chosen not to operate independently in containerised liner trades but instead to amalgamate with others or to join consortia which operate the vessels owned by their members. This development has itself given rise to new and difficult questions of legal liability for loss or damage to goods both as between consortium members and shippers on the one hand and as between consortium members themselves on the other.

A number of other important changes have also occurred since *Heskell* was decided. In UK outbound liner shipping, the mate's receipt is now a comparative rarity. Export cargo to be carried by a line is forwarded for shipment accompanied by a Standard Shipping Note or a Dangerous Goods Note (see Appendix I) prepared in several copies by or on behalf of the shipper. A copy of the Shipping Note is signed and returned to the shipper to acknowledge receipt. And it is now common for the bill of lading to be prepared by the carrier by computer from details supplied when the shipper reserved space on a vessel.

An alternative to a bill of lading is also available. A sea waybill is also a receipt for goods issued by a carrier and may contain evidence of the terms of a contract of affreightment in much the same way as a bill of lading. But unlike a bill of lading, a sea waybill does not have to be presented at destination in order to obtain delivery of the goods. Delivery is made to a nominated consignee against proof of identity. A sea waybill may be used in preference to a bill of lading if, for example, it is likely that goods which have been shipped will reach their destination before a bill of lading (eg on short sea routes in Europe) and if the shipper does not need a bill of lading in order to obtain payment for or to transfer the title to the goods while they are in the possession of the carrier. (See the specimen in Appendix I.)

5 THE CHARTERING PROCESS AND THE CHARTER MARKET

CHARTER PARTIES

Report by the secretariat of UNCTAD

(United Nations Conference on Trade and Development, Geneva)

Published by the United Nations, New York, 1974

(1) The chartering process

A Bargaining position of contracting parties

52 Charterparties are contracts that are negotiated in a free market governed by the prevailing factors of the shipping supply and demand situation. Characteristically, conditions in the freight market are constantly changing, at one stage favouring owners and at another charterers. The state of the market at a particular time is an important factor influencing the bargaining position of the contracting parties.

53 The actual structure of the shipping industry has also an effect on the bargaining position. In chartering, the offer of shipping services in response to an inquiry for shipping space is made by tramp vessel owners who, lacking regular customers, need continuously to find such employment for their vessels as they can under prevailing market conditions. The shipowner's position is not then generally one of domination and the voyage or time charterer is frequently in a position to

negotiate the contract on an equal footing, depending on the state of the market at the time.

54 In some trades, it is not unusual for the charterer to occupy the more powerful position in terms of share of the market and financial strength. Charterers, whether appearing in the voyage market or in the time charter market, are often, through their own organisations, in command of large cargo tonnage, as in some of the grain, coal and ore trades. This concentration of bargaining strength on the cargo shipping side appears to have been growing in recent years. To counter this development, shipowners are forming joint ventures in which owners are chartering their vessels to a jointly owned ship-operating company that, in turn, charters the vessels to shippers. A variety of arrangements as regards the management of individual vessels and other matters are possible in the formation and operation of such shipping pools.

B Standard charterparty forms

55 Voyage and time charterparties are, as a rule, concluded on the basis of standard contract forms, and such documentation therefore plays a role of considerable importance in present chartering practice.

56 A brief account follows of the development of standard charterparty forms, of the organisations dealing with their issue and of the different types in common use, following which some general aspects of these documents are discussed.

THE DEVELOPMENT OF STANDARD CHARTERPARTY FORMS

57 It was in the nineteenth century that shipowners and charterers first concerned themselves with the drafting of standard charterparty forms. Such forms were originally drafted and employed by individual contracting parties, but joint action was later undertaken by groups of shipowners and charterers. An early development began with parties involved in chartering in particular trades co-operating on the joint issue of agreed documents. The establishment in 1862 of the Mediterranean and Black Sea Freight Committee may be cited as an example; this organisation, composed of shipowners, merchants and brokers, issued several standard charterparty forms for the grain trade from the Black Sea and the Mediterranean.

58 In the present century, two organisations have played, and still play, a significant role in the development of internationally utilised standard forms, namely, the Chamber of Shipping of the United Kingdom in London,[2] founded in 1878, and the Baltic and International Maritime Council in Copenhagen (BIMCO), founded in 1905 under the name of the Baltic and White Sea Conference. The work on documentary matters is performed by the Chamber of Shipping through its Documentary Committee and by BIMCO through its Documentary Council. These bodies have issued or approved a great number of standard charterparty

---

2 The General Council of British Shipping (formerly the Chamber of Shipping of the United Kingdom) is no longer directly concerned in developing standard charter forms.

forms many of which are so-called 'agreed' documents, as they result from negotiations between charterer and shipper interests, on the one hand, and shipowner interests, on the other; listed as being in current use are four forms for time chartering, including the much used Baltime form, and more than 60 forms for voyage chartering, comprising special forms for most main commodities, as well as general trade forms. In chartering practice, these documents are generally referred to as 'approved' or 'official' forms.

59 Besides the Chamber of Shipping/BIMCO documents – hereafter called approved forms – there are various long-standing standard charterparty forms which are in widespread use in different trades. Mention might be made of the 'C (Ore)7' form, originally devised by the British government to cover ore imports during the First World War, the 'Americanised Welsh Coal Charter 1953', the 'Africanphos 1950' for shipments of phosphate from Morocco, the 'Sugar CharterParty-Steam (London Form)' in general use for cereal shipments from the United States and Canada, and, for time charters, the 'New York Produce Exchange Time Charter'.

60 A further type of standard charterparty form is the so-called 'private' form (sometimes called 'house charterparty'), which is issued and employed by individual firms, usually charterers enjoying more or less of a monopoly in a particular trade and therefore in a position generally to impose their own form on the shipowner. Such private forms, of which there exist a great number, are common in, for example, the ore, fertilizer and oil trades.

GENERAL ASPECTS OF STANDARD CHARTERPARTY FORMS

61 It is the view of some authorities that where standard forms or particular clauses therein are completed by one party to the contract enjoying a dominant position *vis-à-vis* the other, through protection of his own interests the contract may tend to become unduly favourable to him to the detriment of the other party. In shipping this may be illustrated by the practices which prevailed in respect of liner bills of lading prior to the introduction of the Hague Rules. The situation as regards charterparties does not, however, lend itself to any generalisation of this kind.

62 It is true that some existing charterparty forms may be said to be generally biased in favour of one side, or to contain clauses on particular points which may be considered as unduly detrimental to the interests of one of the parties; in this regard, particular attention needs to be drawn to the so-called private forms mentioned above which, in the main, are documents issued by charterers. On the other hand, many standard forms are considered to represent a fair equilibrium between the interests of the parties; and it should be recalled in this context that many forms in common use are agreed documents, implying that they have been negotiated between owner and charterer interests.

63 As regards the drafting of the standard documentation in current use in chartering, this has been criticised as sometimes lacking in logical and systematic order, and, further, as often containing unclear expressions, lacunae, and provisions of little commercial or legal importance. While this is true in the case of several standard forms of an early origin, attention

should be drawn to the fact that considerable improvement in documentary practice has been achieved by the work done over the last few decades by the Chamber of Shipping and BIMCO. Those two organisations have issued a number of modern documents, most of them agreed documents, which to a great extent have done away with earlier deficiencies.

64 Despite deficiencies of the kind that may still remain in certain documents, it is generally recognised that standard forms – as far as concerns approved or otherwise well known and commonly used forms – serve significant practical purposes and play an important role in maritime commerce as instruments for facilitating and improving the functioning of the contracting procedure.

65 As to the advantages to be derived from the use of such forms, it should be pointed out, firstly, that often the parties to a charter contract are domiciled in different countries and that the negotiations, which to a great extent are carried out through the intermediary of one or several brokers, are often performed under considerable time pressure. By basing the negotiations on a standard form, the contents of which are well known or readily available to both sides, the parties can concentrate their attention on the particular points on which they require an individual regulation, leaving all other questions to be regulated by the terms of the standard form. The use of a standard form, moreover, means that the parties run no risk of being caught out by an unusual clause or a clause imposing unreasonable or unexpected burdens on them; this, in turn, means cheaper freight rates since the owner does not have to reckon on the freight to cover him for such risks. Generally speaking, it reduces the risk of misunderstandings and ensuing disputes arising in respect of the matters covered by the contract.

66 The employment of standard forms in international chartering has an important effect also from a general legal standpoint, in that they contribute to international uniformity; disparities between regulations prescribed in the various legal systems are partly neutralised, so that similar cases taken to litigation or arbitration will tend, to a certain extent, to bring the same result, irrespective of the jurisdiction under which they are decided. Litigation and submission to arbitration is also thereby reduced. The fact that standard forms are very largely drafted in the English language and are based on English legal thinking supports this tendency toward international uniformity.

67 It should be stressed, however, that the charterparty, whether a voyage or a time charter, is an individual contract, and that the widely varying conditions under which chartering is done set a limit to the possibility of using stereotyped contract terms framed to suit a large number of cases. Thus, time charterparties, especially for long charter periods, must to a considerable extent be tailor-made to meet the particular requirements of the parties. As to voyage charterparties, these are often concluded by the charterer pursuant to the conclusion of a sales contract respecting the cargo to be shipped, and their terms are then made to conform with that contract.

Consequently, the standard forms may be amended in various respects, and clauses are often added in order to adapt the contract to the wishes and requirements of the parties. Such amendments, unless made with skill and care, may easily lead to inconsistencies and subsequent difficulties in respect of the construction of the charter; in fact, most charterparty disputes arise from ambiguities created by changes in the standard text or from unclear drafting of additional clauses inserted in the form.

(2) *The charter market*

A The marketplace

110 Finding the right ship or the right cargo among the hundreds of possibilities existing in world shipping at one particular time may seem like searching for the proverbial needle in the haystack. Yet the process of mating cargo with ship can be performed very quickly.

111 The efficiency of the chartering process can be attributed to three dominant characteristics of the charter market:

(a) The large number of shipowners, charterers and shipbrokers the world over;

(b) The availability of rapid modern communications, principally long-distance telex and telephone networks; and

(c) The prevalence of numerous charter market information sources providing late market status reports, as trade newspapers and magazines, shipbrokers' daily information sheets and special studies from a variety of sources.

112 In addition, the world shipping fraternity is an avid reader of the daily news, with special emphasis on weather, economic, trade and crop reports as well as political events. Any current development in those areas may have an important influence on the availability of shipping and on the level of market freight rates. Knowledgeable shipowners and charterers commence a particular chartering transaction with full background information on existing market conditions. Thus, bargaining over freight rates may be limited to a narrow range of rates, with relatively lengthier discussion taking place concerning other specific charter terms.

113 The existence of shipbrokers greatly facilitates the speed and efficiency of the chartering process. The role of the shipbroker is to provide expertise and information at the time these are required by his clients. The expertise takes the form of a knowledge and understanding of ships and trades that enables him to meld the two to the mutual satisfaction of owner and charterer. The shipbroker's information must be highly specific as to the availability of ships and cargoes, together with the freight rates that each may command.

114 A shipbroker is likely to specialise in particular categories of ships and trades. In this process he acquires and maintains an appreciation of the economic factors underlying the trades which he can utilise in interpreting the needs of shipowner and charterer clients alike. The shipbroker's role is that of an intermediary. In this role his communications between principals must reflect the realities of the market place.

115 A standard commission rate for shipbrokers is 2.5 per cent of the gross charter revenue. If the owner and charterer are each represented by a broker normally the commission is equally shared between the two. Many of the larger shipowners and charterers perform their own brokering functions in order to avoid commission, as this can amount to large sums in the case of long-term charters.

116 The charter market is actually composed of many sectoral markets which are generally non-competing. Vessel class distinctions exist for reasons of vessel type or size. Tankers, as a rule, do not engage in the dry cargo trades although they may from time to time enter the grain trades. Ore carriers, whose holds are small, are not suitable for the carriage of lighter commodities such as grain.

117 Specialised vessels, as LNG (liquid natural gas) tankers or other special product tankers, cannot compete with bulk carriers or other vessels of more generalised characteristics. Conversely, combination carriers in the market will cross over between the tanker and dry-cargo trades to seek the employment offering the greatest return. Large tankers and large dry-cargo carriers are most economically employed in long-haul trades. Small vessels cannot compete effectively in these long trades: they are generally most economical in coastal or short deep-sea shipping services. Despite the many differences in vessel sizes and types, a high degree of interchangeability in the employment of vessels does exist at the margin, so that movements in one sector of the market quickly affect the whole chartering market. Small tankers can carry oil even though they are more costly to operate than large tankers.

118 The charter market is also divided by length of charter: the short-term 'spot' market and the longer-term 'period' market. Short-term chartering may take the form of voyage charters or trip time charters (trip charters). The period market includes longer-term time charters, multiple (consecutive) voyage charters and long-term freighting contracts.

119 In contrast with the open charter market, there exists a very sizeable and growing 'closed' or private charter market wherein the fixture details are not publicly reported. In the negotiation of many charters, particularly the long-term sort, owners and charterers are reluctant to publicise the terms of the charter fixtures. For good reason, owners may have agreed to lower rates than might have been expected and widespread knowledge of such rates might 'spoil' the market. Similarly, charterers may not wish their transport costs to become known for reasons of competitiveness. However, the existence of such charters generally becomes known to the market even though information on specific terms may be lacking. The industry 'grapevine' is often very efficient in providing the missing information. Ironically, the level of charter rates negotiated in these non-reported fixtures is believed to be influenced by the reported level of open-market freight rates.

B Comparison of voyage and time charter costs (earnings)

120 Shipowners and charterers each have a choice between chartering on a voyage or on a time charter basis with the selection of the particular form

of charter dependent on a variety of factors. For the shipper (charterer) the frequency, regularity and expected duration of the shipping need are important considerations. The additional workload on the shipper's organisation required by a time charter as compared with a voyage charter will also be considered.

121 For the shipowner, organisational requirements may be a dictating factor since shipowning companies staff, or conversely do not staff, to handle the additional workload associated with voyage charters. However, the shipowner's expectations of future freight market levels as compared with existing levels are frequently an overriding factor in his choice between voyage or time charter. If freight rates are at what the owner considers to be peak levels, he tends to fix his vessels in long-term charters which usually means chartering on a time charter basis, while preferring shorter-term voyage charters when he believes future market rates will rise. For the charterer and shipowner alike, the comparative cost (earnings) of the voyage and the time charter is of great interest. The cost-earnings calculations concerning the two types are not directly comparable since, as has been noted, voyage charters are contracts to transport cargo on a tonnage basis and time charters contract for the lifting capacity of a vessel on a time basis. There exists a need, therefore, for charterers and owners to compare the cost (earnings) relationship of chartering opportunities offered as voyage or time charters. The ability to make such a comparison is basic in the bargaining process associated with the negotiation of a charterparty ...

C Fixing a voyage charter

125 The process of voyage chartering begins with an expression of a shipping requirement by a prospective charterer to his broker for a voyage charter which may be generally described as '25,000 tons of a commodity between ports A and B, loading date ..., ideas $4.50'. The broker will circulate this information to his shipowner clientele and make the information available to the shipping world generally through daily circulars and telex and telephone circuits to the principal chartering centres of the world, as London, New York, Tokyo and Hong Kong.

126 Responses to the charter offering will be received by the charterer's agent in the form of 'indications' which are relayed to the charterer for reaction and instructions. In a voyage charter, the charterer's main concerns are: the suitability of the vessel size and type, the geographical position of the vessel as affecting its ability to meet required loading dates, the charter rate, loading and discharging rates, laytime, and demurrage and dispatch rates.

127 An owner's consideration of a voyage chartering opportunity will particularly include, in addition to the indicated charter rate, the ports of loading and discharge of the voyage in question, the length of the voyage, and the nature of the cargo to be carried. To the owner the offered charter rate is a dominant but by no means the only consideration. If the discharge port is such as to offer further favourable trading possibilities without an unduly long haul in ballast, the owner will be inclined to accept a lower

charter rate. As to voyage length, in general the longer the voyage at a given rate of return, the more attractive the charter to the owner.

128 Owners' responses are usually valid only for a short stated period of time, as 24 hours, so that he may in turn respond to other market offers if the current offer is not accepted. Depending on the 'tone' of the market (ie an indicated plentiful or short supply of tonnage), the charterer will make an early counter-offer or choose to wait if he anticipates that owners may improve their offers.

129 A firm offer for a voyage charter from an owner generally includes the following details:

Period for which the offer is valid

Freight rate

Name of vessel

Lay days

Vessel's carrying capacity of the cargo in question

Loading and discharging ports

Loading/discharge costs

Demurrage/dispatch

Commission

Charterparty form to be used

130 If, after analysis of the owner's offer, the prospective charterer believes that detailed agreement can be reached, he will make a counter-offer specifying the modifications that are desired. As discussed earlier, the effective cost of the voyage charter to the charterer can be reduced not only by lowering the stated charter rate but also by changes in such terms as those concerned with loading and discharging costs, demurrage and dispatch rates, and commission rates.

131 Voyage charters involving more than a single voyage may require extended interchange to reach agreement on the precise timing of each of the voyages, particularly in the case of long-term voyage charters lasting several years. The negotiations on long-term voyage charters will also require agreement on a variety of alternate charter performance conditions (as, acceptable vessel sizes and cargo loading dates, among others), not usually required in single-voyage charters.

132 A firm offer which is accepted within the period of validity binds the offerer and concludes the negotiations, while acceptance after the expiration of the time limit is considered a counter-offer. Indications or counter-offers bind neither party until formulated and accepted as firm offers. The exchange of offers is usually made in written form by telex or telegram and those made and accepted by telephone are usually confirmed afterwards in writing.

133 Often a firm offer is forwarded or accepted subject to special conditions. A typical example may be that of a merchant who wants to secure shipping space for goods he is about to buy or sell. He may find it practical to have

tonnage at hand and negotiate all arrangements for the shipment prior to buying or selling the goods. In such a case his charter offer is made 'subject stem', meaning that he is in no way committed if the purchase or sale of the goods should not materialise. Another example is that of the owner who makes a firm offer 'subject open', meaning that he retains the right to withdraw his offer in case the vessel should be fixed for other business prior to acceptance of the offer in question. Offers with an attached 'subject' proviso should be treated with caution. In general such an offer is no more than an indication. Firm offers given or accepted on this basis do, however, serve a meaningful purpose in keeping the negotiations going and in providing a guide as to why the other party is hesitant.

134 The preparation of the formal voyage charterparty, following agreement on charter terms, is usually an expeditious and straightforward process, particularly for single-voyage charters embodied in a standard form.

135 The administration of the charter during its life requires careful record keeping by both the owner and the charterer to ensure that the payment terms of the various clauses of the charterparty are adhered to. For example, accurate measurement of the cargo loaded must be made in order to compute the charter hire payment. Payments of demurrage or dispatch normally result from each voyage, requiring computations carefully made in accordance with the charterparty terms. Often, agreement on the cost of repairing stevedoring damages does not occur until long after the voyage is completed since the performance of such repairs may not take place until the vessel's next dry-docking period.

D Fixing a time charter

136 The process of searching the market and fixing the charter for vessels to be placed on time charter may vary considerably depending on the contemplated length of the charter. For trip or other short-term charters, the procedures parallel those used for fixing a single-voyage charter. A more selective process is frequently used in the negotiation of time charters of longer duration than, say, one year. Often there is direct negotiation between the charterer and the owner, leaving out shipbrokers to avoid payment of commission.

137 A charterer will have highly specific ideas about the size, type and operating characteristics of the vessel he is seeking to place on time charter for an extended period. In addition, he is likely to have detailed knowledge of the charter status of individual ships of the class he has in mind. Some of those ships may have been employed previously in the charterer's trade and hence he is familiar both with the performance record of the vessel and the reliability of the vessel's owner. Accordingly, the market search may be limited to direct inquiries to one or more owners in order to determine specific vessel availability.

138 The negotiation of a long-term time charter often takes a period of weeks or longer since the wording of each clause will have an important bearing on the overall cost (earnings) under the agreed contract. The negotiation of the rate of hire may well include a series of offers and counter-offers, frequently consisting of varying rates or combinations of rates for different

duration periods or extension options. For time charters involving the 'forward' delivery of the vessel (which may be from, say, six months to several years ahead, as in the case of vessels not yet built), the negotiations on rate of hire become more complicated due to uncertainties as to future market freight rate levels. Current rate levels influence the rate of hire under time charters of both near-term and forward delivery. If, during the charter-negotiating period a turning point in market freight rates is experienced, the process of negotiating the charter rate is further complicated by both owner and charterer having to assess the significance of the change.

139 As discussed in paragraphs 97–99, agreement on the clauses pertaining to the performance of the vessel, in terms of average speeds and fuel consumption, is of basic importance. Equal care is required in the negotiation of other charter clauses. For example, agreement should be reached on the treatment of vessel off hire as this relates to the duration of the charter. Under some time charters, the charter period is extended by the off hire time, although many variations of this method are possible.

140 Careful construction of the time charter clauses affects not only its cost (earnings) value to the charterers and owners but also the ease of administering the charter during its operating life. Time charters require extensive and meticulous record-keeping by both owner and charterer, to ensure that sufficient detail is accumulated to serve as the basis for the adjudication of possible claims, many of which may arise, as is often the case, long after the charter has expired. Owners and charterers must provide for the maintenance of these functions within their respective organisations.

References

Bes, J, *Chartering Practice*, 1960, London: Barker & Howard

Bes, J, *Chartering and Shipping Terms*, 11th edn, 1992, London: Barker & Howard

Branch, Alan E, *Elements of Shipping*, 7th edn, 1996, London: Chapman & Hall

Branch, Alan E, *Economics of Shipping*, 2nd edn, 1988, London: Chapman & Hall

Brodie, PD, *Illustrated Dictionary of Cargo Handling*, 2nd edn, 1996, Lloyd's of London Press

Cufley, CFH, *Ocean Freights and Chartering*, 1972, London: Staples Press, reprinted 1983, London: Granada Press

Farthing, Bruce, *International Shipping*, 3rd edn, 1997, London: Lloyd's of London Press

Graham, MG and Hughes, DO, *Containerisation in the Eighties*, 1985, London: Lloyd's of London Press

Gilmore, G and Black, C, *Law of Admiralty*, 2nd edn, 1975, New York: Foundation Press

Gold, Edgar, *Maritime Transport*, 1984, Centerville, Maryland: Lexington Books

Gorton, Ihre, Sandevarn, *Shipbroking and Chartering Practice*, 4th edn, 1996, London: Lloyd's of London Press

Kendall, Lane C and Buckley, James J, *The Business of Shipping*, 6th edn, 1994, Cambridge, Maryland: Cornell Maritime Press

Spruyt, J, *Ship Management*, 2nd edn, 1994, London: Lloyd's of London Press

Stopford, Martin, *Maritime Economics*, 1992, London: Routledge

Thornton, RH, *British Shipping*, 2nd edn, 1959, Cambridge: Cambridge University Press

Williams, Harvey, *Chartering Documents*, 3rd edn, 1996, London: Lloyd's of London Press.

CHAPTER 2

CARGO CLAIMS

The first part of this book deals with the law which governs the relationship between a sea carrier on the one side and cargo owners on the other. This chapter looks at the basis of responsibility of a sea carrier for goods which are lost, damaged or destroyed. The law in this area is not new. Modern English law developed from cases which were decided long before steel hulls and steam engines began to be used in maritime commerce.

1 PUBLIC CARRIERS

At common law, a distinction is made between the position of public and private carriers. A public or common carrier by sea is someone who holds himself out as willing to carry for reward for anyone who wants to use his services. It does not seem to be necessary for the goods of several persons to be carried in common, or for the carriage to be between English ports, or even for the ship to follow a fixed itinerary. However, a carrier who carries only for particular persons or who genuinely reserves the right to pick and choose his customers is a private carrier.

A public carrier is subject to a stringent legal regime. If space is available, he is bound to carry with reasonable despatch and at a reasonable cost for anyone who wants to make use of his services. Goods which are unreasonable in quantity or weight can be refused, and so can goods not of the type of which he professes to be a carrier. But if goods carried for hire are lost or damaged, a common carrier is absolutely liable, except where the loss or damage is caused by the common law excepted perils, which are losses caused by act of God, the Queen's enemies or by inherent vice of the goods themselves. Loss by general average sacrifice or by the fault of the shipper is also a defence at common law. A common carrier is not, therefore, merely expected to take reasonable care of goods which have been entrusted to him. On the contrary, as the old cases explain, a common carrier is virtually in the position of an insurer of goods against all consequences except the common law excepted perils. Thus he is, for example, liable for loss by theft even if he has not been negligent; and it makes no difference whether the goods are stolen from the carrier by strangers or by his own employees. However, the severity of this approach can be mitigated by the common carrier himself, who is free at common law to limit his responsibilities by contract.

2 PRIVATE CARRIERS

The position of a private carrier by land is very different. A private carrier by land is not absolutely liable for goods which are lost or damaged while in his possession. At common law, where the rights of the parties are not regulated by an express contract, a private land carrier is only liable as a bailee for reward if he deliberately damages goods or if he fails to take reasonable care of them. However, to escape liability, he is obliged to prove that the loss or damage was not caused by his negligence.

The liability at common law of a private carrier by sea for goods which are lost or damaged, but where the rights of the parties are not regulated by an express contract, is more controversial. The cases contain many contradictory statements. One view is that while not all sea carriers are common carriers, they are all nevertheless subject to the same rule of absolute liability as common carriers. The judgment of Lord Justice Brett in *Liver Alkali*, below, is the best known statement of this view, although it is not an isolated instance: see, for example, the judgments of Lopes LJ at trial in *Pandorf v Hamilton* (1885) 16 QBD 635 and of Scott LJ in *Beaumont-Thomas v Blue Star Line* [1939] 3 All ER 127, 131.

However, Chief Justice Cockburn's judgment in *Nugent v Smith*, below, contains a sustained assault on the Lord Justice Brett's views and treats the private carrier by sea as in the same position as a private carrier by land and therefore as being liable only as a bailee for reward to exercise reasonable care. Some commentators find support for this view in dicta such as that of Willes J in *Grill v General Iron Screw Colliery Co* (1866) LR 1 CP 600, 612 that the 'contract is to carry with reasonable care unless prevented by the excepted perils'.

A third possibility mentioned in several cases is that some classes of sea carriers such as lightermen may have a special status as public-but-not-common-carriers and as such have the same liability as common carriers, while all others are liable only to take reasonable care.

Liver Alkali v Johnson (1874) LR 9 Ex 338, Court of Exchequer Chamber, affirming (1872) LR 7 Ex 267, Court of Exchequer

The defendant was a barge owner. He did not ply between fixed termini. With each customer, an agreement was made for carriage at a negotiated rate per ton between the places selected by the customer. His customers (including the plaintiffs) did not normally select or agree on a particular barge. A barge was never used to carry the goods of more than one customer at a time. There was no evidence that the defendant had ever refused to let his vessels to anyone who ever applied to him. The defendant argued that he was not a common carrier.

Blackburn J: It appears by the case stated for this Court on appeal that the defendant was engaged in carrying from Widnes to Liverpool some salt cake of the plaintiffs in a flat on the river Mersey. The goods were injured by reason of the flat getting on a shoal in consequence of a fog. This was a peril of navigation, but could in no sense be called the act of God or of the Queen's enemies.

The jury found that there was no negligence on the part of the defendant.

The question, therefore, raised is, whether the defendant was under the liability of a bailee for hire, *viz*, to take proper care of the goods, in which case he is not responsible for this loss, or whether he has the more extended liability of a common carrier, viz, to carry the goods safe against all events but acts of God and the enemies of the Queen.

We have purposely confined our expressions to the question, 'whether the defendant has the liability of a common carrier', for we do not think it necessary to inquire whether the defendant is a carrier so as to be liable to an action for not taking goods tendered to him.

The rule imposing this extended liability on common carriers was originally established, as Lord Mansfield states, in *Forward v Pittard* (1785) 1 T R 27, 33, on the ground of public policy:

> 'To prevent litigation, collusion, and the necessity of going into circumstances impossible to be unravelled, the law presumes against the carrier, unless he shews it was done by the King's enemies, or by such act as could not happen by the intervention of man.'

And Lord Holt explains it, in the celebrated judgment in *Coggs v Bernard* (1703) 2 Ld Raym 918, as existing in the case of one that exercises a public employment:

> 'And this is the case of the common hoyman, master of a ship, etc, which case of a master of a ship was first adjudged 26 Car 2, in the case of *Morse v Slue* (1671) 1 Vent 190, 238. And this is a politic establishment contrived by the policy of the law for the safety of all persons the necessity of whose affairs oblige them to trust these sort of persons, that they may be safe in their ways of dealing.'

It is too late now to speculate on the propriety of this rule; we must treat it as firmly established that, in the absence of some contract, express or implied, introducing further exceptions, those who exercise a public employment of carrying goods do incur this liability. It appears from the evidence stated that the defendant was the owner of several flats, and that he made it his business to send out his flats under the care of his own servants, different persons as required from time to time, to carry cargoes to or from places in the Mersey, but that it always was to carry goods for one person at a time, and that: 'he carried for any one who chose to employ him, but that an express agreement was always made as to each voyage or employment of the defendant's flats', which means, as we understand the evidence, that the flats did not go about plying for hire, but were waiting for hire by any one. We think that this describes the ordinary employment of a lighterman, and that, both on authority and principle, a person who exercises this business and employment does, in the absence of something to limit his liability, incur the liability of a common carrier in respect of the goods he carries.

It was argued before us that the defendant could not have this liability unless he held himself out as plying between two particular places, or had put up his flat, like a general ship, to go to some particular place, and take all goods brought him for that voyage.

It was urged that in *Morse v Slue* (above) the goods were probably put on board a ship put up as a general ship. It certainly may have been so, but the count is set out in Ventris and is general, that by the law and custom of England charterers and governors of ships which go from London beyond sea are bound, etc, and the ultimate decision was that this count was proved. Hale, CJ, seems to have had a difficulty from the fact that the ship was bound to foreign parts, and that the shipowner would not by the civil law or the maritime law be chargeable for piracy or damnum fatale (a difficulty, it may be remarked, which does not apply to the present case, where the whole transaction is in England), but nothing is in any report said as to the ship being a general ship. And on that count no judgment could have been given on that ground.

The ultimate decision on the special verdict has always been understood to apply equally to all ships employed in commerce and sailing from England, as is shewn from the forms of charterparty and bill of lading in ordinary use in England, which always contain an engagement to deliver the goods in the same condition they were received aboard, and, when Lord Tenterden first wrote, contained only an exception of the dangers of the seas; now the exceptions in each class of instrument are much more extensive. And certainly it is difficult to see any reason why the liability of a shipowner who engages to carry the whole lading of his ship for one person should be less than the liability of one who carries the lading in different parcels for different people.

To come nearer to the particular case, we find that 'lightermen' are specially named in Bacon's Abridgment 'Carrier' (A), and in the notes to *Coggs v Bernard*, 1 Smith's *Leading Cases*, 6th edn, 177. In *Lyon v Mells* (1804) 5 East 428, the course of business of the defendant is thus described:

'The defendant kept sloops for carrying other persons' goods for hire, and also lighters for the purpose of carrying these goods to and from his sloops, and when he had not employment for his lighters in his own business, he let them for hire to such persons as wanted to carry goods to other sloops.'

If there be any difference between the employment of the now defendant, as described in this case, and the employment of the defendant in *Lyon v Mells*, it would seem that the latter was less clearly a public employment. The great point discussed was, whether a notice limiting the liability of the defendant was, as Lord Ellenborough states it, illegal, as being 'to exempt him from a responsibility cast on him by law as a carrier of goods by water for hire', a proposition which could not well have been discussed by any one who did not think that the defendant had, but for the notice, incurred that responsibility. The point actually decided was, that the terms of the notice did not relieve the defendant from liability for furnishing an unseaworthy lighter. As to this Lord Ellenborough says:

> 'Every agreement must be construed with reference to the subject matter, and looking at the parties to this agreement (for so I denominate the notice), and the situation in which they stood in point of law to each other, it is clear beyond a doubt that the only object of the owners of lighters was to limit their responsibility in those cases only where the law would otherwise have made them answer for the neglect of others, and for accidents which it might not be within the scope of ordinary care and caution to provide against.'

We think that Mr James, in arguing for the plaintiff in this case, was right when he relied on *Lyon v Mells* as an important authority in favour of his client.

It is true that the point was not precisely decided in *Lyon v Mells*, and if it had been, it would not have been binding upon us in a Court of Error; but the opinion of Lord Ellenborough, and (as far as we can judge from the report) of every one concerned in the case, was that it was too clear for argument that, but for the notice, the lighterman, acting as the defendant did in that case, would have been liable to the same extent as a common carrier. Lord Abinger, in *Brind v Dale* (1837) 2 Mood & Rob 80, expressed a strong opinion that a town carrier could not be considered a common carrier; but he reserved the point, and as the jury found in favour of the defendant on the question whether the goods were received by him as a common carrier, it never was reviewed in banc.

The ruling of Alderson, B, in *Ingate v Christie* (1850) 3 C & K 61, is in express conformity with what appears to have been Lord Ellenborough's view in *Lyon v Mells* (above) and no English authority has been cited in conflict with this doctrine. We think, therefore, that the judgment below was right, and should be affirmed.

[Mellor, Archibald, and Grove JJ concurred.]

Brett J: I cannot come to the conclusion that the defendant in this case was liable whether he was a common carrier or not, because I conclude that he was liable, notwithstanding that I am clearly of opinion that he was not a common carrier. It seems to me that it is of the very essence of the definition of a common carrier, that he should be one who undertakes to carry the goods (not being dangerous, or of unreasonable weight or bulk) which are first offered to him – he who does not so undertake is not a common carrier. The force of the word 'common' is not that the carrier's business is a public one, or 'in common with others', but that he undertakes to carry for all indifferently in the sense of for the first comer, ie, 'for all in common'. It is clear to my mind that a shipowner who publicly professes to own sloops, and to charter them to any one who will agree with him on terms of charter, is not a common carrier, because he does not undertake to carry goods for or to charter his sloop to the first comer. He wants, therefore, the essential characteristic of a common carrier; he is, therefore, not a common carrier, and therefore does not incur at any time any liability on the ground of his being a common carrier. The defendant in the present case, in my opinion, carried on his business like any other owner of sloops or vessels, and was not a common carrier, and was in no way liable as such. But I think that, by a recognised custom of England – a custom adopted and recognised by the courts in precisely the same manner as the custom of England with regard to common carriers has been adopted and recognised by them – every shipowner who carries goods for hire in his ship, whether by inland navigation, or coastways, or abroad, undertakes to carry them at his own absolute risk, the act of God or of the Queen's enemies alone excepted, unless by agreement between himself and a particular freighter, on a particular voyage, or on particular voyages, he limits his liability by further exceptions.

I think that this liability attaches to shipowners carrying goods, by reason of recognised custom, which may be pleaded as the custom of England, just as the custom of England as to common carriers may be pleaded. But it is a custom wholly independent of the similar custom with regard to common carriers. The similarity of the two customs has occasioned phraseology to be used in some cases which has raised an inaccurate idea that shipowners are common carriers; but I am of opinion that they are not. They are not bound to carry for the first comer. I therefore hold that the defendant is liable as a shipowner, upon the custom applicable to him as such, but not liable as a common carrier, upon the custom applicable to that business or employment.'

Nugent v Smith (1876) 1 CPD 423, Court of Appeal reversing (1876) 1 CPD 19

The plaintiff shipped two horses on board a steamship plying regularly as a general ship between London and Aberdeen. The horses were shipped without any bill of lading. In the course of the voyage one of the horses died from injuries caused partly by the rolling of the vessel in a severe storm and partly from struggling caused by excessive fright. The plaintiff was awarded damages in the High Court. On appeal, the court held that the defendant was a common carrier, but was not liable for a loss caused by a combination of an act of God and inherent vice. One member of the court went on to consider whether the defendant would have been liable if he had not been a common carrier.

> **Cockburn CJ**: ... [A]s the vessel by which the mare was shipped was one of a line of steamers plying habitually between given ports and carrying the goods of all comers as a general ship, and as from this it necessarily follows that the owners were common carriers, it was altogether unnecessary to the decision of the present case to determine the question so elaborately discussed in the judgment of Brett J [(1876) 1 CPD 19] as to the liability of the owner of a ship, not being a general ship, but one hired to carry a specific cargo on a particular voyage, to make good loss or damage arising from inevitable accident. The question being, however, one of considerable importance – though its importance is materially lessened by the general practice of ascertaining and limiting the liability of the shipowner by charterparty or bill of lading – and the question not having before presented itself for judicial decision, I think it right to express my dissent from the reasoning of the court below, the more so as, for the opinion thus expressed, I not only fail to discover any authority whatever,

but find all jurists who treat of this form of bailment carefully distinguishing between the common carrier and the private ship ...

As matter of legal history we know that the more rigorous law of later times, first introduced during the reign of Elizabeth, was, in the first instance, established with reference to carriers by land to whom by the Roman law no such liability attached. It was not till the ensuing reign, in the eleventh of James I, that it was decided, in *Rich v Kneeland* (1613) Cro Jac 330, that the common hoyman or carrier by water stood on the same footing as a common carrier by land, and rightly, for in principle there could be no difference between them.

The next case in point of date, and it is the first case in the books in which the liability of the owner of a sea-going ship comes in question, is the well known case of *Morse v Slue* (1671) 1 Vent 190, 238, in which it was held, after a trial at bar, that where a ship lying in the Thames was boarded by robbers, who took the plaintiff's goods which had been loaded on board, in an action brought against the master, the plaintiff was entitled to recover. And it certainly surprises me that this case should be relied on as an authority for the position that the liability of a common carrier attaches to the shipowner or master where the ship is not a general ship; for though it is not expressly said that the ship in question was a general ship, which has led to the somewhat hasty assumption that she was not, the internal evidence shews conclusively that she was so. In the first place, the declaration is laid on the custom of the realm, and we know that the only custom to which effect had up to that time been given – and that quite in recent times – was in respect of common carriers by land, and still more recently in respect of common carriers by water. Secondly, Hale CJ, in giving judgment, puts the case as on all fours with that of a common carrier or hoyman, and nowhere says that it is to be treated as that of a private ship. 'He who would take off the master from this action,' says the Chief Justice, 'must assign a difference between it and the case of a hoyman, common carrier, or innholder.' Doubtless the counsel for the defendant, if the case had been distinguishable on the ground that the vessel was not a common ship, would have pointed out the difference, and at all events have taken the point; and in the corresponding report of the same case in *Levinz* (1671) 2 Lev 69, the case of *Rich v Kneeland* (above) having been referred to, the Chief Justice is reported to have said that the case 'differed not from that of the hoyman'. But in the case of *Rich v Kneeland* we know that the barge or hoy was a common carrier; and it is obvious that if in *Morse v Slue* (above) the vessel had been a private one, instead of treating the case as identical with that of the common hoyman, the Chief Justice would have put it on the ground that all sea-going vessels were subject to the larger liability. But besides this, there is a circumstance which appears to have been overlooked, which seems decisive to shew that the ship must have been a general ship. It is mentioned in the report in Ventris, that the ship was a vessel of 150 tons burden, bound for Cadiz, and that the goods shipped by the plaintiff consisted of three trunks, containing 400 pairs of silk stockings and 174 lbs of silk. It seems idle to suppose that a ship of that size would have been hired on such a voyage for the purpose of carrying the plaintiff's three trunks as her entire cargo. There seems, therefore, no reasonable doubt that the ship was a general ship.

In like manner, in the case of *Dale v Hall* (1750) 1 Wils 281, although the declaration was not upon the custom of the realm, but upon the implied obligation to carry safely, it appearing that the defendant was a shipmaster or keelman who carried goods from port to port, the court decided in favour of the plaintiff, expressly on the liability of the defendant as a common carrier (though the latter was prepared to shew an absence of negligence on his part), on the ground that the allegation of the duty of a common carrier 'to carry safely' was equivalent to a declaration on the custom of the realm. In the subsequent case of *Barclay v Cuculla y Gana* (1784) 3 Doug 389, which was a case where, as in *Morse v Slue*, goods had been forcibly taken by thieves from a ship lying in the Thames, on the objection being taken on behalf of the defendant that he was not charged in the declaration on the custom of the realm, while there was neither express undertaking nor negligence to make him liable otherwise, the answer of the court was 'that there was no question at the trial as to the ship being a general ship'; and Lord Mansfield adds that it was impossible to distinguish the case from that of a common carrier.

Thus far the reported cases as to carriers by sea have been cases of general vessels. The next in point of time, that of *Lyon v Mells* (1804) 5 East 428, was one in which the defendant kept sloops for carrying other persons' goods for hire, and also lighters for carrying such goods to and from his sloops as well as to and from the sloops of other owners. One of these lighters, in which goods of the plaintiff were being conveyed on board a sloop, proved leaky and took in a quantity of water, and the goods became seriously damaged, and it was also found as a fact that the goods had been negligently stowed. The defendant relied on a notice that he would not be answerable for any loss or damage unless occasioned by want of ordinary care of the master and crew, in which case he would pay 10 per cent on the loss or damage; but that persons desirous of having their goods carried free from any risk in respect of loss or damage, whether arising from the act of God or otherwise, might have them so carried on entering into an agreement to pay extra freight in proportion to the risk. No extra freight having been paid, the question was whether the defendant was protected by this notice from liability for more than 10 per cent of the damage. Nothing in reality turned upon his being a common carrier or subject to the liabilities of a common carrier. Some discussion, it is true, took place on the argument as to whether the defendant was a common carrier or not; but Lord Ellenborough, in giving judgment, put the matter on the right footing, namely, that a carrier by water impliedly engages that his vessel shall be watertight, an obligation obviously applicable to all carriers, whether common carriers or otherwise, and that the defendant could not be taken to have intended by such a notice to claim immunity in respect of his own breach of contract, but only immunity above 10 per cent for loss or damage arising from the negligence of the master and crew, and total immunity in respect of loss or damage from the act of God or other cause, unless extra freight was paid. The owner no doubt thought his liability that of a common carrier, and, as Lord Ellenborough points out, sought to protect himself accordingly; but Lord Ellenborough nowhere treats him as such, but decides the case on a general ground applicable to all carriers, whether common or private. Yet this case is relied on, erroneously as it appears to me, as shewing that a man who lets out a lighter or ship, not to carry the goods of general comers, but to a particular individual on a specific job or contract, if his business be to let out lighters or ships, is a common carrier, or is at all events subject to an equal degree of liability. The last case is that of the *Liver Alkali Co v Johnson* (above), in which the defendant was a barge owner and let out his vessels for conveyance of goods to any customers who applied to him. Each voyage was made under a separate agreement, and a barge was not let to more than one person for the same voyage. The defendant did not ply between any fixed termini, but the customer fixed in each particular case the points of arrival and departure. In an action against the defendant by the plaintiffs for not safely and securely carrying certain goods, the Court of Exchequer Chamber held, affirming the judgment of the Court of Exchequer, that the defendant was a common carrier and liable as such. Mr Justice Brett, differing from the majority, held that the defendant was not a common carrier, but, asserting the same doctrine as in the judgment now appealed from, held him liable upon a special custom of the realm attaching to all carriers by sea, of which custom, however, as I have already intimated, I can find no trace whatever. We are, of course, bound by the decision of the Court of Exchequer Chamber in the case referred to as that of a court of appellate jurisdiction, and which, therefore, can only be reviewed by a court of ultimate appeal; but I cannot help seeing the difficulty which stands in the way of the ruling in that case, namely, that it is essential to the character of a common carrier that he is bound to carry the goods of all persons applying to him, while it never has been held, and, as it seems to me, could not be held, that a person who lets out vessels or vehicles to individual customers on their application was liable to an action for refusing the use of such vessel or vehicle if required to furnish it. At all events, it is obvious that as the decision of the Court of Exchequer Chamber proceeded on the ground that the defendant in that case was a common carrier, the decision is no authority for the position taken in the court below, that all shipowners are equally liable for loss by inevitable accident. It is plain that the majority of the Court did not adopt the view of Mr Justice Brett. Lastly, while it does not lie within our province to criticise the law we have to administer or to question its policy, I cannot but think that we are not called upon to extend a principle of extreme rigour, peculiar to our own law, and the absence of which in the law of other nations has not been found by experience to lead to the evils for the prevention of which the rule of our law was supposed to be necessary, further than it has hitherto been applied. I cannot, therefore, concur in the opinion expressed in the judgment delivered by Mr Justice Brett, that by the law of England all carriers by sea are subject to the liability which by that law undoubtedly attaches to the common carrier whether by sea or by land ...

Notes

1   The decision in *Liver Alkali* was followed in *Hill v Scott* [1895] 2 QB 371, where Lord Russell of Killowen CJ said that there was really no essential difference between the judgments of Blackburn J and Brett J, although he preferred the language of Blackburn J. On appeal, Lord Russell's judgment was affirmed by a Court of Appeal which included Brett. *Liver Alkali* was distinguished in *Consolidated Tea v Oliver's Wharf* [1910] 2 KB 395 where it

was said that to attract the liability of a common carrier it was essential that 'the defendants were exercising a public employment'. In *Watkins v Cottell* [1916] 1 KB 10, Avory J adopted the same explanation as Cockburn CJ had done in *Nugent* of the majority opinion in *Liver Alkali*, *viz*, that the defendant in that case was a common carrier. To complete the range of possible analyses, in *Belfast Ropework v Bushell* [1918] 1 KB 210, *Liver Alkali* was spoken of as a case confined to lightermen.

2   In *Ingate v Christie* (1850) 3 C & K 61, in the course of argument, Baron Alderson said:

Everybody who undertakes to carry for anyone who asks him, is a common carrier. The criterion is, whether he carries for particular persons only, or whether he carries for everyone. If a man holds himself out to do it for everyone who asks him, he is a common carrier; but if he does not do it for everyone, but carries for you and me only, that is a matter of special contract.

3   In *Belfast Ropework Co Ltd v Bushell* [1918] 1 KB 210, it was argued that the defendant was a common carrier. Bailhache J asked:

Did the defendant, while inviting all and sundry to employ him, reserve to himself the right of accepting or rejecting their offers of goods for carriage whether his lorries were full or empty, being guided in his decision by the attractiveness or otherwise of the particular offer and not by his ability or inability to carry having regard to his other engagements? Upon the facts as found by me I answer that question in the affirmative, and in my opinion that answer shows that he is not a common carrier.

4   Act of God:

a mere short way of expressing this proposition. A common carrier is not liable for any accident as to which he can shew that it is due to natural causes directly and exclusively, without human intervention, and that it could not have been prevented by any amount of foresight and pains and care reasonably to be expected from him.

James LJ, *Nugent v Smith*, above, at page 444.

5   King's enemies: in *Russell v Niemann* (1864) 17 CBNS 163 cargo was shipped under a bill of lading containing this exception. The shipowner was a subject of the Duke of Mecklenburg and the ship a Mecklenburg ship; the port of loading was in Russia, the port of discharge in England and the shippers either German or Russian. The ship was seized by Danes with whom the Duke was at war. On the question whether the exception referred to the Emperor of Russia, the Queen of England or the Duke, it was held it included enemies of the sovereign of the carrier, whether or not a King.

6   Inherent vice:

anything which by reason of its own inherent qualities was lost without negligence by any one.

Earl of Halsbury, *Greenshields v Stephens* [1908] AC 431. In *Gould v South Eastern and Chatham Rwy* [1920] 2 KB 186 (a case of inland carriage) Atkin

LJ citing *Story on Bailments* held that the implied liability of a common carrier did not include responsibility for ordinary wear and tear in transit, ordinary loss or deterioration in quality or quantity such as evaporation or loss or damage through insufficiency of packing.

7   For the establishment of the sea carrier's absolute liability at common law in the 16th century, see David Ibbetson, 'Absolute Liability in Contract: the Antecedents of *Paradine v Jayne*', in Rose, F, ed, Consensus ad Idem: *Essays on the Law of Contract in honour of Guenter Treitel*, 1996, Sweet & Maxwell.

3 CARRIAGE UNDER SPECIAL CONTRACT

Uncertainty about the nature of the liability of a sea carrier at common law might seem to be a serious problem. There is little recent case law, although the issue has arisen indirectly from time to time: *The Emmanuel C* [1983] 1 Lloyd's Rep 310, construction of exclusion clause; *The Torenia* [1983] 2 Lloyd's Rep 211, burden of proof of cargo claim. For the most part this is a theoretical rather than an important practical difficulty, since most cargoes are carried today, not on bare common law terms, but under contracts (called 'special contracts' or 'special carriage' in the older cases) which deal expressly with the carrier's obligations.

Under an express contract, the carrier's obligations depend on precise terms of his undertakings and on any terms which must be implied into the contract. Where the contract takes the form of a bill of lading, the carrier's obligation is normally regarded in English courts as an absolute undertaking to deliver the goods at their destination in the same condition in which they were when shipped, unless prevented by causes mentioned in the contract. The common form statement on a bill of lading that the goods are received 'in apparent good order and condition ... for carriage subject to the terms hereof ... from the port of loading to the port of discharge' is not therefore merely a promise to make reasonable efforts. It is an undertaking to deliver the goods in question in the same order and condition in which they were when shipped, subject only to the exceptions in the contract and to any statutory defences to which the carrier may be entitled. To summarise, apart from the effect of legislation, a ship must deliver what she received, as she received it, unless relieved by excepted perils or by legislation.

However, the freedom with which, in the last century, carriers introduced exceptions into contracts to take away responsibility for matters for which they would otherwise have been liable, encouraged a close analysis both of the terms of exclusion clauses and of the nature of carriers' obligations. This process resulted in carriers by sea being regarded as undertaking two distinct implied duties, which would be implied in a contract by way of addition to any express obligations: an implied duty to provide a seaworthy ship, which is the subject of the next chapter; and an implied duty to take reasonable care of cargo, which is considered below together with the meaning of common exceptions clauses.

Notara v Henderson (1872) LR 7 QB 225, Exchequer Chamber

The plaintiffs shipped beans on board the defendants' ship, *The Trojan*, under a bill of lading, from Alexandria to Glasgow, with leave to call at intermediate ports. The ship called at Liverpool and on leaving the port met with a collision (a peril excepted in the bill of lading) and had to put back for repairs. The beans became wet in consequence of the collision and, on arrival at Glasgow, had deteriorated in value. This deterioration could have been prevented if they had been dried at Liverpool. The plaintiffs sued to recover this loss.

Willes J read the judgment of the court:

> ... The question thus raised is a compound one of law and fact; first, of law, whether there be any duty on the part of the shipowners, through the master, to take active measures to prevent the cargo from being spoilt by damage originally occasioned by sea accidents, without fault on their part, and for the proximate and unavoidable effects of which accident they are exempt from responsibility by the terms of the bill of lading; and secondly, of fact, whether, if there be such a duty, there was, under the circumstances of this case, a breach thereof in not drying the beans ...

> That a duty to take care of the goods generally exists cannot be doubted ... the duty imposed upon the master, as representing the shipowner, [is] to take reasonable care of the goods entrusted to him, not merely in doing what is necessary to preserve them on board the ship during the ordinary incidents of the voyage, but also in taking reasonable measures to check and arrest their loss, destruction, or deterioration, by reason of accidents, for the necessary effects of which there is, by reason of the exception in the bill of lading, no original liability.

> The exception in the bill of lading was relied upon in this court as completely exonerating the shipowner; but it is now thoroughly settled that it only exempts him from the absolute liability of a common carrier, and not from the consequences of the want of reasonable skill, diligence, and care, which want is popularly described as 'gross negligence'. This is settled, so far as the repairs of the ship are concerned, by the judgment of Lord Wensleydale in *Worms v Storey* (1855) 11 Ex 427, 430; as to her navigation, by a series of authorities collected in *Grill v General Iron Screw Collier Co* (1866) LR 1 CP 600; (1868) 3 CP 476; and as to her management, so far as affects the case of the cargo itself, in *Laurie v Douglas* (1846) 15 M & W 746; where the court (in a judgment unfortunately not reported at large) upheld a ruling of Pollock, CB, that the shipowner was only bound to take the same care of the goods as a person would of his own goods, *viz*, 'ordinary and reasonable care'. These authorities and the reasoning upon which they are founded are conclusive to shew that the exemption is from liability for loss which could not have been avoided by reasonable care, skill, and diligence, and that it is inapplicable to the case of a loss arising from the want of such care, and the sacrifice of the cargo by reason thereof, which is the subject matter of the present complaint. For these reasons

we think the shipowners are answerable for the conduct of the master, in point of law, if, in point of fact, he was guilty of a want of reasonable care of the goods in not drying them at Liverpool ...

The court held, affirming the judgment of the Court of Queen's Bench, that the facts showed that the beans might have been taken out and dried and then re-shipped, without unreasonably delaying the voyage; that it was, therefore, the master's duty to have done so, and consequently the defendants were liable.

In re Polemis and Furness, Withy and Co [1921] 3 KB 560, CA

Scrutton LJ: The steamship *Thrasyvoulos* was lost by fire while being discharged by workmen employed by the charterers. Experienced arbitrators, by whose findings of fact we are bound, have decided that the fire was caused by a spark igniting petrol vapour in the hold, the vapour coming from leaks from cargo shipped by the charterers, and that the spark was caused by the [stevedores] employed by the charterers negligently knocking a plank out of a temporary staging erected in the hold, so that the plank fell into the hold, and in its fall by striking something made the spark which ignited the petrol vapour.

On these findings the charterers contend that they are not liable ... [*inter alia*, because] they are protected by an exception of 'fire' which in the charter is 'mutually excepted' ...

An excepted perils clause, if fully expanded, runs that one of the parties undertakes to do something unless prevented by an excepted peril, in which case he is excused. But where he has an obligation to do some act carefully, if he fails in his obligation, and by his negligence an excepted peril comes into operation and does damage, the excepted peril does not prevent him from acting carefully, and he is liable for damages directly flowing from his breach of his obligation to act carefully, though the breach acts through the medium of an excepted peril. It is a commonplace of mercantile law that if a peril of the sea is brought into operation by the carelessness of the shipowner or his servants, he is liable, though perils of the sea are excepted perils, unless he has also a clause excepting the negligence of his servants. In the same way, though the charterer has an exception of fire in his favour, he will be liable if the fire was directly caused by his servants' negligence, for it was not fire that prevented them from being careful. This disposes of the first defence ...

Paterson Steamships Limited v Canadian Co-operative Wheat Producers Limited [1934] AC 538, PC

Wheat was shipped on the appellants' steamship *Sarniadoc* under a bill of lading which incorporated the Canadian Water Carriage of Goods Act 1910. The vessel was stranded and the cargo lost during a gale. The Judicial Committee of the Privy Council held that the Act had to be considered in the light of the shipowner's liability at common law and the methods of limiting liability previously in vogue.

Lord Wright: ... It will therefore be convenient here, in construing those portions of the Act which are relevant to this appeal, to state in very summary form the simplest principles which determine the obligations attaching to a carrier of goods by sea or water. At common law, he was called an insurer, that is he was absolutely responsible for delivering in like order and condition at the destination the goods bailed to him for carriage. He could avoid liability for loss or damage only by showing that the loss was due to the act of God or the King's enemies. But it became the practice for the carrier to stipulate that for loss due to various specified contingencies or perils he should not be liable: the list of these specific excepted perils grew as time went on. That practice, however, brought into view two separate aspects of the sea carrier's duty which it had not been material to consider when his obligation to deliver was treated as absolute. It was recognised that his overriding obligations might be analysed into a special duty to exercise due care and skill in relation to the carriage of the goods and a special duty to furnish a ship that was fit for the adventure at its inception. These have been described as fundamental undertakings, or implied obligations. If then goods were lost (say) by perils of the seas, there could still remain the inquiry whether or not the loss was also due to negligence or unseaworthiness. If it was, the bare exception did not avail the carrier ...

But negligence and unseaworthiness of the carrying vessel might generally, by British law, be excepted by express words; in such a case, though the exception of perils of the sea (to take an instance) might not per se for the reasons stated on the facts, avail the carrier, yet he could rely on the exception of negligence or of unseaworthiness, as the case might be, when negligence or unseaworthiness had caused or contributed to the loss. One important object of the Acts under consideration was to limit the use of these general exceptive clauses ...

Notes

1   In *Kay v Wheeler* (1867) LR 2 CP 302, Exchequer Chamber, a consignment of coffee was shipped on the defendants' ship *Victoria*, for carriage from Colombo to London under a bill of lading in common form and containing the exceptions of 'the act of God, the Queen's enemies, fire, and all and every other dangers and accidents of the sea, rivers, and navigation, of what kind and nature soever'. The goods were damaged and partly eaten by rats during the voyage, despite the shipowner's efforts to avoid damage by employing a rat catcher before the ship sailed and equipping her with 'two cats and two mangoose, a species of Cingalese ferret, very destructive to rats'. The defendants argued that they were not common carriers and had used reasonable care, to which Chief Baron Kelly responded:

> in this case the defendants have entered into an express contract to deliver the goods in good condition, except in the four specified cases; and they are therefore liable unless the injury arose from one of the causes so excepted.

2 *Beaumont-Thomas v Blue Star Line* [1939] 3 All ER 127, 130

Scott LJ: The first point is this. In order to construe any exception of liability for events happening in the performance of the contract, where the words of the exception are not so clear as to leave no doubt as to their meaning, it is essential first to ascertain what the contractual duty would be if there were no exception. In the contract of a common carrier by land, or of a shipowner for the carriage of goods by sea, broadly speaking, the carrier is an insurer of the safe delivery of the goods. If they are damaged on the way, he is liable. That is his primary duty. There is also a secondary duty, however – namely, the duty to use skill and care. That duty comes into play in case of the carrier invoking some term of an exception clause as a protection against liability. In such a case, if the excepted peril has been occasioned by the negligence of the carrier's servants, the failure to perform the secondary duty debars him from reliance upon his exception. In the case of a carrier of passengers, no such double liability attaches. He is under a duty to use due skill and care, and no more. The absolute duty of the goods carrier to keep and deliver safely does not apply. This fundamental difference in the basic contract caused the common law courts of England during the last 100 years to make a difference in the interpretation of general words of exception from liability according as the contract to be construed was one imposing the double duty or only one duty ... In the case of the double duty, the courts have treated the exception as *prima facie* directed to the absolute undertaking of safe delivery, but as not applying to the performance of the duty of skill and care. On the other hand, in a contract where there was no duty except the duty of skill and care, the courts have construed the same words of exception in the opposite sense – namely, as directed to the duty of skill and care – for two simple reasons (i) that some meaning must be given, and (ii) that no other meaning than an exception of liability for negligence was left ...

3 Perils of the Sea. In *Thames and Mersey Marine Insurance Co v Hamilton, Fraser & Co* (1887) App Cas 484 Lord Macnaghten said that it was impossible define this expression. But it is clear that a peril or accident is required: something which is fortuitous and unexpected, not something 'due to ordinary wear and tear, nor to the operation of any cause ordinarily incidental to the voyage and therefore to be contemplated', (Lord Herschell, *Hamilton v Pandorf* (1887) App Cas 518 at 530). It has also been said that the peril must be a peril of the sea, not merely a peril on the sea. Perils of the sea 'are those which are peculiar to carrying on business on the sea' (Lord Esher MR, *Pandorf v Hamilton* (1886) 17 QBD 670, 675). Wind and waves are perils of the sea; but fire and lightning are not (Lord Bramwell, *Hamilton v Pandorf*, above, p 527). The accidental incursion of sea water into a vessel at a part of the vessel, and in a manner, where sea water is not expected to enter in the ordinary course of things, is a peril of the sea (Lord Wright, *Canada Rice Mills Ltd v Union Marine* [1941] AC 55, PC). Extraordinary violence of the wind or water is not essential: a collision is a peril of the sea (*The Xantho* (1887) 12 App Cas 503) and can

occur in fine weather. Nor is damage by wind or water necessarily required; overheating of cargo when ventilators are closed to avoid water damage is a peril of the sea. On the other hand, it has also been held that the explosion of machinery and the consumption of the cargo or the ship by rats all lack the necessary connection with the sea: *Thames and Mersey Marine Insurance v Hamilton* (1887) App Cas 484, 491; *Hamilton v Pandorf*, above, p 523. But if a rat eats part of a ship and the sea enters through the hole and harms the cargo, then the damage is done by a peril of the sea.

4　The expression 'perils of the sea' has been held to have the same meaning in a contract of affreightment and a marine insurance policy (*The Xantho*, above) and to describe a proximate cause of loss which may arise with or without negligence. Nevertheless, it has also been held that a shipowner cannot rely on these words in a bill of lading if the loss was the result of his own or his servants' negligence (*The Glendarroch* [1894] P 226; *The Super Servant Two* [1990] 1 Lloyd's Rep 1, CA). In *The Xantho* goods were shipped on the defendants' vessel at Cronstadt for carriage to Hull under bills of lading which were indorsed to the plaintiffs. The bills of lading contained exceptions for dangers and accidents of the sea. *The Xantho* collided with another vessel in fog and was lost. The plaintiffs brought proceedings for non-delivery. In the House of Lords, the appellant shipowners argued that since collision was a peril of the sea in a policy of insurance, it must also be a peril of the sea in a bill of lading. Lord Macnaghten (515):

> My Lords, in this case the bill of lading on which the question arises is in common form. In the usual terms it states the engagement on the part of the shipowner to deliver the goods entrusted to his care. At the same time it specifies, by way exception, certain cases in which failure to deliver those goods may be excused. So much for the express terms of the bill of lading. But the shipowner's obligations are not limited and exhausted by what appears on the face of the instrument. Underlying the contract, implied and involved in it, there is a warranty by the shipowner that his vessel is seaworthy and there is also an engagement on his part to use due care and skill in navigating the vessel and carrying the goods. Having regard to the duties thus cast upon the shipowner, it seems to follow as a necessary consequence, that even in cases within the very terms of the exception in the bill of lading, the shipowner is not protected if any default or negligence on his part has caused or contributed to the loss ...

5　Pirates have also long been regarded as a peril of the sea: *Pickering v Barkley* (1648) Style 132; *Morse v Slue* (1671) 1 Vent 190. Piracy is defined by the *Oxford English Dictionary* (compact edition) as:

> the practice or crime of robbery and depredation on the sea or navigable rivers etc, or by descent from the sea upon the coast, by persons not holding a commission from an established civilised state ...

In *The Andreas Lemos* [1982] 2 Lloyd's Rep 483, Staughton J held (in a marine insurance context) that: (1) piracy requires force or the threat of force and is committed when a crew are overpowered by force or terrified into submission; it does not include clandestine theft:

> It is not necessary that the thieves must raise the pirate flag and fire a shot across the victim's bows before they can be called pirates. But piracy is not committed by stealth (p 491);

and (2) piracy can be committed in territorial waters, although only if the ship in question is 'at sea' or if the attack on her can be described as a 'maritime offence' thus excluding attacks where the vessel or the attack cannot be so described because the vessel is in harbour or moored in a creek or river. Compare *Nesbitt v Lushington ('Restraint of Princes')*, below. See also SJ Hazelwood [1983] 2 LMCLQ 283. For the purposes of any proceedings in a UK court in respect of piracy, the definition of piracy in international law is that:

> Piracy consists of ... any illegal acts of violence or detention, or any act of depredation, committed for private ends by the crew or passengers of a private ship or a private aircraft, and directed – (i) on the high seas, against another ship or aircraft, or against persons or property on board such ship or aircraft; (ii) against a ship, aircraft, persons or property in a place outside the jurisdiction of any State ...

Section 26(1) and Schedule 5 of the Merchant Shipping and Maritime Security Act 1997.

6   Strikes. In *Williams Bros v Naamlooze Ventlootschap WH Berghuys Kolenhandel* (1916) 21 Com Cas 253, shipowners alleged that they had difficulty in maintaining their existing crew or in recruiting a new crew at Rotterdam for a voyage from Hull to Rouen because of the danger of submarine attack, Sankey J said:

> ... I think the true definition of the word 'strike', which I do not say is exhaustive, is a general concerted refusal by workmen to work in consequence of an alleged grievance.

In *The Laga* [1966] 1 Lloyd's Rep 582, the vessel was chartered on terms which provided that time lost through strikes which prevented or delayed discharge would not count against laytime. At Nantes, port labour refused to unload coal importing vessels, including the *Laga*, in an attempt to assist French miners who were on strike. Ships carrying other cargoes were unloaded in the normal way. McNair J:

> ... the word strike is a perfectly good, appropriate word to use to cover a sympathetic strike and a general strike and there is no need today to have any ingredient of grievance between those who are refusing to work and their employers ...

Tramp Shipping v Greenwich Marine, The New Horizon [1972] 2 Lloyd's Rep 314 concerned a vessel chartered for a voyage to St Nazaire with a fixed time for discharge. The charter also provided that time should not count during a strike or lockout of any class of workmen essential to the discharge. The normal course of events at the berth in question was for drivers of cranes and suckers to work round the clock, dividing the 24 hours of the day into three shifts. But when the vessel was ready to discharge, drivers were only working during the day shift in an attempt to improve conditions. The Court of Appeal held that there had been a strike.

Lord Denning MR:

> ... I think a strike is a concerted stoppage of work by men done with a view to improving their wages or conditions, or giving vent to a grievance or making a protest about something or other, or supporting or sympathising with other workmen in such endeavour. It is distinct from a stoppage which is brought about by an external event such as a bomb scare or by apprehension of danger.

Lord Denning MR also said that there could be a strike even though the workmen were not in breach of contract; Stephenson LJ thought there could not be a strike where the employer consents to the stoppage.

7   Robbers, thieves. The first word refers to a taking by force which the carrier could not reasonably resist. It does not include theft by pilferage: *De Rothschild v Royal Mail Steam Packet* (1852) 7 Ex 734. 'Thieves' was said in *Taylor v Liverpool and Great Western Steam* (1874) LR 9 QB 546 to be ambiguous and so was construed against the interests of the carrier to mean a taking by persons from outside the ship and not belonging to it (ie not crew, passengers or, perhaps, others on board with permission). In this context, theft may also require a violent taking: *Shell v Gibbs* [1982] 1 Lloyd's Rep 369, 373.

8   Barratry:

> Where a captain is engaged in doing that which as an ordinary man of common sense he must know to be a serious breach of his duties to the owners, and is engaged in doing that for his own benefit, then he is acting barratrously.

Hamilton J, *Mentz, Decker v Maritime Insurance* (1909) 15 Com Cas 17.

> It is of the essence of barratry that the shipowner is wronged, and he is not wronged when he consents.

Lord Sumner, *Samuel v Dumas* [1924] AC 431, 464.

In *Compania Naviera Bachi v Hosegood* (1938) 60 Ll L Rep 236, the crew prevented the discharge of the vessel in the course of a dispute with the owners over payment of wages. Cargo receivers incurred additional costs in discharging and in obtaining an injunction in an attempt to free the cargo. The bill of lading provided the owners would not be liable for loss or damage occasioned by barratry. Porter J held that the acts of the crew were barratry and that the receivers could recover from the owners neither the amount they spent in obtaining the injunction nor the additional costs of discharge:

> I do not think that for the purpose of barratry the commission of a crime is necessary; it must be a wilful act deliberately done, and to the prejudice of the owners. It is not necessary that the persons doing it should desire to injure the owners if in fact there is an intention to do an act which will

cause injury, even if the act be done to the benefit of persons who are guilty of barratry.

9   Restraint of Princes, Rulers, People. In an action on a policy of insurance, it was held that 'people' in the phrase 'restraints of Kings, princes and people' meant the ruling power of a country. It did not include a riotous mob who came on board the *Industry* in a port of refuge, seized control, stranded the vessel and forced the captain to sell part of the cargo to them at their price. Lord Kenyon CJ indicated that he would have been prepared to hold that the loss in this case was occasioned by a capture by pirates, but the policy did not cover that risk: *Nesbitt v Lushington* (1792) 4 T R 783.

Finlay v Liverpool and Great Western Steamship (1870) 23 LT 251, Court of Exchequer, related to cotton shipped at New York on the defendants' vessel *Idalio*. A bill of lading had been issued to the shipper and indorsed to the plaintiffs. Before the ship sailed, ownership of the cotton was claimed by a third party who alleged that the shipper had obtained the cotton by fraud and successfully sued the master in the New York Supreme Court to recover the goods. The plaintiffs brought proceedings for non-delivery. The bill of lading provided that the defendants would not be liable for non-delivery if delivery were prevented by the acts or restraints of princes or rulers. The Court of Exchequer held that 'acts or restraints of princes' referred to:

> the forcible interference of a state or of the government of a country taking possession of the goods *manu forti*, and do not extend to the legal proceedings which ... took place in the courts at New York. This is an action founded on contract, and I do not see how the act of any court of law, or any judicial tribunal, deciding that the defendants should hold possession of the goods and deliver them to the order of the true owners, can relieve the defendants, the shipowners, from performing their contract, unless such an act or decision of a court or judicial tribunal had been expressly excepted. This is an act of a court, which was not one of the exceptions, and not the 'act or restraint of princes and rulers', which was excepted.

Martin B (p 254), Channell and Cleasby BB, concurring.

The decision in *Rodoconachi v Elliott* (1874) LR 9 CP 518, Exchequer Chamber concerned silk, insured from Shanghai to London against risks including 'arrests, restraints, and detainments of all kings, princes, and people'. In the course of the insured journey, the goods arrived in Paris by train; they could not be forwarded to Boulogne because German forces had seized parts of the railway and, later, because they had laid seige to Paris; the goods became a constructive total loss. The court held that the goods were lost by restraint of kings or princes, even though there had been no specific action on the goods themselves. Restraint of goods included the restraint of persons having custody of the goods. The idea of indirect restraint was carried further in *Nobel's Explosives v Jenkins* [1896] 2

QB 326, a case in which the plaintiffs had shipped explosives on the defendants' vessel *Denbighshire* for carriage from London to Yokohama under a bill of lading. The vessel arrived in Hong Kong in the course of the voyage and on the same day war was declared between China and Japan. The defendants landed the explosives, which had become contraband of war, at Hong Kong and successfully continued the voyage to Yokohama with the remaining cargo. The plaintiffs brought proceedings for breach of contract to carry the goods to Yokohama. Mathew J (330):

> The main ground of defence was the exception in the bill of lading of 'restraint of princes, rulers or people'. A large body of evidence was laid before me to shew that if the vessel sailed with the goods on board she would in all probability be stopped and searched. It was certain in that case that the goods would have been confiscated, and quite uncertain what course the captors would take with the ship and the rest of the cargo. I am satisfied that if the master had continued the voyage with the goods on board he would have been acting recklessly. It was argued for the plaintiffs that the clause did not apply unless there was a direct and specific action upon the goods by sovereign authority. It was said that the fear of seizure, however well founded, was not a restraint, and that something in the nature of a seizure was necessary. But this argument is disposed of by the cases of *Geipel v Smith* (1872) LR 7 QB 404 and *Rodoconachi v Elliott* (above). The goods were as effectually stopped at Hong Kong as if there had been an express order from the Chinese government that contraband of war should be landed. The analogy of a restraint by a blockade or embargo seems to me sufficiently close. The warships of the Chinese government were in such a position as to render the sailing of the steamer with contraband of war on board a matter of great danger, though she might have got away safely. The restraint was not temporary, as was contended by the plaintiffs' counsel. There was no reason to expect that the obstacle in the way of the vessel could be removed in any reasonable time. I find that the captain in refusing to carry the goods farther acted reasonably and prudently, and that the delivery of the goods at Yokohama was prevented by restraint of princes and rulers within the meaning of the exception.

10 Negligence. In *The Raphael* [1982] 2 Lloyd's Rep 42, May LJ said that:

> ... if an exemption clause of the kind we are considering excludes liability for negligence expressly, then the courts will give effect to the exemption. If it does not do so expressly, but its wording is clear and wide enough to do so by implication, then the question becomes whether the contracting parties so intended. If the only head of liability upon which the clause can bite in the circumstances of a given case is negligence, and the parties did or must be deemed to have applied their minds to this eventuality, then clearly it is not difficult for a court to hold that this was what the parties intended – that this is its proper construction. Indeed, to hold otherwise would be contrary to common sense. On the other hand if there is a head of liability upon which the clause could bite in addition to negligence then, because it is more unlikely than not a party will be ready to excuse his other contracting party from the consequences of the latter's negligence, the clause will generally be construed as not covering negligence. If the

parties did or must be deemed to have applied their minds to the potential alternative head of liability at the time the contract was made then, in the absence of any express reference to negligence, the courts can sensibly only conclude that the relevant clause was not intended to cover negligence and will refuse so to construe it. In other words, the court asks itself what in all the relevant circumstances the parties intended the alleged exemption clause to mean.

11 Errors of navigation. In *Industrie Chimiche v Nea Ninemia Shipping, The Emmanuel C* [1983] 1 Lloyd's Rep 310 Bingham J applied the approach adopted in *The Raphael* (above) and concluded that 'errors of navigation' in clause 16 of the NYPE charter form meant 'non-negligent errors of navigation', reasoning that the clause might have been intended to protect the carrier against claims based on the strict liability of a sea carrier at common law, rather than negligent errors of navigation. This decision was approved by the Court of Appeal in *Seven Seas Transportation Ltd v Pacifico Union Marina Corp, The Satya Kailash and Oceanic Amity* [1984] 1 Lloyd's Rep 588.

12 Construction of exemption clauses:

> There is ... another rule of construction which one would one would bring to bear upon this charterparty, and that is, that one must see if this stipulation which we have got to construe is introduced by way of exception or in favour of one of the parties to the contract, and if so, we must take care not to give it an extension beyond what is fairly necessary, because those who wish to introduce words in a contract in order to shield themselves ought to do so in clear words.

Bowen LJ, *Burton & Co v English & Co* (1883) 12 QBD 218, 220.

13 The *TFL Prosperity*, a roll-on/roll-off vessel designed to carry trailers loaded with containers, was time chartered on the Baltime form for use in the charterers' liner service. The form was amended to specify in great detail the description of certain fixed structural features of the vessel; one provision was that the free height of the main deck should be 6.10 metres. In fact, at one critical point the free height was only 6.05 metres. As a result, a Mafi trailer double-stacked with 40ft containers could not be loaded on the main deck. Disponent owners claimed the protection of clause 13 of the form which provided:

> Responsibility and Exemption. The owners only to be responsible for delay in delivery of the vessel or for delay during the currency of the charter and for loss or damage to goods on board, if such delay or loss has been caused by want of due diligence on the part of the owners or their manager in making the vessel seaworthy and fitted for the voyage or any other personal act or omission or default of the owners or their manager. The owners not to be responsible in any other case nor for damage or delay whatsoever and howsoever caused even if caused by the neglect or default of their servants. The owners not to be liable for loss or damage arising or resulting from strikes, lockouts or stoppage or restraint of labour or vehicles (including the master, officers or crew) whether partial or general.

The House of Lords held that the first and second sentences of this clause were linked and that the second only exempted the defendants from claims of the type mentioned in the first, that is, claims relating to delay or loss or damage to goods on board. *Tor Line AB v Alltrans Group, The TFL Prosperity* [1984] 1 WLR 50.

14 Burden of Proof. In *The Glendarroch* [1894] P 226, CA, the plaintiffs were shippers and consignees of cement which was damaged by sea water and became valueless when the *Glendarroch* stranded on St Patrick's Causeway in Cardigan Bay. They brought an action against the defendants for non-delivery. The goods had been shipped under a bill of lading which excepted losses by perils of the sea, but did not relieve the carrier from liability for negligence. The Court of Appeal held that it was for the plaintiffs to prove the contract and for the defendants to prove loss by perils of the sea. If they did so, the burden of proving that the defendants were not entitled to the benefit of the exception on the ground of negligence was on the parties who alleged it, who in this case were the plaintiffs. Lord Esher MR:

> We have to treat this case as if the contract were in the ordinary terms of a bill of lading. The contract being one on the ordinary terms of a bill of lading, the goods are shipped on the terms that the defendant undertakes to deliver them at the end of the voyage unless the loss of the goods during the voyage comes within one of the exceptions in the bill of lading.
>
> ... When you come to the exceptions, among others, there is that one, perils of the sea. There are no words which say 'perils of the sea not caused by the negligence of the captain or crew'. You have got to read those words in by a necessary inference. How can you read them in? They can only be read in, in my opinion, as an exception upon the exceptions. You must read in: 'Except the loss is by perils of the sea, unless or except that loss is the result of the negligence of the servants of the owner'.
>
> That being so, I think that according to the ordinary course of practice each party would have to prove the part of the matter which lies upon him. The plaintiffs would have to prove the contract and the non-delivery. If they leave that in doubt, of course they fail. The defendants' answer is, 'Yes; but the case was brought within the exception – within its ordinary meaning'. That lies upon them. Then the plaintiffs have a right to say there are exceptional circumstances, viz, that the damage was brought about by the negligence of the defendants' servants, and it seems to me that it is for the plaintiffs to make out that second exception ...

15 The decision of the Court of Appeal in *The Glendarroch* was cited with approval in the House of Lords in *Joseph Constantine Steamship Line, Ltd v Imperial Smelting Corporation, Ltd, The Kingswood* [1941] 2 All ER 165, 172, HL. Viscount Simon:

> [I]t is ancient law that, by an implied term of the contract, the shipowner cannot rely on the exception [of perils of the sea] if its operation was brought about either (i) by negligence of his servants, or (ii) by his breach

of the implied warranty of seaworthiness. If a ship sails and is never heard of again, the shipowner can claim protection for loss of the cargo under the express exception of perils of the seas. To establish that, must he go on to prove (i) that the perils were not caused by negligence of his servants, and (ii) were not caused by unseaworthiness? I think clearly not. He proves a prima facie case of loss by sea perils, and then he is within the exception. If the cargo owner wants to defeat that plea, it is for him by rejoinder to allege and prove either negligence or unseaworthiness. The judgment of the Court of Appeal in *The Glendarroch* is plain authority for this ...

16 The *Torenia* was chartered to load a cargo of sugar at Guayabal, Cuba, for carriage to Denmark. In the course of the voyage she developed an uncontrollable leak when a fracture occurred in her hull; she was abandoned and later sank. The cargo was a total loss. The plaintiffs brought proceedings for non-delivery. At trial, the defendants submitted that, on the basis of *Joseph Constantine Steamship v Imperial Smelting Corp* (above) once they had proved the destruction of the goods by a peril of the sea (the fortuitous incursion of sea water), the burden passed to the plaintiffs to prove whatever fault they relied on. The plaintiffs' submission, said Hobhouse J:

> ... sought to treat the fact that the vessel's shell plating fractured in weather conditions of a type which ought to have been, and no doubt were, well within the contemplation and expectation of the vessel's owners and crew as liable to be encountered at some stage during the voyage as a wholly neutral occurrence which carried with it no implication of the unfitness of the vessel for that voyage. Whereas in the days of wooden ships or in the days when the design of steel ships and their construction was less well advanced or the forces they were liable to encounter were less well known and understood there may have been many instances where unexplained losses at sea gave rise to no inference of unseaworthiness, it will now be rare for such an inference not to arise in the absence of some overwhelming force of the sea or some occurrence affecting the vessel from outside. In the present case the shipowners, whilst proving the loss of the cargo, have proved also the loss of the vessel in conditions which ought not to have led to the loss of a seaworthy ship. Similarly in proving that the incursion of sea water was fortuitous they have proved that the structure of the vessel was defective.

Danske Sukkerfabrikker v Bajamar Compania Naviera [1983] 2 Lloyd's Rep 211.

Government of Ceylon v Chandris [1965] 2 Lloyd's Rep 204

The *Agios Vlasios* was chartered to carry rice in bags from Burma to Ceylon. In breach of contract, the charterers detained the vessel on demurrage at Colombo for 120 days. On completion of discharge it was found that some of the bags had been lost or damaged. An umpire found as facts that some of the bags were damaged by sweat and sea water, but that the proportions of damage attributable to each cause could not be stated; that the sweat damage was caused by lack of dunnage, by necessary restriction of ventilation and by the long duration of the voyage, but it was impossible to state the proportions of damage so caused; that the vessel was not adequately fitted with dunnage for the carriage of rice or with adequate tarpaulins. The charter excepted the owners from liability for loss or damage to goods unless caused by personal act or default or personal want of diligence to make the vessel seaworthy. A special case was stated for the opinion of the court.

Mocatta J: Mr Staughton (counsel for the charterers) put forward three propositions, which can more conveniently be reframed or re-stated as four in the following terms: First, the general rule is that the burden of proof rests upon the party claiming relief, be he plaintiff in an action or claimant in an arbitration, and this applies both to the liability of the other party and the damages recoverable. Secondly, in a claim for damages for breach of contract of carriage by sea, once it is proved that the goods in question were shipped in good condition (as is the case here) and that a known quantity of those goods is proved to have been delivered damaged, the carrier is liable to pay damages measured by the difference between the sound and damaged values of the goods at the date and place of delivery unless the carrier can establish, and the burden is on him to do so, that the goods were damaged through the operation of an exception in the contract of carriage. Thirdly, and this is a qualification upon the second proposition, if the carrier can only show that some part of the damage to the goods was due to a cause within the exception, he must also show how much of the damage is comprised in that part, otherwise he is liable for the whole. Fourthly, if part of the damage is shown to be due to a breach of contract by the claimants, then the general rule stated in the first proposition applies, and the claimant must show how much of the damage was caused otherwise than by his breach of contract, failing which he can recover nominal damages only.

The third of the above propositions is based on the well known *dictum* of Viscount Sumner in *Gosse Millerd Ltd v Canadian Government Merchant Marine Ltd* [1929] AC 223, at p 241. The dictum was *obiter*, but was applied by a Divisional Court in Admiralty in *White & Son (Hull) Ltd v 'Hobsons Bay' (Owners)*, (1933) 47 LI L Rep 207, and must have been the basis of innumerable opinions by counsel and solicitors. Mr Staughton did not seek to challenge its validity in this court but reserved his right to do so should the case go higher. His answer to it on the facts of this case was, however, this fourth proposition. Viscount Sumner was dealing with a case in which the carrier could only escape from his *prima facie* liability for the whole of the damage by relying upon an exception clause. No question arose of any part of the damage to the cargo having been caused by the plaintiffs fault or breach of contract. Viscount Sumner did not, therefore, have to consider the application of another principle, namely, that a plaintiff cannot recover damages from a defendant for the consequences of his own breach of contract with the defendant. Where such circumstances arise, and they must necessarily be infrequent, if the quantum of damage due to the plaintiffs own breach of contract cannot be ascertained, the latter principle must, in Mr Staughton's submission, apply to the exclusion of Viscount Sumner's *dictum*, otherwise the plaintiff would recover for the whole of the damage to the goods, notwithstanding that part of such damage, albeit unknown in extent, was due to his own breach.

Counsel for the shipowners was not able, as I understood him, to fault the logic or force of Mr Staughton's argument. He did, however, submit (and with this I have the greatest sympathy) that too ready an application either of Viscount Sumner's dictum or of counsel for the respondent's fourth proposition was to be deprecated because of their rigidity. Thus, on the one hand, a tribunal should be slow, in a case where the carrier has established that part of the damage is due to an excepted peril, to find that he has failed to adduce sufficient facts from which the quantum of such damage can be inferred. Similarly, on the other hand, when some part of a claimant's goods has undoubtedly been damaged by the carrier's breach of contract and some by the claimant's own breach of contract, the tribunal should be slow to award only nominal damages because of the paucity of primary facts from which the quantum of damages due to the claimant's own breach can be inferred. Juries, arbitrators, judges, and even the Court of Appeal (see, for example, *Silver v Ocean Steamship Company* [1930] 1 KB 416, *per* Scrutton LJ at p 429) have not infrequently to make what may in truth be little more than informed guesses at the quantum of damages by drawing inferences from the primary facts proved before them.

In my judgment, Mr Staughton's argument and his fourth proposition are well founded. In so deciding, I am applying no authority because there is none, but the result follows, in my view, from the principles involved. Moreover, if the final view of the facts here be that some part of the sweat damage to the cargo was due to the claimants' breach of contract in keeping the vessel on demurrage for 120 days and some part was due to the respondent's breach of contract in equipping the ship and caring for the cargo, and if there are no primary facts in evidence from which it is possible to draw an inference as to the quantum of damage attributable to either cause, it is, in my view, more consonant with the practice and tradition of the law that the claimants should fail to recover more than nominal damages than that the respondent should pay for the damage caused by her breach of contract and also that caused by the claimants. The law is not unfamiliar with cases where the plaintiff or the claimant fails owing to inability to discharge the burden of proof falling on him ...

CHAPTER 3

STATUTORY EXCLUSION AND LIMITATION OF LIABILITY

The 1976 International Convention on Limitation of Liability for Maritime Claims ('LLMC 1976') permits shipowners and salvors to limit their liability for certain claims to the amounts fixed by the Convention. The Convention is implemented in the UK by s 185 of the Merchant Shipping Act 1995, which re-enacts earlier legislation (s 17 of the MSA 1979). The Convention is set out in Part 1 of Sched 7 of the 1995 Act.

In 1996, a Diplomatic Conference convened in London adopted a Protocol to amend the 1976 Convention and, in particular, to increase the liability limits fixed in 1976. The Merchant Shipping and Maritime Security Act 1997 amends the 1995 Act and provides powers which will enable the revisions made by the Protocol to become law in the UK from a date to be fixed. The Protocol and other proposed amendments are shown in brackets in the following text.

1 MERCHANT SHIPPING ACT 1995

MERCHANT SHIPPING ACT 1995

Limitation of liability of shipowners, etc and salvors for maritime claims

Limitation of liability for maritime claims

185.—(1) The provisions of the Convention on Limitation of Liability for Maritime Claims 1976 as set out in Part I of Sched 7 (in this section and Part II of that Schedule referred to as 'the Convention') shall have the force of law in the United Kingdom.

(2) The provisions of Part II of that Schedule shall have effect in connection with the Convention, and subsection (1) above shall have effect subject to the provisions of that Part.

[*2A–E. Inserted by the Merchant Shipping and Maritime Security Act 1997, s 15(1). These subsections permit revision of the financial limits in Sched 7 and allow Sched 7 to be modified to take account of revisions of the Convention and the amending Protocol of 1996.*]

(3) The provisions having the force of law under this section shall apply in relation to Her Majesty's ships as they apply in relation to other ships.

(4) The provisions having the force of law under this section shall not apply to any liability in respect of loss of life or personal injury caused to, or loss of or damage to any property of, a person who is on board the ship in question or employed in connection with that ship or with the salvage operations in question if:

(a) he is so on board or employed under a contract of service governed by the law of any part of the United Kingdom; and

(b) the liability arises from an occurrence which took place after the commencement of this Act.

In this subsection, 'ship' and 'salvage operations' have the same meaning as in the Convention.

[(5) ...

Exclusion of liability

186.—(1) Subject to sub-s (3) below, the owner of a United Kingdom ship shall not be liable for any loss or damage in the following cases, namely:

(a) where any property on board the ship is lost or damaged by reason of fire on board the ship; or

(b) where any gold, silver, watches, jewels or precious stones on board the ship are lost or damaged by reason of theft, robbery or other dishonest conduct and their nature and value were not at the time of shipment declared by their owner or shipper to the owner or master of the ship in the bill of lading or otherwise in writing.

(2) Subject to sub-s (3) below, where the loss or damage arises from anything done or omitted by any person in his capacity of master or member of the crew or (otherwise than in that capacity) in the course of his employment as a servant of the owner of the ship, sub-s (1) above shall also exclude the liability of:

(a) the master, member of the crew or servant; and

(b) in a case where the master or member of the crew is the servant of a person whose liability would not be excluded by that subsection apart from this paragraph, the person whose servant he is.

(3) This section does not exclude the liability of any person for any loss or damage resulting from any such personal act or omission of his as is mentioned in Article 4 of the Convention set out in Part I of Sched 7.

(4) This section shall apply in relation to Her Majesty's ships as it applies in relation to other ships.

(5) In this section 'owner', in relation to a ship, includes any part owner and any charterer, manager or operator of the ship.

SCHEDULE 7

CONVENTION ON LIMITATION OF LIABILITY FOR MARITIME CLAIMS 1976

PART I

Chapter I

The Right of Limitation

Article 1

Persons entitled to limit liability

1. Shipowners and salvors, as hereinafter defined, may limit their liability in accordance with the rules of this Convention for claims set out in Article 2.

2. The term 'shipowner' shall mean the owner, charterer, manager or operator of a seagoing ship.

3. Salvor shall mean any person rendering services in direct connection with salvage operations. Salvage operations shall also include operations referred to in Article 2, paragraph 1(d), (e) and (f).

4. If any claims set out in Article 2 are made against any person for whose act, neglect or default the shipowner or salvor is responsible, such person shall be entitled to avail himself of the limitation of liability provided for in this convention.

5. In this Convention the liability of a shipowner shall include liability in an action brought against the vessel herself.

6. An insurer of liability for claims subject to limitation in accordance with the rules of this Convention shall be entitled to the benefits of this Convention to the same extent as the assured himself.

7. The act of invoking limitation of liability shall not constitute an admission of liability.

Article 2

Claims subject to limitation

1. Subject to Articles 3 and 4 the following claims, whatever the basis of liability may be, shall be subject to limitation of liability:

(a) claims in respect of loss of life or personal injury or loss of or damage to property (including damage to harbour works, basins and waterways and aids to navigation), occurring on board or in direct connection with the operation of the ship or with salvage operations, and consequential loss resulting therefrom;

(b) claims in respect of loss resulting from delay in the carriage by sea of cargo, passengers or their luggage;

(c) claims in respect of other loss resulting from infringement of rights other than contractual rights, occurring in direct connection with the operation of the ship or salvage operations;

(d) claims in respect of the raising, removal, destruction or the rendering harmless of a ship which is sunk, wrecked, stranded or abandoned, including anything that is or has been on board such ship;

(e) claims in respect of the removal, destruction or the rendering harmless of the cargo of the ship;

(f) claims of a person other than the person liable in respect of measures taken in order to avert or minimise loss for which the person liable may limit his liability in accordance with this Convention, and further loss caused by such measures.

2. Claims set out in paragraph 1 shall be subject to limitation of liability even if brought by way of recourse or for indemnity under a contract or otherwise. However, claims set out under paragraph 1(d), (e) and (f) shall not be subject to limitation of liability to the extent that they relate to remuneration under a contract with the person liable.

Article 3

Claims excepted from limitation

The rules of this Convention shall not apply to:

(a) claims for salvage or contribution in general average; [*The 1996 Protocol replaces this subparagraph with the following: 'claims for salvage, including, if applicable, any claim for special compensation under article 14 of the International Convention on Salvage 1989, as amended, or contribution in general average'.*]

(b) claims for oil pollution damage within the meaning of the International Convention on Civil Liability for Oil Pollution Damage dated 29 November 1969 or of any amendment or Protocol thereto which is in force;

(c) claims subject to any international convention or national legislation governing or prohibiting limitation of liability for nuclear damage;

(d) claims against the shipowner of a nuclear ship for nuclear damage;

(e) claims by servants of the shipowner or salvor whose duties are connected with the ship or the salvage operations, including claims of their heirs, dependants or other persons entitled to make such claims, if under the law governing the contract of service between the shipowner or salvor and such servants the shipowner or salvor is not entitled to limit his liability in respect of such claims, or if he is by such law only permitted to limit his liability to an amount greater than that provided for in Article 6.

Article 4

Conduct barring limitation

A person liable shall not be entitled to limit his liability if it is proved that the loss resulted from his personal act or omission, committed with the intent to cause such loss, or recklessly and with knowledge that such loss would probably result.

Article 5

Counterclaims

Where a person entitled to limitation of liability under the rules of this Convention has a claim against the claimant arising out of the same occurrence, their respective claims shall be set off against each other and the provisions of this Convention shall only apply to the balance, if any.

Chapter II

Limits of Liability

Article 6

The general limits

1. The limits of liability for claims other than those mentioned in Article 7 arising on any distinct occasion, shall be calculated as follows:

(a) in respect of claims for loss of life or personal injury,

    (i) 333,000 Units of Account for a ship with a tonnage not exceeding 500 tons,

    (ii) for a ship with a tonnage in excess thereof, the following amount in addition to that mentioned in (i):

for each ton from 501 to 3,000 tons, 500 Units of Account;

for each ton from 3,001 to 30,000 tons, 333 Units of Account;

for each ton from 30,001 to 70,000 tons, 250 Units of Account; and

for each ton in excess of 70,000 tons, 167 Units of Account,

(b) in respect of any other claims,

    (i) 167,000 Units of Account for a ship with a tonnage not exceeding 500 tons,

    (ii) for a ship with a tonnage in excess thereof the following amount in addition to that mentioned in (i):

for each ton from 501 to 30,000 tons, 167 Units of Account;

for each ton from 30,001 to 70,000 tons, 125 Units of Account; and

for each ton in excess of 70,000 tons, 83 Units of Account.

[The 1996 Protocol replaces Article 6, paragraph 1 of the Convention with the following text:

'1. The limits of liability for claims other than those mentioned in article 7, arising on any distinct occasion, shall be calculated as follows:

(a) in respect of claims for loss of life or personal injury,

    (i) 2 million Units of Account for a ship with a tonnage not exceeding 2,000 tons,

    (ii) for a ship with a tonnage in excess thereof, the following amount in addition to that mentioned in (i):

for each ton from 2,001 to 30,000 tons, 800 Units of Account;

for each ton from 30,001 to 70,000 tons, 600 Units of Account;

for each ton in excess of 70,000 tons, 400 Units of Account,

(b) in respect of any other claims,

    (i) 1 million Units of Account for a ship with a tonnage not exceeding 2000 tons,

    (ii) for a ship with a tonnage in excess thereof the following amount in addition to that mentioned in (i):

for each ton from 2,001 to 30,000 tons, 400 Units of Account;

for each ton from 30,001 to 70,000 tons, 300 Units of Account; and

for each ton in excess of 70,000 tons, 200 Units of Account.]

2. Where the amount calculated in accordance with paragraph 1(a) is insufficient to pay the claims mentioned therein in full, the amount calculated in accordance with paragraph 1(b) shall be available for payment of the unpaid balance of claims under paragraph 1(a) and such unpaid balance shall rank rateably with claims mentioned under paragraph 1(b).

4. The limits of liability for any salvor not operating from any ship or for any salvor operating solely on the ship to, or in respect of which he is rendering salvage services, shall be calculated according to a tonnage of 1,500 tons.

Article 7

The limit for passenger claims

1. In respect of claims arising on any distinct occasion for loss of life or personal injury to passengers of a ship, the limit of liability of the shipowner

thereof shall be an amount of 46,666 Units of Account multiplied by the number of passengers which the ship is authorised to carry according to the ship's certificate, but not exceeding 25 million Units of Account.

[*The 1996 Protocol increases this limit to 175,000 units of account and deletes the cap of 25 million units.*]

2. For the purpose of this Article 'claims for loss of life or personal injury to passengers of a ship' shall mean any such claims brought by or on behalf of any person carried in that ship:

(a) under a contract of passenger carriage, or

(b) who, with the consent of the carrier, is accompanying a vehicle or live animals which are covered by a contract for the carriage of goods.

Article 8

Unit of Account

The Unit of Account referred to in Articles 6 and 7 is the special drawing right as defined by the International Monetary Fund. The amounts mentioned in articles 6 and 7 shall be converted into the national currency of the State in which limitation is sought, according to the value of that currency at the date the limitation fund shall have been constituted, payment is made, or security is given which under the law of that State is equivalent to such payment.

Article 9

Aggregation of claims

1. The limits of liability determined in accordance with Article 6 shall apply to the aggregate of all claims which arise on any distinct occasion:

(a) against the person or persons mentioned in paragraph 2 of Article 1 and any person for whose act, neglect or default he or they are responsible; or

(b) against the shipowner of a ship rendering salvage services from that ship and the salvor or salvors operating from such ship and any person for whose act, neglect or default he or they are responsible; or

(c) against the salvor or salvors who are not operating from a ship or who are operating solely on the ship to, or in respect of which, the salvage services are rendered and any person for whose act, neglect or default he or they are responsible.

2. The limits of liability determined in accordance with Article 7 shall apply to the aggregate of all claims subject thereto which may arise on any distinct occasion against the person or persons mentioned in paragraph 2 of Article 1 in respect of the ship referred to in Article 7 and any person for whose act, neglect or default he or they are responsible.

Article 10

Limitation of liability without constitution of a limitation fund

1. Limitation of liability may be invoked notwithstanding that a limitation fund as mentioned in Article 11 has not been constituted.

2. If limitation of liability is invoked without the constitution of a limitation fund, the provisions of Article 12 shall apply correspondingly.

3. Questions of procedure arising under the rules of this Article shall be decided in accordance with the national law of the State Party in which action is brought.

Chapter III

The Limitation Fund

Article 11

Constitution of the Fund

1. Any person alleged to be liable may constitute a fund with the Court or other competent authority in any State Party in which legal proceedings are instituted in respect of claims subject to limitation. The fund shall be constituted in the sum of such of the amounts set out in Articles 6 and 7 as are applicable to claims for which that person may be liable, together with interest thereon from the date of the occurrence giving rise to the liability until the date of the constitution of the fund. Any fund thus constituted shall be available only for the payment of claims in respect of which limitation of liability can be invoked.

2. A fund may be constituted, either by depositing the sum, or by producing a guarantee acceptable under the legislation of the State Party where the fund is constituted and considered to be adequate by the Court or other competent authority.

3. A fund constituted by one of the persons mentioned in paragraph 1(a), (b) or (c) or paragraph 2 of Article 9 or his insurer shall be deemed constituted by all persons mentioned in paragraph 1(a), (b) or (c) or paragraph 2, respectively.

Article 12

Distribution of the fund

1. Subject to the provisions of paragraphs 1 and 2 of Article 6 and of Article 7, the fund shall be distributed among the claimants in proportion to their established claims against the fund.

2. If, before the fund is distributed, the person liable, or his insurer, has settled a claim against the fund such person shall, up to the amount he has paid, acquire by subrogation the rights which the person so compensated would have enjoyed under this Convention.

3. The right of subrogation provided for in paragraph 2 may also be exercised by persons other than those therein mentioned in respect of any amount of compensation which they may have paid, but only to the extent that such subrogation is permitted under the applicable national law.

4. Where the person liable or any other person establishes that he may be compelled to pay, at a later date, in whole or in part any such amount of compensation with regard to which such person would have enjoyed a right of subrogation pursuant to paragraphs 2 and 3 had the compensation been paid before the fund was distributed, the Court or other competent authority of the State where the fund has been constituted may order that a sufficient sum shall be provisionally set aside to enable such person at such later date to enforce his claim against the fund.

Article 13

Bar to other actions

1. Where a limitation fund has been constituted in accordance with Article 11, any person having made a claim against the fund shall be barred from exercising any right in respect of such a claim against any other assets of a person by or on behalf of whom the fund has been constituted.

2. After a limitation fund has been constituted in accordance with Article 11, any ship or other property, belonging to a person on behalf of whom the fund has been constituted, which has been arrested or attached within the jurisdiction of a State Party for a claim which may be raised against the fund, or any security given, may be released by order of the Court or other competent authority of such State. However, such release shall always be ordered if the limitation fund has been constituted:

(a) at the port where the occurrence took place, or, if it took place out of port, at the first port of call thereafter; or

(b) at the port of disembarkation in respect of claims for loss of life or personal injury; or

(c) at the port of discharge in respect of damage to cargo; or

(d) in the State where the arrest is made.

3. The rules of paragraphs 1 and 2 shall apply only if the claimant may bring a claim against the limitation fund before the Court administering that fund and the fund is actually available and freely transferable in respect of that claim.

Article 14

Governing law

Subject to the provisions of this chapter the rules relating to the constitution and distribution of a limitation fund, and all rules of procedure in connection therewith, shall be governed by the law of the State Party in which the fund is constituted.

Chapter IV

Scope of Application

Article 15

This Convention shall apply whenever any person referred to in Article 1 seeks to limit his liability before the Court of a State Party or seeks to procure the release of a ship or other property or the discharge of any security given within the jurisdiction of any such State.

PART II

PROVISIONS HAVING EFFECT IN CONNECTION WITH CONVENTION

Interpretation

1. In this Part of this Schedule any reference to a numbered article is a reference to the article of the Convention which is so numbered.

Right to limit liability

2. The right to limit liability under the Convention shall apply in relation to any ship whether seagoing or not, and the definition of 'shipowner' in paragraph 2 of article 1 shall be construed accordingly.

Claims subject to limitation

3. (1) Paragraph 1(d) of article 2 shall not apply unless provision has been made by an order of the Secretary of State for the setting up and management of a fund to be used for the making to harbour or conservancy authorities of payments needed to compensate them for the reduction, in consequence of the said paragraph 1(d), of amounts recoverable by them in claims of the kind there mentioned, and to be maintained by contributions from such authorities raised and collected by them in respect of vessels in like manner as other sums so raised by them.

(2) Any order under sub-paragraph (1) above may contain such incidental and supplemental provisions as appear to the Secretary of State to be necessary or expedient.

Claims excluded from limitation

4. (1) The claims excluded from the Convention by paragraph (a) of article 3 include claims under article 14 of the International Convention on Salvage 1989 as set out in Part I of Schedule 11 and corresponding claims under a contract. [*The deletion of this subparagraph is proposed*]

(2) The claims excluded from the Convention by paragraph (b) of article 3 are claims in respect of any liability incurred under section 153 of this Act.

(3) The claims excluded from the Convention by paragraph (c) of article 3 are claims made by virtue of any of sections 7 to 11 of the Nuclear Installations Act 1965.

[*Proposed addition: '(4) Claims for damage within the meaning of the International Convention on Liability and Compensation for Damage in Connection with the Carriage of Hazardous and Noxious Substances by Sea 1996, or any amendment of or Protocol to that Convention, which arise from occurrences which take place after the entry into force of an Order in Council made by Her Majesty under section 182B of the Act shall be excluded from the Convention'.*]

The general limits

5. (1) In the application of Article 6 to a ship with a tonnage less than 300 tons that article shall have effect as if:

(a) paragraph 1(a)(i) referred to 166,667 Units of Account; and

(b) paragraph 1(b)(i) referred to 83,333 Units of Account.

(2) For the purposes of Article 6 and this paragraph a ship's tonnage shall be its gross tonnage calculated in such manner as may be prescribed by an order made by the Secretary of State.

(3) Any order under this paragraph shall, so far as appears to the Secretary of State to be practicable, give effect to the regulations in Annex 1 of the International Convention on Tonnage Measurement of Ships 1969.

[*The LLMC 1976 allows states to regulate by national law the system of limitation of liability applied to ships of up to 300 tons. In June 1997 the Department of Transport invited views on a proposal to increase the UK limits in paragraph 5(1)(a) and 5(1)(b) to 1 million and 500,000 SDR for merchant ships.*]

Limit for passenger claims

6. (1) In the case of a ship for which there is in force a Passenger Ship Safety Certificate or Passenger Certificate, as the case may be, issued under or recognised by safety regulations, the ship's certificate mentioned in paragraph 1 of Article 7 shall be that certificate.

(2) In paragraph 2 of Article 7 the reference to claims brought on behalf of a person includes a reference to any claim in respect of the death of a person under the Fatal Accidents Act 1976, the Fatal Accidents (Northern Ireland) Order 1977 or the Damages (Scotland) Act 1976.

Units of Account

7. (1) For the purpose of converting the amounts mentioned in Articles 6 and 7 from special drawing rights into sterling one special drawing right shall be treated as equal to such a sum in sterling as the International Monetary Fund have fixed as being the equivalent of one special drawing right for:

(a) the relevant date under paragraph 1 of Article 8; or

(b) if no sum has been so fixed for that date, the last preceding date for which a sum has been so fixed.

(2) A certificate given by or on behalf of the Treasury stating:

(a) that a particular sum in sterling has been fixed as mentioned in sub-paragraph (1) above for a particular date; or

(b) that no sum has been so fixed for that date and that a particular sum in sterling has been so fixed for a date which is the last preceding date for which a sum has been so fixed,

shall be conclusive evidence of those matters for the purposes of those articles; and a document purporting to be such a certificate shall, in any proceedings, be received in evidence and, unless the contrary is proved, be deemed to be such a certificate.

Constitution of fund

8. (1) The Secretary of State may, with the concurrence of the Treasury, by order prescribe the rate of interest to be applied for the purposes of paragraph 1 of article 11.

(2) Any statutory instrument containing an order under sub-paragraph (1) above shall be laid before Parliament after being made.

(3) Where a fund is constituted with the court in accordance with article 11 for the payment of claims arising out of any occurrence, the court may stay any proceedings relating to any claim arising out of that occurrence which are pending against the person by whom the fund has been constituted.

Distribution of fund

9. No lien or other right in respect of any ship or property shall affect the proportions in which under article 12 the fund is distributed among several claimants.

Bar to other actions

10. Where the release of a ship or other property is ordered under paragraph 2 of article 13 the person on whose application it is ordered to be released shall be deemed to have submitted to (or, in Scotland, prorogated) the jurisdiction of the court to adjudicate on the claim for which the ship or property was arrested or attached.

Meaning of 'court'

11. References in the Convention and the preceding provisions of this Part of this Schedule to the court are references to the High Court or, in relation to Scotland, the Court of Session.

Meaning of 'ship'

12. References in the Convention and in the preceding provisions of this Part of this Schedule to a ship include references to any structure (whether completed or in course of completion) launched and intended for use in navigation as a ship or part of a ship.

Meaning of 'State Party'

13. An Order in Council made for the purposes of this paragraph and declaring that any State specified in the Order is a party to the Convention shall, subject to the provisions of any subsequent Order made for those purposes, be conclusive evidence that the State is a party to the Convention.

Notes

1   The principle of limited liability is that full indemnity, the natural right of justice, shall be abridged for political reasons.

Dr Lushington, *The Amalia* (1863) 1 Moo PC(NS) 471, 473.

2   (A)nciently the owners were, under the general law, civilly answerable for the total loss occasioned by the negligence or unskilfulness of the persons they employed; but the avowed purpose of the relaxation of this rule of law, was to protect the interests of those engaged in the mercantile shipping of the state, and to remove the terrors which would otherwise discourage people from embarking in the maritime commerce of a country, in consequence of the indefinite responsibility which the ancient rule attached upon them. It was a measure evidently of policy, and established by countries for the encouragement of their own maritime interests.

The Carl Johan 1821, cited in *The Dundee* (1823) 1 Hagg 113.

3   Early legislation in the field, beginning with the Responsibility of Shipowners Act 1733, aimed to remove the terrors by limiting the liability of owners in case of claims for loss or damage to cargo for which they were legally but not personally responsible. In s 503 of the Merchant Shipping Act 1894 (now repealed) this was done by allowing an owner to limit if he could prove that the loss had occurred without 'actual f*ault or privity' on his part. The words 'actual fault or privity' were said to infer something 'personal to the owner, something blameworthy in him, as distinguished from constructive fault or privity such as the fault or privity

of his servants or agents'. Buckley LJ, *Asiatic Petroleum v Leonard's Carrying* [1914] 1 KB 419, CA, affirmed [1915] AC 705.

4 One idea behind the LLMC 1976 was that the liability of a shipowner should be limited in all save exceptional circumstances to levels at which insurance cover was available at reasonable rates. Under the 1976 Convention the limit of liability is therefore significantly greater than under the previous law, but it is more difficult for a claimant to break the limit under article 4: *Caltex Singapore Pte Ltd v BP Shipping Ltd* [1996] 1 Lloyd's Rep 286, 288. Other motives for the adoption of Article 4 included the elimination of uncertainty as to the meaning of 'actual fault or privity' and the abandonment of what were seen by some to be unduly high standards of care required in certain jurisdictions: see generally Arthur M Boal [1979] 53 *Tulane LR* 1276.

5 Burden of proof under article 4:

The effect of articles 2 and 4 is that the claims mentioned in article 2 are subject to limitation of liability unless the person making the claim proves – and the burden of proof is now upon him – that the loss resulted from the personal act or omission of the shipowner ...

The Bowbelle [1990] 1 Lloyd's Rep 532, 535.

6 Article 4: recklessness. One of the provisions on which Article 4 was modelled (Boal [1979] 53 *Tulane L R* 1276) was the 1955 Hague Convention on Carriage by Air: Carriage by Air Act 1961. Article 25 of the Hague Convention is similar though not identical to Article 4 of the LLMC 1976. The leading English case on the meaning of Article 25 is *Goldman v Thai Airways* [1983] 1 WLR 1186, CA, where Eveleigh LJ said that:

... a person acts recklessly [when] he acts in a manner which indicates a decision to run the risk or a mental attitude of indifference to its existence ... One cannot therefore decide whether or not an act or omission is done recklessly without considering the nature of the risk involved ... recklessness involves an element of moral turpitude.

Purchas J said that:

Article 25 ... involves proof of actual knowledge ... at the moment at which the omission occurs, that the omission is taking place and that it does involve probable damage.

7 The claim of a cargo owner for damages consequent on the shipowner's breach of contract is a claim within Article 2 paragraph 1(a): *The Breydon Merchant* [1992] 1 Lloyd's Rep 373.

8 References:

Gaskell, N (ed), *Limitation of Shipowners Liability: the New Law*, 1986

Sheen, Sir Barry (1987) 18 *JMLC* 473

Griggs & Williams, *Limitation of Liability*, 2nd edn, 1991, London: Lloyd's of London Press

Mustill, Lord [1993] *LMCLQ* 490

Steel, D [1995] *LMCLQ* 77.

2 CONDUCT BARRING LIMITATION: COMPANIES

Meridian Global Funds Management Asia Ltd v Securities Commission [1995] 2 AC 500

This appeal to the Privy Council from the Court of Appeal of New Zealand related to an alleged breach by a company of the Securities Amendment Act 1988 (NZ). In the course of his judgment, Lord Hoffmann reviewed the case law dealing with s 503 of the Merchant Shipping Act 1894. Under that legislation, in identifying the individuals whose acts could be considered the acts of the company, the approach adopted by the courts was to look for 'the directing mind and will of the corporation'.

> **Lord Hoffmann**: ... The phrase 'directing mind and will' comes of course from the celebrated speech of Viscount Haldane LC in *Lennard's Carrying Co Ltd v Asiatic Petroleum Co Ltd* [1915] AC 705 at 713. But their Lordships think that there has been some misunderstanding of the true principle upon which that case was decided. It may be helpful to start by stating the nature of the problem in a case like this and then come back to Lennard's case later.

> Any proposition about a company necessarily involves a reference to a set of rules. A company exists because there is a rule (usually in a statute) which says that a *persona ficta* shall be deemed to exist and to have certain of the powers, rights and duties of a natural person. But there would be little sense in deeming such a *persona ficta* to exist unless there were also rules to tell one what acts were to count as acts of the company. It is therefore a necessary part of corporate personality that there should be rules by which acts are attributed to the company. These may be called 'the rules of attribution'.

> The company's primary rules of attribution will generally be found in its constitution, typically the articles of association, and will say things such as 'for the purpose of appointing members of the board, a majority vote of the shareholders shall be a decision of the company' or 'the decisions of the board in managing the company's business shall be the decisions of the company'.

> There are also primary rules of attribution which are not expressly stated in the articles but implied by company law ...

> These primary rules of attribution are obviously not enough to enable a company to go out into the world and do business. Not every act on behalf of the company could be expected to be the subject of a resolution of the board or a unanimous decision of the shareholders. The company therefore builds upon the primary rules of attribution by using general rules of attribution which are equally available to natural persons, namely, the principles of agency. It will appoint servants and agents whose acts, by a combination of the general principles of agency and the company's primary rules of attribution, count as the acts of the company. And having done so, it will also make itself subject to

the general rules by which liability for the acts of others can be attributed to natural persons, such as estoppel or ostensible authority in contract and vicarious liability in tort.

It is worth pausing at this stage to make what may seem an obvious point. Any statement about what a company has or has not done, or can or cannot do, is necessarily a reference to the rules of attribution (primary and general) as they apply to that company. Judges sometimes say that a company 'as such' cannot do anything; it must act by servants or agents. This may seem an unexceptionable, even banal remark. And of course the meaning is usually perfectly clear. But a reference to a company 'as such' might suggest that there is something out there called the company of which one can meaningfully say that it can or cannot do something. There is in fact no such thing as the company as such, no *ding an sich*, only the applicable rules. To say that a company cannot do something means only that there is no one whose doing of that act would, under the applicable rules of attribution, count as an act of the company.

The company's primary rules of attribution together with the general principles of agency, vicarious liability and so forth are usually sufficient to enable one to determine its rights and obligations. In exceptional cases, however, they will not provide an answer. This will be the case when a rule of law, either expressly or by implication, excludes attribution on the basis of the general principles of agency or vicarious liability. For example, a rule may be stated in language primarily applicable to a natural person and require some act or state of mind on the part of that person 'himself', as opposed to his servants or agents. This is generally true of rules of the criminal law, which ordinarily impose liability only for the actus reus and mens rea of the defendant himself. How is such a rule to be applied to a company?

One possibility is that the court may come to the conclusion that the rule was not intended to apply to companies at all; for example, a law which created an offence for which the only penalty was community service. Another possibility is that the court might interpret the law as meaning that it could apply to a company only on the basis of its primary rules of attribution, ie if the act giving rise to liability was specifically authorised by a resolution of the board or a unanimous agreement of the shareholders. But there will be many cases in which neither of these solutions is satisfactory; in which the court considers that the law was intended to apply to companies and that, although it excludes ordinary vicarious liability, insistence on the primary rules of attribution would in practice defeat that intention. In such a case, the court must fashion a special rule of attribution for the particular substantive rule. This is always a matter of interpretation: given that it was intended to apply to a company, how was it intended to apply? Whose act (or knowledge, or state of mind) was for this purpose intended to count as the act etc of the company? One finds the answer to this question by applying the usual canons of interpretation, taking into account the language of the rule (if it is a statute) and its content and policy.

... Against this background of general principle, their Lordships can return to Viscount Haldane. In the *Lennard's* case the substantive provision for which an attribution rule had to be devised was s 502 of the Merchant Shipping Act

1894, which provided a shipowner with a defence to a claim for the loss of cargo put on board his ship if he could show that the casualty happened 'without his actual fault or privity'. The cargo had been destroyed by a fire caused by the unseaworthy condition of the ship's boilers. The language of s 502 excludes vicarious liability; it is clear that in the case of an individual owner, only his own fault or privity can defeat the statutory protection. How is this rule to be applied to a company? Viscount Haldane rejected the possibility that it did not apply to companies at all or (which would have come to the same thing) that it required fault or privity attributable under the company's primary rules. Instead, guided by the language and purpose of the section, he looked for the person whose functions in the company, in relation to the cause of the casualty, were the same as those to be expected of the individual shipowner to whom the language primarily applied. Who in the company was responsible for monitoring the condition of the ship, receiving the reports of the master and ship's agents, authorising repairs etc? This person was Mr Lennard, whom Viscount Haldane described as the 'directing mind and will' of the company. It was therefore his fault or privity which s 502 attributed to the company.

Because Lennard's Carrying Co Ltd does not seem to have done anything except own ships, there was no need to distinguish between the person who fulfilled the function of running the company's business in general and the person whose functions corresponded, in relation to the cause of the casualty, to those of an individual owner of a ship. They were one and the same person. It was this coincidence which left Viscount Haldane's speech open to the interpretation that he was expounding a general metaphysic of companies. In *HL Bolton (Engineering) Co Ltd v TJ Graham & Sons Ltd* [1957] 1 QB 159 at 172 Denning LJ certainly regarded it as a generalisation about companies 'as such' when, in an equally well known passage, he likened a company to a human body:

> It has a brain and a nerve centre which controls what it does. It also has hands which hold the tools and act in accordance with directions from the centre.

But this anthropomorphism, by the very power of the image, distracts attention from the purpose for which Viscount Haldane said he was using the notion of directing mind and will, namely to apply the attribution rule derived from s 502 to the particular defendant in the case:

> For if Mr Lennard was the directing mind of the company, then his action must, unless a corporation is not to be liable at all, have been an action which was the action of the company itself *within the meaning of section 502*. [Original emphasis.]

The true nature of the exercise became much clearer, however, in later cases on the 1894 Act. In *HMS Truculent, The Admiralty v The Divina (owners)* [1951] P 1, an action to limit liability for damage caused by collision under s 503, which also required the owner of the ship which caused the collision to show that the casualty happened without his 'actual fault or privity', the offending ship was a Royal Navy submarine. Her collision with a fishing vessel had been caused by the inadequate system of navigation lights then carried by submarines.

Willmer J held that for this purpose the 'directing mind and will' of the Crown, which owned the submarine, was the Third Sea Lord, to whom the Board of Admiralty had entrusted the function of supervising such matters as the systems of navigation lights carried by warships. That function was one which an individual owner of a ship would be expected to fulfil. In *The Lady Gwendolen, Arthur Guinness, Son & Co (Dublin) Ltd v MV Freshfield (owners)* [1965] P 294 the owners of the ship were Arthur Guinness, Son & Co (Dublin) Ltd. The collision occurred because the master, in accordance with his custom, had taken his vessel laden with stout up the Mersey Channel to Liverpool at full speed in dense fog without more than the odd casual glance at his radar. Owning ships was a very subsidiary part of the company's activities. It had a traffic department which managed the ships under the general supervision of a member of the board who was a brewer and took no interest in the safety of their navigation. The manager of the traffic department knew about railways but took equally little interest in ships. The marine superintendent, one beneath him in the hierarchy, failed to observe that the master of *The Lady Gwendolen* was given to dangerous navigation, although, as Willmer LJ said ([1965] P 294 at 338):

> It would not have required any very detailed examination of the engine room records in order to ascertain that *The Lady Gwendolen* was frequently proceeding at full speed at times when the deck log was recording dense fog.

In applying s 503 of the 1894 Act, Sellers LJ said of the company ([1965] P 294 at 333):

> In their capacity as shipowners they must be judged by the standard of conduct of the ordinary reasonable shipowner in the management and control of a vessel or of a fleet of vessels.

The court found that a reasonable shipowner would have realised what was happening and given the master proper instruction in the use of radar. None of the people in the company's hierarchy had done so.

It is difficult to see how, on any reasonable construction of s 503, these findings would not involve the actual fault or privity of Guinness. So far as anyone in the hierarchy had functions corresponding to those to be expected of an individual owner, his failure to discharge them was attributable to the company. So far as there was no such person, the superior management was at fault in failing to ensure that there was. In either case, the fault was attributable to the company. But the Court of Appeal found it necessary to identify a 'directing mind and will' of the company and lodged it in the responsible member of the board or (in the case of Willmer LJ) the railway expert who managed the traffic department.

Some commentators have not been altogether comfortable with the idea of the Third Sea Lord being the directing mind and will of the Crown or the traffic manager being the directing mind and will of Guinness. Their Lordships would agree that the phrase does not fit the facts of *HMS Truculent* or *The Lady Gwendolen* as happily as it did those of the *Lennard's* case. They think, however, that the difficulty has been caused by concentration on that particular phrase rather than the purpose for which Viscount Haldane was using it. It will often be the most appropriate description of the person designated by the relevant attribution rule, but it might be better to acknowledge that not every such rule has to be forced into the same formula.

Once it is appreciated that the question is one of construction rather than metaphysics, the answer in this case seems to their Lordships to be as straightforward as it did to Heron J ...

SEAWORTHINESS

1 THE IMPLIED WARRANTY OF SEAWORTHINESS

Lyon v Mells (1804) 5 East 428

The defendant agreed to lighter a quantity of yarn owned by the plaintiffs from the quayside at Hull to a vessel in the dock. The lighter leaked and partly capsized, damaging the yarn. The defendant relied on a public notice which purported to limit the liability of lightermen in the Humber area.

> **Lord Ellenborough CJ:** ... In every contract for the carriage of goods between a person holding himself forth as the owner of a lighter or vessel ready to carry goods for hire, and the person putting goods on board or employing his vessel or lighter for that purpose, it is a term of the contract on the part of the carrier or lighterman, implied by law, that his vessel is tight and fit for the purpose or employment for which he offers and holds it forth to the public; it is the very foundation and immediate substratum of the contract that it is so: the law presumes a promise to that effect on the part of the carrier without any actual proof; and every reason of sound policy and public convenience requires it should be so.
>
> ... This brings me to consider the terms of the notice ... Every agreement must be construed with reference to the subject matter; and looking at the parties to this agreement (for so I denominate the notice) and the situation in which they stood in point of law to each other, it is clear beyond a doubt that the only object of the owners of the lighters was to limit their responsibility in those cases only where the law would otherwise have made them answer for the neglect of others, and for accidents which it might not be within the scope of ordinary care and caution to provide against. For these reasons, we are of opinion that the plaintiffs are entitled to have their verdict ...

Steel v State Line Steamship Company (1877) 3 App Cas 72

The plaintiffs were indorsees of a bill of lading in respect of wheat shipped at New York on the *State of Virginia* for carriage to London. The bill of lading contained an exemption for perils of the sea, whether or not caused by negligence of the crew. A lower deck port hole was insufficiently fastened; during the voyage water entered through the port and damaged the cargo.

> **Lord Blackburn:** ... I take it my Lords, to be quite clear, both in England and in Scotland, that where there is a contract to carry goods in a ship, whether that contract is in the shape of a bill of lading, or any other form, there is a duty on the part of the person who furnishes or supplies that ship, or that ship's room, unless something be stipulated which should prevent it, that the ship shall be fit for its purpose. That is generally expressed by saying that it shall be

seaworthy; and I think also in marine contracts, contracts for sea carriage, that is what is properly called a 'warranty', not merely that they should do their best to make the ship fit, but that the ship should really be fit. I think it is impossible to read the opinion of Lord Tenterden, as early as the first edition of Abbott on Shipping, at the very beginning of this century, of Lord Ellenborough, following him, and of Baron Parke, also, in the case of *Gibson v Small* (1853) 4 HLC 353 without seeing that these three great masters of marine law all concurred in that; and their opinions are spread over a period of about forty or fifty years ...

Now, my Lords, taking that to be so, it is settled that in a contract where there are excepted clauses, a contract to carry the goods except the perils of the seas, and except breakage and except leakage, it has been decided both in England and Scotland, that there still remains a duty upon the shipowner, not merely to carry the goods if not prevented by the excepted perils, but also that he and his servants shall use due care and skill about carrying the goods and shall not be negligent ... They may protect themselves against that, and they do so in many cases, by saying, these perils are to be excepted, whether caused by negligence of the ship's crew, or the shipowner's servants, or not. When they do so, of course that no longer applies.

My Lords, I think that exactly the same considerations would arise here as to the implied duty – the duty which, though not expressly mentioned, arises by implication of law – on the part of the shipowner to furnish a ship really fit for the purpose. If that duty is neglected ... the shipowner is liable. If, as is alleged here, a port gives way and the seas come in and wet the wheat, and if it is a consequence of the ship having started unfit that that mischief is produced, it seems to me to be exactly like the case of *Phillips v Clark* (1857) 2 CBNS 156 where negligence, not provided for by the contract, occasioned the breakage or the leakage, which it was said was an exception, but which the court determined was not an exception of which the shipowners could avail themselves, seeing that it was brought about by their negligence. So here I think that if this failure to make the ship fit for the voyage, if she really was unfit, did exist, then the loss produced immediately by that, though itself a peril of the seas, which would have been excepted, is nevertheless a thing for which the shipowner is liable, unless by the terms of his contract he has provided against it.

[Judgments were also delivered by Lord Chancellor Cairns, Lord O'Hagan, Lord Selbourne and Lord Gordon. The case was remitted to the Court of Session to ascertain whether on the facts the ship was seaworthy at the time she sailed and whether the loss was occasioned by the want of seaworthiness.]

2 TIME AT WHICH WARRANTY ATTACHES: THE DOCTRINE OF STAGES

The Vortigern [1899] P 140, CA

The owners of the steamship *Vortigern* sued the defendants to recover the freight due under a charterparty under which shipowners had agreed to carry a cargo of copra to Liverpool from Cebu, Phillipine Islands. The defence was that a portion of the defendants' cargo had been burned as fuel because insufficient coal had been loaded and that shipowners were in breach of the implied warranty of seaworthiness which attached to the contract of affreightment at the commencement of the voyage.

> **AL Smith LJ** (Lord Russell of Killowen CJ concurring): ... The question of law is what implied warranty of seaworthiness attaches to a contract of affreightment upon a voyage such as the present, when, from the necessity of the case, the ship cannot start upon the chartered voyage with an equipment of coal on board sufficient for the whole voyage, if the ship is to be a cargo-carrying vessel, which it clearly was the intention of all parties that it should be.
>
> It cannot be denied that the implied warranty which *prima facie* attaches to a charterparty such as the present is that the ship shall be seaworthy for the voyage at the time of sailing, by which is meant that the vessel shall then be in a fit state as to repairs, equipment, and crew, and in all other respects, sufficient to take her in ordinary circumstances to her port of destination, though there is no warranty that the ship shall continue seaworthy during the voyage.
>
> That coals are part of the equipment of a steamship I do not doubt, and if the voyage in this case had been an ordinary voyage, as to which there was no necessity, as regards taking in coal, for dividing it into stages, it cannot be denied that the steamship was unseaworthy when she started from Cebu on her voyage to Liverpool, for the simple reason that she had not then on board an equipment of coal sufficient to take her in ordinary circumstances to her port of destination.
>
> To obviate this difficulty – and a great difficulty it is in cases of long voyages of cargo-carrying steamships, for it is manifest that no cargo-carrying steamship can ever be seaworthy when she starts upon such a voyage as the present, by reason of the impossibility of her having on board such an equipment of coal as will be sufficient to take her to the port of destination – it has become the practice, by reason of the necessity of the case, for cargo-carrying steamship owners to divide these long voyages into stages for the purpose of replenishing their ships with coal, and thus, as far as practicable, complying with the warranty of seaworthiness which attached when the ship commenced her voyage.
>
> This practice was resorted to in the present case ... [W]hat was the implied warranty, if any – it matters not whether it is called a warranty or an absolute

73

condition – when the ship started upon the second stage from Colombo to Suez? Was there then an implied warranty that she had a sufficiency of coal on board for this second stage, that is, that she was seaworthy for that stage? This is the real point in the case. The shipowners assert that there is no such warranty, and that the sole obligation they were then under to the cargo owners was that their master and crew should not negligently omit to take in coal at Colombo, or during the stages subsequent to the first stage, and that, although the ship might during the second stage in this case have put into Perim and obtained coal, and although it might be negligence for the master and crew not to have done so, as negligence of the master and crew is excepted by the charterparty, the shipowners are not liable to the cargo owners for having burnt up their cargo for fuel as they did.

Now, reduce this contention of the shipowners into a concrete case, to see what in practice it amounts to. Take, for instance, the case of a cargo-carrying steamship commencing a voyage of some 5,000 miles in length, and the shipowners for coaling purposes, by reason of the necessity of the case, having to divide the voyage into five stages of 1,000 miles each. The shipowners must admit that they warrant to the cargo owners that their ship has a sufficiency of coal on board for the whole voyage, when it commences that voyage; but they assert that by reason of their dividing the voyage into stages, although for their own purposes, this warranty is thus cut down to the first stage of 1,000 miles, and that as regards the residue of the stages, 4,000 miles in all, there is no warranty that the ship has a single ton of coal on board, and that the only liability they are under to the cargo owners during the residue of the voyage is for the negligence, if any, of their master and crew, for not taking coal on board when they might have done so; and as the negligence of the master and crew is excepted by the charterparty, the shipowners are under no liability whatever to the cargo owners during the transit of the 4,000 miles. I am asked to hold that this is the true meaning of the charterparty in the present case. I certainly cannot do so. On the other hand, the contention of the cargo owners is that, whether the shipowners divide the chartered voyage into stages or not for coaling purposes, that has nothing to do with them; but if, from the necessity of the case, the shipowners do so, the cargo owners in no way abandon the undoubted warranty they have at the commencement of the voyage.

The only way in which this warranty can be complied with is for the shipowners to extend the existing warranty to the commencement of each stage, and I can see no reason why such a warranty should not be implied, and I have no difficulty in making the implication, for it is the only way in which the clear intention of the parties can be carried out, and the undoubted and admitted warranty complied with. It appears to me to be no answer to say that it is a warranty subsequent to the commencement of the voyage.

In my judgment when a question of seaworthiness arises between either a steamship owner and his underwriter upon a voyage policy, or between a steamship owner and a cargo owner upon a contract of affreightment, and the underwriter or cargo owner establishes that the ship at the commencement of the voyage was not equipped with a sufficiency of coal for the whole of the contracted voyage, it lies upon the shipowner, in order to displace this defence, which is a good one, to prove that he had divided the voyage into stages for coaling purposes by reason of the necessity of the case, and that, at the commencement of each stage, the ship had on board a sufficiency of coal for that stage – in other words, was seaworthy for that stage. If he fails in this he fails in defeating the issue of unseaworthiness which *prima facie* has been established against him. In each case it is a matter for proof as to where the necessity of the case requires that each stage should be, and I think that in the present case the necessity for coaling places at Colombo and Suez has been established.

This question of dividing up voyages into stages, as regards the warranty of seaworthiness, is by no means destitute of authority. There are numerous cases decided upon policies of marine insurance when the voyage is divided into stages, and there is also a case in this court relating to the warranty of seaworthiness upon a contract of affreightment when the voyage was divided into stages.

As regards the first class of cases it suffices to cite from a judgment of Lord Penzance, when delivering the judgment of the Judicial Committee of the Privy Council, consisting of himself, Sir William Erle, and Giffard LJ, in the case of the *Quebec Marine Insurance Co v Commercial Bank of Canada* (1870) LR 3 PC 234 where the numerous prior authorities relating to voyages consisting of different stages are referred to. Lord Penzance says:

> The case of *Dixon v Sadler* (1841) 5 M & W 405 and the other cases which have been cited, leave it beyond doubt that there is seaworthiness for the port, seaworthiness in some cases for the river, and seaworthiness in some cases, as in a case that has been put forward of a whaling voyage, for some definite, well recognised, and distinctly separate stage of the voyage. This principle has been sanctioned by various decisions; but it has been equally well decided that the vessel in cases where these several distinct stages of navigation involve the necessity of a different equipment or state of seaworthiness, must be properly equipped, and in all respects seaworthy for each of these stages of the voyage respectively at the time when she enters upon each stage, otherwise the warranty of seaworthiness is not complied with. It was argued that the obligation thus cast upon the assured to procure and provide a proper condition and equipment of the vessel to encounter the perils of each stage of the voyage, necessarily involves the idea that between one stage of the voyage and another he should be allowed an opportunity to find and provide that further equipment which the subsequent stage of the voyage requires; and no doubt that is so. But that equipment must, if the warranty of seaworthiness is to be complied with – that is, the warranty at the time of the commencement of the voyage – be furnished before the vessel enters upon that subsequent stage of the voyage which is supposed to require it.

Read into this judgment the word 'shipowner' in the place of 'the assured', and the judgment is in point in the present case.

There is no difference between the implied warranty of seaworthiness which attaches at the commencement of the voyage in the case of an assured shipowner and in the case of a shipowner under a contract of affreightment. In each case the shipowner warrants that his ship is seaworthy at the commencement of the voyage ...

3 NATURE OF THE WARRANTY: SEAWORTHINESS AND CARGOWORTHINESS

McFadden v Blue Star Line [1905] 1 KB 697

Cotton was shipped on the *Tolosa* from Wilmington to Bremen under bills of lading which provided, amongst other things, that the shipowners would not be liable for perils of the sea or accidents of navigation even when caused by negligence. In the course of loading, a ballast tank was filled with sea water, after which an attempt was made to close the sea-cock. It appeared that this had been done; but the sea-cock was defective and allowed water to continue to flow. The continued water pressure eventually forced a defective valve chest and water flowed from the valve chest through a sluice door which had not been properly closed and into the cargo hold where the plaintiffs' cotton was damaged.

> **Channell J:** I have to consider whether upon the facts of this case the shipowners are responsible for the damage to the plaintiff's cotton. Mr Bailhache rests his case upon a breach of the implied warranty of seaworthiness, or rather of the implied warranty that the vessel is fit for the reception of the goods and for carrying them upon the voyage in question. Now I think it is clear that ... that warranty is an absolute warranty; that is to say, if the ship is in fact unfit at the time when the warranty begins, it does not matter that its unfitness is due to some latent defect which the shipowner does not know of, and it is no excuse for the existence of such a defect that he used his best endeavours to make the ship as good as it could be made.
>
> And there is also another matter which seems to me to be equally clear – that the warranty of seaworthiness in the ordinary sense of that term, the warranty, that is, that the ship is fit to encounter the ordinary perils of the voyage, is a warranty only as to the condition of the vessel at a particular time, namely, the time of sailing; it is not a continuing warranty, in the sense of a warranty that she shall continue fit during the voyage. If anything happens whereby the goods are damaged during the voyage, the shipowner is liable because he is an insurer except in the event of the damage happening from some cause in respect of which he is protected by the exceptions in his bill of lading. His liability for anything happening after the ship has sailed depends, not upon there being a breach of a warranty that the ship shall continue fit, but upon his position as carrier. So, too, it is clear that the warranty of the ship being fit to encounter the perils of the voyage does not attach before she sails and while she is still loading her cargo. There is, of course, no warranty at the time the goods are put on board that the ship is then ready to start on her voyage; for while she is still loading there may be many things requiring to be done before she is ready to sail. The ordinary warranty of seaworthiness, then, does not take effect before the ship is ready to sail, nor does it continue to take effect after she has sailed: it takes effect at the time of sailing, and at the time of sailing alone.
>
> But Mr Bailhache contends that the warranty with which we are here concerned, namely, that the ship was fit to receive the goods, differs in this

respect from the warranty of fitness to encounter the perils of the voyage: he says that it is a continuing warranty, meaning thereby a warranty that the ship shall continue fit throughout the period of loading. Now there is very little authority about the warranty of fitness to receive the cargo; but when one comes to consider it as a matter of principle, I do not think there is much difficulty about it. In my opinion one must apply the rule which one would have to apply to the warranty of seaworthiness when the voyage is in stages. When a voyage is in stages the warranty is that the ship on starting on each particular stage is fit for that stage. Thus, if she is going to stop at an intermediate port, she must have sufficient coals to take her to that port, but she is not bound to have sufficient coals to take her the whole voyage. It is treated as a separate warranty for each stage of the voyage. I think one must apply exactly the same rule to the loading stage of a vessel whilst she remains in her port of loading. I think the warranty is that at the time the goods are put on board she is fit to receive them and to encounter the ordinary perils that are likely to arise during the loading stage; but that there is no continuing warranty after the goods are once on board that the ship shall continue fit to hold the goods during that stage and until she is ready to go to sea, notwithstanding any accident that may happen to her in the meantime. And the reason for so holding is precisely the same as that which exists with respect to the warranty of fitness to encounter the perils of the voyage; as soon as the goods are on board they are in the custody of the carrier, and he is liable for any accident which then happens because he is an insurer of them unless he is protected by some clause in his bill of lading.

In that view of the matter, then, I proceed to consider whether the facts of the present case shew a breach of the warranty of fitness to receive the cargo. If there was such a breach, I think it is clear that the exceptions in the bill of lading would not apply to exempt the defendants from liability; for *prima facie* words of exception are intended to exempt the shipowner only from his liability as a carrier, and not to affect the warranty that would otherwise be implied. An intention to exclude the warranty must be indicated by express words, and there are no such express words here. Now it is suggested by the plaintiff that there was a breach of the warranty in respect of each of the three apertures through which the water came. The sluice door in the bulkhead was left insufficiently screwed down, and if it had been left in that condition before the goods were loaded I think that that fact would have amounted to a breach of the warranty; for it was an aperture which in the ordinary state of things ought to have been closed except when it was being used, and it was imperfectly closed. It was not obviously left open, and was consequently a source of danger. Thus it is a breach of warranty of seaworthiness to go to sea with a porthole which is improperly closed but is believed to be closed, and which is in such a position that the defect cannot be remedied immediately and in time to prevent the damage being done: *Dobell v Steamship Rossmore Co* [1895] 2 QB 408. But here the opening and imperfect closing of the sluice door only took place the day before the damage happened, and long after the goods were on board. Therefore, in my opinion, it cannot amount to a breach of the warranty as I have interpreted it. The same observations apply to the insufficiently closed sea-cock. It was intended to be closed and was apparently closed, and was consequently in a dangerous condition. But that state of things also was brought about after the goods were on board, and consequently was not a breach of the warranty. Then we come to the defective packing of the valve chest. It may be that that is a defect which points to a certain amount of negligence on the part of the man who packed the joint, but it is immaterial for the present purpose to consider whether there was negligence or not, for, as I have already said, the warranty is ... an absolute warranty. The result shews that in fact there was a defect, in the sense that the packing was not as good as it ought to have been. It resisted the pressure during the three hours that the tank was being hardened up, but was insufficient to resist the subsequent pressure. That defect, unlike those in the sluice door and the sea-cock, existed before the plaintiff's goods were loaded. Whether a particular defect is sufficiently substantial to amount to a breach of the warranty must in all cases be a question of fact; but it is a question of fact which must be determined by certain rules. And the rule applicable to the present case is, I think, correctly stated in a passage in *Carver on Carriage by Sea*, s 18, where it is said that a vessel:

> must have that degree of fitness which an ordinary careful and prudent owner would require his vessel to have at the commencement of her voyage having regard to all the probable circumstances of it. To that extent the shipowner, as we have seen, undertakes absolutely that she is fit, and ignorance is no excuse. If the defect existed, the question to be put is, Would a prudent owner have required that it should be made good before sending his ship to sea had he known of it? If he would, the ship was not seaworthy within the meaning of the undertaking.

Applying that to this case, I cannot doubt that any prudent owner, if he had known that the joint would not resist something more than a three hours' pressure, would have at once ordered the joint to be remade. Therefore, it seems to me that I must hold that the defect was a substantial one, and that as it existed before and at the time of the loading of the goods it amounted to a breach of the warranty ...

A E Reed and Co Ltd v Page, Son and East [1927] 1 KB 743, CA

The plaintiffs were the consignees of 500 tons of wood pulp which arrived at Erith on *The Borgholm*. They employed the defendants to lighter it to Nine Elms. One of the defendants' barges, *The Jellicoe*, had a carrying capacity of 170 tons; 190 tons were put on board. While she was lying alongside the steamer waiting for a tug to tow her to Nine Elms she sank and her cargo was lost. The plaintiffs succeeded in an action for damages. The defendants appealed.

> **Scrutton LJ:** I agree that the appeal should be dismissed, and substantially I am in agreement with the very careful judgment of Roche J. I only add some words of my own as to the law, in deference to the careful and elaborate argument that has been addressed to us by counsel for the appellants.
>
> There is some confusion in the authorities as to the warranty of seaworthiness, due, I think, to two causes: first, the word 'seaworthiness' is used in two senses: (1) fitness of the ship to enter on the contemplated adventure of navigation, and (2) fitness of the ship to receive the contemplated cargo, as a carrying receptacle. A ship may be unfit to carry the contemplated cargo,

because, for instance, she has not sufficient means of ventilation, and yet be quite fit to make the contemplated voyage, as a ship. Secondly, the fact that there are these two meanings of seaworthiness according to different stages of the adventure, has led to some confusion in statements.

As was said in *Cohn v Davidson* (1877) 2 QBD 455:

> Seaworthiness is well understood to mean that measure of fitness which the particular voyage or particular stage of the voyage requires.

A ship, when she sails on her voyage, must be seaworthy for that voyage, that is, fit to encounter the ordinary perils which a ship would encounter on such a voyage. But she need not be fit for the voyage before it commences, and when she is loading in port. It is enough if, before she sails, she has completed her equipment and repair. But she must be fit as a ship for the ordinary perils of lying afloat in harbour, waiting to sail. She must, in my view, be fit as a ship, as distinguished from a carrying warehouse, at each stage of her contract adventure, which may, as in *Cohn v Davidson*, commence before loading. And she may as a ship after loading be unfit to navigate because of her stowage, which renders her unsafe as a ship. *Kopitoff v Wilson* (1876) 1 QBD 377 is a good example of this. There armour plates were so stowed that there was danger of their going through the ship's side, and they did. As Lord Sumner said in *Elder, Dempster & Co v Paterson, Zochonis & Co* [1924] AC 522, 561:

> Bad stowage, which endangers the safety of the ship, may amount to unseaworthiness, of course, but bad stowage, which affects nothing but the cargo damaged by it, is bad stowage and nothing more, and still leaves the ship seaworthy for the adventure, even though the adventure be the carrying of that cargo.

Wade v Cockerline (1905) 10 Com Cas 115 illustrates the latter part of the quotation. The ship was quite fit as a ship to carry the cargo she had on board if properly stowed; the bad stowage did not make the ship unfit as a ship, but did endanger the cargo.

Looked at from the point of view of a ship to sail the sea, the highest measure of liability will be when she starts on her sea voyage, and this is often spoken of as the stage when the warranty attaches; but what is meant is that it is the time when that highest measure of liability attaches. There are previous stages of seaworthiness as a ship, applicable to proceeding to loading port, loading, and waiting to sail when loading is completed.

On the other hand, the highest measure of liability as a cargo-carrying adventure, that is, of 'cargoworthiness', is when cargo is commenced to be loaded. It has been decided that if at this stage the ship is fit to receive her contract cargo, it is immaterial that when she sails on her voyage, though fit as a ship to sail, she is unfit by reason of stowage to carry her cargo safely. Thus, in *The Thorsa* [1916] P 257, where the ship sailed with chocolate and cheese stowed together, so that the chocolate was damaged, the Court of Appeal declined to hold the ship unseaworthy. That case was approved in *Elder Dempster's* case in the House of Lords, where stowage of oil in casks, so that it was damaged by the weight of cargo on top, the stowage not affecting the sailing of the ship, was held not to be unseaworthiness for sailing. This limitation of the warranty of cargoworthiness is expressly made, because negligent stowage of a seaworthy ship is something happening after the warranty of cargoworthiness has been complied with, and, so long as the negligent stowage does not make the ship unseaworthy as a ship, does not affect a warranty which has already been complied with.

It was argued that the doctrine of stages was only a question of difference of equipment, and that overloading was not equipment. But damages unrepaired at the commencement of a new stage, collision during loading, and starting on the voyage with that damage unrepaired, may obviously be unseaworthiness at the commencement of the voyage stage. I see no reason for defining stages only by difference of equipment.

Applying the above statement of the law to the facts of the present case: the barge was sent to the ship's side to carry 170 tons, and she was fit to carry that quantity. The warranty of cargoworthiness was complied with when loading commenced. But then 190 tons were put into her, some 14% more than her proper load. With that cargo in, she had a dangerously low freeboard in calm water. I think at any rate one of her gunwales was awash, and water could continuously enter through cracks, which would be only an occasional source of leakage if she were properly loaded. She had to lie so loaded for some unascertained time in the river till a tug came. The ship was not bound to let the barge lie moored to the ship's side. She might have to navigate under oars to a barge road. She was exposed to all the wash of passing vessels, and the more water she took on board, the more dangerous she would become. It is clear that she was quite unfit to lie in the river for any time exposed to the wash of passing vessels and the natural 'send' of the water. It is still clearer that she was quite unfit to be towed, and that she was in such a condition that she would soon go to the bottom. I am clearly of opinion that the barge was unseaworthy as a barge from the time loading finished, unfit to lie in the river, and still more unfit to be towed. I observe with surprise the suggestion that the surplus of 115 bales might have been put back on the ship. What possible obligation the ship, which had delivered to a barge cargo which the bargeman said she could take, and had got a receipt for it, was under to hoist back by ship's steam and labour 115 bales, or 20 tons, and leave them about on the ship's deck, I cannot understand.

I accept the view of Channell J in *McFadden v Blue Star Line* that the warranty of cargoworthiness, if complied with at the commencement of a stage, is not continuous during the stage, but this view does not negative the position that at the commencement of a new stage of the adventure there is a renewed warranty of seaworthiness as a ship. It seems to me clear that there would be a renewed warranty when the towage started, and that this overloading would be a breach of the warranty. If the leaks found by Channell J in the *Blue Star Line* case had admitted so much water that the safety of the ship was endangered, and if the leaks were incapable of being remedied on the voyage, there would clearly have been a breach of the warranty of seaworthiness as a ship, on sailing on the voyage. It seems equally clear that if an overloaded barge, seaworthy in the calm waters of a dock, went out into the river to wait for a tug, there would be a renewed warranty of fitness to navigate and wait, which would be broken by overloading rendering the barge unfit to lie waiting in the river. And I think in the present case, when the loading was finished and the man in charge, apparently in the ordinary course of his business, left her unattended in the river waiting for a tug, and unfit in fact either to lie in the river or be towed, there was a new stage of the adventure, a new warranty of fitness for that stage, and a breach of that warranty which prevented the exceptions from applying.

[Lord Hewart CJ and Bankes LJ delivered judgments in favour of dismissing the appeal on substantially the same grounds.]

4 UNSEAWORTHINESS OR BAD STOWAGE?

Elder, Dempster and Co Ltd v Paterson, Zochonis and Co Ltd [1924] AC 522

Viscount Cave: My Lords, the appellants Elder, Dempster & Co Ltd, who are managers for the appellants the African Steam Ship Company and the British and African Steam Navigation Company Ltd, run to the West African ports a line of cargo steamers which carry West African produce. These vessels have their holds fitted with 'tween decks, so that goods stored in the lower part of the hold may be relieved from the weight of those stored in the upper part. The appellants Elder, Dempster & Co, requiring an additional vessel for their West African trade, chartered from the appellants the Griffiths Lewis Steam Navigation Company Ltd (whom I will refer to as 'the owners'), the steamship *Grelwen*, a ship of the Isherwood type containing deep holds but no 'tween decks. The *Grelwen* proceeded to the Sherbro River, where she loaded from the respondents Paterson, Zochonis & Co Ltd, 297 casks or butts of palm oil, which were stowed in two or three tiers at the bottom of holds 2, 3 and 4. She also loaded there from the respondents and other shippers about 51,800 bags of palm kernels, which were stowed partly over the casks of palm oil in holds 2 and 4 (thus completely filling those holds) and partly in other parts of the ship. The vessel then proceeded to the port of Konakri, where she loaded from the respondents a further 147 butts of palm oil, which were stowed at the bottom of No 3 hold, and also loaded from the respondents and others about 11,400 more bags of palm kernels, which were stowed partly over the palm oil in No 3 hold (thus filling that hold) and partly elsewhere. She also loaded some piassava and other miscellaneous produce, which was stowed in the space between the main and shelter decks.

When the vessel arrived at Hull, which was her destination, it was found that the casks and butts of palm oil in holds 2, 3 and 4 had been crushed by the palm kernels stored above them, which were very heavy – it was stated in evidence that each cask had to carry 64 bags of palm kernels or nearly six tons in weight and the greater part of the oil was lost or damaged. The casks must have begun to give way immediately after the palm kernels were stowed above them; for the log shows that before the vessel left the Sherbro River she had three feet of palm oil in the bilge well of No 2 hold, and that before she left Konakri the same thing had happened in hold No 3; but it is possible that the leakage continued after the vessel left port and was intensified by the rolling of the ship.

The respondents accordingly commenced this action against the appellants, claiming damages for breach of the contract entered into by the bills of lading under which the palm oil was shipped, or alternatively for negligence or breach of duty. The defendants at the trial attempted to prove that the casks and butts were frail or leaky; but this attempt failed, and it is not now denied that the damage was caused by the altogether unreasonable and excessive weight placed upon the casks. This being so, the contest resolved itself into the question whether the damage was due to bad stowage, or to the fact that the vessel was structurally unfit or unseaworthy for the carriage of the palm oil by reason of the depth of her holds and the absence of 'tween decks. It was not denied that if the damage was due to bad stowage the charterers are protected against liability by the conditions contained in the bills of lading; but if it was due to unseaworthiness, then it was contended (and I think rightly) that the charterers were not protected by any of the conditions of the bills of lading and were liable to make good the damage ...

The general principles which should govern the decision are not in doubt. It is well settled that a shipowner or charterer who contracts to carry goods by sea thereby warrants, not only that the ship in which he proposes to carry them shall be seaworthy in the ordinary sense of the word – that is to say, that she shall be tight, staunch and strong, and reasonably fit to encounter whatever perils may be expected on the voyage – but also that both the ship and her furniture and equipment shall be reasonably fit for receiving the contract cargo and carrying it across the sea. The latter obligation, which is sometimes referred to as a warranty of seaworthiness for the cargo, was formulated by Lord Ellenborough in the year 1804: see *Lyon v Mells* (1804) 5 East 428, and was affirmed by this House in *Steel v State Line Steamship Co* (above) and *Gilroy, Sons & Co v Price & Co* [1893] AC 56. The rule, as it applies to equipment, is well illustrated by such cases as *Owners of Cargo on Ship Maori King v Hughes* [1895] 2 QB 550, where a ship with defective refrigerating machinery was held 'unseaworthy' for a cargo of frozen meat; and *Queensland National Bank v Peninsular and Oriental Steam Navigation Co* [1898] 1 QB 567, where a ship with a bullion room not reasonably fit to resist thieves was held 'unseaworthy' for a consignment of bullion. Reference may also be made to *Hogarth v Walker* [1899] 2 QB 401, where it was said by Bigham J and A L Smith LJ that a ship without dunnage mats (which are usually laid on the floor of a grain ship to protect the grain from being damaged by wet) was unseaworthy for the carriage of a cargo of wheat. It is hardly necessary to add that unseaworthiness and bad stowage are two different things. There are cases, such as *Kopitoff v Wilson* (1876) 1 QBD 377, where, a ship having been injured in consequence of bad stowage, the warrant of seaworthiness of the ship has been held to be broken; but in such cases it is the unseaworthiness caused by bad stowage and not the bad stowage itself which constitutes the breach of warranty. There is no rule that, if two parcels of cargo are so stowed that one can injure the other during the course of the voyage, the ship is unseaworthy: *per* Swinfen Eady LJ in *The Thorsa* [1916] P 257.

Applying these principles to the present case, I have come to the conclusion that the damage complained of was not due to unseaworthiness but to improper stowage. If the fitness or unfitness of the ship is to be ascertained (as was held in *McFadden v Blue Star Line* (above)) at the time of loading, there can be no doubt about the matter. At the moment when the palm oil was loaded the *Grelwen* was unquestionably fit to receive and carry it. She was a well built and well found ship, and lacked no equipment necessary for the carriage of palm oil; and if damage arose, it was due to the fact that after the casks of oil had been stowed in the holds the master placed upon them a weight which no casks could be expected to bear. Whether he could have stowed the cargo in a different way without endangering the safety of the ship is a matter upon which the evidence is conflicting; but if that was impossible, he could have refused to accept some part of the kernels and the oil would then have travelled safely. No doubt that course might have rendered the voyage less profitable to the charterers, but that appears to me for present purposes to be immaterial. The important thing is that at the time of loading the palm oil the ship was fit to receive and carry it without injury; and if she did not do so this was due not to any unfitness in the ship or her equipment, but to another cause.

But it was argued that an owner or charterer loading cargo is to be deemed to warrant the fitness of his ship to receive and carry it, not only at the moment of loading, but also at the time when she sails from the port, and that at the moment when the *Grelwen* left each of her ports of departure she was unfit without 'tween decks to carry the cargo which had then been placed in her holds. My Lords, I think there is some authority for the proposition that the implied warranty of 'seaworthiness for the cargo' extends to fitness for the cargo not only at the time of loading, but also at the time of sailing: see *Cohn v Davidson* (1877) 2 QBD 455, and the observations of Phillimore LJ in *The Thorsa* (above). But it is unnecessary to pursue the point, for the proposition if established will not avail the present respondents. The evidence of the log is conclusive to show that the injury to the casks was caused at or immediately after the time when the cargo was loaded and before the ship sailed, and accordingly that it was not due to any unseaworthiness at the time of sailing. And in any case nothing occurred between the time when the oil was loaded and the time when the ship sailed to make the ship structurally less fit to carry the oil; and it is with reference to the contract cargo – namely, the oil – that the question of fitness must be considered.

It was further argued that, as all the charterers' own ships engaged in the West African trade were fitted with 'tween decks, that equipment must be considered to be reasonably necessary for any vessel engaged in that trade. I do not think that any such universal rule can be properly laid down. It cannot be assumed that every ship running to the West African coast will bring back a cargo of palm oil and palm kernels, or that if she does so it will always be necessary to stow them together in one hold. The *Grelwen*, though without 'tween decks, could have carried a full cargo of West African goods without the oil, or could have carried the oil without the heavy cargo laid upon it. If the oil could not be stowed anywhere except at the bottom of the holds, the master could (as the evidence shows) have stowed four tiers of casks in each hold, and could have utilized the space above them for light cargo or could have left it empty; and the fact that he did not choose to take either of these courses is not sufficient to condemn the ship as unseaworthy.

On this view it becomes unnecessary to consider whether, in the event of unseaworthiness being found, the conditions of the bills of lading would have been sufficient to protect the charterers from liability. It is enough to say that, in my opinion, they are not sufficient for that purpose ...

[Lord Sumner also delivered a full reasoned judgment, with which Lord Dunedin agreed, in which he concluded that the *Grelwen* was not unseaworthy; Lord Carson agreed with both Viscount Cave and Lord Sumner. Lord Finlay dissented on the issue of seaworthiness. On another aspect of this case, see *The Mahkutai*, Chapter 6, Bill of Lading as a Contract.]

5 UNSEAWORTHINESS: NOTES

Competence of crew[1]

Standard Oil v Clan Line [1924] AC 100

Lord Atkinson (at 120): ... It is not disputed, I think, that a ship may be rendered unseaworthy by the inefficiency of the master who commands her. Does not that principle apply where the master's inefficiency consists, whatever his general efficiency may be, in his ignorance as to how his ship may, owing to the peculiarities of her structure, behave in circumstances likely to be met with on an ordinary ocean voyage? There cannot be any difference in principle, I think, between disabling want of skill and disabling want of knowledge. Each equally renders the master unfit and unqualified to command, and therefore makes the ship he commands unseaworthy. And the owner who withholds from the master the necessary information should, in all reason, be as responsible for the result of the master's ignorance as if he deprived the latter of the general skill and efficiency he presumably possessed ...

Lord Parmoor (at 127): ... In the case under appeal I am unable to come to any other conclusion than that a vessel, which requires special precautions of an unusual character to be taken in the maintenance of a sufficient water ballast to ensure conditions of stability which would not be known to a captain of ordinary skill and experience, and which have not been brought to his notice, although they had been specifically indicated to the shipowners in instructions sent to them from the shipbuilders, is not manned so as to be seaworthy, and that there was a duty on the respondents to have brought such instructions to the notice of the captain ...

Lack of necessary documents

In *Toepfer v Tossa Marine, The Derby* [1985] 2 Lloyd's Rep 325, CA, the vessel was chartered on the NYPE form. Line 22 of the charter provided 'vessel on

---

1   See White, R [1995] *LMCLQ* 221.

her delivery to be ready to receive cargo ... and in every way fitted for the service'. The vessel was delayed at Leixoes in Portugal when the ITF (an international workers organisation) discovered the vessel did not have and was not qualified to receive an ITF 'blue card', because the crew were not being paid at European rates.

Lord Justice Croom-Johnson and **Sir Denys Buckley** agreed with **Lord Justice Kerr**: ... The context in which the words 'in every way fitted for the service' occur shows that these words relate primarily to the physical state of the vessel. However, the authorities also show that their scope is wider, in at least two respects. First, in *Hongkong Fir Shipping Co Ltd v Kawasaki Kisen Kaisha Ltd* [1962] 2 QB 26, the words 'she being in every way fitted for ordinary cargo service' in the Baltime form of time charter were treated as forming part of an express warranty that the vessel was seaworthy, and it was held that this warranty required the provision of a sufficient and competent crew to operate the vessel for the purposes of the charter service. I accept that precisely the same reasoning applies to the words 'in every way fitted for the service' in the present case. To that extent, therefore, these words go beyond the purely physical state of the vessel as such. However, I cannot see any basis for any further enlargement of the scope of these words by extracting from them a warranty that the rates of pay and conditions of employment of the crew, with which they expressly declared themselves to be satisfied, must also comply with the requirements, not of any law which is relevant to the vessel, her crew or the vessel's operation under the charter, but also of a self-appointed and extra-legal organization such as the ITF. In my view this is not a meaning which these words can properly bear, let alone in the context in which they appear in the charter.

The second respect in which the scope of these words in line 22 has been held to go beyond the physical state of the vessel is that they have been held to cover the requirement that the vessel must carry certain kinds of documents which bear upon her seaworthiness or fitness to perform the service for which the charter provides. Navigational charts which are necessary for the voyages upon which the vessel may be ordered from time to time are an obvious illustration. For present purposes, however, we are concerned with certificates bearing upon the seaworthiness of the vessel. The nature of such certificates may vary according to the requirements of the law of the vessel's flag or the laws or regulations in force in the countries to which the vessel may be ordered, or which may lawfully be required by the authorities exercising administrative or other functions in the vessel's ports of call pursuant to the laws there in force. Documents falling within this category, which have been considered in the authorities, are certificates concerning the satisfactory state of the vessel which is in some respect related to her physical conditions, and accordingly to her seaworthiness. Their purpose is to provide documentary evidence for the authorities at the vessel's ports of call on matters which would otherwise require some physical inspection of the vessel, and possibly remedial measures – such as fumigation – before the vessel will be accepted as seaworthy in the relevant respect. The nature of description of such certificates, which may accordingly be required to be carried on board to render the vessel seaworthy, must depend on the circumstances and would no doubt raise issues of fact in individual cases. But I do not see any basis for holding that such certificates can properly be held to include documents other than those which may be required by the law of the vessel's flag or by the laws, regulations or lawful administrative practices of governmental or local authorities at the vessel's ports of call. An ITF blue card does not fall within this category, and I can therefore see no reason for including it within the scope of the words in line 22, even in their extended sense as indicated above.

Moreover, I do not consider that the words in line 22 have acquired as a matter of law, any 'expanded meaning', as the arbitrator suggests in para 5 above. The requirement of a deratisation certificate under the laws in force in India in 1957, which was the point at issue in *The Madeleine* [see Chapter 10] and without which the vessel could not sail to any other country, was in no way different in principle from the 'bill of health' required by the law of Sardinia, which fell to be considered in *Levy v Costerton*, (1816) 4 Camp 389. Since a vessel chartered for a voyage from England to Sardinia could not enter and discharge in the port of Cagliari without this document, 'required from all ships even from England', and was consequently delayed by being put under quarantine by the local authorities, it was inevitably held in that case that the vessel had not been '... furnished with everything needful and necessary for such a ship, and for the voyage ...'.

A decision about half way in time between 1816 and the present was *Ciampa v British India Steam Navigation Co Ltd*, [1915] 2 KB 774. On the appeal before us there was considerable controversy whether the reason for the unseaworthiness of the vessel on arrival in Marseilles in that case was the fact that she had previously called at Mombasa, which was contaminated by a plague, or whether she had a 'foul bill of health' in the sense of some deficiency in her proper documentation. In my view this is irrelevant for present purposes. The vessel was clearly unseaworthy at Marseilles in either event, whether on the ground that the local authorities required her to be fumigated because she had recently called at Mombasa, or because she did not have any document certifying a 'clean bill of health', in the same way as the vessel in *Levy v Costerton*. On whichever basis that decision in 1915 falls to be considered, it is wholly in line with the other two cases decided respectively in 1816 and 1967. The same applies to the 'tonnage certificate' required by Swedish law which was in issue in *Chellew Navigation Co Ltd v AR Appelquist Kolinport AG* (1933) 45 Ll L Rep 190 and (1932) 38 Com Cas 218, which the learned Judge also discussed in his judgment. In that case the umpire held, on the facts, that it was no part of the shipowners' obligation to obtain this certificate, or at any rate not by the time when the charterers had obtained it at their own expense.

I can therefore see no basis for the arbitrator's conclusion in the present case that the words in line 22 of this form of charterparty have somehow acquired an expanded meaning in our law so as to lead to the conclusion that a document in the nature of an ITF blue card can nowadays be held to fall within the requirements imposed upon shipowners by virtue of these words.

The only other case to which I think it is necessary to refer is the decision of this court in *Actis Co Ltd v Sanko Steamship Co Ltd, The Aquacharm* [1982] 1 WLR

119. That case was evidently not cited below, but it was strongly relied upon by Mr Kealey on this appeal. It concerned a time charter incorporating the Hague Rules for the carriage of a cargo of coal from Baltimore to Tokyo. The charterparty evidently did not refer expressly to the vessel passing through the Panama Canal, but this was no doubt envisaged by the geographical location of the ports of loading and discharge. The charterers in fact ordered her to pass through the Canal and to load no more coal than to bring her down to a draught 'permissible by the Panama Canal Co'. To that extent she proved to have been overloaded. In the result she was delayed during the charter service, because she had to be lightened to enter the Canal and then reloaded after she had passed through it. One of the issues was whether in these circumstances she had been 'seaworthy' under the Hague Rules when she left Baltimore. It was held by this court that she was, and in the judgment of Lord Denning MR, at p 9, the decisions in *Ciampa* and *The Madeleine* were distinguished, even though the vessel's condition on leaving Baltimore was such that she was bound to be delayed in the course of complying with the charterers' orders. Mr Gaisman expressly reserved the right to question the correctness of this decision if the present case should go further. However that may be, that decision clearly militates against this submission on behalf of the charterers that *any* foreseeable delay in the course of the charter service, due to any reason which is in any way related to the vessel or her crew, has the effect of rendering the vessel unseaworthy and accordingly imports a breach of line 22 of the present form of charter ...

6 CAUSATION AND EXCLUSION OF LIABILITY

Smith, Hogg v Black Sea and Baltic General Insurance [1940] AC 997

The *Lilburn* loaded a cargo of timber for carriage from Soroka to Garston. So much cargo was loaded on deck that on sailing she was dangerously unstable and consequently unseaworthy. When she put into Stornoway to refuel, she fell on her beam ends. Portions of cargo were lost or damaged. The owners claimed a general average contribution. The respondents resisted the claim on the ground that the owners had not exercised due diligence in accordance with the charter to make the vessel seaworthy and that the average act was occasioned by the unseaworthiness. They counterclaimed for loss and damage to cargo. The owners alleged that the accident was the fault of the master (for whose negligence they were not responsible) in taking on bunkers without discharging or reducing the deck cargo.

Lord Wright: ... Sir Robert Aske has strenuously contended on behalf of the appellants, that the master's action, whether or not negligent, was *novus actus interveniens*, which broke the *nexus* or chain of causation, and reduced the unseaworthiness from *causa causans* to *causa sine qua non*. I cannot help deprecating the use of Latin or so-called Latin phrases in this way. They only distract the mind from the true problem which is to apply the principles of English law to the realities of the case ...

Indeed the question what antecedent or subsequent event is a relevant or decisive cause varies with the particular case. If tort, which may in some respects have its own rules, is put aside and the enquiry is limited to contract, the selection of the relevant cause or causes will generally vary with the nature of the contract. I say 'cause or causes' because as Lord Shaw pointed out in *Leyland Shipping Co v Norwich Union Fire Insurance Co* [1918] 1 AC 350, 369, causes may be regarded not so much as a chain, but as a network. There is always a combination of co-operating causes, out of which the law, employing its empirical or common sense view of causation, will select the one or more which it finds material for its special purpose of deciding the particular case. That this is the test of the significance of an event from the standpoint of causation is clearly illustrated by this very doctrine of seaworthiness and its relation to kindred questions of negligence as applied to the two maritime contracts, marine insurance and sea carriage of goods. In the former, unseaworthiness is a condition precedent (at least in voyage policies) and if not complied with the insurance never attaches. In carriage of goods by sea, unseaworthiness does not affect the carrier's liability unless it causes the loss, as was held in *The Europa* [1908] P 84 and in *Kish v Taylor* [1912] AC 604. Again, in marine insurance, negligence causing the loss does not in general affect the insured's right to recover. In carriage of goods by sea, the shipowner will in the absence of valid and sufficient exceptions be liable for a loss occasioned by negligence. Apart from express exceptions, the carrier's contract is to deliver the goods safely. But when the practice of having express exceptions limiting that obligation became common, it was laid down that there were fundamental obligations, which were not affected by the specific exceptions, unless that was made clear by express words. Thus an exception of perils of the sea does not qualify the duty to furnish a seaworthy ship or to carry the goods without negligence: see *Paterson Steamships Ltd v Canadian Co-operative Wheat Producers Ltd* [above, Chapter 2]. From the nature of the contract, the relevant cause of the loss is held to be the unseaworthiness or the negligence as the case may be, not the peril of the sea, where both the breach of the fundamental obligation and the objective peril are co-operating causes. The contractual exception of perils of the seas does not affect the fundamental obligation, unless the contract qualifies the latter in express terms.

To consider these rules, in relation to unseaworthiness, I think the contract may be expressed to be that the shipowner will be liable for any loss in which those other causes covered by exceptions co-operate, if unseaworthiness is a cause, or if it is preferred, a real, or effective or actual cause ...

In truth, unseaworthiness, which may assume according to the circumstances an almost infinite variety, can never be the sole cause of the loss. At least I have not thought of a case where it can be the sole cause. It must, I think, always be only one of several co-operating causes ... In this connection I can draw no distinction between cases where the negligent conduct of the master is a cause and cases in which any other cause, such as perils of the seas, or fire, is a co-operating cause. A negligent act is as much a co-operating cause, if it is a cause at all, as an act which is not negligent. The question is the same in either case, it is, would the disaster not have happened if the ship had fulfilled the obligation of seaworthiness, even though the disaster could not have happened if there had not also been the specific peril or action ...

The sole question, apart from express exception, must then be: 'Was that breach of contract "a" cause of the damage'. It may be preferred to describe it as an effective or real or actual cause though the adjectives in my opinion in fact add nothing. If the question is answered in the affirmative the shipowner is liable though there were other co-operating causes, whether they are such causes as perils of the seas, fire and similar matters, or causes due to human action, such as the acts or omissions of the master, whether negligent or not or a combination of both kinds of cause ...

In cases of the type now being considered, the negligence, if any, must almost inevitably occur in the course of the voyage, and thus intervene between the commencement of the voyage when the duty to provide a seaworthy ship is broken, and the actual disaster. I doubt whether there could be any event which could supersede or override the effectiveness of the unseaworthiness if it was 'a' cause.

This is clearly so in the facts of this case. The acts of the master in bunkering as he did, and in pumping out the forepeak, whether negligent or not, were indeed more proximate in time to the disaster, and may be said to have contributed to the disaster, but the disaster would not have arisen but for the unseaworthiness, and hence the shipowners are liable ...

Lord Porter: ... No doubt those who are either defending themselves or putting forward a counterclaim based upon an allegation of unseaworthiness must prove that the loss was so caused.

But here the loss was, I think, incontestably due to the inability of the ship to take in bunkers by a method which would have been both safe and usual in the case of a seaworthy ship. It was not the coaling that was at fault nor the method adopted: it was the fact that that coaling took place and that method was adopted in a tender ship. If a vessel is to proceed on her voyage, bunkers must be shipped, and though in one sense the change of balance caused by taking in bunkers was responsible for the accident to the *Lilburn*, it was not the dominant cause even if it be necessary to show what the dominant cause was. The master merely acted in the usual way and indeed exercised what he thought was exceptional care in diverting the coal shipped towards the port bunker. In a seaworthy ship his action would have been a safe one. It was the instability of the ship which caused the disaster.

In such circumstances it is unnecessary to decide what would be the result if the loss were attributable partly to the coaling and partly to the unseaworthiness, or to determine whether the fact that the unseaworthiness was a substantial cause even though some other matter relied upon were a substantial cause also, would be enough to make the owners liable for failure to use due care to make the vessel seaworthy.

[Lord Romer agreed with Lord Porter. Lord Atkin agreed with Lord Wright. Lord Maugham agreed with both Lord Porter and Lord Wright.]

7 REMEDIES

Hongkong Fir Shipping v Kawasaki Kisen Kaisha [1962] 2 QB 26, CA

The plaintiff shipowners time chartered the *Hongkong Fir* to the defendants for 24 months. The charter contained off-hire and maintenance clauses. The vessel was placed at the disposal of the charterers at Liverpool and the same day sailed for Newport News to load coal for carriage to Osaka. Between Liverpool and Osaka she was at sea for about 8_ weeks, off hire for about five weeks and had £21,400 spent on her on repairs. While at Osaka, a further 15 weeks and £37,500 were necessary to make her ready for sea. During this period the charterers repudiated the charter and claimed damages for breach of contract. The owners responded that they treated the charterers as having wrongfully repudiated the charter and they too claimed damages. Subsequently the charterers again repudiated the charter and the owners formally accepted the repudiation. In the Court of Appeal, two main issues were argued: (1) Is the seaworthiness obligation a condition the breach of which entitles the charterers to treat the contract as repudiated? (2) Where in breach of contract a party fails to perform it, by what standard does the ensuing delay fall to be measured for the purpose of deciding whether the innocent party is entitled to treat the contract as repudiated?

> **Sellers LJ**: ... By clause 1 of the charterparty the shipowners contracted to deliver the vessel at Liverpool 'she being in every way fitted for ordinary cargo service'. She was not fit for ordinary cargo service when delivered because the engine room staff was incompetent and inadequate and this became apparent as the voyage proceeded. It is commonplace language to say that the vessel was unseaworthy by reason of this inefficiency in the engine room.

> Ships have been held to be unseaworthy in a variety of ways and those who have been put to loss by reason thereof (in the absence of any protecting clause in favour of a shipowner) have been able to recover damages as for a breach of warranty. It would be unthinkable that all the relatively trivial matters which have been held to be unseaworthiness could be regarded as conditions of the contract or conditions precedent to a charterer's liability and justify in themselves a cancellation or refusal to perform on the part of the charterer ...

> If what is done or not done in breach of the contractual obligation does not make the performance a totally different performance of the contract from that intended by the parties, it is not so fundamental as to undermine the whole contract. Many existing conditions of unseaworthiness can be remedied by attention or repairs, many are intended to be rectified as the voyage proceeds, so that the vessel becomes seaworthy; and, as the judgment points out, the breach of a shipowner's obligation to deliver a seaworthy vessel has not been held by itself to entitle a charterer to escape from the charterparty. The charterer may rightly terminate the engagement if the delay in remedying any breach is so long in fact, or likely to be so long in reasonable anticipation, that the commercial purpose of the contract would be frustrated.

Mr Roskill recognised the weight of authority against him in seeking to make seaworthiness a condition of the contract the breach of which, in itself, was to be regarded as fundamental so as to entitle a charterer to accept it as a repudiation of the charterparty and to regard the charterparty as terminated, and he relied more strongly on his second argument.

We were referred to the whole range of authorities from the early 19th century to the present day in support of both contentions ...

In the early part of the last century, before a counterclaim could be raised against a plaintiff's claim, sustained efforts were made, in the problems which arose in the increasing overseas trade, to resist a shipowner's claim by alleging a condition precedent unfulfilled. In *Ritchie v Atkinson* (1808) 10 East 295 it failed. Lord Ellenborough CJ held that the delivery of a complete cargo was not a condition precedent to the recovery of freight ...

The same principle was applied in respect of seaworthiness in *Havelock v Geddes* (1809) 10 East 555 where Lord Ellenborough CJ pointed out that if the obligation of seaworthiness were a condition precedent the neglect of putting in a single nail after the ship ought to have been made tight, staunch, etc, would be a breach of the condition and a defence to the whole of the plaintiff's demand.

By 1810, in *Davidson v Gwynne* (1810) 12 East 381, Lord Ellenborough CJ was saying that it was useless to go over the same subject again 'which has so often been discussed of late' and held the sailing with the first convoy was not a condition precedent, the object of the contract was the performance of the voyage and that had been performed.

Tarrabochia v Hickie (1856) 1 H & N 183 emphasises the same principle and I think is of no less effect because it relates to a voyage charter. Pollock CB, whose succinct judgment provides a complete answer to the appellants' case, cites Lord Ellenborough CJ in *Davidson v Gwynne* 'that unless the non-performance alleged goes to the whole root and consideration of it, the covenant broken is not to be considered as a condition precedent, but as a distinct covenant, for the breach of which the party injured may be compensated in damages' unless by the breach of the stipulation of the fitness of the vessel the object of the voyage is wholly frustrated.

This decision was approved in *Stanton v Richardson* (1872) LR 7 CP 421; (1874) LR 9 CP 390, CA where the shipowner had undertaken to carry a cargo of wet sugar and the ship was not fit to carry it and, as the jury had found, could not be made fit in such time as not to frustrate the object of the voyage. The molasses had drained from the wet sugar into the hold in large quantities and the ship's pumps were unable to deal with it. The cargo was unloaded and the charterers were held entitled to refuse to reload it or to provide any other cargo. If the defect had been or could have been remedied within a reasonable time so as not to frustrate the adventure it would seem that the charterer's right would not have been to terminate the charterparty but to have claimed damages for any loss occasioned by the delay.

Kish v Taylor [1912] AC 604 affirms that a contract of affreightment, in that case a voyage charter, is not put an end to by a breach of the stipulation of seaworthiness. The passage in Lord Atkinson's speech on which the appellants relied:

> The fact that a ship is not in a fit condition to receive her cargo, or is from any cause unseaworthy when about to start on her voyage, will justify the charterer or holder of the bill of lading in repudiating his contract and refusing to be bound by it

does not undermine the principle applied in the case. It applies in terms to the commencement of the voyage and it was not relevant to the case to consider the extent and nature of the unfitness or the time and circumstances in which it could be rectified.

Tully v Howling (1877) 2 QBD 182, although in favour of the charterer, gives no support to the appellants here whether it was decided on the ground of the majority that time was the essence of the contract and that the charterer who had a contract for 12 months' service was not bound to 10 months' service, or, as Brett J held on appeal, that the ship was not fit for the purpose for which she was chartered and could not be made fit within any time which would not have frustrated the object of the adventure.

The argument for the appellants contrasted the decisions on deviation with those on unseaworthiness and submitted that the latter was at least as grave as the former. But deviation amounts to a stepping out of the contract, or may do, and as such it is a repudiation of it and a substitution of a different voyage or engagement.

The formula for deciding whether a stipulation is a condition or a warranty is well recognised; the difficulty is in its application. It is put in a practical way by Bowen LJ in *Bentsen v Taylor, Sons & Co* [1893] 2 QB 274:

> There is no way of deciding that question except by looking at the contract in the light of the surrounding circumstances, and then making up one's mind whether the intention of the parties, as gathered from the instrument itself, will best be carried out by treating the promise as a warranty sounding only in damages, or as a condition precedent by the failure to perform which the other party is relieved of his liability.

In my judgment authority over many decades and reason support the conclusion in this case that there was no breach of a condition which entitled the charterers to accept it as a repudiation and to withdraw from the charter. It was not contended that the maintenance clause is so fundamental a matter as to amount to a condition of the contract. It is a warranty which sounds in damages.

The appellants' argument on the second submission in my judgment equally fails and is to be rejected on many of the authorities already cited ...

In *Universal Cargo Carriers Corporation v Citati* [1957] 2 QB 401 a similar argument was advanced by Mr Ashton Roskill (then appearing for shipowners who had cancelled a voyage charterparty because no cargo had been provided), and he relied on passages in the line of cases which he cited to us here ...

Devlin J said '... But a party to a contract may not purchase indefinite delay by paying damages ... When the delay becomes so prolonged that the breach assumes a character so grave as to go to the root of the contract, the aggrieved party is entitled to rescind. What is the yardstick by which this length of delay is to be measured? Those considered in the arbitration can now be reduced to two: (as in the present appeal) first, the conception of a reasonable time, and secondly, such delay as would frustrate the charterparty ... in my opinion the second has been settled as the correct one by a long line of authorities.'

In my judgment Salmon J was clearly right in the answers he gave to both of the contentions of the charterers relied on in this court, supported as the answers were by established authority and good commercial reason. I would dismiss the appeal.

Diplock LJ: The contract, the familiar 'Baltime 1939' charter, and the facts upon which this case turns have been already stated in the judgment of Sellers LJ, who has also referred to many of the relevant cases. With his analysis of the cases, as with the clear and careful judgment of Salmon J, I am in agreement, and I desire to add only some general observations upon the legal questions which this case involves.

Every synallagmatic contract contains in it the seeds of the problem: in what event will a party be relieved of his undertaking to do that which he has agreed to do but has not yet done? The contract may itself expressly define some of these events, as in the cancellation clause in a charterparty; but, human prescience being limited, it seldom does so exhaustively and often fails to do so at all. In some classes of contracts such as sale of goods, marine insurance, contracts of affreightment evidenced by bills of lading and those between parties to bills of exchange, Parliament has defined by statute some of the events not provided for expressly in individual contracts of that class; but where an event occurs the occurrence of which neither the parties nor Parliament have expressly stated will discharge one of the parties from further performance of his undertakings, it is for the court to determine whether the event has this effect or not.

The test whether an event has this effect or not has been stated in a number of metaphors all of which I think amount to the same thing: does the occurrence of the event deprive the party who has further undertakings still to perform of substantially the whole benefit which it was the intention of the parties as expressed in the contract that he should obtain as the consideration for performing those undertakings?

... What the judge had to do in the present case, as in any other case where one party to a contract relies upon a breach by the other party as giving him a right to elect to rescind the contract, and the contract itself makes no express provision as to this, was to look at the events which had occurred as a result of the breach at the time at which the charterers purported to rescind the charterparty and to decide whether the occurrence of those events deprived the charterers of substantially the whole benefit which it was the intention of the parties as expressed in the charterparty that the charterers should obtain from the further performance of their own contractual undertakings.

One turns therefore to the contract, the Baltime 1939 charter ... Clause 13, the 'due diligence' clause, which exempts the shipowners from responsibility for delay or loss or damage to goods on board due to unseaworthiness, unless such delay or loss or damage has been caused by want of due diligence of the owners in making the vessel seaworthy and fitted for the voyage, is in itself sufficient to show that the mere occurrence of the events that the vessel was in some respect unseaworthy when tendered or that such unseaworthiness had caused some delay in performance of the charterparty would not deprive the charterer of the whole benefit which it was the intention of the parties he should obtain from the performance of his obligations under the contract – for he undertakes to continue to perform his obligations notwithstanding the occurrence of such events if they fall short of frustration of the contract and even deprives himself of any remedy in damages unless such events are the consequence of want of due diligence on the part of the shipowner.

The question which the judge had to ask himself was, as he rightly decided, whether or not at the date when the charterers purported to rescind the contract, namely, 6 June 1957, or when the shipowners purported to accept such rescission, namely, 8 August 1957, the delay which had already occurred as a result of the incompetence of the engine room staff, and the delay which was likely to occur in repairing the engines of the vessel and the conduct of the shipowners by that date in taking steps to remedy these two matters, were, when taken together, such as to deprive the charterers of substantially the whole benefit which it was the intention of the parties they should obtain from further use of the vessel under the charterparty ...

CHAPTER 5

DEVIATION

In the context of a contract for the carriage of goods by sea, the term deviation is used in English law to refer to the voluntary and unjustified departure of a ship from the contractual route. In the last century it came to be treated as a particularly serious breach of contract. If goods were lost during or after a deviation, the shipowner was not permitted to rely on exemption clauses in the bill of lading. An unjustifiable deviation, it was said, deprived the ship of the protection of exceptions. A straightforward explanation for this rule of thumb might have been that exceptions clauses were to be read as applying only to perils which occurred in the course of the voyage on which the parties had agreed and not to departures from that voyage. However, in cases decided around the turn of the last century a more radical doctrine developed.

In *Balian & Sons v Joly, Victoria & Co* (1890) 6 TLR 345, 24 bales of tobacco were shipped on the *Mabel*, a small coaster, under a bill of lading which apparently provided for carriage direct from Thessaly to London. On arrival in London, it was found that 14 bales had been damaged. The goods had not in fact been carried by the *Mabel* direct to London, but in the opposite direction, to Smyrna, where they were transshipped on to a Cunard steamer which discharged them at Liverpool; they finally reached London by rail. The Court of Appeal held that the shipowners could not rely on a clause in the bill of lading which limited their liability to £5.00 per package. The actual decision in this case, in which the damage to cargo occurred at some stage during the deviation, was quite in line with previous practice, which the court expressly followed. Nevertheless, after what can have been only a short hearing and without hearing full argument, the court also indulged in some speculation. Lord Esher MR, with the support of Fry LJ, said (*obiter*) that it:

> might be that the true view was that the deviation made the voyage actually carried out a different voyage from beginning to end from that to which the bill of lading applied, and that therefore the whole bill of lading was gone.

This extempore statement came to be treated in later cases as having decided that a deviation puts a contract of affreightment to an end. In *Joseph Thorley Ltd v Orchis Steamship Co* [1907] 1 KB 660, CA (where cargo was damaged after a deviation), Collins MR supplied a theory to explain how this occurs. In his view, sailing on the contractual route was a condition precedent to the right of a shipowner to rely on the contract evidenced by a bill of lading; by deviating, a shipowner failed to comply with the condition precedent, with the result that the express contract was displaced. In *Orchis*, the vessel deviated in the course of a voyage to London. The cargo of locust beans arrived in London in sound condition, but was damaged during discharge. Notwithstanding the absence of a clear connection between the damage and the deviation, the court held that the shipowner could not rely on an exception clause in the bill of lading.

The effect of the decision in *Orchis Steamship* was that, at least for a time, deviation was thought to make the express contract between the parties void. On this basis, in *Internationale Guano v Macandrew* [1909] 2 KB 360, Pickford J seems to have accepted that a shipowner could not rely on exceptions in a charterparty even in respect of damage to cargo which occurred before the deviation. The effects of the doctrine in *Orchis Steamship* (1907) can be seen at work in several cases included in this chapter: *Kish v Taylor* (1912); *James Morrison v Shaw, Savill and Albion* (1916); and *The Alamosa* (1925).

However, in *Hain Steamship v Tate and Lyle* (1936, below) the House of Lords abandoned the line of reasoning used in *Orchis*. In *Hain*, cargo was lost at a time when, after a deviation, the ship had returned to the contractual route. The House of Lords decided that deviation did not render the contract void ab initio or result in the automatic discharge of the agreement. But it was held that deviation was a serious breach of a contract of affreightment and always gave the innocent party the right to bring the contract to an end, in which case he would not be bound by exclusion clauses or by any other promises in the contract, including the promise to pay freight due on delivery. On the other hand, if the innocent party elected to treat the contract as subsisting, the innocent party would continue to be bound by the contract and in particular the shipowner would continue to be entitled to rely on the contractual excepted perils. In the words of Lord Wright MR:

> In the present case the charterers elected to waive the breach, with the result that the charterparty was not abrogated but remained in force. The appellants were thus entitled to ... rely on the exception of perils of the sea ...

The *Hain* doctrine is capable of producing very odd results. On this approach, if a ship makes a minor and harmless deviation but then returns to the contractual route, it seems that the cargo owner can nevertheless bring the contract to an end and avoid liability for any payments (such as freight payable on delivery or demurrage due at the port of discharge) which become due thereafter. On the other hand, if a vessel deviates, the charterer affirms, and thereafter the vessel and cargo are lost, *Hain* seems to allow the shipowner to rely on exclusion clauses in the contract in every case, even where the loss actually occurs at places other than those which the contract originally contemplated; in this situation, paradoxically, by affirming the contract, the innocent party changes it.

Is *Hain* still good law? The judgments in the case are inconsistent in important respects with the general law of contract as expounded in more recent decisions. In *Photo Production v Securicor* [1980] AC 827, the House of Lords rejected the idea that by rescinding a contract for a serious breach, the innocent party can bring the whole contract, including any exclusion clauses, to an end. In general the question whether an exclusion clause applies to a particular breach of contract depends on the proper meaning of the clause; there is no general rule of the law of contract that an exclusion clause cannot exclude liability for particularly serious or fundamental breaches. Nevertheless, *Hain* has not been formally overruled. In *Photo Production* Lord Wilberforce said of the deviation cases that (at page 845):

> ... I suggested in the *Suisse Atlantique* [1967] 1 AC 361 that these cases can be regarded as proceeding upon normal principles applicable to the law of contract generally, *viz*, that it is a matter of the parties' intentions whether and to what extent clauses in shipping contracts can be applied after a deviation, ie a departure from the contractually agreed voyage or adventure. It may be preferable that they should be considered as a body of authority *sui generis* with special rules derived from historical and commercial reasons ...

In the same case, Lord Diplock spoke of deviation as a breach of condition the effect of which accorded with the general law of contract. Since it is by no means clear that a special rule is needed to deal with the problems of deviation under a contract to carry goods by sea, the view is gaining ground that the law relating to deviation under a contract of affreightment ought to be brought into line with the ordinary law of contract: see *The Antares* [1986] 2 Lloyd's Rep 626, 633; [1987] 1 Lloyd's Rep 424, CA (Chapter 8); *State Trading Corporation of India Ltd v M Golodetz Ltd, The Sara D* [1989] 2 Lloyd's Rep 277, CA.

References

Chorley (1940) 3 *MLR* 287

Tetley & Cleven [1971] 45 *Tulane LR* 810

Lee [1972] 47 *Tulane LR* 155

Mills [1983] 4 *LMCLQ* 587; C Debattista (1989) *JBL* 22

Reynolds, FMB, *The Butterworth Lectures 1990–91*

Baughen, S (1991) *LMCLQ* 70

Wooder, JB (1991) 22 *JMLC* 131 (deck cargo)

Baver, JG (1991) 22 *JMLC* 287 (deck cargo)

Force, R (1996) 1 *Int M L* 14 (carriage on deck under US law)

1 INTENTIONAL DEPARTURE FROM THE CONTRACTUAL ROUTE

Davis v Garrett (1830) 6 Bing 716, Court of Common Pleas

A cargo of lime was delivered to the defendant for carriage on his barge *Safety* from Bewly Cliff, Kent, to the Regents Canal, London, act of God, fire and perils of the sea being excepted. The barge deviated to the East Swale and to Whitstable Bay which was out of the usual and customary route and was caught there in a storm. Sea water reached the cargo, which became heated. The barge caught fire and the master was forced to run her on shore. The lime and the barge were both lost. The plaintiff alleged that the defendant's duty was to carry by the direct usual and customary course without deviation and that the defendant had deviated from the usual and customary route. The defendant argued that he was not liable because (i) the deviation was not a sufficiently proximate cause of the loss, which might have occurred even if the *Safety* had taken a direct course; and (ii) that he was not alleged to have agreed to carry the lime directly to the Regents Canal.

> **Tindal CJ**: ... As to the first point ... [w]e think that the real answer to the objection is that no wrongdoer can be allowed to apportion or qualify his own wrong; and that as a loss has actually happened while his wrongful act was in operation and force, and which is attributable to his wrongful act, he cannot set up as an answer to the action the bare possibility of a loss, if his wrongful act had never been done. It might admit of a different construction if he could show, not only that the same loss might have happened, but that it must have happened if the act complained of had not been done; but there is no evidence to that extent in the present case ...

> [As to the second point] ... We cannot but think that the law does imply a duty in the owner of a vessel, whether a general ship or hired for the special purpose of the voyage, to proceed without unnecessary deviation in the usual and customary course.

Reardon Smith Line v Black Sea and Baltic Insurance [1939] AC 562, House of Lords

The appellants' vessel, the *Indian City*, was chartered to carry a cargo of ore from Poti in the Black Sea to Sparrow's Point, Baltimore, USA. After loading, she sailed first for Constanza on the west coast of the Black Sea for fuel. The vessel grounded at Constanza and was damaged; part of the cargo had to be jettisoned. The charterers refused to contribute to general average expenses on the grounds that in going to Constanza the ship had deviated from her contractual route, which they said was from Poti to Sparrow's Point by the direct route through Istanbul.

> **Lord Porter**: ... It is the duty of a ship, at any rate when sailing upon an ocean voyage from one port to another, to take the usual route between those two ports. If no evidence be given, that route is presumed to be the direct geographical route, but it may be modified in many cases for navigational or other reasons, and evidence may always be given to show what the usual route is, unless a specific route be prescribed by the charterparty or bill of lading. In each case therefore when a ship is chartered to sail or when a parcel is shipped upon a liner sailing from one port to another, it is necessary to inquire what the usual route is. In some cases there may be more than one usual route. It would be difficult to say that a ship sailing from New Zealand to this country had deviated from her course whether she sailed by the Suez Canal, the Panama

Canal, round the Cape of Good Hope or through the Straits of Magellan. Each might, I think, be a usual route. Similarly the exigencies of bunkering may require the vessel to depart from the direct route or at any rate compel her to touch at ports at which, if she were proceeding under sail, it would be unnecessary for her to call.

It is not the geographical route but the usual route which has to be followed, though in many cases the one may be the same as the other. But the inquiry must always be, what is the usual route, and a route may become a usual route in the case of a particular line though that line is accustomed to follow a course which is not that adopted by the vessels belonging to other lines or to other individuals. It is sufficient if there is a well known practice of that line to call at a particular port.

... No doubt *prima facie* the route direct from Poti to Sparrow's Point through Istanbul would be the ordinary course, but I think that in this case we have evidence sufficient to show that the route has been varied and that the practice of proceeding to Constanza to bunker after loading had become a usual one. It is true that a considerable number of vessels proceeding from Black Sea ports do not call at Constanza for bunkers, and that, if one is to take particulars of Poti and Novorossisk alone, only about one-quarter of the ships proceeding on ocean voyages call at Constanza after loading. It is true also that the journey to Constanza lengthens the voyage by some 200 miles, and that shortly after the accident to the *Indian City* the cost of oil at Constanza increased and the appellants thereafter have taken their bunkers from Algiers instead of Constanza.

All these are matters to be considered, but a short usage, particularly where the obtaining of bunkers is concerned, may still be a sufficient usage to create a usual route ...

Rio Tinto v Seed Shipping [1926] 24 Ll L Rep 316

The plaintiff charterers shipped a cargo of coal and coke on the defendants' ship *Marjorie Seed* at Glasgow for Huelva. After leaving the Cubrae the master, not being in perfect health, ordered a course to be steered (SSE) which stranded the ship on rocks off the coast of Ayr. The ordinary course would have been to steer SSW. Ship and cargo were totally lost. The plaintiffs sued for the value of the cargo; the defendants pleaded an excepted peril to which the plaintiffs replied that there had been a deviation.

Roche J: The essence of deviation [is] that the parties contracting have voluntarily substituted another voyage for that which has been insured. A mere departure or failure to follow the contract voyage or route is not necessarily a deviation, or every stranding which occurred in the course of a voyage would be a deviation, because the voyage contracted for, I imagine, is in no case one which essentially involves the necessity of stranding. It is a change of voyage, a radical breach of the contract, that is required to, and essentially does, constitute a deviation ...

Here I am satisfied, and I find as a fact, that the master never intended to leave the route of the voyage, that is to say, the route of the voyage from Glasgow to

Huelva. What he did was to make a mistake as to the compass course which was necessary to take him from the *terminus a quo* to the *terminus ad quem*. To use an analogy which, although analogies are misleading, I think at this stage is in order, he did not adopt another road instead of the road that he had agreed to take, but he got himself into the ditch at the side of the road which he was intending to follow. He was not on another route; he was on the existing route, although he was out of the proper part of the route which he ought to have followed. That is my finding of fact as to what happened; and in my judgment it follows from that that there was not that substitution or change of route which is necessary to constitute a deviation ...

2 JUSTIFIABLE DEVIATION: DEVIATION TO SAVE LIFE

Scaramanga v Stamp (1880) 5 CPD 295, Court of Appeal

Cockburn CJ: ... The steamship *Olympias*, of which the defendants are owners, having been chartered by the plaintiff to carry a cargo of wheat from Cronstadt to Gibraltar, and having started on her voyage, when nine days out, sighted another steamship, the *Arion*, in distress, and, on nearing her, found that the machinery of the *Arion* had broken down, and that the vessel was in a helpless condition. The weather was fine and the sea smooth, and there would have been no difficulty in taking off and so saving the crew; but the master of the *Arion*, being desirous of saving his ship, as well as the lives of his crew, agreed to pay £1,000 to the master of the *Olympias* to tow the ship into the Texel.

Having taken the *Arion* in tow, the *Olympias*, when off the Dutch coast, on the way to the Texel, got ashore on the Terschelling Sands, and with her cargo was ultimately lost.

Under these circumstances the plaintiff claims the value of his goods, alleging that the goods were not lost by perils of the seas, so as to be within the exception in the charterparty, but were lost through the wrongful deviation of the defendants' vessel. The defendants plead that the deviation was justified, because it was for the purpose of saving the *Arion* and her cargo, and the lives of her captain and crew, the ship being in such a damaged condition that she could not be navigated.

That there was here a twofold deviation, which, unless the circumstances were such as to justify it, would entitle the plaintiff to recover, cannot be disputed – in the first place, in the departure of the *Olympias* from her proper course in going to the Texel, secondly, in her taking the *Arion* in tow ... [since] the effect of taking another vessel in tow is necessarily to retard the progress of the towing vessel, and thereby to prolong the risk of the voyage.

[After reviewing the few English authorities on the point, Chief Justice Cockburn said that the effect of American decisions was that] ... deviation for the purpose of saving life is protected, and involves neither forfeiture of insurance nor liability to the goods owner in respect of loss which would otherwise be within the exception of 'perils of the seas'. And, as a necessary consequence of the foregoing, deviation for the purpose of communicating with a ship in distress is allowable, inasmuch as the state of the vessel in distress may involve danger to life. On the other hand, deviation for the sole purpose of saving property is not thus privileged, but entails all the usual consequences of deviation ...

In these propositions I entirely concur ... The impulsive desire to save human life when in peril is one of the most beneficial instincts of humanity, and is nowhere more salutary in its results than in bringing help to those who, exposed to destruction from the fury of winds and waves, would perish if left without assistance. To all who have to trust themselves to the sea, it is of the utmost importance that the promptings of humanity in this respect should not be checked or interfered with by prudential considerations as to injurious consequences, which may result to a ship or cargo from the rendering of the needed aid. It would be against the common good, and shocking to the sentiments of mankind, that the shipowner should be deterred from endeavouring to save life by the fear, lest any disaster to ship or cargo, consequent on so doing, should fall on himself. Yet it would be unjust to expect that he should be called upon to satisfy the call of humanity at his own entire risk.

Moreover, the uniform practice of the mariners of every nation – except such as are in the habit of making the unfortunate their prey – of succouring others who are in danger, is so universal and well known, that there is neither injustice nor hardship in treating both the merchant and the insurer as making their contracts with the shipowner as subject to this exception to the general rule of not deviating from the appointed course. Goods owners and insurers must be taken, at all events in the absence of any stipulation to the contrary, as acquiescing in the universal practice of the maritime world, prompted as it is by the inherent instinct of human nature, and founded on the common interest of all who are exposed to the perils of the seas. What would be the effect of such a stipulation as I have just referred to, if it existed, it is unnecessary for the purpose of the present case to consider.

Deviation for the purpose of saving property stands obviously on a totally different footing. There is here no moral duty to fulfil, which, though its fulfilment may have been attended with danger to life or property, remains unrewarded. There would be much force, no doubt, in the argument that it is to the common interest of merchants and insurers, as well as of shipowners, that ships and cargoes, when in danger of perishing, should be saved, and consequently that, as matter of policy, the same latitude should be allowed in respect of the saving of property as in respect of the saving of life, were it not that the law has provided another, and a very adequate motive for the saving of property, by securing to the salvor a liberal proportion of the property saved – a proportion in which not only the value of the property saved, but also the danger run by the salvor to life or property is taken into account, and in calculating which, if it be once settled that the insurance will not be protected, nor the shipowner freed from liability in respect of loss of cargo, the risk thus run will, no doubt, be included as an element. It would obviously be most unjust if the shipowner could thus take the chance of highly remunerative gain at the risk and possible loss of the merchant or the insurer, neither of whom derive any benefit from the preservation of the property saved. This is strikingly exemplified in the present case, in which, not content with what would have been awarded to him by the proper court on account of salvage, the master made his own terms, and would have been paid a very large sum had the attempt to bring the *Arion* into port proved successful. It is obviously one thing to accord a privilege to one who acts from a sense of duty, without expectation of reward, another to extend it to one who neither acts from a sense of moral duty nor in obedience to what may be thought to be the policy of the law, but solely with a view to his own individual profit.

In the result, I am of opinion that though the deviation of the *Olympias*, so far as relates to her proceeding to the *Arion* in the first instance, was justified, the taking the latter in tow, and departing from the proper course in order to take the ship to the Texel, this not being necessary in order to save the lives of the captain and crew, was an unauthorised deviation; and the loss of the plaintiff's cargo having been the direct consequence of the deviation, or, to use the language of Tindal CJ in *Davis v Garrett* (above), 'the loss having actually happened whilst the wrongful act was in operation and force, and being attributable to the wrongful act', the defendants cannot avail themselves of the exception in the charterparty, and the plaintiff is, therefore, entitled to judgment. The appeal must, therefore, be disallowed.

[Brett and Cotton LJJ agreed with Cockburn CJ. Bramwell LJ also delivered a judgment in favour of allowing the appeal.]

3 DEVIATION TO AVOID IMMINENT PERIL: EXTENT OF PERMISSIBLE DEVIATION

Phelps, James & Co v Hill [1891] 1 QB 605, CA

Tin and iron plates were shipped by the plaintiffs on the *Llanduff City* at Swansea for New York. About five days out the vessel and some of her equipment and cargo were damaged in a storm and it was necessary to put back to a port of refuge. She went first to Queenstown where she was ordered by the defendant owners to return to their own yards in Bristol where suitable spare parts were available and where repairs could have been done more cheaply and quickly than elsewhere. It would also have been possible to sell or transship the cargo there. In the Avon, she was run into by another vessel and was sunk. This risk was excepted by the bill of lading. The question was whether there was an unjustifiable deviation in going to Bristol instead of Swansea. The jury at trial found that there had not been an unjustifiable deviation.

> **Lopes LJ**: The question in this case is whether there was a deviation. If there was a deviation, or, in other words, if the deviation was not justified, the shipowner is liable for a loss by the perils of the sea, and is not protected by the exception of perils in the contract. The voyage must be prosecuted without unnecessary delay or deviation. The shipowner's contract is that he will be

diligent in carrying the goods on the agreed voyage, and will do so directly without any unnecessary deviation. But this undertaking is to be understood with reference to the circumstances that arise during the performance of the contract. He is not answerable for delays or deviations which are occasioned or become necessary without default on his part. Where the safety of the adventure under the master's control necessitates that he should go out of his course, he is not only justified in doing so, but it is his duty in the right performance of his contract with the owners of the cargo. The shipowner through his master is bound to act with prudence and skill and care in avoiding dangers and in mitigating the consequences of any disaster which may have happened. The master is bound to take into account the interests of the cargo owners as well as those of the shipowner. He must act prudently for all concerned ... Going into a port out of the usual course for necessary repairs, and staying till they are completed, is no deviation, provided it plainly appears that such repairs, under the circumstances and at such port, were reasonably necessary, and the delay not greater than necessary for the completion of such repairs, so as to enable the vessel to proceed on her voyage. The deviation must not be greater than a reasonable necessity demands, having regard to the respective interests of shipowner and cargo owner. A reasonable necessity implies the existence of such a state of things as, having regard to the interests of all concerned, would properly influence the decision of a reasonably competent and skilful master ...

4 JUSTIFIABLE DEVIATION AND UNSEAWORTHINESS

Kish v Taylor [1912] AC 604, HL

The *Wearside* was chartered to load a full and complete cargo of timber at Mobile or Pensacola. The charterers failed to provide a full cargo so the master attempted to mitigate by obtained additional cargo from other sources. He was so successful that the *Wearside* was overloaded with deck cargo and became unseaworthy. She sailed, encountered bad weather and had to take refuge in the port of Halifax, where she was repaired and the cargo restowed. On arrival at Liverpool, the shipowners claimed a lien for the charterers' failure to load a full cargo. The cargo owners disputed the existence of the lien, arguing that the deviation to Halifax had been a gratuitous alteration of the voyage and had rendered the contract of affreightment contained in the bill of lading *void ab initio*.

> **Lord Atkinson:** ... it is not disputed that it is *prima facie* not only the right but the duty of the master of a ship to deviate from the course of his voyage and seek a harbour or place of safety, if that be reasonably necessary in order to save his ship and the lives of his crew from the perils which beset them. Neither is it disputed by the appellants that they are answerable in damages to every person who sustains loss or injury by reason of the breach of their warranty of the seaworthiness of their ship, and they further admit that they cannot require the owners of the cargo or any portion of it to recoup them to

any extent for any loss they may have sustained or expense to which they may have been put as a result of this breach of warranty, or of any course they may have had to take in consequence of it. That voluntary or unwarranted deviation may render the contract of affreightment *void ab initio* was decided by the Court of Appeal in *Joseph Thorley Ltd v Orchis Steamship Co* (1907) 1 KB 660. What the appellants contend is, in effect, this, that justifiable deviation does not avoid the contract; that, to use the language of Lord Watson '... it is the presence of the peril and not its causes' which justify it, and that it is, therefore, immaterial whether the unseaworthiness of the ship or her negligent navigation contributed directly to the peril or not. Judged by that test it is not disputed that the deviation in the present case was justifiable, and, if so, that the contract of affreightment was not void ab initio. So that the question for decision resolves itself into this: Is it the presence of the peril and not its cause which determines the character of the deviation, or must the master of every ship be left in this dilemma, that whenever, by his own culpable act, or a breach of contract by his owner, he finds his ship in a perilous position, he must continue on his voyage at all hazards, or only seek safety under the penalty of forfeiting the contract of affreightment? Nothing could, it would appear to me, tend more to increase the dangers to which life and property are exposed at sea than to hold that the law of England obliged the master of a merchant ship to choose between such alternatives ...

On the whole, therefore, I am of opinion that a master, whose ship is, from whatever cause, in a perilous position, does right in making such a deviation from his voyage as is necessary to save his ship and the lives of his crew, and that while the right to recover damages for all breaches of contract, and all wrongful acts committed either by himself or by the owners of his ship, is preserved to those who are thereby wronged or injured, the contract of affreightment is not put an end to by such a deviation, nor are the rights of the owners under it lost ...

Note

In *Monarch Steamship v Karlshamns Oliefabriker* [1949] AC 196 at p 212, Lord Porter referred to *Kish v Taylor* and said:

> Undoubtedly deviation made to remedy unseaworthiness does not amount to unjustifiable deviation or destroy the right to rely upon the terms of the contract of carriage *unless it is established that the owners knew of the vessel's state on sailing* (emphasis supplied) ... no such knowledge has been brought home to the appellants (in the present case) and therefore they continue to be entitled to rely upon the war clause.

5 LIBERTY TO DEVIATE CLAUSES

Leduc v Ward (1888) 20 QBD 475, CA

The plaintiffs were owners of goods shipped on board the defendants' ship and sued for non-delivery of the goods at Dunkirk in accordance with the terms of the bill of lading. The defence was that delivery of the goods was prevented by perils of the sea. To that the plaintiffs replied that the goods were not lost by reason of any perils excepted by the bill of lading, because they were lost at a time when the defendants were committing a breach of their contract by deviating from the voyage provided for by the bill of lading. The bill of lading stated that the ship was 'now lying in the port of Fiume and bound for Dunkirk, with liberty to call at any ports in any order, and to deviate for the purpose of saving life or property'. Instead of proceeding direct to Dunkirk, the vessel had sailed for Glasgow, a total of about 1,200 miles out of the ordinary course of the voyage; ship and cargo were lost near Ailsa Graig, off the mouth of the Clyde.

Fry and **Lopes LJJ** agreed with **Lord Esher MR:**

... In the present case liberty is given to call at any ports in any order. It was argued that that clause gives liberty to call at any port in the world. Here, again, it is a question of the construction of a mercantile expression used in a mercantile document, and I think that as such the term can have but one meaning, namely, that the ports, liberty to call at which is intended to be given, must be ports which are substantially ports which will be passed on the named voyage. Of course such a term must entitle the vessel to go somewhat out of the ordinary track by sea of the named voyage, for going into the port of call in itself would involve that. To 'call' at a port is a well known sea-term; it means to call for the purposes of business, generally to take in or unload cargo, or to receive orders; it must mean that the vessel may stop at the port of call for a time, or else the liberty to call would be idle. I believe the term has always been interpreted to mean that the ship may call at such ports as would naturally and usually be ports of call on the voyage named. If the stipulation were only that she might call at any ports, the invariable construction has been that she would only be entitled to call at such ports in their geographical order; and therefore the words 'in any order' are frequently added, but in any case it appears to me that the ports must be ports substantially on the course of the voyage. It follows that, when the defendants' ship went off the ordinary track of a voyage from Fiume to Dunkirk to a port not on the course of that voyage, such as Glasgow, there was a deviation, and she was then on a voyage different from that contracted for to which the excepted perils clause did not apply; and therefore the shipowners are responsible for the loss of the goods ...

Glynn v Margetson [1891] AC 351

A cargo of oranges were shipped on the *Zena* under a bill of lading on a printed form which had been completed to show that the vessel was lying in the port of Malaga, and bound for Liverpool. The printed form provided that she had 'liberty to proceed to and stay at any ports in any rotation in the Mediterranean, Levant, Black Sea or Adriatic, or on the coasts of Africa, Spain, Portugal, France, Great Britain and Ireland, for the purpose of delivering coals, cargo or passengers, or for any other purpose whatsoever'. The vessel, on leaving Malaga, did not sail towards Liverpool but in the opposite direction and went first to Burriana about 350 miles from Malaga on the east coast of Spain. The oranges were found damaged on arrival at Liverpool because of the delay.

The House of Lords held that the main object and intent of the contract was the carriage of a perishable cargo from Malaga to Liverpool. Since the general words in the printed form (above) would defeat the main purpose of the contract if given full effect, the words were to be given a more limited construction (Lord Herschell) or, if this was not possible, the general words were to be rejected (Lord Halsbury). On the facts, the general words only entitled the owners to call (for the purposes stated) at ports which in a business sense could be said to be on the voyage between Malaga and Liverpool.

James Morrison & Co v Shaw, Savill and Albion [1916] 2 KB 783, CA

Wool worth approximately £4,000 was shipped on the defendants' vessel *Tokomaru* at Napier, New Zealand, for carriage to London. The bills of lading provided for:

> liberty on the way to London to call and stay at any intermediate port or ports to discharge or take on board passengers, cargo, coal or other supplies, with permission, if desired, for the vessel to call at Rio de Janeiro and/or Monte Video and/or La Plata for the purpose of taking on board coal, supplies and/or cargo and/or livestock.

After the plaintiffs' goods were loaded on board and the bills of lading had been issued, a parcel of frozen meat was loaded on board for France. The master received orders on the voyage to deliver the meat at Havre before going to London. The defendants realised that calling at Havre might be a deviation exposing them to claims to the value of the remainder of the cargo (£250,000) should anything happen to the vessel, and decided not to insure against this risk because they thought the premium (10 shillings per cent) was too high.

> **Swinfen Eady LJ:** The plaintiffs are holders for value of two bills of lading for a quantity of wool shipped at Napier, New Zealand, for London by the defendants' steamship *Tokomaru*. This ship was torpedoed on 30 January 1915, by a German submarine when between seven and eight miles from Havre, and ship and cargo were an actual total loss. The plaintiffs sue for breach of the contract evidenced by the bill of lading. The defendants, while admitting the total loss of the goods, dispute their liability. They say that the loss occurred by an excepted peril, the King's enemies. The plaintiffs contend that the defendants are not entitled to rely upon the exception contained in the bill of lading, as they say the *Tokomaru* was deviating from the contract voyage by leaving the direct course for London and proceeding to Havre when the disaster occurred, and that the liberties contained in the bill of lading did not permit that to be done. This raises the first question, namely, whether the *Tokomaru* was deviating in proceeding towards Havre. If not deviating, there is an end of the matter, and the shipowners are protected from liability by the bill of lading. If, however, the *Tokomaru* was deviating, the further question arises

as to the liability of the defendants as carriers under the circumstances. The defendants contend that they incurred no greater liability than that of common carriers, and are therefore not liable for acts of the King's enemies ...

The ordinary route for steamers of this line is, outward bound, via Cape of Good Hope to New Zealand; homeward bound, from New Zealand via Cape Horn and west of the Falkland Islands to Monte Video, then to Teneriffe or Madeira, and thence direct to London ...

On leaving Teneriffe the course, whether for Havre or to London direct, is the same to a point about 10 miles off the Casquets. There the routes diverge. From the point of divergence it is 107 miles to Havre and 118 miles Havre to Dover. Thus from the point of divergence to Dover via Havre it is 225 miles; from the point of divergence to Dover direct it is 171 miles; so by proceeding to Havre the length of the voyage would be increased by 54 miles. From Havre to the nearest point of the ship's ordinary route to Dover is a distance of 68 miles ...

The first question is, can it be said that the ship had liberty to go to Havre to discharge cargo by reason of the 'liberty on the way to London to call and stay at any intermediate port or ports to discharge or take on board passengers, cargo, coal or other supplies'. It must be borne in mind when considering the true construction and effect of bills of lading that it is important to everyone concerned in the carriage of goods by sea – whether shipper, shipowner, or insurer – that the route by which the ship and goods are to pass should be determined, that the risks may be estimated on that basis ...

I am of opinion that it is impossible to lay down any hard and fast rule by which it may be determined whether any particular port is an intermediate port within the meaning of a bill of lading. In construing the document all the surrounding circumstances must be taken into consideration. The size and class of ship, the nature of the voyage, the usual and customary course, the natural or usual ports of call, the nature and position of the port in question. It is a question of fact in each case, and in my judgment Bailhache J was right in deciding that Havre was not an intermediate port on the voyage of this vessel from New Zealand to London, and that the *Tokomaru* in making for that port was deviating from her voyage, and that the defendants thereby lost the benefit of the exceptions in the bill of lading: *Joseph Thorley Ltd v Orchis Steamship Co* [1907] 1 KB 669; *Internationale Guano v Macandrew* [1909] 2 KB 360.

If that be so, the remaining question is whether the defendants are protected from liability as carriers by the fact that the loss occurred through the King's enemies. If they, as carriers, were duly performing their contract of carriage, they would not be liable for loss occasioned by the King's enemies. But they are breaking their contract. They are quite unable to show that the loss must have occurred in any event, and whether they had deviated or not. True it is that there had been no previous warning of danger from submarines, and that the event which occasioned the loss was wholly unexpected, but this does not assist the defendants. The answer to the argument of the defendants on this point is that given by Tindal CJ in *Davis v Garrett* (1830) 6 Bing 716, 724 ...

... In my judgment the appeal fails and should be dismissed.

[Bankes and Phillimore LJJ delivered judgments to the same effect.]

Cunard Steamship v Buerger [1927] AC 1

This was an action for non-delivery of eight cases of textiles shipped by the respondents on the *Verentia* for delivery at Batoum (five cases) and Constantinople (three cases). The ship left Batoum with the five cases still on board, after which nothing more was ever heard of them. The cases for Constantinople were landed at Novorossisk, the last port of call, for reasons unknown. They were retained there for at least two months by the appellants' agents, who wrote that they would be forwarded by the next ship to Constantinople; after which nothing more was heard of them either. The appellants pleaded a contractual limitation of liability: the respondents alleged deviation.

It was held that both the overcarriage of the five cases beyond Batoum and the landing of the three cases at Novorossisk without reloading them at once or promptly forwarding them were deviations unless the appellants could rely on liberty clauses in the bill of lading.

So far as the five Batoum cases were concerned, it was held that the appellants could not rely on a clause which gave a liberty 'before or after proceeding towards her port of discharge', because the acts in question occurred after she left her port of discharge. Nor could they rely on a clause giving liberty to forward from a subsequent port if delivery at the contractual port of discharge was inconvenient or if the goods could not be found, because (a) neither of these circumstances could be proved in the present case and (b) the liberty to forward from a subsequent port was not also a liberty to deviate to a subsequent port.

As to the three cases, the appellants could not rely on a contractual liberty to land and reship because they had (on the facts) landed the goods once and for all with no real intention of reshipping them. While all members of the House agreed that the deviations prevented the appellants relying on a contractual limitation of liability, Lord Parmoor added the explanation that in his view it was a:

> well established principle, that stipulations in a contract of carriage, limiting or negativing the liability of carriers, by land or water, for loss or damage to goods entrusted to them for carriage, do not apply when such damage has occurred outside the route or voyage contemplated by the parties when they entered into the contract of carriage, unless the intention that such limitations should apply is expressed in clear and unambiguous language. (p 13)

Connolly Shaw v Nordenfjeldske Steamship (1934) 50 TLR 418

Lemons were shipped at Palermo on the *Ragnvald Jarl* for carriage to London. The vessel went on to Barcelona and Valencia, where potatoes were loaded which the shipowners agreed to deliver at Hull before going to London. The plaintiffs were indorsees of the bill of lading covering the lemons. They brought an action against the shipowners for delay in deviating to Hull. A clause in the bill of lading covering the lemons provided:

Nothing in this bill of lading (whether written or printed) is to be read as an engagement that the said carriage shall be performed directly or without delays, the ship is to be at liberty, either before or after proceeding towards the port of delivery of the said goods, to proceed to or return to and stay at any ports or places whatsoever (although in a contrary direction to or out of or beyond the route of the said port of delivery) once or oftener in any order backwards or forwards for loading or discharging cargo passengers coals or stores or for any purpose whatsoever whether in relation to her homeward voyage or to her outward voyage or to an intermediate voyage, and all such ports places and sailings shall be deemed included within the intended voyage of the said goods.

Branson J: There could be no question that the clause in the bill of lading in this case was a step forward in the contest between shipowners and ... shippers, the shipowners attempting to keep the order and disposition of their vessels unhampered. The only duty of the courts was to see what was the real contract between the parties. Where two parties, both *sui juris* and at arm's length, entered into a contract which put one at a disadvantage compared with the other they must abide by it, and, provided that the intention was clearly expressed, the court would enforce it.

The present clause ... differed from that in *Leduc and Co v Ward* (1888) 20 QBD 475, *Glynn v Margetson* [1893] AC 351 and *White v Granada Steamship Company Limited* 13 TLR 1. It appeared to have been drawn with the object of avoiding the result of those cases. If the case was put as high as the defendants put it, that they had the right to go anywhere they pleased, there would be a contradiction between the different parts of the contract, and one would then have to reject whatever tended to frustrate the contract, which was to carry a perishable cargo to London. But so far as the liberty could exist without frustrating the contract, it must not be disregarded altogether but must be treated as valid ...

In this case, therefore, the ship had liberty to go where she pleased so long as the purpose of the voyage was not frustrated ... The evidence did not show that the call at Hull before going to London had affected the condition of the lemons, and the action therefore failed.

Renton v Palmyra [1957] AC 149, HL

This appeal arose out of claims under bills of lading issued by the respondent shipowners which provided for the carriage of timber in the vessel *Caspiana* from Canada to London or Hull. While the ship was on passage a dock strike broke out in London followed subsequently by a strike at Hull; shipowners ordered the vessel to proceed to Hamburg where the timber was discharged. The shipowners took no steps to forward it to England but made it available at Hamburg to the holders of the bills of lading on payment of the full freight. In an action against the shipowners for damages for breach of contract, shipowners contended that they had effected due delivery under the bills of lading and relied on the following printed terms:

14 (c) Should it appear that ... strikes ... would prevent the vessel from ... entering the port of discharge or there discharging in the usual manner and leaving again ... safely and without delay, the master may discharge the cargo at port of loading or any other safe and convenient port ...

(f) The discharge of any cargo under the provisions of this clause shall be deemed due fulfilment of the contract ...

The House of Lords rejected an argument that since the main object of the contract was the carriage of timber to London or Hull, clause 14 was inconsistent with that object and could be disregarded.

> **Viscount Kilmuir LC** ... It is necessary in considering the authorities on which Mr Mocatta (counsel for the appellants) relies to consider carefully the form of the deviation clauses in each case. They were invariably in so extensive a form that, if they were fully and literally construed, the shipowners had a complete discretion to delay intolerably and so defeat the main object and intent of the contract if they so desired. The distinction between these cases and that before your Lordships' House has been so well stated by Jenkins LJ [1956] 1 QB 462, 502, that I find it impossible to improve on his words, which I quote:
>
> > ... there is a material difference between a deviation clause purporting to enable the shipowners to delay indefinitely the performance of the contract voyage simply because they choose to do so, and provisions such as those contained in clause 14 (c) and (f) in the present case, which are applicable and operative only in the event of the occurrence of certain specified emergencies. The distinction is between a power given to one of the parties which, if construed literally, would in effect enable that party to nullify the contract at will, and a special provision stating what the rights and obligations of the parties are to be in the event of obstacles beyond the control of either arising to prevent or impede the performance of the contract in accordance with its primary terms.

6 EFFECT OF DEVIATION

Hain Steamship v Tate and Lyle (1936) 41 Com Cas 350, HL

The *Tregenna* was chartered to load a full cargo of sugar in Cuba and San Domingo. The ship loaded a part cargo in Cuba, but having received no orders for San Domingo, sailed for Queenstown. She was recalled by the charterers and directed to complete loading at San Pedro de Macoris in San Domingo, where she arrived a little over a day later than if she had gone direct and after having done 265 miles of extra steaming. On sailing from San Pedro, she stranded and was damaged. Part of the cargo was saved and transshipped. Tate and Lyle, the respondents, were cif purchasers of the whole cargo and bills of lading were indorsed and delivered to them by the charterers. The shipowners refused to deliver the cargo in accordance with the bills of lading until the respondents paid a deposit and entered into a bond relating to the general average contribution claimed by the ship. When the respondents discovered the course the ship had taken on leaving Cuba, they brought proceedings, alleging that in respect of the Cuban cargo, the ship had deviated from the contract voyage. Lord Atkin, Lord Wright and Lord Maugham delivered reasoned judgments.

Lord Atkin: ... My Lords, the effect of a deviation upon a contract of carriage by sea has been stated in a variety of cases but not in uniform language. Everyone is agreed that it is a serious matter. Occasionally language has been used which suggests that the occurrence of a deviation automatically displaces the contract, as by the now accepted doctrine does an event which 'frustrates' a contract. In other cases where the effect of deviation upon the exceptions in the contract had to be considered language is used which Sir Robert Aske (counsel) argued shows that the sole effect is, as it were, to expunge the exceptions clause, as no longer applying to a voyage which from the beginning of the deviation has ceased to be the contract voyage. I venture to think that the true view is that the departure from the voyage contracted to be made is a breach by the shipowner of his contract, a breach of such a serious character that, however slight the deviation, the other party to the contract is entitled to treat it as going to the root of the contract, and to declare himself as no longer bound by any of the contract terms. I wish to confine myself to contracts of carriage by sea, and in the circumstances of such a carriage I am satisfied that by a long series of decisions, adopting in fact commercial usage in this respect, any deviation constitutes a breach of contract of this serious nature. The same view is taken in contracts of marine insurance where there is implied an absolute condition not to deviate. No doubt the extreme gravity attached to a deviation in contracts of carriage is justified by the fact that the insured cargo owner when the ship has deviated has become uninsured. It appears to me inevitable that a breach of contract which results in such momentous consequences well known to all concerned in commerce by sea should entitle the other party to refuse to be bound. It is true that the cargo owner may, though very improbably, be uninsured; it is also true that in these days it is not uncommon for marine insurers to hold the assured covered in case of deviation at a premium to be arranged. But these considerations do not appear to diminish the serious nature of the breach in all the circumstances of sea carriage, and may be balanced by the fact that the ship can and often does take liberties to deviate which prevent the result I have stated. If this view be correct, then the breach by deviation does not automatically cancel the express contract, otherwise the shipowner by his own wrong can get rid of his own contract. Nor does it affect merely the exceptions clauses. This would make those clauses alone subject to a condition of no deviation, a construction for which I can find no justification. It is quite inconsistent with the cases which have treated deviation as precluding enforcement of demurrage provisions. The event falls within the ordinary law of contract. The party who is affected by the breach has the right to say, 'I am not now bound by the contract whether it is expressed in charterparty, bill of lading, or otherwise'. He can, of course, claim his goods from the ship; whether and to what extent he will become liable to pay some remuneration for carriage I do not think arises in this case ... but I am satisfied that once he elects to treat the contract as at an end he is not bound by the promise to pay the agreed freight any more than by his other promises. But, on the other hand, as he can elect to treat the contract as ended, so he can elect to treat the contract as subsisting; and if he does this with knowledge of his rights he must in accordance with the general law of contract be held bound. No doubt one must be careful to see that the acts of the cargo owner are not misinterpreted when he finds that his goods have been taken off on a voyage to which he did not agree. He could not reasonably be expected to recall the goods when he discovers the ship at a port of call presumably still intending to reach her agreed port of destination. There must be acts which plainly show that the shipper intends to treat the contract as still binding. In the present case where the charterer procured the ship to be recalled to a San Domingo port for the express purpose of continuing to load under the charter, an obligation which of course only existed in pursuance of the express contract, and saw that the ship did receive the cargo stipulated under the subcharter provided by persons who had no right to load except under the subcharter, I am satisfied that there is abundant, indeed conclusive, evidence to justify the report of Branson J that the deviation was waived by the charterers.

The result is that at the time the casualty occurred and the general average sacrifice and expenses were incurred the ship was still under the charter. In respect of the Cuban sugar the charterers appear to have been at the time the owners of the goods, and I think it clear that on principle the contribution falls due from the persons who were owners at the time of the sacrifice, though no doubt it may be passed on to subsequent assignees of the goods by appropriate contractual stipulations. The place of adjustment does not seem to have a bearing on the question against whom the contribution has to be adjusted. It must be remembered that, at any rate so far as the Cuban sugar is concerned, at the time of loss and until transfer of the bills of lading in October Messrs Farr were the only persons in contractual relation with the ship. The bills of lading which they held were in their hands merely receipts for shipment and of course symbols of the goods with which they could transfer the right to possession and the property.

It follows that when the [cargo] arrived at Greenock the Hain Company, who were, through their bills of lading, in possession of the goods, had a claim for contribution against the charterers, and for the reasons given by Greer LJ in his admirable judgment, with which I find myself in entire accord, had a lien on the goods for that contribution.

Now the position of the respondents, Tate and Lyle, has to be considered from two points of view: (1) as indorsees of the bills of lading in circumstances in which the rights and liabilities expressed in the bills of lading would devolve upon them as though the contract contained therein had been made with them (under the Bills of Lading Act); (2) as parties to the Lloyd's bond.

(1) In respect of the first, in my opinion, the fact of deviation gives the bill of lading holder the rights I have already mentioned. On discovery he is entitled to refuse to be bound by the contract. Waiver by the charterer seems on principle to have no bearing upon the rights and liabilities which devolve upon the bill of lading holder under the Bills of Lading Act. The consignee has not assigned to him the obligations under the charterparty, nor, in fact, any obligation of the charterer under the bill of lading, for *ex*

hypothesi there is none. A new contract appears to spring up between the ship and the consignee of the terms of the bill of lading. One of the terms is the performance of an agreed voyage, a deviation from which is a fundamental breach. It seems to me impossible to see how a waiver of such a breach by the party to the charterparty contract can affect the rights of different parties in respect to the breach by the same event of the bill of lading contract. I think, therefore, that a deviation would admittedly preclude a claim for contribution arising against parties to a subsisting contract of carriage, though no doubt the claim does not arise as a term of the contract, and as the bill of lading holder is entitled to say that he is not bound by the agreed term as to freight the ship could not, in the present circumstances, claim against Tate and Lyle either contribution or freight if they had to rely on the bill of lading alone.

(2) On the other hand, the terms of the Lloyd's bond appear in the plainest words to give to the ship the right they claim in respect of contribution. The consignees agree to pay to the owners the proper proportion of general average charges 'which may be chargeable upon their respective consignments' or 'to which the shippers or owners of such consignments may be liable to contribute'. General average charges were, as I have said, chargeable by way of lien against the sugar, and the shippers were liable to contribute. The obligation is independent of the bill of lading; there is good consideration in the ship giving up a lien which it claims and giving to the consignees immediate and not delayed delivery. I do not attach any importance in this case to the without-prejudice provisions in the third part of the bond, which affect only the deposit, and would not in any case apply where there was in fact a good claim for contribution against the original shippers. I think, therefore, that the claim of Tate and Lyle which is directed to recovering the deposit made in respect of the Cuban sugar fails, and that the ship's claim for a declaration that there is a valid claim for contribution against the deposit succeeds. On the ship's claim for the balance of freight in respect of the San Domingo sugar I have come to the conclusion that it must fail. That there is no claim on the express contract, the bill of lading, I have already said. An amendment to claim a quantum meruit was, however, allowed, and this has occasioned me some difficulty. I am not prepared at present to adopt the view of Scrutton LJ that in no circumstances can a consignee, whether holder of a bill of lading or not, be liable to pay after a deviation any remuneration for the carriage from which he has benefited. I prefer to leave the matter open, and, in those circumstances, to say that the opinion of the Court of Appeal to the contrary in this case should not be taken as authoritative. In the present case I find that the balance of freight under the charterparty, and therefore under the bill of lading, was to be paid in New York after advice of right delivery and ascertainment of weight. The terms of the cesser clause do not affect this obligation, and consequently the charterer remained and remains still liable for that freight. In these circumstances I am not satisfied that conditions existed under which a promise should be implied whereby the shippers undertook to give to the ship a further and a different right to receive some part of what would be a reasonable remuneration for the carriage. I think, therefore, that the claim for freight fails.

Notes

1   *Effect of deviation: demurrage*

The *Alamosa* was chartered to carry a cargo from the River Plate to Malaga and Seville in that order. After discharging at Malaga within the agreed laytime, she had enough fuel oil to take her to Seville and to discharge there, but not enough to enable her to leave Seville afterwards. The vessel therefore went to Gibraltar having arranged to meet and take on bunkers from a tanker there. After waiting for two days at Gibraltar for the tanker, which did not arrive, the master took the vessel to Lisbon, which was off the geographical route but was the nearest place at which fuel oil could be obtained. The arbitrator found as a fact that the master acted reasonably in doing so. After taking on fuel, the vessel went to Seville where time taken to discharge exceeded the time fixed by the charter. The owners claimed demurrage in arbitration proceedings. The charterers contended that the ship had deviated from the chartered course and that this deprived the owners of the right to demurrage; the charterers also claimed damages for deviation. On a case stated by the arbitrator, Bailhache J held [(1924) 40 TLR 54] that:

> from the point of deviation all clauses in the contract which were in favour of the shipowners come to an end. The fixed lay days for discharge must go, though the charterers will still remain liable to discharge within a reasonable time.

The owners' claim for demurrage failed.

This judgment was affirmed on appeal to the Court of Appeal. In the House of Lords it was not disputed that the trip to Lisbon was a deviation. However, the owners attempted to justify the deviation by arguing that, if the deviation was reasonably necessary in a business sense, then it was in the course of the voyage which the charter prescribed. This argument was rejected on the grounds that it could only aid the shipowners if it had been proved (which it had not) that all necessary steps had been taken to supply the vessel with fuel at the commencement of the voyage. The judgment of the Court of Appeal was affirmed.

[Even if proof had been available on the point in question, it is not certain that the shipowners would have been successful. The House of Lords seems to have doubted whether a deviation could be justified if the object was to take on bunkers, not to get the ship to the port of discharge, but to take her out of that port after discharge had been completed.] (*United States Shipping Board v Bunge and Born* (1925) 42 TLR 174.)

2   *Effect of deviation; statutory limitation of liability*

The appellants were owners of a cargo of flour/cereals laden on board the *Thordoc* for carriage from Port Arthur (Ontario) to Montreal. Before proceeding on her voyage down Lake Superior, the vessel called at the neighbouring port of Fort William to discharge some boats belonging to the respondents. The *Thordoc* then resumed her chartered voyage in the course of which, because of a faulty compass and the incompetence of the steersman, she stranded at Point Porphyry and was wrecked with great loss and damage to cargo. The appellants obtained judgment for damages in respect of that loss and damage. The respondents then brought the present action to limit their liability under s 503 of the Merchant Shipping Act 1894.

The Privy Council, on appeal from the Exchequer Court of Canada, held that since the loss and damage took place without the actual fault or privity of the respondents in respect of that which caused the loss or damage in question, the respondents were entitled to limit their liability. The respondents were not at fault in respect of the improper navigation which caused the stranding merely because there had previously been a deviation. The deviation:

> had nothing whatever to do with the loss of, or damage to, cargo now in question. At the time of the stranding any deviation was over and past, and the ship was at a place and on a course proper for her voyage ...
>
> *per* Lord Roche, *Paterson Steamships v Robin Hood Mills* (1937) 58 Ll L Rep 33, 39.

3   *Deviation and the general law of contract*

In *Suisse Atlantique Societé d'Armement Maritime SA v NV Rotterdamsche Kolen Centrale* [1967] 1 AC 435, Lord Wilberforce said:

> There is a long line of authority the commencement of which is usually taken from the judgment of Tindal CJ in *Davis v Garrett* (1830) 6 Bing 716, which shows that a shipowner who deviates from an agreed voyage, steps out of the contract, so that clauses in the contract (such as exceptions or limitation clauses) which are designed to apply to the contracted voyage are held to have no application to the deviating voyage. The basis for the rule was explained in *Stag Line Ltd v Foscolo, Mango & Co* [1932] AC 328, 347 by Lord Russell of Killowen in these terms:
>
> > it was well settled before the Act [of 1924] that an unjustifiable deviation deprived a ship of the protection of exceptions. They only applied to the contract voyage.

In *The Cap Palos* [1921] P 458, 471, Atkin LJ had applied this principle to contracts generally, adopting for this purpose the formulation of Scrutton LJ in *Gibaud v Great Eastern Railway Company* [1921] 2 KB 426, 435:

> The principle is well known, and perhaps *Lilley v Doubleday* 7 QBD 510, is the best illustration, that if you undertake to do a thing in a certain way, or to keep a thing in a certain place, with certain conditions protecting it, and have broken the contract by not doing the thing contracted for in the way contracted for, or not keeping the article in the place in which you have contracted to keep it, you cannot rely on the conditions which were only intended to protect you if you carried out the contract in the way which you had contracted to do it.

The words 'intended to protect you' show quite clearly that the rule is based on contractual intention.

4   In *Photo Production v Securicor* [1980] AC 827 Lord Wilberforce (Lord Keith of Kinkel and Lord Scarman agreeing) said (at 845):

> ... I must add to this, by way of exception to the decision not to 'gloss' the *Suisse Atlantique* [1967] 1 AC 361 a brief observation on the deviation cases, since some reliance has been placed upon them, particularly upon the decision of this House in *Hain Steamship Co Ltd v Tate and Lyle Ltd* (1936) 155 LT 177 (so earlier than the Suisse Atlantique) ... I suggested in the *Suisse Atlantique* that these cases can be regarded as proceeding upon normal principles applicable to the law of contract generally viz, that it is a matter of the parties' intentions whether and to what extent clauses in shipping contracts can be applied after a deviation, ie a departure from the contractually agreed voyage or adventure. It may be preferable that they should be considered as a body of authority *sui generis* with special rules derived from historical and commercial reasons. What on either view they cannot do is to lay down different rules as to contracts generally from those later stated by this House in *Heyman v Darwins Ltd* [1942] AC 356 ...

In the same case, Lord Diplock spoke of deviation as a breach of condition the effect of which, in accordance with the general law of contract, was that the innocent party was entitled to elect to put an end to all the primary outstanding obligations of both parties:

> ... Where such an election is made (a) there is substituted by implication of law for the primary obligations of the party in default which remain unperformed a secondary obligation to pay monetary compensation to the other party for the loss sustained by him in consequence of their non-performance in the future and (b) the unperformed primary obligations of that other party are discharged. This secondary obligation is additional to the general secondary obligation (ie the obligation to pay damages for any breach of contract): I will call it 'the anticipatory secondary obligation'.
>
> In cases falling within the first exception, fundamental breach, the anticipatory secondary obligation arises under contracts of all kinds by implication of the common law, except to the extent that it is excluded or modified by the express words of the contract. In cases falling within the second exception, breach of condition, the anticipatory secondary obligation generally arises under particular kinds of contracts by implication of statute law; though in the case of 'deviation' from the contract voyage under a contract of carriage of goods by sea it arises by implication of the common law. The anticipatory secondary obligation in these cases too can be excluded or modified by express words.
>
> When there has been a fundamental breach or breach of condition, the coming to an end of the primary obligations of both parties to the contract at the election of the party not in default, is often referred to as the 'determination' or 'rescission' of the contract or, as in the Sale of Goods Act 1893 'treating the contract as repudiated'. The first two of these

expressions, however, are misleading unless it is borne in mind that for the unperformed primary obligations of the party in default there are substituted by operation of law what I have called the secondary obligations.

The bringing to an end of all primary obligations under the contract may also leave the parties in a relationship, typically that of bailor and bailee, in which they owe to one another by operation of law fresh primary obligations of which the contract is the source; but no such relationship is involved in the instant case.

I have left out of account in this analysis as irrelevant to the instant case an arbitration or choice of forum clause. This does not come into operation until a party to the contract claims that a primary obligation of the other party has not been performed; and its relationship to other obligations of which the contract is the source was dealt with by this House in *Heyman v Darwins Ltd* [1942] AC 356.

My Lords, an exclusion clause is one which excludes or modifies an obligation, whether primary, general secondary or anticipatory secondary, that would otherwise arise under the contract by implication of law. Parties are free to agree to whatever exclusion or modification of all types of obligations as they please within the limits that the agreement must retain the legal characteristics of a contract; and must not offend against the equitable rule against penalties ... (at 850).

5   *Deck cargo*

Cargo stowed on the deck of a conventional vessel is exposed to substantially greater risks than cargo stowed in a hold and, if not authorised, is a serious breach of a contract. Unauthorised stowage on deck is sometimes referred to as a quasi-deviation. In *Royal Exchange Shipping Co Ltd v Dixon* (1886) 12 App Cas 11, bales of cotton were shipped on the appellants' screw steamer *Egyptian Monarch* for carriage from New Orleans to Liverpool. In breach of contract, some of the cotton was carried on deck. On the voyage the ship took the ground, and in order to get her off the master properly jettisoned the cotton. The indorsees of the bills of lading brought an action against the shipowners to recover the value of the cotton. The House of Lords held that an exception in the bills of lading of 'jettison' was no defence to the claim. It is not clear from the report whether this was conceived as a decision on the construction of the clause, or the application of a rule of law, but in *The Chanda* [1989] 2 Lloyd's Rep 494 (Chapter 8), it was said that the decision in *Dixon* was based on a principle of construction.

CHAPTER 6

THE BILL OF LADING AS A CONTRACT

The bill of lading is a commercial document with a long history ... it has meant different things at different times. Beginning as a bailment receipt for goods, it has developed into a receipt containing the contract of carriage and acquired in time a third characteristic, that of a negotiable document of title.

Bills of Lading, Report by the Secretariat on the United Nations Conference on Trade and Development, New York, 1971.

1 THE CONTRACT OR EVIDENCE OF THE CONTRACT?

Ardennes (Cargo Owners) v Ardennes (Owners) [1951] 1 KB 55

The plaintiffs shipped 3,000 cases of mandarin oranges on the *Ardennes* at Cartagena after the defendants had orally agreed to carry this cargo direct to London. When the cargo had been loaded, a bill of lading was issued which contained liberty to call at intermediate ports, to proceed by any route directly or indirectly and to overcarry. Instead of sailing direct to London, the vessel went first to Antwerp. By the time she arrived in London there had been an increase in the import tax payable on mandarins and the market price of the fruit had fallen. The plaintiffs were awarded damages in respect of (i) the increase in import duty and (ii) their loss of profit due to the foreseeable fall in the market price.

> **Lord Goddard**: ... The defences raised were in substance that there was no oral agreement, and reliance is placed on one of the conditions in the bill of lading. I have no hesitation in finding that there was a promise made to the shippers' representative that the ship should go direct to London, and that they shipped in reliance on that promise. I therefore have now to consider the defence which arises out of the terms of the bill of lading ...
>
> It is, I think, well settled that a bill of lading is not in itself the contract between the shipowner and the shipper of goods, though it has been said to be excellent evidence of its terms: *Sewell v Burdick* (1884) 10 App Cas 74, 105 *per* Lord Bramwell and *Crooks v Allan* (1879) 5 QBD 38. The contract has come into existence before the bill of lading is signed; the latter is signed by one party only, and handed by him to the shipper usually after the goods have been put on board. No doubt if the shipper finds that the bill contains terms with which he is not content, or does not contain some term for which he has stipulated, he might, if there were time, demand his goods back; but he is not, in my opinion, for that reason, prevented from giving evidence that there was in fact a contract entered into before the bill of lading was signed different from that which is found in the bill of lading or containing some additional term. He is

no party to the preparation of the bill of lading; nor does he sign it. It is unnecessary to cite authority further than the two cases already mentioned for the proposition that the bill of lading is not itself the contract; therefore in my opinion evidence as to the true contract is admissible ...

2 WHOSE CONTRACT? IDENTIFYING THE CARRIER

Sandeman v Scurr (1866) LR 2 QB 86

Cockburn CJ delivered the judgment of the court:

The action is brought against the defendants, who are the owners of the ship *The Village Belle*, for damage and loss occasioned by bad stowage, to certain goods shipped in that vessel by the plaintiffs. The facts upon which the case turns are as follows.

The Village Belle went to Oporto under a charterparty entered into between her master, on behalf of the owners, and a Mr Hodgson, by which the master contracted to load at Oporto from the factors of the affreighter a full cargo of wine or other merchandise, and to carry the same to a safe port in the United Kingdom. Should the cargo consist of wine, the freight was to be 18 shillings per tun of 252 gallons; should other goods than wine be shipped, the freight was to be at the same rate on the quantity of wine the vessel would have carried, the quantity to be ascertained by a stevedore to be appointed by the charterer's agents and the master. The cargo was 'to be brought to and taken from alongside the vessel at the merchant's risk and expense'. The captain was to 'sign bills of lading at any rate of freight, without prejudice to the charter'. The ship was 'to be addressed to the charterer's agents at Oporto on usual terms'.

The ship accordingly proceeded to Oporto, consigned to the agents of the charterer. She was by them put up as a general ship, but without it being at all made known that the vessel was under charter. The plaintiffs delivered their goods on board without any knowledge that the ship was not entirely at the disposition of the owner. Bills of lading for the goods in question were signed by the master in the usual form. The cargo was stowed by stevedores employed and paid by the charterer's agents, but the amount so paid by the latter was repaid to them by the master.

The goods having been damaged by reason of improper stowage, the plaintiffs have brought their action against the defendants, as owners of the vessel; and the question is, whether the defendants, under the circumstances stated, are liable. We are of opinion that they are liable, and that the action against them lies.

On the argument, it was contended on behalf of the defendants, that, as the use of the ship had been made over to Hodgson, the charterer, and the ship had been put up as a general ship by his agents, and the bill of lading had been given by the captain in furtherance of a contract for freight of which the charterer was to have the benefit, the captain must be considered as having given the bill of lading as the agent of the charterer, and the contract as having been made with the latter, and not with the defendants, the owners of the vessel; and that, consequently, the charterer was alone responsible for the negligent stowing of the goods in question.

It is unnecessary to decide whether the charterer would or would not have been liable, if an action had under the circumstances been brought against him. Our judgment proceeds on a ground, wholly irrespective of the question of the charterer's liability, and not inconsistent with it, namely, that the plaintiffs, having delivered their goods to be carried in ignorance of the vessel being chartered, and having dealt with the master as clothed with the ordinary authority of a master to receive goods and give bills of lading on behalf of his owners, are entitled to look to the owners as responsible for the safe carriage of the goods.

The result of the authorities, from *Parish v Crawford* (1746) 2 Str 1251 downwards, and more especially the case of *Newberry v Colvin* (1832) 1 Cl & F 283, in which the judgment of the Court of Exchequer Chamber, reversing the judgment of the Court of Queen's Bench, was affirmed on appeal by the House of Lords, is to establish the position, that in construing a charterparty with reference to the liability of the owners of the chartered ship, it is necessary to look to the charterparty, to see whether it operates as a demise of the ship itself, to which the services of the master and crew may or may not be superadded, or whether all that the charterer acquires by the terms of the instrument is the right to have his goods conveyed by the particular vessel, and, as subsidiary thereto, to have the use of the vessel and the services of the master and crew.

In the first case, the charterer becomes for the time the owner of the vessel, the master and crew become to all intents and purposes his servants, and through them the possession of the ship is in him. In the second, notwithstanding the temporary right of the charterer to have his goods loaded and conveyed in the vessel, the ownership remains in the original owners, and through the master and the crew, who continue to be their servants, the possession of the ship also. If the master, by the agreement of his owners and the charterer, acquires authority to sign bills of lading on behalf of the latter, he nevertheless remains in all other respects the servant of the owners; in other words, he retains that relation to his owners out of which by the law merchant arises the authority to sign bills of lading by which the owner will be bound.

It appears to us clear that the charterparty in the present instance falls under the second of the two classes referred to. There is here no demise of the ship itself, either express or implied. It amounts to no more than a grant to the charterer of the right to have his cargo brought home in the ship, while the ship itself continues, through the master and crew, in the possession of the owners, the master and crew remaining their servants.

It is on this ground that our judgment is founded. We think that so long as the relation of owner and master continues, the latter, as regards parties who ship goods in ignorance of any arrangement whereby the authority ordinarily incidental to that relation is affected, must be taken to have authority to bind his owner by giving bills of lading. We proceed on the well known principle that, where a party allows another to appear before the world as his agent in any given capacity, he must be liable to any party who contracts with such apparent agent in a matter within the scope of such agency. The master of a vessel has by law authority to sign bills of lading on behalf of his owners. A person shipping goods on board a vessel, unaware that the vessel has been chartered to another, is warranted in assuming that the master is acting by virtue of his ordinary authority, and therefore acting for his owners in signing bills of lading. It may be that, as between the owner, the master, and the charterer, the authority of the master is to sign bills of lading on behalf of the charterer only, and not of the owner. But, in our judgment, this altered state of the master's authority will not affect the liability of the owner, whose servant the master still remains, clothed with a character to which the authority to bind his owner by signing bills of lading attaches by virtue of his office. We think that until the fact that the master's authority has been put an end to is brought to the knowledge of a shipper of goods, the latter has a right to look to the owner as the principal with whom his contract has been made ...

Note

In *The Rewia* [1991] 2 Lloyd's Rep 325, the Court of Appeal held that a bill of lading signed for a master could not be a charterer's bill unless the contract was made with the charterer alone and the person signing had authority to sign and did sign on behalf of the charterer and not the owners.

3 THE BILL OF LADING IN THE HANDS OF A CHARTERER

Rodocanachi v Milburn (1886) 18 QBD 67, CA

The plaintiffs chartered the defendants' ship to carry a cargo of cotton seed from Alexandria to the United Kingdom. The cargo was shipped under the charterparty at Alexandria by and on account of the charterers. A bill of lading was issued which contained an exception which was not in the charterparty and which purported to relieve the shipowners from liability for damage arising 'from any act, neglect, or default of the pilot, master, or mariners'. The cargo was lost by the negligence of the master.

Lindley LJ: ... The authorities shew that *prima facie*, and in the absence of express provision to the contrary, the bill of lading as between the charterers and the shipowners is to be looked upon as a mere receipt for the goods. There is nothing here to shew any intention to the contrary; so far from there having been in fact any *animus contrahendi* when the bill of lading was signed, the jury have found upon the evidence that there was none, and that the bill of lading was taken as a mere receipt ...

4 INCORPORATION OF CHARTERPARTIES IN BILLS OF LADING

(a) **Bingham LJ**: Generally speaking, the English law of contract has taken a benevolent view of the use of general words to incorporate by reference standard terms to be found elsewhere. But in the present field a different, and stricter, rule has developed, especially where the incorporation of arbitration clauses is concerned. The reason no doubt is that a bill of lading is a negotiable commercial instrument and may come into the hands of a foreign party with no knowledge and no ready means of knowledge of the terms of the charterparty. The cases show that a strict test of incorporation having, for better or worse, been laid down, the courts have in general defended this rule with some tenacity in the interests of commercial certainty. If commercial parties do not like the English rule, they can meet the difficulty by spelling out the arbitration provision in the bill of lading and not relying on general words to achieve incorporation. (*The Federal Bulker* [1989] 1 Lloyd's Rep 103, 105, CA.)

(b) The language of the bill of lading is the starting point: *The Varenna* [1984] QB 599. The operative words of incorporation must normally be found in the bill of lading itself since incorporation can only be achieved by agreement of the parties to that contract. General words of incorporation in a bill of lading such as 'all terms, conditions and exceptions to be as per charterparty' are normally given a limited meaning and are taken to refer only to those terms, conditions and exceptions in the charter which relate to the main undertakings in a bill of lading agreement, such as the shipment, carriage and delivery of goods and the payment of freight, and not to incorporate collateral matters such as an arbitration agreement.

> I think it would be a sound rule of construction to adopt that when it is sought to introduce into a document like a bill of lading – a negotiable instrument – a clause such as this arbitration clause, not germane to the receipt, carriage, or delivery of the cargo or the payment of the freight – the proper subject matters with which the bill of lading is conversant – this should be done by distinct and specific words, and not by such general words as those written in the margin of the bill of lading in this case. (Lord Atkinson, *TW Thomas and Co Ltd v Portsea Steamship Co Ltd* [1912] AC 1.)

(c) Compare the words of incorporation in the bill of lading in *The Merak* [1965] P 223: 'all terms, conditions, clauses and exceptions ... in the said charterparty', which were held to be wide enough to permit incorporation of an aptly drafted arbitration clause.

(d) In *Manchester Trust v Furness Withy & Co* [1895] 2 QB 539, the bill of lading stated 'paying freight for the same, and other conditions charterparty'. Lindley LJ said (at p 545):

> The effect of that reference has been considered more than once ... the effect of the reference is to incorporate so much of the charterparty as relates to the payment of freight and other conditions to be performed on

the delivery of the cargo. But there is no authority whatever for incorporating more than that.

(e) 'Freight payable as per charterparty' was held in *India Steamship Co v Louis Dreyfus Sugar Ltd, the Indian Reliance* [1997] 1 Lloyd's Rep 52 to incorporate the whole of the relevant charter's terms as to the payment of freight, not only the rate of freight payable but also 'the manner of payment, when and where and to whom freight shall be payable'.

(f) In *The Annefield* [1971] P 178, CA, Lord Denning said that a clause in a charterparty which is not directly germane to the shipment, carriage or delivery of goods should not be incorporated into a bill of lading contract unless it is done by express words. But this has been doubted, since a term which is not germane in this sense may be incorporated if, as in *The Merak*, the language of the incorporation provision is wide enough. On the other hand, a term which is germane may not be incorporated if that is the proper construction of the relevant contract: *Hong Kong Borneo Services Co Ltd v Pilcher* [1992] 2 Lloyd's Rep 593.

(g) Normally, the language of the charterparty only becomes relevant at a second stage of the inquiry: *The Varenna*, above. If the language of a bill of lading is wide enough to effect a *prima facie* incorporation of a clause in a charterparty, the next question is whether that clause makes any sense at all in the context of the bill of lading contract. In *Hamilton & Co v Mackie & Sons* (1889) 5 TLR 677, Lord Esher MR said:

... the conditions of the charterparty must be read verbatim into the bill of lading as though they were printed there *in extenso*. Then, if it was found that any of the conditions of the charterparty on being so read were inconsistent with the bill of lading they were insensible, and must be disregarded.

(h) **Bingham LJ**: In a number of decided cases, as in *Thomas v Portsea* [above] the arbitration clause refers to 'disputes arising under this charter' and such language is obviously inapt for incorporation in a bill of lading. In other cases such as *The Merak* [above] reference is to 'disputes arising out of this charterparty or any bill of lading issued under it'. Language of that kind is plainly apt for incorporation in a bill of lading if the incorporating language is otherwise sufficient. (*The Federal Bulker* [1989] 1 Lloyd's Rep 103, 108, CA.)

(i) Verbal manipulation: if a general incorporation clause in a bill of lading catches terms in a charterparty which are inappropriate in the bill of lading contract, the question then is whether the terms are so clearly inconsistent with the bill of lading contract that they have to be rejected or whether the intention to incorporate a particular clause is so clearly expressed as to require, by necessary implication, some modification of the language incorporated so as to adapt it to the new contract into which it is inserted (Oliver LJ, *The Varenna*, above).

(j) In *Miramar Maritime Corporation v Holborn Oil Trading Ltd* [1984] 1 AC 676 the bill of lading provided for the incorporation of 'all the terms whatsoever of the said charter except the rate and payment of freight'. It was argued, on the basis of *dicta* in *The Annefield*, that this resulted in the incorporation in the bill of lading of the demurrage clause in the charterparty and that, because the clause was directly germane to the shipment, carriage and delivery of goods, a degree of verbal manipulation of the clause was permissible and 'charterer' in the demurrage clause could and should be read as 'consignee' or 'bill of lading holder'. If correct, this argument would have meant that every consignee of every parcel of goods carried on a chartered voyage using the standard forms in question might become liable for an unknown and wholly unpredictable sum for demurrage without any ability on his part to prevent it. The House of Lords rejected the claim.

Lord Diplock: My Lords, I venture to assert that no businessman who had not taken leave of his senses would intentionally enter into a contact which exposed him to a potential liability of this kind; and this, in itself, I find to be an overwhelming reason for not indulging in verbal manipulation of the actual contractual words used in the charterparty so as to give to them this effect when they are treated as incorporated in the bill of lading ...

[W]here in a bill of lading there is included a clause which purports to incorporate the terms of a specified charterparty, there is not any rule of construction that clauses in that charterparty which are directly germane to the shipment, carriage or delivery of goods and impose obligations upon the 'charterer' under that designation, are presumed to be incorporated in the bill of lading with the substitution of (where there is a cesser clause), or inclusion in (where there is no cesser clause), the designation 'charterer', the designation 'consignee of the cargo' or 'bill of lading holder'.

(k) A bill of lading was issued to shippers by shipowners in respect of goods shipped on board a vessel which was under charter. The bill of lading provided that 'all terms and conditions, liberties, exceptions and arbitration clause of the charter party, dated as overleaf, are herewith incorporated'. The arbitration clause in question referred to disputes 'between the Owners and the Charterers'. The Court of Appeal held that by identifying and specifying the charter party arbitration clause, the parties to the bill of lading contract had agreed to arbitrate and that to give effect to that intention, the words in the clause had to be construed as applying to those parties; the words in the clause would therefore be manipulated or adapted so that they covered disputes arising under the bill of lading contract (*The Nerano* [1996] 1 Lloyd's Rep 1, CA).

5 THE BILL OF LADING IN THE HANDS OF A THIRD PARTY

The Pioneer Container [1994] 2 AC 324, PC

The appellants were the owners of goods loaded on board the respondents' ship *Pioneer Container* which sank with all cargo after a collision off the coast of Taiwan. The goods were consigned under bills of lading issued by shipping lines which gave the shipping lines wide authority to subcontract the whole or part of the carriage on any terms. The respondents received the goods as subcontractors of the shipping lines and issued to the lines their own bills of lading ('the feeder bills of lading') which provided for the exclusive jurisdiction of courts in Taiwan. The appellants brought proceedings in Hong Kong. The shipowners sought to rely on the exclusive jurisdiction clauses in the feeder bills of lading to which the appellants were not parties. The Privy Council held that:

(1) there was no contractual relationship between the shipowners and the owners of the goods;

(2) by voluntarily receiving the goods into their custody from the shipping lines with notice that they were owned by other persons, the shipowners assumed the duty to the owners of the goods of a bailee for reward and were obliged to take reasonable care of the goods;

(3) the shipowners could invoke the terms on which the goods were sub-bailed to them, including the exclusive jurisdiction clause, because by agreeing to allow subcontracting on any terms, the owners of the goods had consented to the sub-bailment and its terms.

The Mahkutai [1996] 3 WLR 1, PC

Time charterers of *Mahkutai* issued a bill of lading in respect a cargo of plywood, which was to be carried from Jakarta to Shantou, People's Republic of China. At Shantou the cargo was found to have been damaged by sea water. Cargo owners brought proceedings in Hong Kong against the shipowners. The shipowners sought to stay proceedings on the grounds that the bill of lading provided for the exclusive jurisdiction of the courts of Indonesia and that they were entitled to the benefit of this agreement by virtue of clause 4 of the bill of lading which provided that every 'servant, agent and subcontractor shall have the benefit of all exceptions, limitations, provision, conditions and liberties herein benefiting the carrier as if such provisions were expressly made for their benefit, and, in entering into this contract, the carrier, to the extent of these provisions, does so not only on [his] own behalf, but also as agent and trustee for such servants, agents and subcontractors'.

> **Lord Goff:** There is before their Lordships an appeal by the appellants, the owners of the Indonesian vessel *Mahkutai* (the shipowners), from a decision dated 2 July 1993 of the Court of Appeal of Hong Kong ([1994] 1 HKLR 212) ...

The main issues which arise on the appeal are concerned with the question whether the shipowners, who were not parties to the bill of lading contract, can invoke as against the cargo owners the exclusive jurisdiction clause contained in that contract, the bill of lading being a charterers' bill issued by their agents to the shippers. The shipowners claim to be able to do so, either under a *Himalaya* clause incorporated into the bill ... or alternatively on the principle of bailment on terms ...

The pendulum of judicial opinion

The two principles which the shipowners invoke are the product of developments in English law during the present century. During that period, opinion has fluctuated about the desirability of recognising some form of modification of, or exception to, the strict doctrine of privity of contract to accommodate situations which arise in the context of carriage of goods by sea, in which it appears to be in accordance with commercial expectations that the benefit of certain terms of the contract of carriage should be made available to parties involved in the adventure who are not parties to the contract. These cases have been concerned primarily with stevedores claiming the benefit of exceptions and limitations in bills of lading, but also with shipowners claiming the protection of such terms contained in charterers' bills. At first there appears to have been a readiness on the part of judges to recognise such claims, especially in *Elder Dempster & Co Ltd v Paterson Zochonis & Co Ltd* [1924] AC 522, concerned with the principle of bailment on terms.

Opinion however hardened against them in the middle of the century as the pendulum swung back in the direction of orthodoxy in *Scruttons Ltd v Midland Silicones Ltd* [1962] AC 446; but in more recent years it has swung back again to recognition of their commercial desirability, notably in the two leading cases concerned with claims by stevedores to the protection of a *Himalaya* clause – *The Eurymedon* and *The New York Star*.

In the present case, shipowners carrying cargo shipped under charterers' bills of lading are seeking to claim the benefit of a *Himalaya* clause in the time charterers' bills of lading, or in the alternative to invoke the principle of bailment on terms. However, they are seeking by these means to invoke not an exception or limitation in the ordinary sense of those words, but the benefit of an exclusive jurisdiction clause. This would involve a significantly wider application of the relevant principles; and, to judge whether this extension is justified, their Lordships consider it desirable first to trace the development of the principles through the cases.

The *Elder Dempster* case

The principle of bailment on terms finds its origin in the *Elder Dempster* case. That case was concerned with a damage to cargo claim in respect of a number of casks of palm oil which had been crushed by heavy bags of palm kernels stowed above them in a ship with deep holds but no tween decks to take the weight of the cargo stowed above. The main question in the case was whether such damage was to be classified as damage arising from unseaworthiness of the ship due to absence of tween decks, or as damage arising from bad stowage; in the latter event, no claim lay under the bills of lading, which contained an exception excluding claims for bad stowage. The bills of lading were time charterers' bills, the vessel having been chartered in by the time charterers as an additional vessel for their West African line. The House of Lords (on this point differing from a majority of the Court of Appeal) held that the damage was to be attributed to bad stowage, and as a result the time charterers were protected by the bill of lading exception; but the cargo owners had also sued the shipowners in tort, and the question arose whether the shipowners too were protected by the exception contained in the bill of lading, to which they were not parties.

In the Court of Appeal Scrutton LJ (who alone considered that the damage was to be attributed to bad stowage rather than unseaworthiness) rejected the claim against the shipowners on a suggested principle of vicarious immunity (see [1923] 1 KB 420 at 441–42). This principle was relied on by the shipowners in argument before the House of Lords, and was accepted by Viscount Cave (with whom Lord Carson agreed), and apparently also by Viscount Finlay (see [1924] AC 522). But the preferred reason given by Lord Sumner (with whom Lord Dunedin and Lord Carson agreed) was that:

> in the circumstances of this case the obligations to be inferred from the reception of the cargo for carriage to the United Kingdom amount to a bailment upon terms, which include the exceptions and limitations of liability stipulated in the known and contemplated form of bill of lading. (See [1924] AC 522 at 564.)

The *Midland Silicones* case

This was a test case in which it was sought to establish a basis upon which stevedores could claim the protection of exceptions and limitations contained in the bill of lading contract. Here, the stevedores had negligently damaged a drum of chemicals after discharge at London, to which the goods had been shipped from New York under a bill of lading incorporating the US Carriage of Goods by Sea Act 1936, which contained the Hague Rules limitation of liability to $500 per package or unit. The stevedores sought to claim the benefit of this limit as against the receivers. They claimed to rely on the principle of bailment on terms derived from the *Elder Dempster* case. But they also sought a contractual basis for their contention on various grounds: that they had contracted with the receivers through the agency of the shipowners; that they could rely on an implied contract independent of the bill of lading; or that they could as an interested third party take the benefit of the limit in the bill of lading contract. All these arguments failed. The principle of bailment on terms was given a restrictive treatment; and the various contractual arguments foundered on the doctrine of privity of contract, Viscount Simonds in particular reasserting that doctrine in its orthodox form (see [1962] AC 446 at 467–68). For present purposes, however, three features can be selected as important.

First, the case revealed, at least on the part of Viscount Simonds (here reflecting the view expressed by Fullagar J in *Wilson v Darling Island Stevedoring and Lighterage Co Ltd* (1955) 95 CLR 43 at 78), a remarkable shift from the philosophy which informed the decision in the *Elder Dempster* case. There the point in question was treated very briefly by the members of the Appellate Committee, apparently because it seemed obvious to them that the cargo owners' alternative claim against the shipowners should fail. It was perceived, expressly by Viscount Finlay and, it seems, implicitly by the remainder, that:

> It would be absurd that the owner of the goods could get rid of the protective clauses of the bill of lading, in respect of all stowage, by suing the owner of the ship in tort. (See [1924] AC 522 at 548.)

By contrast, Fullagar J in the *Darling Island* case 95 CLR 43 at 71 condemned 'a curious, and seemingly irresistible, anxiety to save grossly negligent people from the normal consequences of their negligence', a sentiment to be echoed by Viscount Simonds in the concluding sentence of his speech in the *Midland Silicones* case [1962] AC 446 at 472.

Second, the *Elder Dempster* case was kept within strict bounds. Viscount Simonds ([1962] AC 446 at 470) quoted with approval the interpretation adopted by Fullagar J (with whom Dixon CJ agreed) in the High Court of Australia in the *Darling Island* case 95 CLR 43 at 78, where he said:

> In my opinion, what the *Elder Dempster* case decided, and all that it decided, is that in such a case, the master having signed the bill of lading, the proper inference is that the shipowner, when he receives the goods into his possession, receives them on the terms of the bill of lading. The same inference might perhaps be drawn in some cases even if the charterer himself signed the bill of lading, but it is unnecessary to consider any such question.

This approach is consistent with that of Lord Sumner. In the *Midland Silicones* case [1962] AC 446 at 481, 494 Lord Keith of Avonholm and Lord Morris of Borth-y-Gest spoke in similar terms. Lord Reid ([1962] AC 446 at 479) treated the decision on the point as:

> an anomalous and unexplained exception to the general principle that a stranger cannot rely for his protection on provisions in a contract to which he is not a party.

Lord Denning dissented.

It has to be recognised that this reception did not enhance the reputation of the *Elder Dempster* case, as witness certain derogatory descriptions later attached to it, for example by Donaldson J in *Johnson Matthey & Co Ltd v Constantine Terminals Ltd* [1976] 2 Lloyd's Rep 215 at 219 ('something of a judicial nightmare') and by Ackner LJ in *The Forum Craftsman* [1985] 1 Lloyd's Rep 291 at 295 ('heavily comatosed, if not long-interred').

Third, however, and most important, Lord Reid in the *Midland Silicones* case, while rejecting the agency argument on the facts of the case before him, nevertheless indicated how it might prove successful in a future case. He said ([1962] AC 446 at 474):

> I can see a possibility of success of the agency argument if (first) the bill of lading makes it clear that the stevedore is intended to be protected by the provisions in it which limit liability (secondly) the bill of lading makes it clear that the carrier, in addition to contracting for these provisions on his own behalf, is also contracting as agent for the stevedore that these provisions should apply to the stevedore (thirdly) the carrier has authority from the stevedore to do that, or perhaps later ratification by the stevedore

would suffice, and (fourthly) that any difficulties about consideration moving from the stevedore were overcome.

It was essentially on this passage that the *Himalaya* clause (called after the name of the ship involved in *Adler v Dickson* [1955] 1 QB 158) was later to be founded.

The pendulum swings back again

In more recent years the pendulum of judicial opinion has swung back again, as recognition has been given to the undesirability, especially in a commercial context, of allowing plaintiffs to circumvent contractual exception clauses by suing in particular the servant or agent of the contracting party who caused the relevant damage, thereby undermining the purpose of the exception, and so redistributing the contractual allocation of risk which is reflected in the freight rate and in the parties' respective insurance arrangements. Nowadays, therefore, there is a greater readiness, not only to accept something like Scrutton LJ's doctrine of vicarious immunity (as to which see, eg article 4 bis of the Hague-Visby Rules scheduled to the Carriage of Goods by Sea Act 1971) but also to rehabilitate the *Elder Dempster* case itself, which has been described by Bingham LJ, in *Dresser UK Ltd v Falcongate Freight Management Ltd The Duke of Yare* [1992] QB 502 at 511, as 'a pragmatic legal recognition of commercial reality'. Even so, the problem remains how to discover, in circumstances such as those of the *Elder Dempster* case, the factual basis from which the rendering of the bailment subject to such a provision can properly be inferred. At all events, the present understanding, based on Lord Sumner's speech, is that in the circumstances of that case the shippers may be taken to have impliedly agreed that the goods were received by the shipowners, as bailees, subject to the exceptions and limitations contained in the known and contemplated form of bill of lading: see *The Pioneer Container* [1994] 2 AC 324 at 339–40. Their Lordships will however put on one side for later consideration the question how far the principle of bailment on terms may be applicable in the present case, and will turn first to consider the principle developed from Lord Reid's observations in the *Midland Silicones* case in *The Eurymedon* and *The New York Star*.

The Eurymedon and *The New York Star*

Their Lordships have already quoted the terms of clause 4 (the *Himalaya* clause) of the bill of lading in the present case. For the purposes of this aspect of the case, the essential passage reads as follows:

> Without prejudice to the foregoing, every such servant, agent and subcontractor shall have the benefit of all exceptions, limitations, provision, conditions and liberties herein benefiting the Carrier as if such provisions were expressly made for their benefit, and, in entering into this contract, the Carrier, to the extent of these provisions, does so not only on [his] own behalf, but also as agent and trustee for such servants, agents and subcontractors.

The effectiveness of a *Himalaya* clause to provide protection against claims in tort by consignees was recognised by the Privy Council in *The Eurymedon* [1975] AC 154 and *The New York Star* [1981] 1 WLR 138. In both cases, stevedores were sued by the consignees for damages in tort, in the first case on the ground that the stevedores had negligently damaged a drilling machine in the course of unloading, and in the second on the ground that they had negligently allowed a parcel of goods, after unloading onto the wharf, to be removed by thieves without production of the bill of lading. In both cases, the bill of lading contract incorporated a one-year time bar, and a *Himalaya* clause which extended the benefit of defences and immunities to independent contractors employed by the carrier. The stevedores relied upon the *Himalaya* clause to claim the benefit of the time bar as against the consignees.

In *The Eurymedon* the Privy Council held, by a majority of three to two, that the stevedores were entitled to rely on the time bar. The leading judgment was delivered by Lord Wilberforce. He referred to clause 1 of the bill of lading under which the carrier stipulated for certain exemptions and immunities, among them the one-year time bar in art III, r 6, of the Hague Rules, and in addition (in the *Himalaya* clause) the carrier, as agent for (among others) independent contractors, stipulated for the same exemptions. Referring to Lord Reid's four criteria in the *Midland Silicones* case, he considered it plain that the first three were satisfied, the only question being whether the requirement of consideration was fulfilled. He was satisfied that it was. He observed ([1975] AC 154 at 167) that 'If the choice, and the antithesis, is between a gratuitous promise, and a promise for consideration ... there can be little doubt which, in commercial reality, this is'. He then proceeded to analyse the transaction in a way which showed a preference by him for what is usually called a unilateral contract, though he recognised that there might be more than one way of analysing the transaction.

In *The New York Star* the Privy Council again upheld (on this occasion unanimously) the efficacy of a *Himalaya* clause to confer upon the stevedores the benefit of defences and immunities contained in the bill of lading, including a one-year time bar. The judgment of the Judicial Committee was again given by Lord Wilberforce. In the course of his judgment, he stressed:

> It may indeed be said that the significance of *Satterthwaite's* case [ie *The Eurymedon*] lay not so much in the establishment of any new legal principle, as in the finding that in the normal situation involving the employment of stevedores by carriers, accepted principles enable and require the stevedore to enjoy the benefit of contractual provisions in the bill of lading.

(See [1981] 1 WLR 138 at 143.) He continued:

> Although, in each case, there will be room for evidence as to the precise relationship of carrier and stevedore and as to the practice at the relevant port, the decision does not support, and their Lordships would not encourage, a search for fine distinctions which would diminish the general applicability, in the light of established commercial practice, of the principle.

(See [1981] 1 WLR 138 at 144.) Lord Wilberforce in particular expressed the Board's approval of the reasoned analysis of the relevant legal principles in the judgment of Barwick CJ in the court below (the High Court of Australia) ([1979] 1 Lloyd's Rep 298), which in his opinion substantially agreed with, and indeed constituted a powerful reinforcement of, one of the two possible bases put forward in the Board's judgment in *The Eurymedon*. In his judgment, Barwick CJ (at 304–05) saw no difficulty in finding that the carrier acted as the authorised agent of the stevedores in making an arrangement with the consignor for the protection of the stevedores. By later accepting the bill of lading the consignee became party to that arrangement. He could not read the clauses in the bill of lading as an unaccepted but acceptable offer by the consignor to the stevedores. However, the consignor and the stevedores were *ad idem* through the carrier's agency, upon the acceptance by the consignor of the bill of lading, as to the protection the stevedores should have in the event that they caused loss of or damage to the consignment. But that consensus lacked consideration. He continued (at 305):

> To agree with another that, in the event that the other acts in a particular way, that other shall be entitled to stated protective provisions only needs performance by the doing of the specified act or acts to become a binding contract ... The performance of the act or acts at the one moment satisfied the test for consideration and enacted the agreed terms.

Such a contract Barwick CJ was prepared, with some hesitation, to describe as a bilateral contract.

Critique of the *Eurymedon* principle

In *The New York Star* [1981] 1 WLR 138 at 144 Lord Wilberforce discouraged 'a search for fine distinctions which would diminish the general applicability, in the light of established commercial practice, of the principle'. He was there, of course, speaking of the application of the principle in the case of stevedores. It has however to be recognised that, so long as the principle continues to be understood to rest upon an enforceable contract as between the cargo owners and the stevedores entered into through the agency of the shipowner, it is inevitable that technical points of contract and agency law will continue to be invoked by cargo owners seeking to enforce tortious remedies against stevedores and others uninhibited by the exceptions and limitations in the relevant bill of lading contract. Indeed, in the present case their Lordships have seen such an exercise being legitimately undertaken by Mr Aikens QC on behalf of the respondent cargo owners. In this connection their Lordships wish to refer to the very helpful consideration of the principle in *Palmer on Bailment* (2nd edn, 1991) pp 1610–25, which reveals many of the problems which may arise, and refers to a number of cases, both in England and in Commonwealth countries, in which the courts have grappled with those problems. In some cases, notably but by no means exclusively in England, courts have felt impelled by the established principles of the law of contract or of agency to reject the application of the principle in the particular case before them. In others, courts have felt free to follow the lead of Lord Wilberforce in *The Eurymedon*, and of Lord Wilberforce and Barwick CJ in *The New York Star*, and so to discover the existence of a contract (nowadays a bilateral contract of the kind identified by Barwick CJ) in circumstances in which lawyers of a previous generation would have been unwilling to do so.

Nevertheless, there can be no doubt of the commercial need of some such principle as this, and not only in cases concerned with stevedores; and the bold step taken by the Privy Council in *The Eurymedon*, and later developed in *The New York Star*, has been widely welcomed. But it is legitimate to wonder whether that development is yet complete. Here their Lordships have in mind not only Lord Wilberforce's discouragement of fine distinctions, but also the fact that the law is now approaching the position where, provided that the bill of lading contract clearly provides that (for example) independent contractors such as stevedores are to have the benefit of exceptions and limitations contained in that contract, they will be able to enjoy the protection of those terms as against the cargo owners. This is because (1) the problem of consideration in these cases is regarded as having been solved on the basis that a bilateral agreement between the stevedores and the cargo owners, entered into through the agency of the shipowners, may, though itself unsupported by consideration, be rendered enforceable by consideration subsequently furnished by the stevedores in the form of performance of their duties as stevedores for the shipowners; (2) the problem of authority from the stevedores to the shipowners to contract on their behalf can, in the majority of cases, be solved by recourse to the principle of ratification; and (3) consignees of the cargo may be held to be bound on the principle in *Brandt & Co v Liverpool Brazil and River Plate Steam Navigation Co Ltd* [1924] 1 KB 575. Though these solutions are now perceived to be generally effective for their purpose, their technical nature is all too apparent; and the time may well come when, in an appropriate case, it will fall to be considered whether the courts should take what may legitimately be perceived to be the final, and perhaps inevitable, step in this development and recognise in these cases a fully-fledged exception to the doctrine of privity of contract, thus escaping from all the technicalities with which courts are now faced in English law. It is not far from their Lordships' minds that, if the English courts were minded to take that step, they would be following in the footsteps of the Supreme Court of Canada (see *London Drugs Ltd v Kuehne & Nagel International Ltd* (1992) 97 DLR (4th) 261) and, in a different context, the High Court of Australia (see *Trident General Insurance Co Ltd v McNiece Bros Pty Ltd* (1988) 165 CLR 107). Their Lordships have given consideration to the question whether they should face up to this question in the present appeal. However, they have come to the conclusion that it would not be appropriate for them to do so, first, because they have not heard argument specifically directed towards this fundamental question, and second because, as will become clear in due course, they are satisfied that the appeal must in any event be dismissed.

Application of the *Eurymedon* principle in the present case

Their Lordships now turn to the application of the principle in *The Eurymedon* to the facts of the present case. Two questions arose in the course of argument which are specific to this case. The first is whether the shipowners qualify as 'subcontractors' within the meaning of the *Himalaya* clause (cl 4 of the bill of lading). The second is whether, if so, they are entitled to take advantage of the exclusive jurisdiction clause (cl 19). Their Lordships have come to the conclusion that the latter question must be answered in the negative. It is therefore unnecessary for them to answer the first question; and they will proceed to address the question of the exclusive jurisdiction clause on the assumption that the shipowners can be regarded as subcontractors for this purpose.

The exclusive jurisdiction clause

The *Himalaya* clause provides that, among others, subcontractors shall have the benefit of 'all exceptions, limitations, provisions, conditions and liberties herein benefiting the Carrier as if such provisions were expressly made for their benefit'. The question therefore arises whether the exclusive jurisdiction clause (cl 19) falls within the scope of this clause.

In *The Eurymedon* [1975] AC 154 at 169 and *The New York Star* [1981] 1 WLR 138 at 143 Lord Wilberforce stated the principle to be applicable, in the case of stevedores, to respectively 'exemptions and limitations' and 'defences and immunities' contained in the bill of lading. This is scarcely surprising. Most bill of lading contracts incorporate the Hague-Visby Rules, in which the responsibilities and liabilities of the carrier are segregated from his rights and immunities, the latter being set out primarily in Article IV, rr 1 and 2, exempting the carrier and the ship from liability or responsibility for loss of or damage to the goods in certain specified circumstances; though the limitation on liability per package or unit is to be found in Article IV, r 5, and the time bar in art III, r 6. Terms such as these are characteristically terms for the benefit of the carrier, of which subcontractors can have the benefit under the *Himalaya* clause as if such terms were expressly made for their benefit.

It however by no means follows that the same can be said of an exclusive jurisdiction clause, here incorporating, as is usual, a choice of law provision relating to the law of the chosen jurisdiction. No question arises in the present case with regard to the choice of law provision. This already applies to the bill of lading contract itself, and may for that reason also apply to another contract which comes into existence, pursuant to its terms, between the shipper and a subcontractor of the carrier such as the shipowners in the present case. But the exclusive jurisdiction clause itself creates serious problems. Such a clause can be distinguished from terms such as exceptions and limitations in that it does not benefit only one party, but embodies a mutual agreement under which both parties agree with each other as to the relevant jurisdiction for the resolution of disputes. It is therefore a clause which creates mutual rights and obligations. Can such a clause be an exception, limitation, provision, condition or liberty benefiting the carrier within the meaning of the clause?

First of all, it cannot in their Lordships' opinion be an exception, limitation, condition or liberty. But can it be a provision? That expression has, of course, to be considered in the context of the *Himalaya* clause; and so the question is whether an exclusive jurisdiction clause is a provision benefiting the carrier, of which servants, agents and subcontractors of the carrier are intended to have the benefit, as if the provision was expressly made for their benefit. Moreover, the word 'provision' is to be found at the centre of a series of words, *viz* 'exceptions, limitations ... conditions and liberties', all of which share the same characteristic, that they are not as such rights which entail correlative obligations on the cargo owners.

In considering this question, their Lordships are satisfied that some limit must be placed upon the meaning of the word 'provision' in this context. In their

Lordships' opinion, the word 'provision' must have been inserted with the purpose of ensuring that any other provision in the bill of lading which, although it did not strictly fall within the description 'exceptions, limitations ... conditions and liberties', nevertheless benefited the carrier in the same way in the sense that it was inserted in the bill for the carrier's protection, should enure for the benefit of the servants, agents and subcontractors of the carrier. It cannot therefore extend to include a mutual agreement, such as an exclusive jurisdiction clause, which is not of that character.

Their Lordships draw support for this view from the function of the *Himalaya* clause. That function is, as revealed by the authorities, to prevent cargo owners from avoiding the effect of contractual defences available to the carrier (typically the exceptions and limitations in the Hague-Visby Rules) by suing in tort persons who perform the contractual services on the carrier's behalf. To make available to such a person the benefit of an exclusive jurisdiction clause in the bill of lading contract does not contribute to the solution of that problem. Furthermore, to construe the general words of the *Himalaya* clause as effective to make available to servants, agents or subcontractors a clause which expressly refers to disputes arising under the contract evidenced by the bill of lading, to which they are not party, is not easy to reconcile with those authorities such as *TW Thomas & Co Ltd v Portsea Steamship Co Ltd* [1912] AC 1 which hold that general words of incorporation are ineffective to incorporate into a bill of lading an arbitration clause which refers only to disputes arising under the charter.

Furthermore, it is of some significance to observe how adventitious would have been the benefit of the exclusive jurisdiction clause to the shipowners in the present case. Such a clause generally represents a preference by the carrier for the jurisdiction where he carries on business. But the same cannot necessarily be said of his servants, agents or subcontractors. It could conceivably be true of servants, such as crew members, who may be resident in the same jurisdiction; though if sued elsewhere they may in any event be able to invoke the principle of *forum non conveniens*. But the same cannot be said to be true of agents, still less of subcontractors. Take, for example, stevedores at the discharging port, who provide the classic example of independent contractors intended to be protected by a *Himalaya* clause. There is no reason to suppose that an exclusive jurisdiction clause selected to suit a particular carrier would be likely to be of any benefit to such stevedores; it could only conceivably be so in the coincidental circumstance that the discharging port happened to be in the country where the carrier carried on business. Exactly the same can be said of a shipowner who performs all or part of the carrier's obligations under the bill of lading contract, pursuant to a time or voyage charter. In such a case, the shipowner may very likely have no connection with the carrier's chosen jurisdiction. Coincidentally he may do so, as in the present case where the shipowners happened, like Sentosa, to be an Indonesian corporation. This of course explains why the shipowners in the present case wish to take advantage of the exclusive jurisdiction clause in Sentosa's form of bill of lading; but it would not be right to attach any significance to that coincidence.

In the opinion of their Lordships, all these considerations point strongly against the exclusive jurisdiction clause falling within the scope of the *Himalaya* clause. However, in support of his submission that the exclusive jurisdiction clause fell within the scope of the *Himalaya* clause in the present case, Mr Gross QC for the shipowners invoked the decision of the Privy Council in *The Pioneer Container* [1994] 2 AC 324. That case was however concerned with a different situation, where a carrier of goods subcontracted part of the carriage to a shipowner under a 'feeder' bill of lading, and that shipowner sought to enforce an exclusive jurisdiction clause contained in that bill of lading against the owners of the goods. The Judicial Committee held that the shipowner was entitled to do so because the goods owner had authorised the carrier so to subcontract 'on any terms', with the effect that the shipowner as sub-bailee was entitled to rely on the clause against the goods owner as head bailor. The present case is however concerned not with a question of enforceability of a term in a sub-bailment by the sub-bailee against the head bailor, but with the question whether a subcontractor is entitled to take the benefit of a term in the head contract. The former depends on the scope of the authority of the intermediate bailor to act on behalf of the head bailor in agreeing on his behalf to the relevant term in the sub-bailment; whereas the latter depends on the scope of the agreement between the head contractor and the subcontractor, entered into by the intermediate contractor as agent for the subcontractor, under which the benefit of a term in the head contract may be made available by the head contractor to the subcontractor. It does not follow that a decision in the former type of case provides any useful guidance in a case of the latter type; and their Lordships do not therefore find *The Pioneer Container* of assistance in the present case.

In the event, for the reasons they have already given, their Lordships have come to the conclusion that the *Himalaya* clause does not have the effect of enabling the shipowners to take advantage of the exclusive jurisdiction clause in the bill of lading in the present case.

Application of the principle of bailment on terms in the present case

In the light of the principle stated by Lord Sumner in the *Elder Dempster* case [1924] AC 522 at 564, as interpreted by Fullagar J in the *Darling Island* case 95 CLR 43 at 78, the next question for consideration is whether the shipowners can establish that they received the goods into their possession on the terms of the bill of lading, including the exclusive jurisdiction clause (cl 19), ie whether the shipowners' obligations as bailees were effectively subjected to the clause as a term upon which the shipowners implicitly received the goods into their possession (see *The Pioneer Container* [1994] 2 AC 324 at 340 *per* Lord Goff of Chieveley). This was the ground upon which Bokhary JA ([1994] 1 HKLR 212 at 229–30) expressed the opinion, in his dissenting judgment, that the shipowners were entitled to succeed.

Their Lordships feel able to deal with this point very briefly, because they consider that in the present case there is an insuperable objection to the argument of the shipowners. This is that the bill of lading under which the goods were shipped on board contained a *Himalaya* clause under which the shipowners as subcontractors were expressed to be entitled to the benefit of certain terms in the bill of lading but, as their Lordships have held, those terms did not include the exclusive jurisdiction clause. In these circumstances their Lordships find it impossible to hold that, by receiving the goods into their possession pursuant to the bill of lading, the shipowners' obligations as bailees were effectively subjected to the exclusive jurisdiction clause as a term upon which they implicitly received the goods into their possession. Any such implication must, in their opinion, be rejected as inconsistent with the express terms of the bill of lading.

Conclusion

It follows that the shipowners' appeal against the order of the Court of Appeal refusing a stay of proceedings in Hong Kong must fail.

6 *BRANDT* CONTRACTS

The Aramis [1989] 1 Lloyd's Rep 213, CA

The *Aramis* was trip chartered for a voyage from South America to Europe. The ship loaded a cargo of linseed expellers at Necochea in Argentina. Two parcels were to be delivered from this bulk at Rotterdam. One parcel was the subject of bill of lading 5 (204 tonnes), the other of bill of lading 6 (255 tonnes). On discharge at Rotterdam, it became clear that there was a considerable shortage of cargo, possibly because of over delivery at an earlier port of call. No delivery at all was made under bill of lading 5. Only 11.55 tonnes was delivered on presentation of bill of lading 6. Despite the fact that separate bills of lading had been issued, the goods in question were said to have formed part of a single undivided bulk cargo. On this basis, no property in the goods had passed to the plaintiff purchasers, who were not entitled to sue the shipowners on the bill of lading contract under s 1 of the Bills of Lading Act 1855. The plaintiffs alleged that, applying *Brandt v Liverpool, Brazil and River Plate Steam Navigation Co Ltd* [1924] 1 KB 575, CA, an implied contract had arisen, even though the shipowners had no lien over the cargo and were bound to deliver to any holder of these bills of lading claiming delivery. Freight had been pre-paid; no payments were due to the carrier on discharge. The Court of Appeal held that mere presentation of a bill of lading coupled with delivery is not sufficient material on which to find an implied contract.

> **Bingham LJ:** ... Like most important legal decisions, that in *Brandt's* case did not lack ancestors and has not lacked progeny. We were referred to a number of cases before *Brandt* and since, and I think it is of value to see from the authorities how the implication of contracts in this field has grown and developed.
>
> In *Cock v Taylor* (1811) 13 East 399, goods were consigned under a bill of lading which provided for delivery to the consignees or their assigns upon payment of freight. The bill was endorsed to the defendants who obtained the goods. Freight was not demanded or paid at the time of delivery. The shipowner had

a lien on the cargo for the freight and was not bound to part with it until he was paid. The shipowner succeeded in an action to recover the freight. The ratio of the decision most clearly appears in the judgments of Le Blanc and Bailey JJ. Le Blanc J said (at p 401):

> The purchaser must have understood at the time, that the goods were liable to be detained for the payment of the freight, if it were not paid before delivery, and his receiving them from the master, and the master's parting with his lien and giving them up to the purchaser at his request, is evidence of a new contract between them that the purchaser would pay the freight.

Bailey J added (at p 404):

> Here then I think that the purchaser's taking the cargo from the master, who had a lien on it, was evidence of their agreement upon the master's delivering up the goods without receiving the freight, to pay the freight which should be due, and without which they had no right to take the goods.

In *Sanders v Vanzeller* (1843) 4 QB 260 goods were again consigned under bills of lading providing for payment of freight on delivery. The bills were endorsed to the defendants, who obtained the goods without paying the freight. In an action for the freight the shipowner failed. The Court of Exchequer Chamber held that the jury might, on the facts, have found a contract by the defendants to pay the freight; but such a contract would not be implied at law; whether a contract had been made was a question of fact, not law; and the requisite finding of fact had not been made. Ever since this decision it has been accepted that whether a contract is to be implied raises a question of fact for decision by the tribunal of fact. *Wegener v Smith* (1854) 15 CB 285 illustrates the unwillingness of the Court to review the jury's verdict.

In *Stindt v Roberts* (1848) 17 LJ QB 166 the facts were similar to *Cock v Taylor* save that the claim against the endorsees was for demurrage. The jury having found a breach of contract by the defendant endorsees, Erle J upheld the decision:

> The principle on which the consignee is taken to contract for the freight and demurrage mentioned in the bill of lading, applies in respect of other stipulations therein mentioned, and the promise to pay demurrage in case of detention is in effect a promise to discharge within the limited time, or pay for the detention.

In *Young v Moller* (1855) 5 El & Bl 755 a shipowner agreed with a charterer to carry and deliver a cargo at a port of discharge, a certain number of lay days being allowed and demurrage payable thereafter. Bills of lading provided for delivery of the goods to the charterer (and shipper) or his assigns on paying freight as per charterparty but it does not appear whether the charterparty demurrage terms were incorporated in the bill of lading. The bills were indorsed to the defendants. Part of the cargo was discharged. The shipowner demanded payment of freight for the proportion of cargo delivered. The defendant refused to pay until full delivery had been made. Loss of time resulted. Eventually the balance of the cargo was discharged and freight was paid. The shipowner then sued the defendant for freight, losing at first instance, winning in the Court of Queen's Bench and losing in the Court of Exchequer Chamber. Baron Parke said (at pp 760–61):

> No doubt, where a cargo is received under a bill of lading, that, though not necessarily raising a contract in law, is evidence from which a jury may infer a contract to pay freight, in consideration of the captain giving up his lien on the goods: *Sanders v Vanzeller*. But the question here is upon a contract, stated in the declaration to be that, in consideration that the plaintiff, at the request of the defendants, would deliver the wheat to defendants with boats or lighters provided by defendants (and Mr Bovill's argument admits that this means in consideration that the plaintiff undertook to deliver), the defendants promised that within a reasonable time they would accept and receive the wheat into boats and lighters provided by them. The question is, whether there is any evidence to support this averment of a promise by the defendants. There was no such verbal promise; and it is not likely that such a promise would be made, since the plaintiff, under the charterparty, was bound to deliver the wheat to the assignee of the bill of lading, and, if he failed to do so, would break his contract with the charterer. Nevertheless, if there were such an express contract between the captain and the holder of the bill of lading, with whom no contract existed before, it would be valid. But it does not appear to me that there was any evidence of such an undertaking by the captain in the first instance. Then do we find any undertaking by the defendants at any time to unload the vessel in a reasonable time? A part of the wheat is put on board the lighter for the defendants, and received. If that were all, there might be evidence for a jury that the defendants had undertaken to pay for that part. But, if we look at the conduct of the parties from the beginning to the end, it is clear, from first to last, that there was in fact no undertaking by the defendants to pay for any part till all was received.

Williams J (at pp 763–64) held to similar effect:

> The first question is, whether there has been such a contract as that alleged in the declaration. I think there was no evidence of this. The alleged new contract appears to have been implied in the court below, from the presentment of the bill of lading by the indorsee, and the assent by the master. It is the first time that I ever heard such a doctrine laid down; and I can find nothing to support such a novelty. I may observe that the declaration is drawn with considerable subtlety; for, to escape from the difficulty of alleging performance of the condition precedent, it is said that the promise of the defendants was made in consideration that the plaintiff 'would deliver'. But the proof of such a contract has failed.

At this stage in the history the 1855 Act was passed ...

The next important decision is *Allen v Coltart* (1883) 11 QBD 782. The plaintiffs were shipowners. The defendants held bills of lading for goods shipped on the vessel but they held them as security for advances and did not have the property in the goods, so they had not become parties to the contract of carriage under the 1855 Act. The charterparty provided that the vessel should discharge in a dock at Liverpool:

... as ordered on arriving, if sufficient water, or so near thereunto as she may safely get always afloat.

The bills of lading provided for delivery of the cargo to the shipper or his assigns:

... he or they paying freight for the said goods dead freight and demurrage, if any may be shown due, as per charterparty, conforming to all the conditions thereof ...

The vessel arrived in the Mersey. The defendants ordered her to the Canada Dock. The vessel could not enter the Canada Dock for lack of water. So she went into another dock and waited for a month until there was enough water. The jury found that the cause of the delay in Liverpool was the defendants' refusal to take delivery elsewhere than at the Canada Dock. Cave J reviewed the earlier authorities and concluded that by giving directions where the vessel should discharge (a right only exercisable by virtue of the bills and the charterparty) the defendants impliedly offered to adopt the bill of lading terms, an offer which the plaintiffs accepted by complying. The judge said (at pp 785–86):

Is there, then, evidence in this case on which I ought to find that Messrs Coltart & Co agreed to take delivery on the terms of the bill of lading? I am of opinion that there is. It seems to me that if the holder of a bill of lading under which he is entitled to the delivery of goods on certain terms, presents that bill of lading and demands delivery of the goods, he thereby *prima facie* offers to perform those terms of the bill of lading on which alone the goods are deliverable to him. According to the evidence of Mr Castle, which I do not find to have been contradicted, Mr Coltart said he had a right to name the dock according to the charterparty, and he had named the Canada Dock, and wanted delivery there. He named the Canada Dock, not because he refused to perform the conditions of the bill of lading, but because he conceived that under those conditions he was entitled to name the Canada Dock. It is true that at first the plaintiffs refused to accept Mr Coltart's offer to fulfil the conditions of the bill of lading and take delivery; but the jury have found in effect that afterwards the plaintiffs were ready and willing to deliver on the terms of the bill of lading, and that there was a delay caused by the refusal of Messrs Coltart & Co to accept delivery elsewhere than in the Canada Dock. Having regard to this finding of the jury, I think I ought to come to the conclusion that there was an agreement between the plaintiffs and the defendants Messrs Coltart & Co that the former should give and the latter should take delivery under the terms of the bill of lading, and that there was a delay in such delivery by reason of the defendants Messrs Coltart & Co refusing to take delivery elsewhere than in the Canada Dock.

Evans J was not referred to the next authority, *White & Co v Furness Withy & Co Ltd* [1895] AC 40. It turned on the Merchant Shipping Amendment Act 1862 and the facts do not matter, but the speeches of their Lordships contain valuable statements of principle. Lord Herschell LC, said (at pp 43–44):

Now, it is not disputed that where a consignee takes delivery under a bill of lading, and the master of the vessel by giving delivery abandons his lien, there is evidence from which a contract to pay freight may be inferred. This has been regarded as the law ever since the case of *Sanders v Vanzeller*; but in that case it was distinctly stated that it was not a presumption of fact. Inasmuch as a shipowner is entitled to retain goods for the purpose of securing payment of his freight, it is only natural to infer if the goods are parted with to a consignee before the freight is paid, and the lien is thus abandoned, that it could only be on the understanding on both sides that the consignee undertook to pay the freight. And I cannot doubt that in such a case, except under very special circumstances, a jury, or whatever tribunal has to determine the facts, will always find that there was such a contract. But it must be borne in mind that it is only by reason of his lien that the shipowner is entitled to refuse delivery to the owner of the goods or his agent, and I think the abandonment of this right is an essential element in the facts which give rise to the inference of a contract to pay the freight.

Lord Watson said (at pp 51–52):

Before adverting to the provisions of the Act of 1862, it may be useful to consider what, previous to its passing, were the mutual rights arising to parties in the same position as these litigants. The law upon that point does not appear to me to admit of doubt. The holder of the bills, although he was no party to the contract of carriage, and had no property in the goods, had yet a good title to demand delivery; but he could not insist on that demand unless he was prepared, as a condition of obtaining delivery, to satisfy the shipowner's claim for freight. On the other hand, if delivery was not taken on these terms, or, if he delivered the goods without being paid freight, the shipowner could not sue a holder of the bills who was not liable upon the contract of carriage, unless he could shew that such holder incurred an independent obligation to pay freight. The existence of such an obligation was not a matter of legal implication. It required to be proved as a matter of fact. In cases where the goods had been delivered it was frequently held to be matter of reasonable inference that delivery had been given and received, on the mutual understanding that the recipient was to pay the freight in consideration of the surrender of his lien by the shipowner.

Lord Macnaghten said (at pp 53–54):

The appellants, it must be remembered, were not parties to the contract of affreightment. Nor were they liable for the freight under the Bills of Lading Act 1855, being only agents for sale to whom the property in the goods did not pass. No doubt if they had received the goods from the ship one would have inferred a contract on their part to pay the freight in consideration of the shipowner giving up his lien. That would have been only reasonable. The master could not be asked to forego his lien without getting an equivalent. It would involve a breach of duty to his employer. The only possible equivalent short of actual payment would be a binding promise to pay.

One then comes to *Brandt's* case itself. A cargo was shipped at Buenos Aires for carriage to Liverpool under bills of lading which recorded that the goods were shipped in apparent good order and condition and provided for delivery to the order of the shipper or his assigns, he or they paying freight for the goods on delivery. After shipment defects were found in the cargo and it was discharged at Buenos Aires, warehoused, reconditioned and then reshipped to Liverpool. Brandt held the bills of lading as endorsees as security for advances and so, like Coltart, did not have the property in the goods so as to become a party to the contract of carriage under the 1855 Act. When the cargo arrived in Liverpool Brandt paid the freight and also, under protest, a sum of £748 claimed by the shipowner for additional expense incurred at Buenos Aires for which the shipowner asserted a lien on the cargo. Brandt then sued for damages for breach of the contract of carriage and for recovery of the sum of £748 paid under protest. To succeed Brandt had to establish that it had become a party to the contract of carriage so as to gain the benefit of the estoppel arising from the description of the cargo in the bill of lading. Greer J at first instance found for Brandt, summarising his opinion thus ([1924] 1 KB 575 at p 582):

> There can be no doubt that in this case Brandt & Co by presenting the bill of lading and receiving delivery impliedly promised to pay the freight and make any other payments which were payable by the receiver in respect of the goods. What was the consideration for this promise? Was it merely the delivery of the goods which were on the *Bernini*, or was it a promise by the shipowner to perform towards Messrs Brandt all the obligations of the bill of lading? It is not necessary to go as far as to say that the implied consideration was a promise to perform all the obligations of the bill of lading. It is sufficient to say that it was a promise to deliver the goods to Messrs Brandt in the condition in which they ought to be delivered under the bill of lading.

The Court of Appeal supported Greer J's judgment. Having mentioned some of the earlier cases, Bankes LJ said [1924] 1 KB 575 at pp 589–90:

> By those authorities it has been clearly established that where the holder of a bill of lading presents it and offers to accept delivery, if that offer is accepted by the shipowner, the holder of the bill of lading comes under an obligation to pay the freight and to pay the demurrage, if any, and there are general expressions in all those three cases, I think, in which the learned judges have said that the contract so made by that offer and acceptance covers, so as to include, the terms of the bill of lading. In my opinion, in this particular case the contract must include the terms and conditions of the bills of lading and for this reason. In this case the bill of lading holder offered the freight before the goods were delivered; and in fact paid it, and under those circumstances it seems to me that by the acceptance of the freight and the subsequent delivery the shipowners undertook an obligation to deliver the goods as described in the bill of lading. I think from the shipowner's point of view it must necessarily include the whole of the terms of the bill of lading, because he must desire that he should be covered by the exceptions in the bill of lading. I think, therefore, that the learned judge is right when he states his conclusion that on the facts of their case it is sufficient to say there was a promise by the shipowners to deliver the goods to Brandt & Co in the condition in which

they ought to be delivered under the bill of lading. So much for the scope and extent of the contract. I entirely agree with the learned judge's conclusion upon this very important matter.

Scrutton LJ also referred to some of the earlier cases and to the 1855 Act before expressing his conclusion (at p 596):

> When a holder of a bill of lading, who has some property in the goods, presents the bill of lading and accepts the goods, can there be inferred a contract on each side to perform the terms of the bill of lading? The view that Greer J has taken is that such a contract can and ought to be implied in this case, and I take the same view.

Atkin LJ was of the same opinion (at pp 599–600):

> Later on that obligation was extended to paying charges other than freight in cases where those other charges were not specified in the contract expressly as being payable by an assignee, as, for instance, to payment of demurrage or other charges, and there the contract obviously becomes a contract to be implied from the circumstances of the delivery being taken by the assignee of the bill of lading. Then is there any corresponding obligation on the part of the shipowner in that contract? It appears to me that just as plainly as the assignee is bound by an implied contract, so is the shipowner, and the shipowner's obligation in the case where the freight has in fact been paid by the holder of the bill of lading, is that he will deliver the goods. What other contract could be inferred from the fact that an assignee of a bill of lading goes to the shipowner's representative and offers him the freight, which is accepted by the shipowner? The necessary implication when the shipowner says, 'Yes, I will take the bill of lading freight', is that he undertakes in consideration of that to deliver the goods which he has received on board under the bill of lading. Is it a contract to deliver the goods on the terms of the bill of lading? Shipowners would be surprised to hear it suggested that having undertaken to carry goods upon terms in their bill of lading qualifying and limiting their liability they are nevertheless under an absolute obligation to deliver the goods and not an obligation qualified by the exceptions in the bill of lading. They are not accustomed to having a burden put upon them in reference to the carriage of goods except accompanied by the qualification of exceptions, and no other contract could properly be inferred. The bill of lading freight has been assessed and calculated upon the footing of a contract of carriage, qualified by exceptions from liability, and it would be very unfair to say to a shipowner: 'You have received the bill of lading freight which is based upon an obligation to carry qualified by all the exceptions, and now having taken it you must accept an obligation to deliver the goods unqualified by any of the exceptions'. I have no doubt at all that the obligation on the shipowner is to deliver on the terms of the bill of lading. It follows that the contract to be inferred in cases such as this is that the holder of the bill of lading and the shipowner make a contract for the delivery and acceptance of the goods on the terms of the bill of lading, so far as they are applicable to discharge at the port of discharge.

Peter Cremer Westfaelische Central Genossenschaft GmbH v General Carriers SA [1974] 1 WLR 341 concerned a bulk cargo and prior to delivery the buyers owned no part of the undivided bulk. Kerr J regarded the facts as being as strong as they could be in favour of holding that a contract on the bill of lading terms came into being between the shipowners and the buyers (p 350 A–C).

In *The Aliakmon* [1983] 1 Lloyd's Rep 203 at p 207 Staughton J said:

> So I must consider whether a contract should be implied on the facts. The doctrine of *Brandt v Liverpool Steam Navigation Co Ltd* is far more often pleaded than established by judicial decision. The facts in that case were that the bill of lading holder offered the freight before the goods were delivered, and in fact paid it. In those circumstances it was not difficult to imply a contract that the goods should be delivered on the terms of the bill of lading. But here it is as if the buyers had gone to the quay with a gang of stevedores, presented the bill of lading to the master, and asked if they would take delivery of the steel, and the shipowners assented. In those circumstances I do not see any necessary implication of a contract at all, still less one that the goods should be delivered and accepted on the terms of the bill of lading.

When the case reached the Court of Appeal the implied contract issue was argued but it was (as the report of the argument shows) a very subsidiary issue: [1985] QB 350. Sir John Donaldson MR, referred to *Brandt's* case and cited the judgment of Lord Justice Bankes and said (p 364F):

> But for one crucial difference that decision would entitle the buyers to sue the shipowners in the present case. They presented the bill of lading to the shipowners on 12 November 1976, they took delivery of the steel, they paid the discharging costs and they undertook to pay the import duty. The crucial difference between *Brandt's* case and this case is that in the covering letter with which the bill of lading was sent to the ship's agents, the buyers said that the material was to be placed into covered warehouse to the sole order of the sellers, who would be responsible for all discharging costs, adding that they, the buyers, accepted liability for the duty acting as the sellers' agents. In that situation the only contract which, in my judgment, could be implied was a contract between the sellers and the shipowners. This is of no assistance to the buyers. The judge so held and I agree with him.

Robert Goff LJ rejected the implied contract argument for the same reason (p 389A). He did not explicitly say what his view would have been but for the agency point. Oliver LJ agreed (p 368D) that the buyers' claim in contract failed for the reasons given by the Master of the Rolls and Robert Goff LJ. I think it is evident that, quite apart from the agency point, the Master of the Rolls at least did not share Staughton J's view on the application of *Brandt's* case to the facts before the court.

In *The Kelo* [1985] 2 Lloyd's Rep 85 (heard and decided before the Court of Appeal decision in *The Aliakmon*) the issue arose again. Staughton J referred to his earlier observations in *The Aliakmon* (quoted above) and added (at p 88):

> The implication, as I said there, is a question of fact: whether on the facts of a given case one infers a contract. If a person goes to a transporter, hands

him some money and gets a ticket in return, one infers a contract of carriage. If a person at the delivery end goes to the carrier, pays him the freight, hands him the bill of lading, one infers some contract by which he is going to get something in return. But the facts have to be considered in each case. I see no reason to infer any contract because Messrs Elbe went and handed the bill of lading to the ship or ship's agents and took delivery of the goods. If there had been such a contract to be inferred it would further have to be considered whether Elbe were parties to that contract as agents or as principals; about that I need say nothing.

Brandt's case was considered again in *The Elli 2* [1985] 1 Lloyd's Rep 107 (decided before the Court of Appeal decision in *The Aliakmon* and before *The Kelo* was reported). The issue was whether there was a good arguable case, for the purpose of RSC, O 11, r 1, that the defendant had become party to an implied contract on bill of lading terms. Staughton J held that there was a good arguable case. This conclusion was challenged in the Court of Appeal. The defendant had not paid freight, which was pre-paid, but there was evidence of a past course of dealing whereby he had in similar circumstances paid demurrage referable to the bill of lading. Ackner LJ agreed with the judge, relying particularly on the past course of dealing. May LJ also agreed with the judge. In the course of his judgment he said (at p 115):

Finally, Mr Gross submitted that the other minimal condition which has to be satisfied is that usually the freight still remains payable under the contract of carriage. That which may 'usually' be the situation, but *ex hypothesi* may not always be so, cannot in my view properly be described as a condition precedent to the creation of the suggested contract. That the freight is still payable and is paid by the ultimate receiver of the goods may well in a number of cases be the consideration passing from him supporting the relevant contract. Nevertheless, the earlier authority to which I shall refer in a moment, makes it quite clear that other considerations, such as demurrage, will be sufficient.

Nevertheless, I agree that the boundaries of the doctrine are not clear. I would not expect them to be so. As the question whether or not any such contract is to be implied is one of fact, its answer must depend upon the circumstances of each particular case – and the different sets of facts which arise for consideration in these cases are legion. However, I also agree that no such contract should be implied on the facts of any given case unless it is necessary to do so: necessary, that is to say, in order to give business reality to a transaction and to create enforceable obligations between parties who are dealing with one another in circumstances in which one would expect that business reality and those enforceable obligations to exist.

Having cited passages from the judgments in *Brandt's* case and *Allen v Coltart*, May LJ then continued (at p 116):

Such cases, and indeed the instant case, are clearly different from ones where the possession of goods is taken against a bill of lading in circumstances in which nothing remains to be done in performance of the relevant contract of carriage save physically to hand the goods over to the receiver, who comes to the shipowner with the bill of lading in his hand as evidence of his entitlement to take delivery. Such a case was *Leigh and Sillivan & Co Ltd v Aliakmon Shipping Co Ltd* [1983] 1 Lloyd's Rep 203 which, in my opinion correctly, the learned judge distinguished from the instant case but upon which Mr Gross relied in the course of his submissions.

These cases may be said to decide no more than that whether a contract is to be implied is a question of fact and that a contract will only be implied where it is necessary to do so. But the cases certainly show that there is evidence from which a contract may be inferred where a shipowner who has a lien on cargo for unpaid freight or demurrage or other charges makes or agrees to make delivery of the cargo to the holder of a bill of lading who presents it and seeks or obtains delivery and pays outstanding dues or agrees to pay them or is to be taken to agree to pay them. The parties may also (as in *Allen v Coltart*) show an intention to adopt and perform the bill of lading contract in other ways. There does not, however, appear to have been a case in which a contract has been implied from the mere facts (a) that an endorsee, entitled as holder of the bill of lading to demand delivery, does so, and (b) that the shipowner, bound by contract with his shipper (and perhaps his charterer) to deliver goods to any party presenting the bill of lading, duly makes such delivery. Whether on such facts (without more) a contract may be implied must be considered in the light of ordinary contractual principles.

Most contracts are, of course, made expressly, whether orally or in writing. But here, on the evidence, nothing was said, nothing was written. So regard must be paid to the conduct of the parties alone. The questions to be answered are, I think, twofold: (1) whether the conduct of the bill of lading holder in presenting the bill of lading to the ship's agent would be reasonably understood by the agents (or the shipowner) as an offer to enter into a contract on the bill of lading terms; (2) whether the conduct of the ship's agent in accepting the bill or the conduct of the master in agreeing to give delivery or in giving delivery would be reasonably understood by the bill of lading holder as an acceptance of his offer.

I do not think it is enough for the party seeking the implication of a contract to obtain 'it might' as an answer to these questions, for it would, in my view, be contrary to principle to countenance the implication of a contract from conduct if the conduct relied upon is no more consistent with an intention to contract than with an intention not to contract. It must, surely, be necessary to identify conduct referable to the contract contended for or, at the very least, conduct inconsistent with there being no contract made between the parties to the effect contended for. Put another way, I think it must be fatal to the implication of a contract if the parties would or might have acted exactly as they did in the absence of a contract.

If this approach is correct, I think it is impossible to imply a contract on the bare facts of this case. Nothing that the shipowners or the bill of lading holders did need have been different had their intention been not to make a contract on the bill of lading terms. Their business relationship was entirely efficacious without the implication of any contract between them. Although the bill of lading holders had no title to any part of the undivided bulk cargo they had a perfectly good right to demand delivery and the shipowners had no right to refuse or to impose conditions.

Evans J in his judgment ([1987] 2 Lloyd's Rep 58) carefully reviewed the earlier authorities cited to him and then expressed his conclusion (at p 64):

> In my judgment, these authorities show that an implied contract may come into existence before the goods covered by the bill of lading are delivered or discharged, and independently of the payment and acceptance of freight. But I doubt whether it will be possible as a general rule to infer an undertaking by the shipowner that he will deliver goods in accordance with the bill of lading from the mere acceptance of the document by the shipowner or his agent. This would mean that the shipowner would become irrevocably bound to give delivery to that receiver regardless of any subsequent development before discharge takes place. But this does not mean that such a contract cannot be inferred if the circumstances so require.

> I leave this point open, because in my judgment the plaintiffs need not go so far. The evidence here is that the two parcels formed part of a larger bulk. There were other receivers requesting delivery of other parcels from the same bulk. All receivers were represented during discharge by the same supervisor, although he was appointed by different agents. The shipowners gave delivery of whatever quantity of cargo was available on board for delivery against the relevant bills of lading. Taking first bill of lading No 6, under which 11 tons were delivered, it seems to me that these acts by the crew or other agents on behalf of the shipowners were sufficient to constitute an acceptance of the receivers' offer to take delivery of the cargo specified in the bill of lading and on its terms. The shipowners would not contemplate for one moment that the cargo was being delivered, save upon those terms including the exceptions in their favour. Their obligation was to deliver in accordance with the bill of lading, including the quantities specified therein, upon proof that quantity was loaded in fact. The obligation was not 'merely to deliver the goods which he has on board', per Bankes LJ [1924] 1 KB at 589. I therefore hold that the plaintiffs who presented bill of lading No 6 are entitled to claim damages for short delivery of the goods to which it relates.

> The plaintiffs who presented bill of lading No 5 are arguably in a different position, because their complaint is that no goods were delivered to them and therefore they cannot rely upon any act of delivery as an acceptance of the offer which they made. But in my judgment the same actions of the shipowners, through their servants and agents, constitute an acceptance of that offer also. They purported to give delivery of the whole of the bulk cargo, and they did so in conjunction with a representative of all the bills of lading holders. The fact of the matter is that the whole cargo was discharged in bulk and was then delivered in separate parcels to each of the receivers, apart from these plaintiffs. The goods probably were 'ascertained' only after the goods were discharged from the ship. These plaintiffs, who were unlucky, have the same contractual right to claim damages for non-delivery as the other plaintiffs have for the short delivery made to them.

I fully recognise the good sense and the commercial convenience underlying the learned judge's decision. Unless the parties understood s 1 of the 1855 Act (which is not necessarily so) they probably thought that their rights and duties were governed by the bill of lading anyway. It would be perfectly reasonable in a general sense to treat the parties' rights and duties as so governed. Once an intention to contract is found no problem on consideration arises, since there would be ample consideration in the bundle of rights and duties which the parties would respectively obtain and accept. Had the boot been on the other foot it seems very likely that the shipowners would have sought to assert the bill of lading contract. But I do not think these matters entitle one to cast principle aside and simply opt for a commercially convenient solution. Evans J attributed to the bill of lading holders an offer to take delivery 'of the cargo specified in the bill of lading and on its terms', but there is nothing to show that they offered to take the cargo on those terms. He treated the acts of the crew and other agents on behalf of the shipowners as enough to constitute an acceptance, but those acts were in no way referable to the bill of lading terms. If the judge's approach is correct there was in truth no need for the 1855 Act because it is almost impossible to imagine circumstances in which a bill of lading holder could obtain goods without becoming party to the bill of lading contract. It may, of course, be said, and with truth, that the draftsman of the 1855 Act was not concerned to legislate for undivided bulk cargoes consigned or assigned to a number of different consignees or assignees. On that account it may fairly be said that the modern prevalence of undivided bulk cargoes calls for a new, commercially workable, solution. I agree. But the solution is, in my view, to be found in an amendment of the 1855 Act along the lines now under consideration by the Law Commission, rather than in the implication of a contract where the grounds for such implication do not exist.

On this issue I differ from the judge and would allow the shipowners' appeal ...

Stuart-Smith LJ: ... What the court has to determine is whether that is evidence of a new contract between the shipowner and holder of the bill of lading to regulate their dealings on the terms of the bill of lading. Since there is no evidence of any express agreement, it has to be inferred from the conduct of the parties. If their conduct is equally referable to and explicable by their existing rights and obligations, albeit such rights and obligations are not enforceable against each other, there is no material from which the court can draw the inference. It is only if their conduct is unequivocally referable to or explicable by one or more of the rights or obligations contained in the bill of lading that there is factual material from which the court can draw the inference that a contract has been entered into between them ...

Notes

1   The *Captain Gregos* was chartered to carry a cargo of crude oil from Egypt to Rotterdam. Bills of lading incorporating the Hague-Visby rules were issued to shippers. BP, the ultimate purchasers of the cargo, brought proceedings alleging short delivery after the expiry of the Hague-Visby limitation period. The issue for the court was whether BP were bound by

the bill of lading contract. BP were found to have bought the cargo on terms which provided that sellers would pay freight and any demurrage due to shipowners and that the goods might be carried on the terms of the Hague-Visby rules. The cargo was delivered to BP's refinery with 'the active co-operation of both BP and the crew of the vessel'. But BP had not become parties to the bill of lading contract by virtue of the 1855 Act; they did not pay freight or undertake to pay it and they did not presented the bills of lading, which were not available when the vessel discharged. The Court of Appeal held that it was necessary to imply a contract between BP and shipowners:

> to give business reality to the transaction between them and create the obligations which, as we think, both parties plainly believed to exist.
>
> Both sides made reference to the decision of this court in *The Aramis* (above). That decision has been adversely criticised by distinguished commentators (Treitel, 'Bills of Lading and Implied Contracts' (1989) LMCLQ 612; Davenport, 105 LQR 174) and no doubt its correctness may fall to be reviewed hereafter. But whether that decision be right or wrong, the position of BP differs from that of the plaintiffs in *The Aramis* in at least two respects relevant when considering whether a contract should be implied: first, BP were the owners of the cargo before discharge began; and, secondly, BP have very clearly and explicitly consented to the carriage of goods on terms incorporating any of the charterparty conditions normally in use for tankships, which would include the Hague-Visby rules.

Bingham LJ, *The Captain Gregos (No 2)* [1990] 2 Lloyd's Rep 395, CA.

2   In *The Gudermes* [1993] 1 Lloyd's Rep 311, CA, a cargo of fuel oil was loaded on the *Gudermes* at Aden for carriage to Ravenna under a charterparty between the shippers and the shipowners. Bills of lading were issued to the charterers which incorporated the Hague-Visby rules. The charterers sold the oil to the plaintiffs, agreeing that property would pass as the oil was loaded, with the result that the plaintiffs could not take advantage of the Bills of Lading Act 1855. The plaintiffs resold the goods while afloat. At Ravenna, the subpurchasers declined to receive the oil on the grounds that the temperature of the cargo was too low to allow discharge by means of the undersea pipeline and alleging that no other reasonable means of discharge were available. The shipowners declined to accept responsibility for this inability to discharge on the grounds, *inter alia*, that the charterers knew all along that the ship's cargo heating apparatus was not working. In these circumstances the plaintiffs procured and paid for transshipment off Malta to a vessel fitted with heating equipment which thereafter delivered the cargo at Ravenna.

The plaintiffs alleged that a *Brandt* contract was to be inferred on the terms of the bills of lading and that the defendants were in breach of that contract in that the ship was not cargoworthy in that it was unable to heat the cargo. The Court of Appeal rejected this claim and held:

(1) it was not enough to show that the parties had done something more than, or something different from, what they were already bound to do under obligations owed to others. What they do must be consistent only with there being a new contract implied, and inconsistent with there being no such contract;

(2) there had been direct communication between the parties and a very considerable degree of co-operation in the transshipment operation. Nevertheless, decisions on the facts in earlier cases could not compel a particular conclusion on facts unless precisely identical;

(3) that all the facts, both in favour of an implied contract and those pointing against it, should be considered as a single issue in the round;

(4) the shipowner's rejection of liability at Ravenna was significant. '... one does not imply terms which one party has refused to accept'.

References

Debattista, C, 'The Bill of Lading as the Contract of Carriage' (1982) 45 *MLR* 652

Lloyd, Sir Anthony, 'The Bill of Lading: do we really need it' (1989) *LMCLQ* 47

Davenport, B, QC, 'Problems in the Bills of Lading Act 1855: *The Aramis*' (1989) 105 *LQR* 174.

Treitel, GH (1989) *LMCLQ* 162 (Implied contracts)

Clarke, M, 'The Consignee's Right of Action against the Carrier of Goods by Sea: *The Captain Gregos No 2*' (1991) *LMCLQ* 5

Baughen, S, 'Contract and Co-operation: *The Gudermes*' (1991) *LMCLQ* 459

Yiannopoulos, AN, *Ocean Bills of Lading: Traditional Forms, Substitutes and EDI Systems*, Kluwer, Hague, 1995

Wilson, J, 'A flexible contract of carriage' (1996) *LMCLQ* 187

Burrows, A, 'Reforming Privity of Contract' (1996) *LMCLQ* 467

Law Commission, 'Privity of Contract: Contracts for the Benefit of Third Parties', *Law Com No 242*, 1996

CHAPTER 7

THE BILL OF LADING AS A RECEIPT

'THE KEY TO THE WAREHOUSE'

1 Need for production of the bill of lading on delivery[1]

The Stettin (1889) 14 PD 142

The plaintiffs shipped 57 barrels of seed oil on the steamship *Stettin* in London under a bill of lading providing for delivery at a German port to the named consignee or to his assigns. The master delivered the goods at the port of discharge to the consignee without the production of the bill of lading. An attempt was made to prove that under German law, a shipowner was entitled to deliver goods to a named consignee without insisting on the production of the bill of lading.

> **Butt J**: ... German advocates have been called on both sides, but, as they differ, I must, in this divergence of opinion, decide what, in the result, the German law appears to me to be.
>
> Having considered the reasons given by these advocates for their opinions, I have come to the conclusion that, on this point, German law does not essentially differ from English law.
>
> According to English law and the English mode of conducting business, a shipowner is not entitled to deliver goods to the consignee without the production of the bill of lading. I hold that the shipowner must take the consequences of having delivered these goods to the consignee without the production of either of the two parts of which the bill of lading consisted. There will be judgment for the plaintiffs with, if necessary, a reference to the registrar to ascertain the amount of damage.

Carlberg v Wemyss (1915) S C 616

> **Johnson LJ**: A shipowner is not bound to deliver goods except in exchange for the bill of lading. He is not bound to take on trust that he knows the consignee and that no intermediate rights have been created ... Neither the owner, his agent, nor the master can, I think, be called upon to accept a banker's or any other guarantee of indemnity, though such a thing is not unknown, and in the event of total loss of the bill of lading might have to be resorted to, if necessary at the sight of the court.

---

1 And see Wilson, J, 'The Presentation Rules Revisited' [1995] *LMCLQ* 289.

Barclays Bank Ltd v Commissioners of Customs and Excise [1963] 1 Lloyd's Rep 81

Diplock LJ: (at page 88) ... It is clear law that where a bill of lading or order is issued in respect of a contract of carriage by sea, the shipowner is not bound to surrender possession of the goods to any person whether named as consignee or not, except on production of the bill of lading (see *The Stettin*). Until the bill of lading is produced to him, unless at any rate its absence has been satisfactorily accounted for, he is entitled to retain possession of the goods and if he does part with possession he does so at his own risk if the person to whom he surrenders possession is not in fact entitled to the goods.

Kuwait Petroleum Corporation v I & D Oil Carriers Ltd, The Houda [1994] 2 Lloyd's Rep, 541, CA

Neill LJ: [Carriers] do not fulfil their contractual obligations if the cargo is delivered to a person who cannot produce the bill of lading. Of course if such delivery is made and the person to whom the cargo is delivered proves to be the true owner no damages would be recoverable ...

... It is of course open to a shipowner to decide that he is adequately protected by a letter of indemnity and delivery in the absence of the bill of lading, but in my judgment the rights of a time charterer to give orders [see Chapter 15] do not entitle him to insist that cargo should be discharged without production of the bill of lading.

Leggatt LJ: ... Under a bill of lading contract a shipowner is obliged to deliver goods upon production of the original bill of lading. Delivery without production of the bill of lading constitutes a breach of contract even when made to the person entitled to possession. But a shipowner is not discharged by delivery to the holder if he has notice or knowledge of any defect of title ...

In practice, if the bill of lading is not available, delivery is effected against an indemnity. Where the bill of lading is lost, the remedy, in default of agreement, is to obtain an order of the court that on tendering a sufficient indemnity the loss of the bill of lading is not to be set up as a defence ...

The Sormovskiy 3068 [1994] 2 Lloyd's Rep 266

Clarke J: ... In trades where it is difficult or impossible for the bills of lading to arrive at the discharge port in time the problem is met by including a contractual term requiring the master to deliver the cargo against a letter of indemnity or bank guarantee. That is commonplace ...

2 Exemption clauses

Chartered Bank of India, Australia and China v British India Steam Navigation Company Limited [1909] AC 369, PC

The judgment of their Lordships was delivered by Lord Macnaghten:

Lord Macnaghten: ... The carrying vessel was the steamship *Teesta*, one of a line of steamers belonging to the respondent company ... the bills of lading indorsed in blank were held by the bank as security for their advance.

The *Teesta* arrived at Penang on August 10, 1905. On her arrival the cargo intended for Penang was delivered overside into lighters and taken to the wharf.

It is the practice for the owners of steamers calling at Penang to appoint landing agents at that port. The business of the landing agents is to send lighters to meet an incoming vessel belonging to their employers on being furnished with a copy of the ship's manifest. The goods are discharged from the ship's tackle into the lighters. The landing agents give the master a clean receipt, if they are received in good order. The goods are then carried to jetty sheds, held under lease from government, landed there, and assorted by the landing agents ready for delivery to the consignees on production of the bill of lading indorsed by the ship's agents with a delivery order ... The landing agents make out their account of the landing charges and storage rent, if any, according to a scale of charges exhibited in the offices of the ship's agents. They receive payment direct from the consignees. The indorsement of the bill of lading by the ship's agents is required as a release of the ship's lien for freight and expenses incurred on the shipment. Without such indorsement the landing agents are not at liberty to deliver goods to consignees.

This practice, which is obviously for the convenience of all parties concerned, appears to be at present the subject of much controversy in Penang. The shipowners contend that the landing agents are the agents of the merchants. The merchants insist that they are not their agents, but the agents of the shipowners. Neither view perhaps is quite accurate. These landing agents rather seem to be in the position of intermediaries owing duties to both parties – agents for the shipowners as long as the contract of affreightment remains unexhausted, agents for the consignees as soon as the bill of lading is produced with delivery order indorsed. The point, however, is not material for the determination of the question now at issue, and their Lordships therefore do not propose to discuss it further, or to define the exact position of landing agents at the different stages of their employment.

... The appellants produced the bills of lading, with delivery order indorsed, and claimed the goods. The goods were not forthcoming. They had been taken away without the production of a bill of lading or a delivery order by the representative of [cargo receivers] acting in collusion with the representative of [landing agents] and they had been already disposed of, in fraud of the persons entitled. Having thus lost both their money and the goods which had been pledged to them as security, the bank preferred their claim against the respondents ...

Both here and in the courts below the respondent company disclaimed all liability, relying on conditions subject to which the bills of lading were expressed to be issued. They are printed at the foot of the bill of lading, and attention is called to them in the body of the bill. The only conditions material in the present case are those intended to be applicable on the arrival of the carrying vessel at the port of destination. They are contained in the following clause:

> The company is to have the option of delivering these goods or any part thereof into receiving ship or landing them at the risk and expense of the

shipper or consignee as per scale of charges to be seen at the agent's office, and is also to be at liberty until delivery to store the goods or any part thereof in receiving ship, godown, or upon any wharf, the usual charges therefor being payable by the shipper or consignee. The company shall have a lien on all or any part of the goods against expenses incurred on the whole or any part of the shipment. In all cases and under all circumstances the liability of the company shall absolutely cease when the goods are free of the ship's tackle, and thereupon the goods shall be at the risk for all purposes and in every respect of the shipper or consignee.

On behalf of the respondents the contention was that the obligations they undertook were fulfilled by delivering the goods to the landing agents, and that at any rate their liability ceased when the goods were once 'free of the ship's tackle'.

On the other hand it was said on behalf of the bank that the landing agents were neither the assigns nor the agents of the shippers or consignees, and that the goods had never been delivered in accordance with the bills of lading. As regards the provision for cesser of liability, the suggestion was that it applied only to the interval between the removal of the goods from the ship and their being landed on the quay.

... Now it may be conceded that the goods in question were not delivered according to the exigency of the bills of lading by being placed in the hands of the landing agents, and it may be admitted that bills of lading cannot be said to be spent or exhausted until the goods covered by them are placed under the absolute dominion and control of the consignees. But their Lordships cannot think that there is any ambiguity in the clause providing for cesser of liability. It seems to be perfectly clear. There is no reason why it should not be held operative and effectual in the present case. They agree with the learned Chief Justice that it affords complete protection to the respondent company.

Their Lordships therefore will humbly advise His Majesty that the appeal should be dismissed.

Sze Hai Tong Bank Ltd v Rambler Cycle Co Ltd [1959] AC 576, PC

Rambler shipped bicycle parts on *Glengarry* under a bill of lading which provided for delivery to order or assigns. The purchasers of the goods were named as the notify party. After discharge of the goods at Singapore the carrier's agents (relying on an indemnity agreement with the purchasers and their bank) delivered the goods to the purchasers without insisting on production of the bill of lading. The purchasers could not produce the bill of lading because they had not paid the purchase price and taken up the documents.

Lord Denning: ... It is perfectly clear law that a shipowner who delivers without production of the bill of lading does so at his peril. The contract is to deliver, on production of the bill of lading, to the person entitled under the bill of lading. In this case it was 'unto order or his or their assigns', that is to say, to the order of the Rambler Cycle Company, if they had not assigned the bill of lading, or to their assigns, if they had. The shipping company did not deliver the goods to any such person. They are therefore liable for breach of contract unless there is some term in the bill of lading protecting them. And they delivered the goods, without production of the bill of lading, to a person who was not entitled to receive them. They are therefore liable in conversion unless likewise so protected.

In order to escape the consequences of the misdelivery, the appellants say that the shipping company is protected by clause 2 of the bill of lading, which says that:

> During the period before the goods are loaded on or after they are discharged from the ship on which they are carried by sea, the following terms and conditions shall apply to the exclusion of any other provisions in this bill of lading that may be inconsistent therewith, *viz*,' (a) so long as the goods remain in the actual custody of the carrier or his servants' (here follows a specified exception); '(b) whilst the goods are being transported to or from the ship' (here follows another specified exemption); '(c) in all other cases the responsibility of the carrier, whether as carrier or as custodian or bailee of the goods, shall be deemed to commence only when the goods are loaded on the ship and to cease absolutely after they are discharged therefrom'.

The exemption, on the face of it, could hardly be more comprehensive, and it is contended that it is wide enough to absolve the shipping company from responsibility for the act of which the Rambler Cycle Company complains, that is to say, the delivery of the goods to a person who, to their knowledge, was not entitled to receive them. If the exemption clause upon its true construction absolved the shipping company from an act such as that, it seems that by parity of reasoning they would have been absolved if they had given the goods away to some passer-by or had burnt them or thrown them into the sea. If it had been suggested to the parties that the condition exempted the shipping company in such a case, they would both have said: 'Of course not'. There is, therefore, an implied limitation on the clause, which cuts down the extreme width of it: and, as a matter of construction, their Lordships decline to attribute to it the unreasonable effect contended for.

But their Lordships go further. If such an extreme width were given to the exemption clause, it would run counter to the main object and intent of the contract. For the contract, as it seems to their Lordships, has, as one of its main objects, the proper delivery of the goods by the shipping company, 'unto order or his or their assigns', against production of the bill of lading. It would defeat this object entirely if the shipping company was at liberty, at its own will and pleasure, to deliver the goods to somebody else, to someone not entitled at all, without being liable for the consequences. The clause must therefore be limited and modified to the extent necessary to enable effect to be given to the main object and intent of the contract: see *Glynn v Margetson & Co* [1893] AC 351, 357; *GH Renton & Co Ltd v Palmyra Trading Corporation of Panama* [1956] 1 QB 462, 501.

To what extent is it necessary to limit or modify the clause? It must at least be modified so as not to permit the shipping company deliberately to disregard its obligations as to delivery. For that is what has happened here. The shipping company's agents in Singapore acknowledged: 'We are doing something we know we should not do'. Yet they did it. And they did it as agents in such circumstances that their acts were the acts of the shipping company itself. They were so placed that their state of mind can properly be regarded as the state of mind of the shipping company itself. And they deliberately disregarded one of the prime obligations of the contract. No court can allow so fundamental a breach to pass unnoticed under the cloak of a general exemption clause: see *The Cap Palos* [1921] P 458, 471.

The appellants placed much reliance, however, on a case which came before their Lordships' Board in 1909, *Chartered Bank of India, Australia and China v British India Steam Navigation Co Ltd* [1909] AC 369. There was there a clause which said that in all cases and under all circumstances the liability of the company shall absolutely cease when the goods are free of the ship's tackle. The goods were discharged at Penang and placed in a shed on the jetty. Whilst there a servant of the landing agents fraudulently misappropriated them in collusion with the consignees. Their Lordships' Board held that the shipping company were protected by the clause from any liability.

Their Lordships are of opinion that that case is readily distinguishable from the present, as the courts below distinguished it, on the simple ground that the action of the fraudulent servant there could in no wise be imputed to the shipping company. His act was not its act. His state of mind was not its state of mind. It is true that, in the absence of an exemption clause, the shipping company might have been held liable for his fraud, see *United Africa Co Ltd v Saka Owoade* [1955] AC 130. But that would have been solely a vicarious liability. Whereas in the present case the action of the shipping agents at Singapore can properly be treated as the action of the shipping company itself ... their Lordships will humbly advise Her Majesty that this appeal should be dismissed.

3 Delivery to the holder of a bill of lading

Glyn Mills Currie & Co v East and West India Dock Company (1882) 7 App Cas 591

Twenty hogsheads of sugar were shipped in Jamaica on the *Mary Jones* and consigned to Cottam & Co in London. The master signed a set of three bills of lading marked 'First', 'Second', and 'Third', respectively, which made the goods deliverable to Cottam & Co, or their assigns, freight payable in London, 'the one of the bills being accomplished, the others to stand void'. During the voyage Cottam & Co indorsed the bill of lading marked 'First' to a bank in consideration of a loan. Upon the arrival of the ship at London the goods were landed and placed in the custody of a dock company in their warehouses. The dock company bona fide and without notice or knowledge of the bank's claim delivered the goods to other persons upon delivery orders signed by Cottam & Co. *Held*: a shipowner is entitled to deliver to the first person who claims by virtue of an indorsed bill of lading, provided the shipowner has no notice of any better title, even though such person might not, in fact have the legal title to the goods.

> **Lord Blackburn**: ... If there were only one part of the bill of lading, the obligation of the master under such a contract would be clear, he would fulfil the contract if he delivered to Cottam & Co on their producing the bill of lading unindorsed; he would also fulfil his contract if he delivered the goods to anyone producing the bill of lading with a genuine indorsement by Cottam & Co. He would not fulfil his contract if he delivered them to anyone else, though if the person to whom he delivered was really entitled to the possession of the goods, no one might be entitled to recover damages from him for that breach of contract. But at the request of the shipper, and in conformity with ancient mercantile usage, the master has affirmed to three bills of lading all of the same tenor and date, the one of which bills being accomplished the others to stand void.

> ... But where the person who produces a bill of lading is one who – either as being the person named in the bill of lading which is not indorsed, or as actually holding an indorsed bill – would be entitled to demand delivery under the contract, unless one of the other parts had been previously indorsed for value to some one else, and the master has no notice or knowledge of anything except that there are other parts of the bill of lading, and that therefore it is possible that one of them may have been previously indorsed, I think the master cannot be bound, at his peril, to ask for the other parts.

> ... unless this was the practice, the business of a shipowner could not be carried on, unless bills of lading were made in only one part ...

> ... where the master has notice that there has been an assignment of another part of the bill of lading, the master must interplead or deliver to the one who he thinks has the better right, at his peril if he is wrong. And I think it probably would be the same if he had knowledge that there had been such an assignment, though no one had given notice of it or as yet claimed under it. At all events, he would not be safe, in such a case, in delivering without further inquiry. But I think that when the master has not notice or knowledge of anything but that there are other parts of the bill of lading, one of which it is possible may have been assigned, he is justified or excused in delivering according to his contract to the person appearing to be the assign of the bill of lading which is produced to him ...

> [Lord Selborne LC, Lord O'Hagan, Lord Watson and Lord Fitzgerald agreed with Lord Blackburn. Earl Cairns also delivered a judgment in favour of dismissing the appeal.]

4 Indemnity agreements

Brown Jenkinson & Co Ltd v Percy Dalton (London) Ltd [1957] 2 QB 621, CA

The defendants (Dalton) sold 100 barrels of orange juice to a company in Rotterdam who resold to a purchaser in Hamburg. The plaintiffs were loading brokers for the vessel on which the orange juice was to be shipped. They informed the defendants that the barrels were old, frail and leaking and that a claused bill of lading was appropriate. At the defendants' request and on a promise of an indemnity, the plaintiffs signed a clean bill of lading stating that the barrels were 'shipped in apparent good order and condition'. On delivery in Hamburg, the barrels were leaking and the shipowners had to make good the loss. The plaintiffs sued the defendants under the agreement to indemnify, the benefit of which had been assigned to them by the shipowners. The defendants refused to pay, alleging that the contract of indemnity was illegal, because it had as its object the making by the shipowners of a fraudulent misrepresentation.

> **Morris LJ**: The question which is raised in this appeal is whether, on the facts of this particular case, an agreement to indemnify against the consequences of issuing a clean bill of lading is enforceable. The case is one in which the issuing of a clean bill of lading was not justified having regard to the condition of the goods which were shipped ...
>
> To the claim made in the action on the contract of indemnity, the defendants advance the defence that it is unenforceable, because it was founded on an illegal consideration. This plea comes with singular ill grace from those at whose request the procedure at the time of shipment was adopted: they are prepared to condemn their own conduct, in order to save their own pocket. But the legal issue which arises must be determined, and it is perhaps of a nature which transcends in importance and, in any event, cannot be affected by any considerations as to the relative merits of the attitudes of the parties.
>
> It is, I think, clear that the plaintiffs did not desire that anyone should be defrauded. In agreeing with the defendants, they did not have any such desire as their real purpose ... But the question which here arises is whether the contract sued upon was founded upon an illegal consideration. An agreement is illegal and unenforceable if it has as its object the commission of a tort ... It is said that the contract here is illegal because it had as its object the making by the shipowners of a fraudulent misrepresentation. The question arises whether this is so: if so, the further question arises whether the position is effected by the circumstance that the claims made upon the shipowners were satisfied ...
>
> On the facts as found, and indeed on the facts which are not in dispute, the position was therefore that, at the request of the defendants, the plaintiffs made a representation which they knew to be false and which they intended should be relied upon by persons who received the bill of lading, including any banker who might be concerned. In these circumstances, all the elements of the tort of deceit were present. Someone who could prove that he suffered damage by relying on the representation could sue for damages. I feel impelled to the conclusion that a promise to indemnify the plaintiffs against any loss resulting to them from making the representation is unenforceable. The claim cannot be put forward without basing it upon an unlawful transaction. The promise upon which the plaintiffs rely is in effect this: if you will make a false representation, which will deceive indorsees or bankers, we will indemnify

you against any loss that may result to you. I cannot think that a court should lend its aid to enforce such a bargain.

The conclusion thus reached is one that may seem unfortunate for the plaintiffs, for I gain the impression that they did not pause to realise the significance and the implications of what they were asked to do. There was evidence that the practice of giving indemnities upon the issuing of clean bills of lading is not uncommon. That cannot in any way alter the analysis of the present transaction, but it may help to explain how the plaintiffs came to accede to the defendants' request. There may perhaps be some circumstances in which indemnities can properly be given. Thus if a shipowner thinks that he has detected some faulty condition in regard to goods to be taken on board, he may be assured by the shipper that he is entirely mistaken: if he is so persuaded by the shipper, it may be that he could honestly issue a clean bill of lading, while taking an indemnity in case it was later shown that there had in fact been some faulty condition. Each case must depend upon its circumstances. But even if it could be shown that there existed to any extent a practice of knowingly issuing clean bills when claused bills should have been issued, no validating effect for any particular transaction could in consequence result.

... It is said that a result of issuing a clean bill of lading is that a shipowner deprives himself of certain defences to claims that may be made against him. In this way advantage in one sense results for indorsees of the bill of lading and disadvantages for the shipowner. The shipowner deprives himself of the possibility of setting up certain defences, if he is sued. He cannot assert that the goods, which he has carried, were in defective condition when he received them on his ship, if he has stated on the bill of lading that they were in good condition ... It was pointed out by Mr Roche that though there may be an estoppel against the shipowner, the holder of a clean bill of lading may still be in great difficulties if defective goods are shipped. He may have resold the goods and he may find that his purchaser will not accept, and he may sometimes experience great practical difficulties in suing the shipowner if, for example, the shipowner is a foreign shipowner. If he sues the shipowner, the latter may be entitled to rely on some clause in the bill of lading which protects him: furthermore, some time limit may prove fatal to a claim. But in any event buyers and bankers who act on the faith of clean bills of lading are not seeking law suits.

Some of the considerations to which I have referred may denote that in this particular case the plaintiffs, not being actuated by bad intentions, did not realise the viciousness of the transaction. When at the later period inquiries were being made on behalf of the continental underwriters, the plaintiffs acted with commendable frankness and made no attempt to suppress any disclosure ...

But whatever features there are in this case which possibly enable one to approach it with a measure of sympathetic understanding as to how the plaintiffs came to act as they did, the undisputed facts show that a short point is involved. It may be stated thus. Can A, who does what B asks him to do, enforce against B a promise made in the following terms: 'If you will at my request make a statement which you know to be false and which you know will be relied upon by others and which may cause them loss, then, if they hold you liable, I will indemnify you'? In my judgment, the assistance of the courts should not be given to enforce such a promise ...

Pearce LJ agreed with Morris LJ that the appeal should be allowed: ... The real difficulty that arises in the case is due to the fact that the plaintiffs, whatever may have been the defendants' intentions, appear from the evidence not to have contemplated that anybody would ultimately be defrauded. Theirs was a slipshod and unthinking extension of a known commercial practice to a point at which it constituted fraud in law. In the last 20 years it has become customary, in the short-sea trade in particular, for shipowners to give a clean bill of lading against an indemnity from the shippers in certain cases where there is a bona fide dispute as to the condition or packing of the goods. This avoids the necessity of rearranging any letter of credit, a matter which can create difficulty where time is short. If the goods turn out to be faulty, the purchaser will have his recourse against the shipping owner, who will in turn recover under his indemnity from the shippers. Thus no one will ultimately be wronged.

This practice is convenient where it is used with conscience and circumspection, but it has perils if it is used with laxity and recklessness. It is not enough that the banks or the purchasers who have been misled by clean bills of lading may have recourse at law against the shipping owner. They are intending to buy goods, not law suits. Moreover, instances have been given in argument where their legal rights may be defeated or may not recoup their loss. Trust is the foundation of trade; and bills of lading are important documents. If purchasers and banks felt that they could no longer trust bills of lading, the disadvantage to the commercial community would far outweigh any conveniences provided by the giving of clean bills of lading against indemnities.

The evidence seemed to show that, in general, the practice is kept within reasonable limits. In trivial matters and in cases of bona fide dispute, where the difficulty of ascertaining the correct state of affairs is out of proportion to its importance, no doubt the practice is useful. But here the plaintiffs went outside those reasonable limits. They did so at the defendants' request without, as it seems to me, properly considering the implications of what they were doing. They thought that they could trust the defendants' agreement to indemnify them. In that they were in error ...

Lord Evershed MR dissented on the grounds that personal dishonesty, which was not present, was necessary before the misrepresentation could be said to be fraudulent.

THE BILL OF LADING AS EVIDENCE IN A CARGO CLAIM

1 A receipt as to quantity

Legal and evidential burden of proof

Amoco Oil Co v Parpada Shipping Co Ltd [1989] 1 Lloyd's Rep 369, CA

Lord Donaldson of Lymington MR: ... I now turn to the burden of proof. It is trite law that the legal burden lies upon the claimant. He who alleges must prove. The appellants allege a short delivery and consequential loss and they must prove both. How they prove it and the evidential burden involved is another matter. Proof must be met by counter-proof and that in turn by a reinforcement of the original proof (*Smith v Bedouin* [1896] AC 70, *per* Lord Shand at p 79). If at any particular stage in the evidence one party would succeed, it is for the other party to adduce further or better evidence and, if he does so and thereby achieves a contingently winning position, the first party must do likewise or lose. In other words the evidential burden swings or may swing between the parties throughout the hearing, but in the end, in the context of a claim for short delivery, the owner of the cargo must prove the short delivery if he is to succeed in his claim and the shipowner must either prevent his doing so, or prove affirmatively that, although there was indeed a short delivery, it occurred in circumstances for which he was not responsible ...

Anonima Petroli Italiana SpA v Marlucidez Armadora SA, The Filiatra Legacy [1991] 2 Lloyd's Rep 337, CA

Mustill LJ: ... as to the requirement that the plaintiffs shall prove their case, we do not think it profitable to inquire whether the shifting of an evidentiary burden of proof is a useful or reliable guide, especially in a case such as the present where the orthodox adversarial principles of the consecutive presentation of the evidence did not apply, and where the greater part of the evidence for the plaintiffs and defendants alike was adduced simultaneously in writing at the start of the trial and where even the oral evidence did not follow a set pattern. In most cases the plaintiff has the burden of proof and starts from scratch. If he adduces enough evidence to ensure that, if the defendant brings forward no contrary evidence, the plaintiff will win, one can say (if the terminology seems attractive) that the defendant has an evidentiary burden, which means only that, if the defendant wishes to prevent the plaintiff from discharging the burden which rests on him, he must exert himself to do so. But this is all about situations which arise while the trial is in progress and has nothing to do with the position where all the evidence is in and the judge is required to decide the single question, whether on the issue before him the plaintiff has shown that his asserted version of the facts is more likely than not to be correct. Obviously the judge may find it convenient, as we shall here, to look at the evidence in groups to ascertain the parties' strengths and weaknesses in relation to each group. He does not, however, reach a conclusion on one group and then asks himself whether it is displaced by a contrary conclusion on another group, but simply regards the evidence as a whole, weak and strong together and asks what, if any, conclusion can be drawn from it.

We find nothing inconsistent in this approach with cases such as *Smith & Co v Bedouin Steam Navigation Co* [1896] AC 70 and *Sanday v Strath Steamship Co Ltd* (1920) 5 Ll L Rep 448; (1920) 26 Com Cas 277, where the shipowners had issued a bill of lading stating that a certain quantity of goods had been shipped, and sought in the action to controvert it. Nor with *Amoco Oil Co v Parpada Shipping Co (The George S)* [1989] 1 Lloyd's Rep 369 ...

Prima facie *evidence of quantity*

Attorney-General of Ceylon v Scindia Steam Navigation Co Ltd [1962] AC 60, PC

Bills of lading acknowledged receipt of 100,652 bags of rice 'weight, contents and value when shipped unknown' for carriage from Burma to Ceylon. Only 100,417 bags were delivered. The appellants claimed damages. The judgment of their Lordships was delivered by

> **Lord Morris of Borth-y-Gest**: ... The first question which arises is whether the plaintiff established that 100,652 bags were shipped at Rangoon for delivery to the Director of Food Supplies at Colombo. The onus of proving that fact undoubtedly rested upon the plaintiff. It was forcibly pointed out by the respondent that the plaintiff had chosen to rely for proof solely upon producing the bills of lading, and that the plaintiff had not traced the bills of lading to their source or supported them by producing and proving mate's receipts and tally men's books. The respondent further submitted that the bills of lading did not yield *prima facie* evidence of the number of bags that had been shipped.
>
> ... three bills of lading were actually issued. They contained respectively the admissions or acknowledgments that 2,187 bags and 47,992 bags and 50,473 bags 'being marked and numbered as per margin' were shipped. Their Lordships consider that, though these statements in the bills of lading as to the numbers of bags shipped do not constitute conclusive evidence as against the shipowner, they form strong prima facie evidence that the stated numbers of bags were shipped unless it be that there is some provision in the bills of lading which precludes this result. Was there, then, any such provision in the present case? There was a condition in the terms: 'weight, contents and value when shipped unknown'. That meant that in signing a bill of lading acknowledging the receipt of a number of bags there was a disclaimer of knowledge in regard to the weight or contents or value of such bags. There was, however, no disclaimer as to the numbers of bags. Their Lordships cannot agree with the view expressed in the judgment of the Supreme Court that the conditions in the bills of lading disentitled the plaintiff from relying upon the admissions that bags to the numbers stated in the bills of lading were taken on board.

The present case differs from *New Chinese Antimony Co Ltd v Ocean Steamship Co Ltd* [1917] 2 KB 664. In that case a bill of lading for antimony oxide ore stated that 937 tons had been shipped on board: in the margin was a typewritten clause: 'A quantity said to be 937 tons', and in the body of the bill of lading (printed in ordinary type) was a clause: 'weight, measurement contents and value (except for the purpose of estimating freight) unknown'. It was held that the bill of lading was not even prima facie evidence of the quantity of ore shipped, and that in an action against the shipowners for short delivery the onus was upon the plaintiff of proving that 937 tons had in fact been shipped ...

In *Hogarth Shipping Co Ltd v Blyth, Greene, Jourdain & Co Ltd* [1917] 2 KB 534 a captain signed a bill of lading for a specified number of bags of sugar: one of the exceptions and conditions of the bill of lading read 'weight, measure, quality, contents and value unknown'. It was held by Lush J that the bill of lading was conclusive only as to the number of bags in the sense of skins or receptacles and not as to their contents.

Even though the plaintiff called no evidence from Rangoon and took the possibly unusual course of depending in the main upon the production of the bills of lading, their Lordships conclude that the bills of lading did form strong prima facie evidence that the *SS Jalaveera* had received the stated numbers of bags for shipment to Colombo and delivery to the Director of Food Supplies. (See *Henry Smith & Co v Bedouin Steam Navigation Co Ltd* [1896] AC 70, HL.) The shipowners would, however, be entitled to displace the *prima facie* evidence of the bills of lading by showing that the goods or some of them were never actually put on board: to do that would require very satisfactory evidence on their part. In his speech in the case last cited Lord Halsbury said (page 76):

> To my mind, the cardinal fact is that the person properly appointed for the purpose of checking the receipt of the goods has given a receipt in which he has acknowledged, on behalf of the person by whom he was employed, that those goods were received. If that fact is once established, it becomes the duty of those who attempt to get rid of the effect of that fact to give some evidence from which your Lordships should infer that the goods never were on board at all.

Unless the shipowners showed that only some lesser number of bags than that acknowledged in the bills of lading was shipped then the shipowners would be under obligation to deliver the full number of bags. (See *Harrowing v Katz & Co* (1894) 10 TLR 400, CA; *Hain Steamship Co Ltd v Herdman & McDougal* (1922) 11 Ll L Rep 58 and *Royal Commission on Wheat Supplies v Ocean Steam Ship Co*.)

Though by relying upon the bills of lading the plaintiff presented *prima facie* evidence that 100,652 bags (marked and numbered as in the margins of the bills) were shipped, the bills of lading were not even *prima facie* evidence of the weight or contents or value of such bags. This was the result of the incorporation in the bills of lading of the provision above referred to. (See *New Chinese Antimony Co Ltd v Ocean Steamship Co Ltd*, above.) It was for the plaintiff to prove the contents of the bags and the weight of the bags, and it was for him to prove his loss by proving what it was that the bags contained and by proving what was the value of what the bags contained. The respondent company submitted that such proof was lacking. The respondent company further submitted (a) that there was evidence which displaced the *prima facie* evidence of the shipment of 100,652 bags and which led to the conclusion that there never were 235 missing bags, and (b) that if, alternatively, 100,652 bags were in fact shipped, the evidence showed that all the contents of such bags were discharged at Colombo – with the result that the liability of the respondent company would be limited to the value of 235 empty bags.

In support of the respondent company's submission under (a) above it was urged that it was improbable that 235 bags had been put on board at Rangoon and had then been in some manner removed. It was further urged that inasmuch as the ship sailed directly from Rangoon to Colombo and carried no other cargo than was shipped by the State Agricultural Marketing Board Union of Burma, and that it was not suggested that any rice was retained in the ship's hold after discharge at Colombo, the probabilities were that the number of bags shipped was not 100,652 but 100,417. Their Lordships cannot accept the view that these circumstances are of sufficient weight to displace the *prima facie* evidence of the shipment of 100,652 bags. Nor do their Lordships consider that any useful purpose would be served by speculating as to possible explanations as to what might have happened. It was for the shipowners to explain away their acknowledgment of the number of bags that they had received.

On the basis that 100,652 bags were shipped the evidence clearly established a short delivery of 235 bags. The result of the double tally at the time of discharge was that it was satisfactorily proved that only 100,417 bags were discharged. It was not contended by Mr Michael Kerr, appearing for the respondent company, that the 235 original bags were in fact discharged and were missed in the two tallies at Colombo.

It remains to be considered whether the plaintiff proved the loss that he alleged: linked with the points raised in that issue are those which are involved in the submission of the respondent company referred to under (b) above.

It was for the plaintiff to prove what was in the missing bags. Their Lordships consider that there was abundant evidence that the missing bags contained rice ... On the assumption that the bags contained rice the next question is whether there was evidence as to their weight. The provision of the bill of lading which has been quoted above expressly precludes any dependence upon the particulars as to weight which were declared by the shipper ...

In this connection reference may again be made to the decision of Lush J in *Hogarth Shipping Co Ltd v Blyth, Greene, Jourdain & Co Ltd*, above. In his judgment Lush J pointed out that if a certain number of bags had been lost, and if one had to ascertain what was in the bags that were lost, then as a matter of evidence one would almost necessarily infer that the lost bags were bags containing similar goods to those which were not lost ...

In the present case their Lordships consider that it was shown that there was a short delivery of 235 bags and that such bags had been shipped with rice in them, and that each had weighed approximately 160 lbs ...

Carriage of Goods by Sea Act 1992

The Act came into force on 16 September 1992. It repealed the Bills of Lading Act 1855. For the statutory definitions of terms used in this section, see Chapter 8 below.

Section 4 *Representations in bills of lading*

A bill of lading which–

(a) represents goods to have been shipped on board a vessel or to have been received for shipment on board a vessel; and

(b) has been signed by the master of the vessel or by a person who was not the master but had the express, implied or apparent authority of the carrier to sign bills of lading, shall, in favour of a person who has become the lawful holder of the bill, be conclusive evidence against the carrier of the shipment of the goods or, as the case may be, of their receipt for shipment.

2 A receipt as to quality

Cox, Paterson, & Co v Bruce & Co (1886) 18 QBD 147, CA

A bill of lading signed by the master in respect of a shipment of bales of jute stated that a specified proportion of the bales were marked with particular marks. The marks were an indication of their superior quality. On discharge it was found that the number of bales of superior quality had been overstated. The Court of Appeal first rejected an argument by the indorsee of the bill of lading based on breach of a special term of the contract. The court went on to reject a more general argument based on estoppel. Lindley and Lopes LJJ delivered judgments to the same effect as **Lord Esher MR**:

> ... it is said that, because the plaintiffs are indorsees for value of the bill of lading without notice, they have another right, that they are entitled to rely on a representation made in the bill of lading that the bales bore such and such marks, and that there is consequently an estoppel against the defendants. That raises a question as to the true meaning of the doctrine in *Grant v Norway* (1851) 10 CB 665. It is clearly impossible, consistently with that decision, to assert that the mere fact of a statement being made in the bill of lading estops the shipowner and gives a right of action against him if untrue, because it was there held that a bill of lading signed in respect of goods not on board the vessel did not bind the shipowner.[2] The ground of that decision, according to my view, was not merely that the captain has no authority to sign a bill of lading in respect of goods not on board, but that the nature and limitations of the captain's authority are well known among mercantile persons, and that he is only authorised to perform all things usual in the line of business in which he is employed. Therefore the doctrine of that case is not confined to the case where the goods are not put on board the ship. That the captain has authority

---

2   But see now the Carriage of Goods by Sea Act 1992, above.

to bind his owners with regard to the weight, condition, and value of the goods under certain circumstances may be true; but it appears to me absurd to contend that persons are entitled to assume that he has authority, though his owners really gave him no such authority, to estimate and determine and state on the bill of lading so as to bind his owners the particular mercantile quality of the goods before they are put on board, as, for instance, that they are goods containing such and such a percentage of good or bad material, or of such and such a season's growth. To ascertain such matters is obviously quite outside the scope of the functions and capacities of a ship's captain and of the contract of carriage with which he has to do. It was said that he ought to see that the quality marks were not incorrectly inserted in the bill of lading. But, apart from the special terms of the contract with regard to the quality marks, with which I have already dealt, I do not think it was his duty to put in these quality marks at all; all he had to do was to insert the leading marks ...

3 Estoppel

Silver v Ocean Steamship Company Limited [1930] 1 KB 416, CA

Scrutton LJ: This appeal relates to damage done to a large shipment of Chinese eggs while in course of transit from China to London. The transit was from shippers' warehouse in Shanghai to cold stores in London, the defendants' ship being only responsible from delivery on board in Shanghai to delivery overside in London. The liquid content of the eggs was contained in metal cases holding 42 lbs each, cases of a rectangular shape, and, therefore, with 12 right-angled edges. The cases were not covered with any cloth, fibre or cardboard covering. The contents were frozen and the cases carried in refrigerated holds. The more usual method of conveyance was either in rectangular cases covered with some kind of covering, or in circular drums which were sometimes uncovered. In this case the rectangular cases of the size in fact used were used at the request of London purchasers for reasons connected with their own business. They were probably uncovered for cheapness. As to shape, rectangular cases were obviously better for the ship's stowage, as cylindrical cases wasted room in stowage. But the right-angled edges were probably more likely to damage other goods even in careful stowage and handling; and were certainly more likely to do so if there was negligent handling. There was in the whole transit from shippers' warehouse to store very considerable damage to the cases ...

On May 25 a bill of lading is signed stating that a number of tins are shipped 'in apparent good order and condition'. After issuing such a bill can the ship prove that at that time: (1) the tins were perforated or punctured, or (2) that they were insufficiently packed, or must it be taken that on shipment the tins, so far as reasonable inspection would discover, were not perforated or punctured and were by all reasonable inspection sufficiently packed?

... Two questions seem to arise at this stage. First, under the law prior to the Carriage of Goods by Sea Act 1924 [which applied by agreement] a shipowner who received goods which he signed for 'in apparent good order and condition' to be delivered in the like good order and condition, and who delivered them not in apparent good order and condition, had the burden of proving exceptions which protected him for the damage found. The present bill of lading runs 'Shipped in apparent good order and condition for delivery subject to Conditions', etc. Has any difference been made in the old law by this wording? In my opinion no difference has been made. I agree with the view expressed by Wright J in *Gosse Millard v Canadian Government Merchant Marine* [1927] 2 KB 432, on similar words, that there is still an obligation to deliver in the like apparent good order and condition unless the shipowner proves facts bringing him within an exception covering him. Lord Sumner in *Bradley & Sons v Federal Steam Navigation Co* (1927) 27 Ll L Rep 395, 396, appears to express the same view.

The second point of law is this. It has been decided by Channell J in *Compania Naviera Vasconzada v Churchill & Sim* [1906] 1 KB 237 and affirmed by the Court of Appeal in *Brandt v Liverpool, Brazil and River Plate Steam Navigation Co* [1924] 1 KB 575 that the statement as to 'apparent good order and condition' estops (as against the person taking the bill of lading for value or presenting it to get delivery of the goods) the shipowner from proving that the goods were not in apparent good order and condition when shipped and therefore from alleging that there were at shipment external defects in them which were apparent to reasonable inspection. Art III, r 4, of the Carriage of Goods by Sea Act 1924, which says the bill shall be *prima facie* evidence (not *prima facie* evidence only, liable to be contradicted), can hardly have been meant to render the above decisions inapplicable. For the information relates to the shipowner's knowledge; he is to say what is 'apparent', that is, visible by reasonable inspection to himself and his servants, and on the faith of that statement other people are to act, and if it is wrong, act to their prejudice.

I am of opinion that r 4 of Art III has not the effect of allowing the shipowner to prove that goods which he has stated to be in apparent good order and condition on shipment were not really in apparent good order and condition as against people who accepted the bill of lading on the faith of the statement contained in it. Apparent good order and condition was defined by Sir R Phillimore in *The Peter der Grosse* (1875) 1 PD 414, 420 as meaning that 'apparently, and so far as met the eye, and externally, they were placed in good order on board this ship'. If so, on the *Churchill & Sim* decision (above) the shipowner is not allowed to reduce his liability by proving or suggesting contrary to his statement in the bill that the goods in respect of matters externally reasonably visible were not in good condition when shipped.

Now what was reasonably apparent to the shipowner's servants loading at Shanghai at night but under clusters of electric lights? The ultimate damage was classed by the surveyors as (1) serious damage where the tins were gashed or punctured, damage easily discernible in handling each tin; (2) minor damage, pinhole perforations, which on tins covered with rime were not easily discernible but which were found when the tins were closely examined. I have considered the evidence and I find that the first class of damage was apparent to reasonable examination; the second, having regard to business conditions, was not apparent. The result of this is that the shipowner is estopped against certain persons from proving or suggesting that there were gashes or serious damage when the goods were shipped. He may raise the question whether there was not minor or pinprick damage at that time, but having regard to the small quantity of goods rejected for visible damage I should not estimate the amount of such minor damage at shipment as very high.

Canadian and Dominion Sugar Company Limited v Canadian National (West Indies) Steamships Limited [1947] AC 46, PC

The judgment of their Lordships was delivered by **Lord Wright**:

The appellants claimed in the action as holders of a bill of lading in respect of a quantity of sugar shipped at Demerara on the respondents' steamship *Colborne* for delivery at Montreal. In due course the appellants, who had purchased the sugar on cif terms, took up the bill of lading against payment of 95 per cent of the purchase price when it was presented to them in accordance with the terms of the contract, and thereupon became owners of the sugar and duly thereafter paid the balance of the price. The sugar was found to be damaged ...

The bill of lading, dated at Georgetown, BG, on 13 June 1938, and signed by the agents of the shipowners (the respondents) was a 'received for shipment' not a 'shipped' bill of lading. The loading of the sugar in question was completed on June 13, and the ship's receipt was signed on that date. It is not clearly established whether the signing of the bill of lading was before or after the actual completion of the loading, but as the bill of lading bore on its face an endorsement 'Signed under guarantee to produce ship's clean receipt' it would seem reasonable to infer that the ship's receipt had not reached the agents' office when they signed the bill. As will be shown later, this particular point is not material in the final stage of the argument. Evidence was given, and not questioned, that there was a practice at the port to issue bills of lading before the completion of the loading and the issue of the mate's receipt in order to facilitate the shippers' business arrangements by enabling them to catch an earlier mail for the port of destination, so that the document could be presented to the buyer for acceptance and payment before the carrying vessel's arrival. In the present case the Colborne did not arrive until 3 July 1938, but the bill of lading was taken up against payment at Montreal on 29 June 1938.

It was not disputed that the sugar, which had been lying for some time at the wharf at Georgetown, had suffered some damage before shipment. From this resulted the damage found on arrival at Montreal ... The crucial question is what is the true construction of the bill of lading in regard to the matters relevant to this case. The issue is here between the shipowners and the indorsees of the bill, and has to be decided as between these parties on the basis of what appeared on the face of the bill when it was presented at Montreal to the respondents. Their rights and liabilities would not, in a case like this, be affected by what happened at the port of shipment as between the shippers and the shipowners, except in so far as appeared from the bill of lading. Authority for that proposition (if authority be needed at this time of day) is afforded by *Evans v James Webster and Bros Ltd* (1928) 34 Com Cas 172, where it was held that an innocent indorsee for value of a bill of lading is entitled to act on the statements contained in the bill of lading unless he has at the material time clear and definite knowledge from other sources that the statements in the bill are untrue. Any other view would affect the value of a bill of lading as a document of title on the faith of which shipowners and indorsees deal. If the statement at the head of the bill, 'Received in apparent good order and condition', had stood by itself, the bill would have been a 'clean' bill of lading, an expression which means, at least in a context like this, that there was no clause or notation modifying or qualifying the statement as to the condition of the goods. But the bill did in fact on its face contain the qualifying words 'Signed under guarantee to produce ship's clean receipt': that was a stamped clause clear and obvious on the face of the document, and reasonably conveying to any business man that if the ship's receipt was not clean the statement in the bill of lading as to apparent order and condition could not be taken to be unqualified. If the ship's receipt was not clean, the bill of lading would not be a clean bill of lading, with the result that the estoppel which could have been set up by the indorsee as against the shipowner if the bill of lading had been a clean bill of lading, and the necessary conditions of estoppel had been satisfied, could not be relied on. That type of estoppel is of the greatest importance in this common class of commercial transactions; it has been upheld in a long series of authoritative decisions ... But if the statement is qualified, as in the opinion of their Lordships and the judges of the Supreme Court it was, the estoppel fails ...

4 Hague-Visby Rules

Carriage of Goods by Sea Act 1971
SCHEDULE

Article III

3. After receiving the goods into his charge the carrier or the master or agent of the carrier shall, on demand of the shipper, issue to the shipper a bill of lading showing among other things–

(a) The leading marks necessary for identification of the goods as the same are furnished in writing by the shipper before the loading of such goods starts, provided such marks are stamped or otherwise shown clearly upon the goods if uncovered, or on the cases or coverings in which such goods are contained, in such a manner as should ordinarily remain legible until the end of the voyage.

(b) Either the number of packages or pieces, or the quantity, or weight, as the case may be, as furnished in writing by the shipper.

(c) The apparent order and condition of the goods.

Provided that no carrier, master or agent of the carrier shall be bound to state or show in the bill of lading any marks, number, quantity, or weight which he has reasonable ground for suspecting not accurately to represent the goods actually received, or which he has had no reasonable means of checking.

4. Such a bill of lading shall be prima facie evidence of the receipt by the carrier of the goods as therein described in accordance with paragraph 3(a), (b) and (c). However, proof to the contrary shall not be admissible when the bill of lading has been transferred to a third party acting in good faith.

5. The shipper shall be deemed to have guaranteed to the carrier the accuracy at the time of shipment of the marks, number, quantity and weight, as furnished by him, and the shipper shall indemnify the carrier against all loss, damages and expenses arising or resulting from inaccuracies in such particulars. The right of the carrier to such indemnity shall in no way limit his responsibility and liability under the contract of carriage to any person other than the shipper.

CHAPTER 8

THE BILL OF LADING AS A DOCUMENT OF TITLE

1 MERCANTILE CUSTOM

In *Lickbarrow v Mason* (1794) 5 Term Reports 683, the jury on a special verdict found that (p 685):

by the custom of merchants, bills of lading, expressing goods or merchandises to have been shipped by any person or persons to be delivered to order to assigns, have been, and are, at any time after such goods have been shipped, and before the voyage performed, for which they have been or are shipped, negotiable and transferable by the shipper or shippers of such goods to any other person or persons by such shipper or shippers endorsing such bills of lading with his, her, or their name or names, and delivering or transmitting the same so indorsed, or causing the same to be so delivered or transmitted to such other person or persons; and that by such indorsement and delivery, or transmission, the property in such goods hath been, and is transferred and passed to such other person or persons. And that, by the custom of merchants, indorsements of bills of lading in blank, that is to say, by the shipper or shippers with their names only, have been, and are, and may be, filled up by the person or persons to whom they are so delivered or transmitted as aforesaid, with words ordering the delivery of the goods or contents of such bills of lading to be made to such person or persons; and, according to the practice of merchants the same, when filled up, have the same operation and effect, as if the same had been made or done by such shipper or shippers when he, she, or they indorsed the same bills of lading with their names as aforesaid.

2 INTENTION OF THE PARTIES

The law as to the indorsement of bills of lading is as clear as in my opinion the practice of all European merchants is thoroughly understood. A cargo at sea while in the hands of the carrier is necessarily incapable of physical delivery. During this period of transit and voyage, the bill of lading by the law merchant is universally recognised as its symbol, and the indorsement and delivery of the bill of lading operates as a symbolical delivery of the cargo. Property in the goods passes by such indorsement and delivery of the bill of lading, whenever it is the intention of the parties that the property should pass, just as under similar circumstances the property would pass by an actual delivery of the goods. And for the purpose of passing such property in the goods and completing the title of the indorsee to full possession thereof, the bill of lading, until complete delivery of the cargo has been made on shore to some one rightfully claiming under it, remains in force as a symbol, and carries with it not only the full ownership of the goods, but also all rights created by the contract of carriage between the shipper and the shipowner. It is a key which in the hands of a rightful owner is intended to unlock the door of the warehouse, floating or fixed, in which the goods may chance to be.

The above effect and power belong to any one of the set of original bills of lading which is first dealt with by the shipper ...

per Bowen LJ, *Sanders Brothers v Maclean & Co* (1883) 11 QBD 327, CA.

3 NATURE OF THE INTEREST PASSED

The nature of the interest passed depends on the intention of the parties; property in goods on a ship at sea may pass independently of a bill of lading.

In *Sewell v Burdick, The Zoe* (1884) 10 App Cas 74, goods were shipped under bills of lading making them deliverable to the shipper or assigns. Freight was payable at destination. After the goods had arrived and been warehoused the shipper indorsed the bills of lading in blank and deposited them with the defendant bankers as security for a loan. The defendants never took possession or claimed delivery of the goods. The shipowner brought an action against the lender to recover the freight due under the bill of lading. They argued that the indorsement and delivery of a bill of lading necessarily passed the general property in the goods to the defendants, even if this was not what the parties had intended, and that by virtue of the Bills of Lading Act 1855, when the property passed the defendants became subject to the same liabilities as if the contract contained in the bill of lading had been made with themselves.

The House of Lords *held* (i) that the indorsement and delivery of a bill of lading did not necessarily move an absolute or general interest in the property in the goods to the indorsee, but only such an interest in the property as the parties intended to transfer; and (ii) that under the Bills of Lading Act 1855 only a consignee or indorsee who took a general property in the goods became liable on the contract contained in the bill of lading. The result was that the passing of an openly endorsed bill of lading to a lender would only impose liabilities on the lender under the bill of lading contract if and when the latter acquired a general property in the goods by exercising his rights under the pledge.

> **Lord Selborne LC**: ... In principle the custom of merchants as found in *Lickbarrow v Mason* (above) seems to be as much applicable and available to pass a special property at law by the indorsement (when that is the intent of the transaction) as to pass the general property when the transaction is, eg one of sale. In principle also there seems to be nothing in the nature of a contract to give security by the delivery of a bill of lading indorsed in blank, which

requires more in order to give it full effect, than a pledge accompanied by a power to obtain delivery of the goods when they arrive, and (if necessary) to realise them for the purpose of the security. Whether the indorsee when he takes delivery to himself may not be entitled to assume, and may not be held to assume towards the shipowner, the position of full proprietor, is a different question. But, so long at all events as the goods are *in transitu*, there seems to be no reason why the shipper's title should be displaced any further than the nature and intent of the transaction requires.

Lord Blackburn: ... I think that all the judges below were of opinion that if the right reserved was the general right to the property at law, what was transferred being only a pledge (conveying no doubt a right of property and an immediate right to the possession, so that the transferee would be entitled to bring an action at law against anyone who wrongfully interfered with his right), though 'a' property, and 'a' property against the indorser, passed 'upon and by reason of the indorsement', yet the property did not pass. And I agree with them. I do not at all proceed on the ground that this being an indorsement in blank followed by a delivery of the bill of lading so indorsed, had any different effect from what would have been the effect if it had been an indorsement to the appellants by name.

Lord Bramwell: ... I take this opportunity of saying that I think there is some inaccuracy of expression in the statute, It recites that, 'by the custom of merchants a bill of lading being transferable by indorsement the property in the goods may thereby pass to the indorsee'. Now the truth is that the property does not pass by the indorsement, but by the contract in pursuance of which the indorsement is made. If a cargo afloat is sold, the property would pass to the vendee, even though the bill of lading was not indorsed. I do not say that the vendor might not retain a lien, nor that the non-indorsement and non-handing over of the bill of lading would not have certain other consequences. My concern is to shew that the property passes by the contract. So if the contract was one of security – what would be a pledge if the property was handed over – a contract of hypothecation, the property would be bound by the contract, at least as to all who had notice of it, though the bill of lading was not handed over.

4 *NEMO DAT QUOD NON HABET*

... [A] bill of lading is not a negotiable document in the sense in which a bill of exchange is negotiable. It is a document which is transferable by delivery. Since it is not negotiable, the transferee of the bill can only acquire such interest as the transferor is capable of transferring ...

Lloyd LJ, *The Future Express* [1993] 2 Lloyd's Rep 542, 547, CA. See also *Finlay v Liverpool and Great Western Steamship*, Chapter 2, above.

5 NEGOTIABLE AND TRANSFERABLE

In *Kum v Wah Tat Bank Ltd* [1971] 1 Lloyd's Rep 439, PC, it was argued that a mate's receipt was by custom a document of title at a particular place, even though marked 'non-negotiable'.

> **Lord Devlin:** ... It is well settled that 'negotiable', when used in relation to a bill of lading, means simply transferable. A negotiable bill of lading is not negotiable in the strict sense; it cannot, as can be done by the negotiation of a bill of exchange, give to the transferee a better title than the transferor has got, but it can by endorsement and delivery give as good a title. But it has never been settled whether delivery of a non-negotiable bill of lading transfers title or possession at all. The bill of lading obtains its symbolic quality from the custom found in *Lickbarrow v Mason* and that is a custom which makes bills of lading 'negotiable and transferable' by endorsement and delivery or transmission. To the same effect the Bills of Lading Act 1855 recites that a bill of lading is by the custom of merchants 'transferable by endorsement'. There appears to be no authority on the effect of a non-negotiable bill of lading. This is not surprising. When consignor and consignee are also seller and buyer, as they most frequently are, the shipment ordinarily serves as delivery (s 32(1) of the Sale of Goods Act 1893) and also as an unconditional appropriation of the goods (s 18, r 5(2) of the 1893 Act) which passes the property. So as between seller and buyer it does not usually matter whether the bill of lading is a document of title or not.

6 ORDER OR ASSIGNS

In *CP Henderson & Co v The Comptoir D'Escompte de Paris* (1873) LR 5 PC 253, Sir Robert P Collier said that on the facts:

> it appears that a bill of lading was made out, which is in the usual form, with this difference, that the words 'or order or assigns' are omitted. It has been argued that, notwithstanding the omission of these words, this bill of lading was a negotiable instrument, and there is some authority at *nisi prius* for that proposition; but, undoubtedly, the general view of the mercantile world has been for some time that, in order to make bills of lading negotiable, some such words as 'or order or assigns' ought to be in them. For the purposes of this case, in the view their Lordships take, it may be assumed that this bill of lading was not a negotiable instrument.

7 EXHAUSTION OF TRANSFERABILITY

Barclays Bank Ltd v Commissioners of Customs & Excise [1963] 1 Lloyd's Rep 81

A bill of lading was issued at Rotterdam by Bristol Steam Navigation Company Ltd in respect of a consignment of washing machines shipped on the motor vessel *Echo* for delivery at Cardiff to order of shippers or assigns. The goods were landed and warehoused to the order of the shipowners. Two months later B, the holder of the bill of lading, pledged it to the plaintiffs as security. The plaintiffs subsequently presented the bill of lading to the carriers and received a delivery order addressed to the warehouse, but before delivery could be obtained, the goods were seized on behalf of the defendants who were judgment creditors of B. The question for the court was whether on the date of the pledge, the bills of lading were still documents of title to the goods, by indorsement and delivery of which the rights and property in the goods would be transferred.

> **Diplock LJ** (sitting as an additional Judge of the Queen's Bench Division): ... The contention of the Customs and Excise is that as soon as (1) a contract of carriage by sea is complete, or at any rate the contract of carriage evidenced by the bill of lading is complete, and (2), the bill of lading is in the hands of the person entitled to the property in, and possession of, the goods, and is in a form which would entitle him upon mere presentation to obtain delivery of the goods from the shipowner – that is indorsed to him or indorsed in blank – it ceases to be a document of title by delivery and indorsement of which the rights and property in the goods can be transferred. This is indeed a startling proposition of law which, if correct, would go far to destroy the value of a bill of lading as an instrument of overseas credit. It would mean that no bank could safely advance money on the security of a bill of lading without first making inquiries at the port of delivery, which may be at the other side of the world, as to whether the goods had been landed with the shipowner's lien, if any, discharged or released. It would also mean that no purchaser of goods could rely upon delivery and indorsement to him of the bill of lading as conferring upon him any title to the goods without making similar inquiries, for it would follow that once the goods had been landed and any lien of the shipowner released or discharged, the owner of the goods could divest himself of the property in them without reference to the bill of lading. It would also follow that the shipowner, once the goods had been landed in the absence of any lien, could not safely deliver the goods to the holder of the bill of lading upon presentation because the property in and right to possession of the goods, might have been transferred by the owner to some other person. To hold that this was the law would be to turn back the clock to 1794 before the acceptance by the court of the special verdict of the jury as to custom of merchants in the case of *Lickbarrow v Mason* (1794) 5 Term 683, and which laid the foundation for the financing of overseas trade and the growth of commodity markets in the 19th century.

The contract for the carriage of goods by sea, which is evidenced by a bill of lading, is a combined contract of bailment and transportation under which the shipowner undertakes to accept possession of the goods from the shipper, to carry them to their contractual destination and there to surrender possession of them to the person who, under the terms of the contract, is entitled to obtain possession of them from the shipowners. Such a contract is not discharged by performance until the shipowner has actually surrendered possession (that is, has divested himself of all powers to control any physical dealing in the goods) to the person entitled under the terms of the contract to obtain possession of them.

So long as the contract is not discharged, the bill of lading, in my view, remains a document of title by indorsement and delivery of which the rights of property in the goods can be transferred. It is clear law that where a bill of lading or order is issued in respect of the contract of carriage by sea, the shipowner is not bound to surrender possession of the goods to any person whether named as consignee or not, except on production of the bill of lading (see *The Stettin* (1889) 14 PD 142). Until the bill of lading is produced to him, unless at any rate, its absence has been satisfactorily accounted for, he is entitled to retain possession of the goods and if he does part with possession he does so at his own risk if the person to whom he surrenders possession is not in fact entitled to the goods.

... It is not necessary in this case to consider what is a much more difficult question of law ... as to what the position would be if the shipowners had given a complete delivery to B of the goods without production of the bill of lading, at the date when they were entitled under its terms to deliver, and B had subsequently purported to pledge the goods by deposit of the bill of lading. That question does not arise because in this case not only had complete delivery of possession not been given to B, but no delivery of possession at all at the relevant time on 2 June had been given. In my opinion the pledge made on 2 June by deposit of the bill of lading was a valid pledge and as a consequence I think that I can give judgment for the plaintiffs in this case.

Note

In *Enichem Anic SpA v Ampelos Shipping Co Ltd, The Delfini* [1990] 1 Lloyd's Rep 252, Mustill J said that it was clear:

> from *Meyerstein v Barber* (1870) LR 4 HL 317, especially at pp 330 and 335, that when the goods have been actually delivered at destination to the person entitled to them, or placed in a position where the person is entitled to immediate possession, the bill of lading is exhausted 'and will not operate at all to transfer the goods to any person who has either advanced money or has purchased the bill of lading'. It is equally clear that until the buyer has actually received delivery, the fact that the goods have been discharged at destination subject (say) to a lien for freight, does not entail that the bill is exhausted.

At first instance in this case, Phillips J held that where short delivery was alleged, the bill of lading ceased to be a document of title when the majority of the cargo was delivered.

8 STATUTORY TRANSFER OF RIGHTS OF ACTION

The doctrine of privity of contract is distinctly unpopular in some quarters. But it remains part of English law, subject to some real or apparent exceptions ...

In the particular field of bill of lading contracts – as we shall call those contracts which are more accurately described as contained in or evidenced by bills of lading the doctrine has caused trouble for nearly 200 years. By the custom of merchants the property in goods on board a ship can be transferred by endorsement and delivery of the bill of lading. But at common law that did not vest in the endorsee any contractual rights against the shipowner under the bill of lading contract; nor, for that matter, did it vest rights in the shipowner against the endorsee. That was found to be very inconvenient.

Two remedies were developed in parallel, one by the common law and the other by statute. The common law remedy was an implied contract arising from dealings between the endorsee and the shipowner at or about the time of discharge. The statutory remedy was more radical. At first, in 1855, it consisted in the transfer of the rights and liabilities under the bill of lading to the endorsee, in cases where the property in the goods passed to the endorsee 'upon or by reason of ... endorsement'. That may well have been a sufficient remedy in the simpler trading conditions of the 19th century, at any rate in most cases. Then it began to occur that the whole property in the goods did not pass to the endorsee, but only the limited interest of a pledgee; or the endorsee did not acquire property 'upon or by reason of ... endorsement', but at some different stage or for some other reason. To meet those difficulties, the common law continued in many cases (but not all) to provide the remedy of an implied contract. Eventually in the Carriage of Goods by Sea Act 1992, Parliament extended the circumstances in which a statutory transfer of rights, and of liabilities, would occur.

Staughton LJ, reading the judgment of the Court of Appeal in *Mitsui & Co Ltd v Novorossiysk Shipping Co, The Gudermes* [1993] 1 Lloyd's Rep 311, 314.

9 CARRIAGE OF GOODS BY SEA ACT 1992

An Act to replace the Bills of Lading Act 1855 with new provision with respect to bills of lading and certain other shipping documents [16 July 1992, in force 16 September 1992].

1. Shipping documents etc to which Act applies

(1) This Act applies to the following documents, that is to say:

(a) any bill of lading;

(b) any sea waybill; and

(c) any ship's delivery order.

(2) References in this Act to a bill of lading:

(a) do not include references to a document which is incapable of transfer either by indorsement or, as a bearer bill, by delivery without indorsement; but

(b) subject to that, do include references to a received for shipment bill of lading.

(3) References in this Act to a sea waybill are references to any document which is not a bill of lading but:

(a) is such a receipt for goods as contains or evidences a contract for the carriage of goods by sea; and

(b) identifies the person to whom delivery of the goods is to be made by the carrier in accordance with that contract.

(4) References in this Act to a ship's delivery order are references to any document which is neither a bill of lading nor a sea waybill but contains an undertaking which:

(a) is given under or for the purposes of a contract for the carriage by sea of the goods to which the document relates, or of goods which include those goods; and

(b) is an undertaking by the carrier to a person identified in the document to deliver the goods to which the document relates to that person.

(5) The Secretary of State may by regulations make provision for the application of this Act to cases where a telecommunication system or any other information technology is used for effecting transactions corresponding to:

(a) the issue of a document to which this Act applies;

(b) the indorsement, delivery or other transfer of such a document; or

(c) the doing of anything else in relation to such a document.

(6) Regulations under subsection (5) above may:

(a) make such modifications of the following provisions of this Act as the Secretary of State considers appropriate in connection with the application of this Act to any case mentioned in that subsection; and

(b) contain supplemental, incidental, consequential and transitional provision;

and the power to make regulations under that subsection shall be exercisable by statutory instrument subject to annulment in pursuance of a resolution of either House of Parliament.

2. Rights under shipping documents

(1) Subject to the following provisions of this section, a person who becomes:

(a) the lawful holder of a bill of lading;

(b) the person who (without being an original party to the contract of carriage) is the person to whom delivery of the goods to which a sea waybill relates is to be made by the carrier in accordance with that contract; or

(c) the person to whom delivery of the goods to which a ship's delivery order relates is to be made in accordance with the undertaking contained in the order,

shall (by virtue of becoming the holder of the bill or, as the case may be, the person to whom delivery is to be made) have transferred to and vested in him all rights of suit under the contract of carriage as if he had been a party to that contract.

(2) Where, when a person becomes the lawful holder of a bill of lading, possession of the bill no longer gives a right (as against the carrier) to possession of the goods to which the bill relates, that person shall not have any rights transferred to him by virtue of subsection (1) above unless he becomes the holder of the bill:

(a) by virtue of a transaction effected in pursuance of any contractual or other arrangements made before the time when such a right to possession ceased to attach to possession of the bill; or

(b) as a result of the rejection to that person by another person of goods or documents delivered to the other person in pursuance of any such arrangements.

(3) The rights vested in any person by virtue of the operation of subsection (1) above in relation to a ship's delivery order:

(a) shall be so vested subject to the terms of the order; and

(b) where the goods to which the order relates form a part only of the goods to which the contract of carriage relates, shall be confined to rights in respect of the goods to which the order relates.

(4) Where, in the case of any document to which this Act applies:

(a) a person with any interest or right in or in relation to goods to which the document relates sustains loss or damage in consequence of a breach of the contract of carriage; but

(b) subsection (1) above operates in relation to that document so that rights of suit in respect of that breach are vested in another person,

the other person shall be entitled to exercise those rights for the benefit of the person who sustained the loss or damage to the same extent as they could have been exercised if they had been vested in the person for whose benefit they are exercised.

(5) Where rights are transferred by virtue of the operation of subsection (1) above in relation to any document, the transfer for which that subsection provides shall extinguish any entitlement to those rights which derives:

(a) where that document is a bill of lading, from a person's having been an original party to the contract of carriage; or

(b) in the case of any document to which this Act applies, from the previous operation of that subsection in relation to that document;

but the operation of that subsection shall be without prejudice to any rights which derive from a person's having been an original party to the contract contained in, or evidenced by, a sea waybill and, in relation to a ship's delivery order, shall be without prejudice to any rights deriving otherwise than from the previous operation of that subsection in relation to that order.

3. Liabilities under shipping documents

(1) Where subsection (1) of section 2 of this Act operates in relation to any document to which this Act applies and the person in whom rights are vested by virtue of that subsection:

(a) takes or demands delivery from the carrier of any of the goods to which the document relates;

(b) makes a claim under the contract of carriage against the carrier in respect of any of those goods; or

(c) is a person who, at a time before those rights were vested in him, took or demanded delivery from the carrier of any of those goods,

that person shall (by virtue of taking or demanding delivery or making the claim or, in a case falling within paragraph (c) above, of having the rights vested in him) become subject to the same liabilities under that contract as if he had been a party to that contract.

(2) Where the goods to which a ship's delivery order relates form a part only of the goods to which the contract of carriage relates, the liabilities to which any person is subject by virtue of the operation of this section in relation to that order shall exclude liabilities in respect of any goods to which the order does not relate.

(3) This section, so far as it imposes liabilities under any contract on any person, shall be without prejudice to the liabilities under the contract of any person as an original party to the contract.

4. Representations in bills of lading

A bill of lading which:

(a) represents goods to have been shipped on board a vessel or to have been received for shipment on board a vessel; and

(b) has been signed by the master of the vessel or by a person who was not the master but had the express, implied or apparent authority of the carrier to sign bills of lading,

shall, in favour of a person who has become the lawful holder of the bill, be conclusive evidence against the carrier of the shipment of the goods or, as the case may be, of their receipt for shipment.

5. Interpretation etc

(1) In this Act:

'bill of lading', 'sea waybill' and 'ship's delivery order' shall be construed in accordance with section 1 above;

'the contract of carriage':

(a) in relation to a bill of lading or sea waybill, means the contract contained in or evidenced by that bill or waybill; and

(b) in relation to a ship's delivery order, means the contract under or for the purposes of which the undertaking contained in the order is given;

'holder', in relation to a bill of lading, shall be construed in accordance with subsection (2) below;

'information technology' includes any computer or other technology by means of which information or other matter may be recorded or communicated without being reduced to documentary form; and 'telecommunication system' has the same meaning as in the Telecommunications Act 1984.

(2) References in this Act to the holder of a bill of lading are references to any of the following persons, that is to say:

(a) a person with possession of the bill who, by virtue of being the person identified in the bill, is the consignee of the goods to which the bill relates;

(b) a person with possession of the bill as a result of the completion, by delivery of the bill, of any indorsement of the bill or, in the case of a bearer bill, of any other transfer of the bill;

(c) a person with possession of the bill as a result of any transaction by virtue of which he would have become a holder falling within paragraph (a) or (b) above had not the transaction been effected at a time when possession of the bill no longer gave a right (as against the carrier) to possession of the goods to which the bill relates;

and a person shall be regarded for the purposes of this Act as having become the lawful holder of a bill of lading wherever he has become the holder of the bill in good faith.

(3) References in this Act to a person's being identified in a document include references to his being identified by a description which allows for the identity of the person in question to be varied, in accordance with the terms of the document, after its issue; and the reference in section l(3)(b) of this Act to a document's identifying a person shall be construed accordingly.

(4) Without prejudice to sections 2(2) and 4 above, nothing in this Act shall preclude its operation in relation to a case where the goods to which a document relates:

(a) cease to exist after the issue of the document; or

(b) cannot be identified (whether because they are mixed with other goods or for any other reason);

and references in this Act to the goods to which a document relates shall be construed accordingly.

(5) The preceding provisions of this Act shall have effect without prejudice to the application, in relation to any case, of the rules (the Hague-Visby Rules) which for the time being have the force of law by virtue of section l of the Carriage of Goods by Sea Act 1971.

6. Short title, repeal, commencement and extent

(1) This Act may be cited as the Carriage of Goods by Sea Act 1992.

(2) The Bills of Lading Act 1855 is hereby repealed.

(3) This Act shall come into force at the end of the period of two months beginning with the day on which it is passed; but nothing in this Act shall have effect in relation to any document issued before the coming into force of this Act.

(4) This Act extends to Northern Ireland.

10 SECTION 2 OF THE CARRIAGE OF GOODS BY SEA ACT 1992: 'THE CONTRACT OF CARRIAGE'

Leduc & Co v Ward (1888) 20 QBD 475, CA

The plaintiffs were indorsees of a bill of lading which contained the usual exception of sea perils and stated that the goods were shipped:

> in apparent good order and condition on the steamship *Austria*, now lying in the port of Fiume, and bound for Dunkirk, with liberty to call at any ports in any order, and to deviate for the purpose of saving life or property; 3,123 bags of rape seed, being marked and numbered as per margin, and to be delivered in the like good order and condition at the aforesaid port of Dunkirk unto order or assigns.

The ship, instead of proceeding direct for Dunkirk, sailed for Glasgow, and was lost, with her cargo, off the mouth of the Clyde, by perils of the sea. In an action brought by the plaintiffs against the shipowners for non-delivery of the goods, evidence was given to shew that the shippers of the goods, at the time when the bill of lading was given, knew that the vessel was intended to proceed via Glasgow.

> **Lord Esher MR**: In this case the plaintiffs, the owners of goods shipped on board the defendants' ship, sue for non-delivery of the goods at Dunkirk in accordance with the terms of the bill of lading. The defence is that delivery of the goods was prevented by perils of the sea. To that the plaintiffs reply that the goods were not lost by reason of any perils excepted by the bill of lading, because they were lost at a time when the defendants were committing a breach of their contract by deviating from the voyage provided for by the bill of lading. The plaintiffs were clearly indorsees of the bill of lading to whom the property passed by reason of the indorsement; and, therefore, by the Bills of Lading Act [1855], the rights upon the contract contained in the bill of lading passed to them. The question, therefore, arises what the effect of that contract was. It has been suggested that the bill of lading is merely in the nature of a receipt for the goods, and that it contains no contract for anything but the delivery of the goods at the place named therein. It is true that, where there is a charterparty, as between the shipowner and the charterer the bill of lading may be merely in the nature of a receipt for the goods, because all the other terms of the contract of carriage between them are contained in the charterparty; and the bill of lading is merely given as between them to enable the charterer to deal with the goods while in the course of transit; but, where the bill of lading is indorsed over, as between the shipowner and the indorsee the bill of lading must be considered to contain the contract, because the former has given it for the purpose of enabling the charterer to pass it on as the contract of carriage in respect of the goods. Where there is no charterparty, as between the grantee of the bill of lading and the shipowner, the bill of lading is no doubt a receipt for the goods, and as such, like any other receipt, it is not conclusive, for it may be controverted by evidence shewing that the goods were not received; the question whether it will be more than a receipt as

between the shipper and shipowner depends on whether the captain has received the goods, for he has no authority to make a contract of carriage to bind the shipowner, except in respect of goods received by him. If the goods have not been received, the bill of lading cannot contain the terms of a contract of carriage with respect to them as against the shipowner. But, if the goods have been received by the captain, it is the evidence in writing of what the contract of carriage between the parties is; it may be true that the contract of carriage is made before it is given, because it would generally be made before the goods are sent down to the ship: but when the goods are put on board the captain has authority to reduce that contract into writing: and then the general doctrine of law is applicable, by which, where the contract has been reduced into a writing which is intended to constitute the contract, parol evidence to alter or qualify the effect of such writing is not admissible, and the writing is the only evidence of the contract, except where there is some usage so well established and generally known that it must be taken to be incorporated with the contract. In the case of *Fraser v Telegraph Construction Co* (1872) LR 7 QB 566, at p 571. Blackburn J held that a bill of lading must be taken to be the contract under which the goods were shipped. In *Chartered Mercantile Bank of India v Netherlands India Steam Navigation Co* (1883) 10 QBD 531, I expressed the same view that I am now expressing as to the nature of a bill of lading. In *Glyn, Mill & Co v East and West India Dock Co* (1882) 7 App Cas 591, Lord Selborne said, at p 596:

> Every one claiming as assignee under a bill of lading must be bound by its terms, and by the contract between the shipper of the goods and the shipowner therein expressed. The primary office and purpose of a bill of lading, although by mercantile law and usage it is a symbol of the right of property in the goods, is to express the terms of the contract between the shipper and the shipowner.

The terms of the Bills of Lading Act shew that the legislature looked upon a bill of lading as containing the terms of the contract of carriage ...

The Heidberg [1994] 2 Lloyd's Rep 287

Judge Diamond QC: ... Bills of lading are transferrable documents which come into the hands of consignees and indorsees who may be the purchasers of goods or banks. The transferee of the bill of lading does not, however, take precisely the same contract as that made between the shipper and the shipowner (of which the bill of lading is merely the evidence). What is transferred to the consignee or indorsee consists, and consists only, of the terms which appear on the face and reverse of the bill of lading. Thus collateral oral terms are not transferred; see *Leduc v Ward* (1888) QBD 475; *The Ardennes* [1951] 1 KB 55. This rule facilitates the use of bills of lading in international commerce since it enables a prospective transferee of a bill of lading to see, merely by inspecting the bill, whether it conforms to his contract (whether it be a sale contract or a letter of credit) and what rights and obligations will be transferred to him if he takes up the bill. The transferee, or prospective transferee, need not enquire whether any collateral oral agreements have been made between the shipper and the shipowner as, for example, a waiver by the shipper of any obligation undertaken by the shipowner in the bill ...

References

On the 1992 Act, see:

Beatson, J and Cooper, JJ [1991] *LMCLQ* 196

Reynolds, FMB [1993] *LMCLQ* 436

Howard, T (1993) 24 *JMLC* 181

Toh Kian Sing [1994] *LMCLQ* 280

CHAPTER 9

HAGUE-VISBY RULES

1 INTRODUCTION

The early bills of lading did not contain any exceptions at all. The earliest qualifications were either of a general type, such as the 'danger of the sea only excepted' or 'said to be' clauses [ie 'received (5) packages ... said to weigh ...'] However, as a result of eighteenth century judicial decisions, shipowners began generally to amend their bills of lading not only to stipulate the old common law exceptions but also to exempt themselves from liability in respect of all perils of the sea and of navigation 'of whatsoever nature and kind' (UNCTAD, 'Bills of Lading', 1971, para 58).

In the course of the 19th century, reliance by shipowners on exclusion clauses provoked a reaction on the part of cargo interests. It was objected that the only freedom of contract for most shippers was the freedom either to ship on terms dictated by the sea carrier or the freedom not to ship at all. Consignees, indorsees and their bankers usually had even less opportunity than shippers to influence the terms of bills of lading by negotiation. In England, these considerations led to the promotion of model bills of lading. In other jurisdictions, cargo interests were powerful enough to obtain legislation to adjust the balance in their favour. This was done in the United States in the Harter Act in 1893 and later in Australia (Sea Carriage of Goods Act 1904), Canada (Water Carriage of Goods Act 1910) and in New Zealand.

A number of attempts were made to secure a uniform international approach.

After considerable discussion among the representatives of leading shipowners, underwriters, shippers and bankers of the big maritime nations, a set of rules was finally drafted by the Maritime Law Committee of the International Law Association at a meeting held at The Hague in 1921 ... [They] came to be known as the Hague Rules, but ... were not immediately adopted ... The Rules were amended at the London Conference of CMI in 1922. A draft convention drawn up at that conference was amended at Brussels in 1923, and in due course an international Convention was ultimately signed there by the most important trading nations on 25 August 1924. Each State was expected to give the Hague Rules statutory force with regard to all outward bills of lading ... (UNCTAD, 'Bills of Lading', 1971, para 62).

In Great Britain, the draft Convention of 1923 was given statutory effect by the Carriage of Goods by Sea Act 1924. Subsequently, the draft of 1923 was signed at Brussels on 25 August 1924, although only after further amendments, which were not incorporated in the 1924 Act.

The Hague Rules:

> radically changed the legal status of sea carriers under bills of lading. According to the previous law, shipowners were generally common carriers, or were liable to the obligations of common carriers, but they were entitled to the utmost freedom to restrict and limit their liabilities, which they did by elaborate and mostly illegible exceptions and conditions. Under the Act and the Rules, which cannot be varied in favour of the carrier by any bill of lading, their liabilities are precisely determined, and so also are their rights and immunities ...

Wright J, *Gosse Millerd v Canadian Government Merchant Marine Ltd* [1927] 2 KB 432, KBD.

In 1963 the CMI adopted (at Visby on the Swedish island of Gotland) the text of a draft document intended to make limited amendments to the 1924 Convention. This draft was considered at the 12th session of the Brussels Diplomatic Conference on Maritime Law in 1967 and 1968. The result was the Protocol signed on 23 February 1968. In the United Kingdom, the Carriage of Goods by Sea Act 1971 was passed to give effect to that Protocol. The Act was brought into force on 23 June 1977. It repealed the 1924 Act and re-enacted the Hague Rules in their amended Hague-Visby form.

> The Hague Rules (and their successor the Hague-Visby Rules) form an internationally recognised code adjusting the rights and duties existing between shipowners and those shipping goods under bills of lading. As Sir John Donaldson MR said in Leigh & Sillavan Ltd v Aliakmon Shipping Co Ltd [1985] QB 350, 368, 'the rules create an intricate blend of responsibilities and liabilities, rights and immunities, limitations on the amount of damages recoverable, time bars, evidential provisions, indemnities and liberties, all in relation to the carriage of goods under bills of lading'.

Saville LJ, *The Nicholas H* [1994] 1 WLR 1071, 1080.

Although the 1968 Protocol made important changes, it did not radically alter the compromise between the interests of carriers and cargo owners which had been reached in 1924. The case for a more fundamental revision of the Hague Rules was argued in *Bills of Lading*, a report by the secretariat of UNCTAD, published by the United Nations in 1971. The movement for reform, which began with the UNCTAD report, led to the UN Conference on the Carriage of Goods by Sea at Hamburg in 1978 and the adoption of a new convention, the Hamburg Rules. It is uncertain when, if ever, the Hamburg Rules will be enacted into law in the United Kingdom. An extract from the 1971 UNCTAD report and the text of the Hamburg Rules are set out in Appendix 2.

References

Lord Diplock (1969–70) *JMLC* 525

Diamond, A, QC [1978] *LMCLQ* 225

Tetley, W, QC, *Marine Cargo Claims*, 3rd edn, 1988, Montreal: Blais

Davenport, B, QC [1989] 105 *LQR* 521

Clarke, M [1989] *LMCLQ* 394

Debattista, C [1989] *LMCLQ* 403

Sturley, M, *Legislative History of the Carriage of Goods by Sea Act and the* Travaux Preparatoires *of the Hague Rules*, 1990, Rothman & Co

Reynolds, FMB, *The Butterworth Lectures 1990–91*

Sturley, M (1991) *JMLC* 23, (1995) 26 *JMLC* 553

CARRIAGE OF GOODS BY SEA ACT 1971

An Act to amend the law with respect to the carriage of goods by sea [8 April 1971; in force 23 June 1977; printed as amended].

1. Application of Hague Rules as amended

(1) In this Act, 'the Rules' means the International Convention for the unification of certain rules of law relating to bills of lading signed at Brussels on 25 August 1924, as amended by the Protocol signed at Brussels on 23 February 1968, and by the Protocol signed at Brussels on 21 December 1979.

(2) The provisions of the Rules, as set out in the Schedule to this Act, shall have the force of law.

(3) Without prejudice to subsection (2) above, the said provisions shall have effect (and have the force of law) in relation to and in connection with the carriage of goods by sea in ships where the port of shipment is a port in the United Kingdom, whether or not the carriage is between ports in two different States within the meaning of Article X of the Rules.

(4) Subject to subsection (6) below, nothing in this section shall be taken as applying anything in the Rules to any contract for the carriage of goods by sea, unless the contract expressly or by implication provides for the issue of a bill of lading or any similar document of title.

(5) [*Repealed by the Merchant Shipping Act 1981, s 5(3) and schedule.*]

(6) Without prejudice to Article X(c) of the Rules, the Rules shall have the force of law in relation to:

(a) any bill of lading if the contract contained in or evidenced by it expressly provides that the Rules shall govern the contract, and

(b) any receipt which is a non-negotiable document marked as such if the contract contained in or evidenced by it is a contract for the carriage of goods by sea which expressly provides that the Rules are to govern the contract as if the receipt were a bill of lading,

but subject, where paragraph (b) applies, to any necessary modifications and in particular with the omission in Article III of the Rules of the second sentence of paragraph 4 and of paragraph 7.

(7) If and so far as the contract contained in or evidenced by a bill of lading or receipt within paragraph (a) or (b) of subsection (6) above applies to deck

cargo or live animals, the Rules as given the force of law by that subsection shall have effect as if Article I(c) did not exclude deck cargo and live animals.

In this subsection 'deck cargo' means cargo which by the contract of carriage is stated as being carried on deck and is so carried.

1A. Conversion of special drawing rights into sterling

[*Section added by the Merchant Shipping Act 1995, s 314(2), Sch 13, para 45(3). In force 1 January 1996*]

(1) For the purposes of Article IV of the Rules the value on a particular day of one special drawing right shall be treated as equal to such a sum in sterling as the International Monetary Fund have fixed as being the equivalent of one special drawing right:

(a) for that day; or

(b) if no sum has been so fixed for that day, for the last day before that day for which a sum has been so fixed.

(2) A certificate given by or on behalf of the Treasury stating–

(a) that a particular sum in sterling has been fixed as aforesaid for a particular day; or

(b) that no sum has been so fixed for a particular day and that a particular sum in sterling has been so fixed for a day which is the last day for which a sum has been so fixed before the particular day,

shall be conclusive evidence of those matters for the purposes of subsection (1) above; and a document purporting to be such a certificate shall in any proceedings be received in evidence and, unless the contrary is proved, be deemed to be such a certificate.

(3) ... [*Fees for certificates*]

2. Contracting States, etc

(1) If Her Majesty by Order in Council certifies to the following effect, that is to say, that for the purposes of the Rules:

(a) a State specified in the Order is a Contracting State, or is a Contracting State in respect of any place or territory so specified; or

(b) any place or territory specified in the Order forms part of a State so specified (whether a contracting State or not),

the Order shall, except so far as it has been superseded by a subsequent Order, be conclusive evidence of the matters so certified.

(2) An Order in Council under this section may be varied or revoked by a subsequent Order in Council.

3. Absolute warranty of seaworthiness not to be implied in contracts to which Rules apply

There shall not be implied in any contract for the carriage of goods by sea to which the Rules apply by virtue of this Act any absolute undertaking by the carrier of the goods to provide a seaworthy ship.

4. Application of Act to British possessions, etc

...

5. Extension of application of Rules to carriage from ports in British possessions, etc

...

6. Supplemental

(1) This Act may be cited as the Carriage of Goods by Sea Act 1971.

(2) It is hereby declared that this Act extends to Northern Ireland.

(3) The following enactments shall be repealed, that is—

(a) the Carriage of Goods by Sea Act 1924,

(b) section 12(4)(a) of the Nuclear Installations Act 1965,

and without prejudice to section 17(2) of the Interpretation Act 1978, the reference to the said Act of 1924 in section 1(1)(i)(ii) of the Hovercraft Act 1968 shall include a reference to this Act.

(4) It is hereby declared that for the purposes of Article VIII of the Rules section 186 of the Merchant Shipping Act 1995 (which entirely exempts shipowners and others in certain circumstances for loss of, or damage to, goods) is a provision relating to limitation of liability [*Subsection added by s 314(2), Sched 13, para 45(4) of the Merchant Shipping Act 1995, In force 1 January 1996.*]

(5) ... [*Commencement*]

SCHEDULE

THE HAGUE RULES

as amended by the Brussels Protocol 1968

ARTICLE I

In these Rules the following words are employed, with the meanings set out below:

(a) 'Carrier' includes the owner or the charterer who enters into a contract of carriage with a shipper.

(b) 'Contract of carriage' applies only to contracts of carriage covered by a bill of lading or any similar document of title, in so far as such document relates to the carriage of goods by sea, including any bill of lading or any similar document as aforesaid issued under or pursuant to a charter party from the moment at which such bill of lading or similar document of title regulates the relations between a carrier and a holder of the same.

(c) 'Goods' includes goods, wares, merchandise, and articles of every kind whatsoever except live animals and cargo which by the contract of carriage is stated as being carried on deck and is so carried.

(d) 'Ship' means any vessel used for the carriage of goods by sea.

(e) 'Carriage of goods' covers the period from the time when the goods are loaded on to the time they are discharged from the ship.

ARTICLE II

Subject to the provisions of Article VI, under every contract of carriage of goods by sea the carrier, in relation to the loading, handling, stowage, carriage, custody, care and discharge of such goods, shall be subject to the responsibilities and liabilities, and entitled to the rights and immunities hereinafter set forth.

ARTICLE III

1. The carrier shall be bound before and at the beginning of the voyage to exercise due diligence to:

(a) Make the ship seaworthy.

(b) Properly man, equip and supply the ship.

(c) Make the holds, refrigerating and cool chambers, and all other parts of the ship in which goods are carried, fit and safe for their reception, carriage and preservation.

2. Subject to the provisions of Article IV, the carrier shall properly and carefully load, handle, stow, carry, keep, care for, and discharge the goods carried.

3. After receiving the goods into his charge the carrier or the master or agent of the carrier shall, on demand of the shipper, issue to the shipper a bill of lading showing among other things–

(a) The leading marks necessary for identification of the goods as the same are furnished in writing by the shipper before the loading of such goods starts, provided such marks are stamped or otherwise shown clearly upon the goods if uncovered, or on the cases or coverings in which such goods are contained, in such a manner as should ordinarily remain legible until the end of the voyage.

(b) Either the number of packages or pieces, or the quantity, or weight, as the case may be, as furnished in writing by the shipper.

(c) The apparent order and condition of the goods.

Provided that no carrier, master or agent of the carrier shall be bound to state or show in the bill of lading any marks, number, quantity, or weight which he has reasonable ground for suspecting not accurately to represent the goods actually received, or which he has had no reasonable means of checking.

4. Such a bill of lading shall be prima facie evidence of the receipt by the carrier of the goods as therein described in accordance with paragraph 3(a), (b) and (c). However, proof to the contrary shall not be admissible when the bill of lading has been transferred to a third party acting in good faith.

5. The shipper shall be deemed to have guaranteed to the carrier the accuracy at the time of shipment of the marks, number, quantity and weight, as furnished by him, and the shipper shall indemnify the carrier against all loss, damages and expenses arising or resulting from inaccuracies in such particulars. The right of the carrier to such indemnity shall in no way limit his responsibility and liability under the contract of carriage to any person other than the shipper.

6. Unless notice of loss or damage and the general nature of such loss or damage be given in writing to the carrier or his agent at the port of discharge

before or at the time of the removal of the goods into the custody of the person entitled to delivery thereof under the contract of carriage, or, if the loss or damage be not apparent, within three days, such removal shall be *prima facie* evidence of the delivery by the carrier of the goods as described in the bill of lading.

The notice in writing need not be given if the state of the goods has, at the time of their receipt, been the subject of joint survey or inspection.

Subject to paragraph 6 *bis* the carrier and the ship shall in any event be discharged from all liability whatsoever in respect of the goods, unless suit is brought within one year of their delivery or of the date when they should have been delivered. This period may, however, be extended if the parties so agree after the cause of action has arisen.

In the case of any actual or apprehended loss or damage the carrier and the receiver shall give all reasonable facilities to each other for inspecting and tallying the goods.

6 *bis*. An action for indemnity against a third person may be brought even after the expiration of the year provided for in the preceding paragraph if brought within the time allowed by the law of the Court seized of the case. However, the time allowed shall be not less than three months, commencing from the day when the person bringing such action for indemnity has settled the claim or has been served with process in the action against himself.

7. After the goods are loaded the bill of lading to be issued by the carrier, master, or agent of the carrier, to the shipper shall, if the shipper so demands, be a 'shipped' bill of lading, provided that if the shipper shall have previously taken up any document of title to such goods, he shall surrender the same as against the issue of the 'shipped' bill of lading, but at the option of the carrier such document of title may be noted at the port of shipment by the carrier, master, or agent with the name or names of the ship or ships upon which the goods have been shipped and the date or dates of shipment, and when so noted, if it shows the particulars mentioned in paragraph 3 of Article III, shall for the purpose of this article be deemed to constitute a 'shipped' bill of lading.

8. Any clause, covenant, or agreement in a contract of carriage relieving the carrier or the ship from liability for loss or damage to, or in connection with, goods arising from negligence, fault, or failure in the duties and obligations provided in this article or lessening such liability otherwise than as provided in these Rules, shall be null and void and of no effect. A benefit of insurance in favour of the carrier or similar clause shall be deemed to be a clause relieving the carrier from liability.

ARTICLE IV

1. Neither the carrier nor the ship shall be liable for loss or damage arising or resulting from unseaworthiness unless caused by want of due diligence on the part of the carrier to make the ship seaworthy, and to secure that the ship is properly manned, equipped and supplied, and to make the holds, refrigerating and cool chambers and all other parts of the ship in which goods are carried fit and safe for their reception, carriage and preservation in accordance with the provisions of paragraph 1 of Article III. Whenever loss or damage has resulted

from unseaworthiness the burden of proving the exercise of due diligence shall be on the carrier or other person claiming exemption under this article.

2. Neither the carrier nor the ship shall be responsible for loss or damage arising or resulting from:

(a) Act, neglect, or default of the master, mariner, pilot, or the servants of the carrier in the navigation or in the management of the ship.

(b) Fire, unless caused by the actual fault or privity of the carrier.

(c) Perils, dangers and accidents of the sea or other navigable waters.

(d) Act of God.

(e) Act of war.

(f) Act of public enemies.

(g) Arrest or restraint of princes, rulers or people, or seizure under legal process.

(h) Quarantine restrictions.

(i) Act or omission of the shipper or owner of the goods, his agent or representative.

(j) Strikes or lockouts or stoppage or restraint of labour from whatever cause, whether partial or general.

(k) Riots and civil commotions.

(l) Saving or attempting to save life or property at sea.

(m) Wastage in bulk or weight or any other loss or damage arising from inherent defect, quality or vice of the goods.

(n) Insufficiency of packing.

(o) Insufficiency or inadequacy of marks.

(p) Latent defects not discoverable by due diligence.

(q) Any other cause arising without the actual fault or privity of the carrier, or without the fault or neglect of the agents or servants of the carrier, but the burden of proof shall be on the person claiming the benefit of this exception to show that neither the actual fault or privity of the carrier nor the fault or neglect of the agents or servants of the carrier contributed to the loss or damage.

3. The shipper shall not be responsible for loss or damage sustained by the carrier or the ship arising or resulting from any cause without the act, fault or neglect of the shipper, his agents or his servants.

4. Any deviation in saving or attempting to save life or property at sea or any reasonable deviation shall not be deemed to be an infringement or breach of these Rules or of the contract of carriage, and the carrier shall not be liable for any loss or damage resulting therefrom.

5. (a) Unless the nature and value of such goods have been declared by the shipper before shipment and inserted in the bill of lading, neither the carrier nor the ship shall in any event be or become liable for any loss or damage to or in connection with the goods in an amount exceeding [666.67 units of account] per package or unit or [2 units of account per

kilogramme] of gross weight of the goods lost or damaged, whichever is the higher.

(b) The total amount recoverable shall be calculated by reference to the value of such goods at the place and time at which the goods are discharged from the ship in accordance with the contract or should have been so discharged.

The value of the goods shall be fixed according to the commodity exchange price, or, if there be no such price, according to the current market price, or, if there be no commodity exchange price or current market price, by reference to the normal value of goods of the same kind and quality.

(c) Where a container, pallet or similar article of transport is used to consolidate goods, the number of packages or units enumerated in the bill of lading as packed in such article of transport shall be deemed the number of packages or units for the purpose of this paragraph as far as these packages or units are concerned. Except as aforesaid such article of transport shall be considered the package or unit.

[(d) The unit of account mentioned in this Article is the special drawing right as defined by the International Monetary Fund. The amounts mentioned in subparagraph (a) of this paragraph shall be converted into national currency on the basis of the value of that currency on a date to be determined by the law of the court seized of the case.] [*Words in square brackets substituted by s 2(3), (4) of the Merchant Shipping Act 1981, and by s 314(2), Sched 13, para 45(5) of the Merchant Shipping Act 1995; para 45(6) states that Art IV, para 5(d) 'shall continue to have effect as if the date there mentioned were the date of the judgment in question'.*]

(e) Neither the carrier nor the ship shall be entitled to the benefit of the limitation of liability provided for in this paragraph if it is proved that the damage resulted from an act or omission of the carrier done with intent to cause damage, or recklessly and with knowledge that damage would probably result.

(f) The declaration mentioned in subparagraph (a) of this paragraph, if embodied in the bill of lading, shall be prima facie evidence, but shall not be binding or conclusive on the carrier.

(g) By agreement between the carrier, master or agent of the carrier and the shipper other maximum amounts than those mentioned in subparagraph (a) of this paragraph may be fixed, provided that no maximum amount so fixed shall be less than the appropriate maximum mentioned in that subparagraph.

(h) Neither the carrier nor the ship shall be responsible in any event for loss or damage to, or in connection with, goods if the nature or value thereof has been knowingly misstated by the shipper in the bill of lading.

6. Goods of an inflammable, explosive or dangerous nature to the shipment whereof the carrier, master or agent of the carrier has not consented with knowledge of their nature and character, may at any time before discharge be landed at any place, or destroyed or rendered innocuous by the carrier without

compensation and the shipper of such goods shall be liable for all damages and expenses directly or indirectly arising out of or resulting from such shipment. If any such goods shipped with such knowledge and consent shall become a danger to the ship or cargo, they may in like manner be landed at any place, or destroyed or rendered innocuous by the carrier without liability on the part of the carrier except to general average, if any.

ARTICLE IV *bis*

1. The defences and limits of liability provided for in these Rules shall apply in any action against the carrier in respect of loss or damage to goods covered by a contract of carriage whether the action be founded in contract or in tort.

2. If such an action is brought against a servant or agent of the carrier (such servant or agent not being an independent contractor), such servant or agent shall be entitled to avail himself of the defences and limits of liability which the carrier is entitled to invoke under these Rules.

3. The aggregate of the amounts recoverable from the carrier, and such servants and agents, shall in no case exceed the limit provided for in these Rules.

4. Nevertheless, a servant or agent of the carrier shall not be entitled to avail himself of the provisions of this article, if it is proved that the damage resulted from an act or omission of the servant or agent done with intent to cause damage or recklessly and with knowledge that damage would probably result.

ARTICLE V

A carrier shall be at liberty to surrender in whole or in part all or any of his rights and immunities or to increase any of his responsibilities and obligations under these Rules, provided such surrender or increase shall be embodied in the bill of lading issued to the shipper. The provisions of these Rules shall not be applicable to charter parties, but if bills of lading are issued in the case of a ship under a charter party they shall comply with the terms of these Rules. Nothing in these Rules shall be held to prevent the insertion in a bill of lading of any lawful provision regarding general average.

ARTICLE VI

Notwithstanding the provisions of the preceding articles, a carrier, master or agent of the carrier and a shipper shall in regard to any particular goods be at liberty to enter into any agreement in any terms as to the responsibility and liability of the carrier for such goods, and as to the rights and immunities of the carrier in respect of such goods, or his obligation as to seaworthiness, so far as this stipulation is not contrary to public policy, or the care or diligence of his servants or agents in regard to the loading, handling, stowage, carriage, custody, care and discharge of the goods carried by sea, provided that in this case no bill of lading has been or shall be issued and that the terms agreed shall be embodied in a receipt which shall be a non-negotiable document and shall be marked as such.

Any agreement so entered into shall have full legal effect.

Provided that this article shall not apply to ordinary commercial shipments made in the ordinary course of trade, but only to other shipments where the character or condition of the property to be carried or the circumstances, terms and conditions under which the carriage is to be performed are such as reasonably to justify a special agreement.

ARTICLE VII

Nothing herein contained shall prevent a carrier or a shipper from entering into any agreement, stipulation, condition, reservation or exemption as to the responsibility and liability of the carrier or the ship for the loss or damage to, or in connection with, the custody and care and handling of goods prior to the loading on, and subsequent to the discharge from, the ship on which the goods are carried by sea.

ARTICLE VIII

The provisions of these Rules shall not affect the rights and obligations of the carrier under any statute for the time being in force relating to the limitation of the liability of owners of sea-going vessels.

ARTICLE IX

These Rules shall not affect the provisions of any international Convention or national law governing liability for nuclear damage.

ARTICLE X

The provisions of these Rules shall apply to every bill of lading relating to the carriage of goods between ports in two different States if:

(a) he bill of lading is issued in a contracting State, or

(b) the carriage is from a port in a contracting State, or

(c) the contract contained in or evidenced by the bill of lading provides that these Rules or legislation of any State giving effect to them are to govern the contract,

whatever may be the nationality of the ship, the carrier, the shipper, the consignee, or any other interested person.

[*The last two paragraphs of this article are not reproduced. They require contracting States to apply the Rules to bills of lading mentioned in the article and authorise them to apply the Rules to other bills of lading.*]

[*Articles 11 to 16 of the International Convention for the unification of certain rules of law relating to bills of lading signed at Brussels on 25 August 1924 are not reproduced. They deal with the coming into force of the Convention, procedure for ratification, accession and denunciation, and the right to call for a fresh conference to consider amendments to the Rules contained in the Convention.*]

2 APPLICATION OF THE RULES

Pyrene Co Ltd v Scindia Navigation Co Ltd [1954] 2 QB 402

Devlin J: This case raises questions of interest and importance upon the interpretation of the Hague Rules and their applicability to an fob seller. The plaintiffs sold a piece of machinery, a fire tender, to the Government of India (which acted in this matter through a department known for short as ISD) for delivery fob London. ISD nominated the *Jalazad*, one of the defendants' vessels, as the ship to be loaded under the contract of sale, and through their agents, Bahr Behrend & Co, made all the arrangements for the carriage of the goods. While the tender was being lifted on to the vessel by the ship's tackle, and before it was across the rail it was, through the fault of the ship, dropped and damaged. Under the contract of sale the property had not then passed to ISD. The damage to the tender cost £966 to repair and the plaintiffs sue for that sum. The defendants admit liability but claim that the amount is limited under Article 4, r 5, of the Hague Rules. The limit stated in that rule is £100, but this is subject to Article 9 which prescribes that the figure is to be taken to be gold value. There are doubts about the interpretation and effect of this latter article, and they have been very sensibly resolved for the parties to this case by the acceptance of the British Maritime Law Association's Agreement of 1 August 1950, which fixes the limit at £200.

It is therefore for the defendants to establish that they are entitled to limit their liability. To do this they must show privity of contract between themselves and the plaintiffs, that the contract incorporated the rules, and that the rules are effective to limit their liability. The plaintiffs dispute all these points: they claim in tort for the damage done to their goods.

The fire tender was not the only piece of machinery supplied by the plaintiffs for shipment on board this ship, though it was the only piece which was damaged before shipment. A bill of lading had been prepared to cover the whole shipment; and it was issued to ISD in due course but with the fire tender deleted from it. The bill of lading incorporated the Hague Rules and was subject to their provisions, as by s 3 of the Carriage of Goods by Sea Act 1924, it was bound to be. It is not disputed that in this case, as in the vast majority of cases, the contract of carriage was actually created before the issue of the bill of lading which evidences its terms.

I think it is convenient to begin by considering the effect of the rules, for Mr Megaw contends that even if a bill of lading covering the fire tender had been issued incorporating the rules, the holder of the bill would not be subject to immunity in respect of an accident occurring at this stage of the loading. If this is so, it disposes of the defendants' plea. If it is not so, I shall have to consider whether the rules affect the contract of affreightment when no bill of lading is issued, and whether the plaintiffs were a party to that or any similar contract.

Mr Megaw's argument turns upon the meaning to be given to article 1(e), which defines 'carriage of goods' as covering 'the period from the time when the goods are loaded on to the time when they are discharged from the ship'. Mr Megaw says that these goods never were loaded on to the ship. In a literal sense obviously they were not. But Mr Megaw does not rely on the literal sense; there are rules which could hardly be made intelligible if they began to operate only after the goods had been landed on deck. He treats the word 'on' as having the same meaning as in 'free on board'; goods are loaded on the ship as soon as they are put across the ship's rail, which the tender never was. He submits that ... loading is a joint operation, the shipper's duty being to lift the cargo to the rail of the ship (I shall refer to that as the first stage of the loading) and the shipowner's to take it on board and stow it (I shall refer to that as the second stage).

Mr Megaw contends, therefore, that the accident occurred outside the period specified in article I(e). So, he says, Article IV, r 5 (which limits liability), and, indeed, all the other rules which regulate the rights and responsibilities of the shipowner, do not apply. They are made applicable by article II which provides that 'under every contract of carriage of goods by sea the carrier, in relation to the loading, handling, stowage, carriage, custody, care and discharge of such goods, shall be subject to the responsibilities and liabilities, and entitled to the rights and immunities hereinafter set forth'. 'Contract of carriage' is defined in Article I(b); the term 'applies only to contracts of carriage covered by a bill of lading or any similar document of title, in so far as such document relates to the carriage of goods by sea'. Then it is paragraph (e) of this Article I which contains the definition of 'carriage of goods' on which Mr Megaw relies. It is in this way, he argues, that if the casualty does not fall within the period covered by this last definition the rules do not apply to it.

In my judgment this argument is fallacious, the cause of the fallacy perhaps lying in the supposition inherent in it that the rights and liabilities under the rules attach to a period of time. I think that they attach to a contract or part of a contract. I say 'part of a contract' because a single contract may cover both inland and sea transport; and in that case the only part of it that falls within the rules is that which, to use the words in the definition of 'contract of carriage' in Article I(b), 'relates to the carriage of goods by sea'. Even if 'carriage of goods by sea' were given by definition the most restricted meaning possible, for example, the period of the voyage, the loading of the goods (by which I mean the whole operation of loading in both its stages and whichever side of the ship's rail) would still relate to the carriage on the voyage and so be within the 'contract of carriage'.

Article II is the crucial article which for this purpose has to be construed. It is this article that gives the carrier all his rights and immunities, including the right to limit his liability. He is entitled to do that 'in relation to the loading' and 'under every contract of carriage'. Now I shall have to consider later the meaning of 'loading' in Article I and whether it is such as to exclude what I have called the first stage, that is, the operations on the shore side of the ship's rail. For the moment I am concerned only to see whether its meaning is cut down by the definition in Article I(e) on which Mr Megaw relies. The only phrase in Article II that can cut it down is the one I have quoted: 'under every contract of carriage'; it is only in so far as article I(e) operates through the definition of 'contract of carriage' that it can have any effect on Article II. I have already sought to demonstrate that, however limited the period in Article I(e) may be, the loading in both its stages must still relate to it and so be within the definition of contract of carriage.

A precise construction of Article I(e), while not irrelevant, is in no way conclusive of the point I have to decide, which turns, I think, upon the meaning of 'loading' in Article II.

But before I try to elucidate that, let me state my view of Article I(e). For, as I have said, though not dominant, it is not irrelevant; in construing 'loading' in Article II you must have regard to similar expressions throughout the rules, Article I(e) included. In my judgment, no special significance need be given to the phrase 'loaded on'. It is not intended to specify a precise moment of time. Of course, if the operation of the rules began and ended with a period of time a precise specification would be necessary. But they do not. It is legitimate in England to look at section 1 of the Act, which applies the rules not to a period of time but 'in relation to and in connection with the carriage of goods by sea'. The rules themselves show the same thing. The obligations in Article III, r 1, for example, to use due diligence to make the ship seaworthy and man and equip her properly are independent of time. The operation of the rules is determined by the limits of the contract of carriage by sea and not by any limits of time. The function of Article I(e) is, I think, only to assist in the definition of contract of carriage. As I have already pointed out, there is excluded from that definition any part of a larger contract which relates, for example, to inland transport. It is natural to divide such a contract into periods, a period of inland transport, followed perhaps by a period of sea transport and then again by a period of inland transport. Discharging from rail at the port of loading may fall into the first period; loading on to the ship into the second. The reference to 'when the goods are loaded on' in Article I(e) is not, I think, intended to do more than identify the first operation in the series which constitutes the carriage of goods by sea; as 'when they are discharged' denotes the last. The use of the rather loose word 'cover', I think, supports this view.

There is another reason for thinking that it would be wrong to stress the phrase 'loaded on' in Article I(e). It is no doubt necessary for an English court to apply the rules as part of English law, but that is a different thing from assuming them to be drafted in the light of English law. If one is inquiring whether 'loaded on' in Article I(e) has a different meaning from 'loaded' or 'loading' in other parts of the rules, it would be mistaken to look for the significant distinction in the light of a conception which may be peculiar to English law. The idea of the operation being divided at the ship's rail is certainly not a universal one. It does not, for example, apply in Scotland: *Glengarnock Iron and Steel Co Ltd v Cooper & Co*, (1895) 22 R 672, 676 *per* Lord Trayner. It is more reasonable to read the rules as contemplating loading and discharging as single operations. It is no doubt possible to read Article I(e) literally as defining the period as being from the completion of loading till the completion of discharging. But the literal interpretation would be absurd. Why exclude loading from the period and include discharging? How give effect to the frequent references to loading in other rules? How reconcile it with Article VII which allows freedom of contract 'prior to the loading on and subsequent to the discharge from'? Manifestly both operations must be included. That brings me back to the view that Article I(e) is naming the first and last of a series of operations which include in between loading and discharging, 'handling, stowage, carriage, custody and care'. This is, in fact, the list of operations to which Article II is by its own terms applied. In short, nothing is to be gained by looking to the terms of Article I(e) for an interpretation of Article II.

I think, therefore, that Article I(e), which was the spearhead of Mr Megaw's argument, turns out to be an ineffective weapon. But that still leaves it necessary to consider the meaning of 'loading' in Article II. Just how far does the operation of loading, to which Article II grants immunity, extend? Now I have already given reasons against presuming that the framers of the rules thought in terms of a divided operation, and in the absence of such a presumption the natural meaning of 'loading' covers the whole operation. How far can that be pressed? Article III, r 2, for example, provides: 'the carrier shall properly and carefully load', etc. If 'load' includes both stages, does that oblige the shipowner, whether he wants to or not, to undertake the whole of the loading? If so, it is a new idea to English lawyers, though perhaps more revolutionary in theory than in practice. But if not, and 'load' includes only the second stage, then should it not be given a similar meaning in article II with the result that immunity extends only to the second stage?

There is, however, a third interpretation to Article III, r 2. The phrase 'shall properly and carefully load' may mean that the carrier shall load and that he shall do it properly and carefully: or that he shall do whatever loading he does properly and carefully. The former interpretation perhaps fits the language more closely, but the latter may be more consistent with the object of the rules. Their object as it is put, I think, correctly in Carver's Carriage of Goods by Sea, 9th edn (1952), p 186, is to define not the scope of the contract service but the terms on which that service is to be performed. The extent to which the carrier has to undertake the loading of the vessel may depend not only upon different systems of law but upon the custom and practice of the port and the nature of the cargo. It is difficult to believe that the rules were intended to impose a universal rigidity in this respect, or to deny freedom of contract to the carrier. The carrier is practically bound to play some part in the loading and discharging, so that both operations are naturally included in those covered by the contract of carriage. But I see no reason why the rules should not leave the parties free to determine by their own contract the part which each has to play. On this view the whole contract of carriage is subject to the rules, but the extent to which loading and discharging are brought within the carrier's obligations is left to the parties themselves to decide.

I reject the interpretation of loading in Article II as covering only the second stage of the operation ...

Since the shipowner in this case in fact undertook the whole operation of loading it is unnecessary to decide which of the other two interpretations is correct. I prefer the more elastic one, that which I have called the third. There appears to be no binding authority on the point ... However, it is sufficient for me to say that on the facts of this case the rights and immunities under the rules extend to the whole of the loading carried out by the defendants and, therefore, Mr Megaw's first point fails.

I think, if I may so put it, that it is a good thing that it should fail. There must be many cases of carriage to which the rules apply where the ship undertakes the whole of the loading and discharging; and it would be unsatisfactory if the rules governed all but the extremities of the contract. It so happens that in this case (rather unusually) the exemption of the extremities would benefit the shipper. For the form of bill of lading which would have applied is made subject to the rules simpliciter, and does not set out the traditional mass of clauses which the rules have rendered generally ineffective. If they were there the shipper would probably fare worse under them than under the rules. It would certainly be a triumph for the innate conservatism of those who have not scrapped their small print if, though only on the outer fringes, it was to come into its own. But the division of loading into two parts is suited to more antiquated methods of loading than are now generally adopted and the ship's rail has lost much of its 19th-century significance. Only the most enthusiastic lawyer could watch with satisfaction the spectacle of liabilities shifting uneasily as the cargo sways at the end of a derrick across a notional perpendicular projecting from the ship's rail.

The next contention on behalf of the plaintiffs is that the rules are incorporated in the contract of carriage only if a bill of lading is issued. The basis for this is in the definition of Article I(b) of 'contract of carriage'; I have already quoted it, and it 'applies only to contracts of carriage covered by a bill of lading'. The use of the word 'covered' recognises the fact that the contract of carriage is always concluded before the bill of lading, which evidences its terms, is actually issued. When parties enter into a contract of carriage in the expectation that a bill of lading will be issued to cover it, they enter into it upon those terms which they know or expect the bill of lading to contain. Those terms must be in force from the inception of the contract; if it were otherwise the bill of lading would not evidence the contract but would be a variation of it. Moreover, it would be absurd to suppose that the parties intend the terms of the contract to be changed when the bill of lading is issued: for the issue of the bill of lading does not necessarily mark any stage in the development of the contract; often it is not issued till after the ship has sailed, and if there is pressure of office work on the ship's agent it may be delayed several days. In my judgment, whenever a contract of carriage is concluded, and it is contemplated that a bill of lading will, in due course, be issued in respect of it, that contract is from its creation 'covered' by a bill of lading, and is therefore from its inception a contract of carriage within the meaning of the rules and to which the rules apply. There is no English decision on this point; but I accept and follow without hesitation the reasoning of Lord President Clyde in *Harland & Wolff Ltd v Burns & Laird Lines Ltd* (1931) SC 722 ...

I have now arrived at the conclusion that the rules apply to the contract between the defendants and ISD so as to entitle the defendants, if they were sued by ISD, to limit their liability. The plaintiffs' last contention is that they were not a party to the contract between the defendants and ISD or to any similar contract; and that, even if they were, the limitation would not apply to them.

It is convenient to take the last part of this contention first, for it raises only a short point. Even if, so it is argued, the plaintiffs were a party to the contract made by ISD and the rules were a part of the contract, the rules could not affect the plaintiffs; for by their own terms they regulate only the relations between the carrier and the holder of the bill of lading and the plaintiffs were never holders of the bill of lading.

Article II grants rights to and imposes responsibilities upon the carrier 'under any contract of carriage'. *Prima facie* those rights and responsibilities must be against or towards every other party to the contract. But, so it is contended, 'contract of carriage' by its definition excludes all parties except the carrier and the holder of the bill of lading. This contention derives from the concluding words of Article I(b) 'from the moment at which such bill of lading or similar document of title regulates the relations between a carrier and a holder of the same'. In my judgment, those words do not apply to bills of lading generally but only to bills of lading issued under a charterparty; and even then they are intended to define not the parties to the contract but the moment at which the bill of lading becomes a contractual document within the meaning of the rules. I base this conclusion upon the sense of the paragraph as a whole as well as upon its punctuation. If there is any doubt the French text ... makes it quite clear ...

[Devlin J went on to consider whether the plaintiffs were privy to the contract of carriage and concluded that it was the intention of all the parties that 'the seller should participate in the contract of affreightment so far as it affected him'. The result was that the plaintiffs were bound by the Hague Rules and could recover no more than £200.]

Compania Portorafti Commerciale SA v Ultramar Panama Inc, The Captain Gregos [1990] 1 Lloyd's Rep 310, CA

The *Captain Gregos* was chartered for the carriage of a cargo of crude oil from Egypt to Rotterdam. The bills of lading incorporated the Hague-Visby Rules. More than one year after discharge of the cargo, the cargo owners alleged that the ship had made short delivery and that part of the cargo had been deliberately misappropriated. The shipowners commenced proceedings for a declaration that this claim was time-barred under article III, rule 6 of the Rules. Cargo owners argued that the time bar only applied to suits relating to events occurring between loading and discharge and not to complaints relating to later events such as delivery or misdelivery.

Bingham LJ (Stocker and Slade LJJ agreeing): ... The contract of carriage here was of an entirely normal kind. The cargo owners counterclaim as parties to the bill of lading (which I shall at this stage assume them to have been) against the shipowners as carriers. It is a paradigm situation.

The definition in Article I(e) does, I accept, assign a temporal term to the 'carriage of goods' under the rules, supporting an argument that the rules do not apply to events occurring before loading or after discharge. (See also article VII.) I read Article II as defining the scope of the operations to which the responsibilities, rights and immunities in the rules apply. Apart from the obligation of seaworthiness imposed by Article III, r 1 (not in issue here), the carrier's central obligation is (per Article III, r 2) properly and carefully to load, handle, stow, carry, keep, care for and discharge the goods carried.

It seems to me that the acts of which the cargo owners complain are the most obvious imaginable breaches of Article III, r 2. A bailee does not properly and carefully carry, keep and care for goods if he consumes them in his ship's boilers or delivers them to an unauthorised recipient during the voyage. A bailee does not properly and carefully discharge goods if, whether negligently or intentionally, he fails to discharge them and so converts them to his own use. If the cargo owners were to establish the fact they allege, and had brought suit within the year, I cannot see how a claim based on breach of the rules could fail. Both the cargo owners and the judge tended to treat their claim as one of misdelivery, but that does not strike me as an apt or helpful way of characterising it.

Article III, r 6 provides that the carrier and the ship shall: '... *in any event* be discharged from *all liability whatsoever in respect of the goods* (my emphasis) unless suit is brought within the year'. I do not see how any draftsman could use more emphatic language ... I would hold that 'all liability whatsoever in respect of the goods' means exactly what it says. The inference that the one-year time bar was intended to apply to all claims arising out of the carriage (or miscarriage) of goods by sea under bills subject to the Hague-Visby Rules is in my judgment strengthened by the consideration that Article III, r 6 is, like any time bar, intended to achieve finality and, in this case, enable the shipowner to clear his books (*The Aries* [1977] 1 Lloyd's Rep 334 at p 336) ...

If one were to accept that the cargo owners could escape the time bar by declining to sue for breach of the rules and instead framing the claim in tort, one would have also to accept that this was permitted by Article IV *bis*, r 1. This is a provision which the learned judge cited, but did not in this context allude to or discuss. It seems to be specifically directed to answering an argument such as the cargo owners' and I think it effective to do so. The learned editors of *Scrutton* (at 458) describe its principal object as being to ensure that a cargo owner is no better off suing in tort than he would be if he sued in contract. I respectfully agree. But that seems to me to be exactly what the cargo owners are seeking to achieve.

There is an obvious attraction in the argument that a party should not be able to rely on a one-year time bar to defeat a claim based on his own dishonesty. It is, however, to be remembered that claims such as these are made not infrequently (although how often they are established I do not know). I would moreover be slow to suppose that the experienced shipping interests represented at the conferences which led to these rules were not alert to the possibility of almost any form of skulduggery. But I think the rules themselves provide the solution. If damage to the goods is caused by wilful or reckless misconduct the shipowner loses the benefit of the financial limitation (Article IV, r 5(e)). If a servant or agent of the carrier damages the goods by wilful or reckless misconduct he cannot rely on the provisions of Article IV (Article IV *bis*, r 4), although still perhaps able to rely on the time bar (see the commentary in *Scrutton* at p 459). There is, however, no provision which deprives the shipowner of his right to rely on the time bar, even where he has been guilty of wilful or reckless misconduct. I cannot regard the omission as other than deliberate. This approach gains some small support from the Court of Appeal decision in *The Antares* [1978] 1 Lloyd's Rep 424.

I would be more reluctant to accept the shipowners' argument if I thought it would lead to injustice. A limitation provision can lead to injustice if a party's cause of action may be barred before he knows he has it. But that should not, as it seems to me, happen here. A cargo owner should know whether he has received short delivery at or about the time of delivery. With a cargo of crude oil such as this he will quickly be able to consider, and if necessary investigate, whether the shortage is reasonably explicable by evaporation, wastage, clingage, unpumpable residue etc. He can investigate what quantity was loaded. If he finds an unjustifiable shortage during carriage he is in a position to sue, and it is not crucial how or why the shortage occurred. He should be ready to sue well within the year, as the rules intend. The only reason why the cargo owners seek to found on the shipowners' alleged misconduct rather than on the breaches of the rules is, as I infer, that for whatever reason they let the year pass without bringing suit. That is in my view precisely the result the rules were intended to preclude.

For these reasons I differ from the judge and conclude that he was wrong to make the declaration he did on the ground he did. In reaching my conclusion I am not greatly influenced by the *travaux preparatoires*, which seem to me to have been concentrating on a different problem namely delivery to a party who does not present the bills, but I hold the view, if it be relevant, that the *travaux* certainly do disclose the legislative intention which the judge found. I am pleased to find that my conclusions broadly reflect those of Mr Brian Davenport QC in the *Law Quarterly Review* (vol 105, p 521, October, 1989) ...

There were other points raised before the judge ... The cargo owners contend that on the facts they were not, and are not to be treated as, parties to the bills of lading, with the result that they are not bound by the Hague-Visby Rules statutorily incorporated in the bills. To this the shipowners reply ... that on a proper construction of the Act and the rules the cargo owners are bound ...

The shipowners' argument was in essence very brief. They could rely on the time bar in Article III, r 6 because the rules have the force of law and apply to any bill covered by Article X, as these bills admittedly were. Article IV *bis* rule 1 expressly provides that the rules shall apply in any action against the carrier in respect of loss or damage to goods covered by a contract of carriage whether the action be founded in contract or in tort. It would frustrate the purpose of an international convention if its application were to depend on questions of privity to which (as we know) different legal systems may yield different answers. The issue of a bill of lading to which the rules apply is a necessary but also a sufficient condition of the right of shipowner or cargo owner to rely on the rules, even though neither is a party to the bill. Reliance was placed in particular on views expressed by Mr Diamond QC in his article on 'The Hague-Visby Rules' [1978] 2 *LMCLQ* 225 at 248–49) and on *Gillespie Bros v Roy Bowles Ltd* [1973] QB 400 at p 412 where Lord Denning MR cited Article IV *bis* r 1 to show how a non-party could become bound.

The cargo owners' response was even briefer. The effect of the Act is to give statutory force to a mandatory contractual regime. The language of the Act and the rules shows that they were intended to regulate the rights and duties of the parties to the bill of lading contract, not non-parties. That was what Mr Mustill QC thought in 1972 ('Carriage of Goods by Sea Act 1971', *Arkiv for Sjorett* at p 710). The issue of a bill of lading was a necessary, but not in itself a sufficient, condition of the application of the rules.

We are again (no doubt unavoidably) obliged to resolve this issue without the help which the decisions or opinions of foreign judges or jurists might have given us. I have not for my part found it an easy question. I am particularly concerned at the risk that idiosyncratic legal rules on privity might yield different results in different countries. But on balance I prefer the cargo owners' argument for three main reasons:

(1) As section 1(4) of the Act and Articles I(b) and X of the rules in particular make clear, the bill of lading is the bedrock on which this mandatory code is founded. A bill of lading is a contractual document with certain commercially well known consequences when endorsed and transferred. It is not clear to me why the code should treat the existence of a bill of lading as a matter of such central and overriding importance if the code is to apply with equal force as between those who are not parties to the contract which the bill contains or evidences.

(2) Much of the language in the Act and the rules suggests that the code is intended to govern the relations between the parties to the bill of lading contract. Section 1(4) speaks of applying the rules to a contract. Article I(a) defines the carrier as including the party who enters into a contract of carriage with a shipper. Article I(b) speaks of regulating relations between a carrier and a holder of a bill or similar document of title. Most significantly of all, Article II defines the application of the rules 'under every contract of carriage'. Articles V and VI are concerned with agreements between contracting parties. Article X applies the rules to the bill of lading, not the carriage. If it had been intended to regulate relations between non-parties to the bill of lading contract, it is hard to think the language would not have been both different and simpler.

(3) Whatever the law in other jurisdictions, the general principle that only a party to a contract may sue on it is well established here. If the draftsmen of the 1924 or 1971 Acts had intended the respective rules to infringe that principle or appreciated that that was their effect, I think they would have sought to make that clear in the Acts. It would be strange if so fundamental a principle were to be so inconspicuously abrogated.

In reaching this conclusion I recognise the unattractiveness to carriers of exposure to claims by non-parties to bills not subject to limits in time or amount. But the notion that bill of lading terms may be held to regulate relations between those who were not parties to the bills was, as I understand, specifically disavowed by Lord Donaldson MR and the House of Lords in *The Aliakmon* [1985] QB 350 at p 368; [1986] AC 785 at p 818.

I would accordingly determine this second issue in the cargo owners' favour.

3 DEVIATION

Deviation is a breach of the shipowners' undertaking, implied if not expressed, to proceed by a usual and reasonable route (Lord Somervell, *Renton v Palmyra* [1957] AC 149).

Stag Line Ltd v Foscolo, Mango and Co Ltd [1932] AC 328

Lord Buckmaster (Lord Warrington of Clyffe, Lord Russell of Killowen and Lord Macmillan delivered judgments to the same effect): My Lords, the appellants are the owners of the steamship *Ixia* ... The vessel was chartered to carry a cargo of coal ... and to proceed from Swansea, where the coal was to be loaded with all possible despatch, to Constantinople ... The usual and customary route for the voyage was from Swansea, south of Lundy, from thence in a straight line to a point about five miles off Pendeen, on the north coast of Cornwall, and then with a slight alteration to the east to Finisterre and so on.

The ship had been fitted with a heating apparatus designed to make use of the heat which might otherwise be wasted as steam and so to diminish the bill for fuel. This apparatus had not been working satisfactorily, and the owners therefore arranged to send representatives of the engineers to make a test when the vessel started on her next voyage. Two engineers accordingly joined the boat, the intention being that they should leave the ship with the pilot somewhere off Lundy.

The firemen on board the ship were not in possession of their full energies when the boat started at 1.45 in the morning on 31 June 1929, owing to excessive drinking before they joined the ship. The result was that a proper head of steam necessary for making the test was not got up in time to enable the test to be made before the pilot was discharged. Accordingly they proceeded on the voyage until the ship was off St Ives, when the ship was turned about five miles out of its course to enter the St Ives Harbour in order that the engineers might be landed. After landing them, the ship did not go straight back to the recognised route that she ought to have pursued, but hugged too closely the dangerous coast of Cornwall, and ran on a rock called the Vyneck Rock, with the result that the vessel and cargo were totally lost though, fortunately, there was no loss of life. The accident took place at about 3.20 pm, there was a moderate wind from ENE, the weather was cloudy, but visibility was moderately good up to six miles.

The respondents sought to recover damages for loss of their cargo upon the ground that there had been an unlawful deviation from the contracted course. The appellants ... said (that) by the Carriage of Goods by Sea Act 1924, the rules in the Schedule must be regarded as incorporated in the contract and, by those rules, they were entitled to make the deviation which led to the disaster ...

The appellants' argument upon the statute is, firstly, that the accident was a peril of the sea; and, secondly, that the deviation in question was a reasonable deviation and consequently was not an infringement of the contract of carriage ... the first point can, I think, be disregarded. It involves the view that perils and accidents of the sea are not qualified by the provisions as to deviation, and that such perils exempted the shipowner from responsibility for damage if they arise from or in the course of deviation, whether such deviation be reasonable or not. In my opinion clause 4 must be given its full effect without rendering it to a large extent unnecessary by such an interpretation, for it would follow from the arguments that a peril encountered by deviation, wholly unreasonable and wholly unauthorised, would be one for which the shipowner would be exempted from loss. In other words, the reasonable deviation would then only apply to questions of demurrage whatever the deviation might be.

The real difficulty in this case, and it is one by which I have been much oppressed, is whether in the circumstances the deviation was reasonable. It hardly needed the great authority of Lord Herschell in *Hick v Raymond* [1893] AC 22 to decide that in construing such a word it must be construed in relation to all the circumstances, for it is obvious that what may be reasonable under certain conditions may be wholly unreasonable when the conditions are changed. Every condition and every circumstance must be regarded, and it must be reasonable, too, in relation to both parties to the contract and not merely to one ... I do not think elaborate definitions, whether contained in dictionaries or judgments, are of much use in determining the value of a word in common use which means no more in this context than a deviation which where every circumstance has been duly weighed commends itself to the common sense and sound understanding of sensible men ...

Lord Atkin: ... The position in law seems to be that the plaintiffs are *prima facie* entitled to say that the goods were not carried safely: the defendants are then *prima facie* entitled to rely on the exception of loss by perils of the sea: and the plaintiffs are *prima facie* entitled in reply to rely upon a deviation. For unless authorised by the charterparty or the Act the departure to St Ives from the direct course to Constantinople was admittedly a deviation. I pause here to say that I find no substance in the contention faintly made by the defendants that an unauthorised deviation would not displace the statutory exceptions contained in the Carriage of Goods by Sea Act. I am satisfied that the general principles of English law are still applicable to the carriage of goods by sea except as modified by the Act: and I can find nothing in the Act which makes its statutory exceptions apply to a voyage which is not the voyage the subject of 'the contract of carriage of goods by sea' to which the Act applies. It remains therefore for the shipowners to show that the suggested deviation was authorised by the contract including the terms incorporated by the Act ...

(Article IV, r 4 provides that) 'Any deviation in saving or attempting to save life or property at sea, or any reasonable deviation shall not be deemed to be an infringement or breach of these Rules or of the contract of carriage, and the carrier shall not be liable for any loss or damage resulting therefrom'. In approaching the construction of these rules it appears to me important to bear in mind that one has to give the words as used their plain meaning, and not to colour one's interpretation by considering whether a meaning otherwise plain should be avoided if it alters the previous law. If the Act merely purported to codify the law, this caution would be well founded. I will repeat the well known words of Lord Herschell in the *Bank of England v Vagliano Brothers* [1891] AC 107. Dealing with the Bills of Exchange Act as a code he says:

> I think the proper course is in the first instance to examine the language of the statute and to ask what is its natural meaning, uninfluenced by any considerations derived from the previous state of the law, and not to start with inquiring how the law previously stood, and then, assuming that it was probably intended to leave it unaltered, to see if the words of the

enactment will bear an interpretation in conformity with this view ... The purpose of such a statute surely was that on any point specifically dealt with by it, the law should be ascertained by interpreting the language used instead of, as before, by roaming over a vast number of authorities in order to discover what the law was.

He then proceeds to say that of course it would be legitimate to refer to the previous law where the provision of the code was of doubtful import, or where words had previously acquired a technical meaning or been used in a sense other than their ordinary one. But if this is the canon of construction in regard to a codifying Act, still more does it apply to an Act like the present which is not intended to codify the English law, but is the result (as expressed in the Act) of an international conference intended to unify certain rules relating to bills of lading. It will be remembered that the Act only applies to contracts of carriage of goods outwards from ports of the United Kingdom: and the rules will often have to be interpreted in the courts of the foreign consignees. For the purpose of uniformity it is, therefore, important that the courts should apply themselves to the consideration only of the words used without any predilection for the former law, always preserving the right to say that words used in the English language which have already in the particular context received judicial interpretation may be presumed to be used in the sense already judicially imputed to them.

Having regard to the method of construction suggested above, I cannot think that it is correct to conclude, as Scrutton LJ does, that r 4 was not intended to extend the permissible limits of deviation as stated in *The Teutonia* (1872) LR 4 PC 171, 179. This would have the effect of confining reasonable deviation to deviation to avoid some imminent peril. Nor do I see any justification for confining reasonable deviation to a deviation in the joint interest of cargo owner and ship, as MacKinnon J appears to hold, or even to such a deviation as would be contemplated reasonably by both cargo owner and shipowner, as has been suggested by Wright J in *Foreman and Ellams Ltd v Federal Steam Navigation Co* [1928] 2 KB 424, 431, approved by Slesser LJ in the present case. A deviation may, and often will, be caused by fortuitous circumstances never contemplated by the original parties to the contract; and may be reasonable, though it is made solely in the interests of the ship or solely in the interests of the cargo, or indeed in the direct interest of neither: as for instance where the presence of a passenger or of a member of the ship or crew was urgently required after the voyage had begun on a matter of national importance; or where some person on board was a fugitive from justice, and there were urgent reasons for his immediate appearance. The true test seems to be what departure from the contract voyage might a prudent person controlling the voyage at the time make and maintain, having in mind all the relevant circumstances existing at the time, including the terms of the contract and the interests of all parties concerned, but without obligation to consider the interests of any one as conclusive ... The decision has to be that of the master or occasionally of the shipowner; and I conceive that a cargo owner might well be deemed not to be unreasonable if he attached much more weight to his own interests than a prudent master having regard to all the circumstances might think it wise to do.

Applying then this test, was this deviation reasonable? I do not discuss the facts except to say that I see no ground for suggesting that the deviation was due to some default of the shipowner in respect of the firemen. In the absence of evidence directed to that issue it does not seem right to impute blame to the owners in that respect ... I think that Greer LJ is plainly right in applying the test of reasonableness to the deviation as a whole. It could not, however, be laid down that as soon as the place was reached to which deviation was justified, there was an obligation to join the original course as directly as possible. A justified deviation to a port of refuge might involve thereafter a shorter and more direct route to the port of destination compared with a route which took the shortest cut to the original course. On the other hand, though the port of refuge was justifiably reached, the subsequent voyage might be so conducted as to amount to an unreasonable deviation. Taking all the facts into account I am pressed with the evidence which the learned judge accepted, that after St Ives the coasting course directed by the master was not the correct course which would ordinarily be set in those circumstances. It is obvious that the small extra risk to ship and cargo caused by deviation to St Ives, was vastly increased by the subsequent course. It seems to me not a mere error of navigation but a failure to pursue the true course from St Ives to Constantinople which in itself made the deviation cease to be reasonable. For these reasons I agree that this appeal should be dismissed.

4 SEAWORTHINESS

Article III, r 1

An overriding obligation 'before and at the beginning of the voyage'.

Maxine Footwear Co Ltd v Canadian Government Merchant Marine Ltd [1959] AC 589, PC

The appellants were shippers and consignees of cargo loaded on the *Maurienne* at Halifax NS for carriage to Kingston, Jamaica. The contract was subject to the Canadian Water Carriage of Goods Act 1936. Shortly before the vessel was due to sail an attempt was made to thaw a frozen drainpipe with an acetylene torch. A fire was started in the cork insulation around the pipe. The fire eventually forced the master to scuttle the ship.

The judgment of the Privy Council was delivered by **Lord Somervell of Harrow**:

... Before proceeding to consider the arguments it is convenient to state certain conclusions which appear plain to their Lordships. From the time when the ship caught on fire she was unseaworthy. This unseaworthiness caused the damage to and loss of the appellants' goods. The negligence of the respondents' servants which caused the fire was a failure to exercise due diligence.

Logically, the first submission on behalf of the respondents was that in cases of fire Article III never comes into operation even though the fire makes the ship unseaworthy. All fires and all damage from fire on this argument fall to be dealt with under Article IV, r 2(b). If this were right there was at any rate a very strong case for saying that there was no fault or privity of the carrier within that rule, and the respondents would succeed.

In their Lordships' opinion the point fails. Article III, r 1, is an overriding obligation. If it is not fulfilled and the non-fulfilment causes the damage the immunities of Article IV cannot be relied on. This is the natural construction apart from the opening words of Article III, r 2. The fact that that rule is made subject to the provisions of Article IV and r 1 is not so conditioned makes the point clear beyond argument.

The further submissions by the respondents were based, as they had to be, on the construction of Article III, r 1. It was submitted that under that article the obligation is only to exercise due diligence to make the ship seaworthy at two moments of time, the beginning of the loading and the beginning of the voyage.

It is difficult to believe that this construction of the word 'before' could have been argued but for the fact that this doctrine of stages had been laid down in relation to the absolute warranty of seaworthiness in English law.

It is worth, therefore, bearing in mind words used by Lord Macmillan with reference to the English Carriage of Goods by Sea Act 1924, which embodied the Hague Rules, as does the present Act.

> It is important to remember that the Act of 1924 was the outcome of an International Conference, and that the rules in the Schedule have an international currency. As these rules must come under the consideration of foreign courts it is desirable in the interests of uniformity that their interpretation should not be rigidly controlled by domestic precedents of antecedent date, but rather that the language of the rules should be construed on broad principles of general acceptation (*Stag Line Ltd v Foscolo, Mango & Co* [1932] AC 328, 350).

In their Lordships' opinion 'before and at the beginning of the voyage' means the period from at least the beginning of the loading until the vessel starts on her voyage. The word 'before' cannot in their opinion be read as meaning 'at the commencement of the loading'. If this had been intended it would have been said. The question when precisely the period begins does not arise in this case, hence the insertion above of the words 'at least'.

On that view the obligation to exercise due diligence to make the ship seaworthy continued over the whole of the period from the beginning of loading until the ship sank. There was a failure to exercise due diligence during that period. As a result the ship became unseaworthy and this unseaworthiness caused the damage to and loss of the appellants' goods. The appellants are therefore entitled to succeed ...

It becomes therefore unnecessary to consider whether the Supreme Court were justified in holding that the appellants' goods were not stowed until after the commencement of the fire.

It is also unnecessary to consider the earlier cases as to 'stages' under the common law. The doctrine of stages had its anomalies and some important matters were never elucidated by authority. When the warranty was absolute it seems at any rate intelligible to restrict it to certain points of time. It would be surprising if a duty to exercise due diligence ceased as soon as loading began, only to reappear later shortly before the beginning of the voyage.

For these reasons their Lordships will humbly advise Her Majesty that this appeal should be allowed.

Due diligence to make the ship seaworthy

Riverstone Meat Co Pty Ltd v Lancashire Shipping Co Ltd, The Muncaster Castle [1961] AC 807

Cases of canned ox tongue were shipped on board the *Muncaster Castle* for carriage from Sydney to London under a bill of lading which was subject to the Australian Sea Carriage of Goods Act 1924. When the goods were discharged, most of the cases were found damaged by sea water which had entered the hold through storm valves. Shortly before starting the voyage, the storm valve inspection covers had been removed during a survey of the vessel. The covers had not been properly refitted by the independent firm of ship repairers who had been instructed in connection with the survey. The cargo owners alleged that the carriers had not exercise due diligence to make the ship seaworthy.

Viscount Simonds: My Lords, the question, then, is whether the respondents discharged this burden, and it is conceded that they did unless they are to be held responsible for the negligence of the fitter employed by Alexander Stephen & Sons Ltd. This is the single issue in the case ... Its solution depends on the meaning of the words occurring in article III, rule 1, and repeated in article IV, rule 1, 'due diligence to make the ship seaworthy'. To ascertain their meaning it is, in my opinion, necessary to pay particular regard to their history, origin and context ... The Hague Rules, as is well known, were the result of the Conferences on Maritime Law held at Brussels in 1922 and 1923. Their aim was broadly to standardise within certain limits the rights of every holder of a bill of lading against the shipowner, prescribing an irreducible minimum for the responsibilities and liabilities to be undertaken by the latter. To guide them the framers of the rules had amongst other precedents the American Harter Act of 1893, the Australian Sea Carriage of Goods Act 1904, the Canadian Water Carriage of Goods Act 1910, and, though they had no British Act as a model, they had decisions of the English courts in which the language of the Harter Act had fallen to be construed by virtue of its provisions being embodied in bills of lading. In all these Acts the relevant words, 'exercise due diligence to make the ship seaworthy', are to be found. It was in these circumstances that these words were adopted in the Hague Rules.

My Lords, the question how far their meaning should be governed by previous decisions in the courts of America or this country has been more than once discussed in this House. Notwithstanding some apparent qualification of the proposition which is to be found in the speeches of Lords Atkin and Macmillan in *Stag Line Ltd v Foscolo Mango & Co Ltd* [1932] AC 328, I think I am at liberty to adopt emphatically what was said by Lords Sumner and Hailsham in *Gosse Millard Ltd v Canadian Government Merchant Marine Ltd* [1929] AC 223. The former of them said:

> By forbearing to define 'management of the ship' ... the legislature has, in my opinion, shown a clear intention to continue and enforce the old clause as it was previously understood and regularly construed by the courts.

The latter said:

> I am unable to find any reason for supposing that the words as used by the legislature in the Act of 1924 leave any different meaning to that which has been judicially assigned to them when used in contracts for the carriage of goods by sea before that date; and I think that the decisions which have already been given are sufficient to determine the meaning to be put upon them in the statute now under discussion.

Mutatis mutandis these statement I apply to the words we have to construe ...

First I would refer to *G E Dobell & Co v Steamship Rossmore Co Ltd* [1895] 2 QB 408, a case often referred to in the courts of this country and of the United States and never, so far as I am aware, dissented from. In that case the ship was unseaworthy owing to the negligence of the ship's carpenter. Into the bill of lading the words of the Harter Act were introduced, 'which', said Lord Esher MR 'I decline to construe as an Act, but which we must construe simply as words occurring in this bill of lading'. Then he proceeds:

> In section 3 of the Act so incorporated the exception which is to relieve the ship owner is made to depend on the condition that the owner of the ship ... shall exercise due diligence to make the vessel in all respects seaworthy. If he does not do that the exceptions in his favour do not take effect. It is contended that the meaning of the clause is that if the owner personally did all that he could do to make the ship seaworthy when she left America, then, although she was not seaworthy, by the fault of some agent or servant, the owner is not liable.

And the learned Master of the Rolls, after rejecting this contention, went on:

> It is obvious to my mind ... that the words of section 3 which limit the owner's liability if he shall exercise due diligence to make the ship in all respects seaworthy, must mean that it is to be done by the owner by himself or the agents whom he employs to see to the seaworthiness of the ship before she starts out of that port.

So also Kay LJ:

> It seems to me to be plain on the face of this contract that what was intended was that the owner should, if not with his own eyes, at any rate by the eyes of proper competent agents, ensure that the ship was in a seaworthy condition before she left port, and that it is not enough to say that he appointed a proper and competent agent.

I have cited from these judgments at some length because they determine decisively the meaning attached by the courts of this country to the relevant words. It is true that the negligence was that of a servant of the shipowner, but the reasoning and the language of the judgments embrace any agent employed by him. These are wise words.

I turn now to a case decided two years later in the District Court, SD New York, *The Colima* (1897) 82 Fed Rep 665 and I quote at some length from the judgment of Judge Brown. In that case the vessel was unseaworthy owing to negligent loading by the stevedores which was done under the supervision and direction of the master and first officer of the ship. The learned judge said:

> This section [that is, section 3 of the Harter Act] has been in several cases adjudged to require due diligence, not merely in the personal acts of the owner, but also on the part of the agents he may employ, or to whom he may have committed the work of fitting the vessel for sea. The Act requires in other words, due diligence in the work itself ...

> On any other construction, owners would escape all responsibility for the seaworthiness of their ships by merely employing agents of good repute, whether any diligence and care to make their vessels seaworthy were in fact exercised or not. On reason and sound policy no such intent in the statute can be supposed. The context and the pre-existing law indicate that the intent of the Act is to relieve the shipowner from his previous warranty of absolute seaworthiness in fact, and to substitute for that warranty a warranty only of diligence, to make the ship seaworthy. This difference is of great importance, as it avoids responsibility for latent and undiscoverable defects. But the warranty of diligence remains: and this requires the application of the usual rule, that the acts and negligences of the agent are deemed those of the principal.

... My Lords, I have without reluctance ventured on this long quotation because I can find no words more apt to express my own view as to the meaning of words taken from the Harter Act and embodied in the Hague Rules. To one thing in particular I call attention ... Here I may quote words of MacKinnon LJ in *Smith, Hogg & Co Ltd v Black Sea and Baltic General Insurance Co Ltd* [1939] 2 All ER 855:

> The limitation and qualification of the implied warranty of seaworthiness by cutting down the duty of the shipowner to the obligation to use 'due diligence ... to make the ship seaworthy' is a limitation or qualification more apparent than real, because the exercise of due diligence involves not merely that the shipowner personally shall exercise due diligence, but that all his servants and agents shall exercise due diligence. That is pointed out in a note in *Scrutton on Charterparties* (14th edn, p 110) which says that this variation will not be 'of much practical value in face of the dilemma that must constantly arise on the facts. In most cases if the vessel is unseaworthy due diligence cannot have been used by the owner, his servants, or agents; if due diligence has been used the vessel in fact will be seaworthy. The circumstances in which the dilemma does not arise (eg a defect causing unseaworthiness, but of so latent a nature that due diligence could not have discovered it) are not likely to occur often'.

In the same case on appeal to this House, Lord Wright said [1940] AC 997, 1001:

> The unseaworthiness, constituted as it was by loading an excessive deck cargo, was obviously only consistent with want of due diligence on the part of the shipowner to make her seaworthy. Hence the qualified

exception of unseaworthiness does not protect the shipowner. In effect such an exception can only excuse against latent defects. The overloading was the result of overt acts.

... I come, then, to *W Angliss & Co (Australia) Proprietary Ltd v P & O Steam Navigation Co* [1927] 2 KB 456 which is said to be the first case in which the Hague Rules were discussed in an English court ... It is important to note what was the point of decision. It was whether, when the carrier has contracted for the building of a ship, he is liable for lack of due diligence on the part of the shipbuilders or their workmen if he has engaged builders of repute and has adopted all reasonable precautions, such as requiring the builders to satisfy one of the recognised classification societies and engaged skilled naval architects who advise him and skilled inspectors who supervise the work with due diligence. The learned judge, Wright J, as he then was, held that in such circumstances the carrier was not liable. I see no reason to question the correctness of this decision, and need say no more about it, for it does not in the present appeal fall to be reviewed. Of greater significance is that, except in a single passage where the learned judge was dealing with the employment of an inspector to supervise the work, no mention is made of the employment of agents to repair a ship. That passage is as follows: 'Again, the need of repairing a ship may cast on the carrier a special duty to see, as far as reasonably possible, by special advisers for whom he is personally responsible, that the repairs adequately make good the defects.'

It is not possible to extract from this somewhat speculative dictum that the learned judge thought that the carrier would not in any case, with or without inspection, be liable for negligence on the part of those to whom (in the words of Brown J in *The Colima*) 'he committed the work of fitting the vessel for sea'. It was not a matter for his decision and he did not, in my opinion, purport to decide it. But it is upon this authority that the whole fabric of the respondents' case appears to rest. It is a reasonable construction of the words, which once again I quote, 'to exercise due diligence to make the ship seaworthy' to say that in the case of a ship built for the carrier, or newly come into his hands by purchase, the carrier fulfils his obligation if he takes the precautions which the learned judge suggests. Until the ship is his he can have no further responsibility. I am aware of no case either in the United States under the Harter Act or this country when its words fell to be construed in which the contrary has been suggested. But it is far otherwise where the shipowner puts his ship in the hands of third parties for repair. To such a case the words that I have cited from *The Rossmore* and *The Colima* are precisely applicable. An attempt was made to draw a distinction between negligence shown by the shipowner's servants, his agents and independent contractors. But this could but fail. For no sensible reason could be found for such a distinction ...

The plea that the shipowner is not liable for the negligence of an independent contractor failing as a general proposition, as it was bound to fail, it was then urged that it was a question of fact in each case, and that upon the facts of the present case the respondents were not liable for the negligence of the fitter employed by the ship repairers. It was for this reason that I stated the facts fully at the beginning of this opinion. Having done so, I must say at once that I find it impossible to distinguish between one independent contractor and another, or between one kind of repair and another. I have no love for the argumentative question 'Where is the line to be drawn?' but it would be an impossible task for the court to examine the facts of each case and determine whether the negligence of the independent contractor should be imputed to the shipowner. I do not know what criterion or criteria should be used, nor were any suggested. Take the case of repair. Is there to be one result if the necessary repair is slight, another if it is extensive? Is it relevant that the shipowner might have done the work by his own servants but preferred to have it done by a reputable shipyard? These and many other questions that will occur to your Lordships show that no other solution is possible than to say that the shipowner's obligation of due diligence demands due diligence in the work of repair by whomsoever it may be done.

... I will end by categorically repelling the second and third formal reasons in the respondents' case. They did not on the facts of the case by entrusting the vessel to reputable ship repairers perform their duty to exercise due diligence. They were vicariously liable for negligence of a servant of an independent contractor, namely, the fitter of Alexander Stephen & Sons Ltd ...

Lord Keith of Avonholm: My Lords, I agree. I would only add a few words ...

The obligation is a statutory obligation imposed in defined contracts between the carrier and the shipper. There is nothing novel in a statutory obligation being held to be incapable of delegation so as to free the person bound of liability for breach of the obligation, and the reasons for this become, I think, more compelling where the obligation is made part of a contract between parties. We are not faced with a question in the realm of tort, or negligence. The obligation is a statutory contractual obligation. The novelty, if there is one, is that the statutory obligation is expressed in terms of an obligation to exercise due diligence, etc. There is nothing, in my opinion, extravagant in saying that this is an inescapable personal obligation. The carrier cannot claim to have shed his obligation to exercise due diligence to make his ship seaworthy by selecting a firm of competent ship repairers to make his ship seaworthy. Their failure to use due diligence to do so is his failure. The question, as I see it, is not one of vicarious responsibility at all. It is a question of statutory obligation. Perform it as you please. The performance is the carrier's performance ...

[Lord Merriman, Lord Radcliffe and Lord Hodson also delivered reasoned judgments in favour of allowing the appeal.]

Seaworthiness: 'the voyage'

The Makedonia [1962] P 190

The plaintiffs shipped timber on board the vessel for carriage from various British Columbian ports to ports in the United Kingdom. The bills of lading incorporated the Canadian Water Carriage of Goods Act 1936. The *Makedonia* broke down in mid-ocean and had to take salvage assistance. The plaintiffs brought proceedings to recover the shares of the salvage award which they had had to pay.

Hewson J: Before proceeding to the consideration of whether the breakdown was caused by actionable fault on the part of the defendants, I propose to decide first what 'voyage' under Article III (1) of the Hague Rules means. There has been much argument about it. Mr Brandon submitted that the Hague Rules substituted for the absolute warranty of seaworthiness at each bunkering stage at common law a qualified obligation upon the owners to exercise due diligence to make her seaworthy at each bunkering port. If she was unseaworthy on leaving any bunkering port through defective bunkers being shipped there or through loading good fuel oil into tanks already containing sea water, thereby contaminating the fuel and making it unburnable, the owners are responsible for the lack of diligence on the part of the engineers at the beginning of that stage and they cannot, therefore, rely on the exceptions in Article IV (2) of those Rules.

There is no decision on what is meant or implied by 'voyage' in Article III (1) of the Hague Rules ... In *Northumbrian Shipping Co Ltd v E Timm & Son Ltd* [1939] AC 397 Lord Wright said:

> ... the warranty of seaworthiness is subdivided in respect of bunkers. Instead of a single obligation to make the vessel seaworthy in this respect, which must be satisfied once for all at the commencement of the voyage, there is substituted a recurring obligation at each bunkering port at which the owners or those who act for the owners decide she shall bunker, thereby fixing the particular stage of the voyage.

In the *Northumbrian Shipping Co* case, s 6 of the Canadian Water Carriage of Goods Act 1910, applied. This section provided that if the shipowner exercised due diligence to make the ship in all respects seaworthy and properly manned, he should not be responsible for any loss resulting from faults or errors in the navigation of the ship. The House of Lords held that that qualified obligation, referred to by Mr Brandon, applied to the owners at each bunkering stage, that is, the owners were bound to exercise due diligence regarding bunkers at each stage.

Has the different wording of the Hague Rules or the rules of the Canadian Act of 1936 altered the position? Mr Brandon argued that the importation of the words 'before and at the beginning of the voyage' has added nothing, and that the words are simply declaratory of the law as it was at the time or up to the time the Rules were formulated. In my view, the position in this country before the Carriage of Goods by Sea Act 1924, was clear without any further words. Mr Brandon argued that 'seaworthy at the beginning of the voyage' had already been defined by a long line of cases, and therefore the qualified obligations to use due diligence of seaworthiness at each stage should be read into the words.

... I see no obligation to read into the word 'voyage' a doctrine of stages, but a necessity to define the word itself. The word does not appear in the Canadian Act of 1910. 'Voyage' in this context means what it has always meant; the contractual voyage from the port of loading to the port of discharge as declared in the appropriate bill of lading. The rule says 'voyage' without any qualification such as 'any declared stage thereof'. In my view, the obligation on the shipowner was to exercise due diligence before and at the beginning of sailing from the loading port, to have the vessel adequately bunkered for the first stage to San Pedro, and to arrange for adequate bunkers of a proper kind at San Pedro and other selected intermediate ports on the voyage so that the contractual voyage might be performed. Provided he did that, in my view, he fulfilled his obligation in that respect.

I find that the shipowner exercised due diligence to ensure sufficient and proper bunkers at each stage of the voyage ...

5 PROPER CARE

Albacora SRL v Wescott & Laurance Line [1966] 2 Lloyd's Rep 53, HL

Lord Reid: The respondents are the owners of the vessel *Maltasian*. They are sued by the appellants, merchants in Genoa, for £8,180 as damages for deterioration of a consignment of 1,200 cases of wet salted ling fillets during a voyage in that ship from Glasgow to Genoa ...

It is not disputed that the condition of the fish did deteriorate substantially during the voyage which lasted 12 days from 15 September 1961; and the cause of that deterioration is now clearly established by findings of the Lord Ordinary, which both parties accept. The fish, like other sea fish, harboured halophilic bacteria. During the life of the fish these bacteria cause no damage, and after death they remain inactive at temperatures below 41 degrees F. Above that temperature they begin to multiply, and above about 51 degrees F they multiply rapidly. The deterioration or contamination which developed during the voyage was the result of the multiplication of these bacteria.

The holds of the *Maltasian* were not refrigerated and it is now clear that this cargo could not safely be carried on this voyage in September without refrigeration. But no one appears to have realised that ...

The appellants' argument is that the respondents were in breach of Art III, rule 2 of the Schedule to the Carriage of Goods by Sea Act 1924, which was incorporated in the bill of lading:

> Subject to the provisions of Article IV, the carrier shall properly and carefully load, handle, stow, carry, keep, care for and discharge the goods carried.

The argument is that in this Article 'properly' means in the appropriate manner looking to the actual nature of the consignment, and that it is irrelevant that the shipowner and ship's officers neither knew nor could have discovered that special treatment was necessary. The obligation under the Article is to carry goods properly and if that if not done there is a breach of contract. So it is argued that in the present case it is proved that the only proper way to carry this consignment on this voyage was in a refrigerated hold, and there the obligation of the respondents was to do that, even if the appellants' agents who were parties to the contract were aware that there was no refrigeration in this ship.

This construction of the word 'properly' leads to such an unreasonable result that I would not adopt it if the word can properly be construed in any other sense. The appellants argue that, because the article uses the word 'properly' as well as 'carefully', the word 'properly' must mean something more than carefully. Tautology is not unknown even in international conventions, but I think that 'properly' in this context has a meaning slightly different from 'carefully'. I agree with Viscount Kilmuir LC, that here 'properly' means in accordance with a sound system (*GH Renton & Co Ltd v Palmyra Trading Corporation of Panama* [1957] AC 149, at p 166) and that may mean rather more than carrying the goods carefully. But the question remains by what criteria it is to be judged whether the system was sound.

In my opinion, the obligation is to adopt a system which is sound in light of all the knowledge which the carrier has or ought to have about the nature of the goods. And if that is right, then the respondents did adopt a sound system. They had no reason to suppose that the goods required any different treatment from that which the goods in fact received. That is sufficient to dispose of the appellants' case on breach of contract ...

Lord Pearce: ... The word 'properly' presumably adds something to the word 'carefully'. In *GH Renton & Co Ltd v Palmyra Trading Corporation of Panama* [1957] AC 149, this House construed it as meaning 'upon a sound system'. A sound system does not mean a system suited to all the weaknesses and idiosyncrasies of a particular cargo, but a sound system under all the circumstances in relation to the general practice of carriage of goods by sea. It is tantamount, I think, to efficiency ...

Lord Pearson: ... Article III, r 2, is expressly made subject to the provisions of Article IV. The scheme is, therefore, that there is a *prima facie* obligation under Article III, r 2, which may be displaced or modified by some provision of Art IV. Article IV contains many and various provisions, which may have different effects on the *prima facie* obligation arising under Article III, r 2. The convenient first step is to ascertain what is the *prima facie* obligation under Article III, r 2.

It is not an obligation to achieve the desired result, ie the arrival of the goods in an undamaged condition at their destination. It is an obligation to carry out certain operations properly and carefully. The fact that goods, acknowledged in the bill of landing to have been received on board in apparent good order and condition, arrived at the destination in a damaged condition does not in itself constitute a breach of the obligation, though it may well be in many cases sufficient to raise an inference of a breach of the obligation. The cargo owner is not expected to know what happened on the voyage, and, if he shows that the goods arrived in a damaged condition and there is no evidence from the shipowner showing that the goods were duly cared for on the voyage, the court may well infer that the goods were not properly cared for on the voyage.

In *Gosse Millerd v Canadian Government Merchant Marine Ltd* [1927] 2 KB 432, at p 434, Wright J said:

> The words 'properly discharge' in Article III, r 2, mean, I think, 'deliver from the ship's tackle in the same apparent order and condition as on shipment', unless the carrier can excuse himself under Article IV ...

In my view, that is not the right construction of Article III, r 2. Rightly construed, that rule only provides that the operations referred to, including the operation of discharging the goods, shall be carried out properly and carefully. That this is the right construction appears from the judgment of Mr Justice Devlin in *Pyrene Company Ltd v Scindia Navigation Company Ltd* [1954] 2 QB 402 and from the speeches in the House of Lords in *GH Renton & Co Ltd v Palmyra Trading Corporation of Panama* [1957] AC 149.

... The word 'properly' adds something to 'carefully', if 'carefully' has a narrow meaning of merely taking care. The element of skill or sound system is required in addition to taking care. In my opinion, there was no breach of the *prima facie* obligation under Article III, r 2 ...

[Lord Guest and Lord Upjohn agreed with Lord Reid.]

6 FAULT IN NAVIGATION OR MANAGEMENT

Gosse Millerd Ltd v Canadian Government Merchant Marine Ltd [1929] AC 223, HL

The appellants shipped boxes of tinplates on the respondents' ship *Canadian Highlander* at Swansea for carriage to Vancouver. On arrival it was found that the cargo had been damaged by fresh water. The trial judge found that rain entered the hold at a port of call when the hatch cover was removed during discharge of other cargo and during a period in dry dock when there was carelessness in moving and replacing tarpaulins which were supposed to cover the hatch when repair and maintenance work was being done to the vessel.

Lord Hailsham LC: My Lords, this is an action brought by the appellants against the respondents, claiming damages for injury done to their tinplates on a voyage from Swansea to Vancouver in a ship belonging to the respondents and known as the *Canadian Highlander*.

At the trial there was a great conflict as to the cause of the damage to the tinplates; but on the hearing before the Court of Appeal and at your Lordships' bar, both sides accepted the findings of fact of the learned trial judge ...

The appellants relied on rule 2 of Article III of the rules ... but the respondents relied upon rule 2 (a) of Article IV; this rule provides that:

Neither the carrier nor the ship shall be responsible for loss or damage arising or resulting from – (a) Act, neglect, or default of the master, mariner, pilot, or the servants of the carrier in the navigation or in the management of the ship.

... The argument at the bar turned mainly upon the meaning to be placed upon the expression 'management of the ship' in that rule. The words in question first appear in an English statute in the Act now being considered; but nevertheless they have a long judicial history in this country. The same words are to be found in the well known Harter Act of the United States, and as a consequence they have often been incorporated in bills of lading which have been the subject of judicial consideration in the courts in this country. I am unable to find any reason for supposing that the words as used by the

Legislature in the Act of 1924 have any different meaning to that which has been judicially assigned to them when used in contracts for the carriage of goods by sea before that date; and I think that the decisions which have already been given are sufficient to determine the meaning to be put upon them in the statute now under discussion.

In the year 1893, in the case of *The Ferro* [1893] P 38, certain oranges had been damaged by the negligent stowage of the stevedore. It was held by the Divisional Court that the negligent stowage of the cargo was not neglect or default in the management of the ship. Gorell Barnes J says:

> I think it is desirable also to express the view which I hold about the question turning on the construction of the words 'management of the ship', I am not satisfied that they go much, if at all, beyond the word 'navigation'.

Sir Francis Jeune says:

> It would be an improper use of language to include all stowage in such a term [ie 'mismanagement of the ship']. It is not difficult to understand why the word 'management' was introduced, because, inasmuch as navigation is defined as something affecting the safe sailing of the ship ... it is easy to see that there might be things which it would be impossible to guard against connected with the ship itself, and the management of the ship, which would not fall under navigation. Removal of the hatches for the sake of ventilation, for example, might be management of the ship, but would have nothing to do with the navigation.

In the case of *The Glenochil* [1896] P 10, the same two learned judges, sitting as a Divisional Court, held that the words did protect the shipowner for damage done by pumping water into the ballast tank in order to stiffen the ship without ascertaining that a pipe had become broken, and thereby let the water into the cargo. Gorell Barnes J says:

> There will be found a strong and marked contrast in the provisions which deal with the care of the cargo and those which deal with the management of the ship herself; and I think that where the act done in the management of the ship is one which is necessarily done in the proper handling of the vessel, though in the particular case the handling is not properly done, but is done for the safety of the ship herself, and is not primarily done at all in connection with the cargo, that must be a matter which falls within the words 'management of the said vessel'.

Sir Francis Jeune says:

> It seems to me clear that the word 'management' goes somewhat beyond – perhaps not much beyond – navigation, but far enough to take in this very class of acts which do not affect the sailing or movement of the vessel, but do affect the vessel herself.

And referring to his own judgment in *The Ferro*, he says:

> It may be that the illustration I gave in that case, as to the removal of the hatches for the sake of ventilation, was not a very happy one; but the distinction I intended to draw then, and intend to draw now, is one between want of care of cargo and want of care of the vessel indirectly affecting the cargo.

The principles enunciated in this case have repeatedly been cited since with approval in this country and in America ...

In the case of *Hourani v Harrison* (1927) 32 Com Cas 305 the Court of Appeal had to consider the meaning to be attached to the words of Article IV, rule 2, in a case in which loss was caused by the pilfering of the stevedore's men whilst the ship was being discharged. The court held that this did not fall within the expression 'management of the ship'; but both Bankes LJ and Atkin LJ (as he then was) discussed the meaning to be placed on the expression. Bankes LJ reviews the authorities both in this country and in the United States; he points out that the principle laid down in *The Glenochil* has been accepted in the Supreme Court of the United States as being correct, and he adopts and applies that principle to the case which he is then considering. The learned judge expresses the distinction as being between:

> damage resulting from some act relating to the ship herself and only incidentally damaging the cargo, and an act dealing, as is sometimes said in some of the authorities, solely with the goods and not directly or indirectly with the ship herself.

Atkin LJ says:

> that there is a clear distinction drawn between goods and ship; and when they talk of the word 'ship', they mean the management of the ship, and they do not mean the general carrying on of the business of transporting goods by sea.

My Lords, in my judgment, the principle laid down in *The Glenochil* and accepted by the Supreme Court of the United States in cases arising under the American Harter Act, and affirmed and applied by the Court of Appeal in the *Hourani* case under the present English statute, is the correct one to apply. Necessarily, there may be cases on the borderline, depending upon their own particular facts; but if the principle is clearly borne in mind of distinguishing between want of care of cargo and want of care of vessel indirectly affecting the cargo, as Sir Francis Jeune puts it, there ought not to be very great difficulty in arriving at a proper conclusion ...

My Lords, it appears to me plain that if the test which I have extracted from the earlier cases is the correct one, it follows that the appellants are entitled to recover in the present case. It is clear that the tinplates were not safely and properly cared for or carried; and it is for the respondents then to prove that they are protected from liability by the provisions of Article IV, and that the damage was occasioned through the neglect or default of their servants in the management of the ship. In my judgment they have not even shown that the persons who were negligent were their servants; but even if it can be assumed that the negligence in dealing with the tarpaulins was by members of the crew, such negligence was not negligence in the management of the ship, and therefore is not negligence with regard to which Article IV, rule 2 (a), affords any protection ...

Viscount Sumner: ... Now the tarpaulins were used to protect the cargo. They were put over the hatch, as they always are, to keep water out of cargo holds. They should have been so arranged, when the hatch boards were taken off, as to prevent water from getting to the cargo. It was not a question of letting light into the 'tween decks. They were lit by electricity. There is no evidence that an amount of water entered that would have done any harm to an empty hold or to the ship as a ship. Water, sufficient when soaked into the wood of the boxes to rust the tinplates in the course of a voyage through the tropics, might well have been harmless if it merely ran into the bilges. There is neither fact nor finding to the contrary. I think it quite plain that the particular use of the tarpaulin, which was neglected, was a precaution solely in the interest of the cargo. While the ship's work was going on these special precautions were required as cargo operations. They were no part of the operations of shifting the liner of the tail shaft or scraping the 'tween decks ...

7 COMBINED TRANSPORT

Mayhew Foods Ltd v Overseas Containers Ltd [1984] 1 Lloyd's Rep 317

Bingham J: This is a claim by Mayhew Foods Ltd (Mayhew) as shippers against Overseas Containers Ltd (OCL) as carriers. It arises out of the carriage of a cargo of food which was found on arrival at its destination to be unfit to eat. OCL accept that the food became unfit and that they are liable for its deterioration, but seek to limit the damages recoverable against them in reliance on the terms of a standard clause in their bill of lading. Mayhew claim that the relevant carriage was subject to the Carriage of Goods by Sea Act 1971, and the Hague-Visby Rules scheduled thereto and that, accordingly, the contractual limitation of damage clause is of no effect. Whether OCL are entitled to limit their damages in reliance on the contract or whether the contract is superseded by the statutory provisions is the major issue I have to determine.

On about 27 November 1981, Mayhew and OCL made an oral contract for the carriage by OCL of a refrigerated container of Mayhew's products from Mayhew's premises at Uckfield in Sussex to Jeddah in Saudi Arabia. The products in question consisted of 1,100 cartons (weighing 8,685 kilogrammes) of chicken and turkey portions, some cooked, some uncooked, and a few breaded drumsticks which were coated but uncooked. In order that these products should remain in good condition, it was necessary that they should be deep frozen at minus 18 degrees C. It was envisaged that the goods would be carried in a refrigerated container on the vessel *Benalder*. The cartons were collected from Mayhew's premises at Uckfield and stuffed into a refrigerated container on 3 December. They were then, it seems, taken to Shoreham and were, on 5 December, carried from Shoreham to Le Havre on a vessel named *Voline*, arriving in Le Havre very early on the 6th. The container was discharged and remained in Le Havre until it was loaded on *Benalder* on 11 or 12 December. *Benalder* arrived in Jeddah on 21 December, but permission to discharge this container was refused because the contents had decayed and offensive juices were reported to be dripping from it. The reason for this was that the temperature control on the container, instead of being set at minus 18 degrees C, as it should have been, had been set at plus 2 degrees C to plus 4 degrees C. Far from being deep frozen, the goods had been subject to some heating while in the container. OCL accept that, as a result of this failure properly to refrigerate the goods in the container, they were in breach of their contract and of their duty as bailees and at law in failing to take reasonable care of the goods and to carry, keep and care for the same properly and carefully.

When the state of the cargo was discovered and discharge at Jeddah refused, the contents of the container were deep frozen to the required temperature and the container remained aboard the vessel as it continued its journey to the Far East. A cursory inspection of the contents was made in Malaya, but no detailed survey was made until the container was returned to Mayhew on 25 February 1982. The food was then found to be unfit for human consumption and was sold at 2 p per pound for animal food.

OCL's bill of lading showed Mayhew as the shipper. The consignee was to order. The notify party was United Foods Ltd, Jeddah. The place of receipt of the goods was shown as Mayhew's Uckfield premises; the place of delivery as a numbered berth in Jeddah. The intended vessel and voyage number were shown as '*Benalder* 0418'. The 'intended port of loading' was Southampton; the 'intended port of discharge' Jeddah. The place and date of issue were entered as 'London 08 12 81'. The bill bore a signature on behalf of OCL and a stamp which read:

> Shipped on board per ocean vessel *Benalder* on 12 December 1981 for Overseas Containers Ltd ...

followed by a further signature.

The conditions on the reverse of the bill differed in their application depending on whether combined transport shipment or port to port shipment was being undertaken. It is common ground that this was combined transport shipment and I need not refer to the other conditions, save to note that a different scheme applied. Clause 6 provided:

> Carrier's Responsibility – Combined Transport 1/ The Carrier shall be liable for loss or damage to the Goods occurring between the time when he receives the Goods for transportation and the time of delivery.

There follow exceptions irrelevant for present purposes. Clause 7 specified how any compensation recoverable should be calculated and specified an upper limit of:

> ... US $2 per kilo of gross weight of the Goods lost or damaged.

It is this provision, entitling Mayhew to US $17,370, on which OCL rely to limit Mayhew's damages. Clause 8 was a long and involved condition, the effect of which, for present purposes, was to make cl 7 subject to the Hague Rules or any national law or international convention having mandatory effect in respect of the relevant damage. Clause 21, so far as relevant, provided:

> Methods and Routes of Transportation 1/ The Carrier may at any time and without notice to the merchant: -a/ use any means of transport or storage whatsoever, b/ transfer the Goods from one conveyance to another including transhipping or carrying the same on another vessel than the vessel named overleaf or on any other means of transport whatsoever ...

d/ load and unload the Goods at any place or port (whether or not any such port is named overleaf as the Port of Loading or Port of Discharge) and store the Goods at any such place or port. 2/ The liberties set out in sub-clause 1/ may be invoked by the Carrier for any purpose whatsoever ... and anything done in accordance with sub-clause 1 or any delay arising therefrom shall be deemed to be within the contractual carriage and shall not be a deviation.

In seeking to limit the damages recoverable against OCL to the measure prescribed by cl 7 of the bill, Mr Flaux on their behalf submitted: (1) that the 1971 Act and the Hague-Visby Rules did not apply to this carriage until the goods were shipped aboard *Benalder* at Le Havre on 11 or 12 December 1981: (2) that even if the Act and the rules did apply during the period of carriage by sea from Shoreham to Le Havre, they did not apply when the goods were lying ashore at Le Havre before shipment aboard *Benalder*: (3) that during any period when the Act and the rules did not apply, OCL were entitled to limit their damage in accordance with cl 7 of the bill of lading: (4) that by the time the goods were loaded aboard *Benalder* at Le Havre on 11 or 12 December, from which time the 1971 Act and the Hague-Visby Rules admittedly did apply, the goods had already deteriorated to such an extent that Mayhew thereafter suffered no loss and damage as a consequence of OCL's failure to refrigerate.

The first of these submissions rested on the contention that the bill of lading related to shipment on *Benalder* as shown by the reference to the intended vessel and to the stamp. That shipment occurred at Le Havre. No bill of lading was issued in respect of the sea leg from Shoreham to Le Havre and this bill did not cover it. Mayhew could not rely on the Act and the rules before loading aboard the vessel nominated in the bill to undertake the sea carriage.

I cannot accept this submission. As Devlin J pointed out in *Pyrene Co Ltd v Scindia Navigation Co Ltd* [1954] 2 QB 402, at pp 329 and 415, the rights and liabilities under the rules attach to a contract or part of a contract. The contract here was for carriage of these goods from Uckfield to the numbered berth at Jeddah. The rules did not apply to inland transport prior to shipment on board a vessel, because under s 1(3) of the 1971 Act, they are to have the force of law only in relation to and in connection with the carriage of goods by sea in ships. But the contract here clearly provided for shipment at a United Kingdom port, intended to be Southampton but in the event Shoreham, and from the time of that shipment, the Act and the rules plainly applied. It does not matter that the vessel on which the container left this country was not *Benalder*, because OCL had liberty to substitute vessels or tranship and *Benalder* was only the intended vessel. Nor does it matter that the bill of lading was issued some days after the goods had arrived in Le Havre showing *Benalder* and Southampton as the intended vessel and port of shipment. The parties clearly expected and intended a bill of lading to be issued and when issued it duly evidenced the parties' earlier contract. Since this bill was issued in a contracting state and provided for carriage from a port in a contracting state, I think it plain that the rules applied once the goods were loaded on board the vessel at Shoreham.

OCL's second submission took as its starting point fact already noted that the Act and the rules only apply:

... in relation to and in connection with the carriage of goods by sea in ships ...

It was accordingly argued that even if the statutory provisions governed carriage from Shoreham to Le Havre, they did not apply while the goods were lying ashore at Le Havre any more than they applied before the goods were loaded at Shoreham or after they were discharged at Jeddah. In short, it was said that the interval of storage at Le Havre was not carriage by sea and so not covered by the rules ... The answer to this problem is again to be found in the principle that the rights and liabilities under the rules attach to a contract. They do not apply to carriage or storage before the port of shipment or after the port of discharge, because that would be inland and not sea carriage. But between those ports the contract was, despite the wide language of cl 21, for carriage by sea. If, during that carriage, OCL chose to avail themselves of their contractual right to discharge, store and tranship, those were, in my judgment, operations 'in relation to and in connection with the carriage of goods by sea in ships', to use the language of the Act, or were 'within the contractual carriage', to use the language of cl 21(2) of the bill of lading conditions. It would, I think, be surprising if OCL could, by carrying the goods to Le Havre and there storing the goods before transhipment, rid themselves of liabilities to which they would have been subject had they, as contemplated, shipped the goods at Southampton and carried them direct to Jeddah, the more so since Mayhew had no knowledge of any voyage to Le Havre. My conclusion is that the rules, having applied on shipment at Shoreham, remained continuously in force until discharge at Jeddah.

I accept Mr Flaux's third submission, on the construction of the contract if the rules did not apply, but since I conclude that they did apply this does not help him.

If my foregoing conclusions are right, it does not matter whether the damage to the cargo occurred before or after the container was loaded on board *Benalder*, provided only that it occurred only after shipment at Shoreham, as it must have done since, on any showing, the goods needed some time to thaw out and deteriorate. This issue was, however, much debated and expert evidence was called on both sides, so I shall briefly indicate my findings in case I am wrong so far.

I conclude that if the state of the cargo had been discovered at the time when the container was loaded on board *Benalder* on 11 or 12 December, it would, in all probability, have been too late to salve the uncooked products but that the cooked products and breaded drumsticks could at that stage have been frozen and sold at their invoice price ...

8 CHOICE OF FORUM

The Hollandia [1983] 1 AC 565

The respondents shipped machinery on the appellants' vessel *Haico Holwerda* at Leith for carriage to Bonaire in the Netherlands Antilles. A through bill of lading, providing for transhipment at Amsterdam, was issued. The cargo was damaged during the course of discharge at Bonaire as a result of the negligence of the servants of the carrying vessel which for the ocean leg of the voyage was a ship under the Norwegian flag, the *Morviken*, of which the carriers were charterers. The shippers commenced an action *in rem* in the High Court against the *Hollandia*, a sister ship of the *Haico Holwerda*. The carriers sought to stay proceedings on the grounds that the bill of lading included a choice of forum clause which provided for the exclusive jurisdiction of the Court of Amsterdam. The bill of lading also provided that the proper law of the contract should be the law of the Netherlands and stated 'The maximum liability per package is DFL 1,250 (paragraph 1, condition 2). It was common ground that if the dispute was tried by a Dutch court, that court would apply Dutch law and the Hague Rules limit of liability which would limit recovery to £250, but that if an English court tried it, the Hague-Visby limit would be £11,000.

> Lord Keith of Kinkel, Lord Roskill, Lord Brandon and Lord Brightman agreed with **Lord Diplock**: My Lords, the provisions in section 1 of the Act ... appear to me to be free from any ambiguity perceptible to even the most ingenious of legal minds. The Hague-Visby Rules, or rather all those of them that are included in the Schedule, are to have the force of law in the United Kingdom: they are to be treated as if they were part of directly enacted statute law. But since they form part of an international convention which must come under the consideration of foreign as well as English courts, it is, as Lord Macmillan said of the Hague Rules themselves in *Stag Line Ltd v Foscolo, Mango and Co Ltd* [1932] AC 328, 350:
>
>> desirable in the interests of uniformity that their interpretation should not be rigidly controlled by domestic precedents of antecedent date, but rather that the language of the rules should be construed on broad principles of general acceptation.
>
> They should be given a purposive rather than a narrow literalistic construction, particularly wherever the adoption of a literalistic construction would enable the stated purpose of the international convention, *viz*, the unification of domestic laws of the contracting states relating to bills of lading, to be evaded by the use of colourable devices that, not being expressly referred to in the Rules, are not specifically prohibited.
>
> The bill of lading issued to the shippers by the carriers upon the shipment of the goods at the Scottish port of Leith was one to which the Hague-Visby Rules were expressly made applicable by Article X; it fell within both paragraph (a) and paragraph (b); it was issued in a contracting state, the United Kingdom, and it covered a contract for carriage from a port in a contracting state. For good measure, it also fell directly within s 1(3) of the Act of 1971 itself.
>
> The first paragraph of condition 2 of the bill of lading, prescribing as it does for a per package maximum limit of liability on the part of the carriers for loss or damage arising from negligence or breach of contract instead of the higher per kilogram maximum applicable under the Hague-Visby Rules, is *ex facie* a clause in a contract of carriage which purports to lessen the liability of the carriers for such loss or damage otherwise than is provided in the

Hague-Visby Rules. As such it is therefore rendered null and void and of no effect under Article III, paragraph 8. So much indeed was conceded by counsel for the carriers, subject to a possible argument to the contrary which was briefly mentioned but not elaborated upon. I shall have to revert to this argument later, but can do so with equal brevity ...

[The carriers argued for a stay on the grounds that a choice of forum clause] is to be classified as a clause which only prescribes the procedure by which disputes arising under the contract of carriage are to be resolved. It does not *ex facie* deal with liability at all and so does not fall within the description 'Any clause, covenant, or agreement in a contract of carriage ... lessening ... liability', so as to bring it within Article III, paragraph 8; even though the consequence of giving effect to the clause will be to lessen, otherwise than is provided in the Hague-Visby Rules, the liability of the carrier for loss or damage to or in connection with the goods arising from negligence, fault or failure in the duties and obligations provided in the Rules.

My Lords, like all three members of the Court of Appeal, I have no hesitation in rejecting this narrow construction of Article III, paragraph 8, which looks solely to the form of the clause in the contract of carriage and wholly ignores its substance. The only sensible meaning to be given to the description of provisions in contracts of carriage which are rendered 'null and void and of no effect' by this rule is one which would embrace every provision in a contract of carriage which, if it were applied, would have the effect of lessening the carrier's liability otherwise than as provided in the Rules. To ascribe to it the narrow meaning for which counsel contended would leave it open to any shipowner to evade the provisions of Article III, paragraph 8 by the simple device of inserting in his bills of lading issued in, or for carriage from a port in, any contracting state a clause in standard form providing as the exclusive forum for resolution of disputes what might aptly be described as a court of convenience, *viz*, one situated in a country which did not apply the Hague-Visby Rules or, for that matter, a country whose law recognised an unfettered right in a shipowner by the terms of the bill of lading to relieve himself from all liability for loss or damage to the goods caused by his own negligence, fault or breach of contract.

My Lords, unlike the first paragraph of condition 2 a choice of forum clause, such as that appearing in the third paragraph, does not *ex facie* offend against Article III, paragraph 8. It is a provision of the contract of carriage that is subject to a condition subsequent; it comes into operation only upon the occurrence of a future event that may or may not occur, *viz*, the coming into existence of a dispute between the parties as to their respective legal rights and duties under the contract which they are unable to settle by agreement. There may be some disputes that would bring the choice of forum clause into operation but which would not be concerned at all with negligence fault or failure by the carrier or the ship in the duties and obligations provided by article III; a claim for unpaid freight is an obvious example. So a choice of forum clause which selects as the exclusive forum for the resolution of disputes a court which will not apply the Hague-Visby Rules, even after such clause has come into operation, does not necessarily always have the effect of lessening the liability of the carrier in a way that attracts the application of Article III, paragraph 8.

My Lords, it is, in my view, most consistent with the achievement of the purpose of the Act of 1971 that the time at which to ascertain whether a choice of forum clause will have an effect that is proscribed by Article III, paragraph 8 should be when the condition subsequent is fulfilled and the carrier seeks to bring the clause into operation and to rely upon it. If the dispute is about duties and obligations of the carrier or ship that are referred to in that rule and it is established as a fact (either by evidence or as in the instant case by the common agreement of the parties) that the foreign court chosen as the exclusive forum would apply a domestic substantive law which would result in limiting the carrier's liability to a sum lower than that to which he would be entitled if Article IV, paragraph 5 of the Hague-Visby Rules applied, then an English court is in my view commanded by the Act of 1971 to treat the choice of forum clause as of no effect.

The rule itself speaks of a proscribed provision in a contract of carriage as a 'clause, covenant, or agreement in a contract of carriage' and describes the effect of the rule on the offending provision as being to render it 'null and void and of no effect'. These pleonastic expressions occurring in an international convention (of which the similarly pleonastic version in the French language is of equal authenticity) are not to be construed as technical terms of legal art. It may well be that if they were to be so construed the most apt to be applied to a choice of forum clause when brought into operation by the occurrence of a particular dispute would be the expression 'of no effect', but it is no misuse of ordinary language to describe the clause in its application to the particular dispute as being pro tanto 'null' or 'void' or both ...

As foreshadowed at an earlier point in this speech I must return in a brief postscript to an argument based on certain passages in an article by a distinguished commentator, Dr F A Mann, 'Statutes and the Conflict of Laws' which appeared in (1972–73) 46 BYIL 117, and which, it is suggested, supports the view that even a choice of substantive law, which excludes the application of the Hague-Visby Rules, is not prohibited by the Act of 1971 notwithstanding that the bill of lading is issued in and is for carriage from a port in, the United Kingdom. The passages to which our attention was directed by counsel for the carriers I find myself (apparently in respectable academic company) unable to accept. They draw no distinction between the Act of 1924 and the Act of 1971 despite the contrast between the legislative techniques adopted in the two Acts, and the express inclusion in the Hague-Visby Rules of Article X (absent from the Hague Rules), expressly applying the Hague-Visby Rules to every bill of lading falling within the description contained in the article, which article is given the force of law in the United Kingdom by section 1(2) of the Act of 1971. The Act of 1971 deliberately abandoned what may conveniently be termed the 'clause paramount' technique employed in section 3 of the Act of 1924, the Newfoundland counterpart of which provided the occasion for wide-ranging *dicta* in the opinion of the Privy Council delivered by Lord Wright in *Vita Food Products Inc v Unus Shipping Co Ltd* [1939] AC 277. Although the actual decision in that case would have been the same if the relevant Newfoundland statute had been in the terms of the Act of 1971, those dicta have no application to the construction of the latter Act and this has rendered it no longer necessary to embark upon what I have always found to be an unrewarding task of trying to ascertain precisely what those *dicta* meant. I would dismiss this appeal.

Notes

1   *Construction.*

'I take it to be axiomatic that a statute enacted to give legal force to a private law convention should be construed in its international context, unconstrained by technical rules of English law, or by English precedent but on broad principles of general acceptation; further that it should be construed so as to give effect to the purposes which the convention was designed to achieve.' Judge Diamond QC, *The Leni* [1992] 2 Lloyd's Rep 48.

2   *Carrier.* In *The Khian Zephyr* [1982] 1 Lloyd's Rep 73 Robert Goff J said:

I approach the matter as follows. First of all it seems to me, looking at the Hague Rules, that the function of art I(a), in providing that the word 'carrier' includes the owner or charterer who enters into a contract of carriage with a shipper, is to legislate for the fact that you may get a case – for example, under bills of lading – where the bills of lading are charterers' bills; and where there are charterers' bills, of course, the charterer is in a contractual relationship with the cargo owner and is responsible under the bills of lading to the cargo owners. In those circumstances the effect of the definition in Article I(a) is to ensure that provisions which apply to the carrier under the Hague Rules shall likewise apply not only to the shipowner in whose ship the goods are physically being carried and through whose servants and agents, the master and crew of the ship, he is physically in possession of the goods, but shall also apply to a charterer who has contracted as the other party to the bill of lading. That makes good sense, and provides a common sense explanation why the definition of 'carrier' should be so defined in Article I(a) as to include 'the owner or the charterer who enters into a contract of carriage with a shipper'. Of course, the words used in Article III, r 6, and elsewhere in the Hague Rules are not just 'the carrier' but 'the carrier and the ship'. But it has been suggested in Scrutton on Charterparties – I refer in particular to the commentary at p 432 – that references to 'the ship' in the context of the Hague Rules are to cover the situation where there may be a proceeding against the party not as carrier but by virtue of an action *in rem* against the ship as such ...

3   *Deck cargo.* In *Svenska Traktor Aktiebolaget v Maritime Agencies (Southampton) Ltd* [1953] 2 QB 295, Pilcher J said:

The policy of the Carriage of Goods by Sea Act 1924, was to regulate the relationship between the shipowner and the owner of goods along well known lines. In excluding from the definition of 'goods', the carriage of which was subject to the Act, cargo carried on deck and stated to be so carried, the intention of the Act was, in my view, to leave the shipowner free to carry deck cargo on his own conditions, and unaffected by the obligations imposed on him by the Act in any case in which he would, apart from the Act, have been entitled to carry such cargo on deck, provided that the cargo in question was in fact carried on deck and that the bill of lading covering it contained on its face a statement that the particular cargo was being so carried. Such a statement on the face of the hill of lading would serve as a notification and a warning to consignees and indorsees of the bill of lading to whom the property in the goods passed under the terms of s 1 of the Bill of Lading Act 1855, that the goods which they were to take were being shipped as deck cargo. They would thus have full knowledge of the facts when accepting the documents and would know that the carriage of the goods on deck was not subject to the Act. If, on the other hand, there was no specific agreement between the parties as to the carriage on deck, and no statement on the face of the bill of lading that goods carried on deck had in fact been so carried, the consignees or indorsees of the bill of lading would be entitled to assume that the goods were goods the carriage of which could only be performed by the shipowner subject to the obligations imposed on him by the Act. A mere general liberty to carry goods on deck is not in my view a statement in the contract of carriage that the goods are in fact being carried on deck. To hold otherwise would in my view do violence to the ordinary meaning of the words of Article I(c) ...

4   *Non-negotiable receipts*. The defendants operated a cross-channel Ro-Ro ferry between Dover and Calais and, in common with all other English operators in that trade, would not issue a bill of lading for goods loaded on board, but offered only non-negotiable receipts. While entering port during heavy weather, goods overturned and were damaged. The defendants claimed to be entitled to limit their liability under the conditions of carriage to a sum which was less than the amount stated in Article IV, r 5. It was held that the primary statutory application of the 1971 Act was excluded where the shipper was not entitled under the contract of carriage to demand a bill of lading at or after shipment:

> It follows that shipowners, if they are in a strong enough bargaining position, can escape the application of the rules by issuing a notice to shippers that no bills of lading will be issued by them in a particular trade. Subject to the limited restriction introduced by the Unfair Contract Terms Act 1977 in favour of carriage for consumers ... the position is that freedom of contract prevails ...

It was also held that the 1971 Act would only apply by force of law under s 1(6)(b) to a non-negotiable receipt if the contract expressly provided that the whole of the Hague-Visby rules were to govern the contract. Steyn J, *Browner International Ltd v Monarch Shipping Co Ltd, The European Enterprise* [1989] 2 Lloyd's Rep 185.

5   *Unseaworthiness: burden of proof*. In *Ministry of Food v Reardon-Smith Line* [1951] 2 Lloyd's Rep 265 McNair J said that the burden of proving that loss was caused by unseaworthiness lies on the cargo owner and that it is not until that burden has been discharged that any question of any burden of

proof on the carrier under Article IV, r 1 can arise. This decision was followed and applied in *The Hellenic Dolphin* [1978] 2 Lloyd's Rep 336, which was followed in *The Theodegmon* [1990] 1 Lloyd's Rep 52.

6   *Time bar: purpose.*

There were a number of objectives which Article III, r 6 sought to achieve; first, to speed up the settlement of claims and to provide carriers with some protection against stale and therefore unverifiable claims; second, to achieve international uniformity in relation to prescription periods; third, to prevent carriers from relying on 'notice-of-claim' provisions as an absolute bar to proceedings or from inserting clauses in their bills of lading requiring proceedings to be issued within short periods of less than one year.

Judge Diamond QC, *The Leni* [1992] 2 Lloyd's Rep 48.

For a fourth aim, the achievement of finality, see *The Captain Gregos* [1990] 1 Lloyd's Rep 310, CA, above.

7   *Time bar: terminus a quo.* Where goods are not loaded, time begins to run from the moment the goods ought to have been delivered, assuming the loading obligation had been fulfilled: *The Ot Sonja* [1993] 2 Lloyd's Rep 435, CA.

8   *Time bar: 'suit'.* The commencement of an arbitration is a 'suit' within the meaning of Article III, r 6: *The Merak* [1965] P 223, CA.

9   *Time bar: 'brought'.* This means brought by a competent plaintiff (*Compania Columbiana de Seguros v Pacific Steam Navigation Co* [1965] 1 QB 101) in a competent court (*The Nordglimpt* [1988] QB 183) and brought to enforce a relevant claim (*The Leni* [1992] 2 Lloyd's Rep 48).

10   *Time bar: effect.* In *The Aries* [1977] 1 Lloyd's Rep 334, the House of Lords held that the effect of Article III, rule 6 of the Hague Rules is to extinguish the claim, not merely to bar the remedy while leaving the claim against the carrier in existence. Nevertheless, the time bar does not prevent a carrier's negligence being relied on as a defence to a claim by the carrier to be indemnified under Article IV, r 6: *The Fiona* [1994] 2 Lloyd's Rep 506, CA, (above). And see *Goulandris v Goldman* [1958] 1 QB 74, Chapter 17.

11   *Relieving clauses: Article III, r 8.* The holders of bills of lading argued that a liberty clause – which permitted discharge at a substitute port, including the port of loading, in the event of a strike – was a clause which purported to relieve the carrier from loss arising from failure in the duty 'properly to carry ... and discharge the goods carried' (Article III, r 2) and so was rendered null and void by Article III, r 8. The House of Lords rejected this claim on the grounds:

(a) that Article III, r 2 did not require goods to be transported from one place to another if the contract said they need not be moved in a certain event;

(b) that the obligation to 'discharge properly' meant 'in accordance with a sound system' and not at a particular place (Viscount Kilmuir LC);

(c) that the clause did not purport to extend the power to deviate permitted by the Rules, but rather defined the contractual voyage to be performed in certain circumstances. *G H Renton & Co Ltd v Palmyra Trading Corporation of Panama* [1957] AC 149.

(For the facts and the decision of the House of Lords in this case on the construction of the liberty clause, see Chapter 4, 'Deviation'.)

12 *Article IV, r 2 (q): perils of the sea/any other cause.* The plaintiffs shipped tea on the *Chyebassa* for carriage from Calcutta to London, Hull and Amsterdam via Port Sudan. While the vessel was at Port Sudan it discharged other cargo and loaded cotton seed. The work was carried out by stevedores who were the agents of the shipowners. In the course of discharge or loading, one or more of the stevedores stole a brass cover plate from one of the ship's storm valves. As a result, when the vessel left port, water entered the hold and damaged the tea:

> ... The shipowners established that the theft was without their actual fault or privity and they have to establish also that it was without the fault or neglect of their agents or servants. *R F Brown & Co Ltd v T & J Harrison* (1927) 43 TLR 633 held that 'and' has to be substituted for 'or'. ... If a complete stranger had entered the hold unobserved and removed the plate, sub-clause (q) would, I think, apply if the shipowner could prove that it was a stranger who removed the cover and reasonable care had been taken to prevent strangers getting aboard the ship and due diligence generally had been exercised. In the present case the act of the thief ought, I think, to be regarded as the act of a stranger. (Sellers LJ, *Leesh River Tea v British India Steam Navigation* [1967] 2 QB 250, CA.)

13 *Excepted perils: burden of proof.* The burden of proof of an excepted peril under article IV, rule 2, falls on the carrier 'by virtue of the common law principle that he who seeks to rely upon an exception in his contract must bring himself within it'. Staughton LJ, *The Antigoni* [1991] 1 Lloyd's Rep 209, 212, CA.

14 *Excepted peril and concurrent cause: burden of proof.* 'Where the facts disclose that the loss was caused by the concurrent causative effects of an excepted and a non-excepted peril, the carrier remains liable. He only escapes liability to the extent he can prove that the loss or damage was caused by the excepted peril alone.' Hobhouse J, *The Torenia* [1983] 2 Lloyd's Rep 211.

15 *Dangerous goods: article IV, rule 6.* 'Goods of a dangerous nature' in rule 6 means goods which either actually cause physical damage or which pose a threat of physical damage to the ship or to the other cargo on board: *The Giannis NK* [1996] 1 Lloyd's Rep 577, 583.

16 *Dangerous goods: article IV, rules 3 and 6.* The shipment of dangerous goods is an 'act' of the shipper within r 3; r 3 does not import any requirement of

fault or negligence on the part of the shipper into r 6. The carrier's right to an indemnity under r 6 depends on proof of shipment by the defendant; it:

> does not involve any enquiry as to whether the shipper has knowledge of the dangerous nature and character of the goods or was at fault in permitting their shipment or in warning the carrier before shipment ... None of these matters are referred to in the rule as matters on which the carrier's right to an indemnity depends ... (Judge Diamond QC, *The Fiona* [1993] 1 Lloyd's Rep 257, 268, approved by the Court of Appeal in *The Giannis NK* [1996] 1 Lloyd's Rep 577, 582.)

17 *Dangerous goods and unseaworthiness.* An explosion occurred while the *Fiona* was preparing to discharge a cargo of fuel oil. The explosion was caused by the ignition of gasses derived partly (and unknown to the carrier) from the cargo and partly from the remains of a previous cargo which the owners had failed to wash from the ship's ducts and lines. Both the parties were therefore at fault. The shipowners claimed an indemnity under Article IV, r 6, from the shippers of the cargo. The claim failed. It was held that a carrier was not entitled to invoke the indemnity under Article IV, r 6 if he was in breach of his obligation under Article III, r 1 to exercise due diligence to make the vessel seaworthy and that was a total or partial cause of the loss. *Mediterranean Freight Services Ltd v BP Oil International Ltd, The Fiona* [1994] 2 Lloyd's Rep 506, CA.

18 *Deck cargo, deviation and the time bar.* In *Kenya Railways v Antares, The Antares* [1986] 2 Lloyd's Rep 626, 633; [1987] 1 Lloyd's Rep 424, machinery was shipped at Antwerp for carriage to Mombasa under two bills of lading which were subject to the Hague or Hague-Visby rules and which also contained arbitration clauses. On discharge at Mombasa it was found that part of the machinery had been loaded on deck and had been seriously damaged in the course of the voyage. The bills of lading were on the form of the Mediterranean Shipping Company (MSC) but each contained the following demise clause:

> 3(1) If the ship is not owned by or chartered by demise to the Company or Line by whom this Bill of Lading is issued (as may be the case notwithstanding anything that appears to the contrary) this Bill of Lading shall take effect only as a contract with the Owner or Demise Charterer as the case may be as Principal made through the Agency of said Company or Line who act as Agents only and shall be under no personal liability whatsoever in respect thereof.

MSC had chartered the vessel from the defendant owners. The plaintiffs made a claim against MSC by letter and informed MSC that they had appointed an arbitrator under the arbitration clause in the bills of lading. One year and two days after the final discharge of the cargo, MSC's solicitors informed the plaintiffs' solicitors that MSC were not the owners of the vessel. The plaintiffs then attempted to claim against the owners, who asserted that the claim was time barred. The plaintiffs sought a declaration that the owners were in fundamental breach of contract by stowing the goods on deck and that this precluded the owners from relying on the one year time bar in Article III, r 6 of the Hague-Visby rules.

Steyn J held that the question was one of construction of the Article III, r 6 and that the word 'whatsoever' in the rules made it clear that the time limit applied to cases of wrongful stowage of cargo on deck. His Lordship also said that it would be wrong to approach this question of construction by supposing that the Hague-Visby rules were intended to codify or reflect preexisting English law. He concluded that the rule made no distinction between fundamental and non-fundamental breach of contract or between breaches which do and breaches which do not amount to deviations: [1986] 2 Lloyd's Rep 633.

The Court of Appeal agreed that the time limit in Article III, r 6 applied to claims arising from unauthorised carriage on deck, although the question whether the time limit also applied to 'a deviation strictly so called' was not determined. In delivering the leading judgment, Lord Justice Lloyd (Glidewell and O'Connor LJJ concurring) noted that it was 'sometimes said that the so-called "deviation cases" may have survived the abolition (in *Suisse Atlantique*) of the doctrine of fundamental breach' and that the plaintiffs argued that improper loading on deck should be treated in the same way as a geographical deviation. After referring to *Photo Production v Securicor* (see Chapter 5, Deviation) His Lordship said that:

> Whatever may be the position with regard to deviation cases strictly so called, (I would myself favour the view that they should now be assimilated into the ordinary law of contract), I can see no reason for regarding the unauthorised loading of deck cargo as a special case.

The Court of Appeal also held: (a) that MSC were not the authorised agents of the defendants to accept service of the notice of arbitration on behalf of the defendants. The plaintiffs' appointment of an arbitrator could not be treated as commencement of arbitration against the defendants; (b) that since MSC were not the agents of the defendants, the defendants could not be estopped by MSC's silence from relying on the time bar; (c) that the plaintiffs' notice of arbitration could not be amended and treated as a notice of arbitration given to the defendants.

CHAPTER 10

THE VESSEL

Most charters are tied to a single specific vessel. After identifying the parties, charters frequently include a description of the ship, with details such as her name, class, capacity and location: statements such as these are normally terms of the contract. The shipowner must make available to the charterer the vessel on which the parties have agreed and which is the subject of the charter. Unless the parties agree that the shipowner shall have a right to provide a substitute, the charterer cannot be required to accept any other vessel. If a specific vessel is chartered but is lost without fault before the time for performance arrives, the contract will be frustrated: *The Super Servant Two* [1990] 1 Lloyd's Rep 9, CA. It is not unusual for a charterparty also to identify the vessel's builder, country of registration, tonnage and present activities. Forms designed for use in some trades go on to describe the vessel's technical specification in much greater detail.

1 IDENTITY OF SHIP

Reardon Smith Line Ltd v Hansen-Tangen, The Diana Prosperity [1976] 1 WLR 989

Lord Wilberforce: My Lords, these appeals arise out of a charterparty and a subcharterparty both relating to a medium-sized newbuilding tanker to be constructed in Japan. By the time the tanker was ready for delivery the market had collapsed, owing to the oil crisis of 1974, so that the charterers' interest was to escape from their contracts by rejecting the vessel. The ground on which they hoped to do so was that the vessel tendered did not correspond with the contractual description. Both charterparties were on the well known form Shelltime 3. The result of the appeal depends primarily on the view taken of the sub-charterparty between the appellants in the first appeal (Reardon Smith) and the respondents in that appeal (Hansen-Tangen) ...

... the whole case, as regards the first appeal, turns, in my opinion, on the long italicised passage in the subcharter set out above which, for convenience of reference I repeat:

> the good Japanese flag (subject to Clause 41) Newbuilding motor tank vessel called Yard No 354 at Osaka Zosen.

I shall refer to this as the 'box' since it appears enclosed in a typed box on the document.

The contract is in the English language and (cl 40) is to be construed in accordance with English law. But it has been sought to introduce, as an aid to construction, a considerable amount of evidence as to Japanese usages and practice, some of which was in fact taken into account by the Court of Appeal. To decide how far this is legitimate one must make a distinction. When it comes to ascertaining whether particular words apply to a factual situation or, if one prefers, whether a factual situation comes within particular words, it is undoubtedly proper, and necessary, to take evidence as to the factual situation. Thus once one has decided what is meant by 'Yard No 354' or 'to be built at a Yard', it is proper by evidence to establish the characteristics of particular yards, the numbering used at those yards and the 'building' which may have been done, in order to answer, yes or no, the question whether the contractual requirements have been met. There is no difficulty, in law, about this part of the case.

It is less easy to define what evidence may be used in order to enable a term to be construed. To argue that practices adopted in the shipbuilding industry in Japan, for example as to subcontracting, are relevant in the interpretation of a charterparty contract between two foreign shipping companies, whether or not these practices are known to the parties, is in my opinion to exceed what is permissible. But it does not follow that, renouncing this evidence, one must be confined within the four corners of the document. No contracts are made in a vacuum: there is always a setting in which they have to be placed. The nature of what is legitimate to have regard to is usually described as 'the surrounding circumstances' but this phrase is imprecise: it can be illustrated but hardly defined. In a commercial contract it is certainly right that the court should know the commercial purpose of the contract and this in turn presupposes knowledge of the genesis of the transaction, the background, the context, the market in which the parties are operating ...

It is often said that, in order to be admissible in aid of construction, these extrinsic facts must be within the knowledge of both parties to the contract, but this requirement should not be stated in too narrow a sense. When one speaks of the intention of the parties to the contract, one is speaking objectively – the parties cannot themselves give direct evidence of what their intention was – and what must be ascertained is what is to be taken as the intention which reasonable people would have had if placed in the situation of the parties. Similarly, when one is speaking of aim, or object, or commercial purpose, one is speaking objectively of what reasonable persons would have in mind in the situation of the parties ...

... what the court must do must be to place itself in thought in the same factual matrix as that in which the parties were ... [I]n the search for the relevant background, there may be facts, which form part of the circumstances in which the parties contract, in which one or both may take no particular interest, their minds being addressed to or concentrated on other facts, so that if asked they would assert that they did not have these facts in the forefront of their mind, but that will not prevent those facts from forming part of an objective setting in which the contract is to be construed. I shall show that this is so in the present case.

So I ask what was the commercial purpose of these charterparties and what was the factual background against which they were made? The purpose is clear: it was to make available (1) to Hansen-Tangen and (2) to Reardon Smith a medium-sized tanker suitable for use as such, this tanker not being in existence, or even under construction, at the date of either charter and, at the date of the intermediate charter, not even the subject of contracts made by the supplying company. The vessel was to be constructed in a Japanese yard and made available on charter to Sanko as part of a programme. At the date of the subcharter the vessel was identified in contracts for its construction in Japan and had a serial number. In order to ensure that the tanker was suitable for its purpose, a detailed specification was drawn up, by way of a warranted description with which, of course, the vessel must strictly comply.

In addition, since at the time of either charterparty the vessel was not in existence or under construction, some means had to be agreed on for identifying the particular vessel – one out of a programme – which would form the subject matter of the charters. This was indispensable so as to enable those committing themselves to hire the vessel, to subhire it, if they wished, and if necessary to arrange finance. This necessary identification was to be effected by nomination, by Sanko in the first place and then by Hansen-Tangen.

The text of the charterparties confirms beyond doubt that this was what was intended and done. The preamble, in the Shelltime 3 form, provides for the insertion of a name -'being owners of the good ... tank vessel called ... [the box insertion in the subcharter was made in this place] -Yard No 354 at Osaka Zosen'. The intermediate charter, entered into before Sanko had nominated any vessel, provided in its preamble – instead of 'called ...' – for a declaration by the owners together with the hull number, and the addendum, entered into after Sanko had nominated, provided 'to be built by Osaka Shipbuilding Co Ltd and known as Hull No 354, until named'. What is vital about each of these insertions is that they were simple substitutes for a name, serving no purpose but to provide a means whereby the charterers could identify the ship. At the dates when these insertions were made no importance could have been attached to the matters now said to be so significant; they were not a matter of negotiation, but of unilateral declaration. What is now sought is to elevate them into strict contractual terms in the nature of conditions.

The appellants sought, necessarily, to give to the 'box' and the corresponding provision in the intermediate charter contractual effect. They argued that these words formed part of the 'description' of the future goods contracted to be provided, that, by analogy with contracts for the sale of goods, any departure from the description entitled the other party to reject, that there were departures in that the vessel was not built by Osaka and was not Hull No 354. I shall attempt to deal with each of these contentions.

In the first place, I am not prepared to accept that authorities as to 'description' in sale of goods cases are to be extended, or applied, to such a contract as we have here ... The general law of contract has developed along much more rational lines (eg *Hong Kong Fir Shipping Co Ltd v Kawasaki Kisen Kaisha Ltd* [1962] 2 QB 26), in attending to the nature and gravity of a breach or departure rather than in accepting rigid categories which do or do not automatically give a right to rescind, and if the choice were between extending cases under the Sale of Goods Act 1893 into other fields, or allowing more modern doctrine to infect those cases, my preference would be clear. The importance of this line of argument is that Mocatta J and Lord Denning MR used it in the present case so as to reject the appellants' argument on 'description' and I agree with them.

But in case it does not appeal to this House, I am also satisfied that the appellants fail to bring the present case within the strictest rules as to 'description'.

In my opinion, the fatal defect in their argument consists in their use of the words 'identity' or 'identification' to bridge two meanings. It is one thing to say of given words that their purpose is to state (identify) an essential part of the description of the goods. It is another to say that they provide one party with a specific indication (identification) of the goods so that he can find them and if he wishes subdispose of them. The appellants wish to say of words which 'identify' the goods in the second sense, that they describe them in the first. I have already given reasons why I can only read the words in the second sense.

The difference is vital. If the words are read in the first sense, then, unless I am right in the legal argument above, each element in them has to be given contractual force. The vessel must, as a matter of contract, and as an essential term, be built by Osaka and must bear their yard number 354; if not, the description is not complied with and the vessel tendered is not that contracted for. If in the second sense, the only question is whether the words provide a means of identifying the vessel. If they fairly do this, they have fulfilled their function. It follows that if the second sense is correct, the words used can be construed much more liberally than they would have to be construed if they were providing essential elements of the description.

The two significant elements (whether in the 'box', or in the intermediate charter) are (i) the yard number 354, (ii) the expression 'built by Osaka Shipbuilding Co Ltd'. (These words do not appear in the 'box' but I will assume, very much in the appellants' favour, that the 'box' has the same meaning as if the word 'built' were used.) The appellants at one time placed great stress on the yard number provision. They contended that by using it the 'owners' assumed an obligation that the vessel should bear a number which would indicate that it would be constructed in the yard, where that number was appropriate, in sequence after vessels bearing earlier yard numbers (350–53). But this argument broke down in face of the fact, certainly known to Sanko which used and introduced the number into the charterparties, that the sequence through 354 was the sequence used at Osaka's yard at Osaka, which yard could not construct the vessel. Thus the use of the yard number for the contracted vessel must have had some other purpose than indicating construction at a particular yard. This turns the argument against the appellants for it shows the words to be 'labelling' words rather than words creating an obligation.

So the question becomes simply whether, as a matter of fact, it can fairly be said that – as a means of identification – the vessel was 'Yard No 354 at Osaka Zosen' or 'built by Osaka Shipping Co Ltd and known as Hull No 354, until named'. To answer this, regard may be had to the actual arrangements for building the vessel and numbering it before named. My Lords, I have no doubt, for the reasons given by the Court of Appeal, that an affirmative answer must be given. I shall not set out the evidence which clearly makes this good. The fact is that the vessel always was Osaka Hull No 354 – though also Oshima No 004 – and equally it can fairly be said to have been 'built' by Osaka as the company which planned, organised and directed the building and contractually engaged with Sculptor to build it, though also it could be said to have been built by Oshima. For the purpose of the identificatory clause, the words used are quite sufficient to cover the facts. No other vessel could be referred to: the reference fits the vessel in question.

There are other facts not to be overlooked. (1) So long as the charterers could identify the nominated vessel they had not the slightest interest in whatever contracting or subcontracting arrangements were made in the course of the building, a fact which no doubt explains the looseness of the language used in the 'box'. (2) In making the arrangements they did for building the vessel, Osaka acted in a perfectly straightforward and open manner. They cannot be said to be substituting one vessel for another; they have not provided any ground on which the charterers can claim that their bargain has not been fulfilled. The contracts all down the chain were closely and appropriately knitted into what Osaka did. (3) If the market had risen instead of falling, it would have been quite impossible for Osaka or Sculptor, or Sanko, to refuse to tender the vessel in accordance with the charters on the ground that it did not correspond with that contracted for. No more on a falling market is there, in my opinion, any ground on which the charterers can reject the vessel. In the end I find this a simple and clear case ...

2 FLAG

M Isaacs and Sons Limited v William McAllum and Company Limited [1921] 3 KB 377

Rowlatt J: The plaintiffs contend that the defendants committed a breach of the charterparty by selling the steamship during the currency of the charterparty. I do not think that the mere fact that the defendants sold the ship during the currency of the charterparty amounted to a breach of the charterparty, especially as the contract of sale contained a clause reserving to the defendants the right to perform personally the obligations of the charterparty.

The plaintiffs, however, say further, that the defendants have committed a breach of the charterparty by selling the steamship during the charterparty to a foreign subject, and so causing a change in her flag. It is not here necessary to inquire whether that action of the defendants would have entitled the plaintiffs to avoid the charterparty. The plaintiffs did not seek to avoid the charterparty. They kept the steamship and continued to avail themselves of her services during the period of the charterparty which has now expired. The charterparty has been performed in the sense that during its currency the steamship has made the various voyages required by the plaintiffs in accordance with the charterparty.

The complaint of the plaintiffs is that there has been a breach of the charterparty, because the services which have been rendered to them by the steamship have been rendered by a ship not of the British flag but of the Greek flag, and that they have thereby suffered damage.

The case has naturally given rise to some discussion as to the terms which are to be implied in a contract of this kind. It is clear that the fact that in this charterparty the steamship was described by an English name, the *City of Hamburg*, did not imply any warranty that it was, or would continue to be, a British ship: see *Clapham v Cologan* 3 Camp 382, and no claim could be made by the plaintiffs on that ground.

It is said, however, by counsel for the plaintiffs, and it seems to me that they are right in saying so, that where persons enter into a contract for services to be rendered by one of them to the other by means of a specific chattel, there is an implied term in the contract by which the person supplying the chattel undertakes that it shall not be altered so as materially to prejudice the services which are to be rendered by it; and that if it is so altered there is a breach of that term. If a person enters into a contract for the use of a specific thing he does not get what he contracts for if the thing is so altered as to render him services substantially less valuable than, or different from, those contracted for ...

I therefore think that the question here is whether the defendants by selling the steamship to a Greek subject and so causing her flag to be changed from the British to the Greek flag made such an alteration in her as has materially affected the services which she was to render to the plaintiff under the charterparty. The plaintiffs contend that the defendants by so doing gave them the services of a ship different from and less valuable than that for which they had contracted; and the defendants deny this. Many changes can, no doubt, be made in a chartered ship which do not materially affect her position under the charterparty – such, for example, as altering her colour, or her masts. I have here to consider whether a change in the ship's flag is such a change as materially to affect the ship as the subject matter of the charterparty. I think I must deal with the question generally and without drawing any distinction between different nationalities. I do not think that I can treat the question of a change of flag from the British to the French flag, for example, as distinct for this purpose from a change from the British to the Chinese flag or to the flag of some undeveloped power. That distinction is relevant to the question of damages, but not to the question of breach. I have to face the plain question whether a change in the flag of the chartered ship is a breach of the charterparty as being a material change in the nature of the subject matter. It seems to me that it is. I do not think it could possibly be held that it makes no difference under what flag a ship sails. The law of the flag is of direct importance as affecting the status of the ship. It is also of importance in its collateral effects, as, for instance, in determining the nationality and therefore to some extent the discipline and morals of the crew and in many other respects. It seems to me that in any particular case of this kind there can be no question that the change of flag is a breach of the charterparty, and that the only question is what damages, if any, have resulted from the change of flag. I must therefore hold that it was a breach of this charterparty to change the flag of the steamer during the charterparty.

As to damages, these must depend upon the circumstances of the particular case. I cannot conceive that the transfer of a ship from the flag of a civilised power to that of a wholly uncivilised power would not give rise to damages.

Greece, however, is a civilised power and a maritime nation of good standing, and I do not think that the damages in this case can possibly be heavy ...

3 CLASS

French v Newgass (1878) 3 CPD 163, CA

Brett LJ (Bramwell and Cotton LJJ delivered judgments to the same effect): ... The question is one solely of construction, and whatever hardship there may be, we have only to construe the written instrument, which in its terms is elliptical. The document states 'A 1 1/2 Record of American and Foreign Shipping Book'. Now, the ordinary meaning of that language is that it refers to the ship, and that she is, at the time of entering into the charterparty, registered as A 1 1/2. The document further speaks of the ship newly classed as above; that relates to what has been done in the book of the American and Foreign Shipping. I am of opinion that the words amount, not only to a warranty, but to a condition, as to the vessel's classification at the time the charterparty was made, and that they must be construed in their grammatical and natural sense; they cannot be added to. No doubt the meaning of words may be extended by custom, if consistent with the written instrument, but here the words are plain, and no addition can be made to them; construing them according to their grammatical meaning, it is a statement as to the actual registration of the vessel. The only argument that can be urged on behalf of the defendant is the argument which was urged in *Hurst v Usborne* (1856) 18 CBNS 144 unsuccessfully, that it is a continuing warranty, and therefore it must be taken to be a statement that the vessel would continue to be of the same class that she was at the time the charterparty was made. Mr Herschell proposes to add to the statement; he says that the words are to be construed, not merely that she is newly classed, but that she will continue to be of the same class as she was at the time the charterparty was made; but that construction would refer to the future, whereas the words of the charterparty only refer to the present. If the words suggested were added by implication, the shipowner, no doubt, would have failed to offer a proper ship, but that construction adds to the meaning, and if adopted, the shipowner would have warranted, not only the description of the vessel at the time of the charterparty, but he would have made himself liable for the acts of the authorities at New Orleans, over whom he had no control. It is quite clear that we ought to adhere to the words of the charterparty, and give to them their ordinary meaning. The charterparty contains, as a fact, a statement that the ship is A 1 1/2 Record of American and Foreign Shipping at the time the charterparty was made.

4 CARGO CAPACITY

Cargo capacity is normally of great importance to a charterer. If a chartered vessel cannot load all the cargo the charterer wishes to ship, he may be in breach of a contract to sell the goods, miss an intended market or incur extra warehouse or transport expenses on shore as well as the expenses of procuring substitute tonnage. A statement in a charterparty of a vessel's deadweight tonnage (the maximum weight the vessel can lift) or of cubic capacity will usually be treated as a term of the contract. Statements of capacity are often qualified by the word 'about'. Deadweight capacity is sometimes stated generally, although it is often more precisely defined as being measured in certain circumstances (eg on summer salt water) and as being inclusive or exclusive of bunkers, fresh water or stores. It is a question of construction whether a statement in a charterparty of deadweight capacity is to be read as referring to the vessel's abstract lifting capacity (this is the primary meaning) or her capacity to lift a particular type of cargo. For the connection between guaranteed capacity, the charterer's obligation to load a full and complete cargo and the payment of freight, see Chapter 11, 'Loading' and Chapter 12 'Freight'.

Mackill v Wright Brothers & Co Ltd (1888) 14 App Cas 106

Lord Macnaghten: My Lords, the question turns upon the true construction of a charterparty in some respects peculiar. It is a charter for the hire of a vessel for a lump sum from Glasgow to Kurrachee. It has a note in the margin as to the description of part of the proposed cargo, and it contains this guarantee, 'Owners guarantee that the vessel shall carry not less than 2,000 tons dead weight of cargo'. In effect, the charterers say to the owners, 'We want a vessel to carry to Kurrachee a general cargo, including parcels of machinery; we give you the dimensions and number of the largest pieces; will your vessel carry 2,000 tons dead weight?' The owners say 'It will'. That is, I think, something more than a mere guarantee of carrying capacity. It is a guarantee of the vessel's carrying capacity with reference to the contemplated voyage and the description of the cargo proposed to be shipped, so far as that description was made known to the owners ...

... it seems to me that the fair result of the evidence is, that in regard to the machinery which was tendered for shipment and shipped, the cargo was not such a cargo as was contemplated by the charterparty. It contained more large pieces; it was more bulky in comparison to its weight, and it was more awkward for stowage than the terms of the charterparty would naturally have led the owners to expect.

These being the material facts of the case, the clause in the charterparty on which the question turns remains to be considered. The charterparty has this provision: 'Should the vessel not carry the guaranteed dead weight, as above, any expense incurred from this cause to be borne by the owners, and a *pro rata* deduction per ton to be made from the first payment of freight'.

What is the meaning of this provision? What is the event contemplated? Is it the case of the vessel (1) not actually carrying 2,000 tons dead weight from any cause whatever; or (2) not carrying that weight from any cause not attributable to the charterers?

I think it would be unreasonable to read the provision as allowing abatement in the freight in every case of short weight. Such a construction would place the shipowners at the mercy of the charterers. They might fill the whole space at their disposal, and yet the cargo might be much under the contemplated weight, and so the shipowners would lose their full freight without any fault on their part.

I think that the provision was intended to have effect in the event of the vessel not carrying the specified weight, assuming the cargo tendered to be such a cargo as was contemplated by the charterparty, that is, an ordinary general cargo with a fair and reasonable proportion of machinery corresponding as to the largest pieces with the numbers, dimensions, and weights specified in the margin of the charterparty. In other words (to put it most favourably for the charterers), the provision was to come into effect in the event of the vessel not carrying 2,000 tons dead weight from any cause not attributable to the charterers.

I think that the loss of cargo space and the short weight of the cargo carried on the *Lauderdale* were attributable to the charterers. It was their doing ...

Neither the appellants nor the respondents were, I think, conspicuously reasonable. But the respondents were the more unreasonable of the two, and, what is more to the purpose, I think they took a wrong view of the construction of the charterparty, and of their own position. I therefore agree that the appeal ought to be allowed.

[Lord Halsbury LC and Lord Watson also delivered reasoned judgments.]

W Millar & Co Ltd v Owners of SS Freden [1918] 1 KB 611, CA

Swinfen Eady LJ: The charterparty is between the plaintiffs and the defendants for the ship to carry from Durban to a port in the United Kingdom a full and complete cargo of maize in bags. Then there is a rate of freight per ton according to the port of call at which she should be directed to discharge. There are different rates for different ports, but nothing turns upon that. Then comes the clause upon which the whole contest has turned:

> The owners guarantee the ship's deadweight capacity to be 3,200 tons and freight to be paid on this quantity.

So that in order to ascertain the amount to be paid for freight all that one has to do is to multiply the number of tons, 3,200, by the rate per ton according to the port of discharge ultimately selected. It was therefore a contract for a lump sum freight and not for freight so much per ton delivery on arrival. There is no dispute that the vessel was of a deadweight capacity of 3,200 tons – in other words, that she would take on board a cargo to that extent without sinking the ship below her proper loadline. With regard to the particular cargo of maize she was only able to take on board 3,081 tons 560 lbs, but that was not because her deadweight capacity was not as guaranteed, or had been in any way misrepresented. It was because the cubic capacity of the space on board was insufficient to allow of the stowage of more than 3,081 tons 560 lbs of maize in bags. On the one hand it is said on behalf of the appellants, reading the guarantee of the capacity of the ship in connection with the cargo, that the shipowners had notice of what the cargo was to be. It was maize in bags, and it is said that the guarantee must be read as if it meant 'We guarantee that the ship on this voyage will be of a capacity to take, and will be able to carry, 3,200 tons of maize in bags'. On the other hand the respondents say 'That is not the language which is used, and that is not what we meant. What we said was, and what we adhere to is, 'We guarantee that the ship shall be and is of a deadweight capacity of 3,200 tons, and so it is'.' The guarantee is a measure of the capacity of the ship, the general capacity irrespective of the particular cargo that she was to carry on this voyage.

... Reference was made to *Mackill v Wright* (1888) 14 App Cas 106 (above). The dispute there was whether the cargo that was actually shipped corresponded to that which was intended, having regard to the representations made at the time the contract was entered into. But it will be observed that the language of the contract there was very different from what we have to consider here. There it was 'the owners guarantee that the vessel shall carry not less than 2,000 tons dead weight of cargo'. Now that must have been a guarantee that the vessel should carry that amount on the voyage in question; and then there was a subsequent clause: 'and should the vessel not carry' – that is, should the vessel not carry on this particular voyage – 'the guaranteed dead weight as above, then any expense incurred from this cause to be borne by the owners and a *pro rata* reduction per ton to be made from the first payment of freight'. So that there was language there pointing to a guarantee with regard to the weight of cargo to be carried on that particular voyage, and not to the general carrying capacity of the ship. Here it is the opposite. The only guarantee is with reference to the general carrying capacity of the ship – a certain deadweight capacity.

In my opinion the appeal fails and should be dismissed.

[Bankes LJ and Eve J delivered judgments to the same effect.]

Notes

1   A charterparty provided that the ship should 'load a cargo of creosoted sleepers and timbers' and stated that 'charterer has option of shipping 100/200 tons of general cargo' and that 'owners guarantee ship to carry at least about 90,000 cubic feet or 1,500 tons of dead weight of cargo'.

The charterers tendered a cargo of the agreed type which did not exceed 90,000 cubic feet. But because the sleepers were of unequal lengths and many were half-round, the ship could load a cargo of only 64,400 cubic feet, 1,120 tons dead weight. The charterers sought damages. *Held*: the clause was not a guarantee that the ship would carry 90,000 cubic feet of the cargo specified in the charterparty. It was a guarantee of abstract capacity without reference to the particular cargo. *Carnegie v Conner* (1889) 14 QBD 45.

2   Owners guaranteed to place 5,600 tons deadweight cargo capacity and 300,000 cubic feet of bale space at charterer's disposal. The agreed lump sum freight was to be reduced *pro rata* if the deadweight or bale space were less than the guaranteed figures. Charterers claimed a *pro rata* reduction in respect of 32 tons of necessary dunnage used to stow their

cargo. *Held*: the guarantee was of the vessel's abstract lifting capacity, not capacity to lift that weight of the particular type of cargo shipped or of an average or reasonable cargo. *In re Thomson and Brocklebank* [1918] 1 KB 655.

3   Owners guaranteed dead weight as 7,100 tons and grain capacity as 8,450 tons, with a specific right to deduct from freight pro rata for errors. The stated grain capacity was available and was fully utilised by charterers, but deadweight capacity was in fact only 6,728 tons. *Held*: charterers were entitled to deduct *pro rata*. *SA Ungheresi Di Armamento Marittimo Oriente v Tyser Line* (1902) 8 Com Cas 25.

4   *'About'*. The *Resolven* was chartered to carry '2,000 tons or thereabouts'. *Held*: '... words of elasticity are elastic and their extensiveness runs with the subject matter they refer to. I think that in this instance five per cent may be taken as a fair margin.' Sir F Jeune P, *The Resolven* (1892) 9 TLR 75. In *Dreyfus v Parnaso, The Dominator* [1960] 1 Lloyd's Rep 117, Sellers LJ said he would 'regard 331 tons deficiency in a cargo of 10,400 tons, a deficiency of just over three per cent, as fulfilling the obligation to ship about 10,400 tons ... In the absence of any trade evidence on this matter, it is, in my opinion, within a reasonable commercial margin in respect of such cargo'. In *Cargo Ships 'El-Yam' Ltd v Invotra NV* [1958] 1 Lloyd's Rep 39, 52 Devlin J said that if he had to determine whether a margin of 1.2 per cent was within the phrase 'about 478,000 cubic feet bale capacity' it might have been a point requiring careful consideration, but the point did not in fact arise for decision.

5 TIME FOR PERFORMANCE

Modern charterparties provide for the time for start of performance by some means or other. One way is to agree a specific date on which the vessel is to sail or to be ready to receive cargo. But the uncertainties of maritime trade make prudent shipowners reluctant to fix a specific date unless the vessel is ready to begin at once. Another way is to state the present position of the vessel and to agree that the ship will sail for the loading port either forthwith or with reasonable dispatch. A little more precisely, some standard forms require a statement of present position and an estimate of the date the vessel is expected to be ready to load under the charter.

But if it is commercially unreasonable to expect shipowners to be able to promise performance on a specific date in every case, it is equally unrealistic to expect a charterer to be able to use a vessel whenever it manages to arrive. To avoid arguments about what is realistic or reasonable on the part of a charterer or whether delay by a shipowner has been sufficiently long to enable the charterer to throw up the charter and reject the vessel, it is common for charterparties to specify the earliest date on which the charterer is obliged to commence loading (the lay date) and the latest date on which he is obliged to accept the vessel (the cancellation date). These two dates are sometimes referred to as the lay/can spread. Modern forms in some trades go further and require notification of any changes in the date the vessel is expected ready to load and/or advance notice to be given at specified times before arrival.

Firm statements in charters that the vessel is in a certain port or sailed on a certain day or is to sail or be ready to receive cargo on or before a certain date have in the past usually be treated as conditions of the contract. Obligations to proceed with reasonable dispatch and estimates of time of arrival or readiness to load are also treated strictly by English law.

Fixed date obligations

Behn v Burness (1863) 3 B & S 751, Exchequer Chamber

The *Martaban*, described as being 'now in the port of Amsterdam', was chartered to proceed with all possible despatch direct to Newport and load a full cargo of coal for Hong Kong. At the time of the charter, the vessel was unavoidably detained by gales at Niewediep, 62 miles and 12 hours sailing time from Amsterdam. She reached Amsterdam four days later and finally sailed for Newport 28 days after the date of the charter.

> **Williams J** delivered the judgment of the court: ... The question on the present charterparty is confined to the statement of a definite fact – the place of the ship at the date of the contract. Now the place of the ship at the date of the contract, where the ship is in foreign parts and is chartered to come to England, may be the only datum on which the charterer can found his calculations of the time of the ship's arriving at the port of load. A statement is more or less important in proportion as the object of the contract more or less depends upon it. For most charters, considering winds, markets and dependent contracts, the time of a ship's arrival to load is an essential fact, for the interest of the charterer. In the ordinary course of charters in general it would be so: the evidence for the defendant shews it to be actually so in this case. Then, if the statement of the place of the ship is a substantive part of the contract, it seems to us that we ought to hold it to be a condition ... unless we can find in the contract itself or the surrounding circumstances reason for thinking that the parties did not so intend. If it was a condition and not performed, it follows that the obligation of the charterer dependent thereon, ceased at his option and considerations either of the damage to him or of proximity to performance on the part of the shipowner are irrelevant. So was the decision of *Glaholm v Hays* (2 M & G 257), where the stipulation in a charter of a ship to load at Trieste was that she should sail from England on or before the 4 February, and the non-performance of this condition released the charterer, notwithstanding the reasons alleged in order to justify the non-performance. So, in *Ollive v Booker* (1 Exch 416), the statement in the charter of a ship which was to load at Marseilles was that she was 'now at sea, having sailed three weeks ago', and it was held to be a condition for the reasons above stated ... We think these cases well decided, and that they govern the present case ...

Bentsen v Taylor [1893] 2 QB 274, CA

By a charterparty dated 29 March, the *Folkvang* was described as 'now sailed or about to sail from a pitch pine port to the UK'. She did not in fact sail from Mobile until 23 April.

Bowen LJ: ... The first question we have to consider is, What is the true effect and meaning of the words in the charterparty, 'now sailed or about to sail to the United Kingdom'?

... Of course it is often very difficult to decide as a matter of construction whether a representation which contains a promise, and which can only be explained on the ground that it is in itself a substantive part of the contract, amounts to a condition precedent, or is only a warranty. There is no way of deciding that question except by looking at the contract in the light of the surrounding circumstances, and then making up one's mind whether the intention of the parties, as gathered from the instrument itself, will best be carried out by treating the promise as a warranty sounding only in damages, or as a condition precedent by the failure to perform which the other party is relieved of his liability. In order to decide this question of construction, one of the first things you would look to is, to what extent the accuracy of the statement -the truth of what is promised – would be likely to affect the substance and foundation of the adventure which the contract is intended to carry out ...

It was by the application of that train of reasoning that the court in *Behn v Burness* (above) appears to have come to the conclusion, that if a ship, which at the date of a charterparty is in foreign parts, is chartered to come to England, a statement of the place where she is ought *prima facie* to be construed as a condition precedent ...

Now, if that is true as regards the place of a ship which is in foreign parts and is chartered to come to England, the same train of reasoning ought to apply to the time at which a ship is stated to have sailed, or to be about to sail, from the place at which she has been loading, unless the language be so vague as to lead anyone to suppose that it was not intended to be a condition precedent. I quite agree that the vagueness or ambiguity of the statement is one of the elements which would influence the court very much in deciding whether the parties intended that the statement should be a promise the fulfilment of which was to be a condition precedent.

That drives us to consider, what is the real meaning of these words. Is there anything in them so vague or so ambiguous that they cannot fairly be treated as a statement of a condition precedent? I agree that a condition precedent ought to be clearly expressed. The statement is, that the ship 'has now sailed or is about to sail'. Having regard to what we have heard of the history of the port of Mobile, I have not the slightest doubt that, if that statement does not mean that the ship has actually sailed, it does mean that she is loaded, or may at all events for business purposes be treated as actually loaded; that she has got past the embarrassments and dangers attendant on loading, and that her sailing is the next thing to be looked for. And, with regard to the suggested ambiguity in the phrase 'about to sail', when it is read in conjunction with the other words, it seems to me clear that it does not mean that the ship is to sail within a 'reasonable' or indefinite time, a statement which might lead to endless difficulties and expense, but that, if she has not already sailed, she is about to sail forthwith. If that is so, then applying the reasoning which lies at the root of *Behn v Burness*, I have no hesitation in saying that I believe the phrase to be a condition precedent. It is a representation the accuracy of which is made a condition precedent, though I do not doubt that the fulfilment of a promise may be equally made a condition precedent ...

[Lord Esher MR and Kay LJ also delivered reasoned judgments.]

Reasonable despatch

... the implied obligation to proceed with reasonable despatch arises from the nature of the contract and is necessary in order to give it commercial efficacy. Its existence is by now so well established that it can be regarded as an ordinary incident of any contract of carriage by sea which exists unless the parties have expressly or by implication provided otherwise (*The Kriti Rex* [1996] 2 Lloyd's Rep 171, 191, Moore-Bick J).

McAndrew v Adams (1834) 1 Bing NC 31, Common Pleas

The defendant agreed that the *Swallow* would go in ballast from Portsmouth to St Michael's in the Azores and carry a cargo of oranges direct to London. Instead of proceeding direct to St Michael's, the defendant sailed first to Oporto carrying troops. Shore batteries prevented a landing; the vessel returned the troops to Portsmouth. The charterparty fixed 1 December as the earliest date on which the charterer was obliged to load; 35 running days were allowed for loading with a further 10 days on demurrage. The charterer was entitled to cancel if the vessel did not arrive at St Michael's by 31 January. The *Swallow* sailed for St Michael's on 6 December; she loaded there and returned to London, arriving on 1 February, by which time the market price of oranges had fallen.

> **Tindal CJ:** ... And the question here is, whether the defendant sailed within a reasonable time according to the terms of his charterparty. All the authorities concur in stating, that the voyage must be commenced within a reasonable time; and they are all cited and commented upon in *Freeman v Taylor* (1831) 8 Bing 124 and *Mount v Larkins* (1831) 8 Bing 108. If that be the general rule, where there is any delay in a voyage it is incumbent on the party to account for it. In many cases it may be difficult to say what is a reasonable or an unreasonable time for commencing a voyage. It is better, therefore, to refer to the contract itself, and see whether the voyage performed is conformable to that pointed out by the contract.
>
> Now, looking at this contract, I think, with a view to the object of the voyage, its commencement was delayed an unreasonable time. The charterparty was entered into on the 20th of October 1832, and provides, that the *Swallow*:
>
> > being tight, staunch, strong, and in every way fitted for the voyage, shall proceed in ballast to St Michael's.

I do not lay stress on the stipulation for proceeding in ballast, any further than that it seems to refer to a voyage in which the master should not lie by to take in a cargo, which might delay the ship on her voyage. The instrument then goes on:

> shall there receive on board a complete cargo of fruit; and, having been so loaded, shall proceed with the said cargo direct to the port of London.

... Now, inasmuch as the parties have stipulated that the lay days shall commence on the 1st of December, it may be inferred that they contemplated the voyage to St Michael's should terminate by that day. If, indeed, by any accident or unforeseen cause, which should excuse the master, the vessel should arrive later, the charterer would have no just cause of action: but the intention at the time was, that the object of the voyage should, if possible, take effect from the 1st of December. That it might have taken effect from that time, is clear; for the voyage usually lasts a fortnight or three weeks, and the vessel sailed for Oporto on the 7th of November.

The instrument then goes on:

> That, in case the vessel should not be arrived at St Michael's, and in readiness to receive her cargo by the 31st of January next, it shall be optional with the agents of the affreighters whether they load or not; and in case they decline loading, the charterparty shall be null and void.

That was to give the charterer the option of repudiating the contract if the vessel should arrive too late for any useful purpose, although if she had been detained by any justifiable cause, he might have no right of action against the owner.

And all the evidence in the cause goes to show that the intention of the parties in entering into this contract was such as I have described: the course of the trade in London, which requires a speedy voyage, and gives advantages to those who are first in the market; and the letter of the 9th of November, in which the plaintiffs say:

> In having taken the *Swallow* to Oporto with passengers, on her way to St Michael's, instead of proceeding direct, we consider you to have deviated from the due performance of the charterparty entered into with us, and we hold you liable for all loss or injury which may arise to the parties interested in consequence of your not proceeding direct.

I think, therefore, that, as the commencement of the voyage was, without any justifiable cause, delayed till the 6th of December, an action lies for the plaintiffs ...

[The Chief Justice went on to deal with entitlement to damages. Park and Bosanquet JJ delivered judgments to the same effect.]

'Expected ready to load ...'

Maredelanto Compania Naviera SA v Bergbau-Handel GmbH, The Mihalis Angelos [1971] 1 QB 164, CA

The *Mihalis Angelos* was chartered for a voyage from Haiphong to Hamburg. The charterparty described the vessel as 'now trading and expected ready to load under this charter about 1 July 1965'. Lay days were not to commence before 1 July 1965; charterers had the option to cancel if the vessel was not ready to load by 20 July 1965.

Megaw LJ: ... It is not disputed that when a charter includes the words 'expected ready to load ...' a contractual obligation on the part of the shipowner is involved. It is not an obligation that the vessel will be ready to load on the stated date, nor about the stated date, if the date is qualified, as here, by 'about'. The owner is not in breach merely because the vessel arrives much later, or indeed does not arrive at all. The owner is not undertaking that there will be no unexpected delay. But he is undertaking that he honestly and on reasonable grounds believes, at the time of the contract, that the date named is the date when the vessel will be ready to load. Therefore in order to establish a breach of that obligation the charterer has the burden of showing that the owner's contractually expressed expectation was not his honest expectation, or, at the least, that the owner did not have reasonable grounds for it.

In my judgment, such a term in a charterparty ought to be regarded as being a condition of the contract, in the old sense of the word 'condition': that is, that when it has been broken, the other party can, if he wishes, by intimation to the party in breach, elect to be released from performance of his further obligations under the contract; and he can validly do so without having to establish that on the facts of the particular case the breach has produced serious consequences which can be treated as 'going to the root of the contract' or as being 'fundamental' or whatever other metaphor may be thought appropriate for a frustration case. I reach that conclusion for four interrelated reasons.

First, it tends towards certainty in the law. One of the essential elements of law is some measure of uniformity. One of the important elements of the law is predictability. At any rate in commercial law, there are obvious and substantial advantages in having, where possible, a firm and definite rule for a particular class of legal relationship: for example, as here, the legal categorisation of a particular, definable type of contractual clause in common use. It is surely much better, both for shipowners and charterers (and, incidentally, for their advisers), when a contractual obligation of this nature is under consideration, and still more when they are faced with the necessity for an urgent decision as to the effects of a suspected breach of it, to be able to say categorically: 'If a breach is proved, then the charterer can put an end to the contract', rather than that they should be left to ponder whether or not the courts would be likely, in the particular case, when the evidence has been heard, to decide that in the particular circumstances the breach was or was not such as 'to go to the root of the contract'. Where justice does not require greater flexibility, there is everything to be said for, and nothing against, a degree of rigidity in legal principle.

Second, it would, in my opinion, only be in the rarest case, if ever, that a shipowner could legitimately feel that he had suffered an injustice by reason of the law having given to a charterer the right to put an end to the contract because of the breach by the shipowner of a clause such as this. If a shipowner has chosen to assert contractually, but dishonestly or without reasonable grounds, that he expects his vessel to be ready to load on such-and-such a date, wherein does the grievance lie?

Third, it is, as Mocatta J held, clearly established by authority binding on this court that where a clause 'expected ready to load' is included in a contract for the sale of goods to be carried by sea, that clause is a condition, in the sense that any breach of it enables the buyer to reject the goods without having to show that the dishonest or unreasonable expectation of the seller has in fact been prejudicial to the buyer ...

It would, in my judgment, produce an undesirable anomaly in our commercial law if such a clause – 'expected ready to load' – were to be held to have a materially different legal effect where it is contained in a charterparty from that which it has when it is contained in a sale of goods contract ...

The fourth reason why I think that the clause should be regarded as being a condition when it is found in a charterparty is that that view was the view of Scrutton LJ so expressed in his capacity as the author of *Scrutton on Charterparties* ...

Combined effect of reasonable despatch and 'expected ready to load undertakings'

Evera SA Commercial v North Shipping Co Ltd, The North Anglia [1956] 2 Lloyd's Rep 367

Devlin J: A charterer manifestly wants, if he can get it, a fixed date for the arrival of the ship at the port of loading. He has to make arrangements to bring down the cargo and to have it ready to load when the ship arrives, and he wants to know, as near as he can, what that date is going to be. On the other hand, it is to the interest of the shipowner, if he can have it, to have the date as flexible as possible. Because of the inevitable delays due to bad weather or other circumstances that there might be in the course of a voyage, he can never be sure that he can arrive at a port on a fixed and certain day. Therefore, in order to accommodate these two views as far as possible, it has been the general practice for a long time past to have a clause under which the shipowner, without pledging himself to a fixed day, gives a date in the charterparty of expected readiness, that is, the date when he expects that he will be ready to load. The protection that is afforded to the charterer under that type of clause is this. As was clearly settled in *Samuel Sanday & Co v Keighley, Maxted & Co* (1922) 27 Com Cas 296, he is entitled to have that statement of position, as it is called – the statement of expectation as to when the ship arrives or is likely to arrive – made honestly and made on reasonable grounds.

Thus, the result is that, in a perfectly simple case, where at the time when the charterparty was entered into the ship was free to proceed to the port of loading, her obligation is simply to set out in good time so that under normal circumstances she will arrive at the port of loading at or about the day which she has given as being the one when she expects to be ready to load. If something occurs on the voyage to the port of loading which delays the ship without her fault, then the owners under this type of clause are not liable.

The complication arises if the charterparty is made a little ahead so that it is not anticipated by either party that the ship is likely to sail at once for her port of loading. If she is going to have some intervening period, how can she dispose of it?

It was quite clearly settled in *Monroe Brothers Ltd v Ryan* [1935] 2 KB 28 – and I have in mind the point in Greer LJ's judgment (at p 37) where he deals with this particular matter – that the charterers have no right in such circumstances to expect the ship to keep herself free and unoccupied. If the shipowners wish to charter the ship by means of an intervening charterparty, or otherwise to employ her, they are entitled to do so. But if the new engagement into which she enters prevents her from fulfilling her obligations under the next voyage, they take the risk that the will be liable in damages for that. In other words, they take the risk ... of clashing engagements.

But what then happens, the shipowner having entered into the intervening charter, if the intervening charter interferes with the performance of the second voyage. The simplest case, and one that was settled as long ago as 1907, is the case in which the shipowner, having entered into a charterparty, then deliberately enters into an earlier charterparty which he knows is bound to make him late for the following voyage. In those circumstances there is no need, really, to invoke any principle of difficulty. Manifestly in such circumstances the shipowner who has put it out of his power to perform the engagement which he has entered into is liable in damages. That was so decided in *Thomas Nelson & Sons v Dundee East Coast Shipping Co Ltd* [1907] Sess Cas 927.

The next stage, so to speak, is reached when the shipowner enters into a charter which he honestly anticipates, and with reasonable grounds, will be completed in time to fulfil her earlier obligations, and then, through some circumstances for which he is not responsible, he is delayed on the earlier voyage. That situation was considered by the Court of Appeal in this country in the case of *Monroe Brothers Ltd v Ryan*, above, to which I have already referred. There it was held that the shipowner must nevertheless pay damages.

Then the next stage is reached when the shipowner does not enter into an intervening charter, but is in this position, that when he makes his charter with the charterers who are concerned in the case, he is already under charter to another charterer, and, again, making an honest statement of expectation on reasonable grounds, some delay occurs there for which he is not responsible, with the result that he is late with the second charter. That situation was considered in *Louis Dreyfus & Co v Lauro* (1938) 60 Ll L Rep 94.

The present case introduces yet another new feature. Here when the shipowner made his engagement with the plaintiffs as charterers on August 6, 1953, he had already made an earlier engagement, so that in that respect the situation was comparable to that in *Louis Dreyfus & Co v Lauro* above, but he not merely disclosed the circumstance of the earlier engagement to the charterer, but he set out his estimate with regard to them in full in the charterparty. The substantial question, therefore, which has arisen in this case is whether those words in the charterparty affect the position in such a way as to enable me to distinguish it from *Monroe Brothers Ltd v Ryan* ...

It is clear that there are two obligations into which the shipowner enters. He enters into the obligation of making an honest and reasonable statement about his position. That he discharged that is not questioned here. But he also entered into an obligation, which is expressed in the printed words of the charter ... that the ship 'shall with all convenient speed sail and proceed to Fort Churchill'. It is for the breach of that obligation that the ship is being sued in this case, as it was sued in the case of *Monroe Brothers Ltd v Ryan*, above; and the effect of that obligation, it is submitted, combined with the statement of readiness which is made earlier on in the charter, is to impose upon the ship an absolute duty with which ... the ship has not complied. I think the best way of framing the duty ... is to take it as it was framed by Branson J in *Louis Dreyfus & Co v Lauro* ...

> In view of the combination of the expected date and of the implied term that the ship will use all convenient speed to get to her port of loading, the obligation is, as was well put by Mr Mocatta, that she shall start from wherever she may happen to be, at a date when, by proceeding with reasonable dispatch, she will arrive at the port of loading by the expected date.

> ... Under the principle in *Monroe Brothers Ltd v Ryan* the ship is excused if she starts out in good time but something happens on the way to the port of loading. But she is not excused if anything happens before that time which prevents her from starting out upon the expected date.

> ... The question therefore arises: Is there anything in the typed words which demands, or enables, me to alter that construction?

> ... if a shipowner wants to make the beginning of one voyage contingent upon the conclusion of the one before, he must say so in clear terms. There is clearly a number of things that would have to be worked out in order that such an arrangement should be made as would be fair to both sides. It may be that the shipowner had it in mind in this case that that was what he wanted. But, if he did have that in mind, he has not put it into such language as would make it plain to any reasonable charterer that the charterer was being invited to accept the risks of delay under an earlier charterparty in which that charterer was not concerned. To pass those risks on to a person who was not a party to that charter requires, in my judgment, if not express language, at least much clearer language than that which has been adopted in the present case ...

Notes

1 It is a question of construction whether an exclusion clause in a charterparty applies to events occurring before the loading voyage begins. Exclusion clauses do not normally apply before the vessel has begun 'the chartered service'; but chartered service can begin before loading commences. *Barker v McAndrew* (1868) 18 CBNS 759; *Monroe v Ryan* [1935] 2 KB 28; *The Super Servant Two* [1990] 1 Lloyd's Rep 1, 6, CA.

2 In response to the decision in *Evera*, in 1957 BIMCO recommended the following clause, code name ERLOAD:

> Expected ready to load about ... but without obligation to proceed to the loading port hereunder until termination of any voyage on which the vessel may be engaged at the date of the charterparty or of any voyage

which the owners may commit the vessel to undertake after the date of this charterparty.

3   A statement of estimated time of arrival is treated in the same way as a statement of expected readiness to load: *Mitsui v Garnac, The Myrtos* [1984] 2 Lloyd's Rep 449.

4   The approach adopted in *The North Anglia* was approved by the Court of Appeal in *The Baleares* [1993] 1 Lloyd's Rep 215 where it was held that a reasonable despatch obligation does not remain inoperative until a chartered vessel completes discharge under a preceding fixture and the charterer is not obliged to wait until the vessel leaves the last discharge point before treating the owners as being in breach.

5   *The Niizuru* was time chartered on terms which fixed the lay/can spread as 20 February/28 April 1992. It was also agreed that the shipowners would 'narrow lay/can to a 15 day spread 25 days prior to the narrowed lay/can'. It was held that compliance with the lay/can narrowing provision was a condition precedent to the delivery of the vessel. *Hyundai Merchant Marine Co Ltd v Karander Maritime Inc, The Niizuru* [1996] 2 Lloyd's Rep 66.

Cancellation clauses

Cheikh Boutros Selim El-Khoury v Ceylon Shipping Lines Ltd, The Madeleine [1967] 2 Lloyd's Rep 224

The *Madeleine* was fixed on a three-month time charter for world trading. The charterers purported to cancel on the grounds that on the agreed cancellation date the vessel was not in a position in which she could properly be delivered because she did not then possess either a 'deratisation certificate' or a 'deratisation exemption certificate'. Under the law of India, without a certificate she could not sail from Calcutta, the port of delivery, to any port outside India. On the facts, it would have taken two days to obtain the necessary certificate. The charterers purported to cancel at 8.00 am on the cancellation date and again at 8.48 pm on the same day. The shipowners argued that the charterers had no right to cancel in the circumstances or at the times they purported to do so.

> **Roskill J:** ... Plainly it is for the charterers to establish the right which they have sought to exercise. One begins by asking what right it is which clause 22 confers upon the charterers. That must be a question of the true construction of that clause. I therefore turn back to its language:
>
>> Should the Vessel not be delivered by the 2nd day of May 1957 the Charterers to have the option of cancelling.
>
> It is well established that clauses in charterparties cannot be construed in isolation from each other. A charterparty like any other contract must be construed sensibly and in its entirety. Where one has a series of clauses in a standard form which has been in use for a great many years, and which has

been interpreted many times by the courts and by arbitrators, the court must look at the provisions as a whole. It is plain, when one looks at clause 22, that it is referring to the non-performance by the owners of an obligation which they are required elsewhere in the charterparty to perform because the clause starts: 'Should the Vessel not be delivered ...'

Plainly, therefore, that provision has reference to an obligation to deliver and one then turns to see where that obligation is imposed. One turns back to clause 1 in the first instance and one finds there that the vessel is to be delivered and placed at the disposal of the charterers

> ... between 9 am and 6 pm, or between 9 am and 2 pm if on Saturday, at CALCUTTA in such available berth where she can safely lie always afloat, she being in every way fitted for ordinary cargo service.

... One has to see what is the obligation which clause 22 postulates that the owners will not perform. The obligation which clause 22 postulates that the owners will not perform is the owners' obligation under clause 1. That obligation is to deliver the vessel not before April 18, between 9 am and 6 pm on a weekday, or between 9 am and 2 pm on a Saturday (and not, I should add, on Sunday or a legal holiday unless the charterers agree then to take her over) in an 'available berth where she can safely lie always afloat, she being in every way fitted for ordinary cargo service'.

... plainly, as a matter of construction, clause 22 is looking back to clause 1 and it is the owners' failure to deliver in accordance with the provisions of clause 1 which gives the charterers the right to cancel under clause 22.

It is important to emphasise that that which the charterers are claiming to exercise is an express contractual right given by clause 22. Their right to cancel does not in any way depend upon any breach of the charterparty by the owners. Entitlement to cancel under clause 22 depends not on any breach by the owners but upon whether the owners have timeously complied with their obligations under clause 1. If they have, there is no right to cancel. If they have not, there is a right to cancel ...

As I have already said, in my judgment, clause 22 cannot be divorced from clause 1. Clause 1 requires the owners to deliver in a condition in which the vessel was in every way fitted for ordinary cargo service ... There was here an express warranty of seaworthiness and unless the ship was timeously delivered in a seaworthy condition, including the necessary certificate from the port health authority, the charterers had the right to cancel. That right, in my judgment, they possessed, and I think that the umpire was wrong in holding that they did not possess it.

That brings me to the second point in the case, namely, whether that right was exercised timeously. I have already dealt with the question of time. In my judgment, the owners cannot say they had the whole of May 10 in which to deliver to avoid cancellation. They had to deliver, in my judgment, not later than 6 pm on May 10 if they were to avoid the risk of the charterparty being cancelled by the charterers ...

[But] both as a matter of construction of the charterparty and as a matter of authority, it is clear law that there is no contractual right to rescind a charterparty under the cancelling clause unless and until the date specified in that clause has been reached. In other words ... there is no anticipatory right to cancel under the clause. I respectfully agree with the passage in the 17th edn of Scrutton as correctly stating the law. Of course, the fact that there is no contractual right to cancel in advance does not prevent a charterer seeking to claim the right to rescind in advance of the cancelling date, as the learned editors of Scrutton put it 'at common law'... Where the charterer seeks to say that the contract has been frustrated or that there has been an anticipatory breach which entitles him to rescind, then he has such rights as are given to him at common law.

Marbienes Compania Naviera SA v Ferrostaal AG, The Democritos [1976] 2 Lloyd's Rep 149, CA

Lord Denning MR: In November, 1969, the owners of the motor vessel *Democritos* chartered her to a German company, Ferrostaal. The charter was however a time charter and was on the New York produce form. It contains these clauses ...

> That if required by Charterers, time not to commence before 1 December, 1969, and should vessel not have given written notice of readiness on or before 20 December, 1969, but not later than 4 pm charterers or their agents to have the option of cancelling this charter any time not later than the best notice of the vessel's readiness.

The vessel arrived at Durban on 16 December 1969. Her 'tween deck in No 2 hold was found to be collapsed. If the repairs had been done straight away at Durban, they would have taken some days. She might have been delayed so long that she could not have been ready by the cancelling date 20 December 1969. This did not suit anyone. The charterers had steel ready to load. So the repairs were not done at Durban. The master gave a written guarantee that the vessel could load the amount of steel available, namely, 9,230 long tons. She did in fact start loading at Durban on 18 December 1969.

... It is said by the charterers that the owners were under an absolute obligation to deliver the vessel at Durban by the cancelling date, 20 December 1969 – and this is the point – they were bound to deliver her by that date in a fit condition as required by the charter; and that the owners were in breach of that condition because the vessel was not in a fit state then. The 'tween decks were broken. The charterers admit that they may have waived any right to reject the vessel, but nevertheless they claim that they had a right to sue for damages for the vessel being in an unfit condition. The damages would be for loss incurred by her not being able to carry a full cargo, and also by the time occupied later at Seattle in doing the repairs.

Now there is nothing in this charter which binds the owners positively to deliver by 20 December 1969. The only clue to any time of delivery is to be found in the cancelling clause. There is, of course, an implied term that the owners will use reasonable diligence to deliver the ship in a fit condition by 20 December 1969. But that is not an absolute obligation. So long as they have used reasonable diligence, they are not in breach. In this case it is found that reasonable diligence was used, so there is no breach by them of that implied obligation.

Next the cancelling clause. Its effect is that, although there may have been no breach by the owners nevertheless the charterers are, for their own protection, entitled to cancel if the vessel is not delivered in a proper condition by the cancelling date. That is the sole effect.

On this point the Judge referred to the English cases, particularly *Smith v Dart & Son* (1884) 14 QBD 105 at p 110, when A L Smith J said:

> The shipowner does not contract to get there by a certain day, but says: 'If I do not get there you may cancel'.

But we have had the benefit of one or two others. The first is from Scotland, *Nelson & Sons v The Dundee East Coast Shipping Co Ltd* (1907) 44 SLR 661. It was a voyage charter, but Lord M'Laren said this:

> If it can be shown that the shipowners had used their best endeavours and that the delay was due to unavoidable accident or perils of the sea, I should have been of opinion that no damages were due. The contract could be cancelled but damages would not be due, for each party would then be within his rights.

... These authorities show that as long as the owner uses reasonable diligence, he is not in breach, but the charterer is entitled to cancel if the vessel is not delivered by the cancelling date ...

Fercometal SARL v Mediterranean Shipping Co SA, The Simona [1989] 1 AC 788

The *Simona* was chartered to carry a part cargo of steel coils from Durban to Bilbao. The charterers were entitled to cancel the charterparty if the vessel was not ready to load on or before 9 July. On 2 July the owners requested an extension of the cancellation date. The charterers purported to cancel the contract forthwith and fixed alternative tonnage. The owners did not accept the charterers' repudiation. When the vessel arrived in Durban on 8 July the owners tendered notice of readiness although they were not in fact ready to load. The charterers rejected that notice. On 12 July, when the vessel was still not ready to load, the charterers sent a further notice of cancellation. The owners claimed dead freight. Lord Bridge, Lord Templeman, Lord Oliver and Lord Jauncey agreed with Lord Ackner.

> **Lord Ackner**: My Lords, this appeal raises one short question: did the respondents (the charterers), in the circumstances ... lose their right to cancel the charterparty which they had entered into with the appellants (the owners)?
>
> ... It is important at this stage to emphasise that the charterers' right to cancel given by cl 10 was an independent option, only exercisable if the vessel was not ready to load on or before 9 July 1982. Clause 10 did not impose any contractual obligation on the owners to commence loading by the cancellation date.
>
> ... It is common ground that the action of the charterers in giving the notice purporting to cancel the contract was premature. It constituted an anticipatory breach and repudiation of the charterparty, because the right of cancellation could not be validly exercised until the arrival of the cancellation date, some seven days hence. It is equally common ground that this repudiation was not accepted by the owners ...

When one party wrongly refuses to perform obligations, this will not automatically bring the contract to an end. The innocent party has an option. He may either accept the wrongful repudiation as determining the contract and sue for damages or he may ignore or reject the attempt to determine the contract and affirm its continued existence. Cockburn CJ in *Frost v Knight* (1872) LR 7 Ex Ch 111 at 112–13 put the matter thus:

> The law with reference to a contract to be performed at a future time, where the party bound to performance announces prior to the time his intention not to perform it, as established by the cases of *Hochster v De la Tour* (1853) 2 E & B 678 and *The Danube and Black Sea Co v Xenos* (1863) 13 CBNS 825 on the one hand, and *Avery v Bowden* (1855) 5 E & B 714, *Reid v Hoskins* (1856) 6 E & B 953 and *Barwick v Buba* (1857) 2 CBNS 563 on the other, may be thus stated. The promisee, if he pleases, may treat the notice of intention as inoperative, and await the time when the contract is to be executed, and then hold the other party responsible for all the consequences of non-performance: but in that case he keeps the contract alive for the benefit of the other party as well as his own; he remains subject to all the obligations and liabilities under it, and enables the other party not only to complete the contract, if so advised, notwithstanding his previous repudiation of it, but also to take advantage of any supervening circumstance which would justify him in declining to complete it. On the other hand, the promisee may, if he thinks proper, treat the repudiation of the other party as a wrongful putting an end to the contract, and may at once bring his action as on a breach of it and in such action he will be entitled to such damages as would have arisen from the non-performance of the contract at the appointed time, subject, however, to abatement in respect of any circumstances which may have afforded him the means of mitigating his loss.

... The way in which a 'supervening circumstance' may turn out to be to the advantage of the party in default, thus relieving him from liability, is illustrated by *Avery v Bowden*, where the outbreak of the Crimean War between England and Russia made performance of the charterparty no longer legally possible. The defendant, who prior to the outbreak of the war had in breach of contract refused to load, was provided with a good defence to an action for breach of contract, since his repudiation had been ignored. As pointed out by Parker LJ in his judgment ([1987] 2 Lloyd's Rep 236 at 240), the law as stated in *Frost v Knight* and *Johnstone v Milling* has been reasserted in many cases since, and in particular in *Heyman v Darwins Ltd* [1942] AC 356 at 361, where Viscount Simon LC said:

> The first head of claim in the writ appears to be advanced on the view that an agreement is automatically terminated if one party 'repudiates' it. That is not so. As Scrutton LJ said in *Golding v London & Edinburgh Insurance Co Ltd* ((1932) 43 Ll L R 487 at 488): 'I have never been able to understand what effect the repudiation by one party has unless the other accepts it'. If one party so acts or so expresses himself, as to show that he does not mean to accept and discharge the obligations of a contract any further, the other party has an option as to the attitude he may take up. He may, notwithstanding the so-called repudiation, insist on holding his

co-contractor to the bargain and continue to tender due performance on his part. In that event, the co-contractor has the opportunity of withdrawing from his false position, and, even if he does not, may escape ultimate liability because of some supervening event not due to this own fault which excuses or puts an end to further performance.

If an unaccepted repudiation has no legal effect ('a thing writ in water and of no value to anybody': *per* Asquith LJ in *Howard v Pickford Tool Co Ltd* [1951] 1 KB 417 at 421), how can the unaccepted acts of repudiation by the charterers in this case provide the owners with any cause of action? It was accepted in the Court of Appeal by counsel then appearing for the owners that it was an inevitable inference from the findings made by the arbitrators that the *Simona* was not ready to load the charterers' steel at any time prior to the charterers notice of cancellation on 12 July. Counsel who has appeared before your Lordships for the owners has not been able to depart from this concession. Applying the well established principles set out above, the anticipatory breaches by the charterers not having been accepted by the owners as terminating the contract, the charterparty survived intact with the right of cancellation unaffected. The vessel was not ready to load by close of business on the cancelling date, *viz*, 9 July, and the charterers were therefore entitled to and did give what on the face of it was an effective notice of cancellation ...

Towards the conclusion of his able address, counsel for the owners sought to raise what was essentially a new point, argued before neither the arbitrators, Leggatt J nor the Court of Appeal. He submitted that the charterers' conduct had induced or caused the owners to abstain from having the ship ready prior to the cancellation date. Of course, it is always open to A, who has refused to accept B's repudiation of the contract, and thereby kept the contract alive, to contend that, in relation to a particular right or obligation under the contract, B is estopped from contending that he, B, is entitled to exercise that right or that he, A, has remained bound by that obligation. If B represents to A that he no longer intends to exercise that right or requires that obligation to be fulfilled by A and A acts on that representation, then clearly B cannot be heard thereafter to say that he is entitled to exercise that right or that A is in breach of contract by not fulfilling that obligation. If, in relation to this option to cancel, the owners had been able to establish that the charterers had represented that they no longer required the vessel to arrive on time because they had already fixed [another vessel] and, in reliance on that representation, the owners had given notice of readiness only after the cancellation date, then the charterers would have been estopped from contending they were entitled to cancel the charterparty. There is, however, no finding of any such representation, let alone that the owners were induced thereby not to make the vessel ready to load by 9 July. On the contrary, the owners on 5 July on two occasions asserted that the vessel would start loading on 8 July and on 8 July purported to tender notice of readiness ... The non-readiness of the vessel by the cancelling date was in no way induced by the charterers' conduct. It was the result of the owners' decision to load other cargo first.

In short, in affirming the continued existence of the contract, the owners could only avoid the operation of the cancellation clause by tendering the vessel ready to load on time (which they failed to do), or by establishing (which they could not) that their failure was the result of the charterers' conduct in representing that they had given up their option, which representation the owners had acted on by not presenting the vessel on time. I would therefore dismiss the appeal with costs.

6 SPEED AND FUEL CONSUMPTION

Cosmos Bulk Transport Inc v China National Foreign Trade, The Apollonius [1978] 1 Lloyd's Rep 53

By a time charter dated 28 August 1974, *Apollonius* was described as:

> ... when fully loaded, capable of steaming about 14.5 knots in good weather and smooth water on a consumption of about 38 tons of fuel oil [of a certain specification].

The ship was delivered on 1 November 1974 and ordered to load steel at Fukiyama for delivery at Ensenada, Argentina. She made the voyage from Japan to Argentina at an average speed of 10.61 knots and was redelivered to her owners. Thereafter, following cleaning of her hull in dry dock, her average speed returned to a normal 14.5 knots. An arbitrator found that the cause of the speed reduction was that the hull of the vessel had become encrusted with molluscs during a stay at Whampoa, Canton, between the date of the charter and date on which the chartered service had commenced. The charterers made a claim for the loss of 5.821 days, made up of 4.821 days due to fouling of the hull and 24 hours due to unnecessary reduction of engine speed. The questions of law for decision by the court were: (a) were charterers entitled to damages for the loss of 4.821 days due to fouling; (b) were charterers entitled to damages for the loss of one day because of failure to prosecute the voyage with utmost diligence?

> **Mocatta J:** ... I turn now to the first and most important point of all arising in this case, namely whether the speed warranty in the preamble of the charterparty applies only at the date of the charterparty as is contended by the owners or also or in any case applies at the date of the delivery of the vessel under the charter. The strength of the owners' case on this matter rests on the decision of Atkinson J in *Lorentzen v White Shipping Co Ltd* (1942) 74 Ll L Rep 161 which contains an *obiter dictum* favourable to the owners' argument here ...
>
> The first thing to notice about this statement of Atkinson J is that it was obiter, since, as he said, he had to assume that the description in relation to the speed warranty was not true at the date of the charterparty. He was not dealing with a case where there was a breach of a warranty at the date of delivery of a ship under a time charterparty. Secondly, in my judgment little is to be gained from the reference made by Atkinson J to the statement that the classification of a ship as stated in a charterparty is not a condition. In my judgment, the contrary is clearly the case ...
>
> In addition to this mistake, as I consider it to be, in the reference by Atkinson J to the cases on a vessel's class, another criticism of his reasoning, insofar as his

opinion in relation to the speed warranty depended on analogies with the cases on a vessel's class, is that the courts in deciding that a statement as to a vessel's class only applies as at the date that the charterparty is entered into based themselves on very special reasons peculiar to classification ... I cannot think that analogies drawn with ... somewhat ancient cases on classification are of much assistance today in the present problem.

... Counsel for the owners stressed that the *dictum* of Atkinson J on this point had stood unchallenged since 1942 and that no doubt a number of cases in arbitration had been decided on the basis that the *dictum* was good law and, in all probability, an even greater number of cases had been settled on this basis. I do not feel that this argument is of persuasive weight in the circumstances of this case, since it must be relatively rare for there to be a substantial lapse of time between entering into a time charter of an existing vessel and her delivery thereunder, and, in addition, in most cases ... it would be immaterial which date was relevant for the decision whether the warranty had or had not been broken.

Counsel for the owners sought to derive support for the owners' case from the principle *noscitur a sociis*, in that in the preamble to this charterparty, in addition to the statement as to the vessel's class, which has been decided to apply only as at that date, there are other statements descriptive of the vessel which are similarly limited in time. It is true that there is a reference inserted especially in the printed form of this preamble providing for the main holds to be clean and available for dry cargo on delivery. This can be argued to be an unique express reference to the date of delivery and on the basis of this an argument founded on the maxim *expressio unius exclusio alterius* might be mounted. I do not, however, think that there is much weight in this submission. It is noticeable that the various items of description contained in the preamble are not all of the same category ...

The provisions in relation to the ship's capacity in the preamble, which no doubt did apply at the date of the charter, would in my judgment also be applicable at the date of her delivery and it is not impossible that her owners might commit a breach of this term of the charter, if, for example, they were, before delivery, to insert an additional bulkhead or make some other alteration to the structure of the ship which limited the cubic feet grain capacity stated in the preamble. Therefore, I do not think that the associates, if I may so describe them, of the speed warranty in the preamble to this charter are all of one class in respect of the date at which they are applicable. The owners cannot, in my judgment, therefore derive any succour from the well known maxim relied on by counsel ...

On the other hand, it seems to be clear that the whole purpose of the description of the vessel containing a speed warranty is that when the vessel enters on her service, she will be capable of the speed in question, subject of course to any protection which her owners may obtain if there has been some casualty between the date of the charter and the date of delivery affecting her speed which, under an exceptions clause, protects them from liability in relation to a failure to comply with the warranty. From the charterer's point of view the speed warranty is clearly of very great importance in relation to his calculations as to the rate of hire it will be possible for him to pay, a matter on which his decision would be affected by his calculations as to the time which the ship would take to complete the one trip voyage for which this time charter engaged the *Apollonius*. From the business point of view, I think it is clear that commercial considerations require this description as to the vessel's speed to be applicable as at the date of her delivery whether or not it is applicable at the date of the charter. It may well be that at the date of the charter the vessel will have been completing a previous period of service under a time charter or a very long voyage under a voyage charter including stops in tropical ports, with the result that her bottom has become fouled and her speed thereby affected. In order to guard against such a contingency preventing her from attaining the described speed under the present time charter, the latter not unnaturally contained in cl 50 an option given to the owners of dry-docking her before delivery. From the charterer's point of view, the vital date therefore for the purposes of the description of the vessel, with the one exception in relation to her class to which special considerations and a long line of somewhat ancient decided cases apply, is the date of her delivery ...

In my judgment there are overwhelming commercial considerations favouring the charterers' argument that the speed warranty, whenever else it may apply, certainly applies at the date of the delivery of a vessel, subject only to the owners being protected from the consequences of any breach of such warranty by any exception clause that may be applicable. I will deal with this last matter shortly. But for these reasons I decline to follow the *dictum* of Atkinson J on this subject and, but for the question as to the protection afforded by cl 13, ['Responsibility and Exemption'] I would answer the first question of law stated for the decision of the court in the affirmative on the basis of breach of the speed warranty ...

[Mocatta J went on to conclude that the shipowners were protected from the second of the charterers' claims by an exclusion clause and, whether or not they were protected by the same clause against the first claim, on the special facts found by the arbitrator, the vessel was in any event off hire for the relevant period.]

Note

Modern forms of charterparty often contain detailed provisions relating to the speed and fuel consumption of the vessel. These terms are designed to compensate one or other party if the vessel's performance falls below or exceeds stated levels. Clauses may deal in detail with the way in which compliance with agreements about speed and fuel consumption is to be calculated. Promises as to average speed may define the locations and the wind, sea and navigation conditions in which measurements are to be made, perhaps distinguishing between laden and ballast voyages. Forms which exclude, for example, unfavourable weather conditions when calculating a vessel's average performance on a voyage, may thereafter apply the average figure to the vessel's total mileage, making adjustments to take account of actual conditions: points of construction in clauses of this type were considered by the Court of Appeal in *The Didymi* [1988] 2 Lloyd's Rep 108 and *The Gas Enterprise* [1993] 2 Lloyd's Rep 352.

CHAPTER 11

LOADING

1 DUTY TO PROVIDE A CARGO

Grant v Coverdale (1884) 9 App Cas 470

The plaintiff's vessel *Mennythorpe* was chartered to load a cargo of iron at East Bute Dock, Cardiff. The charterers agreed to load in a fixed time subject to frosts or unavoidable accidents. The charterers had intended that part of the cargo should be taken to the ship from the warehouse by canal. They were unable to load within the fixed time because the canal was frozen. A referee found that while the canal was frozen, the iron could not be taken to the dock by any reasonable means.

> **Earl of Selborne LC**: ... it is not denied, and cannot be denied, that unless those words of exception according to their proper construction take this case which has happened out of the demurrage clause, the mere fact of frost or any other thing having impeded the performance of that which the charterer and not the shipowner was bound to perform will not absolve him from the consequences of keeping the ship too long. That was decided under circumstances very similar in many respects, in the case of *Kearon v Pearson* (1861) 7 H & N 386, and decided expressly on the ground, as was pointed out I think by all the learned judges ... that there was no contract as to the particular place from which the cargo was to come, no contract as to the particular manner in which it was to be supplied, or how it was to be brought to the place of loading, and that therefore it could not be supposed that the parties were contracting about any such thing.
>
> This exception in the contract being limited to 'accidents preventing the loading', the only question is, what is the meaning of 'loading'? and whether this particular frost did, in fact, prevent the loading. There are two things to be done – the operation of loading is the particular operation in which both parties have to concur. Taken literally it is spoken of in the early part of this charterparty as the thing which the shipowner is to do. The ship is to 'proceed to Cardiff East Bute Dock', 'and there load the cargo'. No doubt, for the purpose of loading, the charterer must also do his part; he must have the cargo there to be loaded, and tender it to be put on board the ship in the usual and proper manner. Therefore the business of both parties meets and concurs in that operation of loading. When the charterer has tendered the cargo, and when the operation has proceeded to the point at which the shipowner is to take charge of it, everything after that is the shipowner's business, and everything before the commencement of the operation of loading, those things which are so essential to the operation of loading that they are conditions *sine quibus non* of that operation – everything before that is the charterer's part only. It would appear to me to be unreasonable to suppose, unless the words make it

perfectly clear, that the shipowner has contracted that his ship may be detained for an unlimited time on account of impediments, whatever their nature may be, to those things with which he has nothing whatever to do, which precede altogether the whole operation of loading, which are no part whatever of it, but which belong to that which is exclusively the charterer's business. He has to contract for the cargo, he has to buy the cargo, he has to convey the cargo to the place of loading and have it ready there to be put on board; and it is only when he has done those things that the duty and the obligation of the shipowner in respect of the loading arises. These words in the exception are as large as any words can be; they mention 'strikes, frosts, floods, and all other unavoidable accidents preventing the loading'. If therefore you are to carry back the loading to anything necessary to be done by the charterer in order to have the cargo ready to be loaded, no human being can tell where you are to stop. The bankruptcy, for instance, of the person with whom he has contracted for the supply of the iron, or disputes about the fulfilment of the contract, the refusal at a critical point of time to supply the iron, the neglect of the persons who ought to put it on board lighters to come down the canal for any distance or to be brought by sea, or to put it on the railway or bring it in any other way in which it is to be brought; all those things are of course practical impediments to the charterer having the cargo ready to be shipped at the proper place and time; but is it reasonable that the shipowner should be held to be answerable for all those things, and is that within the natural meaning of the word 'loading'? Are those things any part of the operation of loading? Nothing, I suppose, is better established in law with regard to mercantile cases of this kind than the maxim, '*Causa proxima, non remota, spectatur*'; and it appears to me that the fact that this particular wharf was very near the Cardiff East Bute Dock can make no difference in principle if it was not the place of loading. If the cargo had to be brought from this wharf on the Glamorganshire Canal, however near it was, if it had to be brought over a passage which in point of fact was impeded, and over which it was not brought, to the place of loading, to say that the wharf on the Glamorganshire Canal was, upon a fair construction of the words, within the place of loading, appears to me to be no more tenable than if the same thing had been said of a place a mile higher up the canal where, according to the actual contract, the persons were to supply the iron, and where the owner of the iron might have been found.

That really is enough to dispose of the whole argument. The case of *Hudson v Ede* (1868) LR 3 QB 412 was referred to. I understand that case as proceeding upon the same principles, but as containing an admission of this distinction, that where there is, in a proved state of facts, an inevitable necessity that something should be done in order that there should be a loading at the place agreed upon, as for instance that the goods should be brought down part of a river from the only place from which they can be brought, even though that place is a considerable distance off, yet it being practically, according to known mercantile usage, the only place from which they can be brought to be loaded, the parties must be held to have contemplated that the goods should be loaded from that place in the usual manner unless there was an unavoidable impediment. And if the facts had been so about this particular wharf on the Glamorganshire Canal, if that had been the only possible place from which goods could be brought to be loaded at the East Bute Dock, that authority might have applied. But not only was that not the case, but in point of fact cargo not only could be, but actually had been brought up by carts to the East Bute Dock and put on board ship; and I infer from the finding of the referee that the whole might have been done by carting, though I agree that it would have been at an expense which was preposterous and unreasonable if you were to look at the interest of the charterer; but if the charterer has engaged that he will do a certain thing, he must of course pay the damage which arises from his not doing it, whatever the cause of his not doing it may be, whether it be his not being willing to incur an unreasonable expense, or whether it be any other cause.

[Lords Watson, Bramwell and Fitzgerald delivered judgments to the same effect.]

2 A FULL AND COMPLETE CARGO

Hunter v Fry (1819) 2 B & A 421, KB

The plaintiff chartered *Hunter*, which was described in the charterparty as 'of the burden of 261 tons or thereabouts', to the defendants for a circular voyage from London to Madeira, then from Madeira (with an unspecified cargo) to the West Indies, then back to London with 'a full and complete cargo' of coffee and logwood. The defendants failed to load as great a cargo as the vessel could have carried.

Abbott CJ: I am of opinion, that the mention of a ship's burden in the description of a ship in the charterparty, in the manner it is here mentioned, is an immaterial circumstance; although it may be made material by the allegation of fraud or other matter. Here, the freighter has not covenanted to load a cargo equivalent to the burden mentioned in the charterparty: he has covenanted to load and put on board a full and complete cargo, and to pay so much per ton for every ton loaded on board. If the covenant had been to pay a gross sum for the voyage, the freighter (upon the arrival of the ship at the foreign port) might have insisted that the captain should take on board as much as the ship would safely contain; and the owner who had covenanted to take a full and complete cargo, would not be justified in saying, that he would take no more than the register tonnage of the ship. It is, indeed, quite impossible that the burden of the ship (as described in the charterparty) should, in every case, be the measure of the precise number of tons which the ship is capable of carrying. That must depend upon the specific gravity of the particular goods; for a ship of given dimensions would be able to carry a larger number of tons, of a given species of goods, that were of a great specific gravity, than she would of another of a less specific gravity, and the freighter would therefore pay freight in proportion to the specific gravity of the goods. Upon the whole, I am of opinion, that the owner was bound to take on board such a number of tons of goods as the ship was capable of containing without injury; and, therefore, that the plaintiff is entitled to have a verdict for £918, which is the difference between the sum actually paid for freight, and that which would have been payable if the shipper had loaded on board a full and complete cargo.

[Bayley, Holroyd and Best JJ delivered judgments to the same effect. See also Chapter 10, 'Cargo Capacity' and Chapter 12, 'Freight'.]

3 ALTERNATIVE CARGO OPTIONS

Reardon Smith v Ministry of Agriculture [1963] AC 691

Viscount Radcliffe: My Lords, the three consolidated appeals upon which we are now to give judgment arise out of a strike at the port of Vancouver, British Columbia, which prevented any loading work being done at five out of the seven grain elevators at that port between the night of 16–17 February 1953, when the strike began, and 7 May 1953, when the strike came to an end. The dispute to which they relate is between shipowners, who are claiming demurrage, and the Ministry of Agriculture, Fisheries and Food, who were the charterers of the three ships concerned in the appeal ...

There are now only two issues, both, I think, issues of law, which survive for determination: one is concerned with the right of a charterer to adhere to what I will call his preferred cargo under a charterparty which admits of several kinds of cargo when circumstances at the port hold up the loading of that which he prefers to ship, and the other concerns the method and principle of computing laytime when the phrase 'weather working days' is used as the measure of the time allowance.[1]

... The *Queen City*, then, was chartered by the respondents on 12 November 1952, ordered to Vancouver on 12 February 1953, and gave notice of readiness to load on 18 February.

She was chartered on the terms of the Pacific Coast grain charter. The charterparty provided, so far as material (the words in italics being inserted in the printed form in type):

> ... vessel ... shall ... receive on board ... a full and complete cargo ... of wheat in bulk ... and/or barley in bulk, and/or flour in sacks as below which the parties of the second part [*viz*, the charterers] bind themselves shall be shipped ...
>
> *Charterer has the option of loading up to one-third cargo of barley in bulk ...*
> *Charterer has the option of loading up to one-third cargo of flour in sacks ...*

What happened at Vancouver was that ... the *Queen City* gave notice of readiness to load on 18 February 1953. The elevator strike had begun on the night of 16–17 February; so long as it lasted it was impossible for her to load a full and complete cargo of wheat; the respondents made no move to exercise their option to load nor did they load either of their alternative part cargoes of barley or flour; and she lay at the port until, the strike having ended on 7 May, she began loading on that day and completed a full cargo by 12 May.

---

1   On this point, see Chapter 13, 'Laytime'.

... Having regard to what has happened and to the form of the exceptions clause, it is at first sight a little difficult, I think, to see how the shipowners can be justified in their claim to be paid demurrage for 75 days as from February 26, on which date, they say, the lay days expired, since it would seem clear that throughout the period of delay the wheat cargo was held up by the strike which is itself an excepted cause.

The owners meet this, in effect, by saying that the charterers have no right to treat their obligation under this charterparty as being simply one to provide a cargo of wheat in bulk, failing an exercise of their option to ship part alternative cargoes of barley or flour. On the contrary, they say, the obligation is essentially an obligation to provide a full and complete cargo of wheat, barley or flour (up to the permitted proportions) as the charterers may select and the mere fact that one of these possible constituents, wheat, is the subject of delay and so within the exceptions clause does not excuse the charterers from their overriding duty to find and ship a full and complete cargo made up of such proportions of these various commodities as the prevailing conditions at Vancouver made it possible to load during the period of the strike.

... But in my view ... the shipowners' interpretation of the basic obligation of the charterparty is misconceived and the charterers' real promise in the opening clause amounts to nothing else than that of providing a full cargo of wheat, unless they should affirmatively decide to vary the make-up of the cargo by substituting barley or flour up to the permitted proportions ...

... It has been apparent throughout the case that the shipowners' argument on this particular issue depends upon the proposition that the parties' rights under the charterparty are governed by principles laid down by the Court of Appeal in 1924 in *Brightman & Co v Bunge y Born Limitada Sociedad* [1924] 2 KB 619 to which I will refer as the *Brightman* case. I think that the decision in the Brightman case did lay down certain principles, though not so many or so far-reaching as is sometimes supposed, but in my opinion those principles are not applicable to the relationship established by the charterparty which we are now considering. In order to show why that is so I must make some reference to the essential facts of the *Brightman* case.

Like this, it was a dispute between owners and charterers. The terms of the charterparty had bound the charterers to provide:

> a full and complete cargo of wheat and/or maize and/or rye in bags and/or in bulk, which cargo the said charterers bind themselves to ship.

... The decision of the court was to the effect that some demurrage was payable but not to the whole extent claimed by the owners. In arriving at this decision the principles accepted by the court which are relevant to this appeal are, in my opinion, as follows:

(1) If a shipper has undertaken to ship a full and complete cargo made up of alternative commodities, as in the terms 'wheat and/or maize and/or rye', his obligation is to have ready at the port of shipment a complete cargo within the range of those alternatives. Consequently the fact that he is prevented from loading one of the possible types of cargo by a cause within the exceptions clause, even though that is the type that he has himself selected and provided for, is not an answer to a claim for

demurrage. To protect him each of the alternatives or all the alternatives would have to be covered by an excepted cause.

(2) Consistently with this view the shipper's selection of one of the named commodities does not convert the primary obligation to ship a full cargo in one form or the other into a simple obligation to ship a full cargo of the commodity selected. In other words, his selection is not like the exercise of an option to name a port. He may change his mind and alter his choice. He 'retains control of his powers until the final ton is put on the ship', said Atkin LJ [1924] 2 KB 637. This may not be a full statement of the nature or consequences of the right of selection, but I have no doubt that it describes the general situation.

(3) If a shipper finds himself stopped by an excepted cause (eg in that case, the government prohibition) from loading or continuing to load the type of cargo that he has provided for and genuinely intended to ship, he may still rely on delay as covered by the exceptions clause to the extent of a reasonable time 'to consider the position and change [his] cargo' as Scrutton LJ said, or to 'deal with the altered conditions' as Bankes LJ said, or, simply, 'to change over' as Atkin LJ said.

As regards this last principle, I must admit that very careful attention to the three judgments of Bankes, Scrutton and Atkin LJJ has left me uncertain as to its origin or its full implications. I think that on the whole his time for adjustment is better attributed to a term derived from the general position of a shipper under such a charterparty, when confronted with such circumstances, than to a right derived from any possible construction of the exceptions clause itself ...

In my opinion, however, the principle of the *Brightman* case has no application here, because there is here no primary obligation on the charterers to ship a mixed cargo. The primary obligation is to provide a cargo of wheat only, the exceptions clause covers delay in the shipping of wheat, and there is no obligation on the charterers to lose that protection by exercising their option to provide another kind of cargo that is not affected by a cause of delay, even assuming such a cargo to be readily available. Really, that seems to me to contain the whole point of the dispute. There is in this case no duty on the charterers to 'switch' from wheat to barley or flour, because their choice of loading barley or flour is unfettered and is not at any time controlled in their hands by an overriding obligation to put on board by a fixed date a full cargo which must include those commodities, if it cannot consist of wheat alone.

It comes down, then, to a question of construing the opening clause of the charterparty. Under it the vessel is to receive on board 'a full and complete cargo ... of wheat in bulk ... and/or barley in bulk and/or flour in sacks'. There are then added the words in typescript 'as below', and this is a qualification which both affects what has gone before and conditions the meaning of what follows, namely, the charterers' undertaking to ship their cargo. The words 'as below' can only refer to the options which are also added in typescript at the foot of the clause, an option to load up to 'one-third cargo of barley in bulk', subject to an increased rate of freight, and an option to load 'up to one-third cargo of flour in bags', also at an increased freight rate. There is no option relating to wheat: wheat is the one commodity not subject to option.

It is said for the shipowners that there is no special significance in the use of the word option in this clause. Charterers who have stipulated for and undertaken to provide mixed or alternative cargoes have an option anyway, since it is they who retain to the end the right of selecting what cargo they are actually to provide; and it is argued that the total effect of the clause is, just as in the *Brightman* case, to leave the charterers under a primary obligation to put on board at the due date a full cargo made up in one or other of the permitted ways.

I do not think that that is the right construction. I cannot agree that, just because even without mentioning an option the charterers would have had a right of choice, the word 'option', when it is expressly mentioned, means no more than this. Wheat, it is to be noted, though linked indifferently with barley and flour as one of the possible cargoes, is, unlike them, not described as the subject of an option. This supports the view that wheat is to be the basic cargo, displaced only if and as the charterers so decide; just as the rate of freight for wheat is to be the basic rate of which other rates are expressed as a variation. Indeed, if the barley and flour options are not intended to be true options in the sense that only the positive exercise of the holder's choice can ever give him any responsibility to load or the shipowners any right to call for those commodities as part of a cargo, I cannot see how the parties could have expressed the option provisions in the way that they did. For, if the language is understood as the shipowners argue that it should be, the phrases introduced by the words 'charterer has the option' convey nothing more than a restriction on the right of selection among the commodities previously mentioned by tying the range of selection down to the permitted proportions; and what is clearly introduced as a right beneficial to the charterers would amount merely to a limitation on their existing power of selection. Moreover, even a short delay in the shipping of the cargo they wanted would turn their right of choice into a burden to ship a cargo they might never require. I cannot think that this was the bargain of the parties ...

[Lords Cohen, Keith, Evershed and Devlin agreed that the shipowners appeal on this issue should be dismissed.]

4 RESPONSIBILITY

MSC Mediterranean Shipping Co SA v Alianca Bay Shipping Co Ltd, The Argonaut [1985] 2 Lloyd's Rep 216

The *Argonaut* was trip chartered for a voyage from South Africa to the Mediterranean/ Continent/UK. The charter was in the New York Produce Exchange form and provided:

> 8 ... Charterers are to load, stow and ... discharge at their own expense under the supervision and responsibility of the Captain.

The vessel was ordered by the charterers to Durban where she loaded *inter alia* granite blocks for discharge at Marina di Carrara (MDC) and at Sete. The vessel was damaged at both Sete and MDC when granite blocks were dropped by stevedores.

Leggatt J: ... The issue in this appeal is whether, on a proper construction of the charterparty, the owners were responsible for damage to the vessel caused by stevedores employed by the charterers ... Each of the parties argued before the arbitrator that the other was liable for stevedore damage except where the complainants were guilty of active intervention ...

In *Blaikie v Stembridge* (1860) 6 CB(NS) 894 it was held that in the absence of custom or agreement to the contrary, it is the duty of the master, on the part of the owner of a ship, to receive and properly stow on board the goods to be carried; and, for any damage to the goods occasioned by negligence by the performance of this duty, the owner is liable to the shipper. In *Sack v Ford*, (1862) 13 CB(NS) 90, the clause in question provided that the cargoes were to be taken on board and discharged by the charterers, the crew of the vessel rendering customary assistance so far as they might be under the orders of the master; and the charterers were to have liberty to employ stevedores and labourers to assist in the loading, stowage and discharge thereof; but such stevedores and labourers, being under the control and direction of the master, the charterers were not in any case to be responsible to the owners for damage or improper stowage. It was held by the Court of Common Pleas that there was nothing in this charterparty to exonerate the owner from responsibility for negligent and improper stowage by the stevedores employed by the charterers under the clause to which I have referred ... At p 100, Chief Justice Erle said:

> Ordinarily speaking, the shipowner has by law cast upon him the risk of attending the loading, stowing, and unloading of the cargo: and the question is whether by the terms of this charterparty he is exempted from that liability. I think not: on the contrary, it appears to me that the charterer, seeing what were the consequences resulting from the decision in *Blaikie v Stembridge*, has expressly stipulated that the liability of the owner for bad stowage shall continue, notwithstanding that the charterer was to have liberty to employ stevedores and labourers to assist in the loading, stowage, and discharge of the cargo.

The Chief Justice added at p 101 that the clause which provided that the owners should, in every respect, be and remain responsible as if the ship was loading and discharging her cargo was but a repetition of the same idea. At p 103, Byles J said:

> The master is to have the control of the stevedores – to tell them what they are not to do; and he is to have the direction – to tell them what they are to do. If any difference of opinion should arise as to the proper mode of stowage, between the stevedore and the master, that of the latter is to prevail.

In his judgment all possibility of doubt was removed by the additional clause also relied on by the Chief Justice.

In *The Helene* (1865) 167 ER 426, the charterparty provided that the cargo should be taken alongside by the charterer, and be received and stowed by the master as presented for shipment, the charterer being allowed to appoint a head stevedore at the expense and responsibility of the master for proper stowage. After citing this provision, Dr Lushington said at p 431:

These words appear to me to answer the objection, and remove the case out of the authority of *Blaikie v Stembridge* where similar words were not contained in the charterparty, and where the court held the true construction of the charterparty to be, that the cargo was to be brought alongside at the risk and expense of the charterer, and that it was to be shipped and stowed by his stevedore, and consequently at his risk – though at the expense of the shipowner, and subject to the control of the master, on behalf of the shipowner, to protect his interests.

... In *Union Castle Mail Steamship Co Ltd v Borderdale Shipping Co Ltd* [1919] 1 KB 612, the charterparty provided that the charterers should bear the expense of loading and discharging cargo, but:

> ... the stowage shall be under the control of the master, and the owners shall be responsible for the proper stowage and correct delivery of the cargo.

Bailhache J held that this clause did not amount to an absolute warranty by the owners, and that it merely meant that they would not be negligent in the stowage of the cargo. Chloride of lime in iron drums, apparently in good condition, was stowed under deck by the charterers' agents, neither they nor the master knowing, or having any reason to suspect, that it would be likely to do harm by being stowed there. The iron drums were in fact defective, and fumes escaping from them damaged other cargo. In those circumstances the judge was not prepared to impute to the master a state of knowledge which was not shared by the charterers' agents. Since no harm would have been done if the drums had been protected in the way suggested, the judge concluded that no negligence was to be imputed to the master, and negligence being necessary to enable the charterers to succeed, the action failed. I see no warrant for importing that necessity and in that respect I decline to follow that case: see *Carver on Carriage by Sea*, 13th edn, s 1097.

In *Ismail v Polish Ocean Lines* [1976] QB 893, stowage instruction had been given by the charterers under the master's supervision and responsibility. At pp 494 and 902E, after referring to the charterers' obligation to load and stow the cargo at their own expense, Lord Denning said:

> Notwithstanding those provisions, the master has an overriding power to supervise the stowage. He must have this as a matter of course ... The master is responsible for the stowage of the cargo so as to ensure the safety of the ship: and also of the cargo so as to see that it is stowed so as to be able to withstand the ordinary incidents of the voyage. That is the meaning of the last words of cl 49: 'He is to remain responsible for the proper stowage and dunnaging'.

At pp 497 and 907D, Ormrod LJ said of cl 49:

> It would be hard to find a form of words better adapted to promoting disputes between owners and charterers than this. On the fact of it it places the master in the impossible position of being under obligations which are, at least potentially, mutually inconsistent. The first part of the clause requires him to comply with the charterer's instructions as to stowage and dunnaging; the second leaves the responsibility for proper stowing and

dunnaging on him. So, if he declines to comply with his instructions he may be in breach, and if he does comply with them he may also be in breach if damage occurs due to improper stowage.

It may be relevant to observe that in that case the charterer overrode the master with the result that the court held the charterer to be estopped from complaining about stowage.

Finally, in *Filikos Shipping Corporation of Monrovia v Shipmair BV (The Filikos)* [1981] 2 Lloyd's Rep 555, it was held by Lloyd J that, although certain clauses in the charterparty placed duty and responsibility for discharge upon the charterers, the subsequent clause which provided that, notwithstanding anything to the contrary, the owners were to be responsible towards the charterers as carriers rendered it impossible to hold that as between owners and charterers the owners were not liable for the relevant loss. This decision was unequivocally upheld by the Court of Appeal: see [1983] 1 Lloyd's Rep 9 ...

The classic exposition of cl 8, albeit without the addition of the words 'and responsibility', is to be found in *Canadian Transport Co Ltd v Court Line Ltd* [1940] AC 934. In that case the House of Lords held that the requirement that cargo was to be stowed under the supervision of the captain did not relieve the charterers of their primary duty to stow safely. But to the extent that the master did supervise the stowage so as to limit the charterers' control of it their liability was correspondingly limited.

Lord Atkin dealt thus with the charterers' argument at pp 166 and 937:

The first answer which the charterers made was that there was no such liability because the duty of the charterers was expressed to be to stow, etc, 'under the supervision of the captain'. This, it was said, threw the actual responsibility for stowage on the captain; or at any rate threw upon the owners the onus of showing that the damage was not due to an omission by the master to exercise due supervision. This, we were told, was the point of commercial importance upon which the opinion of this House was desired. My Lords, it appears to me plain that there is no foundation at all for this defence; and on this point all the judges so far have agreed. The supervision of the stowage by the captain is in any case a matter of course; he has in any event to protect his ship from being made unseaworthy; and in other respects no doubt he has the right to interfere if he considers that the proposed stowage is likely to impose a liability upon his owners. If it could be proved by the charterers that the bad stowage was caused only by the captain's orders, and that their own proposed stowage would have caused no damage no doubt that might enable them to escape liability. But the reservation of the right of the captain to supervise, a right which in my opinion would have existed even if not expressly reserved, has no effect whatever in relieving the charterers of their primary duty to stow safely ...

At pp 168 and 943, Lord Wright said:

It is, apart from special provisions or circumstances, part of the ship's duty to stow the goods properly, not only in the interests of seaworthiness of the vessel, but in order to avoid damage to the goods, and also to avoid loss of space or dead freight owing to bad stowage. In modern times the work of stowage is generally deputed to stevedores, but that does not generally relieve the shipowners of their duty, even though the stevedores are under the charterparty to be appointed by the charterers, unless there are special provisions which either expressly or inferentially have that effect. But under clause 8 of this charterparty the charterers are to load, stow and trim the cargo at their expense. I think these words necessarily import that the charterers take into their hands the business of loading and stowing the cargo. It must follow that they not only relieve the ship of the duty of loading and stowing, but as between themselves and the shipowners relieve them of liability for bad stowage, except as qualified by the words 'under the supervision of the captain', which I shall discuss later. The charterers are granted by the shipowners the right of performing a duty which properly attaches to the shipowners. Presumably this is for the convenience of the charterers. If the latter do not perform properly the duty of stowing the cargo, the shipowners will be subject to a liability to the bill of lading holders. Justice requires that the charterers should indemnify the shipowners against that liability on the same principle that a similar right of indemnity arises when one person does an act and thereby incurs liability at the request of another, who is then held liable to indemnify. That such a liability on the part of the charterers is contemplated is shown by the last words of clause 8 which supposes that the charterers may incur liability for 'damage to cargo'. So far I think is clear. What then is the effect of the words 'under the supervision of the master'? These words expressly give the master a right, which I think he must in any case have, to supervise the operations of the charterers in loading and stowing. The master is responsible for the seaworthiness of the ship and also for ensuring that the cargo will not be so loaded as to be subject to damage, by absence of dunnage and separation, by being placed near to other goods or to parts of the ship which are liable to cause damage, or in other ways ... But I think this right is expressly stipulated not only for the sake of accuracy, but specifically as a limitation of the charterers' rights to control the stowage. It follows that to the extent that the master exercises supervision and limits the charterers' control of the stowage, the charterers' liability will be limited in a corresponding degree.

... Lord Wright added at pp 169 and 945:

The master's power of supervision is obviously not limited to matters affecting seaworthiness.

Lord Maugham agreed with Lord Atkin, and Lord Romer agreed with Lord Atkin and Lord Wright. Finally, at pp 172 and 951 Lord Porter said:

In my opinion by their contract the charterers have undertaken to load, stow and trim the cargo, and that expression necessarily means that they will stow with due care. Prima facie such an obligation imposes upon them the liability for damage due to improper stowage. It is true that the stowage is contracted to be effected under the supervision of the captain, but this phrase does not, as I think, make the captain primarily liable for the work of the charterers' stevedores. It may indeed be that in certain cases as, eg, where the stability of the ship is concerned the master would be responsible for unseaworthiness of the ship and the stevedore would not. But in such cases I think that any liability which could be established would be due to the fact that the master would be expected to know what method of stowage would affect his ship's stability and what would not, whereas the stevedores would not possess any such knowledge. It might be also that if it were proved that the master had exercised his rights of supervision and intervened in the stowage, again the responsibility would be his and not the charterers. The primary duty of stowage, however, is imposed upon the charterers and if they desire to escape from this obligation they must, I think, obtain a finding which imposes the liability upon the captain and not upon them.

This case was considered by Lord Justice Neill in *AB Marintrans v Comet Shipping Co Ltd* [1985] 1 Lloyd's Rep 568 ... In the course of his judgment, Lord Justice Neill said, referring to *Canadian Transport Co Ltd v Court Line Ltd* (above):

It is apparent from these speeches, however ... that the primary responsibility of the charterers may be affected if the captain in fact intervenes by, for example, insisting on his own system of stowage. But in the present case the contract between the parties included the additional words in typescript 'and responsibility'.

The clause had indeed been altered as it was in the present case. After considering the rival submissions in the case before him Neill LJ said at p 575 of the report:

I have found this question a difficult one to resolve. On the one hand, I see the force of Mr Milligan's submission that the addition of the words 'and responsibility' are apt, when taken in conjunction with cl 32, to transfer responsibility back to the owners and in effect to restore the old rule of maritime law. On the other hand, to limit the responsibility of the charterers to that of providing competent stevedores and paying for them gives little weight to the words in cl 8 ... Charterers are to load, stow, trim and discharge the cargo ... Such a narrow construction may also ignore what happens in practice where stowage is treated as a joint undertaking with both the charterers and the ship playing their part.

In the end I have come to the conclusion that the correct approach is to construe the words 'and responsibility' as effecting a prima facie transfer of liability for bad stowage to the owners, but that if it can be shown in any particular case that the charterers by, for example giving some instruction in the course of the stowage, have caused the relevant loss or damage the owners will be able to escape liability to that extent. In my judgment, this approach is consistent with that of the House of Lords in the *Court Line* case where it was clearly contemplated that the party primarily responsible might be relieved from liability for loss caused by the other party's intervention. There may therefore be cases where it will be necessary to consider the dominant cause of particular damage.

If this analysis is correct, the added words 'and responsibility' will place the primary duty on the master and owners but with the possibility that their liability will be affected by some intervention by the charterers.

Later in his judgment at p 577 of the report, Neill LJ said:

... having regard to the terms of this charterparty, neither the stevedores nor the surveyor can be treated as the agents of the charterers so as to make their acts or conduct the acts or conduct of the charterers.

I respectfully endorse and follow those conclusions.

[Counsel] argues that the correct approach is to consider causation. The test, he says, is whether the charterers, in carrying out the mechanics of loading or other operations, have caused loss or damage or whether the owners, in the exercise of their duty of control, have caused the loss or damage. He relies also on *Union Castle Mail Steamship Co Ltd v Borderdale Shipping Co Ltd* [1919] 1 KB 612. But, for the reasons which I have given earlier, that case will not, in my judgment, avail him.

I agree that the charterers' obligation to load, stow and trim the cargo, and discharge, requires them to do so with due care. The primary responsibility for stowage is, however, imposed on the master. Although in the *Court Line* case 'it was clearly contemplated that the party primarily responsible might be relieved from liability caused by the other party's intervention', the concept of 'intervention' may not be entirely apt where what is being exercised on behalf of the charterers is not a right to supervise, such as may take the form of intervention, but a duty to stow properly. At any rate in a case such as the present, I see no need to ascertain what is 'the dominant cause of particular damage'. Either a party is responsible for a particular operation (or damage caused by it) or he is not. The exercise of a right of supervision may impinge upon, override or detract from a duty to stow properly; but it is difficult to see why the fact that responsibility is conferred on the owners should have a corresponding effect of limiting the charterers' control of stowage operations. The fact that there are duties case upon both parties by cl 8 may militate against a construction which make the owners liable for charterers' breach of their own duty. But the effect of cl 8 was to confer the primary duty on the owners and in the absence of actual intervention by the charterers, as distinct from stevedores employed by them, the owners' liability will not be avoided. A limitation of the scope of the liability accepted by the owners through the master may be implicit in the word 'responsibility' itself. It may be said that if the word is to be reasonably construed, its application must be limited to matters within the power of the master, and that in the sense in which the word is here used, a master cannot properly be said to be 'responsible' for damage which he cannot avoid by the reasonable exercise of his powers of supervision and control. It seems to me that the scope of such powers, which is objectively ascertainable, goes beyond what was regarded by the arbitrators as having been within the master's 'province' ...

... I would wish to reserve the question whether in other circumstances a master, and so owners, should be held liable for damage directly caused by charterers, which it was not within the owners' power to prevent, except by the adoption of unusual precautions. It may be that in such a case, as in *Ismail v Polish Ocean Lines* [1976] QB 893, owners' liability may be avoided by operation of the doctrine of estoppel.

The charterers' appeal from the interim award will accordingly be allowed, and that of the owners dismissed.

Notes

1   *The Argonaut* was followed by Steyn J in *The Alexandros P* [1986] 1 Lloyd's Rep 421:

> ... the words 'and responsibility ...' in clause 8 and the transfer of risk comprehended by it, relate to the entire operation of loading, stowing, trimming and discharging the cargo. Specifically, it covers not only the mechanical process of handling the ship's gear and cargo but also matters of stevedores' negligence in strategic planning of loading and discharge of the cargo.

2   In *The Santamana* (1923) 14 Ll L Rep 159 the court was concerned with claims in respect of a cargo of onions which had been shipped from Alexandria to the UK. The onions were damaged by being in stacks 15 or 16 tiers high with insufficient dunnage. Hill J was referred to a number of earlier authorities on the effect of the knowledge of the shippers about the method of stowage which was being used. At p 163 he said:

> I have considered these cases very carefully. They seem to me to carry the law at least far enough to show that a shipper who takes an active interest in the stowage, and complains of some defects but makes no complaint of others which are patent to him, cannot be heard to complain of that to which he has made no objection. I think that the onions were stowed 15 or 16 tiers high without a temporary deck by the leave and licence of [the shipper] and that he cannot be heard to complain of that. I therefore hold that, for the damage caused by reason of that defect, namely, stowing 15 or 16 tiers high without use of a temporary deck, the [owners] are not answerable to [the shippers]. For the damage caused by the other defects they are answerable.

3   Stowage and estoppel by conduct. In *Ismail v Polish Ocean Lines, The Ciechocinek* [1976] QB 893 CA, the claim related to a cargo of new potatoes shipped from Alexandria to the UK. Lord Denning MR (p 495):

> If a shipper or his representative is present when the goods are loaded – and superintends the stowage – or if he insists on their being stowed in a particular manner, he cannot afterwards complain if they are afterwards damaged by being stowed in a bad manner ... The present case is a classic one of its kind. Here Mr Ismail instructed the master to carry 1,400 tons of potatoes. He told him that no dunnage was necessary, and that the bags were of a new kind, such that the potatoes would not suffer on the voyage. On those representations, I do not see that the master could possibly have refused to load the cargo. If he had refused, he would expose the owners to a claim for damages which they would be quite unable to refute -because they had no evidence that the representations were untrue. Again, Mr Ismail allayed the master's misgivings by promising to get a surveyor's certificate and a guarantee: and on the faith of that promise the master loaded the 1,400 tons. In this situation it would be quite contrary to all fairness and to all justice that the shipper or owner should be able to hold the master liable for improper stowage ...

5 DANGEROUS CARGO

Liability of shippers for loss or damage caused by their goods has been the subject of a number of reported decisions, both ancient and modern. In addition to the possibility of liability in tort for negligence or for breach of a statutory duty, possible bases of liability have been held to include breach of the contract of carriage by failing to ship goods which conform to the contractual description; breach of an implied warranty or of a collateral contract to ship safe goods or to disclose the identity or nature of goods shipped or to pack goods properly. Liability under an express, implied or statutory agreement to indemnify is also possible. The precise scope of a shipper's contractual obligations is a matter of controversy: the current balance of authority seems to favour the view that the shipper's obligation is absolute and is not limited to facts within the shipper's actual knowledge.

Statutory safety regulations taking effect under s 85 of the Merchant Shipping Act 1995 currently include the Merchant Shipping (Dangerous Goods and Marine Pollutants) Regulations 1990 (SI 1990 No 2605) and the Merchant Shipping (Carriage of Cargoes) Regulations 1997 (SI 1997 No 19).

Brass v Maitland (1856) 6 El & Bl 470, QB

The defendants shipped a quantity of chloride of lime packed in 60 casks and described as bleaching powder on the plaintiffs' vessel *Regina* for carriage from Calcutta to London. The chloride of lime corroded and burst the casks and damaged other cargo. The plaintiffs were obliged to make good the losses of the owners of the damaged cargo. The case came before the court on demurrer, with the defendants arguing that the plaintiffs had no cause of action on the facts alleged, while the plaintiffs argued that even if the defendants' pleas were true they did not amount to a defence in law.

> **Lord Campbell CJ**, Wightman J concurring: ... Where the owners of a general ship undertake that they will receive goods, and safely carry them and deliver them at the destined port, I am of opinion that the shippers undertake that they will not deliver, to be carried on the voyage, packages of goods of a dangerous nature, which those employed on behalf of the shipowner may not on inspection be reasonably expected to know to be of a dangerous nature, without expressly giving notice that they are of a dangerous nature. Mr Bovill [counsel for the defendants] denied that there was any warranty whatever on the part of the shipper as to the nature of the article shipped, and contended that it was the duty of the master of the ship to ask for information if he wished to know particularly the nature of the goods, with a view to their stowage, quoting various decisions upon the contract between buyer and seller, and between assured and underwriters. But these contracts are so essentially different from the contract between a carrier and the owner of goods to be carried, that the decisions. upon them can here be of little assistance to us ...

... [T]here is an allegation that the plaintiffs and their servants neither had knowledge nor means of knowledge of the dangerous nature of the goods, or of the defective packing, which increased the danger. If, under these circumstances, there were not a duty incumbent on the shipper to give notice of the dangerous nature of the goods to be shipped, commerce could not be carried on. It would be strange to suppose that the master or mate, having no reason to suspect that goods offered to him for a general ship may not safely be stowed away in the hold, must ask every shipper the contents of every package. If he is not to do so, and there is no duty on the part of the shipper of a dangerous package to give notice of its contents or quality, the consequence is that, without any remedy against the shipper, although no blame is imputable to the shipowners or those employed by them, this package may cause the destruction of the ship and all her cargo and the lives of all who sail in her. In the course of the last term we held [*Gillespie v Thompson* 6 El & Bl 477, note (b)] that the owners of a general ship were liable to a shipper for damage done to the goods from other goods stowed in the hold, without allegation or proof of any wilful or negligent default on the part of the ship; and there can be no doubt that the present plaintiffs were bound to make good (as they allege that they have done) to the other shippers of goods to be carried on board their ship from London to Calcutta, the damage done by the chloride of lime shipped by the defendants. If the plaintiffs and those employed by them did not know, and had no means of knowing the dangerous quality of the goods which caused the calamity, it seems most unjust and inexpedient to say that they have no remedy against those who might easily have prevented it. Although those employed on behalf of the shipowner have no reasonable means during the loading of a general ship to ascertain the quality of the goods offered for shipment, or narrowly to examine the sufficiency of the packing of the goods, the shippers have such means; and it seems much more just and expedient that, although they were ignorant of the dangerous quality of the goods, or the insufficiency of the packing, the loss occasioned by the dangerous quality of the goods and the insufficient packing should be cast upon the shippers than upon the shipowners.

It has been truly observed that there is no express decision to establish the liability of the shipper under such circumstances; but this liability has always hitherto been assumed, and has never been contested. In *Williams v The East India Company* (3 East 192) the court and the bar on both sides thought it clear law that it is the duty of a person putting on board ship a dangerous commodity to give notice to the master or other persons employed in the navigation, of its dangerous nature, without any question being put ...

Crompton J (dissenting): ... What then is the nature and extent of this duty or engagement on the part of shippers of goods? On the one hand it is clearly a tortious act, for the consequences of which the shippers are responsible, to ship goods apparently safe and fit to be carried, and from which the shipowner is ignorant that any danger is likely to arise, without notice of such goods being dangerous, if the shipper is aware of such danger. Such shipment, when the scienter is made out, is clearly wrongful and tortious; and perhaps an action on a contract to give notice in such a case might be supported, though it would seem rather to be the subject of an action in tort. On the other hand, I cannot agree with the doctrine contended for on the part of the plaintiffs, that there is an absolute engagement on the part of the shipper that the goods are safe, and fit to be carried on the voyage. Such a warranty would include the cases where the goods may be openly seen, and are known by the shipowner to be dangerous. It does not seem that there is any authority decisive on the point as to whether the shipper is liable for shipping dangerous goods without a communication of their nature, when neither he nor the shipowners are aware of the danger. It seems very difficult to hold that the shipper can be liable for not communicating what he does not know. Supposing that hay or cotton should be shipped, apparently in a fit state and not dangerous to the knowledge of the shippers or of the shipowners, but really being then in a dangerous state from a tendency to heat, are the shippers to be liable for the consequences of fire from the heating of such goods? This is a most important question; for if this be the law, the underwriters on the ship who really ought to be the persons to suffer from such unexpected fire, might bring an action in the name of the shipowners against the shippers of goods, who would be made responsible for the accidental fire, when they were innocent, and would not be insured against the injury to the ship. Again, suppose that there is a new article of commerce which neither shippers nor shipowners know to be dangerous, is the innocent shipper to be liable? Lord Ellenborough's dictum in *Williams v The East India Company* (above), would tend to shew that knowledge of the party shipping is an essential ingredient. On the other hand, it is stated in the passage from *Abbott on Shipping* (p 402, 8th edition) that the merchant must load no prohibited or uncustomed goods by which the ship may be subjected to detention or forfeiture. And this is laid down without any express qualification as to the knowledge of the shipper. In case of such goods, however, the merchant generally knows, or ought to know, from what he is presumed to be acquainted with as to the nature of his trade, whether the goods he is shipping can properly be sent to their proposed destination; and the passage in question in hardly a sufficient authority for the proposition, that where the shipper is perfectly innocent, and without any means of knowledge, he should be liable to the shipowner for the consequences of a mistake, which neither of them could have avoided. Suppose, for instance, that a shipment was made of goods for a foreign port, to which, according to the information known at the shipping port, such consignments might be properly and safely made, but that by some recent law the foreign country has made such shipment illegal: would the shipper he liable in such case? I entertain great doubt whether either the duty or the warranty extends beyond the cases where the shipper has knowledge, or means of knowledge, of the dangerous nature of the goods when shipped, or where he has been guilty of some negligence as shipper, as by shipping without communicating danger which he had the means of knowing, and ought to have communicated. Probably an engagement or duty may be implied that the shipper will use and take due and proper care and diligence not to deliver goods apparently safe, but really dangerous, without giving notice thereof; and any want of care in the course of the shipment in not communicating what he ought to communicate might he negligence for which he would be liable; but where no negligence is alleged, or where the plea negatives any alleged negligence, I doubt extremely whether any right of action can exist ...

Acatos v Burns (1878) 3 Ex D 282 CA

The plaintiff shipped 5.5 tons of maize on board the defendants' steamship *Sidon* at Constantinople to be carried to Liverpool. The maize was taken alongside the steamer in lighters and winnowed on board; after every 50 kilos were shipped the second officer of the *Sidon* examined it. At Smyrna, a port of call, the master found that the maize had become heated, some of it had sprouted, and that the whole parcel was in bad condition and could not be kept on board without danger to the rest of the cargo. The maize was discharged and sold. The plaintiff sued for non-delivery, alleging that the sale was unlawful; the defendant counterclaimed alleging, on the basis of *Brass v Maitland*, breach of a warranty that the goods were fit to be shipped. The jury found at trial that the maize was not in good order and condition when shipped but that its state could not be ascertained by reasonable means and that all reasonable means had been adopted.

> **Bramwell LJ**: ... The counterclaim is framed on the assumption that, in point of law, the plaintiff warranted that the maize was in a fit state to be carried when shipped. But there was no such warranty. We might admit that *Brass v Maitland* was correctly decided, and yet say that it does not govern this case. For the quality of the maize tendered for shipment was as much known to the one side as the other. Without, however, going further into the question, I am of opinion that there was no warranty.

> **Brett LJ**: ... As to the question of warranty, neither *Brass v Maitland* nor any other case shews that there is a warranty by the shipper that the goods shipped have no concealed defects at the time of shipment.

Bamfield v Goole and Sheffield Transport Co Ltd [1910] 2 KB 94, CA

The plaintiff's husband was the owner of a keel which he operated, with the plaintiff's help, as a common carrier. The defendants were forwarding carriers. They delivered 27 casks which they knew contained a chemical called ferro-silicon to the plaintiff's husband for carriage by him from Goole to Sheffield by canal. The casks were described as general cargo. The deceased was not informed by the defendants and did not know that it was ferro-silicon. None of the parties were aware that, when wet, some ferro-silicon gave off poisonous gasses. The casks gave off gases which killed the plaintiff's husband and injured the plaintiff. The plaintiff claimed, alternatively, for breach of contract, or for negligence or breach of duty and sued both in her own right, and also as administratrix of her husband, to recover damages in respect of her illness and the pecuniary loss occasioned by her husband's death. At trial it was found that knowledge of the dangerous nature of the goods could not be imputed to the defendants. The judge has found a verdict in the plaintiff's favour for £325. On appeal, it was held that the action was maintainable.

Fletcher-Moulton and Farwell LJJ held that a consignor who tenders goods to a common carrier – who is under a common law duty to carry safe but not dangerous goods – must either inform the carrier what the goods are to enable the carrier to decide whether to accept the goods and to assess the risk for himself or be held to impliedly warrant that they are fit to be carried in the ordinary way and are not dangerous. Vaughan Williams LJ refused to imply a warranty that the goods were fit to be carried but found that the defendants were negligent in not communicating the name of the cargo to the carrier.

Mitchell, Cotts v Steel [1916] 2 KB 610

The *Kaijo Maru* was chartered to the defendants to carry a cargo of rice from Bassein to Alexandria. The parties later agreed to substitute Piraeus as the port of discharge. Government authorities detained the vessel at Port Said and refused to allow her to proceed to Piraeus. The cargo was eventually discharged at Alexandria. An umpire found that at the time Piraeus was fixed as the port of delivery, the charterers knew that permission of governmental authorities was necessary, that they did not communicate this to the owners and that they had not obtained the necessary permission. The umpire also found that the shipowners could not reasonably have known that permission was necessary to discharge at Piraeus.

> **Atkin J:** ... I think there is no question that a shipment of goods upon an illegal voyage – ie upon a voyage that cannot be performed without the violation of the law of the land of the place to which the goods are to be carried – a shipment of goods which might involve the ship in danger of forfeiture or delay – is precisely analogous to the shipment of a dangerous cargo which might cause the destruction of the ship. I do not think there is any distinction between the two cases.
>
> Whatever may be the full extent of the shipper's obligations, it appears to me that it amounts at least to this, that he undertakes that he will not ship goods likely to involve unusual danger or delay to the ship without communicating to the owner facts which are within his knowledge indicating that there is such risk, if the owner does not and could not reasonably know those facts. I think that is placing the obligation of the shipper within very moderate limits, and it may be considerably wider ...

The Athanasia Comninos [1990] 1 Lloyd's Rep 277

Coal was shipped on the *Athanasia Comninos* by the defendants, Devco, under bills of lading providing for carriage from Nova Scotia to Birkenhead. Methane gas emitted from the coal after loading mixed with air and exploded in the course of the voyage, injuring members of the crew and damaging the vessel. The holds were not ventilated during the voyage.

> **Mustill J:** ... In essence, the plaintiffs' case ... is founded on the assertion that the gassiness of each cargo on shipment was such as to create a danger which the plaintiffs had not consented to run when they agreed to carry a cargo described as 'coal'; that the excessive gassiness of the coal was not apparent to the master and crew on reasonable examination at the port of shipment, and was not the subject of any sufficient warning by Devco or anyone else; that the

cargo was properly carried in accordance with current practice; and that the casualty was caused by the dangerous nature of the cargo ...

It has been established for more than a century that a shipper, party to a contract of carriage, is under certain contractual obligations as to the suitability for carriage of the goods which he ships, and as to the giving of warnings concerning any dangerous characteristics of the goods: *Williams v East India Company*, (1802) 3 East 192; *Brass v Maitland* (1856) 6 E & B 470. These obligations are not confined to cases where the goods are tendered to a common carrier, but are capable of applying, in appropriate circumstances, to all contracts for the carriage of goods by sea ...

I now turn to the legal problems which are of direct relevance to the present dispute. The first, and most important, is to find a general test which will permit the identification of those cargoes whose shipment is a breach of contract, in the absence of a specific warning as to their characteristics. In my view, it is essential when looking for such a test to remember that we are here concerned, not with the labelling in the abstract of goods as 'dangerous' or 'safe', but with the distribution of risk for the consequences of a dangerous situation arising during the voyage. The character of the goods does, of course, play an important part in creating such a situation. But it is not the only factor. Equally important are the knowledge of the shipowner as to the characteristics of the goods, and the care with which he carries them, in the light of that knowledge. It is true that in some of the reported cases the courts have referred to the goods in question as 'dangerous'. This is perfectly understandable, for the goods were obviously of a type which created extraordinary hazards, and no problems of classification were in issue ... It does not follow that the same approach can be adopted in a case such as the present, where it is impossible to say in the abstract that coal in general, or Devco coal in particular, is either dangerous or safe. Carriage of coal involves hazards greater than those associated with inert goods; but they are hazards which could be overcome if the shipowner had the necessary knowledge, skill and equipment: and this is so even if, as the plaintiffs allege, the particular cargo brings with it a risk greater than that which is usually associated with the carriage of coal. In such a case, I consider that it is not correct to start with an implied warranty as to the shipment of dangerous goods and try to force the facts within it; but rather to read the contract and the facts together, and ask whether, on the true construction of the contract, the risks involved in this particular shipment were risks which the plaintiffs contracted to bear.

If one adopts this approach, the enquiry must obviously begin with the bill of lading. Mr Steyn QC, indeed, maintains for Devco that the enquiry not only begins but ends with that document. The contract was for the carriage of coal; by so contracting, the plaintiffs accepted the risks known to be associated with the carriage of coal; those risks included the hazard that methane emitted from the coal would combine with air to create an explosive mixture; accordingly (so the argument runs) the explosion which occurred here was within the area of risk assumed by the plaintiffs, however gassy the coal might be.

This is a formidable argument, for which support may be found in *Acatos v Burns* (1878) 3 Ex D 282; *Greenshields, Cowie & Co v Stephens & Sons*, [1908] 1 KB 51, *per* Kennedy LJ at p 61, and [1908] AC 431, *per* Lord Halsbury, LC at p 436;

Bamfield v Goole and Sheffield Transport Co, above, *per* Fletcher-Moulton LJ at p 109; and *Brass v Maitland*, above, *per* Lord Campbell CJ at p 487. In my view, however, the submission is not well founded. The decisions and dicta cited were not concerned with situations where it was proved that the cargoes had dangerous characteristics different in degree from those notoriously associated with goods of that type. For my part I can see no reason in principle why a special danger which consists of a difference in degree, rather than in kind, from the known danger should not be regarded as lying outside the area of risk which the shipowner has contracted to bear ...

There still remains the problem of identifying the boundary between those risks which the shipowner contracts to bear and those which he does not. One possibility is to draw the line by reference to the proper method of carriage. According to this view, a shipowner who consents to carry goods of a particular description contracts to perform the carriage in a manner appropriate to goods of that description, and thereby assumes all risks of accidents attributable to a failure to carry in that manner.

This is an attractive proposition, for it neatly solves the question of degree to which I have referred, and enables attention to be concentrated on the means adopted to carry the goods. If the carrier proves that he has used the appropriate means, the claim succeeds, without his having to engage in the often difficult tasks of establishing the precise character of the goods, and the precise respects and degree in which they deviated from the norm. Conversely, if his performance has fallen short of what is appropriate, in a manner which is causative of the loss, his claim must fail. This approach also has the theoretical merit of keeping attention focused on the carriage of the goods, which is the subject matter of the contract from which the liability of both parties mainly, if not exclusively, arises.

This approach will be sufficient to deal with most problems relating to dangerous cargoes, for in respect of the great majority of goods, the 'normal' precautions will suffice to eliminate the risk of carrying normal goods of the description stated in the contract. Leaving outside casualties from wholly extraneous causes, one can say that proper carriage and 'dangerous' nature are opposite sides of the same coin.

There are, however, cases to which this simple analysis cannot be applied: ie those where the nature of the goods is such that even a strict compliance with the accepted methods of carriage will not suffice to eliminate the possibility of an accident. Whether consciously or not, seafarers and those who advise them have chosen to adopt methods of carriage which involve an element of risk. No doubt the risk could be eliminated, if those concerned were to provide complex equipment, and enforce rigorous standards of performance. But for practical reasons, they do not. The existence of this gap between acceptable carriage and safe carriage means that there may be cases where an accident is due, neither to the unusual cargo, nor to any shortcomings in the carrier, but to simple bad luck.

Who is to bear the risks of accidents falling into this category? In my judgment, the risk must fall on the carrier. By contracting to carry goods of a specified description, he assents to the presence on his ship of goods possessing the attributes of the goods so described; and in the case under discussion, those attributes include the capacity to create dangers which the accepted methods are not always sufficient to overcome.

This leaves untouched the problem of identifying boundaries of this middle area of acceptable risks. I do not believe that any general solution can be attempted: everything will depend on description of the goods in the contracts, the size of the gap between proper carriage and completely safe carriage, the knowledge of means of the carrier as to the existence of this gap, and other matters from which the extent of the carrier's assent to the running of the risk can be inferred. All that one can say is that the risks must be of a totally different kind (whether in nature or degree) from those attached to the carriage of the described cargo, before shipment of the particular cargo can be regarded as a breach of duty.

Proof of breach: on the view of the law which I have expressed, it is necessary for the plaintiffs to show that the emission characteristics of the cargoes in question fell outside the range of those contemplated by a contract to carry 'coal' ...

I have come to the clear conclusion that no such case is made out. The plaintiffs have the burden of proving that the shipment of cargoes created risks which they never contracted to bear. At the most, they have raised a suspicion that the cargoes were more gassy on shipment than the majority of coal cargoes. This is not enough ...

Effort Shipping Co Ltd v Linden Management SA, The Giannis NK [1996] 1 Lloyd's Rep 577, CA

A shipment of ground nut pellets was loaded on the vessel at Dakar under a bill of lading which incorporated the Hague Rules. The shipment was infested with Khapra beetle which in its larval form was proved to be capable of consuming a grain cargo. Bulk wheat pellets had been loaded at previous loading ports. The presence of the beetles was discovered and discharge from the vessel was prohibited in the Dominican Republic and Puerto Rico. After unsuccessful attempts to fumigate, the shipowners were required to return the cargo to its port of origin or dump it at sea. The shipowners brought proceedings against the shippers. The Court of Appeal held that the owners were entitled to be indemnified by shippers under Article IV, r 6 of the Hague Rules: see Chapter 9. The court went on to consider an alternative claim that the owners were entitled to rely on an undertaking implied at common law that a shipper will not ship goods of such a dangerous character that they are liable to cause physical damage to the vessel or its cargo, or to cause detention or delay, without giving notice to the owner of the character of the goods.

Hirst LJ (delivering the judgment of the court): ... On the question whether this implied undertaking is absolute or qualified, we were referred to a number of authorities. In *Brass v Maitland* (1856) 6 El & Bl 470 the defendants unwittingly shipped a dangerous cargo on the plaintiffs' vessel, which was a general ship. The majority of the Court of Queen's Bench (Lord Campbell CJ, and Wightman

J) held that the shippers' liability was strict, as illustrated, for example, by the following passage in Lord Campbell's judgment at p 485:

> The merchant must not lade goods of a dangerous nature, which the master and those employed in the navigation of the ship have no means of knowing to be of a dangerous nature, without giving notice of their nature, so that the master and those employed in the navigation of the ship may exercise an option to refuse to accept them, and, if accepted, may stow them where they will not endanger the rest of the cargo.

Crompton J dissented, and held that the implied undertaking of the shipper did not extend beyond the obligation to take proper care not to deliver dangerous goods without notice.

Brass's case was considered in two subsequent Court of Appeal cases, *Bamfield v Goole & Sheffield Transport Co* [1910] 2 KB 94 and *Great Northern Railway Co v LEP Transport* [1922] 2 KB 742. The former case concerned the liability of common carrier, and the latter the liability of a railway company which had similar obligations to a common carrier.

In *Bamfield's* case the majority (Fletcher-Moulton and Farwell LJJ) approved *Brass's* case, while Vaughan Williams LJ preferred the view of Crompton J.

In the *Great Northern Railway Co* case (Bankes, Scrutton and Atkins LJJ) the court unanimously approved *Brass's* case, as exemplified for example in the judgment of Scrutton LJ at p 762 where he stated:

> I will consider first the question which logically comes first, that is the liability of a consignor of dangerous goods, when he sends them to a carrier. That has always been the subject of a difference of judicial opinion, but in my view we are bound by the decision of this court to take our stand on one side of the controversy, and if the controversy is to be finally settled it must be done by a superior tribunal. In *Brass v Maitland*, which in my view was not a case of a common carrier at all, but a shipment of goods on a general ship, the shipper put on board the ship casks of stuff described as bleaching powder. In fact the bleaching powder was of a highly corrosive character; so corrosive that the casks were insufficient to hold it, and the contents ate their way through the casks and damaged other cargo. The question arose, What was the obligation on the shipper? The court was divided. Lord Campbell CJ and Wightman J took the view that there was a warranty by the shipper that he would not deliver dangerous goods so packed that those employed on behalf of the shipowner could not on a reasonable inspection discover their dangerous nature, without expressly giving notice that they were dangerous, and that the warranty was independent of the knowledge of the shipper; if he delivered goods of a dangerous character which when looked at did not show that they were dangerous, and under a name which did not disclose that they were dangerous, there was an absolute warranty that the goods were fit to be carried, and if damage was done because they were not fit to be carried, the consignor or the shipper must pay. Crompton J dissented. I respectfully agree with the comments which have always been made on the judgment of Crompton J. That learned Judge was of opinion that the obligation was only to give notice if it was known that the goods were

dangerous; consequently a forwarding agent, who did not know that the goods were dangerous, was not under liability. That was not a case of a common carrier at all. The duty of the defendants was based on the general obligation of a man who asks somebody else to carry goods for him which, by the nature of them, cannot be openly inspected when they are brought alongside the ship. Those facts are enough to impose a liability on the person making the request.

He then referred to *Bamfield's* case, and at p 764 concluded that the court was bound by the decision of the majority in that case.

In my judgment we are also bound by these two Court of Appeal cases, and I am unable to accept Mr Broadbent's submission that they can be distinguished on the ground that they both dealt with the position of common carriers or the like, seeing that any such distinction was expressly negatived both in the passage quoted above from Scrutton LJ's judgment and by Bankes LJ at p 757.

Finally, Mr Broadbent invited us to regard the two limbs of the common law undertaking as separate principles, and to treat the second limb (legally dangerous goods involving detention or delay to the vessel) as only a qualified obligation. I do not think that this submission is sustainable, since the two limbs have always been treated as two aspects of a single principle ...

I would therefore hold that the common law undertaking in its entirety is absolute, and that the second limb applies here, seeing that, on any view, the shipment of the infested cargo was likely to involve detention and delay of the vessel, as in fact occurred.

References

Bulow, LC, 'Dangerous Cargoes' [US position] [1989] *LMCLQ* 342

Girvin, SD, 'Shipper's Liability for Dangerous Cargoes' [1996] *LMCLQ* 487

Rose, FD, 'Cargo Risks: dangerous goods' [1996] 55 *Camb LJ*

CHAPTER 12

FREIGHT

1 DELIVERY FREIGHT

Freight is the consideration paid to the shipowner for performing his part of the contract of carriage. Typically this means that an agreed rate is payable according to the weight or volume of cargo (eg £10 per long ton) carried to and delivered at its destination. In general, it is open to the parties to make whatever agreement they want about how freight shall be calculated, earned and paid. But unless a special agreement is made, eg for payment in advance, or for a lump sum, payment of freight and delivery of the cargo at the port of discharge are concurrent conditions: *Black v Rose* (1864) 2 Moore PC(NS) 277; *Paynter v James* (1867) LR 2 CP 348. Nevertheless the shipowner is entitled to freight if either he is ready, willing and able to deliver in accordance with the contract of carriage or if he is only prevented from delivering by some act or omission of the cargo owner. But no freight is payable if the shipowner cannot deliver the goods because they have been lost or destroyed. It does not matter how or why the goods are lost or destroyed, or (probably) even if they destroy themselves through inherent vice (see *Matheos v Dreyfus* [1925] AC 655, at 667, Lord Sumner). No freight is payable even where the loss occurs without fault on the part of the shipowner and even if the cause of the loss is an excepted peril: excepted perils may prevent the shipowner from being sued for losing or damaging the cargo, but they do not normally confer a right to freight. Destruction of the merchantable character or commercial identity of a cargo has the same effect on the right to freight as a total destruction of the goods. Where only part of a cargo is delivered, freight is payable on that part; delivery of a complete cargo is not a condition precedent to the recovery of freight: *Ritchie v Atkinson* (1808) 10 East 294. Freight is payable in full on cargo which is delivered damaged. No deductions can be made from or set off against freight which is payable on goods delivered, for the value of other goods which are lost or damaged; but a separate action (or a counterclaim) may be brought to recover damage for which the shipowner is responsible.

Dakin v Oxley (1864) 15 CBNS 647, 660, Court of Common Pleas

Willes J delivered the judgment of the court: This is an action by shipowner against charterer to recover the freight of a cargo of coal carried from Newport to Nassau ... The defendant pleads that, by the fault of the master and crew and their unskilful and negligent navigation of the vessel, the coal was damaged so as upon arrival at the port of discharge to be then there of less value than the freight, and that he abandoned it to the shipowner. The plea, as it does not deny, admits that the cargo arrived as coal, and that it was of some value. The plaintiff demurs: and the question for us to consider is, whether a charterer whose cargo has been damaged by the fault of the master and the crew so as upon arrival at the port of discharge to be worth less than the freight, is entitled to excuse himself from payment of freight by abandoning the cargo to the shipowner. We think not: and we should not have taken time to consider, but for the general importance of the subject, and of its having been suggested that our law was silent upon this question, and that the plea was warranted by the usage and law of other maritime countries, which, it was said, we ought to adopt ...

It ought to be borne in mind, when dealing with such cases, that the true test of the right to freight is the question whether the service in respect of which the freight was contracted to be paid has been substantially performed; and, according to the law of England, as a rule, freight is earned by the carriage and arrival of the goods ready to be delivered to the merchant, though they be in a damaged state when they arrive. If the shipowner fails to carry the goods for the merchant to the destined port, the freight is not earned. If he carry part, but not the whole, no freight is payable in respect of the part not carried, and freight is payable in respect of the part carried unless the charterparty make the carriage of the whole a condition precedent to the earning of any freight – a case which has not within our experience arisen in practice ...

Little difficulty exists in applying the above test where the cargo upon arrival is deficient in quantity. Where the cargo, without loss or destruction of any part, has become accidentally swelled (*Gibson v Sturge* 10 Exch 622), or, perhaps, diminished, as, by drying (*Jacobsen's Sea Laws*, Book 3, ch 2, p 220), freight (usage of trade apart) is payable upon the quantity shipped, because that is what the contract refers to ...

In the case of an actual loss or destruction by sea-damage of so much of the cargo that no substantial part of it remains; as, if sugar in mats, shipped as sugar and paying so much per ton, is washed away, so that only a few ounces remain, and the mats are worthless, the question would arise whether practically speaking any part of the cargo contracted to be carried has arrived ...

Where the quantity remains unchanged, but by sea-damage the goods have been deteriorated in quality, the question of identity arises in a different form, as, for instance, where a valuable picture has arrived as a piece of spoilt canvas, cloth in rags, or crockery in broken shreds, iron all or almost all rust, rice fermented or hides rotten.

In both classes of cases, whether of loss of quantity or change in quality, the proper course seems to be the same, *viz*, to ascertain from the terms of the contract, construed by mercantile usage, if any, what was the thing for the carriage of which freight was to be paid, and by the aid of a jury to determine whether that thing, or any and how much of it, has substantially arrived.

If it has arrived, though damaged, the freight is payable by the ordinary terms of the charterparty; and the question of fortuitous damage must be settled with the underwriters, and that of culpable damage in a distinct proceeding for such damage against the ship captain or owners. There would be apparent justice in allowing damage of the latter sort to be set off or deducted in an action for freight; and this is allowed in some (at least) of the United States, *Parsons on*

Mercantile Law, 172, n. But our law does not allow deduction in that form; and, as at present administered, for the sake perhaps of speedy settlement of freight and other liquidated demands, it affords the injured party a remedy by cross-action only: *Davidson v Gwyne* 12 East 381; *Stinson v Hall* 1 Hurlst & N 831; *Sheels (or Shields) v Davies* 4 Campb 119, 6 Taunt 65; the judgment of Parke B in *Mondel v Steel* 8 M & W 858; *The Don Francisco* 32 LJ Adm 14, *per* Dr Lushington. It would be unjust, and almost absurd that, without regard to the comparative value of the freight and cargo when uninjured, the risk of a mercantile adventure should be thrown upon the shipowner by the accident of the value of the cargo being a little more than the freight; so that a trifling damage, much less than the freight, would reduce the value to less than the freight; whilst, if the cargo had been much more valuable and the damage greater, or the cargo worth a little less than the freight and the damage the same, so as to bear a greater proportion to the whole value, the freight would have been payable, and the merchant have been put to his cross-action. Yet this is the conclusion we are called upon by the defendant to affirm in his favour, involving no less than that that damage, however trifling, if culpable, may work a forfeiture of the entire freight, contrary to the just rule of our law, by which each party bears the damage resulting from his own breach of contract, and no more.

The extreme case above supposed is not imaginary; for, it has actually occurred on many occasions, and notably upon the cessation of war between France and England in 1748, which caused so great a fall in prices that the agreed freight in many instances exceeded the value of the goods. The merchants in France sought a remission of freight or the privilege of abandonment, but in vain. (2 Boulay-Paty, *Cours de Droit Commercial*, 485, 486.)

It is evident enough from this review of the law that there is neither authority nor sound reason for upholding the proposed defence. The plea is naught, and there must be judgment for the plaintiff.

Asfar v Blundell [1896] 1 QB 123, CA

Dates were shipped on the vessel *Govino* under bills of lading which made freight payable to the plaintiffs on right delivery in London. The ship collided with another vessel in the Thames and sank. She was raised but the dates were found to be unfit for human consumption. The trial court found the dates were unmerchantable as dates although a proportion were still recognisable and the cargo was still valuable and was sold for £2,400 for export for distillation. On a claim against underwriters who had insured the carrier against loss of freight, it was held that no freight was payable.

Lord Esher MR (at 127): I am of opinion that this appeal should be dismissed. The first point taken on behalf of the defendants, the underwriters, is that there has been no total loss of the dates, and therefore no total loss of the freight on them. The ingenuity of the argument might commend itself to a body of chemists, but not to businessmen. We are dealing with dates as subject matter of commerce; and it is contended that, although these dates were under water for two days, and when brought up were simply a mass of pulpy matter impregnated with sewage and in a state of fermentation, there had been no change in their nature, and they still were dates. There is a perfectly well known test which has for many years been applied to such cases as the present – that test is whether, as a matter of business, the nature of the thing has been altered. The nature of a thing is not necessarily altered because the thing itself has been damaged; wheat or rice may be damaged, but may still remain the things dealt with as wheat or rice in business. But if the nature of the thing is altered, and it becomes for business purposes something else, so that it is not dealt with by business people as the thing which it originally was, the question for determination is whether the thing insured, the original article of commerce, has become a total loss. If it is so changed in its nature by the perils of the sea as to become an unmerchantable thing, which no buyer would buy and no honest seller would sell, then there is a total loss. That test was applied in the present case by the learned judge in the court below, who decided as a fact that the dates had been so deteriorated that they had become something which was not merchantable as dates. If that was so, there was a total loss of the dates. What was the effect of this upon the insurance? If they were totally lost as dates, no freight in respect of them become due from the consignee to the person to whom the bill of lading freight was payable – that is, to the charterers – and there was a total loss of the bill of lading freight on these dates ...

Notes

1   In *Duthie v Hilton* (1868) 4 CP 138 (an action for freight) the plaintiffs contracted to carry 300 casks of cement on the *John Duthie* from London to Sydney. Freight was to be paid 'within three days after arrival of ship and before delivery of any portion of the goods'. Before delivery and within three days of arrival, the ship was scuttled in Sydney to extinguish an accidental fire. The cement hardened and the casks were destroyed. The parties agreed on these facts that the cement no longer existed as cement. The plaintiffs admitted that this was a case of total loss but alleged that the freight had become payable on arrival of the vessel and before the loss occurred. It was held that the plaintiffs had to be ready to deliver the goods on demand throughout the agreed period. Since they were not, freight was not payable. If no time had been fixed, the shipowner must be ready to deliver for a reasonable time to earn freight.

2   The holders of a respondentia bond on a cargo (for whom the cargo owners were found to be responsible) obtained an order of the Court of Admiralty for the removal and sale of the cargo. It was held that freight was payable as performance of the contract had been (in effect) prevented by the cargo owners: *The Cargo ex The Galam* (1863) 33 LJ Adm 97, Privy Council on appeal from the Court of Admiralty.

3   The *Caspian Sea* was chartered for a voyage from Punta Cardon to Genoa with freight payable on delivery. She was loaded with 'Bachaquero Crude', a Venezuelan crude oil normally free of paraffin. The charterers took physical delivery at the port of discharge, but denied that freight was payable because they alleged that the cargo had been contaminated by paraffinic products from residues of a previous cargo. Arbitrators stated a

case for the opinion of the court. The award was remitted to the arbitrators, the court finding that the owners would be entitled to freight if what they had delivered could in commercial terms, bear a description which sensibly and accurately included the words 'Bachaquero Crude'. The arbitrators had to decide whether 'Bachaquero Crude' meant a 'paraffin-free crude'; if it did, the owners were not entitled to freight. Or did it mean 'a crude from the Bachaquero region which in its natural state contains no paraffin'; in this case, the owners would be entitled to freight unless the cargo was so contaminated that it was not possible to describe it even as 'contaminated Bachaquero Crude': *Montedison v Icroma* [1980] 1 Lloyd's Rep 91, Donaldson J.

4   Is the proper starting point in a case such as the *Caspian Sea* to ask, what description did the shipper apply to the goods? Or should we ask instead, what precisely was it that the parties agreed would be the service on performance of which freight would be paid? Does this mean we must consider not only the words the shipper used to describe the cargo, but also what both parties knew or must be taken to have known about, eg any special susceptibilities of that cargo?

5   The idiosyncratic English rule is that, in the absence of an agreement to the contrary, a claim for loss or damage to cargo cannot be asserted by way of deduction from or equitable set off against freight. There is no general agreement on the reason for this rule, although suggested explanations include: (1) alleged judicial tenderness for shipowners which is suggested to have been appropriate when communications were poor and facilities for transfer of money limited; and (2) a special desire to encourage prompt payment and avoid spurious delaying complaints in case of contracts for carriage by sea. The rule is inconsistent with the law of some other maritime jurisdictions and with the English rule applied to contracts for the sale of goods and for work. Nevertheless, in *Aries Tanker v Total Transport, The Aries* [1977] 1 All ER 398, the House of Lords refused to abandon the rule because the parties had contracted on the basis of and against the background of the established position and to avoid retrospectively disturbing many other contracts similarly entered into. In *Colonial Bank v European Grain & Shipping Ltd, The Dominique* [1989] 1 Lloyd's Rep 431 (noted below) the House of Lords held that a repudiatory breach of a voyage charter, like the non-repudiatory breach considered in *The Aries* (above), was equally incapable of giving rise to a defence by way of equitable set off to a claim for accrued freight under a voyage charterparty. *The Aries* rule is significantly modified in application to time charter hire: see Chapter 15 'Time Charters'. See further Rose, FD [1982] 1 *LMCLQ* 33.

6   It is not unusual in a charterparty for it to be expressly agreed that freight shall be paid in full without deductions for cargo claims, eg by making freight payable 'in cash without discount', as was done in the *Aries* charter,

above. In practice, when a dispute arises, it is common for shipowners to seek payment of freight in full, but for the cargo owner's position to be safeguarded by a guarantee of payment of any damages for which the shipowners are ultimately held responsible to be given by the shipowner's P and I club.

2 LUMP SUM FREIGHT

A lump sum freight is one which is not tied directly to the quantity of cargo actually carried. It is a definite sum agreed to be paid for the hire of a ship for a specified voyage (Lord Lindley, *Williams v Canton Insurance* [1901] AC 462, at 473): for example, £1,000 for a voyage from Y to Z. This may be the easiest way to define the freight obligation when the charterer does not know the exact quantity of cargo which will be loaded or when it is difficult to measure the quantity actually loaded. An alternative, often used in contracts of affreightment which are not tied to a particular vessel, is to fix a rate based on the size of the vessel: eg £10 per deadweight ton. Freight which is computed on intaken quantity and to be paid on that quantity despite a shortage on outturn, shares at least some of the characteristics of lump sum freight: *Shell v Seabridge, The Metula* [1978] 2 Lloyd's Rep 5, CA.

The two basic rules about payment of lump sum freight are, first, that if the ship is put at the disposal of the freighter, the whole of the freight is payable even though no cargo or less than a full cargo is loaded: *Robinson v Knights* (1873) 8 CP 465, at 468. Second, the whole sum is payable if any part of the cargo shipped is delivered, at least if the remainder is lost due to excepted perils. But it is not easy to identity a consistent legal theory which explains these rules. The explanation adopted in *The Norway* (1865) 3 Moore PC(NS) 245 and later followed in *Robinson v Knights* (above) was that a charterparty at a lump sum freight was a contract to pay for the use and hire of a ship for a given voyage, rather than a contract to pay for the carriage and delivery of a particular cargo. On this analysis, the shipowner is clearly entitled to full freight even if he only manages to deliver part of the cargo loaded. He earns freight, it could be said, by making the agreed voyage, not by delivering cargo. But this rationalisation implies that freight can be earned even if no cargo ever arrives, so long as the chartered vessel reached the port of discharge; on the other hand, it also suggests that no freight would be earned if the ship herself does not arrive, even if the whole cargo is in fact delivered in perfect condition. It was largely for these reasons that in *Thomas v Harrowing* (below) a different explanation of the nature of a contract at a lump sum freight was adopted.

Thomas v Harrowing Steamship [1913] 2 KB 171, CA, affirmed (HL) [1915] AC 58

Kennedy LJ (at 184): In this case the plaintiffs chartered their steamship *Ethelwalda* to the defendants to load a cargo of pit props at a place in the Uleaborg district of Finland, and carry it to a dock at Port Talbot for a specified lump sum freight. The freight was payable under article 9 on unloading and right delivery of cargo. The charterparty contained the usual exception of perils of the seas. The *Ethelwalda* arrived with her cargo, which consisted in part of a deckload, outside the port of discharge, when owing to heavy weather she was driven against the breakwater and became a total loss. About two-thirds of the cargo was washed ashore and was collected on the beach by the directions of the master of the *Ethelwalda*, acting on behalf of the plaintiffs, and placed on the dock premises and there delivered to the defendants, the residue of the cargo being lost by perils of the seas. The plaintiffs brought the present action to recover the lump sum freight. Pickford J has held that the plaintiffs, having delivered to the defendants so much of the cargo as they were not prevented by the excepted perils from delivering, had performed their contract, and were entitled to require payment of the lump sum freight. It is against this judgment that the present appeal has been brought ...

[T]wo questions of law, each of which is of considerable general importance, have been raised by the appellants both in this court and before my brother Pickford. They contend, in the first place, that, as the stipulated freight was a lump freight, it could be earned by the plaintiffs only if the cargo was carried to its destination in the *Ethelwalda*, and therefore, inasmuch as she was wrecked outside the breakwater, and the cargo, as it came ashore, was conveyed to the dock in the way in which I have described, no freight could become due, even if the whole cargo had been thus delivered to the defendants. Secondly, they contend that, if they are wrong in this, yet, inasmuch as part of the cargo loaded on board of the *Ethelwalda* was lost and not delivered, that circumstance bars the maintenance of the plaintiffs' claim.

I proceed to consider each of these contentions.

... The only sort of authority which the defendants' counsel put forward for their contention consisted of inferences which they invited us to draw from expressions to be found in the judgments in two reported cases, in each of which the freight reserved by the charterparty under consideration was a lump sum. In the judgment of the Privy Council in *The Norway* (cited above) it was said that the lump sum called freight was not properly so called, but was more properly a sum in the nature of a rent to be paid for the use and hire of the ship. In *Robinson v Knights* (above) Keating J described the freight payable under the charterparty in that case as an entire sum to be paid for the hire of the ship for one entire service, and Brett J, as he then was, in regard to it used the expression 'a stipulated gross sum to be paid for the use of the whole ship for the whole voyage'. It appears to me that none of these statements really afford support to the contention of the present appellants. They must, of course, be read in each case in reference to the particular charterparty which was under the consideration of the court and in reference to the particular question which had to be decided in respect of that charterparty. Neither in *The*

Norway, nor in the case in the Common Pleas, was there any question as to the arrival of the chartered vessel at the port of destination. In each case the vessel had in fact arrived, and therefore the courts had not to consider any question of the shipowner's right, in Lord Ellenborough's words, to earn the whole freight by forwarding the goods by some other means to the place of destination. What they had to decide was the distinct and different question whether under the particular terms of the charterparty before them the shipowner was entitled to claim payment, without deduction, of the whole freight where only part of the cargo was delivered out of the arrived ship – a question involved in the second contention of the defendants which I shall consider presently. Further, it is to be noted that in each of these cases the terms of the charterparty, as I understand the report, were in a material respect different from those of the charterparty with which we are concerned in the present case. In both of them the lump freight was, as to some portion, expressly made payable at a time to be ascertained by reference to the ship's arrival at her destination. In *The Norway*, as is pointed out in the judgment on p 409 of Browning and Lushington's report, one-third in cash was made payable 'on arrival at the port of delivery'. In *Robinson v Knights* the provision was that freight should be paid in cash half on arrival and the remainder on unloading and right delivery of cargo. I must not be understood to say that even such stipulations in a charterparty ought, if that question should ever arise for decision, to be held to affect the shipowner's right, in case of his ship's disablement in the course of the chartered voyage, to forward the cargo and earn the lump sum freight. But the presence of those stipulations in the particular charterparty in each case under consideration cannot properly be left out of sight when we have to consider the expressions in the judgments to which I have referred, and it differentiates the charterparties which contained such stipulations from the charterparty in the present case, which, except that the freight is to be a lump sum and not calculated per standard or per fathom of the timber shipped, in no way differs from the ordinary charterparty for the services of a ship to carry a particular cargo to a particular port, and which expressly provides for the payment of the lump freight, not in reference to the arrival of the ship, but, according to article 9, 'on unloading and right delivery of cargo'. I agree with Pickford J when he says:

> I do not say that there may not be lump sum charters in which the freight, being payable for the use of the particular ship, is not to be paid unless the ship completes her voyage. There may be such charters, but I do not think that this is the effect of the present one.

I may add in this connection that it may be worth noting that by the terms of this charterparty in this case the charterers' agents were to load a full and complete cargo.

I now come to that which I have called the second contention of the defendants, which is that only a part of the cargo was delivered, and, therefore, the contract not having been completely performed by the plaintiffs, they are, according to the principle exemplified by the leading case of *Cutter v Powell* (1795) 6 TR 320, not entitled to claim the lump sum which constituted the agreed remuneration for the performance of the contract of affreightment. Upon this point also I am of opinion that the judgment of Pickford J in favour of the plaintiffs was right. What, under the contract contained in the charterparty, was the condition precedent to the plaintiffs' right to the payment of the lump freight? It was, as I construe the document, the right delivery of the cargo. What is, under this charterparty, meant by 'the cargo'? To ascertain this, we must look at the charterparty, and, so looking, we find that what the shipowner has to deliver is not in all circumstances the quantity of cargo shipped, but all which was shipped and of which delivery was not prevented by any of the excepted perils. This is the law as enunciated in the judgments both of Lord Coleridge CJ and Bramwell B in the case of *Merchant Shipping Co v Armitage* (1873) LR 9 QB 99, in which the charterparty under the consideration of the Exchequer Chamber was in its terms, as to payment of a lump sum freight, excepted perils, and right delivery of cargo, like the charterparty in the present case, and in which, as in the present case, part of the cargo had been lost by excepted perils, and therefore the cargo owner had got only a partial delivery. Lord Coleridge CJ at p 107 dealt with the point in these terms:

> If it were a matter entirely free from authority there might be some ground for saying that 'entire discharge and right delivery of cargo' meant the entire discharge and right delivery of the cargo originally put on board. But the fair and reasonable construction of it, regard being had to the contract being for a lump sum, seems to me to be that which the courts have already put upon similar contracts – that the cargo is entirely discharged and rightly delivered, if the whole of it not covered by any of the exceptions in the contract itself is delivered. Now in this case that which was not delivered and which was not discharged was not so delivered and was not so discharged by reason of perils within the exceptions of the very contract itself; and, therefore, according to these authorities, and according to the reason of the thing, it appears to me that the contract was complied with, and that the lump sum was earned, and that what has not been paid of the lump sum ought to be paid.

... In a comparatively recent case in the House of Lords the law has been laid down in the same way by Lord Lindley. The case was *Williams & Co v Canton Insurance* (above) A lump sum freight, said his Lordship:

> is a definite sum agreed to be paid for the hire of a ship for a specified voyage; and although only payable on the right and true delivery of the cargo, those words are not taken literally, but are understood to mean right and true delivery, having regard to and excluding excepted perils. In other words, the cargo in this clause of the charterparty does not mean the cargo shipped, but the cargo which the shipowner undertakes to deliver. The non-delivery of some of that [namely, the cargo shipped] affords no defence to a claim for a lump sum freight, although such non-delivery, if wrongful, will give rise to a cross-action. This was settled by the Court of Exchequer Chamber in *Merchant Shipping Co v Armitage*, which followed a decision to the same effect by the Privy Council in *The Norway*.

These authoritative pronouncements of the law ... constitute, in my judgment, a sufficient answer to the defendants' second contention. It is common ground that the goods not delivered in the present case were not delivered because they had been lost by excepted perils. The defendants' counsel asked in the course of the argument what, as to the right to freight, ought to be the legal consequence of the chartered ship arriving without any of the cargo on board, so that nothing was delivered, and they further asked whether, if the loss had been caused not by excepted perils, but by the wrongful act or negligence of the shipowner, the lump freight would nevertheless be payable. It is, I think, sufficient to say that it is quite unnecessary for the purpose of our judgment in the present case to decide either of these points which are not involved. But it is clear from his judgment in *Merchant Shipping Co v Armitage* that Bramwell B, for the reason that the delivery of cargo is a condition precedent to payment, would have answered the first of the appellants' questions in favour of the owner of cargo, as he there states; and that in regard to the second question he would have concurred in the opinion expressed by Lord Lindley in the concluding sentence of the passage in his judgment in *Williams & Co v Canton Insurance*, which I have already quoted, that, even if the non-delivery of part of the cargo is due to wrongful conduct or negligence on the part of the shipowner, the proper remedy of the cargo owner is by cross-action. It is, however, in my judgment, as I have already intimated, useless, for the purpose of deciding the present case, to consider how these questions ought to be decided, the relevancy of which is excluded by the facts of the case under consideration.

Notes

1   In *Skibs A/S Trolla v United Enterprises, The Tarva*, [1983] 2 Lloyd's Rep 385 in the Singapore High Court, Chua J held that where the balance of lump sum freight was payable under a voyage charter on 'right and true delivery' the balance became payable when the cargo which had arrived at the ports of discharge had been completely delivered. The shipowners did not have to prove right and true delivery of the whole cargo originally shipped to earn the freight and the charterers had no right to retain the balance against possible cargo claims by consignees.

2   In *Steamship Heathfield Co v Rodenacher* (1896) 2 Com Cas 55, CA, the *Heathfield* was chartered 'guaranteed by owners to carry 2,600 tons dead weight'. It was also provided she would load 'a full and complete cargo of sugar' to be delivered at a stated freight rate 'all per ton dead weight capacity as above'. The ship was given a lien, *inter alia*, for dead freight. The charterer loaded 2,673 tons of sugar, but refused to load the vessel to her actual capacity of 2,950 tons. At first instance (1 Com Cas 446) Mathew J rejected the argument that this was a lump sum freight and held that (1) the owners guarantee meant only that the vessel could carry 2,600 tons at least, not that she could not carry more; (2) that a 'full and complete cargo' meant what it said and was not restricted to 2,600 tons; (3) that the freight rate was to be computed on the basis of a 'full and complete cargo' (2,950 tons), not on the basis of the guaranteed dead weight (2,600 tons). This judgment was upheld on appeal. TE Scrutton was counsel for the successful plaintiffs.

3   In *Rotherfield v Tweedy* (1897) 2 Com Cas 84 the *Rotherfield* was described in the contract (a 'Danube berth note') as 'of the capacity of 4,250 tons'; the owners also guaranteed that the vessel could carry 4,250 tons dead weight. It was agreed that a full cargo would be loaded. Freight was made payable per ton 'on the guaranteed d.-w. capacity of 4,250 tons'. The vessel loaded a full cargo of only 3,947 tons; her stated deadweight capacity included bunkers. The plaintiffs sought freight on 4,250 tons. The court rejected Scrutton's argument as counsel for the unsuccessful plaintiffs that the contract was for a lump sum freight and held freight was payable only on the quantity of cargo actually shipped. Successive editions of Scrutton on *Charterparties*, from the 4th edn, 1899 have stated with justification that both the *Heathfield* and *Rotherfield* decisions seem to strike out of the charters part of their provisions. In *Rotherfield*, the court seems to have been particularly influenced by the fact that, if the parties had intended a lump sum, they could have said so in a simpler way.

4   *Shell v Seabridge* [1977] 2 Lloyd's Rep 5, CA. The *Metula*, a supertanker, was chartered on the Exxonvoy 1969 form to carry a full cargo of petroleum. Freight was to be computed on intake quantity and paid without discount on delivery of cargo at destination. Over 190,000 long tons were loaded at Ras Tanura for carriage to Chile. The vessel stranded in the Magellan Strait and about a third of the cargo was lost; the rest was transhipped and carried to destination. It was held that the owners were entitled to freight on the full amount loaded. The court does not seem to have been impressed by the idea that 'intake quantity' clauses are not intended to deal with accidental losses in known circumstances, but only to avoid disputes where there is, as often occurs, a discrepancy between intake and outturn measurements of bulk cargo because of differences in weighing methods or in the physical circumstances (ie ambient temperature in which the measurements were made); or the normal gains or losses which occur with certain commodities in transit because of, eg evaporation, sedimentation in ship's tanks or absorption of moisture.

3 *PRO RATA* FREIGHT AND THE RIGHT TO FORWARD

Hunter v Prinsep (1808) 10 East 378

The *Young Nicholas* was chartered to carry a cargo of timber from Honduras Bay to London. Freight was payable at agreed rates on or after a right and true delivery of the cargo. The ship and cargo were captured by a French privateer, recaptured by an English sloop but then wrecked at St Kitt's, where the Vice-Admiralty Court (on the master's application) ordered a sale of the cargo. The shipowner claimed to be entitled to freight *pro rata itineris*.

Lord Ellenborough (p 394): The principles which appear to govern the present action are these: the ship owners undertake that they will carry the goods to the place of destination, unless prevented by the dangers of the seas, or other unavoidable casualties: and the freighter undertakes that if the goods be delivered at the place of their destination he will pay the stipulated freight: but it was only in that event, viz, of their delivery at the place of destination, that he, the freighter, engages to pay anything. If the ship be disabled from completing her voyage, the shipowner may still entitle himself to the whole freight, by forwarding the goods by some other means to the place of destination; but he has no right to any freight if they be not so forwarded; unless the forwarding them be dispensed with, or unless there be some new bargain upon this subject. If the shipowner will not forward them, the freighter is entitled to them without paying anything. One party, therefore, if he forward them, or be prevented or discharged from so doing, is entitled to his whole freight; and the other, if there be a refusal to forward them, is entitled to have them without paying any freight at all. The general property in the goods is in the freighter; the shipowner has no right to withhold the possession from him, unless he has either earned his freight, or is going on to earn it. If no freight be earned, and he decline proceeding to earn any, the freighter has a right to possession. The captain's conduct in obtaining an order for selling the goods, and selling them accordingly, which was unnecessary, and which disabled him from forwarding the goods, was in effect declining to proceed to earn any freight, and therefore entitled the plaintiff to the entire produce of his goods, without any allowance for freight. The postea must therefore be delivered to the plaintiff.

St Enoch Shipping v Phosphate Mining [1916] 2 KB 624, at 627

Rowlatt J: There can be no freight *pro rata* unless there is a new contract express or implied to substitute the carriage which has been effected for the carriage originally contracted for. In *Hopper v Burness* (1876) 1 CPD 137, 140, Brett J said:

> What, then, is the principle governing the question whether such freight is payable? It is only payable when there is a mutual agreement between the charterer or shipper and the captain or shipowner, whereby the latter being able and willing to carry on the cargo to the port of destination, but the former desiring to have the goods delivered to him at some intermediate port, it is agreed that they shall be so delivered, and the law then implies a contract to pay freight *pro rata itineris*.

That is a rule clearly stated of what is not only shipping law, but general law, where there is an agreement between two parties that a thing shall be done but no agreement as to the price to be paid for doing it. Park B in *Vlierboom v Chapman* (1844) 3 M & W 230, 238, laid down the law to the same effect:

> To justify a claim for *pro rata* freight, there must be a voluntary acceptance of the goods at an intermediate port, in such a mode as to raise a fair inference, that the further carriage of goods was intentionally dispensed with.

The consignee must accept the goods in such a way as to imply that he and the shipowner agree that the goods have been carried far enough and that the shorter transit shall be substituted for that named in the original contract ... In the present case the defendants, who were consignees, merely took their own goods when they were landed. No agreement to modify the contract of carriage can be inferred from that act.

Note

Lord Ellenborough refers in *Hunter* to the possibility of the shipowner earning freight under a 'new bargain'. Such an agreement may be express or implied. But as Lord Ellenborough's judgment also illustrates, the respective rights of the parties under their original agreement are such that there is little room for the implication of a new contract. It follows from the above decisions that *pro rata* freight will not be payable merely because the owner of the cargo receives it at a place other than the contractual port of discharge. The master is not 'able' to carry or forward cargo if, eg, the cargo has been lost, destroyed or justifiably sold by the master without the cargo owner's consent (*Vlierboom v Chapman, Hopper v Burness*, above).

'Unwillingness' can be demonstrated simply by a wrongful refusal at an intermediate port to carry the cargo to its destination (*Metcalfe v Britannia Ironworks* (1877) 2 QBD 423); it might also be shown if, eg, the crew justifiably abandon the ship and its cargo in a storm, when the cargo owner can treat the contract of carriage as having ended: *The Cito* (1881) 7 PD 5.

The Law Commission provisionally concluded in 1975 (Working Paper No 65 – Pecuniary Restitution on Breach of Contract) that the rules as to payment of *pro rata* freight were so firmly established in the business practice of shipowners and insurers that any interference with them (eg by introducing a general obligation to make a payment in return for any benefit received) would be undesirable. This suggestion was generally approved (Law Com Report No 121, 1983). Compare the approach advocated in (1941) 57 *LQR* 385 (Glanville Williams).

4 ADVANCE FREIGHT

Allison v Bristol Marine Insurance (1876) 1 App Cas 209, HL

The *Merchant Prince* was chartered to carry coal from Greenock to Bombay. The freight rate was 42 shillings a ton, such freight to be paid 'one half in cash on signing bills of lading ... less five per cent for insurance ... and the remainder on right delivery of the cargo'. Half of the freight was paid in London. The shipowner insured the freight which he expected to receive on the delivery of the full cargo. The cargo owner insured his cargo for a sum inclusive of the value of the freight he had prepaid. The ship was wrecked on a reef about eight miles from Bombay. Half the cargo was saved and landed but no further freight was paid. The shipowner claimed on his insurance policies alleging that he had suffered a total loss of half of the freight not paid in advance.

The judges were summoned to assist the House of Lords. After an extensive review of earlier cases Brett J said (at 226):

> I have drawn attention to all the cases, in order to shew how uniform the view has been as to what construction is to be put upon shipping documents in the form of the present charterparty, and as to the uniform, though perhaps anomalous rule, that the money to be paid in advance of freight must be paid, though the goods are before payment lost by perils of the sea, and cannot be recovered back after, if paid before the goods are lost by perils of the sea. Although I have said that this course of business may in theory be anomalous, I think its origin and existence are capable of a reasonable explanation. It arose in the case of the long Indian voyages. The length of voyage would keep the shipowner for too long a time out of money; and freight is much more difficult to pledge, as a security to third persons, than goods represented by a bill of lading. Therefore the shipper agreed to make the advance on what he would ultimately have to pay, and, for a consideration, took the risk in order to obviate a repayment, which disarranges business transactions.

[Of the other judges who attended, Baron Pollock agreed with Brett J; Lord Chief Baron Kelly and Grove J also thought the plaintiff shipowner was entitled to succeed. Blackburn and Mellor JJ thought he was not. The House of Lords unanimously found in favour of the shipowner.]

Notes

1 'Freight due and payable (alternatively: freight to be considered earned) on shipment and non-returnable, ship and/or cargo lost or not lost.' It is very common for bills of lading to make freight payable on or around the date of commencement of the voyage, although there are variations in the precise event (eg receipt of goods by carrier/on shipment/on signing bills of lading/on sailing) on which freight becomes due. Some clauses make a distinction between the date on which freight is 'earned' (on which the freight risk passes from the shipowner) and a later date on which the freight is actually payable. An express statement that advance freight is not repayable might appear to be legally superfluous, at least under English law (many other legal systems require repayment); but it has a commercial advantage. It is easier to resolve a dispute with a shipper by referring him to a clause in a form which he has used than to attempt to demonstrate a general legal principle.

2 Where advance freight is paid and the goods are subsequently lost in circumstances in which the shipowner is liable in an action for damages for non-delivery (ie the loss is not covered by an exclusion clause) then the advance freight paid forms part of the value of the goods at their intended destination and is recoverable as part of their value. *Great Indian Peninsula Rwy v Turnbull* (1885) 53 LT 325.

3 'Final sailing': the *General Chasse* was chartered for a voyage from Cardiff to San Francisco, with a portion of freight payable on final sailing from the port of loading. The ship cleared customs, passed the dock gates, but whilst under tow, she grounded in the ship canal which connected the dock with the open sea. The vessel subsequently became a wreck. It was held that 'sailing' meant the time the vessel is fully fit for sea and breaks ground; but 'final sailing' meant departure from the port and being at sea. The advance freight was not payable: *Roelandts v Harrison* (1854) 9 Ex 447.

4 'On signing bills of lading': one-third of freight was payable on signing bills of lading. The cargo was loaded but the vessel sank before reaching the dock gates and before the bills of lading had been signed. It was held that the charterers had an implied duty to present the bills of lading for signature within a reasonable time and that this obligation did not cease when the ship was lost. The charterers were found to have broken this implied contract and the measure of damages was the amount of the advance freight: *Oriental Steamship v Tylor* [1893] 2 QB 518, CA.

5 'If required': in *Oriental Steamship* (above), the earlier case of *Smith v Pyman* [1891] 1 QB 742 was distinguished. In that case advance freight was payable 'if required' and it was held too late to require it after the ship was lost, because the charterer could then no longer insure it.

6 The *Lorna I* was nominated under a freight contract to lift ore from an Albanian port. The contract provided 'freight non-returnable cargo and/or vessel lost or not lost to be paid ... as follows: 75 per cent ... within five ... days after master signed Bills of lading and the balance after right and true delivery'. Bills of lading were signed but the vessel was lost with all hands, within five days, in a gale in the Black Sea. It was held that freight was not payable because the charterers had been under no obligation to pay any freight until the end of the five-day period and before that time the cargo and the vessel had been lost. Robert Goff J at first instance pointed out that the result would have been different if the parties had chosen to provide that freight was earned on shipment, but was not payable for five days thereafter. *Compania Naviera General v Kerametal* [1983] 1 Lloyd's Rep 373, CA.

7 Plaintiff owners let the *Karin Vatis* for a voyage from Liverpool to India with a cargo of scrap. The charter provided

> Freight deemed earned as cargo loaded ... 95 per cent of freight to be paid within three banking days after completion of loading and surrender of signed bills of lading ... vessel and/or cargo lost or not lost ... Balance of freight to be settled within 20 days after completion of discharge ...

The initial payment was made, the vessel sailed and sank shortly after passing Suez. The charterers denied that the remaining 5 per cent of freight was due on the grounds that no cargo had been discharged. The Court of Appeal held that the entire freight was earned as soon as cargo was loaded. Completion of discharge was not a condition precedent to the recovery of the outstanding amount, which was payable within a reasonable time. *The Karin Vatis* [1988] 2 Lloyd's Rep 330, CA.

8   In *Colonial Bank v European Grain & Shipping Ltd, The Dominique* [1989] 1 Lloyd's Rep 431, shipowners assigned to the plaintiff bank all the earnings of the *Dominique* including all freight. The vessel was chartered to load agricultural produce in bulk at Kakinada, India, for carriage to European ports. The charterparty provided that

> Freight shall be prepaid within five days of signing and surrender of final bills of lading, full freight deemed to be earned on signing bills of lading, discountless and non-returnable, vessel and/or cargo lost or not lost and to be paid to [a named bank in Piraeus].

Cargo was loaded and bills of lading signed. At Colombo the vessel was arrested by suppliers and detained. The charterers justifiably elected to treat the owners' conduct as repudiating the charter. The bills of lading were subsequently surrendered to shippers. The plaintiff bank sued to recover the advance freight from the charterers. The charterers argued that, if the right to freight was held to have accrued before the charterparty was brought to an end, they were nevertheless entitled to set off the damage suffered by them as a result of the owners' repudiation. The House of Lords held that:

(i)   the proper interpretation of the charterparty was that the owners' right to freight accrued on completion of signing of all the bills of lading, with payment being postponed until five days after the signed bills of lading had been delivered to shippers. In the result, the right to freight accrued before the termination of the charter;

(ii) the right to freight was unconditionally acquired before termination of the charter and survived that termination and was not divested or discharged by termination;

(iii) a repudiatory breach of a voyage charter, like the non-repudiatory breach considered in *The Aries* (above), was not capable of giving rise to a defence by way of equitable set off to a claim for accrued freight.

9   In *Krall v Burnett* (1877) 25 W R 305, QB Div Ct, the plaintiff shipped goods in London for carriage to Rouen in the defendant's ship. The ship was lost. The bill of lading stated 'freight payable in London'. It was held that the words meant only that freight was payable in London and not elsewhere, and had no reference to time of payment. The clause was not ambiguous and no evidence of an alleged custom that it meant freight was payable in advance could be given.

5 BACK FREIGHT

Cargo Ex Argos (1873) LR 5 PC 134

The defendant shipped petroleum on the plaintiff's vessel for carriage from London to Le Havre. The bill of lading provided that the petroleum was to be taken out by the defendant within 24 hours of arrival. The vessel arrived at Le Havre, but was ordered to leave the following day by the authorities because of the presence of munitions in the port. The master attempted to land the goods at other local ports but failed. He returned to Le Havre and obtained permission to discharge the petroleum temporarily into a lighter in the outer harbour where it remained under his control. Four days later, the Argos had discharged the rest of her cargo at the quay and was ready to sail. No request for delivery having been made, the master reshipped the petroleum and brought it back to London. It was held that the shipowner had earned the outward freight. But the case is best known for the decision on the shipowner's claim for freight on the return voyage and for expenses.

> **Sir Montague E Smith** (at 164): ... The next question to be considered is, whether the plaintiff is entitled to compensation in the shape of homeward freight for bringing the petroleum back to England. It seems to be a reasonable inference from the facts, that after the four days during which the petroleum had been lying in the harbour had expired, the authorities would not have allowed it to remain there. It was still in the master's possession, and the question is, whether he should have destroyed or saved it. If he was justified in trying to save it, their Lordships think he did the best for the interest of the defendant in bringing it back to England. Whether he was so justified is the question to be considered.

> As pointed out by the judge of the Admiralty Court, the same kind of question arose in *Christy v Rowe* (1808) 1 Taunt 300. In that case Sir James Mansfield says:

>> Where a ship is chartered upon one voyage outwards only, with no reference to her return, and no contemplation of a disappointment happening, no decision, which I have been able to find, determines what shall be done in case the voyage is defeated: the books throw no light on the subject. The natural justice of the matter seems obvious: that a master should do that which a wise and prudent man would think most conducive to the benefit of all concerned. But it appears to be wholly voluntary; I do not know that he is bound to do it; and yet, if it were a cargo of cloth or other valuable merchandise, it would be a great hardship that he might be at liberty to cast it overboard. It is singular that such a question should at this day remain undecided.

> The precise point does not seem to have been subsequently decided; but several cases have since arisen in which the nature and scope of the duty of the master, as agent of the merchant, have been examined and defined. (Amongst others *Tronson v Dent* (1853) 8 Moo PC 419; *Notara v Henderson* (1872) LR 7 QB 225; *Australasian Navigation Company v Morse* (1872) LR 4 PC 222.) It results

from them that not merely is a power given, but a duty is cast on the master in many cases of accident and emergency to act for the safety of the cargo, in such manner as may be best under the circumstances in which it may be placed; and that, as a correlative right, he is entitled to charge its owner with the expenses properly incurred in so doing.

Most of the decisions have related to cases where the accident happened before the completion of the voyage; but their Lordships think it ought not to be laid down that all obligation on the part of the master to act for the merchant ceases after a reasonable time for the latter to take delivery of the cargo has expired. It is well established that, if the ship has waited a reasonable time to deliver goods from her side, the master may land and warehouse them at the charge of the merchant; and it cannot be doubted that it would be his duty to do so rather than to throw them overboard. In a case like the present, where the goods could neither be landed nor remain where they were, it seems to be a legitimate extension of the implied agency of the master to hold that, in the absence of all advices, he had authority to carry or send them on to such other place as in his judgment, prudently exercised, appeared to be most convenient for their owner; and if so, it will follow from established principles that the expenses properly incurred may be charged to him.

Their Lordships have no doubt that bringing the goods back to England was in fact the best and cheapest way of making them available to the defendant, and that they were brought back at less charge in the *Argos* than if they had been sent in another ship.

If the goods had been of a nature which ought to have led the master to know that on their arrival they would not have been worth the expenses incurred in bringing them back, a different question would arise. But, in the present case, their value, of which the defendant has taken the benefit by asking for and obtaining the goods, far exceeded the cost.

The authority of the master being founded on necessity would not have arisen, if he could have obtained instructions from the defendant or his assignees. But under the circumstances this was not possible. Indeed this point was not relied on at the bar.

Their Lordships, for the above reasons, are of opinion that the plaintiff has made out a case for compensation for bringing back the goods to England. But they think the plaintiff is not entitled to recover the amount claimed for demurrage and expenses in attempting to enter the ports of Honfleur and Trouville. These efforts may have been made by him in the interest of the cargo as well as the ship; but they were made before the ship was ready to deliver at all in the port of Havre, and the expenses of this deviation and of the return to Havre, after permission had been obtained to discharge there, must be treated as expenses of the voyage, and not as incurred for the benefit of the defendant.

The charges for the hire of the vessel and of storing the petroleum in her at Havre, after permission had been obtained for its discharge there, stand on different ground. If the ship had then waited in the outer harbour with the petroleum on board, the defendant would have been liable to pay demurrage at £10.10s a day. It was obviously, therefore, to his advantage under the circumstances for the master to hire the vessel, and thus relieve him from the heavy demurrage payable for the detention of the ship. The whole expense of this operation appears to be about £15 only.

In the result their Lordships think the plaintiff is entitled to recover the outward freight, and the charge made for the carriage back to England ... and also the £15 for the above expenses at Havre ...

6 PAYMENT OF FREIGHT, LIENS, CESSER CLAUSES

Domett v Beckford (1833) 5 B & Ad 321

The defendant, by his agent, shipped 15 hogsheads of sugar and 48 puncheons of rum on the plaintiff's ship *William Bryan*. The bill of lading provided for delivery to consignees on payment of freight at agreed rates. The plaintiffs delivered to the consignees without insisting on concurrent payment. The consignees sold the cargo and went bankrupt.

Parke J (Taunton J concurring): As soon as these goods (which were the property of the defendant) were shipped in the plaintiffs' ship, to be carried from Jamaica to London, the defendant, even before any bills of lading were signed, became liable by law to pay freight, unless that liability be controlled by special custom, and of that there is no proof. From the fact, that the goods were laden on a ship to be conveyed from Jamaica to London, the law will imply a contract by the owner of those goods to pay for the carriage. The only difference between the present case and *Shepard v De Bernales* (1811) 13 East 565, is, that in this case a contract to pay freight is implied by law from the fact of the defendant having shipped his goods on board the plaintiffs' ship, to be carried from Jamaica to London. In the other case, there was an express contract by charterparty; but it was there decided, that the clause in the bill of lading, he or they (ie the consignee) paying freight for the said goods', was introduced, not for the benefit of the shipper, but for that of the master or shipowner, and was intended to give the latter the option of insisting, if he thought fit, on receiving the freight before he should make delivery of the goods; and that it did not cast the duty on the captain, at his peril, of obtaining the freight from the consignee at the time of delivery; but that if he did not get it from him, he might insist on receiving it from the consignor. I have not the least doubt, that in this case, the defendant, who is the owner of the goods, is liable to pay freight to the plaintiffs.

Patteson J: *Shepard v De Bernales* shews that the clause in the bill of lading was introduced for the benefit of the master only, and not for that of the consignor, and consequently the master is not bound to the consignor to withhold the delivery of the goods unless the consignee or his assigns pay the freight. In *Christy v Rowe* (1808) 1 Taunt 300, the Court of Common Pleas held, that the master was not bound at his peril to insist upon his freight at the time of delivering the goods; but that if he delivered the goods, and could not afterwards get the freight from the consignee, he might sue the merchant on the charterparty.

Notes

1   Since delivery of cargo to consignees with no attempt to collect freight will not itself relieve a charterer or shipper from liability to pay, even where a clause of the *Domett v Beckford* type is found in the bill of lading, it seems to follow that delivery coupled with an unsuccessful attempt to collect (eg delivery in exchange for a cheque which is dishonoured) will have the same effect. But the position may be different if the consignee offers to pay cash and the master asks for a cheque instead for his own convenience: *Marsh v Pedder* (1815) 4 Camp 257; *Strong v Hart* (1827) 6 B & C 160.

2   *Liens.* At common law, the shipowner is entitled to a possessory lien on cargo for freight payable on delivery. The shipowner is similarly entitled to a lien for general average contributions and for extraordinary expenses which have been justifiably incurred for the protection of cargo: *Hingston v Wendt* (1876) 1 QB 367. These common law liens are all possessory in nature so that the shipowner's right is to retain possession of the goods until the freight due is offered to him. Since the common law lien for freight is only possessory, it can be waived or lost by delivering the goods to the person entitled, without insisting on payment. There is no common law or implied lien in respect of freight which is contractually payable in advance of or after delivery.

> The decision is, that where the agreed time for payment of freight is not contemporaneous with the time of delivery of the cargo, there is no implied right of lien. (Brett J, *Allison v Bristol Marine* [above] referring to *Kirchner v Venus* (1859) 12 Moo P C 361.)

Nor is there any lien at common law for dead freight or for demurrage or damages for detention. But liens for advance freight, demurrage, dead freight and other items ('all other charges') can be and frequently are created by agreement.

3   *Cesser clause.* It is not unusual for a charterparty to provide that, in some circumstances, the charterer shall escape all liability for freight, for example:

> Charterer's liability to cease on steamer being loaded provided the cargo is worth the freight, the owners having an absolute lien on the cargo for all freight, dead freight, demurrage and average.

This example is taken from RN Thornton's evocative *British Shipping* (CUP 1945). Thornton rightly describes the cesser clause as a commercial instrument of real ingenuity and flexibility. He points out that it enables the charterer with a cargo to avoid borrowing and paying interest to finance advance freight charges, and possibly also gives him additional time to sell the cargo; although naturally the cargo must be sold on the basis that the buyer pays the freight. The shipowner for his part is protected by his lien on the cargo. But this is the factor which limits the use of the device: the shipowner is only protected to the extent that the lien is a valid and effective means of securing payment from the receiver in the jurisdiction in which the port of discharge is located. The *Aegis Britannic* (below) although not a case dealing directly with freight, reviews the traditional approach to the construction of cesser clauses.

Action SA v Britannic Shipping, The Aegis Britannic [1987] 1 Lloyd's Rep 119, CA

Dillon LJ: The court has before it an application by charterers for leave to appeal against a decision of Staughton J, given on 7 June 1985, in the Commercial Court.

... As to the facts, by a charterparty in amended Synacomex form dated 23 April 1980, owners chartered the vessel to charterers for the carriage of a cargo of rice from a United State Gulf port to Basrah in Iraq. During discharge by the stevedores, the cargo was partially damaged. In consequence, on 30 November 1982, the owners were held liable to the cargo receivers by an Iraqi court in Basrah in respect of that damage. In the arbitration, the owners claimed damages in so far as they had paid and an indemnity in so far as they had not yet paid, from the charterers in respect of that liability. By his award of 4 December 1984, the arbitrator, Mr Bruce Harris, found the charterers liable to the owners. The question in the arbitration, in the hearing before Staughton J and in the appeal turns on whether the charterers can escape liability by the cesser clause in the charterparty. The argument has turned mainly on three clauses or parts of three clauses in the charterparty.

Firstly, there is cl 5 which imposes the liability on the charterers in the first place. It provides as follows:

5. Cargo to be brought to, loaded, and stowed, respectively discharged at the expense and risk of Shippers/Charterers respectively Receivers/Charterers.

Then there is cl 20, the lien clause. It provides as follows:

20. Owners shall have a lien on the cargo for freight, dead freight and demurrage. Charterers shall remain responsible for dead freight and demurrage incurred at loading port. Charterers shall also remain responsible for freight and demurrage incurred at discharge port.

Then there is the cesser clause, cl 35, which is one of a number of typed additional clauses, starting with cl 22, added to the printed form of the charterparty. Clause 35 provides as follows:

35 Charterers' liability under this charterparty to cease upon cargo being shipped except as regards payment of freight, dead freight and demurrage incurred at both ends.

... Here the lien clause and the cesser clause fit in together, as the judge pointed out, with no difficulty. The owners are to have a lien under the lien clause for freight, dead freight and demurrage. Notwithstanding that lien, the charterers are to remain responsible for freight, dead freight and demurrage. The cesser clause expressly excludes from its scope payment of freight, dead freight and demurrage incurred at both ends. So the lien clause creates no problem as I see it, but the difficulty lies in reconciling the cesser clause with the other provisions of the charterparty, particularly cl 5 which I have read, because if the cesser clause is to be read literally, the liability of the charterers under cl 5, at any rate in respect of discharge, is at once removed by cl 35 of the same document. The same happens with a number of the other additional clauses in the charterparty ...

The courts have long since considered cesser clauses. The leading authority is the decision of this court in *Clink v Radford & Co* [1891] 1 QB 625. There it so happened that the difficulty of construction was concerned with how the lien clause and the cesser clause were to be read together. Lord Esher, it seems to me, put things on a more general basis. He said the following at p 627:

> It seems to me, without going through the cases that have been referred to, that certain rules have been laid down in them which will enable us to decide this particular case. In my opinion, the main rule to be derived from the cases as to the interpretation of the cesser clause in a charterparty, is that the court will construe it as inapplicable to the particular breach complained of, if by construing it otherwise the shipowner would be left unprotected in respect of that particular breach, unless the cesser clause is expressed in terms that prohibit such a conclusion. In other words, it cannot be assumed that the shipowner without any mercantile reason would give up by the cesser clause rights which he had stipulated for in another part of the contract. If that be true, then the question in this particular case, as in every other case, will depend upon this, whether if we apply the cesser clause to the particular breach complained of, and so hold the charterer to be free, the shipowner has any remedy for his loss. If he has, we should construe the cesser clause in its fullest possible meaning, and say that the charterer is released; but if we find that, by so construing it, the shipowner would be left without any remedy whatever for the breach, then we should say that it could not have been the meaning of the parties that the cesser clause should apply to such a breach.

That language seems to me to be directly applicable to treating the liability of the charterers under cl 5 as immediately discharged by the cesser clause, cl 35. Bowen LJ puts the matter similarly. He says, at p 629, the following:

> There is no doubt that the parties may, if they choose, so frame the clause as to emancipate the charterer from any specified liability without providing for any terms of compensation – to the shipowner; but such a contract would not be one we should expect to see in a commercial transaction. The cesser clauses as they generally come before the courts are clauses which couple or link the provisions for the cesser of the charterer's liability with a corresponding creation of a lien.

I interject that here the lien and the cesser clauses are separate from each other. I now continue the citation:

> ... There is a principle of reason which is obvious to commercial minds, and which should be borne in mind in considering a cesser clause so framed, namely, that reasonable persons would regard the lien given as an equivalent for the release of responsibility which the cesser clause in its earlier part creates, and one would expect to find the lien commensurate with the release of liability. That is a sound principle of commercial reasoning which has been sanctioned by the courts in the

cases cited to us, and which has been recognised in the chain of important and valuable judgments of the present Master of the Rolls. That being the principle of construction to apply, one would not expect to find a shipowner placing his ship and himself at the mercy of a charterer without some equivalent, or contracting on a given event to release the charterer from all liability unless there were some other mode of protecting himself against the act of the charterer.

Again, the wording is general and is not limited to finding that the other remedy is given by the lien clause. This, as I see it, is all part of the normal process of construction in which all the various relevant clauses of the contract have to be read together, without taking the wording of one standing on its own and looking no further. The appellant's construction of the cesser clause in effect involves striking out the word 'charterers' wherever it appears in the passage from cl 5 which I have read, at any rate in relation to discharge.

It is submitted, very probably rightly by Mr Priday for the charterers, that the references in that passage in cl 5 to shippers and receivers, envisages that by adoption of clauses of the charterparty into the bills of lading, the owners will have protection against any claims of the receivers of the cargo for damage in discharge. In the present case, the clauses of the charterparty were, we are told, adopted into the bills of lading, but the court in Iraq refused to give effect to those clauses and the arbitrator in his award has said that that is generally the case in Iraq. Hence the liability as held by the Iraqi court of the owners to the receivers of the cargo. But where the question has arisen in a context of reconciling a cesser clause and a lien clause, the court has held that the reconciliation is to be effected by holding that the cesser clause only applies in so far as the lien is effective. This was held first in *Hansen v Harrold Brothers* [1894] 1 QB 612. In that case the charterparty permitted the charterers to recharter the ship. The effect of that was that the owners had a lien on the freight under the recharter, but for various reasons that came out as less than the freight payable under the charterparty and therefore it was not an adequate remedy.

Lord Esher, at p 618, cited from the judgments of the Court in *Clink v Radford &* *Co*. He said the following:

> ... It seems to me that this reasoning has not been and cannot be answered. Therefore the proposition is true that, where the provision for cesser liability is accompanied by the stipulation as to lien, then the cesser of liability is not to apply in so far as the lien, which by the charterparty the charterers are enabled to create, is not equivalent to the liability of the charterers. Where, in such a case, the provisions of the charterparty enable the charterers to make such terms with the shippers that the lien which is created is not commensurate with the liability of the charterers under the charterparty, then the cesser clause will only apply so far as the lien which can be exercised by the shipowner is commensurate with such liability.

Similarly, in the case of *The Sinoe* [1971] 1 Lloyd's Rep 514 – a decision of Donaldson J which was upheld by this court in [1972] 1 Lloyd's Rep 201 – it was held that the cesser clause did not avail charterers where the owners had a lien on cargo which they could not enforce owing to local conditions. I find that reasoning directly applicable in the present case. If the owners had no alternative remedy against the receivers of the cargo or, for that matter anyone else, the cesser clause cannot be construed as immediately cutting out and extinguishing the charterers' primary liability under cl 5 ...

[Lloyd and Nicholls LJJ delivered concurring judgments.]

CHAPTER 13

LAYTIME

CHARTER PARTIES

Report by the Secretariat of UNCTAD

[United Nations Conference on Trade and Development, Geneva]

Published by the United Nations, New York, 1974

221. In principle, any time during which a tramp vessel is not working and earning represents a loss in freight for the owner, since fixed overheads, such as depreciation, insurance, and interest on invested capital – which generally represent the greater part of the running costs – continue to accrue irrespective of whether the vessel is actually employed. The time factor is therefore of major importance to the shipowner.

222. In connexion with the performance of a charter voyage, the time factor comes into particular play where the vessel's stay in port is prolonged. The freight, which must not only cover all the owner's costs but also leave him a reasonable profit margin, is the same irrespective of the duration of the voyage. Every day that the vessel is detained, the owner will incur overheads which will reduce his calculated profit and – in the case of a protracted delay – perhaps turn it into a realised loss. In addition, the owner will lose new business for the time corresponding to the period of detention. His principal concern is therefore to have his vessel working continuously and to limit its stay in port to the shortest possible time.

223. The charterer, on the other hand, must have the vessel available during a long enough period to effect cargo loading and discharge and his concern is to be able to perform his part of the cargo-handling operations at a pace convenient and economical to him.

224. The usual solution in respect of duration of port stay is to allow an appropriate period time to cover loading and discharging, generally called 'laytime' or, sometimes, 'lay days', which is at the charterer's free disposal, and to grant him the possibility, in case of need, of detaining the vessel beyond the agreed time, against payment of compensation to the owner for the use of the additional time; such compensation is called 'demurrage'. Laytime and demurrage thus fulfil functions of fundamental importance, from both an economic and a practical standpoint, and their terms are invariably regulated in standard voyage charter party forms.

225. Laytime and demurrage constitute a complicated field, both from a technical and a legal standpoint. The rules of law provided on these matters diverge on many points under the different legal systems. Moreover, a considerable variation exists in the regulatory terms governing laytime and demurrage under various standard forms; this, however, is to a certain extent unavoidable, since different trades and commodities, as also the particular circumstances of the voyage, may require individual provisions on various

aspects involved. As a consequence of this complexity, laytime and demurrage give rise to many difficulties and frequent disputes.

1 START OF LAYTIME

Unless a different agreement has been made, in general three conditions must be satisfied before laytime will start: the ship must have arrived at her destination – she is then said to be an arrived ship; she must be ready to load and notice of readiness to load must have been given.

Arrival

The time of arrival depends on the destination on which the parties have agreed. In practice, the destination selected is generally either a port, or a specified area within a port such as a dock, or a particular loading place, eg a named berth, quay, wharf, or a mooring. If the stipulated destination is either a dock or a berth, the vessel is an arrived ship when she is in the specified area or at the agreed place. The rule applicable to a port charter has changed over the years. In *Leonis Steamship v Rank* [1908] 1 KB 499, the Court of Appeal held that where a port was referred to in a charterparty – a commercial document – 'the term is to be construed in a commercial sense in relation to the objects of the particular transaction'. On this basis, 'port' meant 'the commercial area of the port'. In *The Aello* [1961] AC 135, the *Leonis* test was held to require that the vessel should be in that part of the port where she was to be loaded when a berth became available, with the result that it was found that the *Aello* had not arrived in the port of Buenos Aires while waiting at a usual waiting area within the port which was 22 miles from the loading area. Influenced by changes 'in the kinds of ships used in maritime commerce, in means of communication and in port facilities and the management of ports' (Lord Diplock) the House of Lords abandoned the *Aello* approach in *The Johanna Oldendorff*, although some phrases and ideas used in the earlier cases continued to be used in the judgments in that case.

EL Oldendorff & Co GmbH v Tradax Export SA, The Johanna Oldendorff [1974] AC 479

The *Johanna Oldendorff* was chartered to carry a bulk grain cargo from the United States to Liverpool/Birkenhead. No berth was available when the vessel arrived on 2 January 1968, and she was ordered by the port authority to anchor at the bar light vessel. Her owners gave notice of readiness. The vessel lay at anchor at the bar from 3 to 20 January ready, so far as she was concerned, to discharge.

Lord Reid: ... The question at issue is who is liable to pay for the delay ... The argument before your Lordships turned on the time when the vessel became an arrived ship. The main contention for the owners is that she became an arrived ship when she anchored at the bar anchorage because that is within the port of Liverpool, it is the usual place where vessels lie awaiting a berth, and it was the place to which she had been ordered to go by the port authority. The reply of the charterers is that that anchorage is at least 17 miles from the dock area, or commercial area of the port, that arrival at that anchorage is not arrival at the port of Liverpool /Birkenhead and that the ship did not arrive until she proceeded to her unloading berth in the Birkenhead docks ...

[T]he essential factor is that before a ship can be treated as an arrived ship she must be within the port and at the immediate and effective disposition of the charterer and that her geographical position is of secondary importance. But for practical purposes it is so much easier to establish that, if the ship is at a usual waiting place within the port, it can generally be presumed that she is there fully at the charterer's disposal.

I would therefore state what I would hope to be the true legal position in this way. Before a ship can be said to have arrived at a port she must, if she cannot proceed immediately to a berth, have reached a position within the port where she is at the immediate and effective disposition of the charterer. If she is at a place where waiting ships usually lie, she will be in such a position unless in some extraordinary circumstances proof of which would lie in the charterer ...

If the ship is waiting at some other place in the port then it will be for the owner to prove that she is as fully at the disposition of the charterer as she would have been if in the vicinity of the berth for loading or discharge ...

Lord Diplock: ... A dock encloses a comparatively small area entered through a gate. There is no difficulty in saying whether a vessel has arrived in it. As soon as a berth is vacant in the dock a vessel already moored inside the dock can get there within an interval so short that for the practical business purpose of loading or discharging cargo it can be ignored. For such purposes she is as much at the disposal of the charterer when at her mooring as she would be if she were already at the actual berth at which the charterer will later make or accept delivery of the cargo, but is unable for the time being to do so.

The area of a port, however, may be much larger. It may sometimes be less easily determinable, because of absence of definition of its legal limits or variations between these and the limits within which the port authority in actual practice exercises control of the movement of shipping; but I do not believe that in practice it is difficult to discover whether a place where ships usually wait their turn for a berth is within the limits of a named port; or is outside those limits as is the case with Glasgow and with Hull ...

... If a port is congested so that on arrival within its limits the chartered vessel cannot proceed immediately to a berth to load or to discharge, it is of no business importance to the charterer where she waits within those limits, so long as it is a place (1) where she counts for turn if the port is one where vacant berths are allotted to waiting vessels in order of arrival; (2) where the charterer can communicate with her as soon as he knows when a berth will become available for the cargo to be loaded or discharged, and (3) from which the vessel can proceed to the available berth when she receives the charterer's communication, so as to arrive there as soon as the berth has become vacant or so shortly thereafter as not to be significant for practical purposes.

... Since it is to the interest of all concerned, of port authorities as well as charterers and shippers, that time should (not) be wasted by leaving berths vacant when they are available for loading or discharging cargo, the usual places for ships to wait their turn for a vacant berth are those which do possess the three characteristics that I have mentioned, if there are any such places within the limits of the port. In days of sailing ships close proximity to berths likely to become vacant may have been necessary in order that a place should possess those characteristics, but distance from the actual berth becomes of less importance as steam and diesel power replaces sail and instantaneous radio communication is available between ship and shore. In modern conditions it is possible for port authorities and charterers to know at least some hours in advance, when a berth presently occupied by a loading or discharging vessel will become vacant and available for use by the chartered vessel. Notice of similar length can be given by the charterer to the waiting vessel so as to enable her to reach the berth as soon as it becomes vacant, if she can make the journey from her waiting place to the berth within that time. And if she can she is as effectively at the disposal of the charterer for loading or discharging while at that waiting place as she would have been if waiting in the immediate vicinity of the berth.

My Lords, this no doubt is why the bar anchorage, which is within the legal limits of the Port of Liverpool and included in the area in which the port authority is entitled to control the movement of shipping, has become the usual place to which vessels are directed by the port authority to wait their turn for a berth. And the same must generally be true of usual waiting places within the limits of other ports where congestion is liable to occur. I would therefore accept as a convenient practical test as to whether a vessel has completed her loading voyage or her carrying voyage under a port charter so as to cast upon the charterer the responsibility for subsequent delay in finding a vacant berth at which her cargo can be loaded or discharged, the test as it is formulated by my noble and learned friend, Lord Reid, at the conclusion of his speech ...

Federal Commerce and Navigation Co Ltd v Tradax Export SA, The Maratha Envoy [1978] AC 2

Lord Diplock: ... My Lords, in *EL Oldendorff & Co GmbH v Tradax Export SA (The Johanna Oldendorff)* [1974] AC 479, the purpose of this House was to give legal certainty to the way in which the risk of delay from congestion at the discharging port was allocated between charterer and shipowner under a port charter which contained no special clause expressly dealing with this matter. The standard form of charterparty used in *The Johanna Oldendorff* was also that used in the instant case – the Baltimore berth grain charterparty – although in each case the destination of the carrying voyage was a port, not a berth. The allocation of this risk under this kind of charterparty depends upon when the vessel becomes an 'arrived ship' so as to enable laytime to start running and demurrage to become payable once laytime has expired ... After a hearing extending over six days in the course of which the position of ports where the usual waiting place lies outside the limits of the port of discharge was fully considered and cases dealing with such ports were cited, this House substituted for the Parker test [*The Aello*, above] a test which I ventured to describe as the 'Reid test', which in its most summary form is stated by Lord Reid thus, at p 535:

> Before a ship can be said to have arrived at a port she must, if she cannot proceed immediately to a berth, have reached a position within the port where she is at the immediate and effective disposition of the charterer.

... The Reid test applies to a port charter in which there is no express provision dealing with how the misfortune risk of delay through congestion at the loading or discharging port is to be allocated between charterer and shipowner. In such a case it allocates the risk to the charterer when the waiting place lies within the limits of the port; but to the shipowner when it lies outside those limits. In a berth charter, on the other hand, it had long been settled law that, in the absence of express provision providing for some other allocation of the risk, the risk is allocated to the shipowner wherever the waiting place lies. In the case of both port and berth charters, however, it is the common practice, by the use of standard clauses, which too have been the subject of judicial exegesis, to provide expressly for the way in which the risk of delay by congestion at the loading or discharging port is to be allocated ...

There are also standard clauses dealing specifically with the commencement of laytime at individual ports at which the usual anchorage for vessels waiting turn lies outside the limits of the port. A typical clause of this kind relating to the ports of Avonmouth, Glasgow and Hull is cited in the judgment of Roskill LJ in *The Johanna Oldendorff* [1974] AC 479, 505. A similar clause is used in the case of the four ports on the River Weser, for all of which the usual waiting place for vessels of considerable draught is an anchorage at the Weser Lightship which lies outside the limits of any of the ports. The Weser Lightship clause runs as follows:

> If vessel is ordered to anchor at Weser Lightship by port authorities, since a vacant berth is not available, she may tender notice of readiness upon arriving at anchorage near Weser Lightship, as if she would have arrived at her final loading/discharging port. Steaming time for shifting from Weser Lightship to final discharging port, however, not to count.

The use of the time lost clause or of standard clauses relating to particular ports whose waiting place is outside the limits of the port may well seem to be particularly appropriate to cases where the charterparty reserves to the charterer an option to choose a loading or discharging place out of a range of ports at some of which the risk of congestion may be greater than at others or at some of which the usual waiting place lies inside and at others outside the limits of the port; for, in the absence of any such express provision, the existence of the option means that the charterer by the way he requires the contract to be carried out may influence the incidence or extent of the risk to be borne by the shipowner.

Nevertheless, even where the extent of the risk is potentially variable according to the way in which the charterer exercises his options, a shipowner may be willing to assume that risk in the course of bargaining rather than to transfer it to the charterer and accept a lower freight rate or demurrage rate or both. He may be content to back his own knowledge and experience of conditions at the ports included in the option range and to rely also on the fact that it will generally be in the charterer's own interest to exercise his options in such a way as to cause as little delay as possible.

The instant case is about a claim to demurrage upon a vessel the *Maratha Envoy* laden with a cargo of grain for which the discharging port nominated by the charterer under a port charter was the port of Brake. This is one of the four ports on the River Weser. The other three are Bremerhaven at the mouth of the river, Nordenham downstream from Brake, and Bremen upstream, for all of which the usual waiting place for vessels of the *Maratha Envoy*'s draught is the Weser Lightship.

... The history of the carrying voyage is set out in detail in the judgments of the courts below. It is sufficient for your Lordships' purpose to mention that the *Maratha Envoy* reached the anchorage at the Weser Lightship on 7 December 1970. She took her turn for discharge at any of the Weser ports on her arrival at the anchorage but no valid nomination of Brake as the discharging port was made by the charterers until 10 December. When this nomination was received, it never crossed the minds of the shipowners or their agents that the *Maratha Envoy* was already an arrived ship while at the Weser Lightship anchorage. They knew she had to get to a place within the limits of the port of Brake itself before she would be entitled to give notice of readiness to discharge. Accordingly on 12 December when the tide was right, she carried out a manoeuvre which has been variously described as 'showing her chimney', 'a charade' and 'a voyage of convenience'. She weighed anchor at the lightship, proceeded up the river until she was opposite the port of Brake, turned round in midstream and went back immediately to the lightship anchorage where she remained until 30 December 1970, when her turn came round and she moved to her discharging berth in Brake. During the ten minutes or so that it took for her to turn round in the river, on 12 December notice of readiness was served upon the charterers' agents.

... Donaldson J held that the voyages of convenience did not serve to make the Maratha Envoy an arrived ship at the port of Brake.

From this judgment the shipowners appealed to the Court of Appeal [which allowed the appeal on the ground that arrival at the Weser Lightship anchorage constituted the *Maratha Envoy* an arrived ship for discharge at the port of Brake].

... My Lords, it is conceded by counsel for the shipowners that the Weser Lightship anchorage is outside the legal, fiscal and administrative limits of the port of Brake. It lies 25 miles from the mouth of the river in an area in which none of the port authorities of Weser ports does any administrative acts or exercises any control over vessels waiting there. It was held by a German court in 1962 that a ship waiting at the Weser Lightship anchorage is not an arrived ship. A similar decision was reached by Donaldson J in *Zim Israel Navigation Co Ltd v Tradax Export SA (The Timna)* [1970] 2 Lloyd's Rep 409, and approved by Megaw LJ when the case came before the Court of Appeal [1971] 2 Lloyd's Rep 91. Counsel also concedes that charterers, shippers and shipowners who use the Weser ports would not regard the waiting area at the lightship as forming part of any of them. All the evidence is to the contrary, the conduct of the parties and their agents, the correspondence and the oral evidence that was accepted by the judge. So is the common use in charterparties of the special Weser Lightship clause, when it is intended that time spent in waiting there for a berth should count as laytime. This way of reconciling loyal adherence to the Reid test with an inclination to find in favour of the shipowners in the instant case is not, in my view, available.

... Your Lordships would be doing a disservice to the shipping community if, so shortly after the Reid test had been laid down by this House in *The Johanna Oldendorff*, you did not reaffirm it and insist upon its application to the instant case.

I turn to the second ground relied on by the Court of Appeal as justifying departing from the Reid test ... The form of charterparty used incorporated as one of the printed clauses dealing with time for discharge:

> Time to count from the first working period on the next day following receipt ... of written notice of readiness to discharge, *whether in berth or not*.

The words italicised are surplusage in a port charter. Their presence, however, is readily explicable. The parties took a printed form appropriate to a berth charter as respects both loading and carrying voyages, and used it for an adventure in which the destination of the carrying, though not the loading voyage, was a range of named ports, not berths. The effect of this well known phrase in berth charters has been settled for more than half a century. Under it time starts to run when the vessel is waiting within the named port of destination for a berth there to become vacant. In effect it makes the Reid test applicable to a berth charter. It has no effect in a port charter; the Reid test is applicable anyway ...

... Finally, there is the voyage of convenience down to Brake and back. This was rejected by Donaldson J and, in the Court of Appeal, by Stephenson and Shaw LJJ. Lord Denning MR characterised it as commercial nonsense but said [1977] QB 324, 341 that he 'would swallow the commercial nonsense if it was the only way in which justice could be done'.

My Lords, I cannot swallow it, nor, for reasons I have stated earlier, do I see that justice would be done if I could bring myself to do so.

Notes

1 *Port charter or berth charter?*

A ship was chartered to 'proceed to one or two safe ports East Canada or Newfoundland, place or places as ordered by charterers and/or shippers ...' It was held that these words conferred an express power to nominate the berth or berths at which the ship should load so that the vessel did not become an arrived ship until she berthed. *Stag Line v Board of Trade* [1950] 2 KB 194, CA.

2 *Demurrage in respect of waiting time*

The *Werrastein* was chartered for a voyage from Australia to Hull to deliver grain at any customary dock, wharf or pier as ordered by the charterers 'provided that if such discharging place is not immediately available, demurrage in respect of all time waiting thereafter shall be paid ...' The only discharging place available for grain at Hull at the relevant time was the King George Dock, which was congested. The *Werrastein* was instructed by port authorities to wait at a customary waiting anchorage off Spurn Head, 22 miles from the King George Dock and outside the geographical, legal and fiscal limits of the port. The charterers had in the circumstances no option as to the dock, but did eventually nominate a particular berth. The shipowner's claim was made against holders and indorsees of bills of lading which incorporated all terms, conditions, clauses and exceptions in the charter. Sellers J said that the claim would have failed if the shipowner had had to show that the *Werrastein* was an arrived ship, but his Lordship held that they did not. The right to 'demurrage' in the clause quoted arose when the vessel was kept waiting because a discharge place was not immediately available; that right was quite independent and distinct from a right to demurrage after lay days had run. *Roland-Linie Schiffart GmbH v Spillers* [1957] 1 QB 109.

3   *Time lost in waiting for a berth to count as laytime*

The *Darrah* was chartered to carry cement from Novorossisk to Tripoli. The charterparty was a port charterparty on the printed Gencon form, with amendments. The fixed laytime was based on an agreed rate of discharge per weather working day of 24 consecutive hours, Fridays and holidays excepted. Time from noon on Thursday or noon on the day before a legal holiday until 8 am on the next working day was not to count. The charter also provided that time lost in waiting for a berth was to count as laytime. The vessel reached the usual waiting place in the port of Tripoli and became an arrived ship. She waited six calendar days for a berth. The shipowners claimed for those six days despite the fact that they included a Friday and a holiday and the periods from noon on the day before each. The House of Lords held (1) that time lost clauses are superfluous in a port charter so far as concerns time spent in waiting in turn within the limits of the port. 'This counts as laytime anyway; it is laytime' (Lord Diplock, p 166). Thus, in a port charter, it is only where the usual waiting area is outside the limits of the port that the clause has any effect; (2) in a berth charter, the effect of the clause is that a waiting vessel which cannot berth because of congestion is treated as though she were in fact in berth. The result is that a waiting vessel cannot count all waiting days against laytime, but only those which would count if she were actually in berth; (3) notice of readiness is not required to start time running under a 'time lost' clause: *Aldebaran Maritima v Aussenhandel* [1977] AC 157.

4   *Time lost to count if cargo inaccessible?*

The Massalia No 2 [1962] 2 QB 416 concerned a dispute relating to demurrage under a charterparty of the vessel for a voyage from Antwerp and Bordeaux to Colombo with a part cargo of flour in bags. The owners had liberty to complete cargo en route, which they exercised at Port Said where a small amount of additional cargo (less than 10 per cent by weight of the flour cargo) was loaded and carried under bills of lading. On arrival at Colombo, the flour was mostly overstowed by the Port Said cargo. The *Massalia* waited six days for a berth. The charter provided that time lost in waiting for a berth was to count as discharging time. Diplock J held that the owners were entitled to rely on this clause and rejected the charterers argument that no time has been 'lost' in waiting for a berth because the vessel was not ready to discharge the flour as soon as she got to berth.'

5   *Time lost and overlapping charters*

In the *Agios Stylianos* [1975] 1 Lloyd's Rep 426 the shipowners entered into two separate charterparties (both in the Gencon form) for the carriage of part cargoes from Constanza. One charter was for carriage of 8,800 metric tons of cement; the other for 450 tons of vehicles. Both charters contained time lost clauses and agreements to pay demurrage at the rate of $1,500 a day. The vessel waited 14 days at the discharge port (Lagos) for a berth. Both cargoes were discharged at the same berth. The owners were awarded demurrage at the agreed rate against the vehicle charterers for the 14-day waiting period. They sought to recover a similar amount from the cement charterers. It was common ground between the parties that laytime did not begin to run under the cement charter until the vehicles had been discharged. Donaldson J held that 'time lost waiting for a berth' meant 'time lost waiting for a cement berth'. The time at Lagos was lost in waiting for a vehicle discharging berth. 'Once the vehicles had been discharged the cement charterers had the right and duty to nominate a berth, but this did not arise at any earlier point in time'. *The Massalia* was to be distinguished because the present point had not been argued in that case.

6   *Berth reachable on arrival*

'Arrival' in the absence of any other agreement between the parties, means the physical arrival of the vessel at the point where the indication or nomination of a particular loading place would become relevant if the vessel were to be able to proceed without being held up: *The Angelos Lusis* [1964] 2 Lloyd's Rep 28. 'Reachable' means able to be reached: *The President Brand* [1967] 2 Lloyd's Rep 338.

7   The *Laura Prima* was chartered on the Exxonvoy 1969 form to load at one safe berth Marsa El Hariga (Libya). Clause 6 of the charterparty provided that on arrival at the port of loading, notice of readiness to load could be given 'berth or no berth' and laytime (agreed at 72 hours) would commence either six hours later or when the vessel arrived at her berth if that occurred earlier. But this clause concluded by stating that 'where delay is caused to vessel getting into berth after giving notice of readiness for any reason over which Charterer has no control, such delay shall not count as used laytime'.

Clause 7 of the form provided that time consumed by the vessel on moving from loading port anchorage to loading berth would not count as laytime. Clause 9 provided that the loading place to be designated or procured by the charterers would be reachable on arrival.

The *Laura Prima* arrived at her loading port and gave the required six hours notice of readiness. She could not reach a loading berth at once since all were occupied by other vessels. She waited nine days for a berth. The shipowners claimed demurrage. The charterers claimed to be protected by clause 6, alleging the reason for the delay (congestion) was something over which they had no control. The House of Lords held that 'reachable on arrival' meant immediately reachable on arrival. Clause 6 only protected the charterers once they had designated a loading place which actually was so reachable. It was only thereafter if some intervening event occurred causing delay over which the charterers had no control that the last sentence of clause 6 would apply: *Nereide v Bulk Oil* [1982] 1 Lloyd's Rep 1.

A different result was reached by the House of Lords in *SA Marocaine de l'Industrie du Raffinage v Notos Maritime* [1987] 1 Lloyd's Rep 503. The *Notos* was chartered on the STB form for a voyage from Ras Tanura (Saudi Arabia) to Mohammedia (Morocco). Clause 6 of the charterparty was in a form similar to that in *The Laura Prima*. But the charter in this case had no 'reachable on arrival' clause. After giving notice of readiness at Mohammedia, the *Notos* was delayed because swell prevented vessels from using the sea line. The shipowners argued that the charterers were obliged to ensure that a berth was available for the vessel on arrival and relied on their right to give notice of readiness 'berth or no berth' under clause 6 of the charter. The House of Lords held those words did no more than provide that a notice of readiness could be given·on arrival whether or not a berth was then available. *The Laura Prima* was distinguished on the grounds that that case was concerned with a charter which was materially different in terms. Swell was held to be a cause of delay over which the charterer had no control within the meaning of clause 6.

8 _Whether in berth or not_

The *Kyzikos* was fixed under a berth charterparty to carry a cargo of steel from Italy to the US Gulf. She was ordered to discharge at Houston. A berth was available on arrival at the port, but she could not proceed to it immediately because the pilot station was closed by fog. The charterparty provided that laytime was to commence whether the vessel was in berth or not. The House of Lord held that WIBON meant 'whether in berth (a berth being available) or not in berth (a berth not being available)'. This agreement did not cause laytime to start in cases where a berth was available on arrival at the port but was unreachable by reason of bad weather. *Seacrystal Shipping Ltd v Bulk Transport Group Shipping Co Ltd, The Kyzikos* [1989] 1 Lloyd's Rep 1.

9   *Charterers' duty to facilitate arrival*

In *Sunbeam Shipping v President of India* [1973] 1 Lloyd's Rep 483 the *Atlantic Sunbeam* was chartered for a voyage from the United States Gulf to one or two safe berths or ports on the east coast of India. She was ordered to discharge at Madras and Calcutta. She could not become an arrived ship at Calcutta until the consignees (who were for this purpose the same as the charterers) obtained a document called a jetty challan from the port commissioners. The owners alleged that a delay in obtaining the jetty challan delayed the ship and this was the responsibility of the charterers. Arbitrators made an award in the form of a special case in favour of the owners.

Kerr J held that a term was to be implied in the charter that 'the charterers were bound to act with reasonable despatch and in accordance with the ordinary practice of the port of Calcutta in doing those acts which had to be done by them as consignees to enable the ship to become an arrived ship' (at 488).

In contrast, in *The Aello* [1961] 1 AC 135 the House of Lords held that if the provision of a cargo is necessary to enable a ship to become an arrived ship, the charterer has an absolute obligation to provide the cargo, or at any rate a reasonable part of it, in time to enable the ship to perform its obligation.

10 *Order not to berth and load*

The *Ulyanovsk* was chartered to carry a cargo of gas oil from Skikda. The charterers had contracted to pay their suppliers by reference to a formula which depended on a market price around the bill of lading date. Anticipating a fall in price, they ordered the vessel not to berth and load on arrival. In disregard of these instructions, on arrival notice of readiness to load was given by the ship to the refinery and shippers and the vessel proceeded to berth and load. It was held that charterers could make use of the total agreed laytime of 72 running hours as they wished and they were entitled to delay the commencement of loading. *Novorossisk Shipping Co v Neopetro Co Ltd, The Ulyanovsk* [1990] 1 Lloyd's Rep 425.

11 References

See (1978) 94 *LQR* 1; Powles, DG [1979] *JBL* 115; Davies, D [1974] *LMCLQ* 1.

Readiness

Compania de Naviera Nedelka SA v Tradax Internacional SA, The Tres Flores [1974] Q B 264

Lord Denning: In October 1970 the *Tres Flores* was chartered for a voyage to go to Varna in Bulgaria, there load a cargo of maize in bulk and carry it to Famagusta in Cyprus ...

On November 22, 1970, the vessel arrived in the roads at the port of Varna. Once she was in the roads she had arrived within the terms of the charterparty. Clause 21 said:

> At loading port, time to commence, whether vessel be in berth or not, whether in free pratique or not, whether in port or not, at 2 pm if written notice is given during usual office hours before noon and at 8 am next working day if notice is given during usual office hours after noon. Master is allowed to give the notice of load readiness by telegram when ship is arrived on the road of loading port.

The vessel arrived at the port of Varna at 05.00 hours on Sunday, 22 November 1970: but no berth was available, so she anchored in the roads. At 10.00 hours on that Sunday morning, the master gave notice of readiness ...

On Monday, 23 November 1970, the charterers had the cargo of maize, 6,500 tons, in the port of Varna ready for loading on the vessel. But the vessel could not be inspected at that time. She was in the roads. There was heavy weather, so that the inspectors of shipping at Varna could not get out to the vessel for some days. They did not get out to her until Friday, 27 November. On that day they inspected her and gave their certificate:

> ... at the survey, made on 27 November 1970, of the hatches of M/V *Tres Flores*, arrived for loading of maize, it was found that there are pests in the hatches. It was ordered by the inspection to be done a fumigation before loading.

The fumigation took place not on that Friday. It was not done until the following Monday, 30 November 1970. It took four and a half hours. Then and then only did the charterers accept the notice of readiness. They accepted it on Tuesday, 1 December. Even then there was no berth available for some days. The vessel berthed on 7 December and then loading commenced at 11.00 hours on that day. Loading was completed at 10.00 hours on 13 December 1970.

The charterparty [clause 6 as amended] contained this provision as to laytimes:

> At both ends from Saturday noon or local equivalents or from 5 pm on days preceding holidays, until following working day at 8 am, time not to count even if used. Any time lost in fitting the shifting boards or other material not to count as laytime. Before tendering notice master has to take necessary measures for holds to be clean, dry, without smell and in every way suitable to receive grain to shippers/charterers' satisfaction.

The dispute is whether laytime commenced at the time for which the master gave his notice of readiness, that is, 14.00 hours on Monday, 23 November, or only at the time when the vessel had been fumigated and was suitable to receive the cargo, that is, at 14.00 hours on Tuesday, 1 December 1970.

It seems to me that this dispute is really covered by the specific sentence in the charterparty which I have already read but which I will repeat now:

> Before tendering notice master has to take necessary measures for holds to be clean, dry, without smell and in every way suitable to receive grain to shippers/charterers' satisfaction.

That lays down a condition precedent to the validity of a notice of readiness to load. That condition precedent was not fulfilled until the fumigation had been completed on 30 November and therefore the notice of readiness could not validly be given until that time.

That is sufficient for the decision of this case; but, as the contrary has been discussed before us, it may be desirable for the members of the court to give their views upon it.

One thing is clear. In order for a notice of readiness to be good, the vessel must be ready at the time that the notice is given, and not at a time in the future. Readiness is a preliminary existing fact which must exist before you can give a notice of readiness: see per Atkin LJ in *Aktiebolaget Nordiska Lloyd v J Brownlie & Co (Hull) Ltd* (1925) 30 Com Cas 307, 315.

The next question, when can a ship be said to be ready? Conversely, if some things are yet to be done, what are the things which make her unready to receive cargo?

The leading case is *Armement Adolf Deppe v John Robinson & Co Ltd* [1917] 2 KB 204, where the hatch covers had not been removed at the time when the notice of readiness was given. It would be necessary for them to be removed before discharging could take place. The notice of readiness was held to be good. Then there is *Sociedad Financiera de Bienes Raices SA v Agrimpex Hungarian Trading Co for Agricultural Products, The Aello* [1961] AC 135, where a police permit was necessary before a ship could be loaded. It was held that the absence of a police permit did not prevent the *Aello* from being 'ready to load' while at the anchorage: see *per* Lord Radcliffe at pp 174–75. And finally *Shipping Developments Corporation v V/O Sojuzneftexport (The Delian Spirit)* [1972] 1 QB 103, where the vessel had not obtained free pratique and would need it before she could load. It was held that she was entitled to give notice of readiness.

In considering the cases, it seems to me that the submission which Mr MacCrindle put forward was correct. In order to be a good notice of readiness, the master must be in a position to say 'I am ready at the moment you want me, whenever that may be, and any necessary preliminaries on my part to the loading will not be such as to delay you'. Applying this test it is apparent that notice of readiness can be given even though there are some further preliminaries to be done, or routine matters to be carried on, or formalities observed. If those things are not such as to give any reason to suppose that they will cause any delay, and it is apparent that the ship will be ready when the appropriate time arrives, then notice of readiness can be given.

In the present case there were pests in the hold such as to make the ship unready to receive cargo. Fumigation was not a mere preliminary, nor a routine matter, nor a formality at all. It was an essential step which had to be taken before any cargo could be received at all. Until the vessel had been fumigated, notice of readiness could not be given. It has always been held that, for a notice of readiness to be given, the vessel must be completely ready in all her holds to receive the cargo at any moment when she is required to receive it ...

So, both under the specific clause and at common law, I am of opinion that the presence of pests in the hold invalidated the notice of readiness. I think the decision of Mocatta J was right and I would dismiss this appeal.

[Cairns and Roskill LJJ agreed that the charter made fumigation a condition precedent to the giving of notice of readiness.]

Notes

1   *Readiness in respect of overstowed cargo*

In *The Massalia No 2* [1962] 2 QB 416 Diplock J held that a requirement under a charterparty to give notice of readiness in respect of 'cargo', means readiness to discharge the cargo which is the subject of the charter, not readiness to discharge other cargo overstowed on it. Notice of readiness in respect of an inaccessible part cargo could not be given until that cargo was actually accessible.

2   *Readiness in respect of the whole of the cargo*

The *Virginia M* was chartered to carry a cargo of bagged calcium ammonium nitrate from Constanza to Lagos. She arrived and gave notice of readiness with insufficient fresh water on board to enable her to discharge the whole cargo by her own steam power. It was held that (1) readiness means readiness in a business and mercantile sense and does not involve the completion of what are mere formalities; (2) the readiness required is readiness to discharge the whole of the cargo that is the subject matter of the charterparty. Readiness to discharge some of the cargo only is not sufficient. The case was remitted to arbitrators to decide, among other things, whether taking more water on board at a discharge berth was a mere formality which would not impede or hold up discharge and not prevent the vessel from being ready to discharge the whole cargo. *Unifert International SAL v Panous Shipping Co Inc, The Virginia M* [1989] 1 Lloyd's Rep 603.

3   *Notice of readiness to load*

The parties to a contract of affreightment can agree on any form of notice they wish (even oral notice: *Franco-British Steamship v Watson & Youell* (1921) 9 Ll L R 282, 283) or they can dispense with notice altogether. In the absence of special agreement or a legally binding custom, the shipowner must give notice of readiness to load: *Stanton v Austin* (1892) LR 7 CP 651. In order to give a valid notice of readiness, then (see above) the ship must first be an arrived ship and must in fact be ready to load: *Nelson v Dahl* (1879) 12 Ch D 581.

4   *Notice of readiness to discharge*

In the absence of agreement a shipowner is not obliged to give notice of readiness to discharge: *Houlder v GSN* (1862) 3 F & F 170. The reason for the distinction between loading and discharge has been said to be that the charterer can be expected to take an interest in the movements of the vessel once his cargo has been loaded which he would not take prior to loading: Donaldson J, *Christensen v Hindustan Steel* [1975] 1 Lloyd's Rep at 398. However, notice of readiness to discharge must be given if the shipowner, as is usual, has contracted to do so, eg as where a bill of lading contains a space for the insertion of the name of the 'party to be notified' and the space has been completed: *Clemens Horst v Norfolk* (1906) 11 Com Cas 141; or where the shipowner intends to rely on a 'near' clause and discharge at a place other than the primary contractual destination: *The Varing* [1931] P 79, 87.

5   *Premature notice of readiness*

Where a charterparty expressly relates the commencement of laytime to the giving of a notice of readiness, and where a notice is given at a time when the vessel is not in fact ready to discharge the cargo in question because it is overstowed with other cargo, the notice does not cause laytime to start automatically when the vessel becomes ready, nor in such a case does laytime start when the charter knows or ought to have known of the readiness. *The Mexico* 1 [1990] 1 Lloyd's Rep 507, CA, where no valid notice ever having been given, the charterers conceded that laytime eventually began when the discharge of their cargo actually commenced.

By a charterparty on the standard form of Richards Bay coal charter, the *Lindaros* was fixed to load a cargo of coal for carriage from Richards Bay, South Africa to Antwerp. The charter provided that laytime would commence 18 hours after notice of readiness and that 'any time lost subsequently by vessels not fulfilling requirements for ... readiness to load in all respects, including Marine Surveyor's Certificate ... shall not count as notice time, or as time allowed for loading'. The vessel gave notice of readiness. After berthing the marine surveyor failed her for loading because of water and rust which he found in her hatches. She was subsequently passed on the following morning. It was argued that while in general a valid notice cannot be given unless and until the vessel is in truth ready to load, it was always open to the parties to alter the position by agreement to the contrary. It was held that the clause contemplated a notice being given at a time when the vessel was not in fact ready to load and that the effect of the clause was to contract out of the normal rule requiring that a vessel must be ready at the time of giving notice. *Cobelfret NV v Cyclades Shipping Co Ltd, The Lindaros* [1994] 1 Lloyd's Rep 28. See also to the same effect *The Jay Ganesh* [1994] 2 Lloyd's Rep 358 (WorldFood charterparty form).

6   *Acceptance of notice of readiness/estoppel*

The effect of provisions in a charterparty relating to the commencement of laytime may be modified by a bilateral agreement to vary the charter inferred from the conduct of the parties, or by waiver, by acceptance of a notice of readiness knowing it to be invalid or by estoppel. In *Surrey Shipping v Compagnie Continentale, The Shackleford* [1978] 1 WLR 1080, CA, the vessel was chartered on the Baltimore form C grain charter for a voyage to Constanza. By a special clause it was agreed that the vessel would obtain customs entry before notice of readiness was given. The master purported to give (to the charterer's agents) notice of readiness before the vessel had been entered with customs at Constanza. The charterer's agents, who had authority to receive a valid notice of readiness, were found also to have authority to accept a premature notice of readiness which, on the facts, they were held to have done. The charterers were estopped from denying that the premature notice of readiness was valid and effective. The shipowners had relied on the acceptance of the notice of readiness to their detriment by not attempting to procure customs entry as soon as they could otherwise have done.

The *Helle Skou* was chartered on the Gencon form to carry a cargo of skimmed milk powder. Her previous cargo had been fish meal. By clause 22 of the berth charter she was 'to be presented with holds clean and dry and free from smell'. Notice of readiness was given although she was not in fact free from smell. The charterers were found to have accepted the invalid notice of readiness when they began to load.

> Whether it is labelled as waiver or estoppel or something else, I do not consider that the charterers can resile from this position, save upon grounds of fraud.

The charterers were not allowed to reject the notice later the same day when the smell became more apparent and it was decided that the milk powder which had been loaded had to be discharged and the vessel cleaned. *Sofial v Ove Skou Rederi* [1976] 2 Lloyd's Rep 205.

2 FIXED LAYTIME

William Alexander & Sons v A/S Hansa [1920] AC 88

Viscount Finlay: ... On this appeal a great many cases were cited laying down the rule that if the charterer has agreed to load or unload within a fixed period of time (as is the case here, for *certum est quod certum reddi potest*), he is answerable for the non-performance of that engagement, whatever the nature of the impediments, unless they are covered by exceptions in the charterparty or arise through the fault of the shipowner or those for whom he is responsible. I am here adopting in substance the language used by Scrutton LJ in his work upon *Charterparties and Bills of Lading*, art 131 ... Although no authority upon the point was cited which would in itself be binding upon your Lordships' House, there has been such a stream of authority to the same effect that I think it would be eminently undesirable to depart in a matter of business of this kind from the rule which has been so long applied, even if your Lordships felt any doubt as to the propriety of these decisions in the first instance. I myself have no doubt as to their correctness, and I understand that this is the opinion of all your Lordships. It seems to me that the appeal on this point must fail ...

Notes

1 *'Exceptions in the charterparty'*

This is a reference to specific exceptions which are expressed to apply to the laytime provisions. A general exceptions clause in a charterparty will not normally be read as applying to provisions for laytime and demurrage unless the language is clear. *The Johs Stove* [1984] 1 Lloyd's Rep 38.

2 *'Whatever the nature of the impediments'*

Charterers have been held liable on an obligation to load or unload within a fixed time notwithstanding that they could not do so because of congestion, as in *Randall v Lynch* (1810) 2 Camp 352; ice, *Barret v Dutton* (1815) 4 Camp 333; bad weather preventing access to the ship, *Thiis v Byers* (1876) 1 QBD 244; strikes of stevedores, *Budgett v Binnington* [1891] 1 QB 35; and even absence of the vessel from the port, the ship having been ordered away by an act of the sovereign authority, *Cantiere Navale Triestina v Soviet Naptha* [1925] 2 KB 172, CA, where it was said that it was just as if the ship had been driven to sea by stress of weather:

> ... there can be no reason why the absence of the ship from the harbour, once the lay days have begun to run, without any fault on the part of the owner, should prevent the lay days from continuing to run and the ship going on demurrage (Atkin LJ, p 207).

However, it seems that the charterer may be excused, on the principle of *Ralli v Compania Naviera* [1920] 2 KB 287, if the loading or unloading becomes illegal by the law of the port of loading or unloading. But it not insufficient if the law applied in the port merely limits the time for loading, as opposed to preventing it completely: *Compania Crystal de Vapores v Herman & Mohatta, The Maria G* [1958] 2 QB 196.

'Fault of the shipowner'

Gem Shipping of Monrovia v Babanaft, The Fontevivo [1975] Lloyd's Rep 399

Donaldson J: The *Fontevivo* is a small Somali flag tanker which was chartered to carry gasoline from Turkey to Lattakia in Syria. She duly arrived at Lattakia and began discharging her cargo. However, when part only had been discharged, she sailed away claiming that the port had become unsafe owing to war risks. Just under three days later, she was persuaded to return and to complete the discharge. The issue raised by this award, in the form of a special case, is whether the time she was away from her berth counts as part of the laytime. Mr Cedric Barclay, sitting as the arbitrator, held that it did not.

In the absence of express exceptions, the charterer's obligation to load and discharge the vessel within the lay days is unconditional, once the vessel has reached the appropriate place. Nevertheless, it is subject to the qualification which applies to all contracts that a party is not liable for the commission of a breach if the breach arose because the other party prevented him from performing the contract and did so without lawful excuse. (See *Budgett & Co v Binnington & Co* [1891] 1 QB 35 *per* Lord Esher MR, at p 38, Lindley LJ at p 40, and Lopes LJ at p 41.)

Mr Pardoe, who has appeared for the shipowners, submits that if the safety of the ship and cargo requires the removal of the vessel from the discharging berth, the removal is lawfully excused and laytime continues to run. (See *Houlder v Weir* [1905] 2 KB 267, and *Compania Crystal de Vapores of Panama v Herman and Mohatta (India) Ltd* [1958] 2 QB 196.) In the former case laytime was held to run although discharge was temporarily interrupted in order to ballast the vessel. In the latter case it continued to run whilst the vessel was temporarily away from the berth in order to avoid the danger of bore tides.

It is at this stage that Mr Hallgarten, for the charterers, introduces a complication by referring me to *Petrinovic & Co Ltd v Mission Française des Transports Maritimes* (1941) 71 Ll L Rep 208. In that case the vessel left Bordeaux, which was the discharging port, because of the danger to both ship and cargo from the advancing German armies. Atkinson J held that demurrage ceased to run and in doing so referred to the fact that the removal was in the interests of ship and cargo, but not of the charterers. Building on this decision Mr Hallgarten submits that Houlder's case is distinguishable since the ballasting was part of the process of discharge and that the *Crystal* case was wrongly decided no doubt because Devlin J was never referred to the *Petrinovic* decision.

I am afraid that I do not accept these submissions. The reasoning underlying both *Houlder's* case and the *Crystal* case is that the mere fact that the shipowner by some act of his prevents the continuous loading or discharging of the vessel is not enough to interrupt the running of the lay days; it is necessary to show also that there was some fault on the part of the shipowner (see the judgment of Devlin J [1958] 2 QB 196, at p 207).

The fundamental distinction between those cases and Petrinovic lies in the fact that in the latter case, the departure of the vessel was intended to be permanent. Such a departure must bring the contact of carriage to an end, whether it be a justified or an unjustified repudiation or whether it merely recognises that in the events which were unfolding the contract had been frustrated. Once the contract of carriage is at an end, laytime must also cease to run.

The issue in this case is, therefore, whether discharge of the vessel was prevented by some action on the part of the shipowner and, if so, whether that action constituted fault on his part. The initial burden of proof lies on the charterers, but this they discharge by proving the removal of the vessel from the berth in the course of discharging. Thereafter the burden lies upon the shipowner of justifying this action or showing that it was involuntary.

[His Lordship then reviewed the facts and continued] ...

The long and the short of it is that the crew of this Somali vessel had a severe attack of cold feet in a hot climate and the master decided that the cure was to leave Lattakia. There is no finding that this was necessary for the safety of ship or cargo or that, had he left the ship at the discharging berth, she would not have been at the disposal of the charterers for the purpose of discharging.

Whatever may be the responsibility of a shipowner for the activity or inactivity of his crew in this context – a point which was left open by Lord Esher in *Budgett v Binnington* [1891] 1 QB 35, at p 39 – there is no doubt as to his responsibility for the actions of the master who decided to leave the discharging berth. On the facts found that cannot be justified and accordingly I hold that time does not run against laytime during the period of the vessel's absence from Lattakia.

Note

In *Overseas Transportation v Mineralimportexport, The Sinoe* [1971] 1 Lloyd's Rep 514, affirmed on appeal [1972] 1 Lloyd's Rep 201, CA, the time allowed for discharging was exceeded because of the incompetence of the stevedores. The owners claimed demurrage.

Sir John Donaldson (at 519): Mr Lloyd [counsel for the plaintiff shipowners] stressed the word 'fault', pointing out that delay by the act or omission of the shipowners which does not amount to a breach of contract or duty remains the liability of the charterers. However, in the present case there can be no doubt that the conduct of the stevedores constituted 'fault', and the real question is whether they were persons for whom the owners were responsible. Mr Lloyd also relied upon a passage in the judgment of Lord Esher MR in *Budgett & Co v Binnington & Co* [1891] 1 QB 35, which suggested that the class of persons for whom the owners were responsible in this context might be very limited indeed – perhaps extending no further than the master. Whatever the basis for this suggestion Lord Esher MR had revised his views two years later in *Harris v Best, Ryley & Co* (1893) 68 LT 75, when he held that charterers were not liable to pay demurrage in respect of delay caused by stevedores employed by the shipowners.

The issue then is by whom were the stevedores employed in such a sense as to make the party concerned vicariously liable for their errors and omissions. This depends upon the terms of the charterparty.

[After considering the terms of the charterparty which provided that the stevedores were to be employed by charterers but 'considered as owners' servants', his Lordship continued at p 520]

If I had to decide this point, I should hold that the charterparty does not sufficiently clearly make the owners responsible for the fault of the stevedores to rebut the prima facie liability of the charterers to pay for the detention of the vessel. Fortunately I do not have to decide it because even if I were to be in the charterers' favour on that point, they have, in my judgment, no answer to the owners' rejoinder, that in employing or causing or allowing these particular stevedores to be employed, the charterers were in breach of their duty to the owners. If this is right, the charterers are unable to rely upon the neglect of the stevedores as barring the owners' claim to demurrage or alternatively are liable to the owners in a like amount as damages for breach of their obligation to employ competent stevedores.

3 CALCULATING FIXED LAYTIME

If a charterparty does not contain an express term fixing the time to be taken in loading and discharging cargo, it is implied that those operations will be carried out within a reasonable time. But it is almost invariable practice today for laytime to be fixed. This can be done directly, eg cargo to be loaded within five days. It can also be fixed a little less directly by an agreement that a specified weight or measurement of cargo will be loaded or discharged in a particular period of time: eg 100 tons per working day 'and as the burden of the ship was known and *id certum est quod certum reddi potest*, this was equivalent to naming a certain number of days' (Lord Blackburn, *Postlethwaite v Freeland* (1880) 5 App Cas 599, 618).

The *prima facie* meaning and effect of a number of words or phrases in common use in calculating laytime were considered by Lord Devlin in *Reardon Smith Line v Ministry of Agriculture* [1963] AC 691.

> *Day*: a calendar day of 24 hours ('*in the beginning a day was a day – a Monday, a Tuesday or a Wednesday, as the case may be*').

> *Conventional day*: a day of 24 hours which starts from the time when a notice of readiness expires. Replaces calendar day when a charter provides, eg, that time for loading shall commence 12 hours after written notice has been given between 9.00 am and 6.00 pm.

> *Working day*: a description of a type of day of 24 hours, not a reference to the part of a day in which work is carried out. A day for work as distinguished from a day for religious observance or for play or rest.

> *Weather working day*: *prima facie* a species of working day. ('It is well established that whether a day is a weather working day or not depends on the character of the day and not on whether work was actually interferred with.') When bad weather occurs, a reasonable apportionment should be made 'according to the incidence of the weather upon the length of day that the parties either were working or might be expected to have been working at the time'.

Notes

1 *Holidays excepted*

A charterparty provided that the vessel should proceed to and load at one safe port US Gulf, loading at the average rate of 1,000 tons per weather working day of 24 consecutive hours Saturday afternoon, Sundays and holidays excepted. The vessel was ordered to Lake Charles, Louisiana. The question stated by the arbitrator for the court was whether at that port Saturday mornings did or did not count as lay time. Donaldson J held: (1) on the evidence, that Saturday was a working day in the port as it was a day on which work was ordinarily done; (2) that a working day could nevertheless be a holiday; and (3) that whether a day was a holiday depended on local law and custom. An act of the Louisiana legislature declared all Saturdays to be holidays in an area which included Lake

Charles and that was conclusive. *Controller of Chartering of the Govt of India v Central Gulf Steamship, The Mosfield* [1968] 2 Lloyd's Rep 173.

2   *Holidays worked*

In *James Nelson v Nelson Line* [1908] AC 108, the House of Lords held that where holidays were excepted from laytime but nevertheless loading continued during the holidays, an agreement to treat a holiday as a working day and count it among the lay days could not be inferred. Such an agreement had to be proved.

3   *Time lost through rain*

The contract provided 'should any time be lost whilst steamer is in a loading berth owing to work being impossible through rain ... the amount of actual time so lost during which it is impossible to work owing to rain ... to be added to the loading time'. *Held*, Greer and Romer LJJ (Scrutton LJ dissenting) that to take advantage of this provision, the charterers must show (1) that rain in fact made work impossible and (2) that, for that reason, time was in fact lost. *Burnett Steamship v Danube and Black Sea Shipping Agencies* [1933] 2 KB 438, CA.

4   *Weather permitting*

It has been held that there is no material difference between a clause which fixes laytime by reference to 'working days weather permitting' and clauses which do so by reference to 'weather permitting working days': *The Camelia* and *The Magnolia* [1978] 2 Lloyd's Rep 182) or to 'running days weather permitting' or 'running hours weather permitting': *Gebr Broere v Saras* [1982] 2 Lloyd's Rep 436. In *Dow Chemical v BP Tanker, the Vorras* [1983] 1 Lloyd's Rep 579 the Court of Appeal held that '72 hours weather permitting' meant '72 hours during which the weather conditions are such that loading or discharging is possible'. In that case, a port charter, the *Vorras* had arrived at the loading port but was awaiting a berth: Sir John Donaldson MR said that in his judgment:

> the weather prohibited any vessel of this general type from loading and it is nothing to the point that owing to the presence of another vessel in the berth, the prohibition was not the operative cause which prevented the vessel from loading (p 584).

5   *Cargo be loaded at the average rate of [100] tons per working hatch*

The alternative expressions working hatch/available working hatch have been held to mean an upper deck hatch which can be worked either because under it is a hold into which cargo can be loaded or a hold out of which cargo can be discharged, in either event being a hatch which the party responsible for loading or discharging is not for any reason disabled from working: *Cargill v Rionda de Pass, the Giannis Xilas* [1982] 2 Lloyd's Rep 511, Bingham J, following the decision of the Court of Appeal in *The Sandgate* [1930] P 30. On this basis, it has been said that a hatch might be unworkable because the loading or discharging of that hatch has been completed or because of physical damage or perhaps because the master insists that the centre holds are loaded first to preserve the vessel's trim. The reference to an average rate of loading means that there is no obligation to load any particular amount on a particular day.

But in considering workability it is necessary to disregard any unevenness in loading (or discharge) which arises from the shippers' choice as opposed to reasons which disable them from working the hatches evenly: *Cargill v Marpro, the Aegis Progress* [1983] 2 Lloyd's Rep 570, 574. If the rule were otherwise, and the laytime calculation was based simply on the way in which the holds are in fact loaded or discharged, then charterers might be able unfairly to influence the total of the lay days. For example, suppose a charterer agrees to load a ship at an average rate of 300 tons per working hatch per day, the vessel has three hatches, and a capacity in tons in No 1 hold of 1,200 tons, No 2 hold, 900 tons and No 3 hold, 600 tons. If the charterer loads at the agreed rate but concentrates on one hold at a time, and each were to be treated as 'unworkable' when filled, the loading could take six days. But if all holds were loaded simultaneously at the average rate, loading might be completed in four days, which is the time taken to load the largest hold. To prevent the length of laytime depending on the whim of the charterer, the laytime calculation under this clause therefore ignores the way in which the charterer in fact chooses to load the vessel: *Compania de Navigacion Zita SA v Louis Dreyfus & Cie, the Corfu Island* [1953] 1 WLR 1399, explaining *The Sandgate* [1930] P 30. The result of this is that in most cases the length of laytime can be found by taking the quantity of cargo passing through the hatch or hold receiving or discharging the largest quantity and then dividing that figure by the average rate figure fixed by the charterparty.

This approach ('the *Sandgate* formula') has to be modified in exceptional cases, such as the *Aegis Progress*, where more than one hatch had to be taken into account in calculating the laytime. In the *Aegis Progress* the vessel loaded at two ports and different holds were workable in the two ports. Permitted laytime was held to consist of the time required to load the critical hold in Port 1 added to the time required to load the hold which was critical in Port 2.

Although this type of clause was described in *The Sandgate* by Scrutton LJ as 'ambiguous and mysterious', more recently Hobhouse J in the *Aegis Progress* (at p 573) has explained that:

> The convenience of such an approach where one is concerned with an fob shipment such as the present is obvious. The vessel is provided by the buyers. The sellers will normally not know at the time of contracting what the vessel is to be, nor what its capacity will be, nor its number of holds. They do not know whether it will be part laden. They do not know whether it will be loading other cargo. They do not know what draft, trim or stability restrictions it may be subject to. They will not normally have

any right to give orders or directions to the vessel. These points are illustrated in the present case. The vessel had seven hatches; she was already partly laden; the master did impose restrictions on the way in which the vessel could be loaded. The workable hatch approach provides a sensible basis for dealing with this situation ...

6   *Cargo to be discharged at the average rate of 1,000 metric tons basis five or more available workable hatches pro rata if less number of hatches per weather working day*

The House of Lords (Lord Templeman dissenting) held that this clause selected an overall rate for the ship which was qualified only to the extent that the overall rate was to be reduced *pro rata* if one or more hatches were unavailable at the start of loading or became unavailable temporarily in the course of discharge. But on this form of words the reference to available workable hatches did not override the overall rate for the ship and substitute a rate per available hatch. The mere fact that discharge of any particular hatch was completed would not itself affect the computation of laytime. Lord Templeman dissented, holding that 'available workable hatch' had an established meaning which could not be ignored. *President of India v Jebsens (UK) Ltd, the General Capinpin* [1991] 1 Lloyd's Rep 1.

7   *Cargo to be loaded at the average rate of 120 metric tons per hatch per weather working day*

The vessel had five hatches. It was held that this clause was no more than a roundabout way of saying that the vessel should be loaded at an average rate of 600 tons per day. *The Sandgate* [1930] P 30 and *Zita v Louis Dreyfus, the Corfu Island* [1953] 1 WLR 1399 (above) were distinguished by the absence of a reference to 'working' or 'available working' hatches: *Lodza Compania de Navigacione SA v Govt of Ceylon, The Theraios* [1971] 1 Lloyd's Rep 209, CA.

8   *Charterers to have right to average the days allowed for loading and discharging*

In the absence of an agreement of this sort, time for loading and discharging have to be considered and calculated separately: *Marshall v Bolckow Vaughan* (1881) 6 QBD 231. Under this clause if the charterer chooses to exercise the right the two calculations are still kept 'entirely separate until the very end when a balance is struck. If time is saved on discharge it is set against the excess time of loading, or vice versa, and in that way, a net result is arrived at' (Devlin J, *Alma v Salgaoncar* [1954] 2 QB 94). The implications of using this method depend on the meaning of 'time saved' and on rates of demurrage and despatch. Where, as is often the case, the despatch rate is half the demurrage rate, it will be in the charterer's interests to be able to average: see Chapter 12.

9   *Loading and discharge time to be reversible*

The words 'to be reversible' give a charterer the right to choose either to draw up separate time sheets for loading and discharge ports and calculate demurrage/despatch accordingly or, if preferred, to draw up one time sheet dealing with both ports and so, in effect, pool or aggregate the laytime at each end of the voyage. *Fury Shipping v State Trading Corp of India, the Atlantic Sun* [1972] 1 Lloyd's Rep 509.

10   *Completion of loading*

The *Argobec* was chartered on the Baltimore berth grain form and ordered to load a cargo of grain at Sorel for carriage to the United Kingdom. The charter provided that the vessel was 'to be loaded according to berth terms, with customary despatch and if detained longer than five days ... charterer to pay demurrage ...' Regulations of statutory force in the port required grain carried in the *Argobec*'s 'tween deck to be in bags. A certificate of the port authorities that the regulations had been complied with was also required before the vessel could sail. At Sorel, the cargo of bulk wheat was put on board by elevators. After the lay days expired, loose grain continued to be poured into the *Argobec*'s 'tween deck where it was bagged by stevedores employed on behalf of the ship. Charterers argued that the vessel was 'loaded' once the elevators had stopped and a full cargo of bulk grain had been put on board. The shipowners claimed that the vessel was not loaded until the grain had also been bagged and stowed. The Court of Appeal, upholding the owner's argument, held that the cargo was not loaded until the cargo was so placed in the ship that the ship could proceed on her voyage in safety. It made no different that this work had to be done at the end of the loading operation or that the shipowner had to pay the costs involved. *Argonaut Navigation v Ministry of Food* [1949] 1 KB 14, CA.

On what seems to be the same principle, Webster J held as an alternative ground of decision in *Total Transport v Amoco Trading, the Altus* [1985] 1 Lloyd's Rep 423 that time spend by a tanker in avoiding pollution by flushing pipelines through which the vessel has been loaded, was part of loading. A reasonable time to disconnect terminal hoses is probably also part of loading, although in tanker charters there is often an express agreement on this point.

11   *Concurrent charterparties*

In *Sarma Navigation v Sidermar* [1982] 1 Lloyd's Rep 13, CA, the *Sea Pioneer* was the subject of two charters in the Gencon form between the same parties, for the carriage of part cargoes of, respectively, steel bars and steel coils. In the event, the port of delivery for both cargoes was the same. At that port (Puerto Cabello, Venezuela) she was delayed for approximately three weeks. Both charters provided that time waiting for a berth should count as discharging time. The freight rates differed under the charters, but both provided for discharge at the rate of 1,000 metric tons per weather working day and both provided for demurrage at the rate of $3,000 per running day. The steel coils were discharged first, followed by the bars: there was an overlap of a few hours during which time both cargoes were being discharged concurrently. The owners claimed demurrage under both charters. The Court of Appeal held that the two charters were complementary and were to be read together. But while the charterers were entitled to the laytime allowed by both charters which was to be added together (ie the rate of discharge per day was *not* doubled), the owners were only entitled to $3,000 per day for detention.

A result which differs from that in *The Sea Pioneer* was reached in *The Oriental Envoy* [1982] 2 Lloyd's Rep 266. In that case, two charters (the 'June' and 'July' charters) were agreed between the same parties: both charters dealt with cargoes of rice in bags. Both cargoes were eventually discharged at the same port. However, the July agreement was made six weeks after the June charter and the freight rates, demurrage rates, and cargo quantities differed as between the two agreements. Neither charter related to a specific vessel, but both gave the owners a right to nominate. The owners, as they were entitled to do, nominated the named vessel to lift the first and part of the second chartered cargo. It was held that the two charterparties had to be read separately. It was also held that the owners became entitled to demurrage under the June charter when laytime expired under that charter (27 December) and under both charters when laytime had also expired under the July charter (7 March).

4 LAYTIME NOT FIXED

Van Liewen v Hollis [1920] AC 239

Lord Atkinson (at 251): If by the terms of the charterparty the charterers have agreed to discharge the chartered ship within a fixed period of time, there is an absolute and unconditional engagement for the non-performance of which they are answerable, whatever be the nature of the impediments which prevented them from performing it, and thereby causing the ship to be detained in their service beyond the time stipulated. If no time be fixed expressly or impliedly by the charterparty the law implies an agreement by the charterers to discharge the cargo within a reasonable time, having regard to all the circumstances of the case as they actually existed, including the custom or practice of the port, the facilities available thereat, and any impediments arising therefrom which the charterers could not have overcome by reasonable diligence: *Postlethwaite v Freeland* (1880) 5 App Cas 599; *Hick v Raymond & Reid* [1893] AC 22; and *Hulthen v Stewart & Co* [1903] AC 389.

Notes

1   *Laytime fixed by implication*

A charterparty in the Chamber of Commerce White Sea Wood form ('Merblanc') provided for discharge 'with customary steamship despatch as fast as the steamer can ... deliver'. It was argued that the shipowner would know and the charterer could ascertain the time required for delivery of the cargo when the ship was working as fast as she could. Since that time could be measured by days and hours, it was contended that, in effect, the time for discharge had been fixed. The House of Lords rejected this argument. The clause was insufficient to fix laytime. Lord Macnaghten said that:

> in order to impose such a liability the language used must in plain and unambiguous terms define and specify the period of time within which delivery of the cargo is to be accomplished (*Hulthen v Stewart* [1903] AC 389).

Similarly, obligations to load or discharge 'with all dispatch according to the custom of the port' (*Postlethwaite v Freeland*, cited above), or 'with all dispatch as customary' (*Castlegate Steamship v Dempsey* [1892] 1 QB 854, CA and *Lyle Shipping v Cardiff Corp* [1900] 2 QB 638) have also been held to be insufficiently definite and free from ambiguity for the charterparty in question to be treated as having a fixed laytime. In all these cases, therefore, the obligation was to load or unload within a reasonable time.

References to 'custom' in this context are taken to refer primarily to the customary or established working practices of the port; they are interpreted as references to the manner of loading or discharge rather than to the time which those activities take: *Dunlop v Balfour, Williamson* [1892] 1 QB 507, CA; *Castlegate Steamship v Dempsey*, cited above.

2   *Reasonable time*

Since 'all the circumstances' are relevant, it is clear that a reasonable time will depend on the terms of the particular contract of affreightment (Lord Herschell, *Carlton v Castle Mail* [1898] AC 486, 491), which must include both the nature of the cargo and the vessel. Both the normal features of the port and any unusual circumstances can also be taken into account. Thus, both delay caused by tides (*Carlton v Castle Mail*, above) and by strikes (*Hick v Raymond*, below) can extend the period which would otherwise be allowed. Delays arising out of the settled and established working practices of the port are also relevant. This is so whether or not the contract expressly incorporates a phrase of the 'according to the custom of the port' type mentioned above: Lord Blackburn, *Postlethwaite v Freeland*, cited above, at p 613; but compare Lord Herschell in *Hick v Raymond*, below, at p 30. But circumstances to be taken into account do not include those caused by a default for which the charterer is held responsible, or which the charterer could be expected to have avoided.

3 A cargo of wheat was shipped under bills of lading on the *Derwentdale* at Taganrog for carriage to London. Time for discharge was not fixed by the bills of lading. The respondents, who were consignees and holders of the bills of lading, employed the dock company to discharge the vessel. After discharge had been commenced, a strike of dock workers began. Completion of discharge was delayed by nearly four weeks. It was admitted that during the strike it was not possible for the respondents either to find any other person to provide the labour or to obtain the necessary labour themselves. It was held that the respondents' obligation was to discharge within a reasonable time under the circumstances as they actually existed, since those circumstances had not been caused or contributed to by them. The respondents were not therefore liable to damages for detention of the vessel: *Hick v Raymond & Reid* [1893] AC 22.

4 The *Cumberland Lassie* was chartered to deliver at East London at a safe wharf or as near thereto as she could safely get, a cargo of steel rails and fastenings. The cargo was 'to be discharged with all dispatch according to the customs of the port'. The vessel had to be lightened before it could cross the harbour bar at East London. Because of the lack of lighters and the number of ships awaiting discharge the vessel had to wait for 24 working days before lightening could begin. No more lighters could have been obtained from any other source in the time available. Discharge was completed as rapidly as possible in all the circumstances. It was held that the shipowner was not entitled to demurrage for the delay.

> Difficult questions may sometimes arise as to the circumstances which ought to be taken into consideration in determining what time is reasonable. If (as in the present case) an obligation, indefinite as to time, is qualified or partially defined by express or implied reference to the custom or practice of a particular port, every impediment arising from or out of that custom or practice, which the charterer could not have overcome by the use of any reasonable diligence, ought (I think) to be taken into consideration (*Postlethwaite v Freeland* (1880) 5 App Cas 599, Lord Selborne LC).

5 The *Ardandearg* was chartered to load a cargo of coal at Newcastle, New South Wales for carriage to Java. Time for loading was not fixed. The cargo was to be loaded in the usual and customary manner. The vessel was delayed for 31 days because the charterers had failed to procure a cargo. Held: the charterers' primary duty to provide a cargo was distinct from their subsequent duty to load that cargo in a reasonable time. The primary duty was, on the facts, absolute and unqualified. An assertion that the charterers did nothing unreasonable was therefore no answer to the shipowners' claims for damages for detention of the vessel where breach of the primary duty caused the delay. *Ardan Steamship v Andrew Weir* [1905] AC 501.

6 The *Julia* was chartered to carry oak logs from Danzig to Millwall Dock. The more usual method of discharge at that dock was to lift the logs direct

into railway trucks. It was found that it was also practicable to discharge into lighters. Discharge took an extra four days because too few trucks and no lighters were provided by the defendants, who were receivers of the cargo. The defendants were held liable in an action for damages for detention because they failed to show that they had used reasonable exertions to get either railway trucks or lighters.

> As the result I come to the conclusion that it has not been shown that the defendants used reasonable care to provide for the discharge, and I am of opinion that they did not exhaust all available means. It is therefore unnecessary to discuss all the cases ... Where there are alternative methods of discharge it is clear that the defendant must use all available methods and exhaust all efforts to effect the discharge. There will, therefore, be judgment for the plaintiffs for four days demurrage (*Rodenacker v May* (1901) 6 Com Cas 37, Mathew J).

CHAPTER 14

DEMURRAGE AND DESPATCH

1 DEMURRAGE

(A) Nature of demurrage

Demurrage ... is not money payable by a charterer as the consideration for the exercise by him of a right to detain a chartered ship beyond the stipulated lay days. If demurrage were that it would be a liability sounding in debt ... It is a liability in damages to which a charterer becomes subject because, by detaining the chartered ship beyond the stipulated lay days, he is in breach of contract. Most, if not all, voyage charters contain a demurrage clause, which prescribes a daily rate at which the damages for such detention are to be quantified. The effect of such a claim is to liquidate the damages payable: it does not alter the nature of the charterer's liability, which is and remains a liability for damages, albeit liquidated damages. In the absence of any provision to the contrary in the charter the charterer's liability for demurrage accrues *de die in diem* from the moment when, after the lay days have expired, the detention of the ship by him begins.

The Lips [1987] 2 Lloyd's Rep 311, 315, Lord Brandon.

A demurrage clause is merely a clause providing for liquidated damages for a certain type of breach. It is presumably the parties' estimate of the loss of prospective freight which the owner is likely to suffer if his ship is detained beyond the lay days. The demurrage rate in this case appears to have been a good deal lower than the freight market rate; and I suppose I need not shut my eyes to the fact that a sum produced by demurrage is generally less than damages for detention, which are presumably assessed by reference to the market rate of freight at the time of the breach. To this extent a demurrage clause may be in practice a concession to the charterer. But I am not, and I do not think I could be, invited to consider it as different in its nature from an ordinary liquidated damage clause.

Chandris v Isbrandtsen-Moller [1951] 1 KB 240, at 249), Devlin J

Compare the following with Devlin J's description (above) of the usual position: 'In many cases, for instance, parties agree upon a low freight, upon a very short laytime, and upon a high demurrage rate, just to keep the freight rate low but to allow the carrier nevertheless to collect sufficient overall remuneration' (Trappe, (1986) LMCLQ 251, 255).

(B) Demurrage or unliquidated damages for detention

A shipowner will be entitled to unliquidated damages for detention for failure to load or discharge within the agreed time, if either:

(a) laytime has expired (either at the end of the period fixed or after a reasonable time) and there is no agreement to pay demurrage; or

(b) a demurrage period is fixed and has expired; eg if the charterparty provides for 72 hours for loading and 72 hours on demurrage and a further delay then occurs. If the demurrage period is not fixed, the demurrage rate applies not just for a reasonable time but for as long as the ship is in fact detained under the contract: *Western Steamship v Amaral Sutherland* [1913] 3 KB 366.

(C) Effect of an agreement to pay demurrage

An agreement to pay demurrage is normally treated as preventing the shipowner recovering from the charterer more than the agreed sum for the wrongful detention of his vessel. This is so however the delay is caused, whether by simply failing to load or discharge within the lay time, even if the delay is deliberate: *Suisse Atlantique v NV Rotterdamsche Kolen Centrale* [1967] AC 361; or by failing to provide a cargo: *Inverkip Steamship v Bunge* [1917] 2 KB 193, CA; or by providing a cargo of the wrong sort: *Chandris v Isbrandtsen-Moller*, above. But while a demurrage clause limits damages recoverable for delay, it does not prevent the recovery of damages of some other character (eg deadfreight) if a breach of contract other than failure to load or discharge within the laytime has also occurred: *A/S Reidar v Arcos* noted below.

(D) A/S Reidar v Arcos [1927] 1 KB 352, CA

The *Sagatind* was chartered to load a full and complete cargo of timber (850 standards) at Archangel. She was to be loaded at an agreed rate per day and demurrage at £25 per day was payable if she was detained beyond the time required to load at the agreed rate. There was no provision for a fixed number of days on demurrage. If she has been loaded at the agreed rate she could have carried a full summer cargo of 850 standards to the discharge port (Manchester) to which she was eventually ordered. Because loading was delayed beyond the agreed time, the master could not lawfully carry more than a winter deck load to a UK port, which was in fact loaded. The Court of Appeal held that the shipowners were entitled to recover damages for loss of freight in addition to demurrage at the agreed rate. Although there is little hostility to the outcome of the case, the basis of the decision has long been a matter of dispute: the three judgments given in the Court of Appeal are impossible to reconcile. In *Suisse Atlantique* in the House of Lords it was said that *Reidar v Arcos* was to be treated as a decision that:

(1) the charterers were in breach of two distinct obligations:

    (a) failure to load a full and complete cargo; and

    (b) detaining the vessel beyond the lay days.

(2) the provisions as to demurrage quantified only the damages arising from the detention of the vessel.

For another analysis of *Reidar v Arcos*, see *The Altus* [1985] 1 Lloyd's Rep 423, 435 and *The Adelfa* [1988] 2 Lloyd's Rep 466, 472, which were not followed in *The Bonde* [1991] 1 Lloyd's Rep 136.

(E) Chandris v Isbrandtsen-Moller [1951] 1 KB 240

A voyage charter provided that the cargo was to consist of lawful general merchandise, excluding dangerous cargo. Demurrage was fixed at £100 per day. A general cargo was loaded, which included 1,546 tons of turpentine. The vessel arrived at the discharge port (Liverpool) and began discharging in dock on 27 May 1941. Because of the dangerous nature of the turpentine, she was ordered by the authorities to move out of the dock and unload in the Mersey into lighters. The discharge took 16 days longer than it otherwise would. In arbitration, the shipowner claimed demurrage, damages for detention for the 16 days, and interest. The arbitrator stated a special case for the court. Devlin J held that turpentine was a dangerous cargo and that the charterers were in breach of contract but that the damages recoverable for the delay were limited by the demurrage clause.

(F) Suisse Atlantique v N V Rotterdamsche Kolen Centrale [1967] AC 361

The appellants chartered the *General Guisan* to the respondents to carry coal from the US to Europe; the charter was for a total of two years' consecutive voyages. Loading and discharge times were fixed with demurrage at $1,000 a day. As a result of failures by charterers to load and discharge within the lay days, the ship did not complete as many voyages as she could have done. The owners claimed damages calculated on the basis of the freights they would have earned if the vessel had not been wrongfully detained. They argued that demurrage provisions ceased to apply where the breach for which a charterer was responsible was such as to entitle the owner to treat the charterparty as repudiated. It was held that (1) that there is no rule of law which deprives demurrage provisions of effect when the breach for which the charterer is responsible is such as to entitle the shipowners to treat the charterparty as repudiated; and (2) it is a question of construction of the contract as a whole whether demurrage provisions apply in the circumstances of a particular breach of contract. The demurrage provisions in this case applied to the whole of the periods of detention.

(G) Once on demurrage, always on demurrage

Dias Compania Naviera v Louis Dreyfus, The Dias [1978] 1 Lloyd's Rep 325, HL

Lord Dilhorne, Lord Edmund-Davies, Lord Fraser of Tullybelton and Lord Scarman agreed with the speech of **Lord Diplock** (at 327):

My Lords, this appeal is about a dispute between shipowners and charterers which arose under a voyage charter for the carriage of 26,500 tons of wheat from the United States to China. As is generally the case with charterparties, the subject of the dispute is laytime and demurrage; and the answer to the question that is involved is to be found by applying well established principles of construction to the particular clauses of the charterparty.

The charterparty, dated 10 August 1973, was a berth charter on the Baltimore berth grain charterparty printed form. The place of discharge was 'one or two safe berths, one or two safe ports, China'. The clauses, numbered 12 to 17, relating to arrival and discharge of the cargo at its destination, were not in standard form. They were typewritten and special to the charterparty; they included a 'time lost' clause, *viz*:

> Time lost in waiting and/or shifting for berth and/or discharge to be counted as discharging time.

The clause which lies at the heart of the dispute is cl 15:

> At discharging, Charterers/Receivers have the option at any time to treat at their expense ship's holds/ compartments/hatchway and/or cargo and time so used to not count. The Master to co-operate with the Charterers/ Receivers or their representative with a view to the treatment being carried out expeditiously.

It is common ground that 'treat' in this clause means fumigate and that fumigation is an operation that has to be performed while the cargo is still on board or at any rate before it has been fully discharged.

What happened was that the vessel was ordered to Hsinkang as the discharging port. She anchored in the roads waiting her turn for a berth. Laytime expired on 26 October 1973. A fortnight later on 9 November fumigation started. It continued for 16 days six hours until 25 November. Discharge into lighters started on 30 November and at berth on 6 December. So no additional delay was caused by the work of fumigation.

The only question in this appeal is whether demurrage is payable for the period of 16 days six hours during which fumigation was being carried out ...

My Lords, the principles that apply to laytime and demurrage under voyage charterparties are clear. What 'laytime' and 'demurrage' mean was stated succinctly by Lord Guest (with the substitution of 'lay days' for 'laytime') in *Union of India v Compania Naviera Aeolus SA* [1964] AC 868 at p 899:

> Lay days are the days which parties have stipulated for the loading or discharge of the cargo, and if they are exceeded the charterers are in breach; demurrage is the agreed damages to be paid for delay if the ship is delayed in loading or discharging beyond the agreed period.

For the purposes of the adventure in four stages contemplated by a voyage charterparty, laytime is that period of time, paid for by the charterer in the freight, for which the shipowner agrees to place the ship at the disposition of the charterer for carrying out the loading operation or the discharging operation. Laytime for discharging is generally based upon an estimate of the time which will be needed to carry out the operation with reasonable diligence if everything else goes well. With dry cargoes the actual discharging of the cargo is not an operation that can be carried on continuously for 24 hours in each successive day, but only intermittently, as weather and working days at the port permit. So the length of time for which the vessel will need to be at the disposition of the charterer for this operation in order to enable him to complete it within the stated period by the exercise of reasonable diligence on his part, is not predictable in advance. It can only be a matter of subsequent calculation by the application of an agreed formula to events that have occurred.

The formula states at what point of time laytime will start and what period of time thereafter shall be excluded from the calculation and so prevent its running continuously. These excluded periods are sometimes expressed as exceptions, eg 'Sundays and holidays excepted', sometimes by some such phrase as that time used for a stated purpose is 'not to count as laytime (or discharging time)' or simply 'not to count'. Similarly, the formula may state that there shall be included in the calculation periods of time spent by the ship in some way or other, which would otherwise not form part of the laytime because during the period so spent the ship had not yet become an arrived ship at the place for loading or discharge, eg a 'time lost' clause. The commonest way of expressing this is to say that time so spent is 'to count as laytime' or simply 'to count'.

As Mocatta J, a judge of great experience in these matters, said in his judgment in the instant case:

> In my experience, so far as it goes, phrases like 'to count' or 'not to count' are generally used in charters in reference to laytime.

If laytime ends before the charterer has completed the discharging operation he breaks his contract. The breach is a continuing one; it goes on until discharge is completed and the ship is once more available to the shipowner to use for other voyages. But unless the delay in what is often, though incorrectly, called redelivery of the ship to the shipowner, is so prolonged as to amount to a frustration of the adventure, the breach by the charterer sounds in damages only. The charterer remains entitled to continue to complete the discharge of the cargo, while remaining liable in damages for the loss sustained by the shipowner during the period for which he is being wrongfully deprived of the opportunity of making profitable use of his ship. It is the almost invariable practice nowadays for these damages to be fixed by the charterparty at a liquidated sum per day and *pro rata* for part of a day (demurrage) which accrues throughout the period of time for which the breach continues.

Since demurrage is liquidated damages, fixed by agreement between the parties, it is possible by apt words in the charterparty to provide that, notwithstanding the continuance of the breach, demurrage shall not be payable in respect of the period when some event specified in the charterparty is happening; but the effect of such an agreement is to make an exception to the ordinary consequences that would flow in law from the charterer's continued breach of his contract, *viz*, his liability in damages. As was said by Scrutton LJ in a passage in his work on charterparties that was cited by Lord Reid in the *Union of India* case (above), at p 879:

> When once a vessel is on demurrage no exceptions will operate to prevent demurrage continuing to be payable unless the exceptions clause is clearly worded so as to have that effect.

This is but an example of the general principle stated by Lord Guest in the same case in continuation of the passage that I have already cited:

> ... an ambiguous clause is no protection. 'If a party wishes to exclude the ordinary consequences that would flow in law from the contract that he is making he must do so in clear terms' (*Szymonowski & Co v Beck & Co* [1923] 1 KB 457 at 466 *per* Scrutton LJ).

With these principles in mind I turn to the clause (cl 15) principally relied upon by the charterers as excluding the accrual of demurrage during the period while fumigation, which did not commence until after the expiration of laytime, was being carried out. Appearing as it does in a set of six clauses dealing with the discharging operation, laytime allowed for it, and demurrage, my immediate reaction, like that of Mocatta J, is that the answer to the question: 'for what purpose is time used in fumigation 'not to count'?' would be: 'for the purpose of calculating laytime'. These words do not seem to me to be an apt way of saying that the time so used is not to be taken into account in assessing the damages payable by the charterer for breach of contract for failing to complete the discharging operation within the stipulated time. Reliance was placed by the charterers on the fact that the words at the beginning of the clause 'at any time' entitled the charterer to carry out the fumigation not only before laytime began to run and while it was running, but also after laytime had run out. For my part, I am unable to attach any significance to this, although Sir John Pennycuick thought it to be decisive. As I have pointed out, the charterers' breach of contract in failing to complete discharge within the laytime sounds in damages only, it does not deprive the charterer of his right to require the shipowner to continue performing his part of the contract. In this respect, the right of the charterer to fumigate after laytime has run out is no different from his right to complete the discharging of the cargo. In the remaining typewritten clauses of the charterparty, the expression 'time so used to count' or 'not to count' appears in cll 12, 16 and 17, in contexts in which, as Browne LJ pointed out, it is plain that it can only mean time to count or not to count as laytime, though the express words 'as laytime' are used only in cl 17. In cl 13, which includes the time lost clause that I have already cited, the words 'time to count' appear in the last sentence, also in a context in which, in my view, they can only mean to count as laytime.

For my part, I think that when construed in the light of established principles, cl 15 is unequivocal. It means that time used in fumigation is not to be taken into account only in the calculation of laytime. The provision that time is 'not to count' has no further application once laytime has expired. But even if I were persuaded that the clause was in some way ambiguous, this would not be enough to save the charterers from their liability to pay demurrage during the period while fumigation was being carried out after laytime had expired. For these reasons, and in agreement with Mocatta J and Browne LJ I would allow this appeal.

(H) The reason for the 'clear exceptions only' rule?

In *Union of India v Compania Naviera Aeolus* [1964] AC 868, the House of Lords considered the meaning of the 'third part' of the Centrocon strike clause. The clause was a single clause but, for convenience, Lord Reid set it out, at page 878 of his judgment, divided into paragraphs:

> If the cargo cannot be loaded by reason of riots, civil commotions, or of a strike or lockout of any class of workmen essential to the loading of the cargo or by reason of obstructions or stoppages beyond the control of the charterers on the railways, or in the docks or other loading places or if the cargo cannot be discharged by reasons of riots, civil commotions or of a strike or lockout of any class of workmen essential to the discharge, the time for loading or discharging, as the case may be, shall not count during the continuance of such causes.

> Provided that a strike or lockout of the shippers' and/or receivers' men shall not prevent demurrage accruing if by the use of reasonable diligence they could have obtained other suitable labour at rates current before the strike or lockout.

> In case of any delay by reason of the before-mentioned causes, no claim for damages or demurrage shall be made by the charterers, receivers of the cargo, or owners of the steamer.

> For the purpose, however, of settling despatch rebate accounts any time lost by the steamer through any of the above causes shall be counted as time used in loading.

The House of Lords, by a majority of three to two, held that the clause as a whole, including the third part, referred to strikes starting during laytime. The third part of the clause did not therefore apply to a strike which began when the lay days had expired. In the course of his judgment, Lord Reid considered the reason for the 'clear exceptions only' rule once a vessel is on demurrage (p 882):

> So in my view the case stands in this position. There is no wholly satisfactory interpretation or explanation of the third part of the clause and one must choose between two almost equally unsatisfactory conclusions. In a case like this where a clause in common use has simply been copied one cannot try to find what the parties intended. They almost certainly never thought about things happening as they did. So I must fall back on the rule which I have already quoted from the work of Scrutton LJ. I do not think that it is an arbitrary rule for this reason. If a strike occurs before the end of the laytime neither party can be blamed in any way. But if it occurs after demurrage has begun to accrue the owner might well say: true, your breach of contract in detaining my ship after the end of the laytime did not cause the strike, but if

you had fulfilled your contract the strike would have caused no loss because my ship would have been on the high seas before it began: so it is more reasonable that you should bear the loss than that I should. So it seems to me right that if the respondents are to escape from paying demurrage during this strike they must be able to point to an exceptions clause which clearly covers this case. And in my judgment they cannot do that.

Notes

1 'Once laytime has been exceeded, there has been a breach and a clause operating at this time may be of a type which excludes or limits the liability in demurrage or it may be one which suspends the continuing obligation to discharge and therefore, *pro tanto*, suspends the breach which would otherwise have given rise to the obligation to pay demurrage. These types of clauses, whether excusing breaches, relieving prima facie obligations, or simply excluding or reducing the liability in liquidated damages are all provisions of the character of exclusion or exceptions clauses and therefore must be clearly expressed if they are to have that effect. Unclear or ambiguous clauses will be ineffective for that purpose. This is an application of the ordinary rules of contractual construction governing such clauses. They must be clearly worded.'

The Forum Craftsman [1991] 1 Lloyd's Rep 81, Hobhouse J.

2 The *Kalliope A* was chartered for the carriage of a cargo of shredded scrap from Rotterdam to Bombay. She was affected by congestion both during laytime and thereafter. The charterers claimed to be excused from any liability to pay demurrage by a clause in the charter which provided that '... unavoidable hindrances which may prevent ... discharging ... always mutually excepted'. It was held that the clause was not clear enough to exempt the charterers from liability in respect of periods when the vessel was on demurrage and they were in breach of contract.

The Kalliope A [1988] 2 Lloyd's Rep 101, CA, applied in *The Lefthero* [1992] 2 Lloyd's Rep 109, CA.

3 A typed addition to a charter in the Pacific Coast Grain form provided by clause 62 that 'Charterers shall not be liable for any delay in ... discharging ... which delay ... is caused in whole or in part by strikes ... and any other causes beyond the control of the charterers'. Other provisions of the charter dealt with causes beyond the charterers' control which interrupted laytime. The vessel came on demurrage at the discharge port and was then delayed for 26 days by a strike of port workers. It was held that clause 62 did relieve the charterers from liability for demurrage.

President of India v N G Livanos Maritime Co, The John Michalos [1987] 2 Lloyd's Rep 188.

(I) Demurrage and owner's default

Blue Anchor Line v Toepfer, The Union Amsterdam [1982] 2 Lloyd's Rep 432

Parker J: This is an appeal from an arbitration award dated 4 September 1981, and is brought pursuant to leave to appeal granted on 18 February 1982. It arises out of a charterparty dated 5 February 1980, between the appellants as time chartered owners and the respondents as charterers. I shall refer to them respectively as owners and charterers.

The charterparty provided by cl 19 for demurrage at loading and discharging ports to be paid at the rate of $ 6,000 per day and *pro rata*.

The chartered vessel duly arrived at the discharge port. Laytime expired while she was still awaiting berth and demurrage had begun to accrue under cl 19 when a berth became available and two pilots boarded in order to take her into that berth. About 90 minutes later she grounded and remained aground from 12.44 hours on 8 March until 18.36 hours on 13 March.

Owners claimed that demurrage continued to accrue during this period. Charterers successfully disputed this claim in the arbitration, which was an arbitration on documents, on the ground that the grounding was due to default, consisting in negligent navigation or management of owners or of those for whom they were responsible, and that the charterers were therefore excused the obligation to pay demurrage during the period the vessel was aground.

It is against the arbitrator's rejection of this claim that owners now appeal. They contend first that the arbitrator's finding of negligence is unsustainable and secondly that even if it stands it does not avail charterers by reason of cl 35 of the charterparty which, so far as immediately material, reads:

> ... neither the vessel nor the Master or Owners shall be or shall be held liable for any loss of or damage or delay to the cargo for causes excepted by the US Carriage of Goods by Sea Act 1936 ...

One of the causes excepted by s 4(2) of that Act is act, neglect or default of the master, mariner, pilot or the servants of the carrier in the navigation or in the management of the ship.

For owners, Mr Pardoe contends that the result of this clause is that any negligence in navigation or management is not actionable and that fault must be actionable before it can excuse charterers from their otherwise absolute obligation to pay demurrage ...

[After considering and upholding the arbitrator's finding of negligence, his Lordship continued] I now come to cl 35. It cannot on its wording avail owners. It excuses them from liability for delay and charterers are not seeking to hold them liable for delay. It is, however, said that the clause makes negligent navigation not actionable and that to stop demurrage running, actionable fault is required. There appears to be no direct authority on the point, although in *The Sinoe* [1971] 1 Lloyd's Rep 514 at p 519, Donaldson J appears to have accepted that delay by act or omission of the owners which does not amount to a breach of contract or duty remains the liability of the charterers. This conflicts with the decision of the Court of Appeal in *Ropner*

Shipping Co Ltd v Cleeves Western Valleys Anthracite Collieries Ltd [1927] 1 KB 879, where it appears to have been accepted that a period of bunkering while the vessel was on demurrage did not involve a breach of the charterparty and where the court proceeded on a very much wider principle.

At p 887 Bankes LJ says:

> In my opinion, this being a claim for demurrage in respect of the detention of the vessel ... it does not lie in the mouth of the owners to say that the vessel was being detained by the charterers during the time that they, the owners, for their own convenience, were bunkering ...

and at p 888 Sargant LJ says:

> ... the owners, for their own convenience, shifted the position of the vessel from the point where she was adapted to receive cargo to a point where she was adapted only to receive bunker coal, and there proceeded, during a number of days, to bunker the vessel, thus rendering it impossible during that period for the charterers to continue the loading of the cargo. The owners now claim that demurrage shall be paid by the charterers during the whole of the period the owners were so using the vessel for their own purposes, and so rendering her unavailable for the purposes of the charterers. That to my mind is an extremely bold claim to say the least of it, and I do not think it is justified. In order that demurrage may be claimed by the owners they must at least do nothing to prevent the vessel being available and at the disposal of the charterers for the purpose of completing the loading of the cargo. That to my mind disposes entirely of the case.

Avory J agreed with both judgments.

In the present case the grounding was due to the negligence of the owners or those for whom they were responsible and what owners are really saying is this: 'although the delay was caused by our negligence you must nevertheless pay for the detention of the vessel because were you claiming damages for delay, which you are not, you would be defeated by cl 35'. This argument cannot, in my judgment, succeed. In the first place on general principles an exceptions clause should be given no wider operation than its words allow. In the second place a breach of duty remains a breach of duty, and therefore fault, notwithstanding that liability for the breach is excluded. In the third place, far from doing nothing to prevent the vessel being available, owners have, by negligent navigation or management, so prevented her and, as Bankes LJ said, it does not lie in their mouths to say that the vessel was being detained by the charterers during the period when by their negligence she was grounded.

The only basis upon which cl 35 could avail owners would be if the true reason for the cessation of demurrage by reason of owners' fault was because, as a result of the fault, the charterers had a claim in damages for delay equal to the demurrage and were entitled to apply that claim in extinguishment of the demurrage claim. There is not a trace of any such principle in the authorities. The question is whether the charterers are released from their obligation to pay, not whether albeit still under that obligation they have a counterclaim. In the result the appeal must be dismissed.

(J) How long must a ship remain on demurrage?

The leading case is *Universal Cargo Carriers v Citati* [1957] 2 QB 401. The facts were that a charterparty in the Gencon form provided that the *Catherine D Goulandris* was to proceed to Basrah and load 6,000 tons of scrap iron for Buenos Aires. The lay/can spread was 5 July to 25 July 1951. The vessel arrived at Basrah on 12 July 1951. The charter allowed six weather working days for loading. Despite repeated enquiries, no shipper or berth was nominated and the cargo did not materialise. The owners purported to cancel the charter on 19 July when the lay days had run for only two-thirds of the time allowed. The question stated by the arbitrator for the opinion of the court was whether the owners were entitled to terminate the charterparty on 18 July. **Devlin J** held:

(1) The charterer was on 18 July in breach of the charter in failing to nominate a berth and in failing to provide a cargo in sufficient time to enable the vessel to be loaded within the lay days (the arbitrator had found that on 18 July the cargo could not have been loaded within the laytime which remained).

(2) For the same reason, the charterer was on 18 July also in anticipatory breach of the express obligation to complete loading by 21 July, or (alternatively) possibly on the same date was in breach of an implied term that he would not by his own act or omission put it out of his power to load by 21 July. 'But whether the breach is said to be an actual breach of an implied term or an anticipatory breach of an express term is not to my mind at all important; and it must be one or the other' (p 429).

(3) The breaches in question were breaches of warranty not of condition.

(4) 'It follows that the owners were not entitled *ipso facto* to rescind on July 18. But a party to a contract may not purchase indefinite delay by paying damages and a charterer may not keep a ship indefinitely on demurrage. When the delay becomes so prolonged that the breach assumes a character so grave as to go to the root of the contract, the aggrieved party is entitled to rescind. What is the yardstick by which this length of delay is to be measured? Those considered in the arbitration can now be reduced to two: first, the conception of a reasonable time, and secondly, such delay as would frustrate the charterparty. The arbitrator, it is clear, preferred the first. But in my opinion the second has been settled as the correct one by a long line of authorities.'

[His Lordship reviewed the earlier cases and continued]

'... Having settled the proper yardstick, the next question that arises for determination could, I think, have been put very conveniently in the form adopted in *Stanton v Richardson* (1872) LR 7 CP 421, namely, was the charterer on July 18, 1951, willing and able to load a cargo within such time as would not have frustrated the object of the venture; and the answer to that question would have determined the case. But in the arbitration the main argument was on anticipatory breach, and the emphasis on one mode of it, namely, renunciation. The chief findings of the arbitrator relate entirely to renunciation. I must therefore consider the nature of anticipatory breach and the findings thereon which the arbitrator has made.

The law on the right to rescind is succinctly stated by Lord Porter in *Heyman v Darwins Ltd* [1942] AC 356 as follows:

> The three sets of circumstances giving rise to a discharge of contract are tabulated by Anson, *Law of Contract*, 20th edition, p 319 as: (1) renunciation by a party of his liabilities under it; (2) impossibility created by his own act; and (3) total or partial failure of performance. In the case of the first two, the renunciation may occur or impossibility be created either before or at the time for performance. In the case of the third, it can occur only at the time or during the course of performance.

The third of these is the ordinary case of actual breach, and the first two state the two modes of anticipatory breach. In order that the arguments which I have heard from either side can be rightly considered, it is necessary that I should develop rather more fully what is meant by each of these two modes.'

(5) 'A renunciation can be made either by words or by conduct, provided it is clearly made. It is often put that the party renunciating must 'evince an intention' not to go on with the contract. The intention can be evinced either by words or by conduct. The test of whether an intention is sufficiently evinced by conduct is whether the party renunciating has acted in such a way as to lead a reasonable person to the conclusion that he does not intend to fulfil his part of the contract.

... Since a man must be both ready and willing to perform, a profession by words or conduct of inability is by itself enough to constitute renunciation. But unwillingness and inability are often difficult to disentangle, and it is rarely necessary to make the attempt. Inability often lies at the root of unwillingness to perform. Willingness in this context does not mean cheerfulness; it means simply an intent to perform. To say: 'I would like to but I cannot' negatives intent just as much as 'I will not' ... If a man says 'I cannot perform', he renounces his contract by that statement, and the cause of the inability is immaterial.'

(6) In considering whether the charterer had renounced by evincing an intention not to perform the charterparty and so committed an anticipatory breach, only events known to the shipowner at the time could be considered.

(7) The arbitration award in the owner's favour on the issue of renunciation could not stand because it was based on an erroneous concept of the length of delay necessary to amount to a repudiation.

(8) Impossibility could arise even if the disability was not deliberately created. However, a party electing to treat 'impossibility' as a repudiatory breach must prove that the inability was still effective at the time fixed for performance.

'In my judgment, therefore, if the owners can establish that in the words of Lord Sumner (*British & Beningtons v N W Cachar Tea* [1923] AC 48, 72) the charterer had on July 18 'become wholly and finally disabled' from finding a cargo and loading it before delay frustrated the venture, they are entitled to succeed. Lord Sumner's words expressly refer to the time of breach as the date at which the inability must exist. But that does not mean in my opinion that the facts to be looked at in determining inability are only those which existed on July 18; the determination is to be made in the light of all the events, whether occurring before or after the critical date, put in evidence at trial.'

(9) The test of impossibility did not depend on how the matter would have appeared to a reasonable shipowner or to a reasonable and well informed person on 18 July.

'An anticipatory breach must be proved in fact and not in supposition. If, for example, one party to a contract were to go to another and say that well informed opinion on the market was that he would be unable to fulfil his obligations when the time came, he might get the answer from his adversary that the latter did not care to have his affairs discussed on the market and did not choose to give any information about them except the assurance that he could and would fulfil his obligations. If that assurance was rejected and the contract rescinded before the time for performance came and the assurance in fact turned out to be well founded, it would be intolerable if the rescinder was entitled to claim that he was protected because he had acted on the basis of well informed opinion.'

(10) His Lordship concluded by dealing with procedural and factual submissions and ordered that the award be remitted to the arbitrator to answer the question whether the charterer was on 18 July 1951 willing and able to perform the charterparty within such time as would not have frustrated the commercial object of the adventure. Subsequent proceedings on these issues are reported at [1957] 1 WLR 979 and [1958] 2 QB 254.

2 DESPATCH

Demurrage and despatch: stick and carrot

The object of demurrage is to encourage the charterer to load or discharge within agreed laytime and, if he does not, to compensate the shipowner for the delay. But the prospect of paying demurrage is no encouragement to a charterer to load or discharge in less than the agreed lay time. Unless the parties have agreed that despatch money will be paid by the shipowner if charterers use less than the agreed time (despatch is only payable by agreement) charterers may find it suits them best to spread loading or discharge – as they are entitled to do – over the whole of the period allowed, even if they could have completed their activities more quickly. Thus, if demurrage is a stick for the charterer, despatch is a carrot.

Agreements for the payment of despatch can give rise to difficult questions of interpretation in charters which provide for lay days subject to exceptions such as Sunday and holidays. How is time to be calculated for the purpose of paying despatch money where the charterparty only refers imprecisely in such cases to 'any time saved in loading and/or discharging' or to 'each clear day saved loading' or 'each running day saved'? As Bailhache J said in *Mawson Shipping v Beyer* [1914] KB 304, 307:

> Is despatch money payable in respect only of lay days saved or in respect of all time saved to the ship? In other words is despatch for this purpose on the same footing as demurrage?

In *Mawson*, Sundays were excluded from lay days; the despatch clause referred to 'all time saved in loading'. In cases before *Mawson*, Bailhache J thought that question he formulated had been decided both ways. *Laing v Hollway* (1878) 3 QBD 437, CA and *In re Royal Mail Steam Packet and River Plate Steamship Co* [1910] 1 KB 600 held that time saved meant all the time saved to the ship; *The Glendevon* [1893] P 269, Div Ct, and *Nelson & Sons v Nelson Line* [1907] 2 KB 705, CA, decided it meant only laytime saved, so that in neither of those two cases was despatch payable in respect of a Sunday which was saved to the ship.

As a judge at first instance, Bailhache J in *Mawson* loyally attempted to reconcile and to follow the earlier decisions. Nevertheless, his personal views were also clear: 'I should, I fear, have decided all the four reported cases in favour of the charterers'. This has commercial logic. In origin exceptions such as Sundays and holidays were carved out of the agreed loading periods because these were days the charterers could not use (or could not use as cheaply) to load or discharge. But a ship which has completed loading or discharge and left port has always been able to make good use of these excepted periods. Consequently, 'one would naturally expect that this despatch money would be proportionate to the advantage derived by the shipowners from the extra speed in loading ...' (Fletcher Moulton LJ, dissenting, in *Nelson & Sons*, above, at p 719).

There is an additional point. Despatch is often dealt with, both in charterparties and in the preceding negotiations, in close relationship with demurrage. And the general rule of construction is that laytime exceptions do not apply while the vessel is on demurrage, in the absence of a clear agreement to the contrary. Since the laytime exceptions do not normally apply when the shipowner is receiving demurrage to compensate for time which is lost, might it not be expected that the exceptions would not normally apply when the shipowner is paying despatch for the advantage of time which he gains?

The conclusion which Bailhache J reached in *Mawson* in his careful reserved judgment was that, on the authorities,

(1) *Prima facie* under this type of despatch clause, shipowners must pay for all time saved to the ship, calculated in the way in which, in the converse

case, demurrage would be calculated; that is, taking no account of lay day exceptions: *Laing v Hollway* and *In re Royal Mail Steam Packet*, above.

(2) The *prima facie* presumption is displaced where either (a) lay days and time saved by despatch are dealt with in the same clause and demurrage in another clause: *The Glendevon*, above; or (b) lay days, time saved by despatch and demurrage are dealt with in the same clause, on construction of which the court is satisfied that 'days saved' are used in the same sense as 'lay days' and not in the same sense as days lost by demurrage: *Nelson & Sons v Nelson Line*, cited above.

In the *Mawson* charterparty, lay time, demurrage and despatch were dealt with in three separate clauses; the case fell within the first of Bailhache J's classes and the charterers succeeded.

The second stage of the *Mawson* approach is probably too mechanical to be generally accepted today. But some recent support for the basic *Mawson* presumption can be found in *Bulk Transport v Sissy Steamship, the Archipelagos* [1979] 2 Lloyd's Rep 289, Com Ct. That case involved a motion to set aside or remit an arbitration award arising out of a dispute as to the calculation of despatch money. Parker J held that the arbitrators ought to have begun with the *prima facie* presumption laid down in *Mawson* and then gone on to consider whether the wording of the clauses rebutted the presumption. The despatch agreement in this case was in the demurrage clause; but the agreement provided for despatch 'on *all laytime* saved'. Looking at the rest of the charterparty, Parker J held that by 'laytime', the parties were referring to 'laytime used for or required to be used for, in the sense of availability for, loading'. Only time that could be counted as laytime could therefore be saved under that despatch agreement.

In *The Themistocles* (1949) 82 Ll LR 232 Morris J took a quite different approach. There too despatch was dealt with in the same clause as demurrage and laytime was dealt with in another clause. The agreement provided for despatch 'on all time saved at port of loading'. **Morris J** said:

> Inasmuch as my task is to construe the particular words of the contract now before me, it does not seem to me that cases which decide the meaning of other words in other contexts can be of governing authority. Indeed, I doubt how far any question of principle is involved in what I have to decide or was involved in the various reported cases ... Unless terms of art are used, or unless the court is bound by some decision relating to a contract in virtually identical form, then, while deriving such assistance as the decisions afford, the task of the court, as it seems to me, is merely one of the construction of particular words as used in their context in a particular contract.

On the point in question, Morris J concluded that despatch was payable not just on loading time saved, but on total saving on the time that the vessel might have stayed in port.

CHAPTER 15

TIME CHARTERS I

1 TERMINOLOGY

Sea & Land Securities Ltd v William Dickinson & Co Ltd [1942] 2 KB 65, CA

MacKinnon LJ: The rights and obligations of the parties to a time charterparty must depend on its written terms, for there is no special law applicable to this form of contract as such. A time charterparty is, in fact, a misleading document, because the real nature of what is undertaken by the shipowner is disguised by the use of language dating from a century or more ago, which was appropriate to a contract of a different character then in use. At that time a time charterparty (now known as a demise charterparty) was an agreement under which possession of the ship was handed by the shipowner to the charterer for the latter to put his servants and crew in her and sail her for his own benefit ... The modern form of time charterparty is, in essence, one by which the shipowner agrees with the time charterer that during a certain named period he will render services by his servants and crew to carry the goods which are put on board his ship by the time charterer. But certain phrases which survive in the printed form now used are only pertinent to the older form of demise charterparty. Such phrases, in the charterparty now before the court, are: 'the owners agree to let', and 'the charterers agree to hire' the steamer. There was no 'letting' or 'hiring' of this steamer. Then it is in terms provided that at the end of the period the vessel shall be 'redelivered' by the time charterers to the shipowners. 'Redelivery' is only a pertinent expression if there has been any delivery or handing over of the ship by the shipowner to the charterer. There never had been any such delivery here. The ship at all times was in the possession of the shipowners and they simply undertook to do services with their crew in carrying the goods of the charterers. As I ventured to suggest quite early in the argument, between the old and the modern form of contract there is all the difference between the contract which a man makes when he hires a boat in which to row himself about and the contract he makes with a boatman that he shall take him for a row ...

2 EMPLOYMENT: THE CHARTERER'S RIGHT TO GIVE ORDERS

Kuwait Petroleum Corp v I & D Oil Carriers Ltd, The Houda [1994] 2 Lloyd's Rep 541, CA

Shipowners let their vessel *Houda* on the Shelltime 4 form. On 2 August 1990 when Iraq invaded Kuwait, *Houda* was loading a cargo of crude oil at Mina Al Ahmadi. She sailed with a part cargo, leaving behind blank bills of lading which had been signed by the master. After the invasion the management of the charterers was moved to London and it was from the London offices that the charterers gave sailing and survey orders to the vessel. The vessel remained at anchor off Fujairah until 27 September. The charterers alleged that the shipowners had refused to comply with orders which were lawfully given.

> **Neill LJ:** ... It was argued on behalf of the charterers ... that subject to three exceptions, the owners and the master were obliged to obey the charterers' orders immediately, or at any rate as soon as practicable. Counsel for the charterers identified these exceptions as follows: (1) where obedience to an order might involve a significant risk of endangering the vessel or its cargo or crew; (2) where it was necessary to seek clarification of an ambiguous order; and (3) where the owners had knowledge of circumstances which were not known to the charterers but which might, if known, affect their orders, and the owners needed confirmation that the orders were to stand. It was submitted that there was no room for the implication of a general term whereby the owners were allowed a reasonable time in which to seek confirmation of the authority of those giving the orders or of the lawfulness of the orders. Furthermore, it was submitted that on the facts of this case the owners' conduct amounted not to delayed compliance but to a refusal to comply with the charterers' orders.
>
> It is clear therefore that it is common ground between the parties that a master is entitled to delay in executing an order if to comply would threaten to expose the ship and cargo to a potential peril or if the circumstances otherwise fall within one of these three exceptions. We were referred to four authorities in support of that proposition. I propose to consider these authorities to see whether one can detect any wider principle on which a right to pause before complying with an order can be founded.
>
> In *Pole v Cetcovitch* (1860) 9 CBNS 430 the master of an Austrian vessel declined to comply immediately with an order to sail from Falmouth to Copenhagen. He relied on the fact that war had broken out between France and Austria and therefore the voyage might expose his vessel to capture by a French cruiser. The Court of Common Pleas upheld a direction to the jury that if they considered that in the circumstances the master was justified in pausing before complying with the order they should find that he was not in breach.
>
> The next case to which we were referred was the decision of the Privy Council in *The Teutonia* (1872) LR 4 PC 171. In giving judgment Mellish LJ said at p 179:
>
>> It seems obvious that, if a Master receives credible information that, if he continues in the direct course of his voyage, his ship will be exposed to some imminent peril, as, for instance, that there are pirates in his course, or icebergs or other dangers of navigation, he must be justified in pausing and deviating from the direct course, and taking any step which a prudent man would take for the purpose of avoiding the danger.
>
> The reference to 'credible information' is of importance because the information which the master had received was premature in the sense that war between France and Prussia was not formally declared until three days

later. Counsel for the charterers treated this case as one where the master had some additional information and where there was a risk of danger to the ship or cargo.

A year later the Privy Council gave judgment in a similar case: *The San Roman* (1873) LR 5 PC 301. In the course of a voyage to Europe *San Roman* put in to Valparaiso for repairs. The repairs were completed on or about 23 September 1870 but the vessel delayed sailing until 23 December because war had broken out between France and Prussia and it was believed that if the vessel sailed there was a risk of capture by the French Navy. In the course of the judgment Sir Montague Smith said at p 306:

> ... the question their Lordships have to determine is entirely a question of fact, namely, whether the German master had during that time such an apprehension of capture founded on circumstances calculated to affect his mind – he being a man of ordinary courage, judgment, and experience – as would justify delay; and their Lordships agree with the judge in the court below that there was a sufficient risk of capture to justify this delay.

> This is not a case where the master has refused to perform the contract at all. No doubt, if the voyage had been abandoned, then it would have been necessary to show that he had been actually prevented from performing it; but this is merely a question of whether there was a reasonable cause for delay.

It was held that the fact that the cargo was an English cargo made no difference. Sir Montague Smith continued at p 307:

> If their Lordships were to look upon this case as a case in which the cargo was German as well as the ship, or a case in which both ship and cargo belonged to the same person, and then were to ask the question: Would a man of reasonable prudence, under such circumstances, have set sail or waited? It appears to their Lordships most clearly that a man of reasonable prudence would have waited.

The fourth case in this quartet was the decision of Donaldson J in *Midwest Shipping Co v DI Henry (Jute) Ltd* [1971] 1 Lloyd's Rep 375. In that case the master under a time charter received orders from the charterers to put back to port. The master did not comply at once because, on the charterers' instructions, he had lied to the port authorities about his destination and he was also concerned as to whether there would be sufficient water to cross the bar at the port. The judge held that the master's actions were justified, but at one point in his judgment he expressed the duty of the master in a way which might suggest that the right to pause may arise in a number of different circumstances including those where there is no threat to expose the ship and cargo to potential peril. Thus at p 379 Donaldson J put the matter in this way:

> ... It is important to remember that the master of a merchant ship occupies a civilian post. He is not the captain of a naval vessel who might well be expected to comply instantly with an order and seek verification or reconsideration afterwards. Furthermore, he is not receiving the instruction from somebody who is his professional superior, as would be the case in the services. He is the representative of his owners and also to some extent of the charterers. He occupies a post of very great

responsibility, and he occupies that post by virtue of long training and experience. If he was the type of man who would immediately act upon any order from charterers without further consideration, he would probably be unfitted for that post. It seems to me that against that background it must be the duty of the master to act reasonably upon receipt of orders. Some orders are of their nature such that they would, if the master were to act reasonably, require immediate compliance. Others would require a great deal of thought and consideration before a reasonable master would comply with them.

... In the course of the argument in this court counsel for the charterers introduced what might be regarded as a fourth category of exception. Thus he accepted that the owners and a master might pause and seek further information if they knew or had reasonable cause to suspect that the instructions had not been given by the charterers. It was not enough, however, it was said, to justify delay if the owners and the master had merely a vague apprehension.

I am unable to accept that the right, or indeed the duty, to pause can safely be confined to specific categories of cases. I consider that it is necessary to take a broad and comprehensive view of the duties and responsibilities of the owners and the master and to ask, as was suggested in *The San Roman*, above: How would a man of reasonable prudence have acted in the circumstances? Thus, for example, the delivery of a cargo pursuant to an order given by the agent of an invading army may pose just as much a threat to cargo and those who have legitimate rights to it as an iceberg or a foreign frigate. It will depend on the circumstances.

... It is not of course for this court to decide whether on the facts the owners had reasonable grounds to pause, but I am satisfied that in a war situation there may well be circumstances where the right, and indeed the duty, to pause in order to seek further information about the source of and the validity of any orders which may be received is capable of arising even if there may be no immediate physical threat to the cargo or the ship.

... it seems to me that it is at least possible that where a country has been invaded prudent owners may be entitled to guard against the risk that their orders may have come from the 'wrong' side ...

Leggatt LJ: It is obvious that lawful orders have to be obeyed, unless to do so would imperil the safety of ship, crew or cargo. It is not obvious that they have to be obeyed unthinkingly. 'Theirs not to reason why' is a creed that neither characterises nor befits masters of chartered vessels. In my judgment when a master receives an order relating to the cargo his duty, which is probably owed to the owners of the cargo as well as the owners of the vessel, is to act reasonably. Orders ordinarily require immediate compliance. But the circumstances in which an order is received or the nature of it may make it unreasonable for the master to comply without further consideration or enquiry. When an order is reasonably regarded as ambiguous, it must be clarified. When the lawfulness of an order is reasonably called in question, it must be established. When the authenticity of an order is reasonably doubted, it must be verified. The delay introduced by any of these processes will usually be brief ...

Millett LJ: ... In my judgment the authorities establish two propositions of general application: (1) the master's obligation on receipt of an order is not one of instant obedience but of reasonable conduct; and (2) not every delay constitutes a refusal to obey an order; only an unreasonable delay does so ...

3 SHIPOWNER'S RIGHT TO AN INDEMNITY

Larrinaga Steamship Co Ltd v The King [1945] AC 246

In 1939 at the start of the war the *Ramon de Larrinaga* was requisitioned by the Crown on the terms of the government form time charter T 99A (incorporating T 773) which provided in clause 9 that:

> The master ... although appointed by the owners ... shall be under the orders and direction of the charterer as regards employment, agency, or other arrangements: and the charterer hereby agrees to indemnify the owners for all consequences or liabilities that may arise from the master or officers ... complying with such orders ...

She was ordered to St Nazaire and notified that after discharge there she would return to South Wales for survey, as she was being released from government service. At St Nazaire written orders were given to her by the Naval Sea Transport Officer that she was to proceed that night to Quiberon Bay and join a convoy to be escorted to the Bristol Channel. The order was repeated orally the same day despite the ship's protest against sailing at night in dangerous navigation conditions and at a time when the weather was worsening. The ship sailed as ordered. Approximately five hours after sailing, during a gale, she anchored on the advice of the pilot. The anchor cable broke and the ship drifted onto a sand bank and was damaged.

The appellants, in a petition of right, claimed that the cost of repair should be borne by the Crown on the grounds, amongst others, that the repair costs were the result of complying with the charterers' orders.

Viscount Simon LC, and Lords Thankerton, Goddard and Wright agreed with Lord Porter.

> **Lord Porter:** My Lords, this appeal calls for a ... consideration of a well known clause in time charterparties by the terms of which the master is placed under the orders and direction of the charterers, as regards employment, agency or other arrangements, and the charterers give the owners an indemnity against the consequences of complying with those orders ...
>
> The argument ... was that the order to leave St Nazaire and to proceed to Cardiff was an order as regards employment, and that though generally a marine loss following on such an order would not be its consequence, yet where, as here, the order was to proceed in the face of the danger of a storm

and against the protests of the master, the damage which the ship suffered was a consequence of the order. Had he not been compelled to leave port the master would not have sailed, and it was, it is said, the natural and a contemplated result of obeying that order that the ship might suffer marine damage; the respondent was therefore under a duty to indemnify the appellants for their loss.

... My Lords, I cannot but think that the word employment in cl 9 does include at any rate certain employments of the ship ... In its natural sense it includes orders to proceed from one port to another or to undertake a voyage or series of voyages, and therefore the original notification of 7 October and the written order of 13 October in so far as it reiterated and confirmed that order, were authorised and covered by the clause. But this order did not in a legal sense, and I doubt if such an order ever could, cause such a loss. Even the order of 13 October specified no exact moment of departure, except that the ship was to sail after the discharge was complete. This wording left it to the master's discretion to sail at a reasonable time thereafter, and in determining what is a reasonable time all such matters as the state of the weather and the exhaustion of the crew would properly be taken into consideration. In these circumstances it cannot be said that either of these orders caused the damage which the ship suffered. A loss is not, under English law, caused by orders to make or by making a voyage because it occurs in the course of it. Such a loss is merely the fortuitous result of the ship being at a particular place at a particular time, and in no legal sense caused by the charterers' choice of port to which the ship is directed or their instructions to her master to proceed to it. But it was said that the ship sailed not by reason of the written order to proceed, but by the subsequent oral order, and that such an order did cause the loss, since it was the probable and contemplated result of sailing in unfavourable weather that the ship might suffer damage which, had the master been free to choose his own time, would probably have been avoided.

Three answers to this argument have been made by the respondent.

(1) That though an order specifying the voyage to be performed is an order as to employment, yet an order as to the time of sailing is not. That order, it is contended, is one as to navigation, or, at any rate, not as to employment. My Lords, this distinction seems to me to be justified: an order to sail from port A to port B is in common parlance an order as to employment, but an order that a ship shall sail at a particular time is not an order as to employment because its object is not to direct how the ship shall be employed, but how she shall act in the course of that employment. If the word were held to include every order which affected not the employment itself but any incident arising in the course of it almost every other liability undertaken by the charterer would be otiose, since the owners would be indemnified against almost all losses which the ship would incur in prosecuting her voyages. In particular war and marine risk insurance would be unnecessary, because the charterers would be liable for the losses which were so covered, since the ship would be proceeding on their orders and entitled to an indemnity for all losses caused by following them ... It would be a further strange consequence of the wide interpretation

contended for, that the first half of cl 9 should impose a liability for (say) stevedores' acts in cases where the charterers directed the owner what stevedoring firm to employ, whereas the second half should exempt them from liability provided they employed the stevedores direct.

The contention that the word bears a limited meaning derives some support from the observations of Lord Davey in *Weir v Union Steamship Co Ltd* [1900] AC 525, 532, a case in which it was suggested that the charterers were under an obligation to provide any ballast necessitated by their order to the chartered vessel to proceed unladen to the loading port. As part of their argument the owners relied upon a clause in the charterparty similar to clause 9, T 99A. Lord Davey rejected this on the ground that the wording, it is true, put the captain under the orders and directions of the charterers as regards employment, agency and other arrangements, but it did not do so as regards navigation. In that case, providing ballast was incidental to the employment, not part of it, as in this sailing at a particular time was only indirectly connected with the employment. It was suggested on behalf of the respondent that a loss or claim due to deviation or change of voyage upon the instructions of the charterers after bills of lading have been signed was the class of order which the clause contemplated and that in any case the charterer cannot be called upon to indemnify the owner in respect of losses for which provision is otherwise made in the charterparty. My Lords, in the present case, I do not think it necessary to determine the exact limitation to be placed on the meaning of the word. It is, I think, enough to say that an order to sail at once, whether wisely or unwisely given, is not within the clause as properly construed.

(2) The second answer of the respondents was that even if it were conceded that orders to sail in a storm were orders in respect of which an indemnity is due, they must still be orders of the charterers as charterers and such as under this charterparty they are entitled to give. The mere instruction to sail may be such an order, but such an instruction leaves it to the discretion of the master who is responsible for the safety of his ship to choose the time and opportunity for starting on his voyage. I know of no right on the part of a charterer to insist that the safety of the ship should be endangered by sailing at a time when seamanship requires her to stay in port. The naval authorities however have this power and, whatever the risk, their orders must be obeyed. The first officer, indeed, recognised the order as that of the naval authorities, when he said in answer to the question 'Why did you leave?', 'Naval orders'. In my view the respondent is right in his contention that the order to put to sea on the night of 13 October was not a charterer's but a naval order, none the less though the Crown is both charterer and the source from which naval authority is derived. The written order to sail, which did not specify any time for compliance except the finish of discharge, left it to the master to choose his time and opportunity but did not cause the loss: the oral order which followed it was not a charterer's but a naval order and therefore not one for which the charterers are responsible.

(3) Finally it was urged that neither the order nor sailing in obedience to it caused the loss. In *Portsmouth Steamship Co Ltd v Liverpool and Glasgow Salvage Association* (1929) 34 Ll L Rep 459, 462, Lord Roche (then Roche J) points out that the clause, where it applies, covers only losses arising directly from charterer's instructions, because, as he says:

> if some act of negligence intervenes or some marine casualty intervenes then the chain of causation is broken and the indemnity does not operate.

I do not think your Lordships are called on to determine the soundness of this argument in the present case. It might be urged that a loss following upon an order to sail into danger which is complied with and results in damage due to the contemplated risk is a consequence of that order, but to decide it in this case is unnecessary and I prefer to express no opinion upon it either in favour or against. For the reasons given above, however, I would dismiss the appeal ...

AB Helsingfors Steamship v Rederiaktiebolaget Rex, The White Rose [1969] 1 WLR 1098

The vessel was trip chartered on the Baltime form and ordered to load grain at Duluth, Minnesota. Clause 9 of the charter provided that '... The master shall be under the orders of the charterers as regards employment, agency or other arrangements. The charterers to indemnify the owners against all consequences or liabilities arising from the master ... complying with such orders ...' The charterers, who were obliged to pay for loading, trimming and stowing of cargo, employed independent contractors to carry out those tasks. During loading, one of the agent's employees fell through an unfenced 'tween deck hatch and was injured. The shipowners settled a claim by the injured man for $3,000 and claimed to recover that sum from the charterers.

> **Donaldson J**: ... Counsel for the shipowners ... submits that the authorities establish that if the shipowner, having complied with an instruction from the charterer, thereby incurs a liability to a third party from which he would be protected had the charterer alone been concerned, he is entitled to an indemnity. He says that the basis of the bargain between the parties was summarised by Devlin J in *Royal Greek Government v Minister of Transport* (1950) 83 Ll L R 228, when he said at p 234:
>
> > If [the shipowner] is to surrender his freedom of choice and put his master under the orders of the charterer, there is nothing unreasonable in his stipulating for a complete indemnity in return.
>
> As applied to a claim by a stevedore for personal injuries, the shipowner, submits counsel, makes good his claim to an indemnity by the following stages: (i) the shipowner established an order to go to a particular port to load a particular cargo; (ii) the terms of the charterparty expressly place the duty of arranging and paying for loading on the charterer, who, in fulfilment of that obligation, engages independent stevedores whom the shipowner is impliedly obliged to accept; (iii) under the terms of the relevant law, that is the local law, a potential liability on the part of the shipowner towards the stevedore is

thereby established; (iv) the charterer fails to clothe the shipowners with the protection against the stevedore's claims which, under cl 13, he would have against similar claims by the charterers. That clause, after dealing with delay in delivery of the vessel, delay during the currency of the charter and loss or damage to goods on board, provides that 'The owners not to be responsible in any other case nor for damage or delay whatsoever and howsoever caused even if caused by the neglect or default of their servants'; (v) as the shipowner has, as a result of complying with the charterers' orders, been placed in a less attractive position than he would have been if the charterers had personally loaded the vessel, he is entitled to an indemnity.

Counsel for the shipowners further submits that this is consistent with the cases in which shipowners have been indemnified against their liability to holders of bills of lading, whose terms were less favourable to the shipowners than were the terms of the time charterparty. (See, for example, *Milburn & Co v Jamaica Fruit Importing & Trading Co of London* [1900] 2 QB 540, where the loss arose from an inability to claim general average contribution from cargo; *Kruger & Co Ltd v Moel Tryvan Ship Co Ltd* [1907] AC 272, where the shipowners became liable for loss of cargo; *Elder Dempster & Co v Dunn & Co* (1909) 15 Com Cas 49, where the cargo was wrongly marked and by the terms of the bills of lading and/or the provisions of the law of the place of discharge the shipowners could not require the receivers to take delivery of the mismarked goods and were liable as if they had lost them; *The Brabant* [1967] 1 QB 588 and *Bosma v Larsen* [1966] 1 Lloyd's Rep 22, further damage to cargo cases.)

He also submits that it is consistent with the decisions in *Lensen Shipping Co Ltd v Anglo-Soviet Shipping Co Ltd* (1935) 40 Com Cas 320, in which a vessel sustained damage as a result of being ordered to load at an unsafe berth; in *Strathlorne Steamship Co Ltd v Andrew Weir & Co* (1934) 40 Com Cas 168, in which the shipowners incurred a liability to the bill of lading holders as a result of their having delivered the cargo on the instructions of the time charterers to persons who could not produce the bills of lading and were not in fact entitled to receive the goods, and in *Portsmouth Steamship Co Ltd v Liverpool & Glasgow Salvage Association* (1929) 34 Ll L R 459, in which the shipowners recovered an indemnity in respect of damage to the vessel caused by the cargo which they loaded on the time charterers' instructions.

Counsel for the charterers accepts much of the submission of counsel for the shipowners, but he says that one vital element has been omitted, namely, that the right to indemnity only arises if and insofar as the loss suffered by the shipowners can be proved to have been caused by the shipowners' compliance with the charterers' instructions. He says that in the bill of lading cases causation is relevant, but it is rarely, if ever, a live issue, because commonly the shipowner is for practical purposes under no liability whatsoever in respect of cargo under the terms of the charterparty and if he is liable under the bills of lading which he has signed under instructions from the charterers, his liability must be caused by his compliance with those instructions. When, however, one looks at the unsafe port cases or cases of damage to the ship resulting from the nature or condition of the cargo (*Portsmouth Steamship Co Ltd v Liverpool & Glasgow Salvage Association*, above, and *Royal Greek Government v Minister of*

Transport, above, the element of causation is all important as it is in the present case).

In my judgment the submission of counsel for the charterers is correct, and it is necessary in every case to establish an unbroken chain of causation, although I would not accept as a generalisation that:

> if some act of negligence intervenes or some marine casualty intervenes, then the chain of causation is broken and the indemnity does not operate

per Roche J, in *Portsmouth Steamship Co Ltd v Liverpool & Glasgow Salvage Association*, 34 Ll LR 459, 462. A loss may well arise in the course of compliance with the charterers' orders, but this fact does not, without more, establish that it was caused by and is in law a consequence of such compliance and, in the absence of proof of such causation there is no right to indemnity.

The shipowners in the present case have undoubtedly established that their 'potential liability' to Mr de Chambeau [the injured employee] and their actual loss of £2,935.5s.5d. were incidents of and occurred in the course of complying with the charterers' orders to load grain at Duluth; but were they caused by such compliance? The judge of fact, the learned umpire, has found that the accident itself was caused partly by the absence of fencing, but it is clear from his conclusion that the charterers themselves were at no time guilty of any improper or negligent act and that they were not responsible for the lack of fencing. He has found that the shipowners were in breach of Finnish law, but I do not think that that is material. What connected the accident with, and gave rise to, a potential liability and an actual loss was the provisions of Minnesota law. Unless it can be said that this law was so unusual as to constitute Duluth a legally unsafe port to which the vessel should not have been ordered – and no such contention was advanced – or that the charterers engaged stevedores who were incompetent by local standards, which is negatived by the findings of fact, I do not consider that it can be said that there is the necessary causal connection between the order to load and the loss. This view is strengthened by, although not dependent on, the finding that at the time of the accident Mr de Chambeau had 'Left his position at No 2 'tween deck hatch, and for his own private purposes unconnected with his employment made his way aft into No 3 'tween deck'. It is also strengthened, and it may be that I am really precluded from reaching any other conclusion, although I have assumed that this is not the case, by the learned umpire's conclusion that 'the accident was not caused by the [shipowners'] complying with orders of the [charterers]', it not being suggested that in reaching this conclusion he misdirected himself in fact or in law. Accordingly in my judgment the claim under cl 9 fails ...

Notes

1   The *Sagona* was time chartered for a period of 38 months during which she was ordered to carry a cargo of gasoil from Sicily to a port on the river Weser. On arrival the vessel was instructed by the charterers to deliver the cargo to receivers without requiring the production of the bill of lading. The cargo was delivered. The vessel was arrested and detained at the suit of the unpaid shippers. The shippers were later reimbursed by one of the string purchasers of the gasoil, but the shipowner sought to recover from

the charterers their loss of earnings while the vessel was under arrest and the expenses of defending the proceedings. It was held that (a) the charterers' order was not one which the shipowners were obliged to obey; (b) nevertheless, the order was not manifestly illegal or such as ought to have caused the master to refuse to act or likely to excite suspicion in the special circumstances of the oil trade; (c) the master had followed the normal practice and his conduct did not sever the causal connection between the order and the loss. *A/S Hansen-Tangen Rederi III v Total Transport Group, The Sagona* [1984] 1 Lloyd's Rep 194.

2   The *Island Archon* was chartered for 36 months on the NYPE form. She was ordered to Basrah where unjustified cargo claims were asserted by the receivers of the cargo under bills of lading. The owners had to provide security before the vessel was allowed to depart. There was no express agreement for an indemnity in the charterparty. An implied agreement to indemnify was alleged. The charterers argued that no promise to indemnify could be implied since the order to carry to Basrah was one which they had a contractual right to give. The Court of Appeal held that, since the charterers had asked the shipowners to sign the bills of lading, a right to an indemnity would be implied in the charter.

> ... the implication is justified ... first by 'business efficacy' in the sense that if the charterer requires to have the vessel at his disposal, and to be free to choose voyages and cargoes and bill of lading terms also, then the owner must be expected to grant such freedom only if he is entitled to be indemnified against loss and liability resulting from it, subject always to the express terms of the charterparty contract; and secondly by the legal principle underlying the 'lawful request' cases such as *Sheffield Corp v Barclay*; in other words, an implication of law. *Triad Shipping Co v Stellar Chartering & Brokerage Inc, The Island Archon*, Evans LJ, [1994] 2 Lloyd's Rep 227).

The rule applied in *Sheffield Corp v Barclay* [1905] AC 392 was that: 'when an act is done by one person at the request of another which act is not in itself manifestly tortious to the knowledge of the person doing it, and such act turns out to be injurious to the rights of a third party, the person doing it is entitled to an indemnity from him who requested that it should be done'.

4 SAFE PORTS

Kodros Shipping Corp of Monrovia v Empresa Cubana de Fletes, The Evia (No 2) [1983] 1 A C 736.

> **Lord Diplock**: My Lords, I agree with the speech to be delivered by my noble and learned friend, Lord Roskill, and with the detailed reasons that he will give for dismissing this appeal.

For my part, I would regard the nature of the contractual promise by the charterer that a chartered vessel shall be employed between safe ports ('the safe port clause') as having been well settled for a quarter of a century at the very least. It was correctly and concisely stated by Sellers LJ in *Leeds Shipping Co Ltd v Société Française Bunge, The Eastern City* [1958] 2 Lloyd's Rep 127 in a classic passage which, in its reference to 'abnormal occurrence', reflects a previous statement in the judgment of Morris LJ in *Compania Naviera Maropan SA v Bowaters Lloyd Pulp and Paper Mills Ltd, The Stork* [1955] 2 QB 68. Sellers LJ said, at p 131:

> a port will not be safe unless, in the relevant period of time, the particular ship can reach it, use it and return from it without, in the absence of some abnormal occurrence, being exposed to danger which cannot be avoided by good navigation and seamanship ...

It is with the prospective safety of the port at the time when the vessel will be there for the loading or unloading operation that the contractual promise is concerned and the contractual promise itself is given at the time when the charterer gives the order to the master or other agent of the shipowner to proceed to the loading or unloading port.

What are the respective rights and duties of charterer and shipowner under a voyage charter if the port becomes prospectively unsafe by reason of some abnormal occurrence actually occurring (whether or not to the knowledge of either of them) during the period of the loading or unloading voyage is not a matter that arises in the instant appeal and I think it would be unwise for your Lordships to express any view about it. In the case of the time charter, however, under which the charterer has power to substitute for his original order to the master to proceed to a particular port and there undertake the loading or unloading operation a fresh order to proceed elsewhere, so long as such fresh order is given at a time when it is possible for the vessel to comply with it, the contractual promise is a continuing one and if an occurrence which at the time of the original order could properly be regarded as abnormal has actually occurred and has rendered the port prospectively unsafe, the charterer could not rely upon the exception of 'abnormal occurrence' in Sellers LJ's statement of the effect of the safe port clause ...

Lord Roskill: My Lords, in preparing this speech I have had the great advantage of the help of my noble and learned friend, Lord Brandon of Oakbrook, and the speech now represents the opinions both of my noble and learned friend and of myself.

My Lords, as a result of the outbreak of hostilities between Iran and Iraq in September 1980, a large number of ships were trapped in the Shatt-al-Arab waterway. The appellants had the misfortune to be the owners of such a ship, the *Evia*, registered in Liberia. The respondents were the time charterers of the *Evia* ...

... In March 1980 the respondents ordered the *Evia* to load a cargo of cement and other building materials for carriage from Cuba to Basrah which is on the west bank of the Shatt-al-Arab waterway ... She finally berthed on 20 August 1980, and, subject to some interruption, completed discharge at 10.00 on 22 September 1980. In the ordinary course of events, she would then have sailed to continue her chartered service. Unhappily she could not do so. By that date, large-scale hostilities had broken out between Iran and Iraq, and the area around the Shatt-al-Arab waterway was in what the umpire called in paragraph 3 of his award 'the thick of those hostilities'. From 22 September 1980, onwards, no ship of the many then in that area was able to escape. All were trapped. Gradually their crews in whole or in part left them. Only the master and a skeleton crew of about a dozen remained on board the *Evia* after 1 October 1980, when the majority of that crew was repatriated ... Your Lordships were told that some 16 months later she and the other ships were still there.

My Lords ... Mr Eckersley [the arbitrator] concluded:

> Basrah was a safe port for the vessel both when she was ordered to proceed there and when she got there. It did not become unsafe until 22 September and by then it was impossible for the vessel to leave.

... Mr Eckersley held, so far as is presently relevant, first that there was no breach of the charterparty by the respondents, secondly, that the charterparty was frustrated, and thirdly, that frustration took place on 4 October 1980. He made a declaration accordingly ...

... [T]he question whether the respondents were in breach of their obligations under the charterparty so as to debar themselves from relying upon frustration on 4 October 1980, depends upon its true construction. Two principal questions of construction arise. First, independently of the provisions of clause 21 [war clause] of the charterparty, were the respondents in breach of the charterparty in ordering the *Evia* to Basrah which, though safe when the order was given, became unsafe on 22 September when the ship was still on her chartered service. It was, as I have already stated, on that date that Basrah and the surrounding area became involved in hostilities of which I have spoken so that she was henceforth trapped. Secondly, if apart from clause 21 of the charterparty the respondents would have been in breach in so ordering the ship to Basrah, is the effect of clause 21 to free the respondents from that liability? A third and subsidiary question, which was briefly argued before your Lordships, was whether clause 21 excludes in any event the application of the doctrine of frustration. As already stated, it is the first of these questions which is of the wide general importance since most charterparties, into whatever class they fall, impose obligations on charterers regarding the safety of the chartered ship during her service under charter. The second question is, of course, of particular importance under this form of time charterparty.

My Lords, I propose to consider first the question which arises on clause 2. It will be convenient to quote again those few words in that clause which are relevant – 'The vessel to be employed ... between good and safe ports ...' Learned counsel were unable to offer any suggestion what in this context the word 'good' added to the word 'safe'. Your Lordships are, I think, all of the like mind. So I will consider only the eight words 'The vessel to be employed ... between ... safe ports ...' The argument for the appellants is simple. The relevant restriction during her employment is to safe ports. Her employment took her to Basrah. Basrah, though safe when nominated, on 22 September 1980, became, and thereafter remained, unsafe. The *Evia* was trapped. Those eight words applied. The respondents were therefore in breach.

... [T]he first question is whether, apart from authority, these words are to be construed in the manner suggested. In order to consider the scope of the contractual promise which these eight words impose upon a charterer, it must be determined how a charterer would exercise his undoubted right to require the shipowner to perform his contractual obligations to render services with his ship, his master, officers and crew, the consideration for the performance of their obligation being the charterer's regular payment of time charter hire. The answer must be that a charterer will exercise that undoubted contractual right by giving the shipowner orders to go to a particular port or place of loading or discharge. It is clearly at that point of time when that order is given that that contractual promise to the charterer regarding the safety of that intended port or place must be fulfilled. But that contractual promise cannot mean that that port or place must be safe when that order is given, for were that so, a charterer could not legitimately give orders to go to an ice-bound port which he and the owner both knew in all human probability would be ice-free by the time that vessel reached it. Nor, were that the nature of the promise, could a charterer order the ship to a port or place the approaches to which were at the time of the order blocked as a result of a collision or by some submerged wreck or other obstacles even though such obstacles would in all human probability be out of the way before the ship required to enter. The charterer's contractual promise must, I think, relate to the characteristics of the port or place in question and in my view means that when the order is given that port or place is prospectively safe for the ship to get to, stay at, so far as necessary, and in due course, leave. But if those characteristics are such as to make that port or place prospectively safe in this way, I cannot think that if, in spite of them, some unexpected and abnormal event thereafter suddenly occurs which creates conditions of unsafety where conditions of safety had previously existed and as a result the ship is delayed, damaged or destroyed, that contractual promise extends to making the charterer liable for any resulting loss or damage, physical or financial. So to hold would make the charterer the insurer of such unexpected and abnormal risks which in my view should properly fall upon the ship's insurers under the policies of insurance the effecting of which is the owner's responsibility under clause 3 unless, of course, the owner chooses to be his own insurer in these respects.

My Lords, it will be seen that in this analysis I have stressed the point of time at which the order is given as the moment when the relevant obligation of the charterer arises, for it is then that the relevant employment of the ship will begin. I venture to think this is plain as a matter of construction. But when one looks at the authorities one sees that they strongly support the view which I have just expressed. As long ago as 1861, *Ogden v Graham* 1 B & S 773, was decided. The charterparty there in question was a voyage charterparty. At that date when the steamship was only beginning to come into general use, the time charterparty was still a rarity. Under that voyage charterparty the ship was chartered to go from England to a safe port in Chile with leave to call at Valparaiso. When she was there, the charterers by their agent ordered her to Carrisal Bojo there to discharge her cargo. At the time of that order that port was closed by government order. The ship could not go there without risk of confiscation. That port was thus 'politically' unsafe to use the adverb often used to describe that type of unsafety. The ship was delayed until, ultimately when that port was opened, she went there and discharged. Her owners claimed damages for delay. The case came before a court comprising Wightman and Blackburn JJ. In agreeing with Wightman J, Blackburn J said, at pp 780–82:

> By the charterparty it is agreed that the vessel shall sail for a safe port in Chile, with leave to call at Valparaiso, and although it is not in terms so stated, it follows by necessary implication that the charterers are to name a safe port to the shipowner, who will then be able to earn his freight by proceeding thither ... Now, in the absence of all authority, I think that, on the construction of this charterparty, the charterers are bound to name a port which, at the time they name it, is in such a condition that the master can safely take his ship into it; but, if a certain port be in such a state that, although the ship can readily enough, so far as natural causes are concerned, sail into it, yet, by reason of political or other causes, she cannot enter it without being confiscated by the government of the place, that is not a safe port within the meaning of the charterparty ... [The charterers] were to name a port which was to be safe at the time they named it. They named a port which had been a safe port, and will probably thereafter become a safe port; but if, at the time they named it, it was a port into which the shipowner could not take his ship and earn his freight, it seems to me that they have not complied with the conditions in the charterparty that they should name a safe port. That being so, they are liable for damages for not naming a safe port within a reasonable time, and the measure of damages will be regulated by the detention of the ship at Valparaiso beyond that time.

It will be seen that the learned judge interpreted the relevant obligation with regard to a safe port in Chile as one which arose at the moment of nomination.

My Lords, I can move forward for nearly a century to the decision of Devlin J in *GW Grace & Co Ltd v General Steam Navigation Co Ltd, The Sussex Oak* [1950] 2 KB 383 ... Devlin J, at pp 396–67, held that it was the giving of the order to go to an unsafe port which constituted a breach of contract. On the facts found by the arbitrator, the charterers had known of the danger from ice which was involved in ordering the *Sussex Oak* to Hamburg, and had given the order to go there knowing of that danger.

But, my Lords, the basic law regarding the nature of the contractual promise to which those eight, or other similar, words gives rise, whether in time or voyage charterparties, remained in doubt until the further decision of Devlin J, affirmed by the Court of Appeal, in *Compania Naviera Maropan SA v Bowaters Lloyd Pulp and Paper Mills Ltd, The Stork* [1955] 2 QB 68. On the facts found by the learned judge in that case, the nominated loading place, Tommy's Arm in Newfoundland, was always inherently unsafe both at the time of nomination and, indeed, later, at least for a ship of the size of the *Stork*, for its permanent characteristics included insufficient room to manoeuvre her in bad weather, which was a regular hazard in that place, and that place was extremely exposed. The ship grounded and was seriously damaged, and her owners sued the charterers for breach of the relevant contractual promise as to safety. The main argument for the charterers, which failed in both courts, was that, even if the loading place were unsafe, as the learned judge ultimately found it to be, they were not liable because an order to go to an unsafe port or place was only a nullity. It was an order which need not be accepted. But once accepted, the shipowner must accept the consequences: see p 73. It was this argument which was emphatically rejected both by the learned judge and by the Court of Appeal, who held that the breach lay in nominating an unsafe port or place, and that when damage followed the obeying of that order, the ordinary rules of the recovery of damages for breach of contract followed. In so holding both the learned judge and the Court of Appeal accepted as correct the dissenting judgment of Sir Owen Dixon CJ in the High Court of Australia in *Reardon Smith Line Ltd v Australian Wheat Board, The Houston City* [1954] 2 Lloyd's Rep 148, a judgment later upheld by the Judicial Committee of the Privy Council [1956] AC 266. I need only refer to, without quoting, the passages in the judgment of the learned Chief Justice at pp 151 and 152, which made it absolutely plain that the relevant breach was the giving of the order to go to an unsafe port or berth. This passage culminated in the statement, at p. 153:

> The point which appears to me to be of capital importance in the decision of the present case is whether the giving of an order to proceed to a port that is unsafe amounts to a breach of obligation on the part of the charterer, and that point appears to me to be definitely covered by what has been determined by the general operation ascribed to such a clause.

That passage summarises the view which was subsequently accepted as correct in the Judicial Committee. But the berth at Geraldton in West Australia, to which the *Houston City* had been ordered by the charterers, was, like the loading place of the *Stork* in Tommy's Arm, inherently unsafe. In both cases the breach lay in giving the respective orders to go there. In neither case were the courts concerned to consider in any way what, if any, were the obligations of the charterer, whether under a time charterparty or a voyage charterparty, where at the time of nomination the port or place was prospectively safe but subsequently became unsafe. Indeed, in delivering the opinion of the Privy Council in *The Houston City*, Lord Somervell of Harrow, at p 284, expressly declined to express any view upon that question which did not there arise.

My Lords, it follows that the passage in the judgment of Morris LJ in *The Stork* [1955] 2 QB 68, 105 and the reference in that passage to 'some abnormal occurrence' – it was this passage which was the foundation of the passage in the judgment of Sellers LJ in *The Eastern City* [1958] 2 Lloyd's Rep 127, 131, to which I have already referred – was directed to a suggested definition of a safe port in the context of a loading port or place which was inherently unsafe at the time the order was given. It was not directed to the situation where a port or place inherently safe when the order was given subsequently, by reason of some unexpected and abnormal occurrence, became unsafe ...

My Lords, even if I had thought some 25 years and more later that those two passages in the judgments of Morris LJ in *The Stork* and of Sellers LJ in *The Eastern City* were in any way open to criticism when properly understood in the context of the issues then before the Court of Appeal in those two cases, which I emphatically do not, I should not after so long a time be bold enough to suggest to your Lordships that they should be overruled. The number of charterparties concluded since those cases were decided with words of the same or of a similar kind included amongst their provisions must be legion. Those who have since concluded such charterparties must be taken to have known the effect of those words as laid down in those cases and to have been content with that interpretation of them. One can often, without the exercise of undue diligence, detect in charterparties typed additions to printed forms designed to circumvent particular decisions on printed clauses the consequence of which the parties to that charterparty seek to avoid. But that has not been the case with the words of the charterparty presently in question.

My Lords, it follows that that passage of the judgment of Sellers LJ in *The Eastern City* is no authority for construing those eight or other similar words as giving rise to an absolute continuing promise of safety by charterers after the order or nomination in question has been given subject only to the qualification of some subsequent unexpected and abnormal occurrence ...

My Lords, on the view of the law which I take, since Basrah was prospectively safe at the time of nomination, and since the unsafety arose after the *Evia*'s arrival and was due to an unexpected and abnormal event, there was at the former time no breach of clause 2 by the respondents, and that is the first ground upon which I would dismiss this appeal.

But, my Lords, since the Court of Appeal gave leave to appeal in order that this branch of the law should be fully explored, I think your Lordships may wish further to consider whether ... there is a residual obligation upon a charterer, whether for time or voyage, given that he has fully complied with his obligation at the time of nomination. My Lords, unless there is something unusual in the relevant express language used in a particular charterparty, the charterer's obligation at the time of nomination which I have been discussing must, I think, apply equally to a voyage charterer as to a time charterer. But in considering whether there is any residual or remaining obligation after nomination it is necessary to have in mind one fundamental distinction between a time charterer and a voyage charterer. In the former case, the time charterer is in complete control of the employment of the ship. It is in his power by appropriate orders timeously given to change the ship's employment so as to prevent her proceeding to or remaining at a port initially safe which has since it was nominated become unsafe. But a voyage charterer may not have the same power. If there is a single loading or discharging port named in the voyage charterparty then, unless the charterparty specifically otherwise provides, a voyage charterer may not be able to order that ship elsewhere. If there is a range of loading or discharging ports named, once the voyage charterer has selected the contractual port or ports of loading or discharge, the voyage charterparty usually operates as if that port or those ports had originally been written into the charterparty, and the charterer then has no further right of nomination or renomination. What, then, is the contractual obligation of such charterers whether for time or voyage if the nominated port becomes unsafe after it was nominated?

My Lords, in the case of a time charterer, I cannot bring myself to think that he has no further obligation to the owner even though for the reasons I have given earlier he is not the insurer of the risks arising from the unsafety of the nominated port. Suppose some event has occurred after nomination which has made or will or may make the nominated port unsafe. Is a time charterer obliged to do anything further? What is a voyage charterer to do in similar circumstances? My Lords, this problem seems never to have been judicially considered in any detail ...

In my opinion, while the primary obligation of a time charterer under clause 2 of this charterparty is that which I have already stated, namely, to order the ship to go only to a port which, at the time when the order is given, is prospectively safe for her, there may be circumstances in which, by reason of a port, which was prospectively safe when the order to go to it was given, subsequently becoming unsafe, clause 2, on its true construction, imposes a further and secondary obligation on the charterer.

In this connection two possible situations require to be considered. The first situation is where, after the time charterer has performed his primary obligation by ordering the ship to go to a port which, at the time of such order, was prospectively safe for her, and while she is still proceeding towards such port in compliance with such order, new circumstances arise which render the port unsafe. The second situation is where, after the time charterer has performed his primary obligation by ordering the ship to go to a port which was, at the time of such order, prospectively safe for her, and she has proceeded to and entered such port in compliance with such order, new circumstances arise which render the port unsafe.

In the first situation it is my opinion that clause 2, on its true construction (unless the cause of the new unsafety be purely temporary in character), imposes on the time charterer a further and secondary obligation to cancel his original order and, assuming that he wishes to continue to trade the ship, to order her to go to another port which, at the time when such fresh order is given, is prospectively safe for her. This is because clause 2 should be construed as requiring the time charterer to do all that he can effectively do to protect the ship from the new danger in the port which has arisen since his original order for her to go to it was given.

In the second situation the question whether clause 2, on its true construction, imposes a further and secondary obligation on the time charterer will depend on whether, having regard to the nature and consequences of the new danger in the port which has arisen, it is possible for the ship to avoid such danger by leaving the port. If, on the one hand, it is not possible for the ship so to leave, then no further and secondary obligation is imposed on the time charterer. This is because clause 2 should not be construed as requiring the time charterer to give orders with which it is not possible for the ship to comply, and which would for that reason be ineffective. If, on the other hand, it is possible for the ship to avoid the new danger in the port which has arisen by leaving, then a further and secondary obligation is imposed on the time charterer to order the ship to leave the port forthwith, whether she has completed loading or discharging or not, and, assuming that he wishes to continue to trade the ship, to order her to go to another port which, at the time when such fresh order is given, is prospectively safe for her. This is again because clause 2 should be construed as requiring the time charterer to do all that he can effectively do to protect the ship from the new danger in the port which has arisen since his original order for her to go to it was given.

My Lords, what I have said with regard to these further and secondary obligations under clause 2 of this charterparty will apply to any other similarly worded 'safe port' clauses.

My Lords, for the reasons I have given I find it much more difficult to say what are the comparable obligations under a voyage charterparty at any rate where there is no express right to renominate ... I think, therefore, in a case where only a time charterparty is involved, that it would be unwise for your Lordships to give further consideration to the problems which might arise in the case of a voyage charterparty, and for my part, I would leave those problems for later consideration if and when they arise.

My Lords, on the basis that time charterers were potentially under the further and secondary obligations which I have held that clause 2 may impose on them, it cannot avail the appellants against the respondents since the events giving rise to the unsafety did not occur until after the *Evia* had entered Basrah, and an order to leave the port and proceed to another port could not have been effective ...

[Lord Roskill went on to conclude that (a) in any event, clause 21 [war clause] of the charterparty freed the respondents from any liability under which they might otherwise be under; (b) the war clause did not exclude the application of the doctrine of frustration and (c) the arbitrator's conclusion as to the date on which the charterparty had become frustrated should be upheld.]

Note

The *Saga Cob* was time chartered for six months' employment in the Red Sea, Gulf of Aden and East Africa. The charterparty provided that the charterers would 'exercise due diligence to ensure that the vessel is only employed between and at safe ports'. She was ordered to Massawa, Ethiopia, with a cargo of aviation fuel. While at anchor she was attacked by Eritrean guerillas; the master was wounded and the ship suffered substantial damage. The Court of Appeal held that 'prospective safety' did not mean 'absolute safety' and that a port should not be regarded as unsafe unless a 'political' risk is sufficient for a reasonable shipowner or master to decline to send or sail his vessel there. *K/S Penta Shipping A/S v Ethiopian Shipping Lines Corp, The Saga Cob* [1992] 2 Lloyd's Rep 545, CA.[1]

Motor Oil Hellas (Corinth) Refineries SA v Shipping Corp of India, The Kanchenjunga1 [1990] [2] Lloyd's Rep 391, HL

In 1978, the *Kanchenjunga* was chartered under a consecutive voyage charter on the Exxonvoy form, with loading at '1/2 safe ports Arabian Gulf'. On 21 November 1980 the charterers ordered the vessel to proceed to the Iranian port of Kharg Island to load a cargo of crude oil. Arbitrators held that on that

---

1   And see [1993] *LMCLQ* 150 (Davenport, B, QC).
2   See Reynolds, FMB [1990] *LMCLQ* 453.

date, Kharg Island was not a prospectively safe port by reason of the Iran/Iraq war. Nevertheless, the vessel undertook the voyage. She arrived and the master gave notice of readiness on 23 November. Before she could berth and load, an Iraqi air attack on 1 December on oil installations on Kharg Island caused the master to sail for a place of safety. Thereafter, the owners called for alternative loading instructions, while the charterers pressed for a return to Kharg; neither side altered its position and both eventually alleged that the other had repudiated the agreement.

Lord Goff: ... There is no dispute between the parties as to the nature of their respective rights and obligations under the contract with regard to the charterers' orders to proceed to Kharg Island to load (I put on one side, of course, the effect of cl 20(vi), which I will consider later). Since these matters are not in dispute, I can state the position very briefly. The arbitrators' finding that Kharg Island was, at the time of its nomination by the charterers, prospectively an unsafe port was not, and indeed could not be, challenged. Kharg Island was not therefore a port which, under the terms of the charter, the charterers were entitled to nominate. It followed that the nomination was a tender of performance which did not conform to the terms of the contract; as such, the owners were entitled to reject it. Even so, by their nomination of Kharg Island the charterers impliedly promised that that port was prospectively safe for the vessel to get to, stay at, so far as necessary, and in due course, leave (see *Kodros Shipping Corporation of Monrovia v Empresa Cubana de Fletes, The Evia (No 2)* [1983] AC 736 at p 757, *per* Lord Roskill). Accordingly if the owners, notwithstanding their right to reject the nomination, complied with it and their ship suffered loss or damage in consequence, they would be entitled to recover damages from the charterers for breach of contract, though the ordinary principles of remoteness of damage and causation would apply to any such claim: see *Compania Naviera Maropan S/A v Bowaters Lloyd Pulp and Paper Mills Ltd, The Stork*, [1955] 2 QB 68, and *Reardon Smith Line Ltd v Australian Wheat Board, The Houston City*, [1956] 1 Lloyd's Rep 1; [1956] AC 266.

This is not, however, a case in which the owners have complied with an order to proceed to an unsafe port, and their ship has proceeded there and suffered damage in consequence. This is a case in which the owners have complied with the charterers' orders to the extent that the vessel has proceeded to the unsafe port and given notice of readiness there, but then the master, having tasted at first hand the danger inherent in the port's unsafety, has persuaded them not to persist in loading there but to sail away. Here the crucial question is whether, before the vessel sailed away, the owners had, by their words or conduct, precluded themselves from rejecting the charterers' nomination as not complying with the contract. Hence the reliance by the charterers on the principles of waiver and estoppel, unsuccessful before the arbitrators, but successful, so far as waiver is concerned, before the judge and the Court of Appeal. The question whether the courts below were correct in their conclusion depends, in my opinion, upon an analysis of these principles, and their proper application to the facts of the present case.

It is a commonplace that the expression 'waiver' is one which may, in law, bear different meanings. In particular, it may refer to a forbearance from exercising a right or to an abandonment of a right. Here we are concerned with waiver in the sense of abandonment of a right which arises by virtue of a party making an election. Election itself is a concept which may be relevant in more than one context. In the present case, we are concerned with an election which may arise in the context of a binding contract, when a state of affairs comes into existence in which one party becomes entitled, either under the terms of the contract or by the general law, to exercise a right, and he has to decide whether or not to do so. His decision, being a matter of choice for him, is called in law an election. Characteristically, this state of affairs arises where the other party has repudiated the contract or has otherwise committed a breach of the contract which entitles the innocent party to bring it to an end, or has made a tender of performance which does not conform to the terms of the contract. But this is not necessarily so. An analogous situation arises where the innocent party becomes entitled to rescind the contract, ie to wipe it out altogether, for example because the contract has been induced by a misrepresentation; and one or both parties may become entitled to determine a contract in the event of a wholly extraneous event occurring, as under a war clause in a charterparty. Characteristically, the effect of the new situation is that a party becomes entitled to determine or to rescind the contract, or to reject an uncontractual tender of performance; but, in theory at least, a less drastic course of action might become available to him under the terms of the contract. In all cases, he has in the end to make his election, not as a matter of obligation, but in the sense that, if he does not do so, the time may come when the law takes the decision out of his hands, either by holding him to have elected not to exercise the right which has become available to him, or sometimes by holding him to have elected to exercise it ... Once an election is made, however, it is final and binding (see *Scarf v Jardine* (1882) 7 App Cas 345, *per* Lord Blackburn, at p 360). Moreover it does not require consideration to support it, and so it is to be distinguished from an express or implied agreement, such as a variation of the relevant contract, which traditionally requires consideration to render it binding in English law.

Generally, however, it is a prerequisite of election that the party making the election must be aware of the facts which have given rise to the existence of his new right ... I add in parenthesis that, for present purposes, it is not necessary for me to consider certain cases in which it has been held that, as a prerequisite of election, the party must be aware not only of the facts giving rise to his rights but also of the rights themselves, because it is not in dispute here that the owners were aware both of the relevant facts and of their relevant rights.

There are numerous examples of the application of this principle of election in English law. Perhaps the most familiar situation is that which arises when one contracting party repudiates the contract. The effect is that the other contracting party then has a choice whether to accept the repudiation (as it is called) and bring the contract to an end; or to affirm the contract, thereby waiving or abandoning his right to terminate it. If, with knowledge of the facts giving rise to the repudiation, the other party to the contract acts (for example) in a manner consistent only with treating that contract as still alive, he is taken in law to have exercised his election to affirm the contract.

The present case is concerned not so much with repudiation as with an uncontractual tender of performance. Even so, the same principles apply. The other party is entitled to reject the tender of performance as uncontractual; and, subject to the terms of the contract, he can then, if he wishes, call for a fresh tender of performance in its place. But if, with knowledge of the facts giving rise to his right to reject, he nevertheless unequivocally elects not to do so, his election will be final and binding upon him and he will have waived his right to reject the tender as uncontractual.

... as Devlin J pointed out in *The Stork* [1955] 2 QB 68 at pp 76–77, the principle of election is applicable in every class of contract. He said:

> ... There is a difference between a contractor who does not discharge his obligation at all and one who does so imperfectly. In the latter case, the contract gives the other party the right to elect to treat the imperfect performance as if it were a fulfilment of the contract (even if he knows that in fact it is not), and to claim damages if any result from the imperfection. This is a right which is, I think, common to every class of contract. The general principle is that the other party is entitled to proceed just as he would have done if the contract had been properly fulfilled, and the risk of any damage that flows from that must be borne by the wrongdoer.

Devlin J was there speaking in the context of the nomination of an unsafe port under a charterparty, and there can be no doubt that the principle of election applies in such circumstances, as it does in other cases.

Election is to be contrasted with equitable estoppel, a principle associated with the leading case of *Hughes v Metropolitan Railway Co* (1877) 2 App Cas 439. Equitable estoppel occurs where a person, having legal rights against another, unequivocally represents (by words or conduct) that he does not intend to enforce those legal rights; if in such circumstances the other party acts, or desists from acting, in reliance upon that representation, with the effect that it would be inequitable for the representor thereafter to enforce his legal rights inconsistently with his representation, he will to that extent be precluded from doing so.

There is an important similarity between the two principles, election and equitable estoppel, in that each requires an unequivocal representation ...

These are the principles which fall to be considered in the present case. Here, as I have already indicated, the situation in which the owners found themselves was one in which they could either reject the charterers' nomination of Kharg Island as uncontractual, or could nevertheless elect to accept the order and load at Kharg Island, thereby waiving or abandoning their right to reject the nomination but retaining their right to claim damages from the charterers for breach of contract. Since the owners were in this situation, it is logical first to consider the question of election before considering (if necessary) equitable estoppel.

The arbitrators addressed themselves to the possibility of election, but unfortunately their rejection of it was founded upon a mistaken appreciation of the law. The judge and the Court of Appeal, however, both held that the owners had elected to waive their right to reject the nomination. In my opinion they were right to reach this conclusion.

Because the arbitrators did not approach the issue of election correctly, they failed to consider the correct questions. In particular, they did not ask themselves whether there had been the necessary unequivocal representation by the owners. It is true that they did ask themselves whether there had been the necessary 'clear and unequivocal promise' when considering the alternative principle of equitable estoppel; they held that there was not, on the basis that the mere acceptance of orders without protest does not amount to such a promise. As a general proposition, this is no doubt correct; and it would equally be true if made with reference to the question whether there had been an unequivocal representation by the owners that they were waiving their right to reject the nomination as uncontractual. Moreover, if the relevant evidence had related only to the communications passing between the parties before the vessel arrived at Kharg Island, the question would have arisen whether, on these communications (set of course in their factual context), there had been such an unequivocal representation. But the matter does not stop there, because on arrival at Kharg Island the master proceeded to serve notice of readiness. Thereafter, as the judge pointed out, the owners were asserting that the vessel was available to load; they were also calling upon the charterers to arrange priority berthing, and referring to the fact that laytime was running. In these circumstances, the owners were asserting a right inconsistent with their right to reject the charterers' orders. The right which they were asserting was that laytime had started to run against the charterers at Kharg Island, with the effect that the charterers had become bound to load the cargo there within the laytime fixed by the charter and, if they failed to do so, to pay demurrage to the owners at the contractual rate. In these circumstances, on the principle stated by Lord Diplock in the *Kammins Ballrooms* case [1971] AC 850, at pp 882–83, the owners must be taken in law to have thereby elected not to reject the charterers' nomination, and so to have waived their right to do so or to call for another nomination ...

No doubt the master was entitled to refuse to endanger his ship and crew in the circumstances in which he found himself; but that did not excuse the owners from their breach of contract, after they had elected not to reject the charterers' nomination of Kharg Island in the knowledge of the facts rendering it prospectively unsafe. Furthermore this is not a case in which a new situation had developed at Kharg Island, or some other danger already existed there. If the known danger had become significantly different; or if a new and different danger had developed; or if some other danger, hitherto unknown, already existed at the port – in such circumstances as these, other questions might have arisen. But your Lordships are not troubled with any such questions in the present case. The arbitrators found as a fact that the safety or unsafety of Kharg Island was not changed in any way by the attack on December 1. This was a finding which they were fully entitled to make, and which cannot be challenged.

For these reasons, I would dismiss the owners' cross-appeal on this issue. It follows that it is unnecessary for the purposes of the cross-appeal to consider the alternative question of equitable estoppel.

I turn then to the charterers' appeal which related to the effect of cl 20(vi) of the charter. Clause 20 (vi) reads, so far as relevant, as follows:

WAR RISKS (a) If any port of loading or of discharge named in this charterparty or to which the vessel may properly be ordered pursuant to the terms of the bills of lading be blockaded, or (b) if owing to any war, hostilities, warlike operations ... entry to any such port of loading or of discharge or the loading or discharge of cargo at any such port be considered by the master or owners in his or their discretion dangerous or prohibited ... the charterers shall have the right to order the cargo or such part of it as may be affected to be loaded or discharged at any other safe port of loading or of discharge within the range of loading or discharging ports respectively established under the provisions of the charterparty (provided such other port is not blockaded or that entry thereto or loading or discharge of cargo thereat is not in the master's or owner's discretion dangerous or prohibited) ...

Both the judge and the Court of Appeal held that this clause was effective to protect the owners from liability in damages, though it did not render the charterers liable in damages in the events which had happened. With this conclusion I agree ...

5 THE NEAR CLAUSE

The Athamas (Owners) v Dig Vijay Cement Co Ltd [1963] 1 Lloyd's Rep 287, CA

The *Athamas* was chartered to carry cement in bags to Saigon and to Pnom-Penh or 'so near thereto as she may safely get and lie ... afloat and there deliver the cargo'. Pilotage was compulsory on the River Mekong. The Pilotage Authority refused to take the vessel to Pnom-Penh believing she did not have sufficient power to navigate the river safely in the condition it was then in. After giving notice to the charterers, the carriers discharged the Pnom-Penh cargo at Saigon. At that time, it would not have been legal or safe for the vessel to make the river voyage for a further five months. There was no other place between Saigon and Pnom-Penh at which the cargo could have been discharged. Arbitrators found that the insistence of the Pilotage Authority on a minimum speed could not have been reasonably foreseen.

> **Pearson LJ**: The owners claim demurrage on the ground that they duly completed their voyage and fully performed their contract by discharging the Pnom-Penh cargo at Saigon, because Saigon was, in relation to Pnom-Penh, 'so near thereto as she may safely get and lie ... afloat and there deliver the cargo'. The charterers say that the owners are not entitled to demurrage, because they were not entitled to discharge the Pnom-Penh cargo at Saigon.
>
> ... In order to establish that they were entitled to discharge the Pnom-Penh cargo at Saigon, the owners have to show that four conditions were fulfilled, namely: (i) the vessel was prevented from going to Pnom-Penh; (ii) the prevention was sufficiently permanent, and not merely temporary; (iii) there was no port or place, nearer than Saigon, to which the vessel could safely go and lie afloat and discharge the remaining cargo; (iv) Saigon was for the

purposes of this charterparty in the vicinity of Pnom-Penh or within a reasonable range of proximity to it. There is no doubt that the first and third conditions were fulfilled. The vessel was prevented by a legal obstacle from going to Pnom-Penh, and there was no suitable port or discharging place nearer than Saigon.

As to the second condition, involving the question whether the prevention was sufficiently permanent, or merely temporary, the arbitrators, in para 45 of the special case, said this:

> We find (if this be a matter of fact) that it would be wholly unreasonable to expect that the *Athamas* should, with 2,100 tons (or any quantity) of cargo for Pnom-Penh on board, wait from 21 March to mid-August in order to proceed to Pnom-Penh and there discharge it; and that what she did – namely to give notice to the charterers and receivers on 21 March 1959 that she was discharging [her] Pnom-Penh cargo at Saigon and to do so – was, from a commercial point of view, reasonable. But we find ourselves, with reluctance, obliged to accept the guidance given us by *Schilizzi v Derry* (1855) 4 EdB 873 ... and *Metcalfe v Britannia Iron Works* (1876) 1 QBD 613 ... and to hold accordingly that the *Athamas* was obliged to wait those five months ...

In my judgment the arbitrators should have given effect to their own view of what was reasonable and should have come to the conclusion that the obstacle was sufficiently permanent. The authorities taken as a whole did not require them to hold that the vessel was obliged to wait those five months. The proposition which can be derived from the authorities is concisely stated by Lord Watson in *Dahl v Nelson, Donkin* (1881) 6 App Cas 38, at pp 59 and 60. Referring to the judgment of Brett LJ in the court below ((1879) 12 Ch D, at p 593), he said:

> ... I adopt the view of Brett LJ that the shipowner must bring his ship to the primary destination named in the charterparty, 'unless he is prevented from getting his ship to that destination by some obstruction or disability of such a character that it cannot be overcome by the shipowner by any reasonable means, except within such a time as, having regard to the adventure of both the shipowner and the charterer, is, as a matter of business, wholly unreasonable'.

When that test is applied all the relevant matters have to be taken into account, including (i) the carrying capacity of the vessel, shown by the charterparty to be more than 9,000 tons; (ii) the earning capacity of the vessel, shown by the charterparty to be in this case about $17,000 in a period which normally would have been less than four months from 29 December 1958, to about the end of March or early April, 1959; (iii) the fact that the remaining cargo was only a little over 2,000 tons, less than a quarter of the total cargo; (iv) the prohibitive expense, as shown by the special case, of storing the remaining cargo at Saigon with a view to carrying it on to Pnom-Penh later; and (v) the fact that the remaining cargo could be carried by lighters from Saigon to Pnom-Penh at an expense which, though substantial, would not be prohibitive. Clearly the arbitrators' view of what was reasonable was amply justified, and, if they had applied the right test in law, they must have decided this point in favour of the owners.

There remains the difficult question whether, for the purposes of this charterparty, Saigon was within the vicinity of Pnom-Penh or within a reasonable range of proximity to it. On this question the arbitrators' finding is in para 43 of the special case, where they say:

> In so far as this be a matter of fact we find that if the applicability of the phrase 'or so near thereto as she can safely get' is still dependent upon the ship being within the 'ambit' of the intended discharging place then 'ambit' must, in regard to this voyage of the *Athamas*, include Saigon as within the 'ambit' of Pnom-Penh.

The condition as to vicinity or proximity is not an express term of the charterparty, but is read into it by necessary implication. Partly it is derived from the word 'near', which requires the substitute destination not to be too far away, but there are other reasons also. The intended destination is that which is named, in this case Pnom-Penh. The parties intend that the cargo shall be carried to Pnom-Penh, and the receivers will be expecting it there, and will make their arrangements accordingly. If by reason of some obstruction the ship cannot get to Pnom-Penh, the receivers must be content with a second-best destination, as near to Pnom-Penh as the ship can safely get. The substitute destination is thus an unnamed destination, described only in general terms, and it is the second-best in relation to Pnom-Penh as the chosen destination. If the words 'so near thereto as she may safely get' were taken literally without any implied limitation, a situation might arise in which the owners could claim to have completed the voyage and fully performed the contract by the vessel discharging the cargo after sailing only a small fraction of the distance to the named port, or even at the loading port if the vessel were prevented from leaving the loading port. To avoid absurdity some limitation has to be implied, and that is what the authorities show, but they do not supply any precise definition of the limitation. In *Schilizzi v Derry* (1855) 4 E & B 873, the charterers required the ship to proceed from London to Galatz or Ibrail or so near thereunto as she might safely get and there load. Galatz and Ibrail are respectively 95 and 115 miles up river from the mouth of the Danube at Sulina. On 5 November she arrived at Sulina, but could not go up the river because there was not enough water over the bar. After remaining at Sulina from 5 November to 11 December she went to Odessa, 100 miles from Sulina, and loaded a cargo there. On and after 7 January there was enough depth of water over the bar at the mouth of the Danube. Another ship had gone to Constantinople and returned to Sulina and crossed the bar on February 10. Two questions arose: (1) whether the ship completed her voyage by going 'so near thereunto as she might safely get', (2) whether she was prevented from completing the voyage. It was held that she had not completed her voyage, and that she was not prevented from doing so as the obstruction was only temporary. On the first point, Lord Campbell CJ said (at p 886):

> ... the meaning of the charterparty must be that the vessel is to get within the ambit of the port, though she may not reach the actual harbour. Now could it be said that the vessel, if she was obstructed in entering the Dardanelles, had completed her voyage to Galatz. There can therefore be no doubt as to the first issue.

Wightman J said (p 887):

> I am of the same opinion as to both issues. As to the first, I think the vessel did not, within the meaning of the charterparty, complete the voyage. It might as well, as has indeed been suggested, be said that she had completed her voyage if she had been stopped in the Dardanelles.

In *Metcalfe v Britannia Ironworks Company* (1876) 1 QBD 613; (1877) 2 QBD 423, CA, a cargo of railway bars was shipped under a charterparty from a port in England to Taganrog in the Sea of Azov or so near thereto as the ship could safely get. Taganrog is at the north-eastern end of the Sea of Azov. On the arrival of the ship at Kertch in the straits leading from the Black Sea into the Sea of Azov, it was found that the Sea of Azov was blocked with ice until the ensuing spring, and the cargo was unloaded at Kertch. The Queen's Bench Court assumed, as appears from the judgment of Chief Justice Cockburn (at p 617), that Kertch was about 30 miles distant from Taganrog. Chief Justice Cockburn (p 618) said:

> Upon these facts I entirely concur in thinking that the plaintiff is not entitled to recover the full freight. The case of *Schilizzi v Derry* established that when a charterparty speaks of a vessel, bound to a particular port, discharging 'as near as she can get' to such port, this must be taken to mean some place 'within the ambit' of the port; and Kertch certainly cannot be said to be within the ambit of the port of Taganrog.

There is a passage to the same effect in the judgment of Mellor and Quain JJ (p 631). On appeal, the Court of Appeal did not deal with the question of 'ambit'. Lord Coleridge CJ said ((1877) 2 QBD at p 426):

> On the first point the court below decided unanimously against the plaintiff and we are of opinion that the court below was clearly right. It is not necessary to say more than that the obstruction was only temporary, and is such as must be incident to every contract for a voyage to a frozen sea, and it cannot be said that in all these contracts the words 'at that time', or 'then and there', are to be inserted after the words 'as near thereto as the ship can safely get'.

The Court of Appeal had been informed that the distance from Kertch to Taganrog is about 300 miles.

In *Capper & Co v Wallace Brothers* (1880) 5 QBD 163, the ship was directed to Koogerpolder, lying at the end of a canal, and the ship's draught was deeper than the canal. It was held that Nieuwediep, situated at the entrance to the canal and about 30 miles from Koogerpolder, was 'as near thereto as she may safely get'.

Similarly in *Hayton v Irwin* (1879) 5 CPD 130, the vessel could not reach Hamburg, because her draught was deeper than the river, and it was held that Stade, about 30 miles distant from Hamburg, was 'so near thereto as she may safely get'.

In *Dahl v Nelson*, above, the distance between the named docks and the substitute place for unloading was only about half a mile. Lord Blackburn (at pp 50–51) referred to *Schilizzi v Derry*, above, and *Metcalfe v Britannia Ironworks Company*, above, and said:

... I think it plain that neither of those decisions touches the present case. Whether the language which Lord Campbell uses is quite the most accurate to express his idea may be doubted ...

Lord Watson said, at p 57:

Both parties seemed to concede, and I think it may be taken as settled law, that when, by the terms of a charterparty, a loaded ship is destined to a particular dock, or as near thereto as she may safely get, the first of these alternatives constitutes a primary obligation; and, in order to complete her voyage, the vessel must proceed to and into the dock named, unless it has become in some sense 'impossible' to do so. It is only in the case of her entrance into the dock being barred by such 'impossibility' that the owners can require the charterers to take delivery of her cargo to a place outside the dock. When a vessel in the course of her voyage is stopped, by an impediment occurring at a distance from the primary place of discharge, it has been decided that she cannot be held to have got 'as near thereunto as she could safely get', and therefore cannot claim to have completed the voyage in terms of the second alternative: *Schilizzi v Derry* ... also *Metcalfe v Britannia Ironworks Company*, above. It was observed by Lord Chief Justice Campbell in Schilizzi v Derry, above, that the meaning of these words in the charterparty 'so near the port of landing as the ship may safely get', 'must be that she should get within the ambit of the port, though she may not be able to enter it'.

In *Horsley v Price* (1883) 11 QBD 244 (North J), the decision turned on special wording in the particular charterparty, and does not, I think, give guidance as to the general effect of the words 'so near thereto as she may safely get'. The charterparty in that case said 'at all times of the tide'.

In *Castel and Latta v Trechman* (1884) 1 C & E 276, the charterparty provided that the ship should go to Glasgow to load, and having so laden should proceed 'to Tonapse (Black Sea) with the bricks and clay, Poti with the ironwork, and Taganrog with the pig iron in whatever order of ports owners may approve (cargo to be brought to and taken from alongside) or so near thereto as she may safely get, and there deliver the same'. Tonapse is the same as Tuapse and is on the north-east coast of the Black Sea. Poti is on the east coast of the Black Sea. Taganrog is at the north-eastern end of the Sea of Azov. On 5 May 1877, the Turkish government proclaimed a blockade, presumably of all the Russian ports in the Black Sea and the Sea of Azov and gave time for a neutral vessel to leave a blockaded port up to 17 May. On 17 May the ship left Poti and was unable to proceed to Taganrog owing to the blockade. She, accordingly, proceeded to Constantinople, and refused to deliver the cargo except on payment of freight. The charterers paid the freight under protest, and sued to recover it. Stephen J said (at p 277):

... the defendants contend that in going to Constantinople the vessel got as near to Tonapse and Taganrog 'as she could safely get', and so they are entitled to the chartered freight. That phrase no doubt meets the case of the vessel not being able to get absolutely to the very place or spot or dock stipulated; but it cannot, in my opinion, enable the vessel to go to any port which, under the circumstances, it is a reasonable course for the master to go to. The authorities are numerous, but I need only refer to the judgments in the recent decision, *Nelson v Dahl*, in the House of Lords.

In *East Asiatic Company Ltd v SS Tronto Company Ltd* (1915) 31 TLR 543, at p 544, Bailhache J said that two questions arose upon the facts – first, whether Amsterdam was a safe port, and secondly, if not, was Hull as near thereto as the *Tronto* could safely get within the meaning of those words in the bill of lading? He held that Amsterdam was in the existing situation a safe port. He then said that the second question therefore did not arise, but he would have had great difficulty in holding, both on principle and on the authorities, that the words 'so near thereto as she may safely get' covered the port of Hull some 200 miles from Amsterdam and separated from it by the North Sea.

This examination of the authorities has not yielded any precise definition of the range of proximity or vicinity within which the substitute destination must lie in order to be, in relation to the named destination for the ship, 'as near thereto as she may safely get'. I do, however, derive from these authorities an impression that the range is fairly narrow, and that in an ordinary case a substitute destination 250 miles by water from the named destination would be outside the range of proximity. This, however, is an extraordinary case in that Saigon, though 250 miles by water away from Pnom-Penh, is nevertheless the nearest port to Pnom-Penh at any rate for the purpose of unloading the cargo concerned. It is helpful to consider the question as at the date of the conclusion of the charterparty. The parties would not be deemed necessarily to know that Saigon is the nearest port to Pnom-Penh, but they should be deemed to have general maritime knowledge and therefore to know that that part of the world is sparsely provided with ports, so that there might well be a long distance between the named port and any possible substitute. That differentiates this case from, at any rate, any case where the named port is on the west coast of Europe or in the Mediterranean Sea or in the Black Sea. The question is largely one of degree and to be decided mainly on a basis of commercial knowledge and experience. I have read the findings of the arbitrators. McNair J said ([1962] 2 Lloyd's Rep, p 130):

> ... The limit of the word 'ambit' clearly did not arise for consideration or discussion in *Dahl v Nelson, Donkin*, above. The use of the word 'near' clearly connotes some idea of proximity. But, just as Lord Blackburn (at p 52) and Lord Watson (at pp 58 and 59), when considering the question whether an obstacle is temporary or permanent, import the element of reasonableness in relation to time, so here it seems to me that, in considering whether a substitute discharging place or port is within the phrase 'so near thereto as she may safely get', the court should apply the conception of reasonableness in relation to distance. There clearly will come a point at which the substituted port cannot properly be said to be near or within the ambit of the primary port, but is to be held to be at such a distance that it cannot be assumed to be within the contemplation of the parties as fair and reasonable men. What is a reasonable distance clearly has to be determined in the light of all the circumstances and of the particular adventure.

He said also (*ibid*):

Where the line is to be drawn is essentially a question of fact for the tribunal of fact properly directed (or, in the case of an arbitration, for the arbitrators properly directing themselves) on the question of law, and I am not satisfied that the arbitrators in their carefully phrased finding in para 43 have in any way misdirected themselves. They had the advantage of a full discussion of the authorities above referred to by counsel, who also appeared before me. They have in effect found that, for the Pnom-Penh cargo, Saigon, in the events which happened, and in relation to this particular voyage, was the nearest reasonably practical port of discharge, and, as I read their finding, that Saigon was within the ambit of Pnom-Penh in the sense of being in an area or zone or within a range of proximity not beyond the reasonable contemplation of the parties as fair and reasonable men.

I have found the question difficult, but on the whole I agree with McNair J that the arbitrators' decision on the point should be accepted ...

[Sellers LJ delivered a judgment agreeing that the effect of the arbitrators' decision was that discharge on the Pnom-Penh cargo at Saigon was a fulfilment of the voyage and that the demurrage was recoverable. Harman LJ agreed generally with Pearson LJ, although his Lordship thought that in a two-port charter, as a matter of construction, the first port of discharge could not also be the 'nearest' port to the second port of discharge.]

6 OFF-HIRE

The only general rule that can be laid down is that one must consider the wording of the off-hire clause in every case (Staughton LJ, *The Berg Sund* [1993] 2 Lloyd's Rep 453, 459).

Off-hire clauses operate as exceptions

The cardinal rule, if I may call it such, in interpreting such a charterparty as this, is that the charterer will pay hire for the use of the ship unless he can bring himself within the exceptions. I think he must bring himself clearly within the exceptions. If there is a doubt as to what the words mean, then I think those words must be read in favour of the owners because the charterer is attempting to cut down the owners' right to hire.

Royal Greek Government v Minister of Transport, The Ann Stathatos (1948) 82 Ll L Rep 196, 199, Bucknill LJ.

Off-hire events must cause loss of time

Hogarth v Miller, The Westfalia [1891] AC 48

While the vessel was on a voyage from West Africa to Harburg and Antwerp, under charter, her high pressure engine broke down and it was necessary to put back about 100 miles to Las Palmas, which she reached with the aid of a low pressure engine assisted by her sails. As repairs could not be effected in that port, the appellants and respondents agreed that a tug should be employed to tow the ship to Harburg, and that the expense, £1,100, should be treated as general average on cargo, ship, and freight. As their proportion of this expense the respondents eventually paid £867. The ship left Las Palmas on 18 October 1887, towed by the tug and assisted by her own low pressure engine. She arrived at Harburg on 31 October and discharged the cargo with her own power. Repairs to her main engine were completed on 10 November. The charterparty provided that:

> In the event of loss of time from deficiency of men or stores, breakdown of machinery, want of repairs, or damage, whereby the working of the vessel is stopped for more than 48 consecutive working hours, the payment of hire shall cease until she be again in an efficient state to resume her service.

The shipowner admitted that the vessel was off-hire while at Las Palmas, but claimed payment of hire for the whole period of the voyage from Las Palmas to Harburg; the charterer denied liability to pay anything for the period before completion of repairs.

Lord Halsbury LC: ... My Lords, the whole of this case, as it appears to me, turns upon the true construction of the contract which regulates the relations between the parties ...

What the parties to this contract contemplated was this: the hirer of the vessel wants to use the vessel for the purpose of his adventure, and he is contemplating the possibility that by some of the causes indicated in the clause itself ... the efficient working of the vessel may be stopped, and so loss of time may be incurred; and he protects himself by saying, that during such period as the working of the vessel is stopped for more than 48 consecutive hours, payment shall cease; and now come the words upon which such reliance is placed: 'until she be again in an efficient state to resume her service'. If the contention which has been put forward at your Lordships' Bar were well founded one might have expected that the parties in contemplating what upon that view was said to be the intention of the parties if they had intended that the test should be the efficient state of the vessel as it originally was might very readily have used the words, 'until such time as the deficiency of men or stores has been removed, or the breakdown of the machinery has been set to rights, or the want of repairs has been supplied, or the damage has been remedied', and so forth; or the terms might have been inserted that the resumption of the payment shall be dependent upon the vessel being restored to full efficiency in all respects, as to seaworthiness and otherwise, as she was at the time when she was originally handed over. But the parties have not used such language. On the contrary, the test by which the payment for the hire is to be resumed is the efficient state of the vessel to resume her service; so that each of those words, as it appears to me, has relation to that which both of the parties must be taken to have well understood, namely, the purpose for which the vessel was hired, the nature of the service to be performed by the vessel, and the efficiency of the vessel to perform such service as should be required of her in the course of the voyage.

As to the first part of the claim which has been insisted upon here, I confess that I entertain no doubt whatever that the vessel was not efficient in any sense for the prosecution of her voyage from Las Palmas to Harburg ... As a matter of fact, this vessel did not and could not pursue her voyage as a vessel from Las Palmas to Harburg. That another vessel took her in tow, that another vessel accomplished the voyage and brought this vessel, not as an efficient steamer, but as a floating barge, whereby the goods were brought to Harburg, seems to me to be nothing to the purpose. I use that phrase because, although I am aware that it is suggested that the low pressure engine was used for the purpose of easing the work of the tug, that appears to me to be entirely irrelevant when one is ascertaining whether this vessel of its own independent power was efficient for the purpose of prosecuting the voyage. All that is suggested is that the tug was assisted by the use of the low pressure engine. I find, as a matter of evidence, as each court I think has found, that the vessel was not seaworthy for the purpose of accomplishing her voyage without the assistance of a tug; she did not accomplish her voyage without the assistance of a tug; and in truth, as it appears to me, upon these facts it is clear that the voyage which was accomplished, and the service which it was contemplated this hired vessel was to perform, was performed by another vessel, and that the auxiliary assistance which she gave to that other vessel was not making the vessel herself an efficient vessel for the working of which the hirer was to pay.

... That is conclusive upon the first part of the case, and therefore no payment for the hire was due during the period that she was passing from Las Palmas to Harburg.

With reference to the second question which has been argued it appears to me that one has again to refer to each of these clauses of the contract to see what the parties were bargaining for. I should read the contract as meaning ... that she should be efficient to do what she was required to do when she was called upon to do it; and accordingly, at each period, if what was required of her was to lie at anchor, if it was to lie alongside the wharf, upon each of those occasions, if she was efficient to do it at that time she would then become, in the language of the contract, to my mind 'efficient', reading with it the other words, 'for the working of the vessel'. How does a vessel work when she is lying alongside a wharf to discharge her cargo? She has machinery there for the purpose. It is not only that she has the goods in the hold, but she has machinery there for the purpose of discharging the cargo. It is not denied that during the period that she was lying at Harburg there was that machinery at work enabling the hirer to do quickly all that this particular portion of her employment required to be done. It appears to me, therefore, that at that period there was a right in the shipowner to demand payment of the hire, because at that time his vessel was efficiently working; the working of the vessel was proceeding as efficiently as it could with reference to the particular employment demanded of her at the time.

Under these circumstances, it appears to me that the pursuer here was entitled to payment for the hire of the vessel during the period of discharge ...

My Lords, I wish to say one word as to the other view which has been presented, that the shipowner was not entitled to anything in respect of the period during which she was discharging. It has been put in various forms by the learned counsel. What reason or good sense would there be in construing a mercantile contract so that all right for payment should cease when the other party to the contract was getting everything he could out of the use of the vessel if the vessel was in an efficient state? I can see none. And what was put this morning seems to me conclusive: if some other part of the steam-gearing not used for the purpose of navigation had gone out of working in mid-ocean, and there had been no longer any use for that particular thing, the reason why such a breakdown of the machinery in mid-ocean would not have created a cesser of payment under the contract would, I suppose, have been this – it would have been argued, and argued justly, 'It is very true that there has been a breakdown of machinery; but that breakdown of machinery is not the only event contemplated; it does not of itself entitle you to a cesser of payment. There must be to entitle you to a cesser of payment a loss of time arising from a breakdown of machinery. Not even then does the cesser of payment arise; but there must be a loss of time by the breakdown of the machinery whereby the working of the vessel is stopped for the contracted time'. That appears to me to reflect great light upon the other question – What was the breakdown of the machinery which was contemplated by both the parties? It appears to me that the resumption of the right of payment is correlative with that; and inasmuch as when the vessel got to Harburg the vessel became 'efficient' for the purpose for which alone she was wanted at that time, it appears to me that the right of payment arose ...

[Lord Watson held that (a) the vessel was not in an efficient state to resume her service when she started from Las Palmas under tow and that she remained off-hire until she reached that port; (b) that a quantum meruit might be payable in some cases while a vessel is off-hire where the charterer was benefiting from the use of the vessel, although not in the present case because of the arrangement made to pay for the tow; (c) hire was payable again when the vessel berthed at Harburg because the vessel was then in an efficient state for the service then required.

Lord Herschell agreed with the Lord Chancellor and Lord Watson. Lord Morris thought that the vessel was off-hire at Las Palmas and the hire only became payable again when she had been repaired. Lord Bramwell thought that the vessel was efficient at Las Palmas; the charterers had had the benefit of their cargo being taken to Harburg and ought to pay for it.]

Mareva Navigation Co Ltd v Canaria Armadora SA, The Mareva AS [1977] 1 Lloyd's Rep 368

The *Mareva AS* was chartered on the NYPE form. During the charter, a cargo of wheat in bulk became wet because of a breach of the seaworthiness obligation by the shipowner in failing to ensure that the hatch covers were watertight. The shipowners accepted that they were liable to the charterers in damages for the consequent loss of 15 days. But they argued that this liability arose only in damages and not under the off-hire clause. This enabled them to go on and argue that the damages for which they were liable should be reduced by the amount of demurrage received by the charterers in respect of the same period under a subcharter. Kerr J rejected the owner's claim to a credit for the demurrage under the subcharter. His Lordship went on to consider whether the vessel had been off-hire.

> **Kerr J**: ... Since in my judgment the owners' claim for demurrage must fail ... I am tempted not to decide the off-hire point. But it raises a well known problem under a widely used form of charter and was fully argued before me. I therefore feel bound to deal with it in case I am wrong on the first point and the matter goes further.

> The crucial words are:

>> ... in the event of the loss of time from ... detention by average accidents to ship or cargo ... or by any other cause preventing the full working of the vessel, the payment of hire shall cease for the time thereby lost.

> ... It is settled law that *prima facie* hire is payable continuously and that it is for the charterers to bring themselves clearly within an off-hire clause if they contend that hire ceases. This clause undoubtedly presents difficulties of construction and may well contain some tautology, eg in the reference to damage to hull, machinery or equipment followed by 'average accidents to ship'. But I think that the object is clear. The owners provide the ship and the crew to work her. So long as these are fully efficient and able to render to the charterers the service then required, hire is payable continuously. But if the ship is for any reason not in full working order to render the service then required from her, and the charterers suffer loss of time in consequence, then hire is not payable for the time so lost. The word 'other' in the phrase 'or by any other cause preventing the full working of the vessel' in my view shows that the various events referred to in the foregoing provisions were also only intended to take effect if the full working of the vessel in the sense just described was thereby prevented and time was lost in consequence. But if, for instance, the cargo is damaged as the result of an accident, but the vessel's ability to work fully is not thereby prevented or impaired, because the vessel in herself remains fully efficient in all respects, then I do not think that the charterers bring themselves within the clause. On this analysis, in view of the [arbitrators'] finding that the vessel was fully capable of performing every service that was required of her] ... I therefore consider that the vessel was not off-hire.

> But even if I be wrong about this construction, I think that the same result follows because the charterers cannot bring the facts of this case within the word 'detention'. I think that some more specific meaning must be given to this word than mere delay, in which case it would be tautologous with 'loss of time'. It is not used in relation to any of the other events referred to, and must, I think, be given some specific and additional meaning. I think that it is intended to refer to some physical or geographical constraint upon the vessel's movements in relation to her service under the charter. On this basis there was no 'detention' in the present case ...

Note

The *Ira* was time chartered on the NYPE form. The parties agreed that after discharging cargo at Ravenna, the vessel would drydock in Greece. The vessel proceeded to Piraeus where it was drydocked. When the vessel was ready to resume chartered service, the charterers fixed the vessel to load a cargo at Novorossiysk in the Black Sea. Charterers contended that the vessel was off-hire from dropping the outward pilot at Ravenna; owners argued that almost none of the duration of the voyage from Ravenna to Piraeus was lost since Piraeus is, with a very slight deviation, on the route from Ravenna to the Black Sea. The off-hire clause provided that 'In the event of loss of time from drydocking preventing the full working of the vessel the payment of hire shall cease for the time thereby lost'. Tuckey J held that:

> A net time clause, such as this clause is, requires the charterer to prove the happening and the duration of the off-hire event, and that time has been lost to him thereby. So it is a two-stage operation and it does not follow merely by proof of the off-hire event and its duration that he is able to establish a loss of time to him. That must depend on the circumstances of the particular case.

The drydocking had not caused the charterers to lose the whole of the time occupied by the voyage from Ravenna to Piraeus and the vessel was not therefore off-hire for the whole of that period. *Forestships International Ltd v Armonia Shipping and Finance Corp, The Ira* [1995] 1 Lloyd's Rep 103.

Partial inefficiency

Tynedale Steam Shipping Co Ltd v Anglo-Soviet Shipping Co Ltd, The Hordern [1936] 1 All ER 389

The *Hordern* was chartered on the Baltime 1920 form. In the course of a voyage from Archangel to Liverpool with a deckload of timber, she was struck by a heavy squall; part of the deck cargo fell overboard carrying away the foremast to which the forward winches were attached. Discharge took six days longer than it would normally have taken. The shipowners claimed hire for the period during which the vessel was delayed. Baltime 1920 provided:

> Clause 10 – In the event of loss of time caused by dry-docking or by other necessary measures to maintain the efficiency of steamer, or by deficiency of men or owners' stores, breakdown of machinery, damage to hull or other accident preventing the working of the steamer and lasting more than 24 consecutive hours, hire to cease from commencement of such loss of time until steamer is again in efficient state to resume service. Should steamer be driven into port, or to anchorage by stress of weather, or in the event of steamer trading to shallow harbours, rivers or ports with bars, or in case of accident to cargo, causing detention to steamer, time so lost and expenses incurred shall be for charterers' account even if caused through fault or want of due diligence by owners' servants.

The shipowners argued that the ship was partly efficient and that the clause only put the ship off-hire in the event of complete or total prevention from working the ship, not if there was a mere interference with working. Scott LJ and Eve J delivered judgments agreeing with Lord Roche.

Lord Roche: ... There is one fatal objection to that argument, and that is that it has come about 45 years too late. In the year 1890 a clause which I am unable in any way to distinguish from the present clause came up for decision in ... *Hogarth v Miller, Brother & Co* [above]. I say that the language of that clause cannot in my view be distinguished from the language of the clause in this case. The only difference was that the word 'stopped' occurred in that case instead of the word 'preventing' in this case.

... Here, the mast being damaged did not prevent or hinder the ship steaming, but it did hinder or prevent her discharging in the sense that prevention was construed in the House of Lords in *Hogarth v Miller* as preventing discharge or the working of the ship happening in accordance with the contract. That is the full point, it seems to me, between the parties in this case, as it was between the majority of the House in the case of *Hogarth v Miller* and the dissenting Lord Bramwell.

Let me go a little further into the judgments in order to make good my point. I recognise that the facts in *Hogarth v Miller* were in a sense different to those in this case. It was held there that the ship could not have got to a port without a tug. Mr Le Quesne says in this case that they could have discharged slowly and did discharge slowly, but that they did discharge. I am afraid that the answer to that part of the case is that it is a finding of fact. There is a finding of fact here that discharge of the forward part of the ship was impossible by the ship herself by means of her winches and derricks ...

... It seems to me that it follows from [the reasoning in *Hogarth v Miller*] that the vessel was not fit or able to work for the services required and stipulated for by the initial words of the charterparty, and in those circumstances two results follow. Under clause 2 it was the duty of the owners then to put her back into an efficient state in hull and machinery for that purpose. Under clause 10 events had happened which put into operation the cesser of hire clause ...

Now it is really sufficient to dispose of this case to indicate the reasons why I think on this part of the case the learned judge was right and why the appeal fails. There are two matters to be added. We must only answer the questions put by the arbitrators, and it is important in answering them not to be ambiguous. The first question is: 'Whether upon the true construction of the charter and upon the facts as herein found the shipowners are entitled to hire for the vessel in respect of the time occupied in discharge'.

... The answer that I give is this: that upon the true construction of the charter and upon the facts as here found – that is to say, found in the case – the ship-owners' right to be paid hire ceased in respect of the time occupied in discharge; that is to say, they should get no further than that during the continuance of that period.

That answer is really sufficient to dispose of the argument which was developed by Mr Le Quesne in reply: namely, that there should be a sort of assessment of the amount of time lost by reason of the inefficiency, and that for that net loss of time so ascertained hire should be deemed to cease. With respect to that argument, it is sufficient to say that I regard every word which I have read from the judgments of Lord Halsbury and the other noble Lords who formed the majority [in *Hogarth v Miller*] as negativing that argument, which in my view is opposed to the proper construction of the clause, that construction being a stipulation that, if certain events happen, then *ipso facto* hire is to cease and is not to begin again until that state of affairs has ceased to exist. The ascertainment of the net loss is something foreign to the clause as drawn ...

Scott LJ: I agree with the whole of the judgment delivered by Lord Roche and with a little hesitation only add one or two observations ...

Mr Le Quesne submitted to us that in [*Hogarth v Miller*] ... the House accepted as a principle that hire had ceased by reason of prevention within the meaning of the charter before the vessel reached the port of refuge at Las Palmas and before the voyage home with a tug assisting began. He said, therefore, that the House was not considering what caused the charter hire to cease, but what entitled the shipowner to say that the right to charter hire had re-attached. That argument had at first its attractions, but on further reflection, apart from the *obiter dicta* – to which we have to pay the very greatest possible attention in this court – which fell from their Lordships in the House of Lords, I do feel this very strongly: that from a commercial point of view the distinction between what causes the charter hire to go off and what causes it to come on again is, to the commercial man, a distinction which is rather apt to worry him; and I am very loath to construe an ordinary commercial clause in a way that is not simple to the commercial mind if the clause can properly be interpreted in a simple way. And this clause, I think, can be interpreted simply, for this reason: the clause provides that in the event of loss of time caused by damage to hull or other accident preventing the working of the steamer, then hire for a minimum length of time is to cease until the steamer is again in an efficient state to resume the service. As Lord Roche has said, the word 'again' indicates the former state of the ship and the latter state of the ship. The state before she went off-hire and the state to which she must have returned before she goes on hire again are intended to be the same ...

Canadian Pacific (Bermuda) Ltd v Canadian Transport Co Ltd, The HR Macmillan [1974] 1 Lloyd's Rep 311, CA

By a time charterparty in the New York Produce Exchange form, the owners of the *HR Macmillan*, which was fitted with three Munck gantry cranes, chartered her to the charterers for eight years from the date of delivery. In April 1968 the trolley of the No 1 crane fell overboard and the crane was not operational for nearly three and a half months. The charter contained a special clause to cover a breakdown of the Munck cranes. But in the course of his judgment, Lord Denning also referred to the off-hire clause which provided:

That in the event of the loss of time from deficiency and/or default of men or deficiency of stores, fire, breakdown or damages to hull, machinery or equipment, grounding, detention by average accidents to ship or cargo, drydocking for the purpose of examination or painting bottom, or by any other cause preventing the full working of the vessel, the payment of hire shall cease for the time thereby lost ...

Lord Denning MR: ... Taking that clause by itself, it would mean that, if one crane broke down, there would have to be an inquiry as to the time lost thereby. That would be a most difficult inquiry to undertake. For instance, if one broke down and the other two cranes were able to do, and did do, all the work that was required, there would be no 'time lost thereby'; and there would be no cessation of hire. But if there was work for three cranes, and there was some loss of time owing to the one crane breaking down, there would have to be an assessment of the amount of time lost. In that event, as the judge pointed out, the question would have to be asked: 'How much earlier would the vessel have been away from her port of loading or discharge if three Munck cranes, instead of two, had been available throughout?' The judge called that a 'net loss of time' clause ...

Inefficiency and external causes

Actis Co Ltd v Sanko Steamship Co Ltd, The Aquacharm [1982] 1 WLR 119, CA

Shaw LJ agreed with **Lord Denning MR**: In 1974 the owners of the *Aquacharm* let her to Japanese charterers on a time charter. She was to carry a cargo of coal on a trip from Baltimore to Tokyo. This necessitated her passing through the Panama Canal. The charterers ordered her to load up to the draught 'permissible by the Panama Canal Company of 39 ft 6 in TFW'. TFW stands for tropical fresh water.

The master took on board 43,000 tons of coal. That was too much for safety through the canal. When a vessel is in transit through the Panama Canal she has to sail through a lake called Gatun Lake. It is a fresh water lake. Now, when a vessel passes from salt water into fresh water, there is a tendency for the bow to go down relative to the stern. The master knew this, but he did not allow for it when he loaded at Baltimore. He was at fault in loading the vessel. She was already down by the head when she reached Cristobal, at the entrance to the canal. This gave rise to a risk that, when her bow went down on entering the Gatun Lake, she might touch bottom. He ought to have loaded less cargo so as to allow for the tendency of the bow to go down.

When the vessel arrived at the entrance to the canal, the Panama Canal Company refused to allow her to go through. They said that she exceeded the permitted draught as prescribed by their regulations. To get over the difficulty, it was decided to discharge 636 tons of coal into another vessel called *Mini Lux*. She followed the *Aquacharm* through the canal. The 636 tons were then reloaded at the other end.

This delay held up the vessel for eight days 23 hours and 45 minutes. Nine days all but a quarter of an hour. The hire for that period came to $ 86,344.89. The charterers refused to pay. They invoke the 'off-hire' clause to excuse them from paying ...

off-hire or not?

The charterparty was on the New York Produce Exchange form, but with arbitration in London instead of New York. The 'off-hire' clause 15 said:

... in the event of the loss of time ... by any other cause preventing the full working of the vessel, the payment of hire shall cease for the time thereby lost ...

... In seeing whether clause 15 applies, we are not to inquire by whose fault it was that the vessel was delayed. We are to inquire first whether the 'full working of the vessel' has been prevented. Only if it has, do we consider the 'cause'. I do not think the lightening of cargo does 'prevent the full working of the vessel'. Often enough cargo has to be unloaded into a lighter – for one reason or another – to get her off a sandbank – or into a basin. The vessel is still working fully, but she is delayed by the need to unload part of the cargo. It is rather like *Court Line Ltd v Dant and Russell Inc* (1939) 44 Com Cas 345. The vessel was still working fully, but she was delayed by the boom across the Yangtze River. This vessel was, therefore, still on hire for nearly nine days ...

Griffiths LJ: ... The charterers submit that they are not liable to pay for the period of delay as the *Aquacharm* was off-hire during that time ...

The charterers rely upon the words, 'any other cause preventing the full working of the vessel'. Mr Phillips, founding himself upon a passage in the judgment of Kerr J in *Mareva Navigation Co Ltd v Canaria Armadora SA* [1977] 1 Lloyd's Rep 368 submits that the excess draught caused by the amount of cargo she was carrying prevented the full working of the *Aquacharm* because she was unable in that condition to perform the service required of her, namely to pass through the canal. I do not read Kerr J's judgment as supporting the proposition that a ship which is sound in herself is prevented from 'full working' because it has loaded too much cargo to pass through a particular waterway, or to enter a particular harbour.

Kerr J was not considering a situation such as has arisen in this case, and the whole emphasis of his judgment directs one to consider the efficiency of the ship herself in deciding whether or not it is capable of 'full working': see in particular the passage where he said [1977] 1 Lloyd's Rep 368, 382:

> But if, for instance, the cargo is damaged as the result of an accident, but the vessel's ability to work fully is not thereby prevented or impaired, because the vessel in herself remains fully efficient in all respects, then I do not think the charterers bring themselves within the clause.

The *Aquacharm* remained at all times in herself fully efficient in all respects. She could not pass through the canal because the canal authorities decided she was carrying too much cargo, but that decision in no way reflected upon the *Aquacharm*'s efficiency as a ship.

By contrast, in *Sidermar SpA v Apollo Corporation* [1978] 1 Lloyd's Rep 200, a ship was held up by the port health authorities because two of the crew had been taken to hospital with suspected typhus, and the health authority insisted that the ship be disinfected before they would issue a free pratique. Mocatta J held that the vessel was off-hire during that period of delay. A ship suspected of carrying typhus is prevented from working fully until it is cleared, for no responsible person would use it in such a condition. The incapacity of the ship to work in such a case is directly attributable to the suspected condition of the ship itself, and in my view is clearly distinguishable from the present case.

Although obviously not on all fours, the present case is nearer to *Court Line Ltd v Dant and Russell Inc* 44 Com Cas 345 when the ship although sound in herself was delayed by a boom across the Yangtze River, and it was held that it remained on hire.

As the *Aquacharm* remained at all times an efficient ship, she was capable of 'full working' within the meaning of the off-hire clause and the charterers do not succeed under this head ...

Andre & Cie SA v Orient Shipping Rotterdam BV, The Laconian Confidence [1997] 1 Lloyd's Rep 139

The *Laconian Confidence* was chartered on the NYPE form for one time charter trip from Yangon to Bangladesh. Authorities at Chittagong refused to allow the vessel to proceed to her next business following discharge of her cargo of 10,000 metric tonnes of rice in bags because of the presence remaining on board of 15 tonnes of residue sweepings. As a result the vessel was delayed for nearly 18 days until she was allowed to dump these residues and thereafter to sail. Charterers argued that the vessel was off-hire during this period.

> **Rix J:** This is, for the present, the latest in a line of cases arising out of the New York Produce Exchange's off-hire clause and the problem created by the interference of authorities. As a result of such interference, the vessel, although entirely sound and efficient in herself, is prevented from working, that is to say from performing the next task required of her. Is the vessel off-hire, on the ground that she has been prevented from working by some 'other cause', ie by some cause other than the named causes in the clause? Or does she remain on hire, because the vessel remains entirely efficient in herself, and/or because the ejusdem generis principle curtails 'any other cause' to causes similar to the named causes?
>
> My reader will recall that the NYPE's off-hire clause (clause 15) provides as follows:
>
>> That in the event of the loss of time from deficiency of [*and/or default*] men or stores, fire, breakdown or damages to hull, machinery or equipment, grounding, detention by average accidents to ship or cargo, dry-docking for the purpose of examination or painting bottom, or by any other cause preventing the full working of the vessel, the payment of hire shall cease for the time thereby lost ...
>
> The words in italics 'and/or default' were added to the standard clause in the instant case, as they often are. (They were in error slightly misplaced: the obvious intent is that the clause should read 'deficiency and/or default of men'; but nothing turns on that.) The word 'whatsoever' is sometimes added to the phrase 'or by any other cause', but not in the instant case. It is established that the phrase 'preventing the full working of the vessel' qualifies not only the phrase 'any other cause' but also all the named causes: *The Mareva AS* [1977] 1 Lloyd's Rep 368 at 382. It has therefore been said that the first question to be answered in any dispute under the clause is whether the full working of the vessel has been prevented; for if it has not, there is no need to

go on to ask whether the vessel has suffered from the operation of any named cause or whether the phrase 'any other cause [whatsoever]' is or is not limited in any way: *The Aquacharm* [1982] 1 Lloyd's Rep 7, at p 9; *The Roachbank* [1987] 2 Lloyd's Rep 498, at p 507.

The Mareva AS is also cited for the proposition that the qualifying condition 'preventing the full working of the vessel' is not met if 'the vessel in herself remains fully efficient in all respects'.

Ten years later, by time of *The Roachbank*, this had become:

> a judicial gloss ... so that the question which has to be asked, according to the authorities, is whether the vessel is fully efficient and capable in herself of performing the service immediately required by the charterers ...

Nevertheless, this judicial gloss has caused problems in cases where the cause of delay is the interference of authorities operating on a vessel which is herself fully efficient. Four cases in particular illustrate this problem. In *The Apollo* [1978] 1 Lloyd's Rep 200 the vessel was denied free pratique and thus prevented from berthing and discharging while the suspicion of typhus in two of her crew members was investigated and, as it turned out, eliminated. In *The Aquacharm* [1980] 2 Lloyd's Rep 237, Lloyd J, [1982] 1 Lloyd's Rep 7, CA, the vessel was delayed by the authorities at the entrance to the Panama Canal until she had lightened part of her cargo. In *The Mastro Giorgis* [1983] 2 Lloyd's Rep 66 the vessel was arrested by receivers as a result of alleged cargo damage on the voyage. In *The Roachbank* the vessel was delayed in being permitted to enter port because of the presence on board her of 293 Vietnamese refugees. In the first and third of those cases the vessel was held to be off-hire, in the second and fourth on hire. The word 'whatsoever' lies on both sides of that divide for, although it was absent in *The Aquacharm*, it was present in the other cases ...

The authorities

... I would ... observe at the outset of my discussion of those authorities that there appear to be two interrelated concepts which run here and there through them. One is that the typical off-hire clause does not cover an 'extraneous' cause, by which is, I think, meant a cause extraneous to the vessel itself. This concept I suppose relates to the meaning or possible width of meanings of 'cause' in the expression 'any other cause' or 'any other cause whatsoever'. The other concept is that a vessel cannot be off-hire unless there is some defect or incapacity of or in the vessel itself which affects her working. This concept relates of course to the phrase 'preventing the full working of the vessel'.

Both concepts may be said to go back to what in a sense is for these purposes the leading case of *Court Line Limited v Dant and Russell Incorporated* (1939) 44 Com Cas 345. That concerned a vessel, the *Errington Court*, which got caught by a boom placed in the Yangtze River by Chinese forces. For a leading case the relevant part of the judgment is brief. At pp 352–53 Branson J merely opined that the words 'any other cause preventing the full working of the vessel':

> are not apt to cover a case where the ship is in every way sound and well found, but is prevented from continuing her voyage by such a cause as this.

... The concept of an extraneous cause was not ... in issue in *The Mareva AS*, nor was that expression used in the *Court Line* case. But in *The Apollo* counsel for shipowners based a submission upon *Court Line* and *The Mareva AS* to the effect that:

> the off-hire clause applied to matters internal to the ship and her crew and not to external interferences or delays (at p 205).

However, Mocatta J rejected that submission. He said (*ibid*):

> I find it very difficult to lay down criteria of this kind. For example if a surveyor from a classification society required tests to be made to the machinery, would the delay consequent upon this bring the off-hire clause into play?

So far the concept of extraneous or external cause had not perhaps got very far: but in *The Aquacharm* [1980] 2 Lloyd's Rep 237 at p 240 Lloyd J relied expressly on *Court Line* to eliminate 'some external cause, such as the boom' as a possible off-hire cause at any rate when the vessel remained 'fully efficient in herself'. Those decisions were in turn relied on by the Court of Appeal in *Harmony Shipping Co SA v Saudi-Europe Line Ltd, The Good Helmsman* [1981] 1 Lloyd's Rep 377 at p 422.

Then in *The Mastro Giorgis* Lloyd J held that a distinction should be made, in deciding whether a cause prevents the full working of a vessel:

> between causes which are totally extraneous, such as the boom in *Court Line Ltd v Dant & Russell Inc*, and causes which are attributable to the condition of the ship itself, such as engine breakdown (at p 69).

Lloyd J then went on to decide that a vessel's susceptibility to arrest by reason of an allegation of cargo damage was sufficient to prevent the arrest itself being totally extraneous ...

... It follows that in *The Mastro Giorgis* Lloyd J was not giving to the words 'preventing the full working of the vessel' a meaning that required the vessel to be inefficient in herself. Her full working was only prevented inasmuch as she was under arrest ...

... *The Mastro Giorgis* is therefore a decision to the effect that a vessel's inability to perform the service immediately required of her by reason of the interference of authorities fulfils the requirements of the words 'preventing the full working of the vessel', at any rate if the authorities' interference is not totally extraneous. A vessel may of course be susceptible to the interference of authorities for a whole variety of reasons: the arrest jurisdiction is one such reason, but in truth any vessel visiting a port becomes immediately subject to the law of the country in which the port is situated and to the requirements and directives of the local authorities.

The off-hire clause in *The Mastro Giorgis* contained the word 'whatsoever'. That meant, said Lloyd J at p 92, that any cause may suffice to put the vessel off-hire, whether physical or legal. Lloyd J's reasoning thereafter appears to be concerned with the qualification of 'preventing the full working of the vessel'. The effect of his reasoning, however, appears to be that under a 'whatsoever' clause outside interference which prevents the vessel performing her service, provided that it is not 'totally extraneous', will put the vessel off-hire.

I would comment that, if Lloyd J was wrong in his conclusion that an efficient vessel may be prevented from working by the action of the authorities, then it would be odd if the addition of the word 'whatsoever' could make any difference. If a vessel efficient in herself cannot be within the words 'preventing the full working of the vessel', then it does not seem to me that the nature of the cause which operates on such a vessel can alter the fact that the vessel is efficient in herself. In such a case, widening the ambit of 'cause' by adding the word 'whatsoever' ought not in logic to affect the position.

In *The Roachbank*, however, Lloyd J's conclusion in *The Mastro Giorgis* was not applied. In that case the vessel was prevented for a while from entering port by the authorities because of the presence on board of Vietnamese refugees who had been rescued in pitiful condition at sea during the vessel's voyage. The off-hire clause contained the word 'whatsoever' ... Webster J felt required by previous authorities to place upon the words 'preventing the full working of the vessel' a judicial gloss:

> so that the question which has to be asked, according to the authorities, is whether the vessel is fully efficient and capable in herself of performing the service immediately required by the charterers (at p 507).

In the circumstances it was inevitable that he should uphold the award, for he was bound by the arbitrators' finding on that question. Equally, it would be irrelevant for him that the vessel could not work in the different sense that she was prevented from entering port and discharging by the action of the port authorities. In the circumstances, having been asked by counsel (see at p 502) to differ from the conclusions of Lloyd J in *The Mastro Giorgis,* he expressed his diffident disagreement with that decision in these terms (at p 507):

> ... for two reasons; first, because it seems to me to give undue emphasis to the cause of the prevention of the full working, as distinct from the fact that full working is prevented; and, secondly because, for the reasons that I have already expressed, in the case of an amended clause in my view it is probably unnecessary to consider the nature of the cause at all, something which Lloyd J himself acknowledged in the way in which he stated his second reason: 'any cause may suffice'. Moreover, for my own part, I do not think it either necessary or helpful to attempt to categorise causes with a view to distinguishing between totally extraneous and other causes.

I feel bound to say, however, with equal diffidence, that in my judgment the real point of difference between Lloyd J and Webster J (and perhaps both of them, reading this, would disagree with me) was that Lloyd J was willing to say that a vessel wholly efficient in herself might nevertheless, under certain circumstances, come within the words 'preventing the full working of the vessel', whereas Webster J was of the view, based upon his reading of the authorities, that such a reading was not possible where the vessel was fully efficient and capable in herself ...

So, as it seems to me, the critical question may well be whether Webster J was right to say that a judicial gloss had been put upon the phrase so as to require, for a vessel to be off-hire, that she should not be efficient in herself to perform the next service required. The authorities considered by Webster J were *Court Line*, *The Mareva AS*, *The Apollo*, and *The Aquacharm*.

I have already considered *Court Line* and *The Mareva AS*. In my opinion there is nothing in those cases to require the judicial gloss which Webster J found to exist. *Court Line* differed perhaps from all other cases in that the boom there was a totally extraneous matter – I know of no other way in which to point up that idiosyncrasy. Although it was man-made, it was akin to a geographical impediment. A vessel is not off-hire just because she cannot proceed upon her voyage because of some physical impediment, like a sand bar, or insufficiency of water, blocking her path. While remarking that the vessel was 'in every way sound and well found' Branson J ultimately founded his reasoning, it seems to me, on the fact that 'such a cause as this' was not within the clause. As for *The Mareva AS*, I have already made the point that that case was not concerned at all with the interference of authorities. The language of a vessel's inherent efficiency is there found, but in circumstances where there was no interference with the vessel's service, and the distinction that had to be made was between the efficiency of the vessel herself and the increased time involved in the discharge of a damaged cargo. In such circumstances it comes as no surprise that Kerr J used the language which he did, nor that he found that the cargo damage had not prevented the full working of the vessel. The vessel, after all, was working fully.

Similarly I do not think that *The Apollo* supports the judicial gloss determined by Webster J, nor did he found any reliance on it. On the contrary, Mocatta J said (at 205):

> In my judgment the action taken by the port health authorities did prevent the full working of the vessel and did bring the off-hire clause into play.

It seems to me that in saying this Mocatta J was recognising that a vessel could be prevented from working by an outside bar on her working. That is not consistent with glossing the critical phrase as requiring some failure of the vessel's efficiency in herself. Of course I bear in mind that in that case there was suspected typhus of the crew.

The last case considered by Webster J was *The Aquacharm*. It was Lloyd J himself who, at first instance, introduced the judicial test of whether:

> the vessel is fully efficient in herself, that is to say, whether she is fully capable of performing the service immediately required of her (at p 240).

I would comment in passing first that the test of 'fully efficient in herself' is not necessarily the same as the test of 'fully capable of performing the service immediately required of her' as Lloyd J was himself to recognise in *The Mastro Giorgis*; and secondly, that on the facts of that case, once the vessel had to be lightened to transit the Panama Canal, there could have been no difference between the service required by the charterers and that required by the canal authorities, *viz*, the lightening of the vessel.

In the Court of Appeal in *The Aquacharm*, Lord Denning MR did not adopt the gloss of 'fully efficient in herself'. He merely said (at 9):

> I do not think the lightening of the vessel does 'prevent the full working of the vessel'. Often enough cargo has to be unloaded into a lighter – for one reason or another – to get her off a sandbank – or into a basin. The vessel is still working fully, but she is delayed by the need to unload part of the cargo.

Griffiths LJ did, however, adopt the judicial gloss. For instance he said (at p 11):

> *Aquacharm* remained at all times in herself fully efficient in all respects. She could not pass through the canal because the canal authorities decided she was carrying too much cargo, but that decision [in] no way reflected upon the *Aquacharm*'s efficiency as a ship. By contrast, in *The Apollo* ... A ship suspected of carrying typhus is prevented from working fully until it is cleared, for no responsible person would use it in such a condition. The incapacity of the ship to work in such a case is directly attributable to the suspected condition of the ship itself ...

Shaw LJ said that he agreed entirely with the judgments of Lord Denning and of Lloyd J and would dismiss the appeal for the reasons stated in the judgment of Lord Denning (at p 12).

The judgment of Griffiths LJ and his explanation of *The Apollo* have been influential; but the reasoning of the majority in the Court of Appeal is that contained in the judgment of Lord Denning, and that in my view does not support, and a fortiori does not require, the judicial gloss found by Webster J. Of course, *The Aquacharm* was fully efficient in herself, that was one of the facts of the case. Equally, it was a fact of the case that the vessel was fully working when she was waiting to lighten and actually lightening. That, however, may be contrasted with the situation in *The Apollo*, where the vessel was not working at all during the period when free pratique was refused; and could also be contrasted perhaps with a hypothetical situation where the Panama Canal authorities perversely refused entrance to the canal on grounds of draught, even though the vessel plainly was not overladen, a problem with which the Court of Appeal did not have to contend ...

In these circumstances I would for my part respectfully differ from Webster J's conclusion that he was bound by authority to impose the judicial gloss he adopted upon the phrase 'preventing the full working of the vessel'. I would prefer myself to accept that it could be legitimate to find that the full working of a vessel had been prevented by the action of authorities in preventing her working ...

Two further decisions cited to me but not mentioned by Webster J are *The Manhattan Prince* [1985] 1 Lloyd's Rep 140 and *The Bridgestone Maru No 3* [1985] 2 Lloyd's Rep 62. It may be that they were not cited to Webster J, or if cited not mentioned in his judgment, because they are both decisions on the Shelltime 3 clause with its slightly different language 'preventing the *efficient* working of the vessel' (emphasis added). The efficiency of the vessel is mentioned twice in the clause, thus:

> In the event of loss of time ... due to deficiency of ... or any other cause preventing the efficient working of the vessel ... hire shall cease to be payable from the commencement of such loss of time until the vessel is again ready and in an efficient state to resume her service ...

In *The Manhattan Prince* the vessel was arrested by the ITF on the ground that her owners were in breach of their agreement with the ITF to employ crew in accordance with ITF rates for worldwide trading. Leggatt J considered the authorities down to *The Maestro Giorgis* and held that the vessel remained on hire. He said (at p 146):

It is plain that what the charterers have to show is that the efficient working of the vessel was indeed prevented by the ITF. One starts then by asking: What is the natural meaning of the words in that context? One may take account of the *ejusdem generis* principle in the sense that the causes of loss of time which are specified may indeed throw light upon the proper meaning to be ascribed to the phrase 'efficient working of the vessel'.

It seems to me that the true interpretation of the phrase in its context demands that it should apply, and apply only, to the physical condition of the vessel, with the result that, as Mr Phillips contends, the phrase 'efficient working' must enjoy the connotation of efficient physical working. In my judgment the vessel worked, even though she was prevented from working in the way the charterers would have wished by the action of the ITF. She was indeed fully operational and as such was not within the scope of the off-hire clause.

In *The Bridgestone Maru No 3* it will be recalled that the vessel was unable to remain and discharge at Livorno because her booster pump was not a fixed installation as required by local RINA regulations. She was nevertheless in every way an efficient vessel. Hirst J considered the same authorities and held that the vessel was off-hire on the ground that the delay was attributable to the suspected condition of the ship ...

I find nothing in these two cases, or in their examination of the NYPE authorities, to alter the view I have formed of those authorities. On the contrary, it seems to me that the Shelltime 3's emphasis upon the efficiency of the vessel is a real difference from the language of the NYPE, fully justifying Leggatt J's conclusion that the former's off-hire clause applies only to the physical condition of the vessel or at any rate to her efficiency as a vessel (including, I would readily accept, her suspected efficiency). It seems to me that Leggatt J pointed up the difference in the language of the two forms when he said:

> the vessel worked, even though she was prevented from working in the way the charterers would have wished ...

In my judgment therefore, the qualifying phrase 'preventing the full working of the vessel' does not require the vessel to be inefficient in herself. A vessel's working may be prevented by legal as well as physical means, and by outside as well as internal causes. An otherwise totally efficient ship may be prevented from working. That is the natural meaning of those words, and I do not think that there is any authority binding on me that prevents me from saying so. The question remains, of course, whether a ship has been prevented from working by a cause within the clause. Moreover, it will generally be relevant to find whether the ship is efficient in herself: either, as in *The Mareva AS*, because, even on the assumption of the operation of a named cause, it may be relevant to point out that the vessel's working had not been prevented; or, as in *Court Line*, because, in considering whether an alleged cause of off-hire is a cause within the clause, it may be very pertinent to point out that the vessel was otherwise efficient in herself.

Those comments bring me back to consider the phrase 'any other cause' in the light of the authorities. In my judgment it is well established that those words, in the absence of 'whatsoever', should be construed either *ejusdem generis* or at any rate in some limited way reflecting the general context of the charter and clause: see *The Apollo* at p 205, *The Aquacharm* at p 239 (Lloyd J), *The Maestro Giorgis* at p 68, *The Manhattan Prince* at p 146, *The Roachbank* at p 507. A consideration of the named causes indicates that they all relate to the physical condition or efficiency of either vessel (including its crew) or, in one instance, cargo. There is, moreover, the general context, emphasised for instance by Kerr J in *The Mareva AS* (at p 382), that it is for the owners to provide an efficient ship and crew. In such circumstances it is to my mind natural to conclude that the unamended words 'any other cause' do not cover an entirely extraneous cause, like the boom in *Court Line*, or the interference of authorities unjustified by the condition (or reasonably suspected condition) of ship or cargo. Prima facie it does not seem to me that it can be intended by a standard off-hire clause that an owner takes the risk of delay due to the interference of authorities, at any rate where that interference is something beyond the natural or reasonably foreseeable consequence of some named cause. Where, however, the clause is amended to include the word 'whatsoever', I do not see why the interference of authorities which prevents the vessel performing its intended service should not be regarded as falling within the clause, and I would be inclined to say that remains so whether or not that interference can be related to some underlying cause internal to the ship, or is merely capricious. That last thought may be controversial, but it seems to me that if an owner wishes to limit the scope of causes of off-hire under a clause which is deliberately amended to include the word 'whatsoever', then he should be cautious to do so.

The decision

It follows in my judgment that, although I would for my part accept Mr Kendrick's submission that the full working of a vessel may be prevented for legal as well as physical reasons, this appeal must nevertheless fail. In the absence of the word 'whatsoever', the unexpected and unforeseeable interference by the authorities at Chittagong at the conclusion of what was found to be a normal discharge was a totally extraneous cause, (save in a 'but for' sense) unconnected with, because too remote from, the merely background circumstance of the cargo residues of 15.75 tonnes. There was no accident to cargo, and there was nothing about the vessel herself, her condition or efficiency, nor even anything about the cargo, which led naturally or in the normal course of events to any delay. If the authorities had not prevented the vessel from working, she would have been perfectly capable of discharging the residues or of sailing and dumping them without any abnormal delay. In such circumstances I reject Mr Kendrick's submission that the action of the authorities was in any sense *ejusdem generis* any of the named causes within the clause. There is no finding that they suspected an average accident to cargo, or, to pick up the award's reference to a certificate for non-radioactivity, that there was any suspected problem in regard to radioactive contamination. I would be extremely doubtful in any event that a capricious suspicion could bring their action within the clause. As it is we do not know why on this occasion the authorities delayed the vessel for so long, other than the arbitrators' finding that their procedures were remarkably bureaucratic.

Having decided the issue before me, I should perhaps go no further. But out of deference to the submissions made to me, I would venture the following thoughts, but emphasising their *obiter* nature.

I would suggest that if the clause had been amended to contain the word 'whatsoever', then the position would probably have been otherwise. The vessel would have been prevented from working, albeit in unexpected circumstances. The cause would not have been ejusdem generis, but with the addition of the word 'whatsoever' would not have to be. It would not seem to me to matter that the authorities' actions may have been capricious.

The authorities suggest, moreover, that where the authorities act properly or reasonably pursuant to the (suspected) inefficiency or incapacity of the vessel, any time lost may well be off-hire even in the absence of the word 'whatsoever'. Thus in *The Apollo* (albeit the presence of 'whatsoever' may have facilitated the decision) Mocatta J stressed that there was good cause for the careful testing and disinfection that was carried out before free pratique was granted (at p 205); and Griffiths LJ pointed out (in *The Aquacharm* at p 11) that no responsible person would use a ship suspected of carrying typhus. Moreover in *The Bridgestone Maru No 3* Hirst J held that the vessel was off-hire even in the absence of the word 'whatsoever' on the basis that the regulations had been properly applied and that the failure of the pump to comply with the regulations was a potential (sc and reasonable) challenge to the efficiency of the ship herself.

Finally, suppose time lost due to the detention of a vessel by, the authorities arising out of the discovery of contraband on board her, an example debated before me. In such a case the position may well depend on who was responsible for the presence of the contraband. If the owners (or their crew) were responsible, the vessel might well be off-hire, particularly under an amended clause, but even perhaps in the absence of amendment. If, however, the charterers were responsible, it would seem to be absurd to hold the vessel off-hire: how would that square under an amended clause with my construction, seeing that the detention by the authorities under my construction would be 'any other cause whatsoever preventing the full working of the vessel'? It seems to me that there would be an implicit exclusion of causes for which the charterers were responsible.

Considerations such as these indicate that there will always be difficult decisions to make in borderline cases or unusual combinations of circumstances. In many if not most cases the ultimate decision will depend on findings of fact or mixed fact and law made by the arbitrators, which could not be easily, if at all, faulted. So in the present case, even upon the construction of the words 'preventing the full working of the vessel' which I have preferred, and even after taking into account the charterers' shift of position, it seems to me that ultimately my decision is concluded for me by the arbitrators' findings.

Notes

1   In the absence of a breach of contract by the owner, if the natural result of following charterers' orders is that it is necessary for a ship to spend time bunkering, ballasting, lightening or cleaning, the vessel will not go off-hire unless the contract so provides.

If the charterer orders the vessel to load coal on one voyage and sugar in bulk on the next, he can hardly expect the necessary cleaning to be done in the owner's time.

Time spent on those activities is, in the ordinary way, to be paid for in hire. The charterer has acquired the services of the vessel, and has the right to determine what cargoes she shall carry on what voyages. If, as a result of his orders, any of those measures become necessary, hire must be paid for the time so spent ...

Staughton LJ, *The Berg Sund* [1993] 2 Lloyd's Rep 453, 460.

2   The *Trident Beauty* was subchartered for a single time chartered trip, with hire payable in advance in respect of each period of 15 days. The disponent owners assigned the right to receive hire to the defendants and charterers then made one payment of semi-monthly hire to them. At about the end of that hire period, the vessel was withdrawn by head owners, the ship having in fact been off-hire for the whole of the last hire period under the subcharter. Disponent owners were unable to make a repayment for the period when the vessel was off-hire. The charterers sought to recover the last instalment of hire from the assignees. It was held that the charterers had no right to repayment from the assignees in contract and that there was no basis for the charterers to recover in restitution on the grounds of a total failure of consideration.

Pan Ocean Shipping Co Ltd v Creditcorp Ltd, The Trident Beauty [1994] 1 Lloyd's Rep 365, House of Lords.

CHAPTER 16

TIME CHARTERS II

1 HIRE AND WITHDRAWAL

Tankexpress A/S v Compagnie Financière Belge des Petroles SA, The Petrofina [1949] AC 76

Lord Porter: My Lords, the case for the appellants can be put in the simplest possible terms. The charterparty, they say, requires payment on a specific date, which, in the events which happened, is the twenty-seventh of each month, with the right of withdrawal of the ship if payment is not made on that date: the respondents failed to pay on the due date, and consequently the ship was rightly withdrawn. It matters not that the respondents carried out their part in the way usually adopted: their duty was to pay in London on the due date, and they have not done so.

The respondents ... say, first, that the right of withdrawal only arises if they are in default, and, having paid in the usual and recognised way, they are not in default, though in fact their cheque did not reach Hambro's Bank on the twenty-seventh of the month ...

... I think that the respondents are entitled to succeed in their first contention. This result must follow, if it is to follow at all, from the findings of the arbitrator. He states them in cls 5, 7 and 9 of the award. He says in cl 5 that the charterers dispatched their cheque to Hambro's Bank in London from Brussels on 25 September and on the same day wrote to the owners at Oslo and their brokers in Paris of the dispatch of the cheque. All this, as he finds, was in accordance with the procedure which had previously been adopted; the delay in delivery in London resulted from the outbreak of war. In cl 7 he sets out the practice between owner and charterers during the currency of the charter under which hire was paid on the twenty-seventh of each month, but from the gross sum was deducted any reduction for time off-hire during the previous month. Clause 9 sets out the method accepted by both parties for payment of hire, which was effected by sending a cheque in favour of Hambro's Bank to be placed by them to the credit of the owners. The arbitrator adds 'the payment of hire had been regularly and properly paid in this way during the currency of the charter and had always been paid on its due date until this payment ...' The last part of this sentence I take to mean that the cheque had always hitherto been received in London on the twenty-seventh of each month. In a contract between charterers and shipowners when the former are in Brussels, the latter in Oslo and their brokers in Paris, and when the contract stipulates for payment in cash in London, obviously some further terms are required to regulate its performance. Admittedly Hambro's Bank was nominated as the place of payment, a cheque drawn on a foreign bank substituted for cash, and receipt by post accepted at any rate when the letter arrived by or before the twenty-seventh of the month, the twenty-fifth being apparently the accepted day for posting. In these circumstances I think the true inference to be drawn is that the method of performance of the contract was varied by an arrangement for payment to Hambro's Bank by cheque posted at such time as would in the ordinary course of post reach London on the twenty-seventh of the month. 'Regularly and properly' are the words used by the arbitrator, and 'properly', I think, means in accordance with the accepted practice. No doubt the appellants could at any time have insisted upon a strict performance of the contract after due notice, but they were not, in my view, entitled suddenly to vary the accepted method of performance without first notifying the respondents in time to enable them to perform the contract in strict conformity with the terms of the charterparty. I think, therefore, that payment was duly made in accordance with the practice adopted and accepted between the parties and in the way and at the time stipulated ...

[Lord Wright, Lord Uthwatt, Lord Du Parcq and Lord Morton all delivered reasoned judgments in favour of dismissing the appeal.]

Mardorf Peach & Co Ltd v Attica Sea Carriers Corp of Liberia, The Laconia [1977] AC 850

Lord Wilberforce: My Lords, the appellants are the owners of the ship *Laconia* which they chartered, in January 1970, to the respondents on a time charter for three months 15 days more or less in charterers' option. The charterparty, on a New York Produce Exchange form, provided that the hire was to be paid in cash in US currency semi-monthly in advance:

> to the owners ... into their account with First National City Bank of New York, 34, Moorgate, London, EC2 to the credit of OFC Account No 705586.

and that 'failing the punctual and regular payment of the hire' the owners should be at liberty to withdraw the vessel.

The seventh and final instalment became due on Sunday, 12 April 1970. It was conceded by the charterers, and this case has been conducted on the footing, that, as London banks are closed on Sunday and Saturday, the due date for payment of this instalment was Friday, 10 April 1970. It was not paid on that day but was tendered or paid to the owners' bank (this will be discussed later), about 3 pm on Monday, 13 April 1970. At 6.55 pm on the same day the owners withdrew the vessel. The question is whether they had the right to do so ...

The result of this appeal turns, in my opinion, upon the answer to two and only two questions. First, what is the meaning of the withdrawal clause. Second, whether the owners have waived the default of the charterers in not making punctual payment ...

The clause which regulates the payment of hire and the right to withdraw is, in full, as follows:

> 5. Payment of said hire to be made in New York in cash in United States currency, semi-monthly in advance, and for the last half month or part of same the approximate amount of hire, and should same not cover the actual time, hire is to be paid for the balance day by day, as it becomes due, if so required by owners, unless bank guarantee or deposit is made by the charterers, otherwise failing the punctual and regular payment of the hire, or bank guarantee, or on any breach of this charterparty, the owners shall

be at liberty to withdraw the vessel from the service of the charterers, without prejudice to any claim they (the owners) may otherwise have on the charterers.

The provision as to payment was altered by a typed addendum (clause 52) which produced the results I have previously stated.

My Lords, I cannot find any difficulty or ambiguity in this clause. It must mean that once a punctual payment of any instalment has not been made, a right of withdrawal accrues to the owners. Conversely, it is incapable of meaning that a charterer who has failed to make a punctual payment, can (unless the owners have waived the default) avoid the consequences of his failure by later tendering an unpunctual payment. He would still have failed to make a punctual payment, and it is on this failure and by reason of it that the owners get the right to withdraw ...

This leaves the second question, which is whether the right of withdrawal was waived by the owners. The submission of the charterers was that on Monday, 13 April 1970, before the owners purported to withdraw the ship, they accepted the charterers' late payment of the instalment and so affirmed the contract. The arbitrators found that there had not been any waiver, so that the charterers must undertake the task of showing that, upon the facts found, the only possible conclusion must have been there had.

In order to understand the argument, it is necessary to go into the facts in some detail. At about 3 pm, at which time London banks closed for the day, a messenger from the Midland Bank, acting for the charterers, delivered to the owners' bank, the First National City Bank, 34, Moorgate, London (FNCB), a 'payment order' for the amount of the seventh instalment. A payment order is a document issued by one bank to another under a scheme (LCSS) by which banks maintain dollar suspense accounts in which they credit or debit each other with sums in dollars and make periodical settlements. As between banks, a payment order is the equivalent of cash, but a customer cannot draw upon it. The amount must first be credited to his account, but he can, of course, make special arrangements for earlier drawing. At about 3.10 or 3.15 pm the payment order was received and stamped in the sorting office of FNCB. It was then taken to the transfer department. There an official called an editor wrote on the face of the order the formula CR ADV & TT Lausanne, an instruction (to be carried out elsewhere in the bank) meaning 'credit advice and telegraphic transfer Lausanne'. Not perhaps quite simultaneously, but at about the same time, another official telephoned to the owners' agents and said that the bank had received a payment order for the amount of the hire: this was in accordance with instructions received by the bank earlier in the day from the owners' agents. This official was immediately told to refuse the money and to return it. Thereupon the editor deleted the annotation he had made on the payment order and wrote on it: 'Beneficiary has refused payment. Advise remitter by phone'. There was no direct evidence that this was done but such may be presumed. The next day FNCB sent to the Midland Bank a payment order for the same amount as that which the Midland Bank had sent the previous day.

My Lords, much ingenuity and effort was used in order to show that this series of actions, or some part of it, constituted acceptance and waiver by the owners of the right to withdraw. But in my opinion it did not approach success. Although the word 'waiver', like 'estoppel', covers a variety of situations different in their legal nature, and tends to be indiscriminately used by the courts as a means of relieving parties from bargains or the consequences of bargains which are thought to be harsh or deserving of relief, in the present context what is relied on is clear enough. The charterers had failed to make a punctual payment but it was open to the owners to accept a late payment as if it were punctual, with the consequence that they could not thereafter rely on the default as entitling them to withdraw. All that is needed to establish waiver, in this sense, of the committed breach of contract, is evidence, clear and unequivocal, that such acceptance has taken place, or, after the late payment has been tendered, such a delay in refusing it as might reasonably cause the charterers to believe that it has been accepted.

My Lords, if this is, as I believe, what would have to be proved in order to establish a waiver in the situation under review, it must be obvious that the facts in the present case do not amount to it. Looked at untechnically, the facts were that the money was sent to the bank, taken into the banking process or machinery, put in course of transmission to the owners, but rejected by the latter as soon as they were informed of its arrival and as soon as they were called upon, or able, to define their position. Put more technically, the bank, though agents of the owners, had a limited authority. It is not necessary to decide whether, in general, and in the absence of specific instructions, bankers in such situations as these have authority to accept late payments ... here it is clear that the bankers had no such authority and still less any authority to make business decisions as to the continuance or otherwise of the charterparty but that *per contra* they had express instructions to refer the matter to the owners' agents. On this basis they receive the order (they clearly had no right to reject it out of hand), and, while provisionally starting to process it into the owners' possession, at the same time seek the owners' directions in accordance with the owners' previous instructions. On those directions, they arrest the process and return the money. The acts of the editors – the annotation on the payment order – were internal acts (Brandon J, of a similar situation in *The Brimnes* [1973] 1 WLR 386, 411 called them 'ministerial', ie acts done without any intention or capacity to affect legal relations with third parties), not irrevocable, but provisional and reversible acts, consistent with an alternative decision of the customer which might be to accept or reject. The customer chose to reject, he did so as rapidly as the circumstances permitted, and he could have given no ground to the charterer for supposing that the payment had been accepted. The charterer did not act upon any such supposition.

The pattern of action is to me so clear that I do not find it necessary to decide the rather technical question whether, as regards the owners, there was payment 'in cash' as required by the charterparty, or not. Whatever it was it was not punctual payment, and not accepted in waiver of the unpunctuality. I think then that there is no basis on which the arbitrators' finding against waiver can be attacked.

The result of my conclusions on these two points leaves the matter as follows:

1 Under the withdrawal clause, as under similar clauses, including the Baltime clause properly interpreted, a right of withdrawal arises as soon as

default is made in punctual payment of an instalment of hire. Whether or not this rule is subject to qualification in a case of punctual but insufficient payment as some authorities appear to hold, is not an issue which now arises and I express no opinion upon it.

2   The owners must within a reasonable time after the default give notice of withdrawal to the charterers. What is a reasonable time – essentially a matter for arbitrators to find – depends on the circumstances. In some, indeed many cases, it will be a short time – *viz*, the shortest time reasonably necessary to enable the shipowner to hear of the default and issue instructions. If, of course, the charterparty contains an express provision regarding notice to the charterers, that provision must be applied.

3   The owners may be held to have waived the default, *inter alia*, if when a late payment is tendered, they choose to accept it as if it were timeous, or if they do not within a reasonable time give notice that they have rejected it ...

Lord Simon agreed with Lord Wilberforce. Lord Salmon, Lord Fraser and Lord Russell also delivered full reasoned judgments.

Afovos Shipping Co SA v Pagnan, The Afovos [1983] 1 WLR 195

Lord Hailsham LC: My Lords, on 18 June 1979, in circumstances hereafter to be described, the appellants as shipowners purported to withdraw the ship *Afovos* from a time charter dated 8 February 1978 on the New York Produce Exchange form by which she was let to the respondents as charterers for two years three months more or less at charterers' option from delivery date on 14 February 1978. The purported ground was a right of withdrawal conferred by a clause in the charter. The formal question in this appeal is whether the owners were entitled so to act, and whether their action was effective to achieve its purpose.

The commercial reality is, as happens not seldom, somewhat different. By a without prejudice agreement the ship remained on charter to the respondents for the rest of the charter period. The real question in dispute is whether the hire is to be at the original rate of US $1.975 per ton or an enhanced rate reflecting the market at the time of the purported withdrawal. The difference is about US $2.5m.

The result of the appeal depends on the construction of two clauses in the charter and the effect to be given to the purported notice of withdrawal. It will be convenient to deal first with the terms of the two clauses to be construed, and then to recite the facts, of which the purported notice of withdrawal was one.

The arrangements for payment and the right of withdrawal were contained in cl 5 of the charter which provided as follows:

Payment of said hire to be made in London, to the First National Bank of Chicago ... for the credit of Angelicoussis Shipholding Group Limited ... in cash in United States Currency, semi-monthly in advance ... otherwise failing the punctual and regular payment of the hire ... the Owners shall be at liberty to withdraw the vessel from the service of the Charterers ...

This is the first of the two clauses which falls to be construed. The severity of the right of the withdrawal contained in the last phrase was mitigated by an 'anti-technicality clause' contained in cl 31 of the charter.

This anti-technicality clause was in the following terms:

> When hire is due and not received the Owners, before exercising the option of withdrawing the vessel from the CharterParty, will give Charterers 48 hours notice, Saturdays, Sundays and Holidays excluded and will not withdraw the vessel if the hire is paid within these 48 hours.

This is the second clause to be construed.

In the events which happened, the hire was punctually paid up to and including 11 June 1979 when there occurred a chapter of accidents, for so only can it be described, which gave rise to the present dispute. On that date the charterers gave instructions in good time to their bankers, the Padua branch of the Credito Italiano, to pay the instalment then currently due for payment on or before 14 June 1979 in accordance with the charter to the London branch of the First National Bank of Chicago for the credit of Angelicoussis Shipholding Group Ltd. This the Padua bank purported to do by telex on 13 June. Both banks were in funds and were in account with one another. But for one unfortunate circumstance there was no reason why the transaction should not have been completed in due time.

The London branch of the Chicago bank had originally possessed three telex call numbers, the last two digits of which were respectively 16, 17 and 18. But that numbered 18 had been abandoned in 1975 and by 1979 had been allotted to a third party. Nevertheless, in the relevant directories for 1976, 1977 and 1978 the old call number had continued to be recorded under the name of the Chicago bank, and as at 14 June 1979 the Padua bank was using the 1978 edition. By a singular mischance the Padua branch tried first to connect with 16 and 17 and found, in the first case, that there was no reply and, in the second, that the number was engaged. The third time the Padua bank connected with the number 18 and there was a reply from the third party; and though the answering call was wrong the Padua bank transmitted the telex to the third party and the error was not discovered and corrected until 19 June, when the payment of the instalment was admittedly overdue.

In the meantime, on 14 June 1979, which was the last day for paying the instalment, the owners had purported to exercise their rights under cl 31. At 16.40 hrs (London time) on that day, which was a Thursday, they sent to the charterers through their London agents the following telex:

> Owners have instructed us that in case we do not receive the hire which is due today, to give charterers notice as per cl 31 of the charterparty for withdrawal of the vessel from their service.

The telex, we were told, was received five minutes later. Allowing for the intervening Saturday and Sunday, 48 hours from the receipt of this telex would have expired at 16.45 hrs on Monday, 18 June. At 19.20 hrs on that day the owners sent to the charterers a telex purporting to withdraw the vessel from their service.

This resulted in a dispute giving rise to the present proceedings ...

A number of questions arose for debate at one time or another. Only a small number of these were still alive by the time of the appeal before your Lordships, and, in my view, the case can be disposed of by considering only two, *viz*: (1) at what point of time on 14 June 1979, apart from the mitigation of cl 31, would the right of withdrawal have arisen under cl 5 of the charter? and (2) on the assumption that, at 16.40 or 16.45 hrs on 14 June 1979, the point of time indicated by the answer to the first question had not been reached, were the owners entitled to send a notice exercising their option under cl 31 in advance of that point of time?

... Of the two questions which must be decided, the second appears to me to be plain beyond argument. Both the grammatical meaning of cl 31 and the policy considerations underlying the contract require that the moment of time at which the 48 hours' notice must be given did not arise until after the moment of time at which, apart from the clause, the right of withdrawal would have accrued. I agree with the judgment of the Court of Appeal that both the expression 'due and received', and the reference to the right as an 'option', really only admit of this sense ... The notice can only be given 'when hire is due and not received', which cannot arise before the time postulated by the answer given to the first question (whatever that answer may be), and the notice can only be given when there is (or apart from cl 31 would be) already in existence, an 'option' capable of exercise of 'withdrawing the vessel from the CharterParty', and that option can only be exercised after the arrival of the same point of time ...

Quite obviously the clause was inserted in order to save the charterer, who may (as in this case) be quite innocent even of the knowledge that his payment had not been received, from the extremely onerous effects (in this case a cost of $2.5m) of cl 5, and equally obviously if the owners' arguments be accepted a premature notice would have the effect of allowing the shipowner to reduce the effective period of 48 hrs notice by anything up to 24 hours ...

In the result, I conclude that the crux of this case depends on the answer given to the first of the two questions I have posed. This was: at what point of time apart from the mitigation of cl 31 would the right of withdrawal under cl 5 of the charter have arisen? To put the question in the terms of cl 5: at what point of time can the charterers be said to have been 'failing the punctual and regular payment of the hire'? Since the punctual payment of only one instalment is in question, for the purpose of the present appeal one need only ask the question in the simpler form: what is the latest point of time on 14 June 1979 which would have constituted punctual payment of the instalment? To this question I believe that, in principle, only one answer is possible, namely at midnight on the last day available to them for the due and punctual payment of the hire, ie 14 June. I take it to be a general principle of law not requiring authority that where a person under an obligation to do a particular act has to do it on or before a particular date he has the whole of that day to perform his duty. No doubt as the hours pass it becomes less and less probable that he will be able to do it. That is the risk he runs. But he is not actually in default until the time arrives ...

Scandinavian Trading Tanker Co AB v Flota Petrolera Ecuatoriana, The Scaptrade [1983] 2 AC 694

Lord Keith, Lord Scarman, Lord Roskill and Lord Bridge agreed with Lord Diplock.

Lord Diplock: My Lords, in this appeal between the appellant ('the charterers') and the respondent ('the owners') of the tanker *Scaptrade*, your Lordships have heard argument upon one question only: 'Has the High Court any jurisdiction to grant relief against the exercise by a shipowner of his contractual right, under the withdrawal clause in a time charter, to withdraw the vessel from the service of the charterer upon the latter's failure to make payment of an instalment of the hire in the manner and at a time that is not later than that for which the withdrawal clause provides?'

... The time charter concerned was on the standard printed Shelltime 3 form with typed additions that are not material to the question that your Lordships have to decide. This form of charterparty is expressed to be governed by the law of England, and to be subject to the jurisdiction of the English court. The relevant wording of the payment of hire clause, which, as is usual in most standard forms of time charter, incorporated the withdrawal clause, was:

> Payment of the said hire shall be made in New York monthly in advance ... In default of such payment owners may withdraw the vessel from the service of charterers, without prejudice to any claim owners may otherwise have on charterers under this charter.

The charter had become by extension a three-year charter. In July 1979 when it had still a year to run the freight market was rising steeply. The charterers were unfortunate enough, through some slip up in their own office, to fail to pay on 8 July 1979, the instalment of hire due upon that date. Four days later, on 12 July the owners gave notice to the charterers withdrawing the vessel. Tender of the overdue hire was made on the following day but was refused. After negotiations had taken place, the vessel was rechartered by the owners to the charterers on a 'without prejudice' agreement of the usual kind, the rate of hire (ie charter rate or market rate) to abide the result of litigation, which in the event came before Lloyd J ...

A time charter, unless it is a charter by demise, with which your Lordships are not here concerned, transfers to the charterer no interest in or right to possession of the vessel; it is a contract for services to be rendered to the charterer by the shipowner through the use of the vessel by the shipowner's own servants, the master and the crew, acting in accordance with such directions as to the cargoes to be loaded and the voyages to be undertaken as by the terms of the charterparty the charterer is entitled to give to them. Being a contract for services it is thus the very prototype of a contract of which before the fusion of law and equity a court would never grant specific performance: *Clarke v Price* (1819) 2 Wils 157; *Lumley v Wagner* (1852) 1 De GM & G 604. In the event of failure to render the promised services, the party to whom they were to be rendered would be left to pursue such remedies in damages for breach of contract as he might have at law. But as an unbroken line of uniform authority in this House, from *Tankexpress* [1949] AC 76 to *The Chikuma* [1981] 1 WLR 314, has held, if the withdrawal clause so provides, the shipowner is entitled to withdraw the services of the vessel from the charterer if the latter fails to pay an instalment of hire in precise compliance with the provisions of the charter. So the shipowner commits no breach of contract if he does so; and the charterer has no remedy in damages against him.

To grant an injunction restraining the shipowner from exercising his right of withdrawal of the vessel from the service of the charterer, though negative in form, is pregnant with an affirmative order to the shipowner to perform the contract; juristically it is indistinguishable from a decree for specific performance of a contract to render services; and in respect of that category of contracts, even in the event of breach, this is a remedy that English courts have always disclaimed any jurisdiction to grant. This is, in my view, sufficient reason in itself to compel rejection of the suggestion that the equitable principle of relief from forfeiture is juristically capable of extension so as to grant to the court a discretion to prevent a shipowner from exercising his strict contractual rights under a withdrawal clause in a time charter which is not a charter by demise.

... All the analogies that ingenuity has suggested may be discovered between a withdrawal clause in a time charter and other classes of contractual provisions in which courts have relieved parties from the rigour of contractual terms into which they have entered can in my view be shown upon juristic analysis to be false. *Prima facie* parties to a commercial contract bargaining on equal terms can make 'time to be of the essence' of the performance of any primary obligation under the contract that they please, whether the obligation be to pay a sum of money or to do something else. When time is made of the essence of a primary obligation, failure to perform it punctually is a breach of a condition of the contract which entitles the party not in breach to elect to treat the breach as putting an end to all primary obligations under the contract that have not already been performed. In *Tankexpress A/S v Compagnie Financière Belge des Petroles SA* [1949] AC 76 this House held that time was of the essence of the very clause with which your Lordships are now concerned where it appeared in what was the then current predecessor of the Shelltime 3 charter. As is well known, there are available on the market a number of so-(mis)called 'anti-technicality clauses', such as that considered in *The Afovos*, which require the shipowner to give a specified period of notice to the charterer in order to make time of the essence of payment of advance hire; but at the expiry of such notice, provided it is validly given, time does become of the essence of the payment.

My Lords, quite apart from the juristic difficulties in the way of recognising a jurisdiction in the court to grant relief against the operation of a withdrawal clause in a time charter there are practical reasons of legal policy for declining to create any such new jurisdiction out of sympathy for charterers. The freight market is notoriously volatile. If it rises rapidly during the period of a time charter, the charterer is the beneficiary of the windfall which he can realise if he wants to by subchartering at the then market rates. What withdrawal of the vessel does is to transfer the benefit of the windfall from charterer to shipowner.

The practical objections to any extension to withdrawal clauses in time charters of an equitable jurisdiction to grant relief against their exercise are so convincingly expressed by Robert Goff LJ in the judgment of the Court of Appeal [1983] QB 529, 540–41 in the instant case that I can do no better than to incorporate them in my own speech for ease of reference:

Parties to such contracts should be capable of looking after themselves: at the very least, they are capable of taking advice, and the services of brokers are available, and are frequently used, when negotiating terms. The possibility that shipowners may snatch at the opportunity to withdraw ships from the service of time charterers for non-payment of hire must be very well known in the world of shipping: it must also be very well known that anti-technicality clauses are available which are effective to prevent any such occurrence. If a prospective time charterer wishes to have any such clause included in the charter, he can bargain for it. If he finds it necessary or desirable to agree to a charter which contains no such clause, he can warn the relevant section of his office, and his bank, of the importance of securing timeous payment. But the matter does not stop there. It is of the utmost importance in commercial transactions that, if any particular event occurs which may affect the parties' respective rights under a commercial contract, they should know where they stand. The court should so far as possible desist from placing obstacles in the way of either party ascertaining his legal position, if necessary with the aid of advice from a qualified lawyer, because it may be commercially desirable for action to be taken without delay, action which may be irrevocable and which may have far-reaching consequences. It is for this reason, of course, that the English courts have time and again asserted the need for certainty in commercial transactions – for the simple reason that the parties to such transactions are entitled to know where they stand, and to act accordingly. In particular, when a shipowner becomes entitled, under the terms of his contract, to withdraw a ship from the service of a time charterer, he may well wish to act swiftly and irrevocably. True, his problem may, in any particular case, prove to be capable of solution by entering into a without prejudice agreement with the original time charterer, under which the rate of hire payable in future will be made to depend upon a decision, by arbitrators or by a court, whether he was in law entitled to determine the charter. But this is not always possible. He may wish to refix his ship elsewhere as soon as possible, to take advantage of a favourable market. It is no answer to this difficulty that the ship may have cargo aboard at the time, so that her services cannot immediately be made available to another charterer ... For one thing, the ship may not have cargo on board, and for another she can be refixed immediately under a charter to commence at the end of her laden voyage. Nor is it an answer that the parties can immediately apply to arbitrators, or to a court, for a decision, and that both maritime arbitrators and the Commercial Court in this country are prepared to act very quickly at very short notice. For, quite apart from the fact that some delay is inherent in any legal process, if the question to be decided is whether the tribunal is to grant equitable relief, investigation of the relevant circumstances, and the collection of evidence for that purpose, cannot ordinarily be carried out in a very short period of time.

For all these reasons I would dismiss this appeal. I do so with the reminder that the reasoning in my speech has been directed exclusively to time charters that are not by demise. Identical considerations would not be applicable to bareboat charters and it would in my view be unwise for your Lordships to express any views about them.

Note

In *Antaios Compania Naviera SA v Salen Rederierna AB, The Antaios* [1985] AC 191, shipowners purported to withdraw the vessel on the grounds of the charterers' breach of an innominate term in the charterparty relating to the charterers' right to issue bills of lading on behalf of the master, arguing that this breach fell within the words 'any breach of this charterparty' in the NYPE withdrawal clause.

> **Lord Diplock**: ... The arbitrators decided this issue against the shipowners. The 78 pages in which they expressed their reasons for doing so contained an interesting, learned and detailed dissertation on the law, so lengthy as to be, in my view, inappropriate for inclusion in the reasons given by arbitrators for an award. Their reasons can be adequately summarised as being ... that 'any other breach of this charter party' in the withdrawal clause means a repudiatory breach – that is to say: a fundamental breach of an innominate term or breach of a term expressly stated to be a condition, such as would entitle the shipowners to elect to treat the contract as wrongfully repudiated by the charterers, a category into which in the arbitrators' opinion the breaches complained of did not fall ...
>
> To the semantic analysis, buttressed by generous citation of judicial authority, which led the arbitrators to the conclusions as to the interpretation of the wording of the withdrawal clause that I have summarised, the arbitrators' added an uncomplicated reason based simply upon business common sense:
>
> > We always return to the point that the owners' construction is wholly unreasonable, totally uncommercial and in total contradiction to the whole purpose of the NYPE time charter form. The owners relied on what they said was 'the literal meaning of the words in the clause'. We would say that if necessary, in a situation such as this, a purposive construction should be given to the clause so as not to defeat the commercial purpose of the contract.
>
> ... your Lordships would not be trespassing on the field of a discretion that a judge upon whom it was conferred had in fact exercised if you were to take this opportunity of stating ... that the arbitrators in the passage in their award that I have cited earlier were not obviously wrong but were obviously right in their decision on the 'repudiatory breach' question ...

2 HIRE AND SET OFF

Federal Commerce & Navigation Co Ltd v Molena Alpha Inc, The Nanfri [1978] QB 927, CA

> **Lord Denning MR**: ... On 1 September 1977, the monthly hire due on all three vessels together was $530,000. The charterers deducted $109,000 for various reasons of which they gave detailed justifications. On September 13, 1977, the owners agreed that these deductions were justified save for $38,000. So all was paid except $38,000 – that is about seven per cent.

The owners contested these deductions. They did so on the ground:

> the charterers were not entitled to make any deduction from hire by way of off-hire or set off (even if the same was in fact due to the charterers) unless prior to such deduction either the owners had accepted the validity thereof or it was supported by vouchers signed by the master or a proper tribunal had pronounced on its validity.

This contention was founded on the proposition that hire payable under a time charterparty is in the same position as freight payable under a voyage charterparty: and that under a settled rule of law freight is payable in full without deduction. Even if cargo is short-delivered, or delivered damaged, there can be no deduction on that account. Any cross-claim must be left to be decided later by the courts or by arbitration. That is well established now for 'freight' in such cases as *Henriksens Rederi A/S v T H Z Rolimpex (The Brede)* [1974] QB 233 and *Aries Tanker Corporation v Total Transport Ltd, The Aries* [1977] 1 WLR 185.

At one time it was common to describe the sums payable under a time charterparty as 'freight'. Such description is to be found used by judges and textbook writers of great distinction. But in modern times a change has come about. The payments due under a time charter are usually now described as 'hire' and those under a voyage charter as 'freight'. This change of language corresponds, I believe, to a recognition that the two things are different. 'Freight' is payable for carrying a quantity of cargo from one place to another. 'Hire' is payable for the right to use a vessel for a specified period of time, irrespective of whether the charterer chooses to use it for carrying cargo or lays it up, out of use. Every time charter contains clauses which are quite inappropriate to a voyage charter, such as the off-hire clause and the withdrawal clause. So different are the two concepts that I do not think the law as to 'freight' can be applied indiscriminately to 'hire'. In particular the special rule of English law whereby 'freight' must be paid in full (without deductions for short delivery or cargo damage) cannot be applied automatically to time charter 'hire'. Nor is there any authority which says that it must. It would be a mistake to suppose that the House of Lords had time charter hire and so forth in mind when they decided *The Aries* [1977] 1 WLR 185 or the *Nova (Jersey) Knit Ltd v Kammgarn Spinnerei GmbH* [1977] 1 WLR 713, or that anything said in those cases can bind this court. Many of us, I know, in the past have assumed that the rule as to 'freight' does apply: and some judges have said so. But now, after full argument, I am satisfied that the 'freight' rule does not apply automatically to 'time charter' hire: and we have to consider the position on principle.

Equitable set off in general

... one thing is quite clear: it is not every cross-claim which can be deducted. It is only cross-claims that arise out of the same transaction or are closely connected with it. And it is only cross-claims which go directly to impeach the plaintiff's demands, that is, so closely connected with his demands that it would be manifestly unjust to allow him to enforce payment without taking into account the cross-claim ...

Equitable set off in this case

So I turn to the problem here. A shipowner has contracted to give a charterer the right to use the vessel for a period of time – six years in fact. In return the charterer has agreed to pay a stated sum of hire monthly in advance. Then let us suppose that, after the charterer has paid his month's hire in advance, the shipowner wrongly declines to allow the charterer to have the use of the vessel for some days during the ensuing month. He may put the vessel perhaps to some more profitable use. He, by his conduct, deprives the charterer of part of the consideration for which the hire was paid. I should have thought it plain that the charterer should in fairness be able to recoup himself by making a deduction from the next month's hire -so as to compensate him for the loss of use for those days – equivalent to the hire of those lost days. Likewise if the shipowner has been guilty of some other wrongful conduct which has deprived the charterer of the use of the ship during some days – or prejudiced the charterer in the use of the ship – then the charterer should in fairness be able to recoup himself by making a deduction from the next month's hire. If the charterer quantifies his loss by a reasonable assessment made in good faith – and deducts the sum quantified – then he is not in default. The shipowner cannot withdraw his vessel on account of non-payment of hire nor hold him guilty at that point of any breach of contract. If it subsequently turns out that he has deducted too much, the shipowner can of course recover the balance. But that is all. This point of view is supported by a score of judges versed in commercial matters over the last 30 to 40 years ...

... I would hold that, when the shipowner is guilty of a breach of contract which deprives the time charterer of part of the consideration for which the hire has been paid in advance, the charterer can deduct an equivalent amount out of the hire falling due for the next month.

I would as at present advised limit the right to deduct to cases when the shipowner has wrongly deprived the charterer of the use of the vessel or has prejudiced him in the use of it. I would not extend it to other breaches or default of the shipowner, such as damage to cargo arising from the negligence of the crew ...

The special clauses

Thus far I have considered only cases where the shipowner has himself been guilty of a breach of contract in depriving the charterer of the use of the vessel. Now I come to cases where the shipowner has not been guilty of any breach of contract, or is protected by exceptions clauses. In such cases the charterer is often given a right of deduction by express clauses such as the off-hire clause or a clause allowing deductions for disbursements. There is no doubt that the charterer can make the deduction, but the question is when? Have they to be agreed or established before he can make the deduction? There is no authority that I know of to that effect. It seems to me that he is entitled to quantify his loss by a reasonable assessment made in good faith – and deduct the sum so quantified from the hire. Then the actual figures can be ascertained later: either by agreement between the parties: or, failing agreement, by arbitration. That was what the parties did in the present case for the first three years of the charters. The right to deduct would be useless to the charterer if he had to wait until a figure was agreed or established – for then it might be postponed indefinitely ...

Note

Shipowners let the *Aditya Vaibhav* to charterers on the Shelltime 3 form. The charterers alleged that a failure by the owners to clean the holds properly in breach of the charterparty had resulted in a delay to the vessel of 14 days when the vessel was not available for the service required and had caused them consequential loss and expense which they claimed to deduct from hire due to the owners. Saville J held that the maximum amount which could be deducted by the charterers, applying *The Nanfri*, was the amount of hire payable for the period during which the vessel was off-hire.

> What is needed is something so closely connected with the owners' claim for hire that it would offend justice to require the charterers to pay hire and then to pursue their own claims.

> To my mind that close connection exists in relation to a claim for hire which is in effect a claim in respect of a period during which the owners, in breach of the charter, have failed to provide the very thing for which that hire was payable ... However, in respect of other periods when the owners are providing that for which hire is payable, such manifest injustice does not appear. The reason for this is that a claim for hire in respect of such periods cannot be impeached by saying that the owners are in any sense asking to be paid for a service for which they have not provided. In other words, the cross-claim has no connection with the period when the vessel is at the service of the charterers other than that it arises out of the same transaction. This, however, only satisfies the first and not the second requirement for equitable set off. *Century Textiles and Industry Ltd v Tomoe Shipping Co (Singapore) Pte Ltd, The Aditya Vaibhav* [1991] 1 Lloyd's Rep 573.

3 DATE FOR REDELIVERY: THE LEGITIMATE FINAL VOYAGE

Alma Shipping Corp of Monrovia v Mantovani, The Dione [1975] 1 Lloyd's Rep 115, CA

Lord Denning MR: ... The point is really a short point of construction. What is the meaning of the words 'for a period of six months time charter 20 days more or less' ... I will first state some propositions which can be derived from the cases:

(a) *Implied margin or allowance*

When a charterparty is for a stated period – such as 'three months' or 'six months' – without any express margin or allowance, then the court will imply a reasonable margin or allowance. The reason is because it is not possible for anyone to calculate exactly the day on which the last voyage will end. It is legitimate for the charterer to send her on a last voyage which may exceed the stated period by a few days. If the vessel does exceed the stated period – and the market rate has gone up – nevertheless the charterer is only bound to pay the charter rate until she is actually redelivered, see *Gray and Co v Christie* (1889) 5 TLR 577: *Watson Steamship Co v Merryweather & Co* (1913) 18 Com Cas 294 at p 300 (without the handwritten words).

(b) *No margin or allowance express or implied*

But it is open to the parties to provide in the charterparty – by express words or by implication – that there is to be no margin or allowance. In such a case the charterer must ensure that the vessel is redelivered within the stated period. If he does not do so – and the market rate has gone up – he will be bound to pay the extra. That is to say, he will be bound to pay the charter rate up to the end of the stated period, and the market rate thereafter, see *Watson v Merryweather* (1913) 18 Com Cas 294 (with the handwritten words).

(c) *Express margin or allowance*

It is also, in my opinion, open to the parties themselves to fix expressly what the margin or allowance shall be. In that case the charterer must ensure that the vessel is redelivered within the permitted margin or allowance. If he does not do so – and the market rate has gone up – he will be bound to pay the extra. That is to say, he will be bound to pay the charter rate up to the end of the expressly permitted margin or allowance, and the market rate for any overlap thereafter ...

In view of those three propositions, when I speak of the 'charter period', I mean the stated period plus or minus any permitted margin or allowance, express or implied. There follows these two propositions:

(d) If the charterer sends the vessel on a legitimate last voyage – that is, a voyage which it is reasonably expected will be completed by the end of the charter period, the shipowner must obey the directions. If the vessel is afterwards delayed by matters for which neither party is responsible, the charter is presumed to continue in operation until the end of that voyage, even though it extends beyond the charter period. The hire is payable at the charter rate until redelivery, even though the market rate may have gone up or down, see *Timber Shipping Co SA v London & Overseas Freighters Ltd* [1972] AC 1.

(e) If the charterer sends the vessel on an illegitimate last voyage – that is, a voyage which it cannot be expected to complete within the charter period, then the shipowner is entitled to refuse that direction and call for another direction for a legitimate last voyage. If the charterer refuses to give it, the shipowner can accept his conduct as a breach going to the root of the contract, fix a fresh charter for the vessel, and sue for damages. If the shipowner accepts the direction and goes on the illegitimate last voyage, he is entitled to be paid – for the excess period – at the current market rate, and not at the charter rate, see *Meyer v Sanderson* (1916) 32 TLR 428. The hire will be payable at the charter rate up to the end of the charter period, and at the current market rate for the excess period thereafter.

... If this clause had said simply 'six months time charter' without any express margin or allowance, I should have thought that there would be implied a reasonable margin or allowance. But this clause expressly defines the margin as '20 days more or less'. That leaves no room for any implied margin or allowance. The express margin is greater than any period which would normally be implied ...

Torvald Klaveness A/S v Arni Maritime Corp, The Gregos [1994] 1 WLR 1465, HL

Lord Ackner, Lord Slynn and Lord Woolf agreed with Lord Mustill.

Lord Mustill: My Lords, in merchant shipping time is money. A cargo ship is expensive to finance and expensive to run. The shipowner must keep it earning with the minimum of gaps between employments. Time is also important for the charterer, because arrangements must be made for the shipment and receipt of the cargo, or for the performance of obligations under subcontracts. These demands encourage the planning and performance of voyages to the tightest of margins. Yet even today ships do not run precisely to time. The most prudent schedule may be disrupted by regular hazards such as adverse weather or delays in port happening in an unexpected manner or degree, or by the intervention of wholly adventitious events.

Where the charterparty is for a period of time rather than a voyage, and the remuneration is calculated according to the time used rather than the service performed, the risk of delay is primarily on the charterer. For the shipowner, so long as he commits no breach and nothing puts the ship off-hire, his right to remuneration is unaffected by a disturbance of the charterer's plans. It is for the latter to choose between cautious planning, which may leave gaps between employments, and bolder scheduling with the risk of setting aims which cannot be realised in practice.

This distribution of risk holds good during most of the chartered service. As the time for redelivery approaches things become more complicated. (The word 'redelivery' is inaccurate, but it is convenient, and I will use it.) If the market is rising, the charterer wants to have the use of the vessel at the chartered rate for as long as possible. Conversely, the shipowner must think ahead to the next employment, and if, as is common, he has made a forward fixture he will be in difficulties if the vessel is retained by the charterer longer than had been foreseen. This conflict of interest becomes particularly acute when there is time left for only one more voyage before the expiry of the charter, and disputes may arise if the charterer orders the ship to perform a service which the shipowner believes will extend beyond the date fixed for redelivery.

Disputes of this kind have given rise to a considerable body of authority, not entirely easy to reconcile. In the first place there are judgments which lay down rules for deciding what, in the light of the words used in the individual charterparty, is the last permissible date for redelivery. In its early stages, the present case raised an issue of this kind. Next, the courts have discussed the 'legitimacy', as it is often called, of the final voyage (that is, the question whether the charterer's order to perform the voyage is one which the shipowner must obey) in terms of the likelihood that the voyage will end in time to permit redelivery by the last permissible date. Finally, some of the legal consequences of late redelivery have been worked out.

There remain a number of unanswered questions, with some of which your Lordships are now concerned. The context is a dispute between the owners and the charterers of the vessel Gregos. This was referred to arbitration. In the reasons for his award the arbitrator succinctly described the issues as follows:

> This arbitration concerned a claim by the registered owners for damages flowing from the time charterers' orders for a final allegedly 'illegitimate' voyage, in other words, one that could not reasonably be expected to allow redelivery by the end of the charter period. The owners had refused to accept the orders. The parties had then entered into a without prejudice agreement under which the last voyage was performed. I had to determine whether or not the orders for the last voyage were ones that the charterers were entitled to give and, if not, what consequences flowed from the giving of those orders.

... The facts of the dispute were as follows. The *Gregos* was chartered by Arni Maritime Corporation (the owners) to Torvald Klaveness A/S (the charterers) on terms which, so far as material, were as follows:

> Witnesseth, That the said Owners agree to let and the said Charterers agree to hire the said vessel, from the time of delivery, for about 50 to maximum 70 days ... Vessel ... to be employed in carrying lawful merchandise ... in such lawful trades ... between safe port and ... as the Charterers or their Agents shall direct, on the following conditions ...

> 8. That the Captain shall prosecute his voyages with the utmost despatch ... The Captain (although appointed by the Owners), shall be under the orders and directions of the Charterers as regards employment and agency ...

> 11. That the Charterers shall furnish the Captain from time to time with all requisite instructions and sailing directions ...

... The charterers' original contemplation was to employ the vessel first by ballasting her from Antwerp to Trombetas in Brazil to carry a cargo of bauxite to Matanzas, a port in Venezuela on the Orinoco River. Thence the vessel was to proceed up river in ballast to Puerto Ordaz where she would load a cargo of iron ore for Italy, prior to redelivery. Later, this plan was revised in two respects. First, the charterers interposed a second voyage from Matanzas to Trombetas in ballast with a return leg to Matanzas with bauxite, between the first bauxite voyage and the final voyage to Europe. Secondly, this final voyage was now to be from Palua, also on the Orinoco, with iron ore for Fos. The first element of this changed schedule was notified to the owners and complied with. The vessel did lift a second bauxite cargo. The other element, namely the substitution of a laden voyage from Palua to Fos, was notified by the charterers to the master of the vessel on 9 February 1988. If judged when the order was given, compliance with the order could reasonably have been anticipated to allow redelivery by 18 March, the last permissible date.

Three days later things began to go wrong. Another vessel grounded with unusual severity in the Orinoco, causing delays to river traffic which led the owners to warn the charterers that if the plan was adhered to the *Gregos* could not be redelivered in time. As the arbitrator was later to find, this warning was justified. Even if all had gone well thereafter there would have been a late redelivery of between two and four days. The vessel nevertheless proceeded on the very short ballast leg to Palua from Matanzas. On 25 February 1988 the owners advised the charterers that they declined to perform the laden voyage from the Orinoco to Fos, and called upon the charterers to give revised orders for the final voyage. No such orders were given, and a dispute arose, the charterers insisting and the owners denying that the order of 9 February for a voyage from Palua to Fos remained valid ... In the event, the deadlock was broken by a without prejudice agreement between the owners and the charterers. The terms were not before the House, but it was explained in argument that the agreement provided for the performance of the laden voyage to Fos on terms that if, in subsequent proceedings, it was held that the owners were justified in refusing to perform the voyage they would be entitled to a sum reflecting the difference between the chartered rate of hire and the more advantageous terms of [a] proposed substitute fixture ... Pursuant to the without prejudice agreement the vessel loaded the cargo of iron ore and prepared to sail from Palua, but her departure was further delayed because another vessel grounded in the river ahead of her. In the event, the last laden voyage was not completed until 23 March, and the actual redelivery took place on 26 March – eight days late.

On these facts the matter went to arbitration. The clear and thorough reasons given by the arbitrator for his award reflected a distinction drawn in the arguments before him, and still drawn in the submissions before the House, between two issues. (1) Should the validity of the order for the final voyage be judged as at the time when it was given or as at the time when it fell to be complied with; or on some other date? (2) If the validity of the order was to be judged in the light of matters as they stood on 25 February, so that the voyage was not one for which a legitimate order could be given, what was the effect of (a) the charterers having given the order and (b) their refusal to replace it by another? Two decisions by the arbitrator are no longer challenged. First, that the wording of the charter left no room for a margin beyond the end of the stipulated 70 days. Second, as regards the order for the voyage from Palua to Fos, his conclusion was that if judged as at 9 February the order was reasonable but that due to the intervening delays by 25 February this was no longer the case ...

I begin with the first issue, concerning the date for judging the validity of the charterers' order. Here, it seems to me that the inquiry has been led astray by concentrating too much on the order and too little on the shipowner's promise to furnish the services of the vessel, which is what the contract is about. Initially, the practical implications of the promise are undefined, since they depend on how in the future the charterer decides to employ the vessel; but they are not unlimited, being constrained from the start as to duration, nature and extent by express terms in the charter (concerning for example the types of cargo to be carried and the geographical limits of trade) and also by important implied terms. Later, when the time for performance has arrived, this broad promise is converted to a series of specific obligations by the charterer's orders for employment, but the constraints expressly or impliedly accepted by the charterer in the original contract continue to apply. Whatever the charterer may order, a service which falls outside the range encompassed by the owner's original promise is not one which he can be compelled to perform; and this is so as regards not only the duration of the chartered service, but also all the other limitations imposed by the charterparty on the charterer's freedom of choice. There is thus to be a measuring of the service called for against the service promised. As a matter of common sense, it seems to me that the time for such measurement is, primarily at least, the time when performance falls due.

My Lords, I have qualified this statement with the words 'primarily at least' because in practice the interests of both parties demand that the charterer is entitled to give orders in advance of the time for performance; and this must entail at least a provisional judgment on the validity of the order. If it can be seen at this early stage that compliance will involve a service which lies outside the shipowner's undertaking the latter can say so at once, and reject the order. But if the order is apparently valid its validity is no more than contingent, since the time for matching the service against the promise to serve does not arrive until the nature of the service is definitively known; and this will not usually be until the service is due to begin, or in some instances until it is already in progress. Thus, if and for so long as the service required conforms with those which the shipowner promised in advance to render the specific order creates a specific obligation to perform them when the time arrives. But only for so long as that state of affairs persists. If circumstances change, so that compliance with the order will call for a service which in the original contract the shipowner never undertook, the obligation to comply must fall away. As I see it, the charterers' order in advance amounts to a continuing requirement, the validity of which may change with the passage of time.

My Lords, this much I conclude simply by considering the general nature of a time charterparty. The conclusion must however be tested by recourse to the authorities and (with appropriate caution) to its practical implications. On the former I need not dwell. Great care has properly been taken in the courts below to see whether there can be found in the decided cases any judicial pronouncement which points unequivocally to a conclusion. For my part I can find none. Certainly, there are several turns of phrase which suggest one or another assumption about when the question of validity should be judged, but I am quite satisfied that in no case was the choice of date in issue, or even in most instances present to the mind of the judges, and I will therefore not stay to quote from them.

Turning to the practicalities, I entirely share the opinion of Saville J in *The Peonia* [1991] 1 Lloyd's Rep 100 that questions of this kind are better decided by looking at what the contract says than by speculating on the practical outcome of preferring one solution to another ... if the matter is to be decided according to balance of convenience the owners' argument appears to have much the better of it. But I prefer to concentrate on the charterparty itself; and here, for the reasons stated, the analysis leads directly to the conclusion that, as the arbitrator and Evans J decided, the correct date for assessment was 25 February. By then, an order originally permissible had become illegitimate.

I turn to the issue of repudiation. Although the appeal is concerned with an invalid order for a final voyage this is only a special case of an order issued for the performance of a service which lies outside the scope of the shipowner's promise. Since orders for employment and compliance with them lie at the heart of a time charter the question is of general importance, and the solution arrived at should hold good for all types of order ...

The original order having become ineffectual the charterers were obliged by cl 11 to replace it with one which they were entitled to give. Whether at the time of the cancellation they had committed an actual breach of this obligation is debatable, but at all events the breach was not final, since (if I correctly understand the arbitrator's reasons) there would have been time if all else failed for the charterers to ballast the vessel back to the redelivery area before the final date, or conceivably to issue an order for a revised laden voyage. But it is plain from the facts stated by the arbitrator that the charterers had no intention of doing this, and that the critical time would pass without any valid orders being given. This is the significance of the changed circumstances which rendered the original order invalid. Not that the order constituted a repudiation in itself, but that the charterers' persistence in it after it had become invalid showed that they did not intend to perform their obligations under the charter. That is to say, they 'evinced an intention no longer to be bound' by the charter. This was an anticipatory breach, which entitled the owners to treat the contract as ended ...

4 REDELIVERY IN DISREPAIR

Attica Sea Carriers Corp v Ferrostaal Poseidon Bulk Reederei GmbH, The Puerto Buitrago [1976] 1 Lloyd's Rep 250, CA

Lord Denning MR: This is an urgent case. A vessel – the *Puerto Buitrago* – is lying at Kiel with only a caretaker on board. She was let on a bareboat charter, which expired three months ago. She is out of repair. So much so that it would cost more to repair her than she is worth, even after the repairs have been done. The cost of repairs is said to be twice as much as her value when repaired. The shipowners say that it is the charterer's duty to repair her, whatever the cost, and that the charterers must pay the charter hire until she is repaired, even to the crack of doom. The charterers say that that is absurd: and that they are entitled to hand her back to the shipowners at this very moment, just as she is, out of repair: and that the shipowners should sell her for what they can get. The shipowners, they say, can get damages for the delivery up out of repair, but not the charter hire.

The *Puerto Buitrago* is a fairly old vessel ... In August 1974, she was surveyed and passed for classification without any recommendations of qualifications. Soon afterwards there was trouble with her engines. She was repaired temporarily. But more serious trouble arose in March, 1975, when she was at Rio Grande in Brazil. She had loaded a cargo of soya bean meal for Europe ... The charterers then decided that the only thing to do was to have her towed all the way to Europe. This was done. On 18 June 1975, the vessel, full of a cargo of soya bean meal, was towed out of Rio and then for six weeks across the oceans till she reached Gdynia in Poland on 1 August 1975. Her cargo was there discharged. She was then towed to Kiel, where she arrived on 7 September 1975.

At Kiel a survey was commenced by the surveyors for the parties. The owners produced a specification for drydocking and repairs. If these repairs were all done, they would cost, it is said, about $2 million, whereas the value of the vessel, when repaired, would only be $1 million. Her scrap value would be about $0.5 million. The charterers admit that repairs to the tune of $400,000 are their responsibility: but they dispute the rest ...

The first question

The first question is as to the true construction of the charterparty. I will not set it out in full, but in substance the question is whether or not, on the wording of the charterparty, the charterers are entitled to redeliver the vessel now: or must wait until after the ship has been surveyed and all repairs done (ordinary wear and tear excepted) and passed in class without recommendations ...

... it is plain that the charterer is under an obligation to put the vessel in good repair before redelivery. But the question is whether that stipulation is a condition precedent to his right to redeliver the vessel (so that he is not entitled to redeliver the vessel until he has performed it): or whether it is merely a stipulation which, if broken, gives a remedy in damages but does not prevent him from redelivering the vessel to the owner. This is the sort of question which has come before the courts for the last 200 or 300 years. I summarised the history in *Cehave NV v Bremer mbH* [1975] 3 WLR 447 at pp 453–54.

The parties can, by clear words, provide that complete performance of a particular stipulation can be a condition precedent: but, in the absence of clear words, the court looks to see which of the rival interpretations gives the more reasonable result. Lord Reid said so in *Wickman v Schuler* [1974] AC 235 at p 251E. He said:

> The fact that a particular construction leads to a very unreasonable result must be a relevant consideration. The more unreasonable the result, the more unlikely it is that the parties can have intended it, and if they do intend it, the more necessary it is that they shall make that intention abundantly clear.

There are only two cases in the books where the courts have had to apply this principle to the obligation to repair a ship. They were both cases of ordinary time charters (not by demise). The first is the *Wye Shipping* case [1922] 1 KB 617. McCardie J looked to see what was reasonable. He said:

> In my opinion they [the charterers] are not liable for hire after they have tendered redelivery at the proper time. If the rule were otherwise, it seems to me that absurd situations would arise.

and he gave an illustration of such an absurdity. That case was followed in *Black Sea v Goeland* (1942) 74 Ll L Rep 192 by Atkinson J, who regarded it as authority that 'the contract terminated on redelivery whether the repairs had been effected or not'.

Those were both cases of ordinary time charters in which the word 'redelivery' is used in a different sense from that in a demise charterparty ... But the distinction makes no difference to our present question. The illustration given by McCardie J of an absurdity can be applied equally to a charterparty by demise. Another illustration was given in the present case. Suppose some spare parts were needed for the turbo-generator (so as to maintain classification without recommendations or qualifications), and it would take some months to get them. It would be most unreasonable to require the charterer to keep the vessel – and pay the hire – for the months that would elapse. It was suggested that the doctrine of frustration would apply, but I do not think it would. The correct answer is that the obligation to repair in cl 15 (in class without recommendations) was not a condition precedent to the right to redeliver, but only a stipulation giving a remedy in damages ...

Finally, on this question of construction, the charterparty itself defines the period of the charter as 'until 28th May, 1975, one month more or less at charterer's option' ... I do not see that it can be extended to cover the drydocking and survey, and subsequent repairs. These are expressly covered in cl 4. If the vessel has been properly maintained, the owner has to bear the expense of them. If not, the time and expense are for the charterer's account.

In my opinion, therefore, on the true construction of the charterparty, the answer to the first question is this: the redelivery of the vessel on 23 September 1975, was effective, notwithstanding the fact that the surveys had not been completed, or the fact that the vessel was not in class without recommendations, and was not in proper repair ...

5 REDELIVERY AT THE WRONG PLACE

Santa Martha Baay Scheepvaart and Handelsmaatschappij NV v Scanbulk A/S, The Rijn [1981] 2 Lloyd's Rep 267

Mustill J: Several disputes have arisen between ... the owners and Scanbulk A/S (the charterers) concerning the charter of the vessel *Rijn* ...

Delivery under the time charter took place at Kobe on 17 October 1974. The vessel then proceeded in ballast to Lourenco Marques, arriving on 8 November. She remained there until 29 January 1975, and then sailed for Baltimore with a cargo of chrome ore ...

While the vessel was on passage to Baltimore, the charterers informed the owners that the vessel had been fixed for a further voyage after completion of discharge. At a later stage of the voyage they said that the vessel would load a cargo of grain in the US Gulf for Japan ...

Meanwhile, on 14 March the vessel had sailed from Wilmington for the US Gulf, and on 17 March the charterers nominated Galveston as the port of loading. During the passage to Galveston, there was an engine stoppage amounting to one day 11 hours. This imperilled the cancelling date under the subcharter, but the charterers said that they would do their utmost to persuade the subcharterers to accept the vessel for the voyage to Japan.

The vessel arrived at Galveston on 23 March. Early on the following day she was rejected by the authorities because of excessive loose rust in the holds; this rust had been present from the outset of the chartered service. After two days' cleaning, for which the charterers paid, the vessel was passed by the authorities. Notice of readiness was tendered under the subcharterparty on 26 March but was rejected as being out of time.

On the same day, the charterers notified the owners that the time charter was terminated 'as is, where is'. They never thereafter provided employment for the vessel, which was ultimately fixed by the owners for a substitute voyage.

From this event there stemmed a major dispute between the parties; namely, whether the shortcomings of the vessel's condition and performance amounted to a repudiatory breach of contract. The arbitrators have found that it did not, and the argument in the High Court has proceeded on the basis that the charterers were themselves in repudiation by terminating the charter.

Of the two items remaining in issue, the first concerns the measure of damage recoverable in respect of this repudiation. Here the question is whether, as the charterers maintain, the owners are entitled to no more than compensation for the redelivery of the vessel at Galveston rather than at a Japanese port, as required by the charter; or whether they can recover the difference between the net profit which they would have earned if the voyage had continued, and their net receipts under the substitute fixture.

For the charterers it is pointed out that where a charterer has tendered the vessel for redelivery at a port within the redelivery range, the tender is valid even 'if the vessel is not, as she ought to be, in the same good order and condition as on delivery': *Wye Shipping Co Ltd v Compagnie du Chemin de Fer Paris-Orleans* (1922) 10 Ll L Rep 55, and *The Puerto Buitrago* [1976] 1 Lloyd's Rep 250. They say that there should be a similar result where the complaint is reversed. If the charter terminates when the ship is redelivered at the right port in the wrong condition, then it should equally come to an end when she is redelivered at the wrong port in the right condition.

This argument sounds attractive, but I do not accept it. There is no true analogy between the two situations. Both legal and commercial considerations demand that the charter shall come to an end, even if the condition of the vessel on redelivery is unsatisfactory. So far as concerns the law, the contractual service is defined in terms of the place or time, or both, at which the vessel is redelivered. The stipulation concerning the vessel's condition on redelivery is not part of this definition. Once the stated time has expired, or the stated port or range has been reached, the period of hiring is accomplished, even if the charterer is in breach at the time. Equally, from a commercial point of view, it would be absurd if the charter were to run on indefinitely, with the charterer obliged to retain the ship in service, even though there was no longer any voyage upon which she could permissibly be sent.

The position is quite different where the ship is tendered at a port which is not within the redelivery range. Here there is no question of the charterer breaking a collateral obligation attaching at the moment of redelivery, nor is it the owner's sole complaint that the ship has been returned to him in the wrong place. He has a contractual right to have the ship kept in employment at the charter rate of hire until the service is completed. This does not happen until the ship reaches the redelivery range, and the voyage to that range forms part of the chartered service. In a case such as the present, therefore, the tender is not only in the wrong place but also at the wrong time; and full compensation for the breach requires the charterer to restore to the owner the hire which he would have earned if the voyage had in fact been performed.

I therefore consider that the arbitrators were right in basing their award of damages on the cost of a notional final voyage to Japan. I am fortified in this view by the decision of Parker J in *Malaysian International Shipping Corporation v Empresa Cubana de Fletes* [1981] 1 Lloyd's Rep 518, the reasoning of which I respectfully adopt.

This is not the end of the question of damages, for there remains a dispute as to the basis on which to calculate loss of hire on the notional redelivery voyage. For how long should that voyage be presumed to have lasted?

Apart from any express agreement as to the nature of the voyage, there is little room for doubt. It is quite clear that where a promisor has the choice of how his promise shall be performed, it is presumed for the purpose of calculating damages that he would have chosen the way which would have brought least benefit to the promisee. This principle, that an option is presumed to have been exercised in the way which reduces damages to a minimum, is too well established to require citation in support. Applying this approach to the present case yields the conclusion that the loss should be assessed in terms of the voyage which would have yielded the least hire. This was a voyage to the nearest safe port within the redelivery range, namely, Yokohama; and it would have been a voyage in ballast, because this would have saved time which would otherwise have been occupied in loading and discharge ...

6 CONSTRUCTION OF CONTRACTS OF AFFREIGHTMENT

1   Charterparties are like any other contract and must be construed as such. Their true construction is a question of law not fact. The duty of the court is to ascertain the presumed common intention of the parties, to be deduced from the words used and the background to the transaction: Donaldson J, *The Aragon* [1975] 2 Lloyd's Rep 216.

2   The basic English rule for the construction of contracts is to examine the words the parties have used in the context in which they have used them, in order to try and ascertain objectively what bargain the parties intended to make. The contract must be looked at as a whole in its context, rather than seeking to construe provisions in isolation, for to do otherwise is in effect to shut one's eyes to what the parties themselves actually did: Saville LJ, *The Nerano* [1996] 1 Lloyd's Rep 1, 3/4.

3   *The words used*: all the words used must be considered: the contract must be construed as a whole: *The Madeleine* [1967] 2 Lloyd's Rep 224. The relevant clause must be looked at as a whole: *The TFL Prosperity* [1984] 1 WLR 50.

4   It is not necessary that every word should add something to the contract. Surplusage ('some tautology') is not necessarily a good objection to a possible construction: *The Mareva AS* [1977] 1 Lloyd's Rep 368; *The TFL Prosperity*, above.

5   It cannot be assumed that parties will always choose to express their intention in the simplest or most straightforward way possible: consider *Heathfield v Rodenacher* and *Rotherfield v Tweedy*, Chapter 12, 'Freight'.

6   There must be ascribed to the words a meaning that would make good commercial sense not just in the case before the court but in any of the circumstances in which the words could fall to be applied: *Miramar Maritime Corp v Holborn Oil Trading Ltd* [1984] AC 676, 682.

7   Familiar expressions which have a well established meaning should be consistently construed; a well established meaning should not be departed from in the absence of compelling surrounding circumstances or a context strongly suggestive of some other meaning: *The Varenna* [1984] 1 QB 599, 621.

8   The form in which the words appear may indicate the intention of the parties. Words which are written/typed/stamped on a printed form should be preferred to an inconsistent printed clause: Mocatta J, *The Athinoula* [1980] 2 Lloyd's Rep 481, 487.

9   There are well established rules of construction which permit the court to disregard printed words when they are inconsistent with written words or with the paramount object which the document appears from its language to be designed to achieve. But these rules can be used only when there is a conflict between one part of the document and another or between the effect of a part and the effect of the whole. They are rules for reconciling different expressions in or of the document itself. They cannot be used to introduce into the document, either by implication or by force of custom, what is outside it.

Lord Devlin: *Kum v Wah Tat Bank* [1971] 1 Lloyd's Rep 439, PC.

10 Deletions:

There is a controversy as to whether one can ever look at deleted words in an agreement. If the words were first inserted by the draftsman of the agreement and then deleted before signature then I have no doubt that they must not be considered in construing the agreement. They are in the same position as any other preliminary suggestion put forward and rejected before the final agreement was made. But it appears to me that striking out words from a printed form is quite a different matter. The process of adapting a printed form to make it express the parties' intentions requires two things to be done. Those parts which are not to be part of the agreement are struck out and words are inserted to complete the rest of the form so as to express the agreement. There is no inference that in striking out words the parties had second thoughts: the words struck out were never put there by the parties or any of them or by their draftsman. I must not express a concluded opinion because for some reason this question was not argued by counsel on either side. But fortunately in this case the result is the same on any view ...

Lord Reid, *London & Overseas v Timber Shipping* [1972] AC 1, 14.

11 In the course of the hearing a brief but interesting discussion took place whether I could properly look at the ... clause deleted from the charterparty

form in this case as showing the intention of the parties ... The owners argued that I could not, relying on *Inglis v Buttery & Co* (1878) 3 App Cas 552, 569 and 576, *Sasson & Sons Ltd v International Banking Corp* [1927] AC 711, 721 and *Compania Naviera Termar SA v Tradax Export SA* [1965] 1 Lloyd's Rep 198 at 204. The authorities relied on by the owners are of such persuasive weight that I do not feel entitled to disregard them ...

Bingham J, *The C Joyce* [1986] 2 Lloyd's Rep 285.

12 The background

Courts will never construe words in a vacuum. To a greater or lesser extent, depending on the subject matter, they will wish to be informed of what may variously be described as the context, the background, the factual matrix or the mischief. To seek to construe any instrument in ignorance or disregard of the circumstances which gave rise to it or the situation in which it is expected to take effect is in my view pedantic, sterile and productive of error. But that is not to say that an initial judgment of what an instrument was or should reasonably have been intended to achieve should be permitted to override the clear language of the instrument, since what an author says is usually the surest guide to what he means. To my mind construction is a composite exercise, neither uncompromisingly literal nor unswervingly purposive: the instrument must speak for itself, but it must do so *in situ* and not be transported to the laboratory for microscopic analysis:

Arbuthnot v Fagan, unreported, 30 July 1993, Sir Thomas Bingham MR, cited in *The Fina Samco* [1995] 2 Lloyd's Rep 344, 348, CA.

13 Dictionaries never solve concrete problems of construction. The meaning of words cannot be ascertained divorced from their context. And part of the contextual scene is the purpose of the provision:

Arbuthnot v Fagan, unreported, 30 July 1993, Steyn LJ, cited in *The Fina Samco* [1995] 2 Lloyd's Rep 344, 348, CA.

14 What the court must do must be to place itself in thought in the same factual matrix as that in which the parties were.

Lord Wilberforce, *The Diana Prosperity* [1976] 1 WLR 989, HL.

15 The factual matrix includes the commercial purpose of the contract, which presupposes knowledge of the genesis of the transaction, the background, the context, the market in which the parties are operating. Specific contextual factors identified as relevant in reported cases include: the nature of the adventure in question, the nature of the trade, the legal and historical background, the commercial background and the knowledge and experience which the parties can be assumed to have.

16 The *Miramar* Rule:

if detailed semantic and syntactical analysis of words in a commercial contract is going to lead to a conclusion that flouts business commonsense, it must be made to yield to business commonsense.

Lord Diplock, *The Antaios* [1984] 2 Lloyd's Rep 235, 238 referring to the approach to questions of construction of commercial documents that was adopted by the House of Lords in *Miramar Maritime Corp v Holborn Oil Trading* [1984] 2 Lloyd's Rep 129.

17 *Judging by results*. The fact that a particular construction leads to a very unreasonable result must be a relevant consideration. The more unreasonable the result the more unlikely it is that the parties can have intended it, and if they do intend it the more necessary it is that they should make their intention abundantly clear: *Wickman Tools v Schuler AG* [1974] AC 235, 251; *The Fina Samco* [1995] 2 Lloyd's Rep 344, 348.

CHAPTER 17

GENERAL AVERAGE

1 INTRODUCTION

The term 'general average' refers to those rules and principles of maritime law which govern the sharing of losses caused to the interests of ship and cargo by the intentional sacrifice of cargo or extraordinary expenditure by one or other of those interests in the face of exposure to a common danger.

The concept of general average was known as early as 900 BC when under Rhodian Law it was provided that if one party's cargo had to be jettisoned to save ship and cargo in a situation of common danger, the ship and remaining cargo had to contribute to those losses. The Romans knew of general average and the concept appears in the *Digest* of Justinian.

A general average loss is said to give rise to the duty to make a general average contribution but the definition of loss and the extent of the duty have not been without controversy. While the laws of most mercantile states made (and make) provision in one form or another for general average, there were considerable divergences. In the second half of the 19th century various international efforts culminated in the adoption of the York-Antwerp Rules of 1877. These rules established a uniform approach to the calculation of general average contribution and remain, as periodically amended, the most important source on general average today. The latest rules known as the York-Antwerp Rules 1994 were adopted during a meeting of the Comité Maritime International (CMI) held in Sydney, Australia.

The York-Antwerp Rules 1994 consist of a rule paramount, a rule of interpretation, seven lettered rules setting out general principles and 22 numbered rules covering particular issues. The Rules have been amended over the years principally to take account of technological changes and while they now cater for most situations they are not free from problems of interpretation as the cases below will reveal. The Rules have always been a voluntary code and never an international treaty. They are only thus relevant to the regulation of a claim for general average if the contractual documentation for the voyage (usually the charterparty or bill of lading) incorporates them.

English law has allowed claims for general average independently of the Rules since the 18th century (*Da Costa v Newnham* (1788) 2 TR 407, 100 ER 219). It is not clear whether the right to claim arises as a matter of contract (implied or otherwise) or as a matter of law. In practice however most contracts of affreightment incorporate the York-Antwerp Rules. This is not to belittle the debate however or dismiss the privity problem which arises between two shippers (cargo interests) who have contracts with the shipowner but not each other.

The words 'general average' are used to refer to the act which gives rise to the loss, the loss itself and the contribution which is claimed. The process of establishing the extent of the loss is known as general average adjustment and the professional adjusters who are employed for this purpose are average adjusters.

Examples of general average sacrifices include the jettison of cargo to enable a vessel to float off after being grounded and water damage caused by attempts to put out a fire. Expenses can include port of refuge expenses and other third party expenses such as those payable for towage.

Not all sacrifices and expenditures give rise to valid claims for general average contribution however and both under the York-Antwerp Rules 1994 and at common law certain conditions must be met. Very generally the act giving rise to the loss alleged to found the duty to contribute must be: extraordinary in nature; voluntarily and deliberately undertaken but reasonably incurred at a time of general peril caused by a real and imminent danger; undertaken for the common safety of a common maritime adventure and result in some saving from which contribution can be made.

It is not always clear what relationship exists between general average and the other international maritime agreements regulating the rights of ship, cargo and freight. The Hague Rules and the Hague-Visby Rules may often have a role in a fact situation out of which a claim for general average contribution is also made. The extent to which the shipowner may claim for general average contribution where his own negligence has caused the loss and the opposability of limitation clauses are the subjects of the case of *Goulandris Bros Ltd v B Goldman Sons Ltd* [1957] 2 Ll L Rep 20 extracted below.

The interface between general average and insurance law is not always an easy one either. The cargo owner will normally be insured against the risks of loss or damage to his goods caused by a general average loss and against the liability to contribute in respect of such a loss. The Marine Insurance Act 1906 provides explicitly for such recovery in s 66. In practice underwriters pay cargo for a general average loss well before adjustment and are then subrogated in respect of any contribution claim. Underwriters will normally provide the so-called general average bond required by the shipowner before release of the cargo pursuant to his lien.

2 THE YORK-ANTWERP RULES 1994

Rule of interpretation. In the adjustment of general average the following Rules shall apply to the exclusion of any Law and Practice inconsistent therewith.

Except as provided by the Rule Paramount and the numbered Rules, general average shall be adjusted according to the lettered Rules.

Rule Paramount. In no case shall there be any allowance for sacrifice or expenditure unless reasonably made or incurred.

Rule A. There is a general average act, when, and only when, any extraordinary sacrifice or expenditure is intentionally and reasonably made or incurred for the common safety for the purpose of preserving from peril the property involved in a common maritime adventure.

General average sacrifices and expenditures shall be borne by the different contributing interests on the basis hereinafter provided.

Rule B. There is a common maritime adventure when one or more vessels are towing or pushing another vessel or vessels, provided that they are all involved in commercial activities and not in a salvage operation.

When measures are taken to preserve the vessels and their cargoes, if any, from a common peril, these Rules shall apply.

A vessel is not in common peril with another vessel or vessels if by simply disconnecting from the other vessel or vessels she is in safety; but if the disconnection is itself a general average act the common maritime adventure continues.

Rule C. Only such losses, damages or expenses which are the direct consequence of the general average act shall be allowed as general average.

In no case shall there be any allowance in general average for losses, damages or expenses incurred in respect of damage to the environment or in consequence of the escape or release of pollutant substances from the property involved in the common maritime adventure.

Demurrage, loss of market, and any loss or damage sustained or expense incurred by reason of delay, whether on the voyage or subsequently, and any indirect loss whatsoever, shall not be admitted as general average.

Rule D. Rights to contribution in general average shall not be affected, though the event which gave rise to the sacrifice or expenditure may have been due to the fault of one of the parties to the adventure, but this shall not prejudice any remedies or defences which may be open against or to that party in respect of such fault.

Rule E. The onus of proof is upon the party claiming in general average to show that the loss or expense claimed is properly allowable as general average.

All parties claiming in general average shall give notice in writing to the average adjuster of the loss or expense in respect of which they claim contribution within 12 months of the date of the termination of the common maritime adventure.

Failing such notification, or if within 12 months of a request for the same any of the parties shall fail to supply evidence in support of a notified claim, or particulars of value in respect of a contributory interest, the average adjuster shall be at liberty to estimate the extent of the allowance or the contributory value on the basis of the information available to him, which estimate may be challenged only on the ground that it is manifestly incorrect.

Rule F. Any additional expense incurred in place of another expense which would have been allowable as general average shall be deemed to be general average and so allowed without regard to the saving, if any, to other interests, but only up to the amount of the general average expense avoided.

Rule G. General average shall be adjusted as regards both loss and contribution upon the basis of values at the time and place when and where the adventure ends.

This Rule shall not affect the determination of the place at which the average statement is to be made up.

When a ship is at any port or place in circumstances which would give rise to an allowance in general average under the provisions of Rules X and XI, and the cargo or part thereof is forwarded to destination by other means, rights and liabilities in general average shall, subject to cargo interests being notified if practicable, remain as nearly as possible the same as they would have been in the absence of such forwarding, as if the adventure had continued in the original ship for so long as justifiable under the contract of affreightment and the applicable law.

The proportion attaching to cargo of the allowances made in general average by reason of applying the third paragraph of this Rule shall not exceed the cost which would have been borne by the owners of cargo if the cargo had been forwarded at their expense.

Rule I. *Jettison of cargo*. No jettison of cargo shall be made good as general average, unless such cargo is carried in accordance with the recognised custom of the trade.

Rule II. *Loss or Damage by sacrifices for the common safety*. Loss of or damage to the property involved in the common maritime adventure by or in consequence of a sacrifice made for the common safety, and by water which goes down a ship's hatches opened or other opening made for the purpose of making a jettison for the common safety, shall be made good as general average.

Rule III. *Extinguishing fire on shipboard*. Damage done to a ship and cargo, or either of them, by water or otherwise, including damage by beaching or scuttling a burning ship, in extinguishing a fire on board the ship, shall be made good as general average; except that no compensation shall be made for damage by smoke however caused or by heat of the fire.

Rule IV. *Cutting away wreck*. Loss or damage sustained by cutting away wreck or parts of the ship which have been previously carried away or are effectively lost by accident shall not be made good as general average.

Rule V. *Voluntary stranding*. When a ship is intentionally run on shore for the common safety, whether or not she might have been driven on shore, the consequent loss or damage to the property involved in the common maritime adventure shall be allowed in general average.

Rule VI. *Salvage remuneration*.

(a) Expenditure incurred by the parties to the adventure in the nature of salvage, whether under contract or otherwise, shall be allowed in general average to the extent that the salvage operations were carried out for the purpose of preserving from peril the property involved in the common maritime adventure.

Expenditure allowed in general average shall include any salvage remuneration in which the skill and efforts of the salvors in preventing or minimising damage to the environment such as is referred to in Article 13 paragraph 1 (b) of the International Convention on Salvage, 1989 have been taken into account.

(b) Special compensation payable to a salvor by the shipowner under Article 14 of the said Convention to the extent specified in paragraph 4 of that Article or under any other provision similar in substance shall not be allowed in general average.

Rule VII. *Damage to machinery and boilers.* Damage caused to any machinery and boilers of a ship which is ashore and in a position of peril, in endeavouring to refloat, shall be allowed in general average when shown to have arisen from an actual intention to float the ship for the common safety at the risk of such damage; but where a ship is afloat no loss or damage caused by working the propelling machinery and boilers shall in any circumstances be made good as general average.

Rule VIII. *Expenses lightening a ship when ashore, and consequent damage.* When a ship is ashore and cargo and ship's fuel and stores or any of them are discharged as a general average act, the extra cost of lightening, lighter hire and reshipping (if incurred), and any loss or damage to the property involved in the common maritime adventure in consequence thereof, shall be admitted as general average.

Rule IX. *Cargo, ship's materials and stores used for fuel.* Cargo, ship's materials and stores, or any of them, necessarily used for fuel for the common safety at a time of peril shall be admitted as general average, but when such an allowance is made for the cost of the ship's materials and stores the general average shall be credited with the estimated cost of the fuel which would otherwise have been consumed in prosecuting the intended voyage.

Rule X. *Expenses at port of refuge etc.*

(a) When a ship shall have entered a port or place of refuge or shall have returned to her port or place of loading in consequence of accident, sacrifice or other extraordinary circumstances which render that necessary for the common safety, the expenses of entering such port or place shall be admitted as general average; and when she shall have sailed thence with her original cargo, or part of it, the corresponding expenses of leaving such port or place consequent upon such entry or return shall likewise be admitted as general average.

When a ship is at any port or place of refuge and is necessarily removed to another port or place because repairs cannot be carried out in the first port or place, the provisions of this Rule shall be applied to the second port or place as if it were a port or place of refuge and the cost of such removal including temporary repairs and towage shall be admitted as general average. The provisions of Rule XI shall be applied to the prolongation of the voyage occasioned by such removal.

(b) The cost of handling on board or discharging cargo, fuel or stores whether at a port or place of loading, call or refuge, shall be admitted as general average, when the handling or discharge was necessary for the common safety or to enable damage to the ship caused by sacrifice or accident to be repaired, if the repairs were necessary for the safe prosecution of the voyage, except in cases where the damage to the ship is discovered at a port or place of loading or call without any accident or other extraordinary circumstance connected with such damage having taken place during the voyage.

The cost of handling on board or discharging cargo, fuel or stores shall not be admissible as general average when incurred solely for the purpose of restowage due to shifting during the voyage, unless such restowage is necessary for the common safety.

(c) Whenever the cost of handling or discharging cargo, fuel or stores is admissible as general average, the costs of storage, including insurance if reasonably incurred, reloading and stowing of such cargo, fuel or stores shall likewise be admitted as general average. The provisions of Rule XI shall be applied to the extra period of detention occasioned by such reloading or restowing.

But when the ship is condemned or does not proceed on her original voyage, storage expenses shall be admitted as general average only up to the date of the ship's condemnation or of the abandonment of the voyage or up to the date of completion of discharge of cargo if the condemnation or abandonment takes place before that date.

Rule XI. *Wages and maintenance of crew and other expenses bearing up for and in a port of refuge, etc.*

(a) Wages and maintenance of master, officers and crew reasonably incurred and fuel and stores consumed during the prolongation of the voyage occasioned by a ship entering a port or place of refuge or returning to her port or place of loading shall be admitted as general average when the expenses of entering such port or place are allowable in general average in accordance with Rule X(a).

(b) When a ship shall have entered or been detained in any port or place in consequence of accident, sacrifice or other extraordinary circumstances which render that necessary for the common safety, or to enable damage to the ship caused by sacrifice or accident to be repaired, if the repairs were necessary for the safe prosecution of the voyage, the wages and maintenance of the master, officers, and crew reasonably incurred during the extra period of detention in such port or place until the ship shall or should have been made ready to proceed upon her voyage, shall be admitted in general average.

Fuel and stores consumed during the extra period of detention shall be admitted as general average, except such fuel and stores as are consumed in effecting repairs not allowable in general average.

Port charges incurred during the extra period of detention shall likewise be admitted as general average except such charges as are incurred solely by reason of repairs not allowable in general average.

Provided that when damage to the ship is discovered at a port or place of loading or call without any accident or other extraordinary circumstance connected with such damage having taken place during the voyage, then the wages and maintenance of master, officers and crew and fuel and stores consumed and port charges incurred during the extra detention for repairs to damages so discovered shall not be admissible as general average, even if the repairs are necessary for the safe prosecution of the voyage.

When the ship is condemned or does not proceed on her original voyage, the wages and maintenance of the master, officers and crew and fuel and stores consumed and port charges shall be admitted as general average only up to the date of the ship's condemnation or of the abandonment of the voyage or up to the date of completion of discharge of cargo if the condemnation or abandonment takes place before that date.

(c) For the purpose of this and the other Rules wages shall include all payments made to or for the benefit of the master, officers and crew, whether such payments be imposed by law upon the shipowners or be made under the terms or articles of employment.

(d) The cost of measures undertaken to prevent or minimise damage to the environment shall be allowed in general average when incurred in any or all of the following circumstances:

(i) as part of an operation performed for the common safety which, had it been undertaken by party outside the common maritime adventure, would have entitled such party to a salvage reward;

(ii) as a condition of entry into or departure from any port or place in the circumstances prescribed in Rule X (a);

(iii) as a condition of remaining at any port or place in the circumstances prescribed in Rule XI (b), provided that when there is an actual escape or release of pollutant substances the cost of any additional measures required on that account to prevent or minimise pollution or environmental damage shall not be allowed as general average;

(iv) necessarily in connection with the discharging, storing or reloading of cargo whenever the cost of those operations is admissible as general average.

Rule XII. *Damage to cargo in discharging, etc.* Damage to or loss of cargo, fuel or stores sustained in consequence of their handling, discharging, storing, reloading and stowing shall be made good as general average, when and only when the cost of those measures respectively is admitted as general average.

Rule XIII. *Deductions from cost of repairs.* Repairs to be allowed in general average shall not be subject to deductions in respect of 'new for old' where old material or parts are replaced by new unless the ship is over 15 years old in which case there shall be a deduction of one third. The deductions shall be regulated by the age of the ship from 31 December of the year of completion of construction to the date of the general average act, except for insulation, life and similar boats, communications and navigational apparatus and equipment, machinery and boilers for which the deductions shall be regulated by the age of the particular parts to which they apply.

The deductions shall be made only from the cost of the new material or parts when finished and ready to be installed in the ship.

No deduction shall be made in respect of provisions, stores, anchors and chain cables.

Drydock and slipway dues and costs of shifting the ship shall be allowed in full.

The costs of cleaning, painting or coating of bottom shall not be allowed in general average unless the bottom has been painted or coated within the twelve months preceding the date of the general average act in which case one half of such costs shall be allowed.

Rule XIV. *Temporary repairs*. Where temporary repairs are effected to a ship at a port of loading, call or refuge, for the common safety, or of damage caused by general average sacrifice, the cost of such repairs shall be admitted as general average.

Where temporary repairs of accidental damage are effected in order to enable the adventure to be completed, the cost of such repairs shall be admitted as general average without regard to the saving, if any, to other interests, but only up to the saving in expense which would have been incurred and allowed in general average if such repairs had not been effected there.

No deductions 'new for old' shall be made from the cost of temporary repairs allowable as general average.

Rule XV. *Loss of freight*. Loss of freight arising from damage to or loss of cargo shall be made good as general average, either when caused by a general average act, or when the damage to or loss of cargo is so made good.

Deduction shall be made from the amount of gross freight lost, of the charges which the owner thereof would have incurred to earn such freight, but has, in consequence of the sacrifice, not incurred.

Rule XVI. *Amount to be made good for cargo lost or damaged by sacrifice*. The amount to be made good as general average for damage to or loss of cargo sacrificed shall be the loss which has been sustained thereby based on the value at the time of discharge, ascertained from the commercial invoice rendered to the receiver or if there is no such invoice from the shipped value. The value at the time of discharge shall include the cost of insurance and freight except insofar as such freight is at the risk of interests other than the cargo.

When cargo so damaged is sold and the amount of the damage has not been otherwise agreed, the loss to be made good in general average shall be the difference between the net proceeds of sale and the net sound value as computed in the first paragraph of this Rule.

Rule XVII. *Contributory values*. The contribution to a general average shall be made upon the actual net value of the property at the termination of the adventure except that the value of cargo shall be the value at the time of discharge, ascertained from the commercial invoice rendered to the receiver or if there is no such invoice from the shipped value. The value of the cargo shall include the cost of insurance and freight unless and insofar as such freight is at the risk of interests other than the cargo, deducting therefrom any loss or damage suffered by the cargo prior to or at the time of discharge. The value of the ship shall be assessed without taking into account the beneficial or detrimental effect of any demise or time charterparty to which the ship may be committed.

To these values shall be added the amount made good as general average for property sacrificed, if not already included, deduction being made from the freight and passage money at risk of such charges and crew's wages as would not have been incurred in earning the freight had the ship and cargo been totally lost at the date of the general average act and have not been allowed as general average; deduction being also made from the value of the property of all extra charges incurred in respect thereof subsequently to the general average act, except such charges as are allowed in general average or fall upon the ship by virtue of an award for special compensation under Article 14 of the International Convention on Salvage, 1989 or under any other provision similar in substance.

In the circumstances envisaged in the third paragraph of Rule G, the cargo and other property shall contribute on the basis of its value upon delivery at original destination unless sold or otherwise disposed of short of that destination, and the ship shall contribute upon its actual net value at the time of discharge of cargo.

Where cargo is sold short of destination, however, it shall contribute upon the actual net proceeds of sale, with the addition of any amount made good as general average.

Mails, passengers' luggage, personal effects and accompanied private motor vehicles shall not contribute in general average.

Rule XVIII. *Damage to ship*. The amount to be allowed as general average for damage or loss to the ship, her machinery and/or gear caused by a general average act shall be as follows:

(a) When repaired or replaced.

   The actual reasonable cost of repairing or replacing such damage or loss subject to deduction in accordance with Rule XIII;

(b) When not repaired or replaced.

   The reasonable depreciation arising from such damage or loss, but not exceeding the estimated cost of repairs. But where the ship is an actual total loss or when the cost of repairs of the damage would exceed the value of the ship when repaired, the amount to be allowed as general average shall be the difference between the estimated sound value of the ship after deducting therefrom the estimated cost of repairing damage which is not general average and the value of the ship in her damaged state which may be measured by the net proceeds of sale, if any.

Rule XIX. *Undeclared or wrongfully declared cargo*. Damage or loss caused to goods loaded without the knowledge of the shipowner or his agent or to goods wilfully misdescribed at time of shipment shall not be allowed as general average, but such goods shall remain liable to contribute, if saved.

Damage or loss caused to goods which have been wrongfully declared on shipment at a value which is lower than their real value shall be contributed for at the declared value, but such goods shall contribute upon their actual value.

Rule XX. *Provision of funds*. A commission of two per cent of general average disbursements, other than the wages and maintenance of master, officers and crew and fuel and stores not replaced during the voyage, shall be allowed in general average. The capital loss sustained by the owners of goods sold for the purpose of raising funds to defray general average disbursements shall be allowed in general average.

The cost of insuring general average disbursements shall also be admitted in general average.

Rule XXI. *Interest on losses made good in general average*. Interest shall be allowed on expenditure, sacrifices and allowances in general average at the rate of seven per cent, per annum, until three months after the date of issue of the general average adjustment, due allowance being made for any payment on account by the contributory interests or from the general average deposit fund.

Rule XXII. *Treatment of cash deposits*. Where cash deposits have been collected in respect of cargo's liability for general average, salvage or special charges, such deposits shall be paid without any delay into a special account in the joint names of a representative nominated on behalf of the shipowner and a representative nominated on behalf of the depositors in a bank to be approved by both. The sum so deposited, together with accrued interest, if any, shall be held as security for the payment to the parties entitled thereto of the general average, salvage or special charges payable by cargo in respect to which the deposits have been collected. Payments on account or refunds of deposits may be made if certified to in writing by the average adjuster. Such deposits and payments or refunds shall be without prejudice to the ultimate liability of the parties.

Notes

The key changes made in 1994 were:

(a) the introduction of the Rule Paramount with its overriding requirement of reasonableness. The need for such a rule was clearly demonstrated by the first instance decision of *Corfu Navigation Co and Bain Clarkson Ltd v Mobil Shipping Co Ltd Zaire SEP and Petroca SA, The Alpha* [1991] 2 Lloyd's Rep 515 in which a contribution in general average was allowed despite a finding that the master's conduct in causing the general average act had been 'unskilful and unreasonable';

(b) a new Rule C on environmental liabilities to exclude pollutant substances;

(c) a new Rule XI(D) about the costs of measures undertaken in relation to environmental damage;

(d) a new Rule B (tug and tows/push boat and barges);

(e) new paragraphs in Rule E to reduce delays in the preparation of adjustments; and

(f) incidental amendments to Rules G, II, V, VIII, IX, XVII and in the relation to the calculation of interest.

References

Lowndes and Rudolf, *The Law of General Average and the York-Antwerp Rules*, 12th edn, Wilson, DJ and Cooke, JHS (eds) 1996, London: Sweet & Maxwell.

For a discussion of the changes to the Rules agreed in 1994 see (1995) 26 *JMLC* 465; Geoffrey Hudson, N, *The York-Antwerp Rules*, 2nd edn, 1996, London: Lloyd's of London Press; Macdonald, John (1995) *LMCLQ* 480; and Geoffrey Hudson, N (1996) 27 *JMLC* 469.

3 CAUSATION

Australian Coastal Shipping Commission v Green [1971] 1 QB 456, CA

Lord Denning's judgment in this case concerning causation and Rules A and C of the York-Antwerp Rules 1950 is set out below almost in its entirety as it provides a comprehensive survey of the law on the subject.

Lord Denning MR:

1   Introductory

We so rarely have to consider the law of general average that it is as well to remind ourselves of it. It arises when a ship, laden with cargo, is in peril on the sea, such peril indeed that the whole adventure, both ship and cargo, is in danger of being lost. If the master then, for the sake of all, throws overboard some of the cargo, so as to lighten the ship, it is unjust that the owner of the goods so jettisoned should be left to bear all the loss of it himself. He is entitled to a contribution from the shipowner and the other cargo owners in proportion of their interests. See the exposition by Lord Tenterden quoted in *Hallett v Wigram* (1850) 9 CB 580, at pp 607 to 608; and *Burton & Co v English & Co* (1883) 12 QBD 218. Likewise, if the master, for the sake of all, at the height of a storm, cuts away part of the ship's tackle (as in *Birkley and Others v Presgrave* (1801) 1 East 220); or cuts away a mast (as in *Atwood and Others v Sellar & Co* (1880) 5 QBD 286), or, having sprung a leak, puts into a port of refuge for repairs and spends money on them (as in *Svendsen and Others v Wallace Bros* (1885) 10 App Cas 404), it is unfair that the loss should fall on the shipowner alone. He is entitled to contribution from the cargo owners for the loss or expenditure to which he has been put. In all such cases the act done by the master is called a 'general average act': and the loss incurred is called a 'general average loss'.

The principles underlying these cases have been codified in the Marine Insurance Act 1906, which defines a 'general average act' in s 66(2):

> There is a general average act where any extraordinary sacrifice or expenditure is voluntarily and reasonably made or incurred in time of

peril for the purpose of preserving the property imperilled in the common adventure.

And it defines a 'general average loss in s 66(1):

A general average loss is a loss caused by or directly consequential on a general average act. It includes a general average expenditure as well as a general average sacrifice.

These definitions, however, have been supplemented by the York-Antwerp Rules, 1950, which replaced the 1924 Rules, and which by agreement, apply in the two cases now before us. In those rules a 'general average act' is defined by rule A:[1]

There is a general average act when, and only when, any extraordinary sacrifice or expenditure is intentionally and reasonably made or incurred for the common safety for the purpose of preserving from the peril the property involved in a common maritime adventure.

And a 'general average loss' is defined by rule C:[2]

Only such losses, damages or expenses which are the direct consequence of the general average act shall be allowed as general average.

Loss or damage sustained by the ship or cargo through delay, whether on the voyage or subsequently, such as demurrage, and any indirect loss whatsoever, such as loss of market, shall not be admitted as general average.

2   *The two cases before us*

(i) *The Bulwarra*: On 13 July 1960, the motor vessel *Bulwarra* was moored in a port in New South Wales, laden with steel products. A violent storm arose. Her after-mooring carried away. Her owners had an officer on shore. He saw the danger. He signalled for help to the master of a tug called the *Hero*. The tug got a line on board and towed the *Bulwarra* for about 10 minutes. Then the towline parted. It wrapped itself around the propeller of the tug and stopped it revolving. The tug drifted helplessly. Her anchors were useless. They were inboard and securely lashed to the bulwarks. They had no chains attached to them. The tug grounded and became a total loss. But the *Bulwarra* managed to get to safety.

The tugowners had thus lost their tug by their own negligence. But they claimed to be indemnified by the owners of the *Bulwarra*. They said that they were engaged on the terms of the United Kingdom Standard Towing Conditions which contain this provision:

3. The Tugowner shall not, whilst towing, bear or be liable for damage of any description done by or to the tug ... or for loss of the tug ... arising from any cause, including negligence at any time of the Tugowner's servants or agents ... and the Hirer shall pay for all loss or damage ... and shall also indemnify

---

1   Unchanged by the York-Antwerp Rules 1994.

2   Materially unchanged under the York-Antwerp Rules 1994 apart from a reference to environmental liabilities and an amendment to the position of 'loss of market' (see the note at the end of this section).

the Tugowner against all consequences thereof ... Provided that any such liability for loss or damage as above set out is not caused by want of reasonable care on the part of the Tugowner to make his tugs seaworthy ...

The owners of the *Bulwarra* acknowledged that, by the course of dealing, they hired the tug on those conditions. But they resisted the claim on the ground that the loss of the tug was caused by want of reasonable care on the part of the tugowners to make the tug seaworthy. They succeeded in the defence and were awarded costs against the tugowners. But in that action the shipowners recovered only party and party costs. The shipowners had to pay to their own lawyers, the solicitor and client costs. This left them out of pocket A\$3,396.31 or £1,313.5s.4d. They claim that this was a general average expenditure. If this is right, they can recover their own proportion from the insurers and the rest from the cargo owners. But the insurers say it was not general average expenditure, and is, therefore, not recoverable from them.

At first sight, it seems strange that such costs should be regarded as general average expenditure. But I must notice an important arrangement that the parties have made. The insurers have agreed that, if the shipowners had lost the case brought by the tugowners (and thus became liable to indemnify the tugowners for the loss of the tug): and, if in that case the expenditure by way of indemnity would have been general average expenditure, then this sum of £1,313.5s.4d for costs (which they had to pay their own solicitors) should be treated as general average expenditure. The reason for this agreement is, no doubt, to encourage shipowners in like case to resist a claim by the tugowners.

(ii) *The Wangara*: On 17 November 1961, the motor vessel *Wangara* sailed from Melbourne with a cargo of steel products for carriage to Auckland, New Zealand. Next day she grounded. Two shore officers of the owners engaged the tug *Walumba* to tow her off. While the tug was towing the *Wangara*, the towrope parted and wrapped itself round the propeller of the tug and the tug was damaged. A pilot vessel came to the assistance of the tug and towed it to safety. The *Wangara* also got to safety. The pilot vessel claimed salvage remuneration from the owners of the tug and was awarded it.

The tugowners then claimed to be indemnified by the owners of the *Wangara*. They relied on the United Kingdom Standard Towage Conditions ... The owners of the Wangara resisted the claim but were found liable. Their total expenditure came to \$50,446.71 (£20,098.5s.9d), made up of: (a) the damage to the tug herself; (b) the salvage award payable by the tug to the pilot vessel; (c) the costs payable to the tugowners; (d) their own costs of resisting the claim of the tugowners.

The owners of the *Wangara* say that expenditure was general average expenditure and that they can recover their own proportion from the insurers and the rest from the cargo owners. The insurers say it was not general average expenditure. In each of the two cases, we must ask, first, what was the general average act? Second, what was the general average loss?

3   The general average act

The 'general average act' was I think the contract made by the shipowners with the tug. In each case the vessel was in dire peril and the shipowners called upon the tug for help. If the tug had rendered salvage services on the usual terms of 'no cure-no pay', the contract would undoubtedly have been a 'general average act'. If the services had been successful, the owners would have been liable to pay a very high reward: which would count as 'general average expenditure'. If the services had been unsuccessful, they would have had to pay nothing, see *NV Bureau Wijsmuller v Tojo Maru (Owners)* [1969] 2 Lloyd's Rep 193, at p 199; [1969] 3 WLR 902, at p 913. Instead of entering into such a contract, the shipowners made a towage contract on the United Kingdom Standard Towage Conditions. That was a very reasonable contract to make for both sides. It is well known that there is a substantial risk in towage operations that the towrope may break and foul the propeller of the tug: and that, if that happens, the tug may run aground or be damaged and have to be rescued. In a salvage agreement, the tugowners take that risk on themselves in return for the chance of a very high salvage reward. In a hiring agreement, at a fixed rate of hire, they cannot be expected to take the risk on themselves. It is only right and fair that they should ask for and receive an indemnity. The benefit to the shipowners is that, if the service is successful, he pays much less than he would under a salvage award: but, in return, he has to give an indemnity to the tugowner. In these circumstances, I have no doubt that the towage contract is a 'general average act'. It was intentionally and reasonably made for the common safety: just as was the contract in *The Gratitudine* (1801) 3 C Rob 240 (for the hypothecation of the cargo); and in *Anderson Tritton & Co v Ocean Steamship Company* (1884) 10 App Cas 107, (for towage service).

4   The general average loss

The next question is: What was the general average loss? If the towline had not parted, and the tug had completed her task in safety, the hiring charge would certainly have been a general average expenditure. But the towline did part. It wrapped itself round the propeller of the tug. The result was that, in the case of the *Bulwarra*, the tug became a total loss: and, in the case of the *Wangara*, the tug was salved at great expense. The shipowners have become bound under the indemnity clause to indemnify the tug owners. Is this expenditure under the indemnity clause, a 'general average loss'?

This depends on whether the expenditure was the 'direct consequence' of the general average act within rule C of the York-Antwerp Rules. At the time when the rules were made in 1924, all lawyers thought that they could tell the difference between 'direct' and 'indirect' consequences ... But 40 years later the Privy Council poured scorn upon it. It was in *Overseas Tankship (UK) Ltd v Morts Dock & Engineering Company Ltd (The Wagon Mound)* [1961] AC 388, when Viscount Simonds said (at pp 423 ...) that the test of the 'direct consequence' leads to nowhere but the never-ending and insoluble problem of causation. To add to the confusion, rule C of the York-Antwerp Rules gives 'loss of market' as a typical instance of indirect loss, following, no doubt, *The Parana* (1877) 2 PD 118; whereas in *Koufos v C Czarnikow Ltd* [1969] 1 AC 350, at p 385 ... Lord Reid says that the loss of market there was 'directly caused' by the defendants' breach of contract.[3]

---

3   See the note at the end of this section.

In these circumstances I propose to go back to the concept, as I understood it in 1924, when the York-Antwerp Rules were made. 'Direct consequences' denote those consequences which flow in an unbroken sequence from the act: whereas 'indirect consequences' are those in which the sequence is broken by an intervening or extraneous cause. I realise that this is not very helpful: because the metaphor of 'breaking the chain' of causation means one thing to one man and another thing to another. But still we have to do the best we can with it.

Direct consequences

Applying this test, I would start with the engagement of the tug on the towage conditions. That was the 'general average act'. From that act we have this sequence: (i) the making fast of the towline and the subsequent towage; (ii) the snapping of the towline and its fouling the propeller; (iii) the loss, or salvage, of the tug; (iv) the claim for indemnity.

Is that a direct sequence in unbroken line? Or is the sequence broken? The only two points at which it may be broken are at (ii) and (iv). I will consider them separately.

(i) *The subsequent accident*: It was a most unfortunate thing that the towline snapped and fouled the propeller. That was an intervening cause of much importance. Without it, the loss and expenditure would never have happened. But did it break the chain of causation?

There is a passage in the German author Ulrich (Grosse-Haverei) which seems to say that, when, after a general average act, there is a 'subsequent accident' which results in loss or damage, it breaks the chain of causation: so that such loss or damage is never the direct consequence of the general average act. It was quoted with approval by Bigham J in *Anglo-Argentine Live Stock and Produce Agency v Temperley Shipping Company* [1899] 2 QB 403, at p 410; and by Bailhache J in *Austin Friars Steamship Company Ltd v Spillers & Bakers Ltd* [1915] 1 KB 833, at p 836.

I cannot accept this view. If the master, when he does the 'general average act' ought reasonably to have foreseen that a subsequent accident of the kind might occur – or even that there was a distinct possibility of it – then the subsequent accident does not break the chain of causation. The loss or damage is the direct consequence of the original general average act.

A good instance was given by Lord Tenterden in his book on shipping:

> So, if, to avoid an impending danger, or to repair the damage occasioned by a storm, the ship be compelled to take refuge in a port to which it was not destined, and into which it cannot enter without taking out a part of her cargo, *and the part taken out to lighten the ship on this occasion happens to be lost in the barges employed to convey it to the shore*, this loss also, being occasioned by the removal of the goods for the general benefit, must be repaired by general contribution. [Emphasis supplied.]

This passage was quoted with approval by Cresswell J in *Hallett v Wigram* (1850) 9 CB, at p 608; and by Mathew J in *McCall & Co Ltd v Houlder Bros* (1897) 2 Com Cas 129. Another instance is the case before Roche J of *Anglo-Grecian Steam Trading Company Ltd v T Beynon & Co* (1926) 24 Ll L Rep 122. The vessel was in peril and was taken in tow. The intention was to beach the vessel in the centre of Whitmore Bay. On the way she grounded, the towropes parted, and she got on the rocks and suffered damage. This subsequent accident, said Roche J at p 127, was 'at all times a possibility'. It did not

> ... break the chain of causation and prevent the plaintiffs from recovering in respect of the damage done by the rocks.

If, however, there is a subsequent accident which was only a remote possibility, it would be different. Thus Lowndes (Lowndes & Rudolf: *Law of General Average*) gave the illustration of a sailing vessel, when the master cuts away the mast and thus reduces her speed; and afterwards she is captured by the enemy. Her loss is not the direct consequence of the general average act. It is due to the intervening capture.

In both cases before us, the master, when he engaged the tug, should have envisaged that it was distinctly possible that the towline might break and foul the propeller. When it happened, therefore, it did not break the chain of causation.

(ii) *The indemnity clause*: The indemnity clause was most stringent. It was an extraneous cause of much importance. Without it, the expenditure by the shipowners would never have been incurred. But did it break the chain of causation?

If the indemnity clause had been unreasonable and such that the master ought never, in justice to the cargo owners, to have agreed to it, then I think that the expenditure would not flow from the general average act. It would flow from the onerous clause in the towage agreement: see *Moss Steamship Company Ltd v Board of Trade* [1924] AC, at p 141 by Viscount Cave LC, and Lord Sumner; and at p 145 ... by Viscount Haldane. But, seeing that the indemnity clause here was reasonable, and such that the master, quite justly and fairly, agreed to it, then I think the expenditure flowed directly from the general average act. That is borne out by *The Gratitudine* (1801) 3 C Rob 240, at pp 272 to 276, when there was a most onerous contract under which the master hypothecated both ship and cargo to a moneylender – so as to pay for repairs – but, as the master had no practicable alternative but to accept the contract, the loss under it was held to be a general average loss.

This, I think, gives the clue to *Anderson Tritton & Co v Ocean Steamship Company* (1884) 10 App Cas 107. If the master of the *Achilles* agreed to pay an exorbitant charge, such that he ought never, in justice to the cargo owners, to have agreed to, then the excess of the charge (over and above a reasonable charge) would not flow from the general average act, but from the onerous clause which the master had agreed to. The only amount allowable as a 'general average loss' would be a reasonable charge. We were taken right through that case in its course through every court and through the record of the House of Lords. But counsel do not seem to have discovered the later stages of the case on the retrial. It is reported in (1885) 1 TLR, at pp 324, 413, and 615. The jury found that there was no agreement for an exorbitant sum, but only for a fair remuneration, ie a *quantum meruit*. So all the nice points of law disappeared. But, if there had been an agreement by the master to pay an exorbitant charge, then it would have to be scaled down to a reasonable figure and that only allowed as general average expenditure. That appears from *The Gratitudine*

(1801) 3 C Rob at p 277, where Lord Stowell thought that the commission charged might be excessive; and, if it was more than a proper charge, it would have to be scaled down.

None of those refinements need worry us here. The indemnity was quite reasonable. So was the expenditure under it. It was the direct consequence of the general average act and must be accepted as a general average loss ...

6   Conclusion

The classical writers stress that general average arises when the master of a vessel gives something for the sake of all (*quod pro omnibus datum est*). In these cases the master gave, for the sake of all, his agreement to a towage contract containing an indemnity to the tugowner in case the tug was lost or damaged. He must be taken to have realised that there was a distinct possibility that the towline might part and that the tug would be lost or damaged: and that, if that happened, the tugowner would be entitled to an indemnity. Such expenditure was the direct consequence of his act in hiring the tug on those terms. It is, therefore, general average loss.

I would dismiss this appeal.

[Phillimore and Cairns LJJ also delivered judgments in favour of dismissing the appeal but neither was concerned about causation where the expenditure was incurred under a contract which was itself the general average act. Both judges did however accept Ulrich's test which Lord Denning questioned.]

Note

The York-Antwerp Rules 1994 add a reference in Rule C to the exclusion of environmental liabilities and amend the wording of the last paragraph of the rule so as to exclude 'loss of market' from 'indirect loss' as such which had been the source of the confusion under earlier versions of the rules.

4   WHO CAN SUE AND WHEN? BASIS OF CLAIM IN ENGLISH LAW / SHIPOWNERS' LIEN / LIMITATION

Castle Insurance v Hong Kong Islands Shipping [1984] 1 AC 226, PC

The Privy Council decided in this case that a shipowner's claim under a bill of lading for a general average contribution arose when the sacrifice was made or incurred and not when the adjustment was delivered. The judgment of their Lordships was delivered by **Lord Diplock**:

> The immediate question in this interlocutory appeal and cross-appeal from an order of the Court of Appeal of Hong Kong is whether the original plaintiffs in the action, Hong Kong Islands Shipping Co Ltd (the ship managers), should be allowed to join Hong Kong Atlantic Shipping Co Ltd (the shipowners) as second plaintiffs in an action brought by writ issued on 25 October 1978, against 85 defendants, of whom 74 (the consignees) were consignees of cargo carried upon a general ship *Potoi Chau* owned by the shipowners and managed

by the ship managers and the remaining 11 defendants (the cargo insurers) are insurers of the cargo. The plaintiffs' claims in the action are for general average contributions to losses consequential on general average sacrifices made and general average expenditures incurred in the course of a voyage from ports in the Far East to Jeddah, Hodeidah, Aden and Bombay. The claims against the consignees are not made against them at common law as owners of the cargo at the time of the sacrifices and expenditure but are based upon the contracts contained in the bills of lading or, in the preferred alternative, upon agreements in one or other of the forms that are usually, though inaccurately, referred to as Lloyd's average bonds. The claims against the cargo insurers are based upon agreements contained in what are usually, and again inaccurately, called letters of guarantee.

The Court of Appeal, upholding in this respect the order of Mr Commissioner Mayo at first instance, refused to allow the joinder of the shipowners as plaintiffs in the claim against the consignees of the cargo. This refusal is the subject of the cross-appeal by the plaintiffs. The Court of Appeal, however, reserving in this respect the order of the Commissioner, allowed the joinder of the shipowners as additional plaintiffs in the claims against the cargo insurers. This is the subject of the appeal. The grounds of the Court of Appeal's decision were that as against the cargo owners the shipowners' claims were barred by the expiry of the six-year limitation period; whereas against the cargo insurers the shipowners' claims were not.

[His Lordship set out the relevant events and dates]

... The significance of these dates is that the original writ was issued within six years of the first general average act and within six years of the execution of the average bonds by each of the consignees and of the letters of guarantee by each of the cargo insurers. On the other hand the application to join the shipowners as plaintiffs in the action was made more than six years after the last of these events.

Under that branch of English common law into which the lex mercatoria has long ago become absorbed, the personal liability to pay the general average contribution due in respect of any particular consignment of cargo that had been preserved in consequence of a general average sacrifice or expenditure lies, in legal theory, upon the person who was owner of the consignment at the time when the sacrifice was made or the liability for the expenditure incurred. In practice, however, the personal liability at common law of whoever was the owner of the contributing consignment of cargo at the time of the general average act is hardly ever relied upon. There are two reasons for this. The first is that the contract of carriage between the shipowner and the owner of the consignment, whether the contract be contained in a charterparty or a bill of lading, invariably nowadays (so far as the decided cases show) contains an express clause dealing with general average and so brings the claim to contribution into the field of contract law. The second, and this has in practice been the decisive reason, is that there attaches to all cargo that has been preserved in consequence of a general average sacrifice or expenditure a lien in favour of those concerned in ship or cargo who have sustained a general average loss. The lien attaches to the preserved cargo at the time when the sacrifice is made or the liability to the expenditure incurred. The lien is a possessory lien and it is the duty of the master of the vessel to exercise the lien at the time of discharge of the preserved cargo in such a way as will provide equivalent security for contributions towards general average sacrifices made or expenditure incurred not only by those concerned in the ship but also by those concerned in cargo in respect of which a net general average loss has been sustained. The lien, being a possessory one and not a maritime lien, is exercisable only against the consignee, but it is exercisable whether or not the consignee was owner of the consignment at the time of the general average sacrifice or expenditure that gave rise to the lien: a fact of which the shipowner may well be unaware. At the time of discharge the sum for which the lien is security (save in the simplest cases, which do not include that of a general ship) is unquantifiable until after there has been an average adjustment. Indeed in the case of some consignees of cargo that has been preserved in part only or damaged in consequence of a general average loss, so far from being liable to a net general average contribution they may eventually turn out to be entitled to a net payment in general average. The disadvantages and legal complications which would result from the master's actually withholding delivery to its consignee of cargo preserved by general average acts are conveniently set out in Lowndes & Rudolf, *General Average and York-Antwerp Rules* (*British Shipping Laws*, vol 7), 10th edn (1975), para 453 and need not be repeated here.[4] In practice what happens is what happened in the instant case; the master, acting on behalf of the shipowner and of any persons interested in cargo who will be found on the adjustment to be entitled to a net general average payment, releases the preserved cargo to the consignees upon the execution by each consignee of an average bond in one or other of Lloyd's standard forms accompanied, in the comparatively rare cases of cargo that is uninsured or underinsured, by a deposit in a bank in joint names of money as security or, more usually, by a letter of guarantee from the insurer of the cargo.

Although the instant case is not concerned with the common law liability to general average contribution of the owner of the cargo at the time of the general average act, the bills of lading contained an express clause dealing with general average which was in the following terms:

> 28 (General Average). General Average shall be adjusted, stated and settled according to York-Antwerp Rules 1950.

This creates a contractual liability on the part of the consignee as indorsee of the bill of lading to pay general average contribution, if there be any chargeable on the cargo shipped, whether it was he, the shipper or some intermediate indorsee of the bill of lading, who happened to be owner of the goods at the time when a general average sacrifice took place or a liability for a general average expenditure was incurred. Since this liability arises under a simple contract, the period of limitation is six years from the accrual of the cause of action; but the clause is intended to regulate, and to transfer to whoever acquires title to the consignment of cargo under the bill of lading, what would otherwise be a common law liability of the owner of the cargo at the time of the general average act; so for the purposes of the instant case a

---

4   The reference in the 12th edition (1997) is para 30.38-30.41.

necessary starting point is first to determine when, at common law, a cause of action for a general average contribution would have accrued against the owner of cargo, and then to see whether the wording of the clause is apt to postpone the accrual of a cause of action for such contribution against a holder of the bill of lading or to create some different cause of action accruing at a later date than that of the general average act in respect of which contribution was claimed.

The relevant cases as to the time of accrual of a cause of action for a general average contribution at common law are scanty. They are the subject of close analysis in the judgments of Sir Alan Huggins VP and Leonard JA in the Court of Appeal. Scanty though the cases may be, their Lordships are of opinion that the law is plain and was correctly stated by Greer LJ in his dissenting judgment in *Tate & Lyle Ltd v Hain Steamship Co Ltd* (1934) 49 Ll L Rep 123, 135:

> I cannot find that these questions have ever been definitely settled in any of the decided cases, but the law has been frequently stated by judges and jurists of authority in commercial matters in words which lead me to conclude that both the liability and the lien come into existence as soon as the sacrifice has been made or the expenses have been incurred, but that the liability and lien are subject to be defeated by the non-arrival of the cargo at the port of destination.

... Although the claim to general average contribution against the consignees in the instant appeal appears in the points of claim to be based primarily upon the average bonds executed by them upon discharge of the cargo at its port of destination, a claim based upon the general average clause in the bills of lading was permitted to be argued in the Court of Appeal where it is discussed in the judgment of Leonard JA. The Court of Appeal rejected it; but it was renewed, albeit with a justifiable air of diffidence, before this Board.

Upon a claim so framed the judgment in *Chandris v Argo Insurance Co Ltd* [1963] 2 Lloyd's Rep 65 is very much in point. That was a single judgment given in six test cases that were heard together and involved, *inter alia*, claims by assureds against insurers to be indemnified against general average contributions under a hull policy of insurance which incorporated a provision that:

> 8. General average and salvage to be adjusted according to the law and practice obtaining at the place where the adventure ends, as if the contract of affreightment contained no special terms upon the subject; but where the contract of affreightment so provides the adjustment shall be according to York-Antwerp Rules 1890 ... or York-Antwerp Rules 1924.

The contracts of affreightment did provide that general average should be 'adjusted according to York-Antwerp Rules'. The actions were commenced more than six years after the general average acts in respect of which the liability to general average contribution arose, but less than six years after an average adjustment had been completed by average adjusters and the average statement published. The relevant provision of the Marine Insurance Act 1906 dealing with the assured's right to recover general average contribution from the insurer under the policy is contained in section 66(5) which reads:

Subject to any express provision in the policy, where the assured has paid, or is liable to pay, a general average contribution in respect of the subject insured, he may recover therefor from the insurer.

So the question for the learned judge in the *Chandris* case was: when does a shipowner become liable to pay a general average contribution to a consignee of cargo under a contract of affreightment which provides for adjustment of general average according to York-Antwerp Rules? The argument for the assured in the *Chandris* case was that since the contract of affreightment, and hence the policy, contemplated that there would be an adjustment of general average according to York-Antwerp Rules, and since those rules contemplate that the adjustment will lead to the making by average adjusters of a general average statement, this statement, the argument goes, will for the first time quantify the net amount of the general average contribution due from each individual contributor, which up to that time had been only an unliquidated and unascertained sum, so a fresh cause of action thereupon arises for recovery of the amount so quantified.

The difficulty in this argument lies in that part of the judgment of the Privy Council delivered in *Wavertree Sailing Ship Co Ltd v Love* [1897] AC 373 that states what for more than a century had been the accepted law of general average. Their Lordships do not refer to this authority for the purpose of relying upon the opinion of the Board that it was not an implied term of the contract of affreightment that in the event of the occurrence of a general average act in the course of the voyage the shipowner would procure an average adjustment and statement to be prepared by a professional average adjuster. There is nothing in the instant appeal that makes it necessary for their Lordships to consider whether changes in mercantile practices which have taken place since 1897 have made such an implication necessary, at any rate in cases of contracts contained in bills of lading for carriage in a general ship. In the instant case this question cannot arise; there was a prolonged and complex average adjustment and statement made by professional average adjusters. But the Board's other reason for allowing the appeal in *Wavertree Sailing Ship Co Ltd v Love* [1897] AC 373 in the view of their Lordships, presents insuperable difficulties to the consignees' claims so far as they are based upon the general average clause in the bills of lading. It is that an average statement under the York-Antwerp Rules prepared by average adjusters appointed by shipowners is not binding upon cargo owners either as respects any net general average contribution or any net general average claim. Cargo owners can not only dispute entire liability upon such grounds as that the vessel was unseaworthy at the beginning of the voyage owing to failure by the shipowner to exercise due diligence, or that sacrifices or expenses claimed were not made or incurred to preserve from a common peril the property involved in the adventure and therefore did not amount to general average acts, but they can also dispute the quantum of any contribution or claim attributed to their consignment by the average statement. If there were any such dispute it would fall to be determined by a court of justice of competent jurisdiction or, if the contract of affreightment contained an arbitration clause, by arbitration.

So, as a matter of law, in the absence of any agreement to the contrary, the publication of the average statement settles nothing: it has no other legal effect than as an expression of opinion by a professional man as to what are the appropriate sums payable to one another by the various parties interested in ship and cargo. It is just not capable of giving rise to any fresh cause of action or of postponing the accrual of an existing cause of action for an unliquidated sum.

Causes of action for unliquidated sums that, in the absence of earlier agreement as to quantum reached between the parties themselves, will only become quantified by the judgment of a court or the award of an arbitrator, accrue at the time that the events occur which give rise to the liability to pay to the plaintiff compensation in an amount to be subsequently ascertained. They are commonplace in the field of contract as well as in the field of tort. Unliquidated damages for breach of contract, claims on a quantum meruit, claims for salvage services under Lloyd's open form of salvage agreement are examples and in their Lordships' view it was rightly decided in *Chandris v Argo Insurance Co Ltd* [1963] 2 Lloyd's Rep 65, that claims for contributions in general average under contractual provisions which do no more than require general average to be adjusted according to York-Antwerp Rules fall within this class and that, accordingly, the cause of action under such a contractual provision in a bill of lading accrues at the time when each general average sacrifice was made or general average expense incurred.

It was submitted that a distinction could be drawn between the more common form of general average clause in bills of lading which refers only to general average being 'adjusted' according to York-Antwerp Rules and the general average clause in bills of lading in the instant case which refers to general average being 'adjusted, stated and settled' according to York-Antwerp Rules 1950. In their Lordships' view, however, the inclusion of the additional words 'stated and settled' makes no difference. The York-Antwerp Rules do not make the average adjuster's assessments of liability to contribute contained in his general average statement binding upon cargo owners nor do the rules impose any legal obligation on cargo owners to settle general average claims by paying the amount so assessed; so in the context the additional words add nothing to what would already be comprehended in 'adjusting according to York-Antwerp Rules'.

The judgment in *Chandris v Argo Insurance Co Ltd* [1963] 2 Lloyd's Rep 65 in what were intended to be test cases has stood unchallenged for 20 years. In the interests of business certainty their Lordships would have been very reluctant to overrule it; but so far as claims in general average between parties to the maritime adventure are concerned, the almost invariable use of average bonds eliminates the need to rely directly on the general average clause in the contract of affreightment.

Their Lordships turn now to the average bonds executed by the consignees upon delivery to them of their respective consignments at the port of destination. The Court of Appeal held that the contracts thereby created did not give rise to a fresh cause of action which did not accrue until the amount of the contribution chargeable to the consignment had been ascertained and stated in a general average statement prepared by an average adjuster. It is this decision of the Court of Appeal that is the principal subject of challenge in the ship managers' and the shipowners' appeal.

The average bonds, to give them their common though legally inaccurate description, were in the usual Lloyd's forms which appear to have been in use in substantially the same terms for well over a century: *Svendsen v Wallace* (1885) 10 App Cas 406, 410. There are two varieties one of which provides for security in the form of a cash deposit on joint account in a bank, the other does not call for any cash deposit but it is stated on its face that it is: 'To be used in conjunction with underwriters' guarantee'. In both varieties the wording of the preamble and the mutual promises is the same. As respects the bonds providing for cash deposits, of which there were very few in the instant case, it is only necessary for their Lordships to draw attention to the fact that the provisions relating to the cash deposit deal with interim payments on account out of the deposit of sums certified to be proper 'by the adjuster or adjusters who may be employed to adjust the said ... general average'. The implication from this is clear: it was the mutual intention of the parties that there should be an average adjustment undertaken by professional average adjusters ...

[Lord Diplock then set out the terms of average bonds omitting only those relating to the cash deposit in the bonds which were not accompanied by an insurer's guarantee.]

[The bond is] a fresh agreement which stands on its own independently of the bill of lading and is for fresh consideration on either side: the release by the shipowner of his claim to any possessory lien for a general average contribution (also referred to as a 'charge') he may have on the consignment, and the assumption by the consignee of a personal liability, secured by a cash deposit or an insurer's guarantee, to pay such general average contribution/charge which may have been payable, at common law, by the owner of the consignment at the time of the general average act or, under the contract of affreightment, by the shipper (each of whom, particularly in the case of a general ship, may well be someone other than the consignee). Their Lordships draw attention to the statement in the preamble [to the bond] that the general average contribution (if there be one) 'cannot be immediately ascertained'. The agreement then goes on to deal with what is to be done by the parties until it is ascertained. First of all the consignment is to be delivered 'on payment of freight payable on delivery if any', ie against payment to be made immediately. This is to be contrasted with the promise by the consignee which immediately follows expressed in the future tense that he 'will pay' his proper general average contribution. This is a promise to make a payment of a liquidated sum at some date in the future which cannot arrive until what is his proper general average contribution/charge has been ascertained. The contrast between this promise to do something in the future and a promise to do something immediately is again apparent from the succeeding promise by the consignee to furnish particulars of the value of the consignment 'forthwith' in order that something further may be done in the future that is needed to enable the liquidated sum that the consignee has promised he will pay to be ascertained. What is to be done is in order that the general average contribution/charge 'may be ascertained and adjusted *in the usual manner*'. The words italicised are crucial. They direct one to the procedure that is in actual practice followed when general average is adjusted according to York-Antwerp Rules even though such practice may involve the non-insistence by persons interested in the adventure upon their strict legal rights. The usual practice, in the case of a general ship at any rate, is for the shipowner to employ a professional average adjuster to determine and set out in a general average statement his determination on the one hand of the sums payable as a contribution from each party to the adventure who is liable to contribute to general average and on the other hand of the sums in respect of general average sacrifices or expenditures which are recoverable by way of reimbursement by each party to the adventure by whom such sacrifices were made or expenditures incurred. The usual practice is for actual payment of contributions/charges to be deferred until completion of the general average statement, unless, as did not happen in the instant case, the average adjuster has given a certificate providing for some interim reimbursement to be made to a claimant for a general loss without prejudice to ultimate liability.

In their Lordships' view, although, from the point of view of clarity, the draftsmanship of the Lloyd's forms of average bond leave much to be desired, the application of commercial common sense to the language used makes clear the intention of the parties to it as respects payments by the consignees. The contractual obligation assumed by the consignee is to make a payment of a liquidated sum at a future date which will not arrive until the general average statement has been completed by an average adjuster appointed by the shipowners. That in the instant case, where no question of the issue by the adjuster of certificates for interim reimbursements arose, was the earliest date at which the shipowners' cause of action against the consignees under the average bond for payment of general average contribution arose. It was not time barred at the date of the application of 19 July 1979 to add the shipowners as additional plaintiffs.

Since the average bond provided that the consignees' general average contributions should be adjusted in the usual manner, which in the instant case meant according to York-Antwerp Rules, the consignees were not thereby deprived of any defence they might have on the ground that the statement had not been drawn up according to such rules, as for instance that they were excused from liability owing to the unseaworthiness of the *Potoi Chau* resulting from the failure of the shipowners to exercise due diligence – a defence which it appears from the affidavit evidence they intend to raise.

For these reasons their Lordships are of the opinion that the plaintiffs' cross-appeal should be allowed as against the consignees ...

Notes

1   The 1994 amendments to the Rules have had no impact on the status of this case which remains authoritative on the Lloyd's bond.

2   The case has been criticised on the issue of the contract: see Lowndes and Rudolf paras 00.29–30.

5 FAULT/RULE D/UNSEAWORTHINESS

Goulandris Brothers v Goldman & Sons [1958] 1 QB 74

Pearson J read the following judgment:

This is an award stated in the form of a special case pursuant to section 21(1)(b) of the Arbitration Act 1950. It raises questions of law which are intricate and difficult.

The claimants were at all material times the owners of a ship called the *Granhill*, which sailed from Liverpool on 26 October 1950, under a time charterparty to ports in West Africa. From 11 to 23 November 1950, she was at Sapele where a part cargo was loaded, and unfortunately some river water was used for filling the boilers. From 25 November to 3 December 1950, the ship was at Lagos and loaded cargo, including the respondents' goods which were for delivery in London under the bill of lading. When the ship was on the way to London in January, 1951, serious troubles developed in the boilers and she had to be towed first to Falmouth and then to London, where the cargo was discharged. The goods were undamaged but expenditure of a general average nature was incurred by the ship. A general average adjustment was duly prepared and it showed the respondents' proportion of the general average expenditure incurred by the claimants to be £22.10s.4d. The claimants claimed that sum from the respondents, but the respondents denied liability, contending that the ship was unseaworthy and that due diligence had not been exercised to make her seaworthy before and at the beginning of the voyage from Lagos. The claimants denied these contentions ...

[On the issues of unseaworthiness and due diligence the arbitrator found that the claimants, their servants or agents had failed to exercise due diligence to make the vessel seaworthy and that this was the cause of the general average expenditure in question being incurred.]

The respondents' contention is that those findings of unseaworthiness and failure to exercise due diligence the claimants' claim for contribution in general average must be rejected. The claimants, however, contend that they are still entitled to maintain their claim by virtue of the operation of rule D of the York-Antwerp Rules 1950,[5] and the third paragraph of article III, rule 6, of the Hague Rules ...

The first paragraph of clause 9 of the bill of lading provides: 'General average payable according to the York-Antwerp Rules 1950, and any amendment thereof'. Rule D of the York-Antwerp Rules 1950, provides: 'Rights to contribution in general average shall not be affected, though the event which gave rise to the sacrifice or expenditure may have been due to the fault of one of the parties to the adventure; but this shall not prejudice any remedies which may be open against that party for such fault'.

By virtue of a clause in the bill of lading and the Nigerian Carriage of Goods by Sea Ordinance, No 1 of 1926, the bill of lading was subject to the Hague Rules.

---

5   Minor amendments to rule D in the 1994 Rules have no impact on this decision.

The third paragraph of article III, rule 6, of the Hague Rules, provides: 'In any event the carrier and the ship shall be discharged from all liability in respect of loss or damage unless suit is brought within one year after delivery of the goods or the date when the goods should have been delivered'.

The argument put forward by Mr Donaldson for the claimants was to this effect: (1) Under the first part of rule D the claimants have a right to contribution in general average which is not affected by the fact that the event which gave rise to the general average expenditure was due to the fault of the claimants. (2) The remedy, which was originally open to the respondents for the fault of the claimants, and was preserved by the second part of rule D, was to sue the claimants for damages for breach of the contract of carriage, claiming as damages the amount of the general average contribution payable by the respondents to the claimants. (3) So long as the respondents' claim for damages for breach of contract remained enforceable, an action by the claimants against the respondents for the general average contribution could be met and defeated by the respondents setting up their claim for damages equal to the amount of the contribution, and the court in such a case would give judgment for the respondents on the claimants' claim in order to avoid circuity of action. (4) But the respondents' claim for damages for breach of contract has become unenforceable because it was a claim 'in respect of loss or damage' within the meaning of the third paragraph of rule 6 of article III of the Hague Rules, and, as no suit was brought within the year after the delivery of the goods, or the date when the goods should have been delivered, the claimants have been discharged from all liability in respect of the loss or damage. (5) Therefore, now the position is that the claimants still have their right to general average contribution and the respondents no longer have anything to set against it, so that no question of circuity arises, and the claimants are entitled to recover from the respondents the amount of the contribution, which is £22.10s.4d. That was Mr Donaldson's argument for the claimants.

It was suggested to Mr Donaldson that his argument, if correct, would produce unreasonable results, in that the cargo owner has originally a good defence to the shipowners' claim on the ground that the general average expenditure was caused by the fault of the shipowners but the shipowner, by merely deferring the issue of his writ for a year, can deprive the cargo owner of that defence. Mr Donaldson's answer was that the cargo owner could protect his interest by bringing an action within the year against the shipowner, even though the shipowner had not yet brought any action or made any claim against the cargo owner. As to the nature of such action by the cargo owner, Mr Donaldson had two suggestions. First, he suggested that the cargo owner's action should be for a declaration of non-liability ... One difficulty is that if Mr Donaldson's other contentions are right, the possible future claim, though invalid at an early date, would become valid at a later date after the lapse of time had destroyed the defence to it.

The second suggestion was that the cargo owner should bring against the shipowner an action for damages for breach of the charterparty, and should include in the damages the amount of the cargo owner's liability to the shipowner for general average contribution. That is a more promising method and safer on the legal side, because if a breach of contract could be proved, the plaintiff would be entitled to at least nominal damages. However, this method is not free from difficulties because the plaintiff would be unable to quantify his claim until after the compilation of the average adjustment, and normally he should not start an action unless he intended to proceed with it, and proceeding with it would involve the expense of proving that there was a fault on the part of the ship, and that fault caused the casualty. Moreover, in some cases, where there was both damage to the ship and damage to the cargo, it might be impossible to know, until after the average adjustment had been compiled, which party would on balance be owing a contribution to the other. Also a cargo owner, if he did not happen to take legal advice at the earliest stage, would not be expected to realise that he had to bring an action forthwith, not for the purpose of gaining any positive relief or because he had any complaint as to the existing situation, but for the purpose of maintaining unimpaired the validity of his just defence against a possible future claim not yet made or threatened. In my view, there are elements not only of inconvenience but even of absurdity in the results which would follow if the claimants' contentions were accepted. That is not, in itself, a sufficient reason for rejecting the contentions but does prompt a careful scrutiny of them.

Questions were raised in the special case and in the argument as to the relationship between the York-Antwerp Rules and the English common law. Mr Donaldson contended that the York-Antwerp Rules are in the nature of a code ...

It was further argued that the York-Antwerp Rules, being an international set of rules drawn up by an international convention, are for that reason also not to be presumed to have the same effect as the English common law, and should not be artificially construed in an endeavour to make them conform to the English common law. In my view, those contentions are right in principle. But I also agree with Mr Megaw when he says that, on examining the provisions of the York-Antwerp Rules, you find that they do not constitute a complete or self-contained code, and need to be supplemented by bringing into the gaps provisions of the general law which are applicable to the contract. I will give examples of that later. The York-Antwerp Rules have not in themselves any legal force. The parties to a contract can, if they so choose, agree that general average shall be payable according to the York-Antwerp Rules. But the parties have freedom of contract: they could agree not to adopt the York-Antwerp Rules or agree to adopt them with express modifications or agree to adopt them with implied modifications. In this case there is no express modification and I do not think that there is any implied modification.

[His Lordship cited the rule of interpretation and rule D of the York-Antwerp Rules 1954 and continued:]

There is not in these rules any definition of the word 'fault', and, therefore, the meaning which the word is to bear in these rules as applying to the present contract must be determined by the general law covering the present contract. If different general laws give different meanings to the word 'fault' that is an unavoidable lack of uniformity. Similarly the rules do not give any definition or list or indication of the remedies which may be open against a party whose fault has caused the event which gave rise to the general average sacrifice or expenditure. To ascertain what the remedies are you must go to the general law covering the contract, which in the present case is English law.

Another question is as to the relationship between the first part of rule D and the second part of it. In my view the manifest objects of rule D are to keep all questions of alleged fault outside the average adjustment and to preserve unimpaired the legal position at the stage of enforcement. The effect of the first part of the rule is that the average adjustment is compiled on the assumption that the casualty has not been caused by anybody's fault. The convenience of this arrangement appears when regard is had to the size and complexity that an average adjustment may attain. The average adjustment in the present case covers 183 pages and the compilation would involve much collection of information and many calculations. I understand that the task of compiling an average adjustment in a complicated case may take years. It is highly convenient and desirable, almost necessary, that the task should not be further enlarged and complicated by questions whether the casualty was caused by some fault or faults of one or more of the parties. Moreover, such questions would naturally be settled by litigation arbitration, as they go beyond the sphere of general average and may affect other matters. The average adjusters ought to be able to produce figures which, so far as they are concerned, are final figures. When they have produced their final figures, the question of enforcement arises, and it is at this stage that the second part of rule D comes into play. The average adjustment shows X owing to Y £100, but that showing is without prejudice to any remedies which may be open to X for Y's fault having caused the casualty. In my view that is clearly the intended mode of operation of the two parts of rule D, and it affords the clue to the interpretation of the rule. The first part refers to the rights to contribution in general average as they will be set out in the average adjustment, and these are properly and naturally called 'rights', because normally the holder of such rights is entitled to receive payment. But the second part of the rule provides that the first part is not to prejudice remedies for faults. That implies that in some cases the remedies referred to in the second part of the rule will override the rights referred to in the first part; in other words, the second part operates as a proviso, qualifying, overriding, cutting down or derogating from the first part. The rights may be nullified or defeated or diminished or otherwise affected by the remedies. In that sense the rights referred to in the first part of the rule are prima facie rights because they are subject to the remedies.

The position, therefore, is that the claimants have their prima facie right to recover from the respondents contribution in general average, but the respondents may be able to defeat that right by using their 'remedies' for the claimants' 'fault'. As I have said, the York-Antwerp Rules are silent as to what are the remedies and what is a fault, and for elucidation of those matters it is necessary to have resort to the English law.

There is the case of *Schloss v Walter Heriot* (1863) 14 CBNS 59, and the headnote, so far as material, states:

> To an action by a shipowner against a shipper of goods to recover his proportion of average loss, the defendant pleaded ... that the ship was unseaworthy at the commencement of the voyage, and that the average

loss was occasioned and arose from and in consequence of such unseaworthiness. Held: a good plea, inasmuch as it showed that the plaintiff's actionable negligence and misconduct produced the very damage for which he sought to recover contribution from the defendants; and (probably) also on the ground of avoidance of circuity of action.

There is an interesting citation in the argument from Kent's *Commentaries*, vol 3, p 232, where it says:

By the Rhodian Law, as cited in the Pandects (Dig 14.2.1), if goods were thrown overboard, in a case of extreme peril, to lighten and save the ship, the loss, being incurred for the common benefit, was to be made good by the contribution of all. The goods must not be swept away by the violence of the waves, for then the loss falls entirely upon the merchant or his insurer, but they must be intentionally sacrificed by the mind and agency of man, for the safety of the ship and the residue of the cargo. The jettison must be made for sufficient cause, and not from groundless timidity. It must be made in a case of extremity, when the ship is in danger of perishing by the fury of a storm, or is labouring upon rocks or shallows, or is closely pursued by pirates or enemies; and then, if the ship and the residue of the cargo be saved by means of the sacrifice, nothing can be more reasonable than that the property saved should bear its proportion of the loss. The doctrine of general average is one of those rules of the marine law which is built upon the plainest principles of justice; and it has, accordingly, recommended itself to the notice and adoption of all the commercial nations of the world.

Then Erle CJ gave judgment as follows:

The fourth plea I think is a good one. It shows that the plaintiff was himself the cause of the loss, that this actionable negligence and misconduct produced the very damage for which he seeks to recover contribution from the defendants. Further, I am of opinion, that, if necessary, the plea is sustainable on the ground that the defendants would be entitled in a cross-action to recover back the whole sum claimed by the plaintiff in this action.

Willes and Keating JJ concurred.

The next in the case law is *The Ettrick* (1881) 6 PD 127. The headnote states:

The payment into court of £8 a ton under 25 and 26 Vict cl 63, s 54, does not place the shipowner in the position of a person who has not done wrong. The owner of a ship sunk by a collision in the Thames admitted it to be his fault, and paid into court £8 a ton in a suit to limit his liability. The Thames Conservators, having powers under the Removal of Wrecks Act 1877, and the Thames Conservancy Acts, raised the ship and delivered the ship and cargo to the owner, he undertaking to pay the expense of raising. Part of the cargo was some wool, which was damaged by being sunk. Held: that the shipowner was bound to deliver the wool to the owner of the wool without claiming from him, by way of contribution to salvage, any part of the expenses of raising the ship and cargo.

Brett LJ said (page 135):

> A general average contribution is a contribution in money paid to a person who has been obliged to pay for a general average loss. If the plaintiff had not been in any fault, I am inclined at present to think that he would have been entitled to claim from the defendant if it was a general average contribution. But he has been in fault, and the authorities are decisive that if the general average contribution which he claims is a general average contribution, which arose by reason of a default of his, he cannot claim anything. Therefore, taking it to be a claim for a general average contribution, he is ousted by the authorities, because the loss was a loss occasioned by his own default.

Cotton LJ said (page 137):

> Then, independently of the contract, what are the rights of the parties? I take it, first of all, without reference to the Thames Conservancy Act, but treating this as in the nature of a general average contribution, that the claim is one founded on equity, namely, that where a person has incurred expense for the general benefit of the whole adventure he shall claim contribution from all those who are interested. But it would be against equity to say that the person who himself has done the wrongful act which caused the expenditure shall claim thereupon from anybody else, and the cases have decided accordingly that where the expense has been incurred in consequence of the wrongful act of the person who incurred it, he cannot claim contribution in the way of general average.

In that case there would not have been circuity of action because the shipowner had limited his liability. Therefore, the decision rested on the ground that a person shall not recover from any other person in respect of the consequences of his own wrong. That may be called for convenience the equitable defence, although it has no special connexion with the Court of Chancery. Clearly it is a matter of defence and not of cross-claim.

Then there is the case of *Burton & Co v English & Co* (1883) 12 QBD 218. The headnote is:

> It was stipulated in a charterparty that the 'ship should be provided with a deck cargo if required at full freight, but at merchant's risk'. Held: reversing the decision of the Queen's Bench Division, that the words 'at merchant's risk' did not exclude the right of the charterers to general average contribution from the shipowners in respect of deck cargo, shipped by the charterers, and necessarily jettisoned to save the ship and the rest of the cargo.

The interest of the case for the present purpose is in what is said about the foundation of law of general average contribution, whether it is essentially of a contractual nature or whether it really rests on the old law of the sea and is based upon what Cotton LJ called the equitable considerations. Brett MR said (page 220):

> By what law does the right arise to general average contribution? Lord Bramwell in his judgment in *Wright v Marwood* (1881) 7 QBD 62 considers it to arise from an implied contract, but although I always have great doubt when I differ from Lord Bramwell, I do not think that it forms any part of

the contract to carry, and that it does not arise from any contract at all, but from the old Rhodian laws, and has become incorporated into the law of England as the law of the ocean. It is not as a matter of contract, but in consequence of a common danger, where natural justice requires that all should contribute to indemnify for the loss of property which is sacrificed by one in order that the whole adventure may be saved. If this be so, the liability to contribute does not arise out of any contract at all, and is not covered by the stipulation in the charterparty on which the defendants rely. I therefore disagree with the decision of the Divisional Court in this case.

Bowen LJ said (page 223), with regard to this question:

But does it cover this claim for general average contribution? What is this claim, and how does it arise? In the investigation of legal principles the question whether they arise by way of implied contract or not often ends by being a mere question of words. General average contribution is a principle which comes down to us from an anterior period of our history, and from the law of commerce and the sea. When, however, it is once established as part of the law, and as a portion of the risks which those who embark their property upon ships are willing to take, you may if you like imagine that those who place their property on board a ship on the one side, and the shipowner who puts his ship by the quay to receive the cargo on the other side, bind themselves by an implied contract which embodies this principle, just as it may be said that those who contract with reference to a custom impliedly make it a portion of the contract. But that way, although legally it may be a sound way, nevertheless is a technical way of looking at it. This claim for average contribution, at all events, is part of the law of the sea.

Then there is another case, *Strang, Steel & Co v A Scott & Co* (1889) 14 App Cas 601, before the Judicial Committee. The essence of the problem which faced the court appears in a sentence which states (page 605): 'The learned judge found, as matter of fact, that the stranding of the ship upon the Baragua Flats was occasioned by the negligent navigation of the master; and he held, as matter of law, that no claim for general average arises to the owners of cargo jettisoned when the peril which necessitated jettison is induced by the fault of the ship.' One finds in later passages (page 610) that there was considerable textbook authority for the view which the judge of first instance (the Recorder of Rangoon) had taken, but his view was not accepted by the Judicial Committee. Lord Watson, delivering the opinion of the Judicial Committee, said (page 607):

Whether the rule ought to be regarded as matter of implied contract, or as a canon of positive law resting upon the dictates of natural justice, is a question which their Lordships do not consider it necessary to determine. The principle upon which contribution becomes due does not appear to them to differ from that upon which claims of recompense for salvage services are founded. But, in any aspect of it, the rule of contribution has its foundation in the plainest equity. In jettison, the rights of those entitled to contribution, and the corresponding obligations of the contributors, have their origin in the fact of a common danger which threatens to destroy the property of them all; and these rights and obligations are mutually perfected whenever the goods of some of the shippers have been advisedly sacrificed, and the property of the others has been thereby preserved. There are two well established exceptions to the rule of contribution for general average, which it is necessary to notice. When a person who would otherwise have been entitled to claim contribution has, by his own fault, occasioned the peril which immediately gave rise to the claim, it would be manifestly unjust to permit him to recover from those whose goods are saved, although they may be said, in a certain sense, to have benefited by the sacrifice of his property. In any question with them he is a wrongdoer, and, as such, under an obligation to use every means within his power to ward off or repair the natural consequences of his wrongful act. He cannot be permitted to claim either recompense for services rendered, or indemnity for losses sustained by him, in the endeavour to rescue property which was imperilled by his own tortious act, and which it was his duty to save. *Schloss v Heriot* (above) is the leading English authority upon the point. In that case, which was an action by the shipowner against the owners of cargo for contribution in an average loss, a plea stated in defence, to the effect that the ship was unseaworthy at the commencement of the voyage, and that the average loss was occasioned by such unseaworthiness, was held to be a good answer to the claim by Chief Justice Erle and Willes and Keating JJ.

Then he went on to say (14 App Cas 608): 'The second exception is in the case of deck cargo', and I need not refer to that. Then he said (page 609):

It appears from the proceedings in this suit that the average claim at the instance of cargo owners exceed $30,000, and that there is a small claim on account of ship. The fault of the master being matter of admission, it seems clear, upon authority, that no contribution can be recovered by the owners of the *Abington*, unless the conditions ordinarily existing between parties standing in that relation have been varied by special contract between them and their shippers. But the negligent navigation of the master cannot, in the opinion of their Lordships, afford any pretext for depriving those shippers whose goods were jettisoned of their claim to a general contribution. They were not privy to the master's fault, and were under no duty, legal or moral, to make a gratuitous sacrifice of their goods, for the sake of others, in order to avert the consequences of his fault. The Rhodian Law, which in that respect is the law of England, bases the right of contribution not upon the causes of the danger to the ship and cargo, but upon its actual presence; and such exceptions as that recognised in *Schloss v Heriot* are in truth limitations on the rule, which have been introduced, from equitable considerations, in the case of actual wrongdoers, or of those who are legally responsible for them. The owners of goods thrown overboard having been innocent of exposing the *Abington* and her cargo to the sea peril which necessitated jettison, their equitable claim to be indemnified for the loss of their goods is just as strong as if the peril had been wholly due to the action of the winds and waves.

... As to the scope of the word 'remedies' in rule D, clearly it is wide enough to cover the respondents' cross-claim for the same amount as the claimants are claiming. If the cross-claim is still open, the claimants' claim can be defeated by it because judgment should be given for the respondents in order to avoid circuity of action. That has not been disputed. The question which is disputed at this stage of the argument is whether the word 'remedies' in rule D is wide enough to cover the so-called 'equitable' defence, that the casualty was caused by the claimants' own fault. Mr Donaldson argued that the word 'remedies' refers only to positive legal steps which may be taken to assert and enforce a claim, and does not include a mere defence to a claim. Using a very familiar metaphor, one can say that according to his argument a remedy is in the nature of a spear, which a man uses to attack somebody else, and is not in the nature of a shield, with which he seeks to repel somebody else's attack on him.

... Mainly I am influenced by the evident objects of rule D, which are to keep the whole question of alleged fault outside the average adjustment and to leave the legal 'remedies' in respect of fault unimpaired. There is no reason to suppose an intention to destroy defences while keeping alive cross-claims. The intention which may reasonably be inferred is an intention to preserve the legal position intact at the stage of enforcement. Suitable effect is given to that intention by construing the word 'remedies' in rule D as wide enough to cover defences as well as cross-claims, shields as well as spears, pleas as well as counts.

Next one has to consider what is, for the purposes of a case such as this, the meaning of the word 'fault' in English law. There is the case of *The Carron Park* (1890) 15 PD 203. The headnote states:

> By a charterparty it was agreed that the defendants' steam vessel should go to New Fairwater, and there load from the agents of the plaintiffs a cargo of sugar and proceed therewith to Greenock, the defendants not to be responsible 'for any act, neglect, or default whatsoever of their servants during the said voyage'. The agents commenced loading the vessel with sugar belonging to the plaintiffs, and during the loading the cargo was damaged by water through a valve in the engine-room having been negligently left open by one of the engineers of the vessel ... The defendants counterclaimed for a general average contribution from the plaintiffs. Held: that their right to contribution was not affected by the negligence of their servants, for which by the terms of the exception they were not responsible, and that they were entitled to recover.

Hannen P said (page 207):

> With regard to the counterclaim for general average, I think the defendants are entitled to recover. The claim for contribution as general average cannot be maintained where it arises out of any negligence for which the shipowner is responsible; but negligence for which he is not responsible is as foreign to him as to the person who has suffered by it. The loss would not have fallen on the shipowner, and the expenditure or sacrifice made by him is not made to avert loss from himself alone, but from the cargo owner. This question was considered in the case of *Strang, Steel & Co v A Scott & Co*. That was a case of jettisoned cargo; Lord Watson, in delivering judgment, says (14 App Cas 601, 609): 'The fault of the master being matter of admission, it seems clear upon authority that no compensation can be recovered by the owners of the (ship) unless the conditions ordinarily

existing between the parties standing in that relation have been varied by special contract between them and their shippers'. Here it appears to me that the relation of the goods owner to the shipowner has been altered by the contract – that the shipowner shall not be responsible for the negligence of his servants in the events which have happened.

Then there was another case of *Milburn & Co v Jamaica Fruit Importing and Trading Co of London* [1900] 2 QB 540. There the headnote reads:

Where a contract for carriage of goods by sea contains an exception of negligence of the master and crew, the shipowner is entitled to a contribution from the owner of the goods to general average expenses, though the necessity for the same has been occasioned by the negligence of the master: – So held by A L Smith and Romer LJJ, Vaughan Williams LJ dissenting.

The first relevant passage is where A L Smith LJ, after a citation from the judgment of Lord Esher in *Burton & Co v English & Co* (above) said (page 546):

But, although general average is not the creature of contract, that does not settle the question in the present case; for what the contract of carriage is becomes an important factor when considering, not whether a general average claim for contribution has arisen, but in considering, assuming that such claim has arisen, whether it can be taken away by the cargo owner showing that, as between him and the shipowner, the latter, to use Lord Watson's words, has been a wrongdoer. To create the shipowner a wrongdoer as regards the cargo owner there must be the breach of some duty, and, if by agreement between the two it has been agreed that it shall be no breach of duty for the master to be guilty of negligence, in other words, that as between the two the negligence of the master shall be always excepted, it cannot be said that it is a breach of duty towards the cargo owner for the master to be guilty of that which the cargo owner and shipowner have agreed shall be no breach of duty at all.

Then he said that raised the question whether *The Carron Park* (above) is good law, and, having made a citation from that case, said (page 547): 'This decision of Sir James Hannen has been acted upon in practice in this country ever since it was given, and we are asked now to overrule it'. He states:

When read it will be seen that these cases do not deal with the question whether, where a general average expenditure has been incurred, the right to contribute thereto can be taken away by showing that the party incurring the expenditure was a wrongdoer as regards the person called upon to contribute. Whether he be such a wrongdoer must, as it seems to me, depend upon the contract which existed between the parties. This is not, as before stated, a case in which the question is whether a general average claim has arisen, for that in this case is not disputed, but the question is whether the shipowner has been a wrongdoer to the cargo owner. The shipowner says to the cargo owner, a general average loss has occurred to which you must contribute, and you cannot show that I have been guilty of negligence so as to absolve you from contributing thereto, for by express contract between us negligence is excepted.

Then Romer LJ said (page 554):

> Between shipowners and charterers such negligence was to be 'mutually excepted', so that both parties could be regarded as equally blameless in respect of it. Let me then first consider how the case would have stood between the parties to the charterparty if all the goods on board the vessel during a voyage had been the property of the charterers, and then by the master's negligence a condition arose necessitating a sacrifice at the expense of the shipowners for the common good, so that prima facie a claim for general average contribution against the owners of the cargo had arisen. In my opinion there could have been no answer to the claim. The charterers could not have brought themselves within the exception to general average claims which is so well known, and was discussed by Lord Watson in the case cited (14 App Cas 601) in the judgments already delivered. For the charterers could not have said as against the shipowners that the negligence of the master was to be attributed to the shipowners, so as to place the latter in the position of persons who had brought about the peril necessitating the common sacrifice by their own wrong. There would have been no ground for treating the shipowners and the charterers as standing on a different footing at the moment when the common sacrifice became necessary. As between themselves they stood at that moment on a footing of equality. Neither the goods as against the ship, nor the ship as against the goods, had any claim by reason of any peril arising, or loss which might have resulted, from the master's negligence; and the position of equality is the very essence of the right to contribution. It would in my opinion, be matter for regret if the opposite view were upheld, for the result would be that, though, if loss ensued to the goods by the peril, the shipowners could not be made responsible for the loss, yet, if to avoid that peril a sacrifice is made at the expense of the ship, there would be no right of contribution.

In *Tempus Shipping Co Ltd v Louis Dreyfus & Co Ltd* [1931] 1 KB 195, which I have already mentioned, in the Court of Appeal Greer LJ said (page 211):

> It seems to me that the question which has to be asked in cases of this kind is: 'Is the danger which occasions the sacrifice or the expense sought to be recovered one for which the shipowner is responsible to the cargo owners, so that it can be said that he has made the sacrifice or incurred the expense not for the benefit of all concerned, but for his own benefit only?'

In the same case in the House of Lords Lord Warrington of Clyffe said [1931] AC 726, 742:

> The next question is how does the contract between the shipowner and the cargo owner affect the right of the former to contribution by the latter to general average expenses. I agree with Greer LJ that the right to contribution arises whenever the expenditure is incurred or the sacrifice made in the interest of both the parties and not of one of them alone. In the present case, inasmuch as the whole of the loss of or damage to the cargo falls on the cargo owner, the expenditure in question is incurred in the interest of both parties, and a due proportion thereof in the shape of contribution in general average would be recoverable by the shipowner.

Then Lord Atkin [referring to *Milburn & Co v Jamaica Fruit Importing and Trading Co of London*] said (page 748):

> The defence argued by Mr Carver KC and Mr Scrutton was that if the bills of lading had contained a negligence clause still the shipowner would not have been entitled to contribution, and that the decision in *The Carron Park* was wrong. The court by a majority (AL Smith LJ and Romer LJ; Vaughan Williams LJ dissenting), gave judgment for the shipowner and affirmed *The Carron Park*. AL Smith LJ, a judge of large experience in these matters, said: 'To create the shipowner a wrongdoer as regards the cargo owner there must be the breach of some duty, and if by agreement between the two it has been agreed that it shall be no breach of duty for the master to be guilty of negligence, in other words, that as between the two the negligence of the master shall be always excepted, it cannot be said that it is a breach of duty towards the cargo owner for the master to be guilty of that which the cargo owner and the shipowner have agreed shall be no breach of duty at all'. Romer LJ expressed the same reasoning, pointing out that, with the negligence clause, at the moment of the sacrifice shipowner and cargo owner between themselves stood on a footing of equality.

It appears, therefore, in my opinion, from the citations which have been given, that for the relevant purpose a 'fault' is a legal wrong which is actionable as between the parties at the time when the general average sacrifice or expenditure is made.

In the present case there was a legal wrong, and it was actionable as between the parties at the time when the general average expenditure was made. There was, therefore, a 'fault' in this case. Whatever effect the third paragraph of article III, rule 6, of the Hague Rules may have upon the rights of the parties in other ways, it did not deprive the legal wrong of its character as a 'fault'.

Now I have to consider what effect, if any, the third paragraph of article III, rule 6, of the Hague Rules has had upon the legal position. Has it destroyed the respondents' equitable defence, and has it destroyed their cross-claim? In my view clearly it has not destroyed the equitable defence because it brings about only a discharge of liabilities and not a barring of defences. Therefore, if I am right in my conclusion that the equitable defence is one of the 'remedies' preserved by the second part of rule D of the York-Antwerp Rules, that defence is unaffected by the third paragraph of article Ill, rule 6, of the Hague Rules, and defeats the claimants' claim.

What effect, if any, does the third paragraph of article III, rule 6, have upon the respondents' cross-claim? This is a rather elusive problem because the cross-claim is in a sense artificial, being intended ultimately to have only the effect of repelling the claimants' claim if any. The problem can be stated in this form. Have the claimants been discharged under the said third paragraph from liability on the respondents' cross claim for damages equal to the amount of the claimants' claim against the respondents for general average contribution? There is a gap in the wording of the said third paragraph, which reads: 'In any event the carrier and the ship shall be discharged from all liability in respect of loss or damage unless suit is brought within one year after delivery of the goods or the date when the goods should have been delivered'. There are no express words to provide a subject matter for the 'loss or damage', and there are no express words to identify 'the goods'. But in my view there is an implied reference to the cargo owner's goods. The liability of the carrier and the ship must be a liability to the cargo owner, who is the other party to the contract of carriage, and the loss or damage arising out of the contract for the carriage of the cargo owner's goods, and the goods of which the date of delivery or non-delivery is significant for the cargo owner must be his goods. In my view the loss or damage referred to must be loss or damage which is related to the cargo owner's goods, and the delivery of the goods must mean the delivery of his goods. But how close is the relation required between the loss or damage and the cargo owner's goods? Can the loss or damage be confined to actual loss of or physical damage to the cargo owner's goods? That can be plausibly suggested when regard is had to the provisions of article III, rule 6, taken as a whole, but it is difficult to maintain in the face of the decision of the House of Lords in *GH Renton & Co Ltd v Palmyra Trading Corporation of Panama* [1957] AC 149, that the 'loss or damage to or in connexion with the goods' referred to in article III, rule 6, is not confined to actual loss or physical damage, and the decision of Devlin J in *Anglo-Saxon Petroleum Co Ltd v Adamastos Shipping Co Ltd* [1957] 2 QB 333, that the 'loss or damage' referred to in article IV, rules 1 and 2, is not confined to actual loss and physical damage.

It can be argued for the claimants that there is a sufficient connexion between the damage in this case, which is the respondents' liability to pay general average contribution, and the respondents' goods, because the liability arises from the fact that those goods were carried on the voyage on which the casualty occurred, and that they could be held under lien for general average contribution until a general average bond was given or some equivalent arrangement was made. That is certainly arguable, but in my view the connexion is too remote. The liability to pay general average contribution is not related to the respondents' goods but to the ship's expenditure in the present case, and it might in some other case be related to the jettison or the damage to some other person's goods.

The respondents' goods were duly delivered, and there was no loss or damage of or to in connexion with them. There is this further consideration: If the cargo owner has sustained loss or damage at or about the date of delivery, and it is not unreasonable that time should run against him from that date. But if his goods have been duly and safely carried, discharged and delivered and for, some reason or in some way not connected with his goods, a general average contribution is required for ship's expenses or jettison of or damage to some other person's goods, the date for delivery of his goods has no adequate significance or relevance to the claim for general average contribution or his liability in respect of it or his cross-claim for the shipowner's fault, and in regard to those matters it is not fair or reasonable that the time should start running against him as from the date when his goods are delivered to him. At that date, and for long afterwards, he may have little or no knowledge of the ship's expenses or the other person's goods or what happened to them. The cases of *Schmidt v Royal Mail SS Co* (1876) 45 LJQB 646 and *Greenshields, Cowie & Co v Stephens & Sons Ltd* [1908] AC 431 help to show that matters related to general average contribution are outside the scope of provisions such as this.

I therefore decide that the claimants have not been discharged under the third paragraph of article III, rule 6, from liability on the respondents' cross-claim. The cross-claim is available and can be set against the claimants' proposed claim, and to avoid circuity of action judgment would be given for the respondents.

I will merely mention two other points which were argued for the respondents: (1) That the so-called 'New Jason clause', which is the second paragraph of clause 9 of the bill of lading, affects the interpretation of rule D of the York-Antwerp Rules, 1950; and (2) that the word 'fault' in rule D does not cover unseaworthiness or failure to exercise due diligence to make the ship seaworthy. Having reached a decision on other grounds, I will not deal with those two points.

The decision of the court upon the question of law stated in the special case is in the negative. Upon the facts found and upon the true construction of the contract, the claimants are not entitled to recover the said sum of £22.10s.4d or any sum from the respondents in respect of contribution to general average. The award of the arbitrator is affirmed.

6 RULE XIV AND RULE X

Marida Ltd v Oswal Steel, The Bijela [1994] 1 WLR 615, HL

In November 1985, the *Bijela* loaded a cargo of scrap iron in Providence, Rhode Island for carriage to an Indian port pursuant to contracts of carriage that incorporated the York-Antwerp Rules, 1974. The vessel sailed but while still in Rhode Island Sound she grounded and seriously damaged her double bottom tanks. Temporary repairs were completed at Jamestown, the nearest anchorage, and the vessel proceeded to her original destination of Kandla and discharged her cargo. She then sailed to Singapore where permanent repairs were carried out.

The plaintiff shipowners alleged that the cost of temporary repairs were allowable in general average as substituted expenses under the second paragraph of Rule XIV of the York-Antwerp Rules, 1974. The shipowners' argument was that if temporary repairs had not been completed at Jamestown, the vessel would have had to proceed to New York for permanent repairs which would have entailed discharging, storing and reloading the cargo at a cost of more than US $ 500,000. They argued that this cost would have been allowed under Rule X (b) and (c) whereas doing the temporary repairs at Jamestown resulted in a very substantial saving and that they were entitled to recover the appropriate proportion of the sum actually incurred in carrying out the temporary repairs as substituted expense under the York-Antwerp Rules, 1974.

The defendants argued that had permanent repairs been carried out at New York none of the expenses of such repairs would have been recoverable in general average because the alternative of the temporary repairs existed and was all that was required to enable the vessel to complete the original voyage.

> **Lord Lloyd of Berwick:** My Lords, the issue in this appeal is whether the owners of *Bijela* can claim general average contribution in respect of the cost of temporary repairs carried out in the course of a voyage from Providence, Rhode Island to Kandla, in India. The question turns on the construction of the second paragraph of rule XIV of the York-Antwerp Rules 1974.

> ... It is accepted that the cost of entering Jamestown, as a port of refuge, and her detention there, is allowable in general average under rules X and XI of the York-Antwerp Rules. The question is whether the cost of the temporary repairs should also be admitted. This depends, as I have said, on the second paragraph of rule XIV.

> ... The second paragraph of rule XIV obliges us to suppose that the temporary repairs had not been effected at Jamestown. What then would have happened? The answer is simple. She would have gone into drydock in New York. Was the discharge of the cargo necessary to enable the damage to the ship to be repaired in drydock? The answer is clearly yes. Were those repairs necessary to enable the vessel to proceed safely from New York to India, always assuming that she had not already been repaired in Jamestown? The answer, again, is clearly yes. The assumption required by rule XIV must be carried through when applying rule X. It is not necessary to assume that the vessel could not have been repaired in Jamestown in order to give effect to the two rules. It is necessary only to assume that she was not so repaired, as rule XIV requires. In this way effect can be given to the clear intention of the opening words of the second paragraph of rule XIV, that the cost of temporary repairs of accidental damage are admissible in general average, subject only to the limit imposed by the second half of the paragraph.

Notes

1   The second paragraph of Rule XIV survived the 1994 amendments intact despite a proposal to delete it.

2   The problem for the shipowners was that the cost of temporary repairs is not normally allowable in general average at common law. The case decided that incorporation of the York-Antwerp Rules 1974 had the effect of giving the shipowners a claim.

3   See the comment by Gaskell, N on the case and its importance for adjusters in [1995] *LMCLQ* 342.

4   Cross references: see also Chapter 2 'Cargo Claims', Chapter 5 'Deviation' and Chapter 9 'Hague-Visby Rules'.

SPECIMEN DOCUMENTS

1 Standard Shipping Note and Dangerous Goods Note

IMPORTANT USE THE DANGEROUS GOODS NOTE IF THE GOODS ARE CLASSIFIED AS DANGEROUS ACCORDING TO APPLICABLE REGULATIONS SEE BOX 10A

(c) SITPRO 1991 — STANDARD SHIPPING NOTE – FOR NON-DANGEROUS GOODS ONLY

Exporter: **1**	Customs reference/status: **2**
	Booking number **3** / Exporter's reference **4**
	Forwarder's reference **5**
6	
Freight Forwarder **7**	International carrier **8**
	For use of receiving authority only
Other UK transport details (eg, ICD, terminal, vehicle bkg. ref. receiving dates) **9**	
	10A
Vessel/flight no. and date Port/airport of loading **10**	The Company preparing this note declares that, to the best of their belief, the goods have been accurately described, their quantities, weights and measurements are correct and at the time of despatch they were in good order and condition, that the goods are not classified as dangerous in any UK, IMO, ADR, RID, or IATA/ICAO regulation applicable to the intended modes of transport.
Port/airport of discharge Destination **11**	TO THE RECEIVING AUTHORITY – Please receive for shipment the goods described below subject to your published regulations and conditions (including those as to liability).

Shipping marks	Number and kind of packages; description of goods' non-hazardous special stowage requirements **12**	Gross wt (kg) of goods **13A**	Cube (m³) of goods **14**
For use of Shipping company only.		Total gross weight of goods	Total cube of goods

PREFIX and container/trailer number **16**	Seal number(s) **16A**	Container/trailer size(s) and type(s) **16B**	Tare wt(kg) as marked on CSC plate **16C**	Total of boxes 13A and 16C **16D**

DOCK/TERMINAL RECEIPT — Received the above number of packages/containers/
RECEIVING AUTHORITY REMARKS — trailers in good order and condition unless stated hereon

Hauliers' name

Vehicle reg. no.

DRIVER'S SIGNATURE   SIGNATURE AND DATE

Name of company preparing this note **17**

Date

(Indicate name and telephone number of contact)

130 Non-completion of any boxes is a subject for resolution by the contracting parties   SITPRO Licensee No. 000.

DANGEROUS GOODS DECLARATION, SHIPPING NOTE & CONTAINER/VEHICLE PACKING CERTIFICATE
© SITPRO 1995

DANGEROUS GOODS NOTE

Exporter: [1]	Customs reference/status: [2]
	Booking number [3] / Exporter's reference [4]
	Forwarder's reference [5]
Consignee [6]	DSHA Notification given by: [6A]
	Shipper / Cargo agent / Transport operator / Shipping line
	(in accordance with the DSHA Regulations)
Freight Forwarder [7]	International carrier [8]
Other UK transport details (eg, ICD, terminal, vehicle bkg. ref. receiving dates) [9]	For use of receiving authority only
Vessel / Port of loading [10]	
Port of discharge / Destination [11]	TO THE RECEIVING AUTHORITY – Please receive for shipment the goods described below subject to your published regulations and conditions (including those as to liability).

Shipping marks Number and Kind of packages; description of goods [12] SPECIFY: PROPER SHIPPING NAME †, IMO HAZARD CLASS, UN No. Additional information (if applicable, see overleaf)	Net wt (kg) [13]	Gross wt (kg) [13A]	Cube (m³) of goods [14]

CONTAINER/ VEHICLE PACKING CERTIFICATE
I hereby declare that the goods described above have been packed/loaded into the container/vehicle identified below in accordance with the provisions shown overleaf

MUST BE COMPLETED AND SIGNED FOR ALL CONTAINER/ VEHICLE LOADS BY PERSON RESPONSIBLE FOR PACKING/ LOADING

† PROPER SHIPPING NAME – TRADE NAMES ALONE ARE UNACCEPTABLE

Name of company	**DANGEROUS GOODS DECLARATION** [15] I hereby declare that the contents are fully and accurately described above by the proper shipping name(s), that the shipment is packaged in such a manner as to withstand the ordinary risks of handling and transport by sea, having regard to the properties of the goods to be carried, and that the goods are classified, marked and labelled, and are in all respects in accordance with applicable international and national governmental regulations. I further declare that, if appropriate, the goods are classified, packaged and marked to comply with the requirements of the European Agreement concerning the International Carriage of Dangerous Goods by Road (ADR) and of Annex 1 (RID) to the Uniform Rules concerning the Contract for International Carriage of Goods by Rail (CIM) or special arrangements made between the contracting parties to these Agreements. The shipper must complete and sign box 17.	Total gross weight of goods / Total cube of goods
Name/Status of declarant		
Place and date		
Signature of declarant		

Prefix and container/vehicle reg. number [16]	Seal number(s) [16A]	Container/vehicle size & type [16B]	Tare wt (kg) as marked on CSC plate [16C]	Total of boxes 13A and 16C [16D]

DOCK/TERMINAL RECEIPT Received the above number of packages/containers/trailers in apparent good order and condition unless stated hereon
RECEIVING AUTHORITY REMARKS

Name and telephone no. of shipper preparing this note [17]

Haulier's Name

Name/status of declarant

Place and date

Vehicle reg No.

Signature of declarant

DRIVER'S SIGNATURE	SIGNATURE AND DATE

2 Demise Charterparty

First issued by
The Baltic and International Maritime Council (BIMCO), Copenhagen
in 1974 as "Barecon 'A'" and "Barecon 'B'"
Revised and amalgamated 1989

Adopted by
the Documentary Committee of The
Japan Shipping Exchange, Inc, Tokyo

Copyright, published by
The Baltic and International Maritime Council
(BIMCO), Copenhagen, September 1989

1. Shipbroker	THE BALTIC AND INTERNATIONAL MARITIME COUNCIL (BIMCO) STANDARD BAREBOAT CHARTER CODE NAME "BARECON 89" PART I
	2. Place and date
3. Owners/Place of business	4. Bareboat charterers (Charterers/Place of business)
5. Vessel's name, Call Sign and Flag (Cl. 9(c))	
6. Type of Vessel	7. GRT/NRT
8. When/Where built	9. Total DWT (abt.) in metric tons on summer freeboard
10. Class (Cl. 9)	11. Date of last special survey by the Vessel's classification society
12. Further particulars of Vessel (also indicate minimum number of months' validity of class certificates agreed acc. to Cl. 14)	

13. Port or Place of delivery (Cl. 2)	14. Time for delivery (Cl. 14)	15. Cancelling date (Cl. 4)
	16. Port or Place of redelivery (Cl. 14)	
17. Running days' notice if other than stated in Cl. 3	18. Frequency of dry-docking if other than stated in Cl. 9(f)	

19. Trading Limits (Cl. 5)	
20. Charter period	21. Charter hire (Cl. 10)
22. Rate of interest payable acc. to Cl. 10(f) and, if applicable, acc. to PART IV	23. Currency and method of payment (Cl. 10)

(continued)

24. Place of payment; also state beneficiary and bank account (Cl. 10)	25. Bank guarantee/bond (sum and place) (Cl. 22) (optional)
26. Mortgage(s), if any, (state whether Cl. 11(a) or (b) applies; if 11(b) applies state date of Deed(s) of Covenant and name of Mortgagee(s)/Place of business) (Cl. 11)	27 Insurance (marine and war risks) (state value acc. to Cl. 12(f) or, if applicable, acc to Cl. 13(k)) (also state if Cl. 13 applies)
28. Additional insurance cover, if any, for Owners' account limited to (Cl. 12(b)) or, if applicable, (Cl. 13(g))	29. Additional insurance cover, if any, for Charterers' account limited to (Cl. 12(b)) or, if applicable, (Cl. 13(g))
30. Latent defects (only to be filled in if period other than stated in Cl. 2)	31. War cancellation (indicate countries agreed) (Cl. 24)
32. Brokerage commission and to whom payable (Cl. 25)	
33. Law and arbitration (state 26.1, 26.2, or 26.3 of Cl. 26 as agreed; if 26.3 agreed, also state place of arbitration) (Cl. 26)	34. Number of additional clauses covering special provisions, if agreed
35. Newbuilding Vessel (indicate with "yes" or "no" whether Part III applies) (optional)	36. Name and place of Builders (only to be filled in if Part III applies)
37. Vessel's Yard Building No. (only to be filled in if Part III applies)	38. Date of Building Contract (only to be filled in if Part III applies)
39. Hire/Purchase agreement (indicate with "yes" or "no" whether Part IV applies) (optional)	40. Bareboat Charter Registry (indicate with "yes" or "no" whether Part V applies((optional)
41. Flag and Country of the Bareboat Charter Registry (only to be filled in if Part V applies)	42. Country of the Underlying Registry (only to be filled in if Part V applies)

PREAMBLE – It is mutually agreed that this Contract shall be performed subject to the conditions contained in this Charter which shall include PART I and PART II. In the event of a conflict of conditions, the provisions of PART I shall prevail over those of PART II to the extent of such conflict but no further. It is further mutually agreed that PART III and/or PART IV and/or PART V shall only apply and shall only form part of this Charter if expressly agreed and stated in the Boxes 35, 39 and 40. If PART III and/or PART IV and/or PART V apply, it is further mutually agreed that in the event of a conflict of conditions, the provisions of PART I and PART II shall prevail over those of PART III and/or PART IV and/or PART V to the extent of such conflict but no further.

Signature (Owners)	Signature (Charterers)

Printed and sold by Fr. G. Knudtzons Bogtrykkeri A/S, 55 Toldbodgade, DK-1253 Copenhagen K, Telefax +45 33 93 11 84
by authority of The Baltic and International Maritime Council (BIMCO), Copenhagen

Appendix I

PART II
'BARECON 89' Standard Bareboat Charter

1. Definitions
In this Charter, the following terms shall have the meanings hereby assigned to them:
'The Owners' shall mean the person or company registered as Owners of the Vessel.
'The Charterers' shall mean the Bareboat charterers and shall not be construed to mean a time charterer or a voyage charterer.

2. Delivery (*not applicable to newbuilding vessels*)
The Vessel shall be delivered and taken over by the Charterers at the port or place indicated in Box 13, in such ready berth as the Charterers may direct. The Owners shall before and at the time of delivery exercise due diligence to make the Vessel seaworthy and in every respect ready in hull, machinery and equipment for service under this Charter. The Vessel shall be properly documented at time of delivery.
The delivery to the Charterers of the Vessel and the taking over of the Vessel by the Charterers shall constitute a full performance by the Owners of all the Owners' obligations under Clause 2, and thereafter the Charterers shall not be entitled to make or assert any claim against the Owners on account of any conditions representations or warranties expressed or implied with respect to the Vessel but the Owners shall be responsible for repairs or renewals occasioned by latent defects in the Vessel, her machinery or appurtenances, existing at the time of delivery under the Charter, provided such defects have manifested themselves within 18 months after delivery unless otherwise provided in Box 30.

3. Time for Delivery (*not applicable to newbuilding vessels*)
The Vessel to be delivered not before the date indicated in Box 14 unless with the Charterers' consent.
Unless otherwise agreed in Box 17 the Owners to give the Charterers not less than 30 running days' preliminary and not less than 14 days' definite notice of the date on which the Vessel is expected to be ready for delivery.
The Owners to keep the Charterers closely advised of possible changes in the Vessel's position.

4. Cancelling (*not applicable to newbuilding vessels*)
Should the Vessel not be delivered latest by the cancelling date indicated in Box 15, the Charterers to have the option of cancelling this Charter without prejudice to any claim the Charterers may otherwise have on the Owners under this Charter.
If it appears that the Vessel will be delayed beyond the cancelling date, the Owners shall, as soon as they are in a position to state with reasonable certainty the day on which the Vessel should be ready, give notice thereof to the Charterers asking whether they will exercise their option of cancelling, and the option must then be declared within one hundred and sixty-eight (168) hours of the receipt by the Charterers of such notice. If the Charterers do not then exercise their option of cancelling, the seventh day after the readiness date stated in the Owners' notice shall be regarded as a new cancelling date for the purpose of this Clause.

5. Trading Limits
The Vessel shall be employed in lawful trades for the carriage of suitable lawful merchandise within the trading limits indicated in Box 19.
The Charterers undertake not to employ the Vessel or suffer the Vessel to be employed otherwise than in conformity with the terms of the instruments of insurance (including any warranties expressed or implied therein) without first obtaining the consent to such employment of the Insurers and complying with such requirements as to extra premium or otherwise as the Insurers may prescribe. If required, the Charterers shall keep the Owners and the Mortgagees advised of the intended employment of the Vessel.
The Charterers also undertake not to employ the Vessel or suffer her employment in any trade or business which is forbidden by the law of any country to which the Vessel may sail or is otherwise illicit or in carrying illicit or prohibited goods or in any manner whatsoever which may render her liable to condemnation, destruction, seizure or confiscation.
Notwithstanding any other provisions contained in this Charter it is agreed that nuclear fuels or radioactive products or waste are specifically excluded from the cargo permitted to be loaded or carried under this Charter. This exclusion does not apply to radio-isotopes used or intended to be used for any industrial, commercial, agricultural, medical or scientific purposes provided the Owners' prior approval has been obtained to loading thereof.

6. Surveys (*not applicable to newbuilding vessels*)
Survey on Delivery and Redelivery – The Owners and Charterers shall each appoint surveyors for the purpose of determining and agreeing in writing the condition of the Vessel at the time of delivery and redelivery hereunder. The Owners shall bear all expenses of the On-Survey including loss of time, if any, and the Charterers shall bear all expenses of the Off-Survey including loss of time, if any, at the rate of hire per day or pro rata, also including in each case the cost of any docking and undocking, if required, in connection herewith.

7. Inspection
Inspection. – The Owners shall have the right at any time to inspect or survey the Vessel or instruct a duly authorised surveyor to carry out such survey on their behalf to ascertain the condition of the Vessel and satisfy themselves that the Vessel is being properly repaired and maintained. Inspection or survey in dry-dock shall be made only when the Vessel shall be in dry-dock for the Charterers' purpose. However the Owners shall have the right to require the Vessel to be dry-docked for inspection if the Charterers are not docking her at normal classification intervals. The fees for such inspection or survey shall in the event of the Vessel being found to be in the condition provided in Clause 9 of

this Charter be payable by the Owners and shall be paid by the Charterers only in the event of the Vessel being found to require repairs or maintenance in order to achieve the condition so provided. All time taken in respect of inspection, survey or repairs shall count as time on hire and shall form part of the Charter period.
The Charterers shall also permit the Owners to inspect the Vessel's log books whenever requested and shall whenever required by the Owners furnish them with full information regarding any casualties or other accidents or damage to the Vessel. For the purpose of this Clause, the Charterers shall keep the Owners advised of the intended employment of the Vessel.

8. Inventories and Consumable Oil and Stores
A complete inventory of the Vessel's entire equipment, outfit, appliances and of all consumable stores on board the Vessel shall be made by the Charterers in conjunction with the Owners on delivery and again on redelivery of the Vessel. The Charterers and the Owners, respectively, shall at the time of delivery and redelivery take over and pay for all bunkers, lubricating oil, water and unbroached provisions, paints, oils, ropes and other consumable stores in the said Vessel at the then current market prices at the ports of delivery and redelivery, respectively.

9. Maintenance and Operation
(a) The Vessel shall during the Charter period be in the full possession and at the absolute disposal for all purposes of the Charterers and under their complete control in every respect. The Charterers shall maintain the Vessel, her machinery, boilers, appurtenances and spare parts in a good state of repair, in efficient operating condition and in accordance with good commercial maintenance practice and, except as provided for in Clause 13 (I), they shall keep the Vessel with unexpired classification of the class indicated in Box 10 and with other required certificates in force at all times.
The Charterers to take immediate steps to have the necessary repairs done within a reasonable time failing which the Owners shall have the right of withdrawing the Vessel from the service of the Charterers without noting any protest and without prejudice to any claim the Owners may otherwise have against the Charterers under the Charter.
Unless otherwise agreed, in the event of any improvement, structural changes or expensive new equipment becoming necessary for the continued operation of the Vessel by reason of new class requirements or by compulsory legislation costing more than 5 per cent. of the Vessel's marine insurance value as stated in Box 27, then the extent, if any, to which the rate of hire shall be varied and the ratio in which the cost of compliance shall be shared between the parties concerned in order to achieve a reasonable distribution thereof as between the Owners and the Charterers having regard inter alia, to the length of the period remaining under the Charter, shall in the absence of agreement, be referred to arbitration according to Clause 26.
The Charterers are required to establish and maintain financial security or responsibility in respect of oil or other pollution damage as required by any government, including Federal, state or municipal or other division or authority thereof, to enable the Vessel without penalty or charge lawfully to enter, remain at, or leave any port, place, territorial or contiguous waters of any country, state or municipality in performance of this Charter without any delay. This obligation shall apply whether or not such requirements have been lawfully imposed by such government or division or authority thereof. The Charterers shall make and maintain all arrangements by bond or otherwise as may be necessary to satisfy such requirements at the Charterers' sole expense and the Charterers shall indemnify the Owners against all consequences whatsoever (including loss of time) for any failure or inability to do so.
TOVALOP SCHEME. (Applicable to oil tank vessels only). - The Charterers are required to enter the Vessel under the **TOVALOP SCHEME** or under any similar compulsory scheme upon delivery under this Charter and to maintain her so during the currency of this Charter.
(b) The Charterers shall at their own expense and by their own procurement man, victual, navigate, operate, supply, fuel and repair the Vessel whenever required during the Charter period and they shall pay all charges and expenses of every kind and nature whatsoever incidental to their use and operation of the Vessel under this Charter including any foreign general municipality and/or state taxes. The Master officers and crew of the Vessel shall be the servants of the Charterers for all purposes whatsoever, even if for any reason appointed by the Owners.
Charterers shall comply with the regulations regarding officers and crew in force in the country of the Vessel's flag or any other applicable law.
(c) During the currency of this Charter, the Vessel shall retain her present name as indicated in Box 5 and shall remain under and fly the flag as indicated in Box 5. Provided, however, that the Charterers shall have the liberty to paint the Vessel in their own colours, install and display their funnel insignia and fly their own house flag. Painting and re-painting, instalment and re-instalment to be for the Charterers' account and time used thereby to count as time on hire.
(d) The Charterers shall make no structural changes in the Vessel or changes in the machinery, boilers, appurtenances or spare parts thereof without in each instance first securing the Owners' approval thereof. If the Owners so agree, the Charterers shall, if the Owners so require, restore the Vessel to its former condition before the termination of the Charter.
(e) The Charterers shall have the use of all outfit, equipment, and appliances on board the Vessel at the time of delivery, provided the same or their substantial equivalent shall be returned to the Owners on redelivery in the same good order and condition as when received, ordinary wear and tear excepted. The Charterers shall from time to time during the Charter period replace such

477

items of equipment as shall be so damaged or worn as to be unfit for use. The Charterers are to procure that all repairs to or replacement of any damaged, worn or lost parts or equipment be effected in such manner (both as regards workmanship and quality of materials) as not to diminish the value of the Vessel. The Charterers have the right to fit additional equipment at their expense and risk but the Charterers shall remove such equipment at the end of the period if requested by the Owners.
Any equipment including radio equipment on hire on the Vessel at time of delivery shall be kept and maintained by the Charterers and the Charterers shall assume the obligations and liabilities of the Owners under any lease contracts in connection therewith and shall reimburse the Owners for all expenses incurred in connection therewith, also for any new equipment required in order to comply with radio regulations.
(f) The Charterers shall dry-dock the Vessel and clean and paint her underwater parts whenever the same may be necessary, but not less than once in every eighteen calendar months after delivery unless otherwise agreed in Box 18.

10. Hire
(a) The Charterers shall pay to the Owners for the hire of the Vessel at the lump sum per calendar month as indicated in Box 21 commencing on and from the date and hour of her delivery to the Charterers and at and after the agreed lump sum for any part of a month. Hire to continue until the date and hour when the Vessel is redelivered by the Charterers to her Owners.
(b) Payment of Hire, except for the first and last month's Hire, if sub-clause (c) of this Clause is applicable, shall be made in cash without discount every month in advance on the first day of each month in the currency and in the manner indicated in Box 23 and at the place mentioned in Box 24.
(c) Payment of Hire for the first and last month's Hire if less than a full month shall be calculated proportionally according to the number of days in the particular calendar month and advance payment to be effected accordingly.
(d) Should the Vessel be lost or missing, Hire to cease from the date and time when she was lost or last heard of. Any Hire paid in advance to be adjusted accordingly.
(e) Time shall be of the essence in relation to payment of Hire hereunder. In default of payment beyond a period of seven running days, the Owners shall have the right to withdraw the Vessel from the service of the Charterers without noting any protest and without interference by any court or any other formality whatsoever, and shall, without prejudice to any other claim the Owners may otherwise have against the Charterers under the Charter, be entitled to damages in respect of all costs and losses incurred as a result of the Charterers' default and the ensuing withdrawal of the Vessel.
(f) Any delay in payment of Hire shall entitle the Owners to an interest at the rate per annum as agreed in Box 22. If Box 22 has not been filled in the current market rate in the country where the Owners have their Principal Place of Business shall apply.

11. Mortgage
*) (a) Owners warrant that they have not effected any mortgage of the Vessel.
*) (b) The Vessel chartered under this Charter is financed by a mortgage according to the Deed(s) of Covenant annexed to this Charter and as stated in Box 26. By their counter-signature on the Deed(s) of Covenant, the Charterers undertake to have acquainted themselves with all terms, conditions and provisions of the said Deed(s) of Covenant. The Charterers undertake that they will comply with all such instructions or directions in regard to the employment, insurances, repairs and maintenance of the Vessel, etc., as laid down in the Deed(s) of Covenant or as may be directed from time to time during the currency of the Charter by the Mortgagee(s) in conformity with the Deed(s) of Covenant.
(c) The Owners warrant that they have not effected any mortgage(s) other than stated in Box 26 and that they will not effect any other mortgage(s) without the prior consent of the Charterers.
) (<u>Optional</u>, Clauses 11 (a) and 11 (b) are alternatives; indicate alternative agreed in Box 26*).

12. Insurance and Repairs
(a) During the Charter period the Vessel shall be kept insured by the Charterers at their expense against marine, war and Protection and Indemnity risks in such form as the Owners shall in writing approve, which approval shall not be unreasonably withheld. Such marine, war and P. and I. insurances shall be arranged by the Charterers to protect the interests of both the Owners and the Charterers and mortgagees (if any), and the Charterers shall be at liberty to protect under such insurances the interests of any managers they may appoint. All insurance policies shall be in the joint names of the Owners and the Charterers as their interests may appear.
If the Charterers fail to arrange and keep any of the insurances provided for under the provisions of sub-clause (a) above in the manner described therein, the Owners shall notify the Charterers whereupon the Charterers shall rectify the position within seven running days, failing which Owners shall have the right to withdraw the Vessel from the service of the Charterers without prejudice to any claim the Owners may otherwise have against the Charterers.
The Charterers shall, subject to the approval of the Owners and the Underwriters effect all insured repairs and shall undertake settlement of all costs in connection with such repairs as well as insured charges, expenses and liabilities (reimbursement to be secured by the Charterers from the Underwriters) to the extent of coverage under the insurances herein provided for.
The Charterers also to remain responsible for and to effect repairs and settlement of costs and expenses incurred thereby in respect of all other repairs not covered by the insurances and/or not exceeding any possible franchise(s) or deductibles provided for in the insurances.
All time used for repairs under the provisions of sub-clause (a) of this Clause and for repairs of latent defects according to Clause 2 above including any deviation shall count as time on hire and shall form part of the Charter period.
(b) If the conditions of the above insurances permit additional insurance to be placed by the parties, such cover shall be limited to the amount for each party set out in Box 28 and Box 29, respectively. The Owners or the Charterers as the case may be shall immediately furnish the other party with particulars of any additional insurance effected, including copies of any cover notes or policies and the written consent of the insurers of any such required insurance in any case where the consent of such insurers is necessary.
(c) Should the Vessel become an actual, constructive, compromised or agreed total loss under the insurances required under sub-clause (a) of Clause 12, all insurance payments for such loss shall be paid to the Mortgagee, if any, in the manner described in the Deed(s) of Covenant, who shall distribute the moneys between themselves, the Owners and the Charterers according to their respective interests. The Charterers undertake to notify the Owners and the Mortgagee, if any, of any occurrences in consequence of which the Vessel is likely to become a Total Loss as defined in this Clause.
(d) If the Vessel becomes an actual, constructive, compromised or agreed total loss under the insurances arranged by the Charterers in accordance with sub-clause (a) of this Clause, this Charter shall terminate as of the date of such loss.
(e) The Owners shall upon the request of the Charterers promptly execute such documents as may be required to enable the Charterers to abandon the Vessel to insurers and claim a constructive total loss.
(f) For the purpose of insurance coverage against marine and war risks under the provisions of sub-clause (a) of this Clause, the value of the Vessel is the sum indicated in Box 27.

13, Insurance, Repairs and Classification
(*<u>Optional</u>, only to apply if expressly agreed and stated in Box 27, in which event Clause 12 shall be considered deleted*).
(a) During the Charter period the Vessel shall be kept insured by the Owners at their expense against marine and war risks under the form of policy or policies attached hereto. The Owners and/or insurers shall not have any right of recovery or subrogation against the Charterers on account of loss of or any damage to the Vessel or her machinery or appurtenances covered by such insurance, or on account of payments made to discharge claims against or liabilities of the Vessel or the Owners covered by such insurance. All insurance policies shall be in the joint names of the Owners and the Charterers as their interests may appear.
(b) During the Charter period the Vessel shall be kept insured by the Charterers at their expense against Protection and Indemnity risks in such form as the Owners shall in writing approve which approval shall not be unreasonably withheld. If the Charterers fail to arrange and keep any of the insurances provided for under the provisions of sub-clause (b) in the manner described therein, the Owners shall notify the Charterers whereupon the Charterers shall rectify the position within seven running days, failing which the Owners shall have the right to withdraw the Vessel from the service of the Charterers without prejudice to any claim the Owners may otherwise have against the Charterers.
(c) In the event that any act or negligence of the Charterers shall vitiate any of the insurance herein provided, the Charterers shall pay to the Owners all losses and indemnify the Owners against all claims and demands which would otherwise have been covered by such insurance.
(d) The Charterers shall, subject to the approval of the Owners or Owners' Underwriters, effect all insured repairs, and the Charterers shall undertake settlement of all miscellaneous expenses in connection with such repairs as well as all insured charges, expenses and liabilities, to the extent of coverage under the insurances provided for under the provisions of sub-clause (a) of this Clause. The Charterers to be secured reimbursement through the Owners' Underwriters for such expenditures upon presentation of accounts.
(e) The Charterers to remain responsible for and to effect repairs and settlement of costs and expenses incurred thereby in respect of all other repairs not covered by the insurances and/or not exceeding any possible franchise(s) or deductibles provided for in the insurances
(f) All time used for repairs under the provisions of sub-clause (d) and (e) of this Clause and for repairs of latent defects according to Clause 2 above, including any deviation, shall count as time on hire and shall form part of the Charter period.
The Owners shall not be responsible for any expenses as are incident to the use and operation of the Vessel for such time as may be required to make such repairs.
(g) If the conditions of the above insurances permit additional insurance to be placed by the parties such cover shall be limited to the amount for each party set out in Box 28 and Box 29, respectively. The Owners or the Charterers as the case may be shall immediately furnish the other party with particulars of any additional insurance effected, including copies of any cover notes or policies and the written consent of the Insurers of any such required insurance in any case where the consent of such Insurers is necessary.
(h) Should the Vessel become an actual, constructive, compromised or agreed total loss under the insurances required under sub-clause (a) of this Clause, all insurance payments for such loss shall be paid to the Owners, who shall distribute the moneys between themselves and the Charterers according to their respective interests.
(i) If the Vessel becomes an actual, constructive, compromised or agreed total loss under the insurances arranged by the Owners in accordance with sub-clause (a) of this Clause, this Charter shall terminate as of the date of such loss.
(j) The Charterers shall upon the request of the Owners, promptly execute such documents as may be required to enable the Owners to abandon the Vessel to Insurers and claim a constructive total loss.

Appendix I

(k) For the purpose of insurance coverage against marine and war risks under the provisions of sub-clause (a) of this Clause, the value of the Vessel is the sum indicated in Box 27.

(l) Notwithstanding anything contained in Clause 9 (a), it is agreed that under the provisions of Clause 13 if applicable the Owners shall keep the Vessel with unexpired classification in force at all times during the Charter period.

14. Redelivery

The Charterers shall at the expiration of the Charter period redeliver the Vessel at a safe and ice-free port or place as indicated in Box 16. The Charterers shall give the Owners not less than 30 running days' preliminary and not less than 14 days' definite notice of expected date, range of ports of redelivery or port or place of redelivery. Any changes thereafter in Vessel's position shall be notified immediately to the Owners.

Should the Vessel be ordered on a voyage by which the Charter period may be exceeded the Charterers to have the use of the Vessel to enable them to complete the voyage provided it could be reasonably calculated that the voyage would allow redelivery about the time fixed for the termination of the Charter.

The Vessel shall be redelivered to the Owners in the same or as good structure, state, condition and class as that in which she was delivered, fair wear and tear not affecting class excepted.

The Vessel upon redelivery shall have her survey cycles up to date and class certificates valid for at least the number of months agreed in Box 12.

15. Non-Lien and Indemnity

The Charterers will not suffer, nor permit to be continued, any lien or encumbrance incurred by them or their agents, which might have priority over the title and interest of the Owners in the Vessel.

The Charterers further agree to fasten to the Vessel in a conspicuous place and to keep so fastened during the Charter period a notice reading as follows:

'This Vessel is the property of (name of Owners). It is under charter to (name of Charterers) and by the terms of the Charter Party neither the Charterers nor the Master have any right, power or authority to create, incur or permit to be imposed on the Vessel any lien whatsoever.'

The Charterers shall indemnify and hold the Owners harmless against any lien of whatsoever nature arising upon the Vessel during the Charter period while she is under the control of the Charterers, and against any claims against the Owners arising out of or in relation to the operation of the Vessel by the Charterers. Should the Vessel be arrested by reason of claims or liens arising out of her operation hereunder by the Charterers, the Charterers shall at their own expense take all reasonable steps to secure that within a reasonable time the Vessel is released and at their own expense put up bail to secure release of the Vessel.

16. Lien

The Owners to have a lien upon all cargoes and sub-freights belonging to the Charterers and any Bill of Lading freight for all claims under this Charter, and the Charterers to have a lien on the Vessel for all moneys paid in advance and not earned.

17. Salvage

All salvage and towage performed by the Vessel shall be for the Charterers' benefit and the cost of repairing damage occasioned thereby shall be borne by the Charterers.

18. Wreck Removal

In the event of the Vessel becoming a wreck or obstruction to navigation the Charterers shall indemnify the Owners against any sums whatsoever which the Owners shall become liable to pay and shall pay in consequence of the Vessel becoming a wreck or obstruction to navigation.

19. General Average

General Average, if any, shall be adjusted according to the York-Antwerp Rules 1974 or any subsequent modification thereof current at the time of the casualty.

The Charter Hire not to contribute to General Average.

20. Assignment and Sub-Demise

The Charterers shall not assign this Charter nor sub-demise the Vessel except with the prior consent in writing of the Owners which shall not be unreasonably withheld and subject to such terms and conditions as the Owners shall approve.

21. Bills of Lading

The Charterers are to procure that all Bills of Lading issued for carriage of goods under this Charter shall contain a Paramount Clause incorporating any legislation relating to Carrier's liability for cargo compulsorily applicable in the trade; if no such legislation exists, the Bills of Lading shall incorporate the British Carriage of Goods by Sea Act. The Bills of Lading shall also contain the amended New Jason Clause and the Both-to-Blame Collision Clause.

The Charterers agree to indemnify the Owners against all consequences or liabilities arising from the Master, officers or agents signing Bills of Lading or other documents.

22. Bank Guarantee

The Charterers undertake to furnish, before delivery of the Vessel, a first class bank guarantee or bond in the sum and at the place as indicated in Box 25 as guarantee for full performance of their obligations under this Charter.

(*Optional*, only to apply if Box 25 filled in).

23. Requisition/Acquisition

(a) In the event of the Requisition for Hire of the Vessel by any governmental or other competent authority (hereinafter referred to as 'Requisition for Hire') irrespective of the date during the Charter period when 'Requisition for Hire' may occur and irrespective of the length thereof and whether or not it be for an indefinite or a limited period of time, and irrespective of whether it may or will remain in force for the remainder of the Charter period, this Charter shall not be deemed thereby or thereupon to be frustrated or otherwise terminated and the Charterers shall continue to pay the stipulated hire in the manner provided by this Charter until the time when the Charter would have terminated pursuant to any of the provisions hereof always provided however that in the event of 'Requisition for Hire' any Requisition Hire or compensation received or receivable by the Owners shall be payable to the Charterers during the remainder of the Charter period or the period of the 'Requisition for Hire' whichever be the shorter.

The Hire under this Charter shall be payable to the Owners from the same time as the Requisition Hire is payable to the Charterers.

(b) In the event of the Owners being deprived of their ownership in the Vessel by any Compulsory Acquisition of the Vessel or requisition for title by any governmental or other competent authority (hereinafter referred to as 'Compulsory Acquisition'), then, irrespective of the date during the Charter period when 'Compulsory Acquisition' may occur, this Charter shall be deemed terminated as of the date of such 'Compulsory Acquisition'. In such event Charter Hire to be considered as earned and to be paid up to the date and time of such 'Compulsory Acquisition'.

24. War

(a) The Vessel unless the consent of the Owners be first obtained not to be ordered nor continue to any place or on any voyage nor be used on any service which will bring her within a zone which is dangerous as the result of any actual or threatened act of war, war hostilities warlike operations, acts of piracy or of hostility or malicious damage against this or any other vessel or its cargo by any person body or State whatsoever, revolution, civil war, civil commotion or the operation of international law, nor be exposed in any way to any risks or penalties whatsoever consequent upon the imposition of Sanctions nor carry any goods that may in any way expose her to any risks of seizure, capture, penalties or any other interference of any kind whatsoever by the belligerent or fighting powers or parties or by any Government or Ruler.

(b) The Vessel to have liberty to comply with any orders or directions as to departure, arrival, routes, ports of call, stoppages, destination, delivery or in any other wise whatsoever given by the Government of the nation under whose flag the Vessel sails or any other Government or any person (or body) acting or purporting to act with the authority of such Government or by any committee or person having under the terms of the war risks insurance on the Vessel the right to give any such orders or directions.

(c) In the event of outbreak of war (whether there be a declaration of war or not) between any two or more of the countries as stated in Box 31, both the Owners and the Charterers shall have the right to cancel this Charter, whereupon the Charterers shall redeliver the Vessel to the Owners in accordance with Clause 14, if she has cargo on board after discharge thereof at destination, or if debarred under this Clause from reaching or entering it at a near open and safe port as directed by the Owners, or if she has no cargo on board, at the port at which she then is or if at sea at a near open and safe port as directed by the Owners. In all cases hire shall continue to be paid in accordance with Clause 10 and except as aforesaid all other provisions of this Charter shall apply until redelivery.

25. Commission

The Owners to pay a commission at the rate indicated in Box 32 to the Brokers named in Box 32 on any Hire paid under the Charter but in no case less than is necessary to cover the actual expenses of the Brokers and a reasonable fee for their work. If the full Hire is not paid owing to breach of Charter by either of the parties the party liable therefor to indemnify the Brokers against their loss of commission.

Should the parties agree to cancel the Charter, the Owners to indemnify the Brokers against any loss of commission but in such case the commission not to exceed the brokerage on one year's Hire.

26. Law and Arbitration

*) 26.1. This Charter shall be governed by English law and any dispute arising out of this Charter shall be referred to arbitration in London one arbitrator being appointed by each party, in accordance with the Arbitration Acts 1950 and 1979 or any statutory modification or re-enactment thereof for the time being in force. On the receipt by one party of the nomination in writing of the other party's arbitrator, that party shall appoint their arbitrator within fourteen days failing which the decision of the single Arbitrator appointed shall apply. If two Arbitrators properly appointed shall not agree they shall appoint an umpire whose decision shall be final.

*) 26.2. Should any dispute arise out of this Charter the matter in dispute shall be referred to three persons at New York, one to be appointed by each of the parties hereto, and the third by the two so chosen, their decision or that of any two of them shall be final, and for purpose of enforcing any award, this agreement may be made a rule of the Court.

The arbitrators shall be members of the Society of Maritime Arbitrators Inc. of New York and the proceedings shall be conducted in accordance with the rules of the Society.

*) 26.3. Any dispute arising out of this Charter shall be referred to arbitration at the place indicated in Box 33, subject to the law and procedures applicable there.

26.4. If Box 33 in Part 1 is not filled in, sub-clause 26.1. of this Clause shall apply.

*) 26.1., 26.2. and 26.3. are alternatives; indicate alternative agreed in Box 33.

479

'BARECON 89' Standard Bareboat Charter

PART III

PROVISIONS TO APPLY FOR NEWBUILDING VESSELS ONLY

(Optional, only to apply if expressly agreed and stated in box 35)

OPTIONAL PART

Specifications and Building Contract
(a) The Vessel shall be constructed in accordance with the Building Contract (hereafter called 'the Building Contract') as annexed to this Charter, made between the Builders and the Owners and in accordance with the specifications and plans annexed thereto, such Building Contract, specifications and plans having been countersigned as approved by the Charterers.
(b) No change shall be made in the Building Contract or in the specifications or plans of the Vessel as approved by the Charterers as aforesaid, without the Charterers' consent.
(c) The Charterers shall have the right to send their representative to the Builders' Yard to inspect the Vessel during the course of her construction to satisfy themselves that construction is in accordance with such approved specifications and plans as referred to under sub-clause (a) of this Clause.
(d) The Vessel shall be built in accordance with the Building Contract and shall be of the description set out therein provided nevertheless that the Charterers shall be bound to accept the Vessel from the Owners on the date of delivery by the Builders as having been completed and constructed in accordance with the Building Contract and the Charterers undertake that after having so accepted the Vessel they will not thereafter raise any claims against the Owners in respect of the Vessel's performance or specification or defects if any except that in respect of any repair or replacement of any defects which appear within the first 12 months from delivery the Owners shall use their best endeavours to recover any expenditure incurred in remedying such defects from the Builders, but shall only be liable to the Charterers to the extent the Owners have a valid claim against the Builders under the guarantee clause of the Building Contract (a copy whereof has been supplied to the Charterers) provided that the Charterers shall be bound to accept such sums as the Owners are able to recover under this clause and shall make no claim upon the Owners for any difference between the amounts so recovered and the actual expenditure incurred on repairs or replacements or for any loss of time incurred thereby.

Time and Place of Delivery
(a) Subject to the Vessel having completed her acceptance trials including trials of cargo equipment in accordance with the Building Contract and specifications to the satisfaction of the Charterers, the Owners shall give and the Charterers shall take delivery of the Vessel afloat when ready for delivery at the Builders' Yard or some other safe and readily accessible dock, wharf or place as may be agreed between the parties hereto and the Builders. Under the Building Contract the Builders have estimated that the Vessel will be ready for delivery to the Owners as therein provided but the delivery date for the purpose of this Charter shall be the date when the Vessel is in fact ready for delivery by the Builders after completion of trials whether that be before or after as indicated in the Building Contract. Notwithstanding the foregoing, the Charterers shall not be obliged to take delivery of the Vessel until she has been classed and documented as provided in this Charter and free for transfer to the flag she has to fly. Subject as aforesaid the Charterers shall not be entitled to refuse acceptance of delivery of the Vessel and upon and after such acceptance the Charterers shall not be entitled to make any claim against the Owners in respect of any conditions, represen-

tations or warranties, whether express or implied, as to the seaworthiness of the Vessel or in respect of delay in delivery or otherwise howsoever.
(b) If for any reason other than a default by the Owners under the Building Contract, the Builders become entitled under that Contract not to deliver the Vessel to the Owners the Owners shall upon giving to the Charterers written notice of Builders becoming so entitled, be excused from giving delivery of the Vessel to the Charterers and upon receipt of such notice by the Charterers this Charter shall cease to have effect.
(c) If for any reason the Owners become entitled under the Building Contract to reject the Vessel the Owners shall, before exercising such right of rejection, consult the Charterers and thereupon
i)   if the Charterers do not wish to take delivery of the Vessel they Shall inform the Owners within seven (7) days by notice in writing and upon receipt by the Owners of such notice this Charter shall cease to have effect; or
ii) if the Charterers wish to take delivery of the Vessel they may by notice in writing within seven (7) days require the Owners to negotiate with the Builders as to the terms on which delivery should be taken and/or refrain from exercising their right to rejection and upon receipt of such notice the Owners shall commence such negotiations and/or take delivery of the Vessel from the Builders and deliver her to the Charterers;
iii) in no circumstances shall the Charterers be entitled to reject the Vessel unless the Owners are able to reject the Vessel from the Builders;
iv) if this Charter terminates under sub-clause (b) or (c) of this Clause the Owners shall thereafter not be liable to the Charterers for any claim under or arising out of this Charter or its termination.

Guarantee Works
If not otherwise agreed, the Owners authorise the Charterers to arrange for the guarantee works to be performed in accordance with the building contract terms and hire to continue during the period of guarantee works. The Charterers have to advise the Owners about the performance to the extent the Owners may request.

Name of Vessel
The name of the Vessel shall be mutually agreed between the Owners and the Charterers and the Vessel shall be painted in the colours, display the funnel insignia and fly the house flag as required by the Charterers.

Survey on Redelivery
The Owners and the Charterers shall appoint surveyors for the purpose of determining and agreeing in writing the condition of the Vessel at the time of redelivery.
Without prejudice to Clause 14 (Part II), the Charterers shall bear all survey expenses and all other costs, if any, including the cost of docking and undocking if required, as well as all repair costs incurred.
The Charterers shall also bear all loss of time spent in connection with any docking and undocking as well as repairs, which shall be paid at the rate of Hire per day or pro rata.

- -

PART IV
HIRE/PURCHASE AGREEMENT
(Optional, only to apply if expressly agreed and stated in Box 39)

On expiration of this Charter and provided the Charterers have fulfilled their obligations according to Part I and II as well as Part III, if applicable, it is agreed, that on payment of the last month's hire instalment as per Clause 10 the Charterers have purchased the Vessel with everything belonging to her and the Vessel is fully paid for.
If the payment of the instalment due is delayed for less than 7 running days or for reason beyond the Charterers' control, the right of withdrawal under the terms of Clause 10(e) of Part II shall not be exercised. However, any delay in payment of the instalment due shall entitle the Owners to an interest at the rate per annum as agreed in Box 22. If Box 22 has not been filled in the current market rate in the country where the Owners have their Principal Place of Business shall apply.

In the following paragraphs the Owners are referred to as the Sellers and the Charterers as the Buyers.

The Vessel shall be delivered by the Sellers and taken over by the Buyers on expiration of the Charter.

The Sellers guarantee that the Vessel, at the time of delivery, is free from all encumbrances and maritime liens or any debts whatsoever other than those arising from anything done or not done by the Buyers or any existing mortgage agreed not to be paid off by the time of delivery. Should any claims which have been incurred prior to the time of delivery be made against the Vessel, the Sellers hereby undertake to indemnify the Buyers against all consequences of such claims to the extent it can be proved that the Sellers are responsible

for such claims. Any taxes, notarial, consular and other charges and expenses connected with the purchase and registration under Buyers' flag, shall be for Buyers' account. Any taxes, consular and other charges and expenses connected with closing of the Sellers register, shall be for Sellers' account.
In exchange for payment of the last month's hire instalment the Sellers shall furnish the Buyers with a Bill of Sale duly attested and legalized together with a certificate setting out the registered encumbrances, if any. On delivery of the Vessel the Sellers shall provide for deletion of the Vessel from the Ship's Register and deliver a certificate of deletion to the Buyers.
The Sellers shall, at the time of delivery, hand to the Buyers all classification certificates (for hull, engines, anchors, chains, etc.), as well as all plans which may be in Sellers' possession.

The Wireless Installation and Nautical Instruments, unless on hire, shall be included in the sale without any extra payment.

The Vessel with everything belonging to her shall be at Sellers' risk and expense until she is delivered to the Buyers, subject to the conditions of this Contract and the Vessel with everything belonging to her shall be delivered and taken over as she is at the time of delivery, after which the Sellers shall have no responsibility for possible faults or deficiencies of any description.

The Buyers undertake to pay for the repatriation of the Captain, officers and other personnel if appointed by the Sellers to the port where the Vessel entered the Bareboat Charter as per Clause 2 (Part II) or to pay the equivalent cost for their journey to any other place.

Appendix I

PART V
PROVISIONS TO APPLY FOR VESSELS REGISTERED IN A BAREBOAT CHARTER REGISTRY
(*Optional*, only to apply if expressly agreed and stated in Box 40)

Definitions
For the purpose of this PART V, the following terms shall have the meanings hereby assigned to them:
'The Bareboat Charter Registry' shall mean the registry of the State whose flag the Vessel will fly and in which the Charterers are registered as the bareboat charterers during the period of the Bareboat Charter.
'The Underlying Registry' shall mean the registry of the State in which the Owners of the Vessel are registered as Owners and to which jurisdiction and control of the Vessel will revert upon termination of the Bareboat Charter Registration.

Mortgage
The Vessel chartered under this Charter is financed by a mortgage and the provisions of Clause 11 (b) (Part II) shall apply.

Termination of Charter by Default
If the Vessel chartered under this Charter is registered in a Bareboat Charter Registry as stated in Box 41 and if the Owners shall default in the payment of any amounts due under the mortgage(s) specified in Box 26, the Charterers shall, if so required by the mortgagee, direct the Owners to re-register the Vessel in the Underlying Registry as shown in Box 42.
In the event of the Vessel being deleted from the Bareboat Charter Registry as stated in Box 41, due to a default by the Owners in the payment of any amounts due under the mortgage(s), the Charterers shall have the right to terminate this Charter forthwith and without prejudice to any other claim they may.have against the Owners under this Charter

3 Voyage Charterparties

Copyright, published by The Baltic and International Maritime Council (BIMCO), Copenhagen

1. Shipbroker	RECOMMENDED THE BALTIC AND INTERNATIONAL MARITIME COUNCIL UNIFORM GENERAL CHARTER (AS REVISED 1922, 1976 and 1994) (To be used for trades for which no specially approved form is in force) CODE NAME "GENCON"　　　　　　　　　　　　　　PART I
	2. Place and date
3. Owners/Place of business (Cl. 1)	4. Charterers/Place of business (Cl 1)
5. Vessel's name (Cl. 1)	6. GT/NT (Cl. 1)
7. DWT all told on summer load line in metric tons (abt.) (Cl.1)	8. Present position (Cl. 1)
9. Expected ready to load (abt.) (Cl. 1)	
10. Loading port or place (Cl. 1)	11. Discharging port or place (Cl. 1)
12. Cargo (also state quantity and margin in Owners' option, if agreed, if full and complete cargo not agreed state "part cargo" (Cl. 1)	
13. Freight rate (also state whether freight prepaid or payable on delivery) (Cl. 4)	14. Freight payment (state currency and method of payment, also beneficiary and bank account) (Cl. 4)
15. State if vessel's cargo handling gear shall not be used (Cl. 5)	16.Laytime (if separate laytime for load, and disch. is agreed fill in a) and b). If total laytime for load, and disch., fill in c) only) (Cl. 6)
17. Shippers/Place of business (Cl. 6)	(a) Laytime for loading
18. Agents (loading) (Cl. 6)	(b) Laytime for discharging
19. Agents discharging) (Cl. 6)	(c) Total laytime for loading and discharging
20. Demurrage rate and manner payable (loading and discharging) (Cl. 7)	21. Cancelling date (Cl. 9)
	22. General Average to be adjusted at (Cl. 12)
23. Freight Tax (state if for the Owners' Account (Cl. 13(c))	24. Brokerage commission and to whom payable (Cl. 15)
25. Law and Arbitration (state 19 (a), 19 (b) or 19 (c) of Cl. 19; if 19(c) agreed also state Place of Arbitration) (if not filled in 19(a) shall apply) (Cl. 19)	
(a) State maximum amount for small claims/shortened arbitration (Cl. 19)	26. Additional clauses covering special provision, if agreed

If mutually agreed that this contract shall be performed subject to the conditions contained in this Charter Party which shall include Part I as well as Part II. In the event of a conflict of conditions, the provisions of Part I shall prevail over those of Part II to the extent of such conflict.

Signature (Owners)	Signature (Charterers)

Printed and sold by Fr. G. Knudtzon Ltd., 55 Toldbodgade, DK-1253 Copenhagen K, Telefax +45 33 93 11 84
by authority of The Baltic and International Maritime Council (BIMCO), Copenhagen

Appendix I

PART II
'Gencon' Charter (As Revised 1922, 1976 and 1994)

1. It is agreed between the party mentioned in Box 3 as the Owners of the Vessel named in Box 5, of the GT/NT indicated in Box 6 and carrying about the number of metric tons of deadweight capacity all told on summer loadline stated in Box 7, now in position as stated in Box 8 and expected ready to load under this Charter Party about the date indicated in Box 9, and the party mentioned as the Charterers in Box 4 that:
The said Vessel shall, as soon as her prior commitments have been completed, proceed to the loading port(s) or place(s) stated in Box 10 or so near thereto as she may safely get and lie always afloat, and there load a full and complete cargo (if shipment of deck cargo agreed same to be at the Charterers' risk and responsibility) as stated in Box 12, which the Charterers bind themselves to ship, and being so loaded the Vessel shall proceed to the discharging port(s) or place(s) stated in Box 11 as ordered on signing Bills of Lading, or so near thereto as she may safely get and lie always afloat, and there deliver the cargo.

2. Owners' Responsibility Clause
The Owners are to be responsible for loss of or damage to the goods or for delay in delivery of the goods only in case the loss, damage or delay has been caused by personal want of due diligence on the part of the Owners or their Manager to make the Vessel in all respects seaworthy and to secure that she is properly manned, equipped and supplied, or by the personal act or default of the Owners or their Manager.
And the Owners are not responsible for loss, damage or delay arising from any other cause whatsoever, even from the neglect or default of the Master or crew or some other person employed by the Owners on board or ashore for whose acts they would, but for this Clause, be responsible, or from unseaworthiness of the Vessel on loading or commencement of the voyage or at any time whatsoever.

3. Deviation Clause
The Vessel has liberty to call at any port or ports in any order, for any purpose, to sail without pilots, to tow and/or assist Vessels in all situations, and also to deviate for the purpose of saving life and/or property.

4. Payment of Freight
(a) The freight at the rate stated in Box 13 shall be paid in cash calculated on the intaken quantity of cargo.
(b) *Prepaid.* If according to Box 13 freight is to be paid on shipment it shall be deemed earned and non-returnable, Vessel and/or cargo lost or not lost.
Neither the Owners nor their agents shall be required to sign or endorse bills of lading showing freight prepaid unless the freight due to the Owners has actually been paid.
(c) *On delivery.* If according to Box 13 freight, or part thereof, is payable at destination it shall not be deemed earned until the cargo is thus delivered. Notwithstanding the provisions under (a), if freight or part thereof is payable on delivery of the cargo the Charterers shall have the option of paying the freight on delivered weight/quantity provided such option is declared before breaking bulk and the weight/quantity can be ascertained by official weighing machine, joint draft survey or tally.
Cash for Vessel's ordinary disbursements at the port of loading to be advanced by the Charterers, if required, at highest current rate of exchange, subject to two (2) per cent to cover insurance and other expenses.

5. Loading/Discharging
(a) *Costs/Risks*
The cargo shall be brought into the holds, loaded, stowed and/or trimmed, tallied, lashed and/or secured and taken from the holds and discharged by the Charterers, free of any risk, liability and expense whatsoever to the Owners. The Charterers shall provide and lay all dunnage material as required for the proper stowage and protection of the cargo on board, the Owners allowing the use of all dunnage available on board. The Charterers shall be responsible for and pay the cost of removing their dunnage after discharge of the cargo under this Charter Party and time to count until dunnage has been removed.
(b) *Cargo Handling Gear*
Unless the Vessel is gearless or unless it has been agreed between the parties that the Vessel's gear shall not be used and stated as such in Box 15, the Owners shall throughout the duration of loading/discharging give free use of the Vessel's cargo handling gear and of sufficient motive power to operate all such cargo handling gear. All such equipment to be in good working order. Unless caused by negligence of the stevedores, time lost by breakdown of the Vessel's cargo handling gear or motive power - pro rata the total number of cranes/winches required at that time for the loading/discharging of cargo under this Charter Party - shall not count as laytime or time on demurrage.
On request the Owners shall provide free of charge cranemen/winchmen from the crew to operate the Vessel's cargo handling gear, unless local regulations prohibit this, in which latter event shore labourers shall be for the account of the Charterers. Cranemen/winchmen shall be under the Charterers' risk and responsibility and as stevedores to be deemed as their servants but shall always work under the supervision of the Master.
(c) *Stevedore Damage*
The Charterers shall be responsible for damage (beyond ordinary wear and tear) to any part of the Vessel caused by Stevedores. Such damage shall be notified as soon as reasonably possible by the Master to the Charterers or their agents and to their Stevedores, failing which the Charterers shall not be held responsible. The Master shall endeavour to obtain the Stevedores' written acknowledgement of liability.
The Charterers are obliged to repair any stevedore damage prior to completion of the voyage, but must repair stevedore damage affect-

ing the Vessel's seaworthiness or class before the Vessel sails from the port where such damage was caused or found. All additional expenses incurred shall be for the account of the Charterers and any time lost shall be for the account of and shall be paid to the Owners by the Charterers at the demurrage rate.

6. Laytime
* (a) *Separate laytime for loading and discharging*
The cargo shall be loaded within the number of running days/hours as indicated in Box 16, weather permitting, Sundays and holidays excepted, unless used, in which event time used shall count.
The cargo shall be discharged within the number of running days/hours as indicated in Box 16, weather permitting, Sundays and holidays excepted unless used, in which event time used shall count.
* (b) *Total laytime for loading and discharging*
The cargo shall be loaded and discharged within the number of total running days/hours as indicated in Box 16, weather permitting Sundays and holidays excepted, unless used, in which event time used shall count.
(c) *Commencement of laytime (loading and discharging)*
Laytime for loading and discharging shall commence at 13.00 hours, if notice of readiness is given up to and including 12.00 hours, and at 06.00 hours next working day if notice given during office hours after 12.00 hours. Notice of readiness at loading port to be given to the Shippers named in Box 17 or if not named, to the Charterers or their agents named in Box 18. Notice of readiness at the discharging port to be given to the Receivers or, if not known, to the Charterers or their agents named in Box 19.
If the loading/discharging berth is not available on the Vessel's arrival at or off the port of loading/discharging, the Vessel shall be entitled to give notice of readiness within ordinary office hours on arrival there, whether in free pratique or not, whether customs cleared or not. Laytime or time on demurrage shall then count as if she were in berth and in all respects ready for loading/discharging provided that the Master warrants that she is in fact ready in all respects. Time used in moving from the place of waiting to the loading/discharging berth shall not count as laytime.
If, after inspection, the Vessel is found not to be ready in all respects to load/discharge time lost after the discovery thereof until the Vessel is again ready to load/discharge shall not count as laytime.
Time used before commencement of laytime shall count.
* *Indicate alternative (a) or (b) as agreed, in Box 16.*

7. Demurrage
Demurrage at the loading and discharging port is payable by the Charterers at the rate stated in Box 20 in the manner stated in Box 20 per day or pro rata for any part of a day. Demurrage shall fall due day by day and shall be payable upon receipt of the Owners' invoice.
In the event the demurrage is not paid in accordance with the above, the Owners shall give the Charterers 96 running hours written notice to rectify the failure. If the demurrage is not paid at the expiration of this time limit and if the vessel is in or at the loading port, the Owners are entitled at any time to terminate the Charter Party and claim damages for any losses caused thereby.

8. Lien Clause
The Owners shall have a lien on the cargo and on all sub-freights payable in respect of the cargo, for freight, deadfreight, demurrage, claims for damages and for all other amounts due under this Charter Party including costs of recovering same.

9. Cancelling Clause
(a) Should the Vessel not be ready to load (whether in berth or not) on the cancelling date indicated in Box 21, the Charterers shall have the option of cancelling this Charter Party.
(b) Should the Owners anticipate that, despite the exercise of due diligence the Vessel will not be ready to load by the cancelling date, they shall notify the Charterers thereof without delay stating the expected date of the Vessel's readiness to load and asking whether the Charterers will exercise their option of cancelling the Charter Party, or agree to a new cancelling date.
Such option must be declared by the Charterers within 48 running hours after the receipt of the Owners' notice. If the Charterers do not exercise their option of cancelling, then this Charter Party shall be deemed to be amended such that the seventh day after the new readiness date stated in the Owners' notification to the Charterers shall be the new cancelling date.
The provisions of sub-clause (b) of this Clause shall operate only once, and in case of the Vessel's further delay, the Charterers shall have the option of cancelling the Charter Party as per sub-clause (a) of this Clause.

10. Bills of Lading
Bills of Lading shall be presented and signed by the Master as per the 'Congenbill' Bill of Lading form, Edition 1994, without prejudice to this Charter Party, or by the Owners' agents provided written authority has been given by Owners to the agents, a copy of which is to be furnished to the Charterers. The Charterers shall indemnify the Owners against all consequences or liabilities that may arise from the signing of bills of lading as presented to the extent that the terms or contents of such bills of lading impose or result in the imposition of more onerous liabilities upon the Owners than those assumed by the Owners under this Charter Party.

11. Both-to-Blame Collision Clause
If the Vessel comes into collision with another vessel as a result of the negligence of the other vessel and any act, neglect or default of the Master, Mariner, Pilot or the servants of the Owners in the navigation or in the management of the Vessel, the owners of the cargo carried hereunder will indemnify the Owners against all loss or liability to the other or non-carrying vessel or her owners in so far as

such loss or liability represents loss of, or damage to, or any claim whatsoever of the owners of said cargo, paid or payable by the other or non-carrying vessel or her owners to the owners of said cargo and set-off, recouped or recovered by the other or non-carrying vessel or her owners as part of their claim against the carrying Vessel or the Owners.
The foregoing provisions shall also apply where the owners, operators or those in charge of any vessel or vessels or objects other than, or in addition to, the colliding vessels or objects are at fault in respect of a collision or contact.

12. General Average and New Jason Clause
General Average shall be adjusted in London unless otherwise agreed in Box 22 according to York-Antwerp Rules 1994 and any subsequent modification thereof. Proprietors of cargo to pay the cargo's share in the general expenses even if same have been necessitated through neglect or default of the Owners' servants (see Clause 2).
If General Average is to be adjusted in accordance with the law and practice of the United States of America, the following Clause shall apply: 'In the event of accident, danger, damage or disaster before or after the commencement of the voyage, resulting from any cause whatsoever, whether due to negligence or not, for which, or for the consequence of which, the Owners are not responsible, by statute contract or otherwise, the cargo shippers, consignees or the owners of the cargo shall contribute with the Owners in General Average to the payment of any sacrifices, losses or expenses of a General Average nature that may be made or incurred and shall pay salvage and special charges incurred in respect of the cargo. If a salving vessel is owned or operated by the Owners, salvage shall be paid for as fully as if the said salving vessel or vessels belonged to strangers. Such deposit as the Owners, or their agents, may deem sufficient to cover the estimated contribution of the goods and any salvage and special charges thereon shall, if required, be made by the cargo, shippers consignees or owners of the goods to the Owners before delivery.'.

13. Taxes and Dues Clause
(a) On Vessel - The Owners shall pay all dues, charges and taxes customarily levied on the Vessel, howsoever the amount thereof may be assessed.
(b) On cargo - The Charterers shall pay all dues, charges, duties and taxes customarily levied on the cargo, howsoever the amount thereof may be assessed.
(c) On freight - Unless otherwise agreed in Box 23, taxes levied on the freight shall be for the Charterers' account.

14. Agency
In every case the Owners shall appoint their own Agent both at the port of loading and the port of discharge.

15. Brokerage
A brokerage commission at the rate stated in Box 24 on the freight, dead-freight and demurrage earned is due to the party mentioned in Box 24.
In case of non-execution 1/3 of the brokerage on the estimated amount of freight to be paid by the party responsible for such non-execution to the Brokers as indemnity for the latter's expenses and work. In case of more voyages the amount of indemnity to be agreed.

16. General Strike Clause
(a) If there is a strike or lock-out affecting or preventing the actual loading of the cargo, or any part of it, when the Vessel is ready to proceed from her last port or at any time during the voyage to the port or ports of loading or after her arrival there, the Master or the Owners may ask the Charterers to declare, that they agree to reckon the laydays as if there were no strike or lock-out. Unless the Charterers have given such declaration in writing (by telegram, if necessary) within 24 hours, the Owners shall have the option of cancelling this Charter Party. If part cargo has already been loaded, the Owners must proceed with same, (freight payable on loaded quantity only) having liberty to complete with other cargo on the way for their own account.
(b) If there is a strike or lock-out affecting or preventing the actual discharging of the cargo on or after the Vessel's arrival at or off port of discharge and same has not been settled within 48 hours, the Charterers shall have the option of keeping the Vessel waiting until such strike or lock-out is at an end against paying half demurrage after expiration of the time provided for discharging until the strike or lock-out terminates and thereafter full demurrage shall be payable until the completion of discharging, or of ordering the Vessel to a safe port where she can safely discharge without risk of being detained by strike or lock-out. Such orders to be given within 48 hours after the Master or the Owners have given notice to the Charterers of the strike or lock-out affecting the discharge. On delivery of the cargo at such port, all conditions of this Charter Party and of the Bill of Lading shall apply and the Vessel shall receive the same freight as if she had discharged at the original port of destination, except that if the distance to the substituted port exceeds 100 nautical miles, the freight on the cargo delivered at the substituted port to be increased in proportion.
(c) Except for the obligations described above, neither the Charterers nor the Owners shall be responsible for the consequences of any strikes or lock-outs preventing or affecting the actual loading or discharging of the cargo.

17. War Risks ('Voywar 1993')
(1) For the purpose of this Clause, the words:
(a) The 'Owners' shall include the shipowners, bareboat charterers, disponent owners, managers or other operators who are charged with the management of the Vessel, and the Master; and
(b) 'War Risks' shall include any war (whether actual or threatened), act of war, civil war, hostilities, revolution, rebellion, civil commotion, warlike operations, the laying of mines (whether actual or reported), acts of piracy, acts of terrorists, acts of hostility or malicious damage, blockades (whether imposed against all Vessels or imposed selectively against Vessels of certain flags or ownership, or against certain cargoes or crews or otherwise howsoever), by any person, body, terrorist or political group, or the Government of any state whatsoever which, in the reasonable judgement of the Master and/or the Owners, may be dangerous or are likely to be or to become dangerous to the Vessel, her cargo, crew or other persons on board the Vessel.
(2) If at any time before the Vessel commences loading, it appears that, in the reasonable judgement of the Master and/or the Owners, performance of the Contract of Carriage, or any part of it, may expose, or is likely to expose, the Vessel, her cargo, crew or other persons on board the Vessel to War Risks the Owners may give notice to the Charterers cancelling this Contract of Carriage, or may refuse to perform such part of it as may expose, or may be likely to expose, the Vessel, her cargo, crew or other persons on board the Vessel to War Risks; provided always that if this Contract of Carriage provides that loading or discharging is to take place within a range of ports, and at the port or ports nominated by the Charterers the Vessel, her cargo, crew, or other persons onboard the Vessel may be exposed, or may be likely to be exposed, to War Risks, the Owners shall first require the Charterers to nominate any other safe port which lies within the range for loading or discharging, and may only cancel this Contract of Carriage if the Charterers shall not have nominated such safe port or ports within 48 hours of receipt of notice of such requirement.
(3) The Owners shall not be required to continue to load cargo for any voyage, or to sign Bills of Lading for any port or place or to proceed or continue on any voyage, or on any part thereof, or to proceed through any canal or waterway, or to proceed to or remain at any port or place whatsoever, where it appears, either after the loading of the cargo commences, or at any stage of the voyage thereafter before the discharge of the cargo is completed, that, in the reasonable judgement of the Master and/or the Owners, the Vessel, her cargo (or any part thereof), crew or other persons on board the Vessel (or any one or more of them) may be, or are likely to be, exposed to War Risks. If it should so appear, the Owners may by notice request the Charterers to nominate a safe port for the discharge of the cargo or any part thereof, and if within 48 hours of the receipt of such notice, the Charterers shall not have nominated such a port, the Owners may discharge the cargo at any safe port of their choice (including the port of loading) in complete fulfilment of the Contract of Carriage. The Owners shall be entitled to recover from the Charterers the extra expenses of such discharge and, if the discharge takes place at any port other than the loading port, to receive the full freight as though the cargo had been carried to the discharging port and if the extra distance exceeds 100 miles, to additional freight which shall be the same percentage of the freight contracted for as the percentage which the extra distance represents to the distance of the normal and customary route, the Owners having a lien on the cargo for such expenses and freight.
(4) If at any stage of the voyage after the loading of the cargo commences, it appears that, in the reasonable judgement of the Master and/or the Owners, the Vessel, her cargo, crew or other persons on board the Vessel may be, or are likely to be, exposed to War Risks on any part of the route (including any canal or waterway) which is normally and customarily used in a voyage of the nature contracted for, and there is another longer route to the discharging port, the Owners shall give notice to the Charterers that this route will be taken. In this event the Owners shall be entitled, if the total extra distance exceeds 100 miles, to additional freight which shall be the same percentage of the freight contracted for as the percentage which the extra distance represents to the distance of the normal and customary route.
(5) The Vessel shall have liberty:-
(a) to comply with all orders, directions, recommendations or advice as to departure, arrival, routes, sailing in convoy, ports of call, stoppages, destinations, discharge of cargo, delivery or in any way whatsoever which are given by the Government of the Nation under whose flag the Vessel sails, or other Government to whose laws the Owners are subject, or any other Government which so requires, or any body or group acting with the power to compel compliance with their orders or directions;
(b) to comply with the orders, directions or recommendations of any war risks underwriters who have the authority to give the same under the terms of the war risks insurance;
(c) to comply with the terms of any resolution of the Security Council of the United Nations, any directives of the European Community, the effective orders of any other Supranational body which has the right to issue and give the same, and with national laws aimed at enforcing the same to which the Owners are subject, and to obey the orders and directions of those who are charged with their enforcement;
(d) to discharge at any other port any cargo or part thereof which may render the Vessel liable to confiscation as a contraband carrier;
(e) to call at any other port to change the crew or any part thereof or other persons on board the Vessel when there is reason to believe that they may be subject to internment, imprisonment or other sanctions;
(f) where cargo has not been loaded or has been discharged by the Owners under any provisions of this Clause, to load other cargo for the Owners' own benefit and carry it to any other port or ports whatsoever, whether backwards or forwards or in a contrary direction to the ordinary or customary route.
(6) If in compliance with any of the provisions of sub-clauses (2) to (5) of this Clause anything is done or not done, such shall not be deemed to be a deviation, but shall be considered as due fulfilment of the Contract of Carriage.

18. General Ice Clause
Port of loading
(a) In the event of the loading port being inaccessible by reason of ice when the Vessel is ready to proceed from her last port or at any time during the voyage or on the Vessel's arrival or in case frost sets in after the Vessel's arrival, the Master for fear of being

frozen in is at liberty to leave without cargo, and this Charter Party shall be null and void.

(b) If during loading the Master, for fear of the Vessel being frozen in, deems it advisable to leave, he has liberty to do so with what cargo he has on board and to proceed to any other port or ports with option of completing cargo for the Owners' benefit for any port or ports including port of discharge. Any part cargo thus loaded under this Charter Party to be forwarded to destination at the Vessel's expense but against payment of freight, provided that no extra expenses be thereby caused to the Charterers, freight being paid on quantity delivered (in proportion if lumpsum), all other conditions as per this Charter Party.

(c) In case of more than one loading port, and if one or more of the ports are closed by ice, the Master or the Owners to be at liberty either to load the part cargo at the open port and fill up elsewhere for their own account as under section (b) or to declare the Charter Party null and void unless the Charterers agree to load full cargo at the open port.

Port of discharge

(a) Should ice prevent the Vessel from reaching port of discharge the Charterers shall have the option of keeping the Vessel waiting until the reopening of navigation and paying demurrage or of ordering the Vessel to a safe and immediately accessible port where she can safely discharge without risk of detention by ice. Such orders to be given within 48 hours after the Master or the Owners have given notice to the Charterers of the impossibility of reaching port of destination.

(b) If during discharging the Master for fear of the Vessel being frozen in deems it advisable to leave, he has liberty to do so with what cargo he has on board and to proceed to the nearest accessible port where she can safely discharge.

(c) On delivery of the cargo at such port, all conditions of the Bill of Lading shall apply and the Vessel shall receive the same freight as if she had discharged at the original port of destination, except that if the distance of the substituted port exceeds 100 nautical miles, the freight on the cargo delivered at the substituted port to be increased in proportion.

19. Law and Arbitration

* (a) This Charter Party shall be governed by and construed in accordance with English law and any dispute arising out of this Charter Party shall be referred to arbitration in London in accordance with the Arbitration Acts 1950 and 1979 or any statutory modification or re-enactment thereof for the time being in force. Unless the parties agree upon a sole arbitrator, one arbitrator shall be appointed by each party and the arbitrators so appointed shall appoint a third arbitrator, the decision of the three-man tribunal thus constituted or any two of them, shall be final. On the receipt by one party of the nomination in writing of the other party's arbitrator, that party shall appoint their arbitrator within fourteen days, failing which the decision of the single arbitrator appointed shall be final.

For disputes where the total amount claimed by either party does not exceed the amount stated in Box 25** the arbitration shall be conducted in accordance with the Small Claims Procedure of the London Maritime Arbitrators Association.

* (b) This Charter Party shall be governed by and construed in accordance with Title 9 of the United States Code and the Maritime Law of the United States and should any dispute arise out of this Charter Party, the matter in dispute shall be referred to three persons at New York, one to be appointed by each of the parties hereto, and the third by the two so chosen; their decision or that of any two of them shall be final, and for purpose of enforcing any award, this agreement may be made a rule of the Court. The proceedings shall be conducted in accordance with the rules of the Society of Maritime Arbitrators, Inc..

For disputes where the total amount claimed by either party does not exceed the amount stated in Box 25** the arbitration shall be conducted in accordance with the Shortened Arbitration Procedure of the Society of Maritime Arbitrators, Inc..

* (c) Any dispute arising out of this Charter Party shall be referred to arbitration at the place indicated in Box 25, subject to the procedures applicable there. The laws of the place indicated in Box 25 shall govern this Charter Party.

(d) If Box 25 in Part I is not filled in, sub-clause (a) of this Clause shall apply.

* *(a), (b) and (c) are alternatives; indicate alternative agreed in Box 25.*
** *Where no figure is supplied in Box 25 in Part I, this provision only shall be void but the other Provisions of this Clause shall have full force and remain in effect.*

Issued July 1987

Code word for this Charter Party

'SHELLVOY 5'
Voyage Charter Party
LONDON,   19

PREAMBLE

IT IS THIS DAY AGREED between

of   (hereinafter referred to as 'Owners') being owners/disponent

owners of the motor/steam tank vessel called

(hereinafter referred to as 'the vessel')

and   of

(hereinafter referred to as 'Charterers')

that the service for which provision is herein made shall be subject to the terms and conditions of this charter which includes Part I and Part II. In the event of any conflict between the provisions of Part I and Part II hereof, the provisions of Part I shall prevail.

PART I

(A) Description of vessel   Owners guarantee that at the date hereof the vessel:

(i)   Is classed

(ii)   Has a deadweight of tonnes (1000 kg.) on a salt-water draft on assigned summer freeboard of   m.

(iii) Has a capacity available for the cargo of tonnes (1000 kg.) 5% more or less in Owners' option.

(iv)   Is fully fitted with heating systems for all cargo tanks capable of maintaining cargo at a temperature of up to degrees Celsius.

(v)   Has tanks coated as follows:-

(vi)   Is equipped with cranes/derricks capable of lifting to and supporting at the vessel's port and starboard manifolds submarine hoses of up to   tonnes (1000 kg.) in weight.

(vii) Has cargo pumps capable of discharging a full cargo within   hours or maintaining a back pressure of   at the vessel's manifold (provided shore facilities permit and the cargo does not have a kinematic viscosity exceeding 600 centistokes at the discharge temperature required by Charterers).

(viii) Has or will have carried the following three cargoes immediately prior to loading under this charter:-

Last

2.

3.

(ix)   Has a crude oil washing system complying with the requirements of the International Convention for the Prevention of Pollution from Ships 1973 as modified by the Protocol of 1978 ('MARPOL 73/78').

(x)   Has an operational inert gas system.

(xi)   Has on board all papers and certificates required by any applicable law, in force as at the date of this charter, to enable the vessel to perform the charter service without any delay.

(xii) Is entered in   P&I Club.

(B) Position/ Readiness   Now   Expected ready to load

(C) Laydays

Commencing Noon Local Time on   (Commencement Date)

Terminating Noon Local Time on   (Termination Date)

Appendix I

PART I

(D Loading
   Port(s)/
   Range

                                             one or more ports at Charterers' option

(E) Discharging
    Port(s)/
    Range

                                             one or more ports at Charterers' option

(F) Cargo
    description

                                             Charterers' option

        Maximum temperature on loading   degrees Celsius

(G) Freight rate   At   % of the rate for the voyage as provided for in the Worldwide Tanker Nominal Freight Scale current at the date of commencement of loading (hereinafter referred to as 'Worldscale') per ton (2240 lbs)/tonne (1000 Kg).

(H) Freight
    payable to

(I) Laytime

                                             running hours

(J) Demurrage
    per day (or
    pro rata)

(K) ETAs

    All radio messages sent by the master to Charterers shall be addressed to

(L) Special pro-
    visions

Signatures

    IN WITNESS WHEREOF, the parties have caused this charter consisting of the Preamble, Parts I and II to be executed as of the day and year first above written.

        By

        By

Issued July 1987   'SHELLVOY 5'

PART II

Condition of vessel

1.   Owners shall exercise due diligence to ensure that from the time when the obligation to proceed to the loading port(s) attaches and throughout the charter service –
(a)   the vessel and her hull, machinery, boilers, tanks, equipment and facilities are in good order and condition and in every way equipped and fit for the service required; and
(b)   the vessel has a full and efficient complement of master, officers and crew;
and to ensure that before and at the commencement of any laden voyage the vessel is in all respects fit to carry the cargo specified in Part I(F).

Cleanliness of tanks

2.   Whilst loading, carrying and discharging cargo the master shall at all times use due diligence to keep the tanks, lines and pumps of the vessel clean for the cargo specified in Part I(F). It shall be for the master alone to decide whether the vessel's tanks, lines and pumps are suitably clean. However, the decision of the master shall be without prejudice to the right of Charterers, should any contamination or damage subsequently be found, to contend that the same was caused by inadequate cleaning and/or some breach of this or any other Clause of this charter.

Voyage

3. Subject to the provisions of this charter the vessel shall perform her service with utmost despatch and shall proceed to such berths as Charterers may specify, in any port or ports within Part I(D) nominated by Charterers, or so near thereunto as she may safely get and there, always safely afloat, load a full cargo, but not in excess of the maximum quantity consistent with the International Load Line Convention for the time being in force and, being so loaded, proceed as ordered on signing bills of lading to such berths as Charterers may specify, in any port or ports within Part I(E) nominated by Charterers, or so near thereunto as she may safely get and there, always safely afloat, discharge the cargo.

Charterers shall nominate loading and discharging ports, and shall specify loading and discharging berths, in sufficient time to avoid delay or deviation to the vessel. Subject to the foregoing, and provided it does not cause delay or deviation to the vessel, Charterers shall have the option of ordering the vessel to safe areas at sea for wireless orders.

In this charter, 'berth' means any berth, wharf, dock, anchorage, submarine line, a position alongside any vessel or lighter or any other loading or discharging point whatsoever to which Charterers are entitled to order the vessel hereunder, and 'port' means any port or location at sea to which the vessel may proceed in accordance with the terms of this charter.

Safe berth

4.   Charterers shall exercise due diligence to order the vessel only to ports and berths which are safe for the vessel and to ensure that transhipment operations conform to standards not less than those set out in the latest edition of ICS/OCIMF Ship-to-Ship Transfer Guide (Petroleum). Not withstanding anything contained in this charter, Charterers do not warrant the safety of any port, berth or transhipment operation and Charterers shall not be liable for loss or damage arising from any unsafety if they can prove that due diligence was exercised in the giving of the order.

Freight

5.   Freight shall be earned concurrently with delivery of cargo at the nominated discharging port or ports and shall be paid by Charterers to Owners without any deductions in United States Dollars at the rate(s) specified in Part I(G) on the gross Bill of Lading quantity as furnished by the shipper (subject to Clauses 8 and 40), upon receipt by Charterers of notice of completion of final discharge of cargo, provided that no freight shall be payable on any quantity in excess of the maximum quantity consistent with the International Load Line Convention for the time being in force.

If the vessel is ordered to proceed on a voyage for which a fixed differential is provided in Worldscale, such fixed differential shall be payable without applying the percentage referred to in Part I(G).

If cargo is carried between ports and/or by a route for which no freight rate is expressly quoted in Worldscale, then the parties shall, in the absence of agreement as to the appropriate freight rate, apply to Worldscale Association (London) Ltd., or Worldscale Association (NYC) Inc, for the determination of an appropriate Worldscale freight rate.

Save in respect of the time when freight is earned, the location of any transhipment at sea pursuant to Clause 26(2) shall not be an additional nominated port for the purposes of this charter (including this Clause 5) and the freight rate for the voyage shall be the same as if such transhipment had not taken place.

Dues and other charges

6.   Dues and other charges upon the vessel, including those assessed by reference to the quantity of cargo loaded or discharged, and any taxes on freight whatsoever shall be paid by Owners, and dues and other charges upon the cargo shall be paid by Charterers. However, notwithstanding the foregoing, where under a provision of Worldscale a due or charge is expressly for the account of Owners or Charterers then such due or charge shall be payable in accordance with such provision.

Loading and discharging cargo

7.   The cargo shall be loaded into the vessel at the expense of Charterers and, up to the vessel's permanent hose connections, at Charterers' risk. The cargo shall be discharged from the vessel at the expense of Owners and, up to the vessel's permanent hose connections, at Owners' risk. Owners shall, unless otherwise notified by Charterers or their agents, supply at Owners' expense all hands, equipment and facilities required on board for mooring and unmooring and connecting and disconnecting hoses for loading and discharging.

Deadfreight

8.   Charterers need not supply a full cargo, but if they do not freight shall nevertheless be paid as if the vessel had been loaded with a full cargo.
The term 'full cargo' as used throughout this charter means a cargo which, together with any collected washings (as defined in Clause 40) retained on board pursuant to the requirements of MARPOL 73/78, fills the vessel to either her applicable deadweight or her capacity stated in Part I(A)(iii), whichever is less, while leaving sufficient space in the tanks for the expansion of cargo.

Shifting

9. Charterers shall have the right to require the vessel to shift at ports of loading and/or discharging from a loading or discharging berth within port limits and back to the same or to another such berth once or more often on payment of all additional expenses incurred. For the purposes of freight payment and shifting the places grouped in Port and Terminal Combinations in Worldscale are to be considered as berths within a single port. If at any time before cargo operations are completed it becomes dangerous for the vessel to remain at the specified berth as a result of wind or water conditions, Charterers shall pay all additional expenses of shifting from any such berth and back to that or any other specified berth within port limits (except to the extent that any fault of the vessel contributed to such danger).

Subject to Clause 14(a) and (c) time spent shifting shall count against laytime or if the vessel is on demurrage for demurrage.

Charterers' failure to give orders

10. If the vessel is delayed due to Charterers' breach of Clause 3 Charterers shall, subject to the terms hereof, compensate Owners in accordance with Clause 15(1) and (2) as if such delay were time exceeding the laytime.

The period of such delay shall be calculated
(i) from 6 hours after Owners notify Charterers that the vessel is delayed awaiting nomination of loading port until such nomination has been received by Owners, or
(ii) from 6 hours after the vessel gives notice of readiness at the loading port until commencement of loading
as the case may be, subject always to the same exceptions as those set out in Clause 14. Any period of delay in respect of which Charterers pay compensation pursuant to this Clause 10 shall be excluded from any calculation of time for laytime or demurrage made under any other Clause of this charter.

Periods of delay hereunder shall be cumulative for each port, and Owners may demand compensation after the vessel has been delayed for a total of 20 running days, and thereafter after each succeeding 5 running days of delay and at the end of any delay. Each such demand shall show the period in respect of which compensation is claimed and the amount due. Charterers shall pay the full amount due within 14 days after receipt of Owners' demand. Should Charterers fail to make any such payments Owners shall have the right to terminate this charter by giving written notice to Charterers or their agents, without prejudice to any claims which Charterers or Owners may have against each other under this charter or otherwise.

Laydays/ Termination

11. Should the vessel not be ready to load by noon local time on the termination date set out in Part I(C) Charterers shall have the option of terminating this charter unless the vessel has been delayed due to Charterers' change of orders pursuant to Clause 26, in which case the laydays shall be extended by the period of such delay.

However, if Owners reasonably conclude that, despite the exercise of due diligence, the vessel will not be ready to load by noon on the termination date, Owners may, as soon as they are able to state with reasonable certainty a new date when the vessel will be ready, give notice to Charterers declaring the new readiness date and asking Charterers to elect whether or not to terminate this charter. Unless Charterers within 4 days after such notice or within 2 days after the termination date (whichever is earlier) declare this charter terminated, Part I(C) shall be deemed to be amended such that the new readiness date stated shall be the commencement date and the second day thereafter shall be the termination date.

The provisions of this Clause and the exercise or non-exercise by Charterers of their option to terminate shall not prejudice any claims which Charterers or Owners may have against each other.

Laytime

12. The laytime for loading, discharging and all other Charterers' purposes whatsoever shall be the number of running hours specified in Part I(I). Charterers shall have the right to load and discharge at all times, including night, provided that they shall pay for all extra expenses incurred ashore.

Notice of readiness/Running time

13. (1) Subject to the provisions of Clauses 13(3) and 14, if the vessel loads or discharges cargo other than by transhipment at sea

(a) Time at each loading or discharging port shall commence to run 6 hours after the vessel is in all respects ready to load or discharge and written notice thereof has been tendered by the master or Owners' agents to Charterers or their agents and the vessel is securely moored at the specified loading or discharging berth. However, if the vessel does not proceed immediately to such berth time shall commence to run 6 hours after (i) the vessel is lying in the area where she was ordered to wait or, in the absence of any such specific order, in a usual waiting area and (ii) written notice of readiness has been tendered and (iii) the specified berth is accessible. A loading or discharging berth shall be deemed inaccessible only for so long as the vessel is or would be prevented from proceeding to it by bad weather, tidal conditions, ice, awaiting daylight pilot or tugs, or port traffic control requirements (except those requirements resulting from the unavailability of such berth or of the cargo).

If Charterers fail to specify a berth at any port, the first berth at which the vessel loads or discharges the cargo or any part thereof shall be deemed to be the specified berth at such port for the purposes of this Clause.

Notice shall not be tendered before commencement of laydays and notice tendered by radio shall qualify as written notice provided it is confirmed in writing as soon as reasonably possible.

(b) Time shall continue to run
(i) until cargo hoses have been disconnected, or
(ii) if the vessel is delayed for Charterers' purposes for more than one hour after disconnection of cargo hoses, until the termination of such delay provided that if the vessel waits at any place other than the berth, time on passage to such other place, from disconnecting of hoses to remooring/anchorage at such other place, shall not count.

(2) If the vessel loads or discharges cargo by transhipment at sea time shall count from the arrival of the vessel at the transhipment area or from commencement of the laydays, whichever is later, and, subject to Clause 14(c), shall run until transhipment has been completed and the vessels have separated.

(3) Notwithstanding anything else in this Clause 13, if Charterers start loading or discharging the vessel before time would otherwise start to run under this charter, time shall run from commencement of such loading or discharging.

(4) For the purposes of this Cause 13 and of Clause 14 'time' shall mean laytime or time counting for demurrage, as the ease may be.

Suspension of time

14. Time shall not count when

(a) spent on inward passage from the vessel's waiting area to the loading or discharging berth specified by Charterers, even if lightening occurred at such waiting area; or

(b) spent in handling ballast except to the extent that cargo operations are carried on concurrently and are not delayed thereby; or

(c) lost as a result of
   (i) breach of this Charter by Owners; or
   (ii) any cause attributable to the vessel, including breakdown or inefficiency of the vessel; or
   (iii) strike, lock-out, stoppage or restraint of labour of master, officers or crew of the vessel or tug boats or pilot.

Demurrage

15. (1) Charterers shall pay demurrage at the rate specified in Part I(J).

If the demurrage rate specified in Part I(J) is expressed as a percentage of Worldscale such percentage shall be applied to the demurrage rate applicable to vessels of a similar size to the vessel as provided in Worldscale or, for the purpose of clause 10 and/or if this charter is terminated prior to the commencement of loading, in the Worldwide Tanker Nominal Freight Scale current at the termination date specified in Part I(C).

Demurrage shall be paid per running day or pro rata for part thereof for all time which, under the provisions of this charter, counts against laytime or for demurrage and which exceeds the laytime specified in Part I(I). Charterers' liability for exceeding the laytime shall be absolute and shall not in any case be subject to the provisions of Clause 32.

(2) If, however, all or part of such demurrage arises out of or results from fire or explosion at ports of loading and/or discharging in or about the plant of Charterers, shippers or consignees of the cargo (not being a fire or explosion caused by the negligence or wilful act or omission of Charterers, shippers or consignees of the cargo or their respective servants or agents), act of God, act of war, riot, civil commotion, or arrest or restraint of princes rulers or peoples, the rate of demurrage shall be reduced by half for such demurrage or such part thereof.

(3) Owners shall notify Charterers within 60 days after completion of discharge if demurrage has been incurred and any demurrage claim together with supporting documentation shall be submitted within 90 days after completion of discharge. If Owners fail to give notice of or to submit any such claim within the time limits aforesaid, Charterers' liability for such demurrage shall be extinguished.

Vessel inspection

16. Charterers shall have the right, but no duty, to have a representative attend on board the vessel at any loading and/or discharging ports (except locations at sea) and the master and Owners shall co-operate to facilitate his inspection of the vessel and observation of cargo operations. However, such right, and the exercise or non-exercise thereof, shall in no way reduce the master's or Owners' authority over, or responsibility to Charterers and third parties for, the vessel and every aspect of her operation, nor increase Charterers' responsibilities to Owners or third parties for the same.

Cargo inspection

17. Without prejudice to Clause 2 hereof, Charterers shall have the right to require inspection of the vessel's tanks at loading and/or discharging ports (except locations at sea) to ascertain the quantity and quality of the cargo, water and residues on board. Depressurisation of the tanks to permit inspection, shippers or ullaging shall be carried out in accordance with the recommendations in the latest edition of the International Safety Guide for Oil Tankers and Terminals. Charterers shall also have the right to inspect and take samples from the bunker tanks and other non-cargo spaces. Any delay to the vessel caused by such inspection and measurement or associated depressurising/repressurising of tanks shall count against laytime, or if the vessel is on demurrage, for demurrage.

Cargo measurement

18. The master shall ascertain the contents of all tanks before and after loading and before and after discharging, and shall prepare tank-by-tank ullage reports of the cargo, water and residues on board which shall be promptly made available to Charterers or their representative if requested. Each ullage report shall show actual ullage/dips, and densities at observed and standard temperature (15^0 Celsius). All quantities shall be expressed in cubic metres at both observed and standard temperature.

Inert gas

19. The vessel's inert gas system (if any) shall comply with Regulation 62, Chapter II-2 of the 1974 Safety of Life at Sea Convention as modified by the Protocol of 1978 and Owners warrant that such system shall be operated in accordance with the guidance given in the IMO publication 'Inert Gas Systems (1983)'. Should the inert gas system fail, Section 8 (Emergency Procedures) of the said IMO publication shall be strictly adhered to and time lost as a consequence of such failure shall not count against laytime or, if the vessel is on demurrage, for demurrage.

Crude oil washing

20. If the vessel is equipped for crude oil washing Charterers shall have the right to require the vessel to crude oil wash those tanks in which the cargo is carried. If crude oil washing is required by Charterers or any competent authority, any additional discharging time thereby incurred shall count against laytime or, if the vessel is on demurrage, for demurrage, and the number of hours specified in Part I(A)(vii) shall be increased by 0.75 hours per cargo tank washed.

Appendix I

Over age insurance

21. Any additional insurance on the cargo required because of the age of the vessel shall be for Owners' account.

Ice

22. The vessel shall not be required to force ice or to follow icebreakers. If the master finds that a nominated port is inaccessible due to ice, the master shall immediately notify Charterers requesting revised orders and shall remain outside the ice-bound area; and if after arrival at a nominated port there is danger of the vessel being frozen in, the vessel shall proceed to the nearest safe and ice free position and at the same time request Charterers to give revised orders.

In either case if the affected port is
 (i) the first or only loading port and no cargo has been loaded, Charterers shall either nominate another port, or give notice cancelling this charter in which case they shall pay at the demurrage rate in Part I(J) for the time from the master's notification aforesaid or from notice of readiness on arrival, as the case may be, until the time such cancellation notice is given;
 (ii) a loading port and part of the cargo has been loaded, Charterers shall either nominate another port, or order the vessel to proceed on the voyage without completing loading in which case Charterers shall pay for any deadfreight arising therefrom;
 (iii) a discharging port, Charterers shall either nominate another port or order the vessel to proceed to or return to and discharge at the nominated port. If the vessel is ordered to proceed to or return to a nominated port, Charterers shall bear the risk of the vessel being damaged whilst proceeding to or returning to or at such port, and the whole period from the time when the master's request for revised orders is received by Charterers until the vessel can safely depart after completion of discharge shall count against laytime or, if the vessel is on demurrage, for demurrage.

If, as a consequence of Charterers revising orders pursuant to this clause, the nominated port(s) or the number or rotation of ports is changed freight, shall nevertheless be paid for the voyage which the vessel would otherwise have performed had the orders not been so revised, such freight to be increased or reduced by the amount by which, as a result of such revision of orders,
 (a) the time used including any time awaiting revised orders (which shall be valued at the demurrage rate in Part I(J)),
 (b) the bunkers consumed (which shall be valued at the bunker costs at the port at which bunkers were last taken) and
 (c) the port charges
for the voyage actually performed are greater or less than those that would have been incurred on the voyage which, but for the revised orders under this Clause, the vessel would have performed.

Quarantine

23. Time lost due to quarantine shall not count against laytime or for demurrage unless such quarantine was in force at the time when the affected port was nominated by Charterers.

Agency

24. The vessel's agents shall be nominated by Charterers at nominated ports of loading and discharging.

Such agents, although nominated by Charterers, shall be employed and paid by Owners.

Charterers' obligation at shallow draft port/ Lightening in port

25. (1) (a) If the vessel, with the quantity of cargo then on board, is unable due to inadequate depth of water in the port safely to reach any specified discharging berth and discharge the cargo there always safely afloat. Charterers shall specify a location within port limits where the vessel can discharge sufficient cargo into vessels or lighters to enable the vessel safely to reach and discharge cargo at such discharging berth, and the vessel shall lighten at such location.

(b) If the vessel is lightened pursuant to Clause 25(1)(a) then, for the purposes of the calculation of laytime and demurrage, the lightening place shall be treated as the first discharging berth within the port where such lightening occurs.

Charterers orders/ Change of orders/ Part cargo transhipment

26. (1) If, after loading and/or discharging ports have been nominated, Charterers wish to vary such nominations or their rotation, Charterers may give revised orders subject to Part I(D) and/or (E), as the case may be. Charterers shall reimburse Owners at the demurrage rate provided in Part I(J) for any deviation or delay which may result therefrom and shall pay at replacement price for any extra bunkers consumed.

Charterers shall not be liable for any other loss or expense which is caused by such variation unless promptly on receipt of the revised orders Owners notify Charterers of the expectation of such loss or expense in which case, unless Charterers promptly revoke such orders, Charterers shall be liable to reimburse Owners for any such loss or expense proven.

(2) Subject to Clause 33(6), Charterers may order the vessel to load and/or discharge any part of the cargo by transhipment at sea in the vicinity of any nominated port or en route between two nominated ports, in which case Charterers shall reimburse Owners at the demurrage rate specified in Part I(J) for any additional steaming time and/or delay which may be incurred as a consequence of proceeding to and from the location at sea of such transhipment and, in addition, Charterers shall pay at replacement price for any extra bunkers consumed.

Heating of cargo

27. If Charterers require cargo heating the vessel shall, on passage to and whilst at discharging port(s), maintain the cargo at the loaded temperature or at the temperature stated in Part I(A)(iv), whichever is the lower. Charterers may request that the temperature of the cargo be raised above or lowered below that at which it was loaded, in which event Owners shall use their best endeavours to comply with such request and Charterers shall pay at replacement price for any additional bunkers consumed and any consequential delay to the vessel shall count against laytime or, if the vessel is on demurrage, for demurrage.

ETA

28.   Owners undertake that, unless Charterers require otherwise, the master shall:
- (a) advise Charterers by radio immediately on leaving the final port of call on the previous voyage or within 48 hours after the time and date of this charter, whichever is the later, of the time and date of the vessel's expected arrival at the first loading port or, if the loading range is in the Arabian Gulf, the time of her expected arrival off Quoin Island;
- (b) confirm or amend such advice not later than 72 hours and again not later than 24 hours before the vessel is due at the first loading port or, in the case of a loading range in the Arabian Gulf, off Quoin Island;
- (c) advise Charterers by radio immediately after departure from the final loading port, of the vessel's expected time of arrival at the first discharging port or the area at sea to which the vessel has been instructed to proceed for wireless orders, and confirm or amend such advice not later than 72 hours and again not later than 24 hours before the vessel is due at such port or area;
- (d) immediately radio any variation of more than six hours from expected times of arrival at loading or discharging ports, Quoin Island or such area at sea to Charterers;
- (e) address all radio messages in accordance with Part I(K).

Owners shall be responsible for any consequences or additional expenses arising as a result of non-compliance with this Clause.

Packed cargo

29.   Charterers have the option of shipping products and/or general cargo in available dry cargo space, the quantity being subject to the master's discretion. Freight shall be payable at the bulk rate in accordance with Clause 5 and Charterers shall pay in addition all expenses incurred solely as a result of the packed cargo being carried. Delay occasioned to the vessel by the exercise of such option shall count against laytime or, if the vessel is on demurrage, for demurrage.

Subletting/
Assignment

30.   Charterers shall have the option of sub-chartering the vessel and/or of assigning this charter to any person or persons, but Charterers shall always remain responsible for the due fulfilment of all the terms and conditions of this charter.

Liberty

31.   The vessel shall be at liberty to tow or be towed, to assist vessels in all positions of distress, to call at any port or ports for bunkers, to sail without pilots, and to deviate for the purpose of saving life or property or for the purpose of embarking or disembarking persons spares or supplies by helicopter or for any other reasonable purpose.

Exceptions

32. (a) The vessel, her master and Owners shall not, unless otherwise in this charter expressly provided, be liable for any loss or damage or delay or failure arising or resulting from any act, neglect or default of the master, pilots, mariners or other servants of Owners in the navigation or management of the vessel; fire unless caused by the actual fault or privity of Owners; collision or stranding; dangers and accidents of the sea; explosion, bursting of boilers, breakage of shafts or any latent defect in hull, equipment or machinery; provided, however, that Part I(A) and Clauses 1 and 2 hereof shall be unaffected by the foregoing. Further, neither the vessel, her master or Owners, nor Charterers shall, unless otherwise in this charter expressly provided, be liable for any loss or damage or delay or failure in performance hereunder arising or resulting from act of God, act of war, act of public enemies, seizure under legal process, quarantine restrictions, strikes, lock-outs, restraints of labour, riots, civil commotions or arrest or restraint of princes rulers or people.

(b) Nothing in this charter shall be construed as in any way restricting, excluding or waiving the right of Owners or of any other relevant persons to limit their liability under any available legislation or law.

(c) Clause 32(a) shall not apply to or affect any liability of Owners or the vessel or any other relevant person in respect of
- (i) loss of or damage caused to any berth, jetty, dock, dolphin, buoy, mooring line, pipe or crane or other works or equipment whatsoever at or near any port to which the vessel may proceed under this charter, whether or not such works or equipment belong to Charterers, or
- (ii) any claim (whether brought by Charterers or any other person) arising out of any loss of or damage to or in connection with the cargo. Any such claim shall be subject to the Hague-Visby Rules or the Hague Rules, as the case may be, which ought pursuant to Clause 37 hereof to have been incorporated in the relevant bill of lading (whether or not such Rules were so incorporated), or, if no such bill of lading is issued, to the Hague-Visby Rules.

Bills of lading

33. (1) Subject to the provisions of this Clause Charterers may require the master to sign lawful bills of lading for any cargo in such form as Charterers direct.

(2) The signing of bills of lading shall be without prejudice to this charter and Charterers hereby indemnify Owners against all liabilities that may arise from signing bills of lading to the extent that the same impose liabilities upon Owners in excess of or beyond those imposed by this charter.

(3) All bills of lading presented to the master for signature, in addition to complying with the requirements of Clauses 35, 36 and 37, shall include or effectively incorporate clauses substantially similar to the terms of Clauses 22, 33(7) and 34.

(4) All bills of lading presented for signature hereunder shall show a named port of discharge. If when bills of lading are presented for signature discharging port(s) have been nominated hereunder, the discharging port(s) shown on such bills of lading shall be in conformity with the nominated port(s). If at the time of such presentation no such nomination has been made hereunder, the discharging port(s) shown on such bills of lading must be within Part I(E) and shall be deemed to have been nominated hereunder by virtue of such presentation.

(5) Article III Rules 3 and 5 of the Hague-Visby Rules shall apply to the particulars included in the bills of lading as if Charterers were the shippers, and the guarantee and indemnity therein contained shall apply to the description of the cargo furnished by or on behalf of Charterers.

(6)   Notwithstanding any other provisions of this charter, Owners shall not be obliged to comply with any orders from Charterers to discharge all or part of the cargo
- (i)   at any port other than that shown on the bills of lading (except as provided in Clauses 22 or 34) and/or
- (ii)   without presentation of an original bill of lading

unless they have received from Charterers both written confirmation of such orders and an indemnity acceptable to Owners.

(7)   The master shall not be required or bound to sign bills of lading for any blockaded port or for any port which the master or Owners in his or their discretion consider dangerous or impossible to enter or reach.

(8)   Charterers hereby warrant that on each and every occasion that they issue orders under Clauses 22, 26, 34 or 38 they will have the authority of the holders of the bills of lading to give such orders, and that such bills of lading will not be transferred to any person who does not concur therein.

War risks   34.   (1)   If
- (a)   any loading or discharging port to which the vessel may properly be ordered under the provisions of this charter or bills of lading issued pursuant to this charter be blockaded, or
- (b)   owing to any war, hostilities, warlike operation, civil commotions, revolutions, or the operation of international law (i) entry to any such loading or discharging port or the loading or discharging of cargo at any such port be considered by the master or Owners in his or their discretion dangerous or prohibited or (ii) it be considered by the master or Owners in his or their discretion dangerous or impossible or prohibited for the vessel to reach any such loading or discharging port,

Charterers shall have the right to order the cargo or such part of it as may be affected to be loaded or discharged at any other loading or discharging port within the ranges specified in Part I(D) or (E) respectively (provided such other port is not blockaded and that entry thereto or loading or discharging of cargo thereat or reaching the same is not in the master's or Owners' opinion dangerous or impossible or prohibited).

(2)   If no orders be received from Charterers within 48 hours after they or their agents have received from Owners a request for the nomination of a substitute port, then
- (a)   if the affected port is the first or only loading port and no cargo has been loaded, this charter shall terminate forthwith;
- (b)   if the affected port is a loading port and part of the cargo has already been loaded, the vessel may proceed on passage and Charterers shall pay for any deadfreight so incurred;
- (c)   if the affected port is a discharging port, Owners shall be at liberty to discharge the cargo at any port which they or the master may in their or his discretion decide on (whether within the range specified in Part I(E) or not) and such discharging shall be deemed to be due fulfilment of the contract or contracts of affreightment so far as cargo so discharged is concerned.

(3)   If in accordance with Clause 34(1) or (2) cargo is loaded or discharged at any such other port, freight shall be paid as for the voyage originally nominated, such freight to be increased or reduced by the amount by which, as a result of loading or discharging at such other port,
- (a)   the time on voyage including any time awaiting revised orders (which shall be valued at the demurrage rate in Part I(J)),
- (b)   the bunkers consumed (which shall be valued at the bunker costs at the port at which bunkers were last taken), and
- (c)   the port charges

for the voyage actually performed are greater or less than those which would have been incurred on the voyage originally nominated Save as aforesaid, the voyage actually performed shall be treated for the purpose of this Charter as if it were the voyage originally nominated.

(4) The vessel shall have liberty to comply with any directions or recommendations as to departure, arrival, routes, ports of call, stoppages, destinations, zones, waters, delivery or in any otherwise whatsoever given by the government of the nation under whose flag the vessel sails or any other government or local authority including any de facto government or local authority or by any person or body acting or purporting to act as or with the authority of any such government or authority or by any committee or person having under the terms of the war risks insurance on the vessel the right to give any such directions or recommendations. If by reason of or in compliance with any such directions or recommendations anything is done or is not done, such shall not be deemed a deviation.

If by reason of or in compliance with any such directions or recommendations the vessel does not proceed to the discharging port or ports originally nominated or to which she may have been properly ordered under the provisions of this charter or bills of lading issued pursuant to this charter, the vessel may proceed to any discharging port on which the master or Owners in his or their discretion may decide and there discharge the cargo. Such discharging shall be deemed to be due fulfilment of the contract or contracts of affreightment and Owners shall be entitled to freight as if discharging had been effected at the port or ports originally nominated or to which the vessel may have been properly ordered under the provisions of this charter or bills of lading issued pursuant to this charter. All extra expenses involved in reaching and discharging the cargo at any such other discharging port shall be paid by Charterers and Owners shall have a lien on the cargo for all such extra expenses.

Both to blame clause

35.　If the liability for any collision in which the vessel is involved while performing this charter falls to be determined in accordance with the laws of the United States of America, the following clause, which shall be included in all bills of lading issued pursuant to this charter shall apply:

'If the vessel comes into collision with another vessel as a result of the negligence of the other vessel and any act, neglect or default of the master, mariner, pilot or the servants of the Carrier in the navigation or in the management of the vessel, the owners of the cargo carried hereunder will indemnify the Carrier against all loss or liability to the other or non-carrying vessel or her owners in so far as such loss or liability represents loss of, or damage to, or any claim whatsoever of the owners of the said cargo, paid or payable by the other or non-carrying vessel or her owners to the owners of the said cargo and set off, recouped or recovered by the other or non-carrying vessel or her owners as part of their claim against the carrying vessel or the Carrier.

The foregoing provisions shall also apply where the owners, operators or those in charge of any vessel or vessels or objects other than, or in addition to, the colliding vessels or objects are at fault in respect of a collision or contact.'

General average/ New Jason Clause

36.　General average shall be payable according to the York/Antwerp Rules, 1974, and shall be adjusted in London, but should the adjustment be made in accordance with the law and practice of the United States of America, the following clause, which shall be included in all bills of lading issued pursuant to this charter, shall apply:

'In the event of accident, danger, damage or disaster before or after the commencement of the voyage, resulting from any cause whatsoever, whether due to negligence or not, for which, or for the consequence of which, the Carrier is not responsible, by statute, contract or otherwise, the cargo, shippers, consignees or owners of the cargo shall contribute with the Carrier in general average to the payment of any sacrifices, losses or expenses of a general average nature that may be made or incurred and shall pay salvage and special charges incurred in respect of the cargo.

If a salving vessel is owned or operated by the Carrier, salvage shall be paid for as fully as if the said salving vessel or vessels belonged to strangers. Such deposit as the Carrier or its agents may deem sufficient to cover the estimated contribution of the cargo and any salvage and special charges thereon shall, if required, be made by the cargo, shippers, consignees or owners of the cargo to the Carrier before delivery.'

Clause paramount

37. The following clause shall be included in all bills of lading issued pursuant to this charter:

'CLAUSE PARAMOUNT

(1)　Subject to sub-clause (2) hereof, this bill of lading shall be governed by, and have effect subject to, the rules contained in the International Convention for the Unification of Certain Rules relating to Bills of Lading signed at Brussels on 25th August 1924 (hereafter the 'Hague Rules') as amended by the Protocol signed at Brussels on 23rd February 1968 (hereafter the 'Hague-Visby Rules'). Nothing herein contained shall be deemed to be either a surrender by the Carrier of any of his rights or immunities or an increase of any of his responsibilities or liabilities under the Hague-Visby Rules.

(2)　If there is governing legislation which applies the Hague Rules compulsorily to this bill of lading, to the exclusion of the Hague-Visby Rules, then this bill of lading shall have effect subject to the Hague Rules. Nothing herein contained shall be deemed to be either a surrender by the Carrier of any of his rights or immunities or an increase of any of his responsibilities or liabilities under the Hague Rules.

(3)　If any term of this bill of lading is repugnant to the Hague-Visby Rules, or the Hague Rules if applicable, such term shall be void to that extent but no further.

(4)　Nothing in this bill of lading shall be construed as in any way restricting, excluding or waiving the right of any relevant party or person to limit his liability under any available legislation and/or law.'

Back loading

38.　Charterers may order the vessel to load a part cargo at any nominated discharging port, and to discharge such part cargo at a port(s) to be nominated by Charterers within the range specified in Part I(E) and within the rotation of the discharging ports previously nominated, provided that such part cargo is of the description specified in Part I(J) and that the master in his absolute discretion determines that this cargo can be loaded, segregated and discharged without risk of contamination by, or of, any other cargo remaining on board.

Charterers shall pay a lump sum freight in respect of such part cargo calculated at the demurrage rate specified in Part I(J) on any additional time used by the vessel as a result of loading, carrying or discharging such part cargo.

Any additional expenses, including port charges, incurred as a result of loading or discharging such part cargo shall be for Charterers' account.

Bunkers

39.　Owners shall give Charterers or any other company in the Royal Dutch/Shell Group of Companies first option to quote for the supply of bunker requirements for the performance of this charter.

Oil pollution prevention

40.　(1)　Owners shall ensure that the masters shall:
　　　　(a)　comply with MARPOL 73/78 including in particular and without limitation Regulation 9, Chapter II of the International Convention for the Prevention of Pollution from Ships 1973;
　　　　(b)　collect the drainings and any tank washings into a suitable tank or tanks and, after maximum separation of free water, discharge the bulk of such water overboard, consistent with the above regulations; and
　　　　(c)　thereafter notify Charterers promptly of the amounts of oil and free water so retained on board and details of any other washings retained on board from earlier voyages (together called the 'collected washings').

(2) On being so notified, Charterers, in accordance with their rights under this Clause (which shall include without limitation the right to determine the disposal of the collected washings), shall before the vessel's arrival at the loading berth (or if already arrived as soon as possible thereafter) give instructions as to how the collected washings shall be dealt with. Owners shall ensure that the master on the vessel's arrival at the loading berth (or if already arrived as soon as possible thereafter) shall arrange in conjunction with the cargo suppliers for the measurement of the quantity of the collected washings and shall record the same in the vessel's ullage record.

(3) Charterers may require the collected washings to be discharged ashore at the loading port, in which case no freight shall be payable on them.

(4) Alternatively Charterers may require either that the cargo be loaded on top of the collected washings and the collected washings be discharged with the cargo, or that they be kept separate from the cargo in which case Charterers shall pay for any deadfreight incurred thereby in accordance with Clause 8 and shall, if practicable, accept discharge of the collected washings at the discharging port or ports.

In either case, provided that the master has reduced the free water in the collected washings to a minimum consistent with the retention on board of the oil residues in them and consistent with sub-Clause (1)(a) above, freight in accordance with Clause 5 shall be payable on the quantity of the collected washings as if such quantity were included in a bill of lading and the figure therefor furnished by the shipper provided, however, that

    (i)   if there is provision in this charter for a lower freight rate to apply to cargo in excess of an agreed quantity, freight on the collected washings shall be paid at such lower rate (provided such agreed quantity of cargo has been loaded) and

    (ii)   if there is provision in this charter for a minimum cargo quantity which is less than a full cargo, then whether or not such minimum cargo quantity is furnished, freight on the collected washings shall be paid as if such minimum cargo quantity had been furnished provided that no freight shall be payable in respect of any collected washings which are kept separate from the cargo and not discharged at the discharge port.

(5) Whenever Charterers require the collected washings to be discharged ashore pursuant to this Clause, Charterers shall provide and pay for the reception facilities, and the cost of any shifting therefor shall be for Charterers' account. Any time lost discharging the collected washings and/or shifting therefor shall count against laytime or, if the vessel is on demurrage, for demurrage.

TOVALOP   41.   Owners warrant that the vessel:
    (i)   is a tanker owned by a Participating Owner in TOVALOP and
    (ii)   is entered in the P&I Club stated in Part I(A)(xii)
and will so remain during the currency of this charter.

When an escape or discharge of Oil occurs from the vessel and causes or threatens to cause Pollution Damage, or when there is the Threat of an escape or discharge of Oil (i.e. a grave and imminent danger of the escape or discharge of Oil which, if it occurred, would create a serious danger of Pollution Damage, whether or not an escape or discharge in fact subsequently occurs), then Charterers may, at their option upon notice to Owners or master, undertake such measures as are reasonably necessary to prevent or minimise such Pollution Damage or to remove the Threat, unless Owners promptly undertake the same. Charterers shall keep Owners advised of the nature and result of any such measures taken by them and, if time permits, the nature of the measures intended to be taken by them. Any of the aforementioned measures taken by Charterers shall be deemed taken on Owners' authority and as Owners' agents, and shall be at Owners' expense except to the extent that:

    (1)   any such escape or discharge or Threat was caused or contributed to by Charterers, or

    (2)   by reason of the exceptions set out in Article III, paragraph 2, of the 1969 International Convention on Civil Liability for Oil Pollution Damage or any protocol thereto, Owners are or, had the said Convention applied to such escape or discharge or to the Threat, would have been, exempt from liability for the same, or

    (3)   the cost of such measures together with all other liabilities, costs and expenses of Owners arising out of or in connection with such escape or discharge or Threat exceeds the maximum liability applicable to the vessel under TOVALOP as at the time of such escape or discharge or threat, save and insofar as Owners shall he entitled to recover such excess under either the 1971 International Convention on the Establishment of an International Fund for Compensation for Oil Pollution Damage or under CRISTAL

PROVIDED ALWAYS that if Owners in their absolute discretion consider said measures should be discontinued, Owners shall so notify Charterers and thereafter Charterers shall have no right to continue said measures under the provisions of this Clause and all further liability to Charterers under this Clause shall thereupon cease.

The above provisions are not in derogation of such other rights as Charterers or Owners may have under this charter or may otherwise have or acquire by law or any international convention or TOVALOP.

The term 'TOVALOP' means the Tanker Owners' Voluntary Agreement Concerning Liability for Oil Pollution dated 7th January 1969, as amended from time to time, and the term 'CRISTAL' means the Contract Regarding an Interim Supplement to Tanker Liability for Oil Pollution dated 14th January 1971, as amended from time to time The terms 'Participating Owner', 'Oil' and, 'Pollution Damage' shall for the purposes of this clause have the meanings ascribed to them in TOVALOP.

Lien   42.   Owners shall have an absolute lien upon the cargo and all subfreights for all amounts due under this charter and the cost of recovery thereof including any expenses whatsoever arising from the exercise of such lien.

**Law and
litigation**

43. (a)   This charter shall be construed and the relations between the parties determined in accordance with the laws of England.

    (b)   Any dispute arising under this charter shall be decided by the English Courts to whose jurisdiction the parties hereby agree.

    (c)   Notwithstanding the foregoing, but without prejudice to any party's right to arrest or maintain the arrest of any maritime property, either party may, by giving written notice of election to the other party, elect to have any such dispute referred to the arbitration of a single arbitrator in London in accordance with the provisions of the Arbitration Act 1950, or any statutory modification or re-enactment thereof for the time being in force.

        (i)   A party shall lose its right to make such an election only if:
           (a)   it receives from the other party a written notice of dispute which
              (1) states expressly that a dispute has arisen out of this charter;
              (2) specifies the nature of the dispute; and
              (3) refers expressly to this clause 43(c) and;
           (b)   it fails to give notice of election to have the dispute referred to arbitration not later than 30 days from the date of receipt of such notice of dispute.

        (ii)   the parties hereby agree that either party may
           (a)   appeal to the High Court on any question of law arising out of an award;
           (b)   apply to the High Court for an order that the arbitrator state the reasons for his award;
           (c)   give notice to the arbitrator that a reasoned award is required; and
           (d)   apply to the High Court to determine any question of law arising in the course of the reference.

    (d) It shall be a condition precedent to the right of any party to a stay of any legal proceedings in which maritime property has been, or may be, arrested in connection with a dispute under this charter, that that party furnishes to the other party security to which that other party would have been entitled in such legal proceedings in the absence of a stay.

Construction

44. The side headings have been included in this charter for convenience of reference only and shall in no way affect the construction hereof.

Appendix I

SHELL 1st December 1996 amendments/additions/deletions to Shellvoy 5 Charter Party Issued July 1987.

Part I

(A) Preamble delete and insert

    (A)   I   Description of vessel – Owners guarantee that at the date hereof, and from the time when the obligation to proceed to the loadport (s) attaches, the vessel

         iii)   delete and insert – Has capacity for cargo of _____ m3

         vii)   delete and insert – Discharges a full cargo (whether homogenous or multi grade) within 24 hours or can maintain a back pressure of 100 PSI at the vessel's manifold and Owners guarantee such minimum performance provided shore facilities permit. The discharge guarantee shall only be applicable provided the kinematic viscosity does not exceed 600 centistokes at the discharge temperature required by Charterers. If the kinematic viscosity only exceeds 600 centistokes on part of the cargo or particular grade(s) then the discharge guarantee shall continue to apply to all other cargo/grades.

    (A)   II   insert – Maintenance/Restoration – throughout the Charter service, Owners shall ensure that the vessel shall be maintained, or that they shall take all steps necessary to promptly restore vessel to be, within the description in Part 1 (A) I and any questionnaires requested by Charterers or within information provided by Owners.

    (G)   Insert in line 51 'New' before 'Worldwide Tanker Nominal Freight Scale'

    (K)   ETA's – add

(Each Charterer to insert own instruction here .... for STASCO as Charterers)

STASCO LONDON OTA/421 TELEX G919651 SHEL A G, copied to other parties as advised in Charterers' voyage instructions.

All telexes must begin with the vessel name at the start of the subject line (no inverted commas, ', MT/SS preceding the name)

Part II

Clause 2 – Cleanliness of tanks – delete and insert

Whilst loading, carrying and discharging the cargo the Master shall at all times keep the tanks, lines and pumps of the vessel always clean for the cargo. Unless otherwise agreed between Owners and Charterers the vessel shall present for loading with cargo tanks ready and, if vessel fitted with Inert Gas System (IGS), fully inerted.

Charterers shall have the right to inspect vessel's tanks prior to loading and the vessel shall abide by Charterers' instructions with regard to tank or tanks which the vessel is required to present ready for entry and inspection. If Charterers' inspector is not satisfied with the cleanliness of the vessel's tanks, Owners shall clean them in their time and at their expense to the satisfaction of Charterers' inspector, provided that nothing herein shall affect the responsibilities and obligations of the Master and Owners in respect of the loading, carriage and care of cargo under this Charter nor prejudice the rights of Charterers, should any contamination or damage subsequently be found, to contend that the same was caused by inadequate cleaning and/or some breach of this or any other clause of this Charter.

Notwithstanding that the vessel, if equipped with IGS, shall present for loading with all cargo tanks fully inerted, any time used for re-inerting those tanks that, at Charterers' specific request, were gas freed for inspection shall count as laytime or if on demurrage for demurrage provided tank or tanks inspected were found to be suitable. If vessel's tanks are inspected and rejected laytime or demurrage time shall not commence or recommence to run until the tanks have been re-inspected, approved by Charterers' inspector and re-inerted.

Clause 4 – Safe Berth – add

Charterers shall not be held in breach of their due diligence obligation under this Clause 4 as a consequence of loss, damage or delay from any warlike act occurring within the Arabian Gulf and Gulf of Oman north of Latitude 24 Degrees North and the occurrence or threat of such acts shall not constitute unsafety for the purposes of this clause.

Clause 8 – Deadfreight – add

If under part 1 (F) vessel is chartered for a minimum quantity and the vessel is unable to load such quantity due to having reached her capacity as stated in Part 1 (A) (iii), always leaving sufficient space for expansion of cargo, then without prejudice to any claims which Charterers may have against Owners, no deadfreight between the quantity loaded and the quantity shown in part 1 (F) shall be due.

Clause 13 – Notice of readiness/running time

Delete in line 177/178 words 'if the vessel loads or discharges cargo other than by transhipment at sea'

Insert in line 189 a 'comma' between 'daylight' and 'pilot'

Clause b) delete and insert:

     Time shall:-

     i)   Continue to run until the cargo hoses have been disconnected

     ii)   Recommence two hours after disconnection of hoses if the vessel is delayed for Charterers purposes and shall continue until the termination of such delay provided that if the vessel waits at any place other than the berth, any time or part of the time on passage to such other place that occurs after two hours from disconnection of hoses shall not count.

(2)   Delete and insert -

     If the vessel loads or discharges cargo by transhipment at sea time shall commence in accordance with Clause 13 (I) (a) as amended, and run until transhipment has been completed and the vessels have separated, always subject to Clause 14(c).

Clause 15 Demurrage

(1)   Insert in line 226 'New' before 'Worldwide Tanker Nominal Freight Scale'

(2)   Insert in line 231 after explosion 'or strike or failure/breakdown of plant and/or machinery'

(3) Delete and insert

Owners shall notify Charterers within 60 days after completion of discharge if demurrage has been incurred and any demurrage claim shall be fully and correctly documented, and received by Charterers, within 90 days after completion of discharge. If Owners fail to give notice of or to submit any such claim with documentation, as required herein, within the limits aforesaid, Charterers' liability for such demurrage shall be extinguished.

Clause 20 – delete and insert

If the vessel is equipped for crude oil washing Charterers shall have the right to require the vessel to crude oil wash, concurrently with discharge, those tanks in which Charterers' cargo is carried. If crude oil washing is required by Charterers or any competent authority, any additional discharge time thereby incurred, always subject to the next succeeding sentences, shall count against laytime or, if the vessel is on demurrage, for demurrage. The number of hours specified in Part I (A) (vii) as amended shall be increased by 0.6 hours per cargo tank washed, always subject to a maximum increase of 8 hours. If vessel fails to maintain 100 PSI throughout the discharge then any time over 24 hours, plus the additional discharge performance allowance under this clause, shall not count as laytime or demurrage, if on demurrage. This does not reduce Owners' liability for vessel to perform her service with utmost despatch.

Clause 32 Exceptions – delete (C) (ii) and insert

'any claim (whether brought by Charterers or any other person) arising out of any loss of or damage to or in connection with the cargo. Any such claim shall be subject to The Hague Visby Rules or The Hague Rules or the Hamburg Rules as the case may be, which ought pursuant to Clause 37 hereof to have been incorporated in the relevant bill of lading (whether or not such Rules were so incorporated), or if no such bill of lading is issued to The Hague Visby Rules unless the Hamburg Rules compulsorily apply in which case to the Hamburg Rules.'

Clauses 36 General Average/New Jason Clause – delete first paragraph and insert

General average shall be payable according to the York-Antwerp Rules as amended 1994 and shall be adjusted in London. All disputes relating to General Average shall be resolved in London in accordance with English Law. Without prejudice to the foregoing, should the adjustment be made in accordance with the Law and practise of the United States of America the following clause, which shall be included in all Bills of Lading issued pursuant to this Charter, shall apply:-

Clause 37 Clause Paramount – delete and insert.

The following clause shall be included in all bills of lading issued pursuant to this charter:

(1) Subject to sub-clauses (2) or (3) hereof, this bill of lading shall be governed by, and have effect subject to, the rules contained in the International Convention for the Unification of Certain Rules relating to Bills of Lading signed at Brussels on 25th August 1924 (hereafter the 'Hague Rules') as amended by the Protocol signed at Brussels on 23rd February 1968 (hereafter The 'Hague Visby Rules'). Nothing contained herein shall be deemed to be either a surrender by the carrier of any of his rights or immunities or any increase of any of his responsibilities or liabilities under the Hague-Visby Rules.

(2) If there is governing legislation which applies the Hague Rules compulsory to this bill of lading, to the exclusion of the Hague Visby Rules, then this bill of lading shall have effect subject to the Hague Rules. Nothing herein contained shall be deemed to be either a surrender by the carrier of any of his rights or immunities or an increase of any of his responsibilities or liabilities under the Hague Rules.

(3) If there is governing legislation which applies the Hamburg rules compulsory to this Bill of Lading to the exclusion of the Hague Visby rules, then this Bill of Lading shall have effect subject to the Hamburg rules. Nothing herein contained shall be deemed to be either a surrender by the carrier of any of his rights or immunities or an increase of any of his responsibilities or liabilities under the Hamburg Rules.

(4) If any term of this bill of lading is repugnant to the Hague Visby Rules, or Hague Rules, or Hamburg Rules, if applicable, such term shall be void to that extent but no further.

(5) Nothing in this bill of lading shall be construed as in any way restricting, excluding or waiving the right of any relevant party or person to limit his liability under any available legislation and/or law.

Clause 38 Backloading – delete and insert

Charterers may order the vessel to discharge and/or backload a part or full cargo at any nominated port within the loading/discharging ranges specified within Part 1 (D/E) and within the rotation of the ports previously nominated, provided that any cargo loaded is of the description specified in Part 1 (F) and that the Master in his reasonable discretion determines that the cargo can be loaded, segregated and discharged without risk of contamination by, or of any other cargo.

Charterers shall pay in respect of loading, carrying and discharging such cargo

1) A lumpsum freight calculated at the demurrage rate specified in Part 1 (J) on any additional port time used by the vessel; and

2) any additional expenses, including port charges incurred, and

3) if the vessel is fixed on a Worldscale rate in Part 1 (A) then freight shall always be paid for the whole voyage at the rate(s) specified in Part 1 (G) on the largest cargo quantity carried on any ocean leg.

Clause 40 (i) Oil Pollution prevention

Insert new sub paragraph (d) 'Not to load on top of such 'collected washing' without specific instructions from Charterers'

Appendix I

Recommended by
The Documentary Committee of
THE BALTIC and INTERNATIONAL MARITIME COUNCIL, (BIMCO)
Copenhagen

Copyright, published by
WORLD FOOD PROGRAMME, Rome
1 October 1986

1. Shipbroker		**THE WORLD FOOD PROGRAMME** **VOYAGE CHARTER PARTY** **CODE NAME "WORLDFOOD"** PART I		
		2. Place and date		
3. Owners/Disponent Owners/Time-chartered Owners/ Place of business (also state full address & telex number)		4. Charterers/Place of business **World Food Programme Via delle Terme di Caracalla, I – 00100 Rome. Tlx: 626675 WFP I Cables: "WORLDFOOD" ROME**		
5. Vessel's name	6. Type of vessel	7. Flag	8.When built	9. Call signs
10. Class (Cl 1(B))	11. GRT/NRT	12. DW-cargo capacity on summer loadline	13. Draft fully loaded	14. T.P.I on loaded draft
15. Vessel's speed (abt.)	16. Length overall and beam	17. No. of decks	18. No. of holds	19. No. of hatches
20. Size of hatches	21. Cubic feet grain/bale capacity	22. No. of winches and S.W.L. of derricks/cranes	23. Owners' P. & I. Club (Cl. 1(a))	
24. Loading port(s) or place(s) (if applicable, also state number of days prior declaration of actual loading port(s) or place(s)) (Cl. 3)		25. Discharging port(s) or place(s) (if applicable, also state number of days prior declaration of actual discharging port(s) or place(s)) (Cl. 2(a))		
26. Cargo (also state quantity and margin in Owners' option, if agreed; if full and complete cargo not agreed state "part cargo") (Cl. 3)		27. Laydays Date (Cl. 4(a))	28. Present position with ETA first loading port (Cl. 4(b))	
		29. Cancelling date (Cl. 5(a))		
30. Advance notices (loading) (Cl.6) to be given to Charterers (cable- and telex address as per Box 4) and to:		31. Advance notices (discharging) (Cl. 7) to be given to Charterers (cable- and telex address as per Box 4) and to:		
32. Laytime for loading (Cl. 10(a))		33. Laytime for discharging (Cl. 10(b))		
34. Demurrage (loading and discharging) (Cl. 11(a))		35. Separation (indicate alternative (b) or (c) of Cl. 14)		
36. Freight rate (Cl. 23(a))		37. Freight payment (state currency and method of payment; also state beneficiary and bank account) (Cl. 23(f))		
38. General average shall be adjusted/settled at (Cl. 33)		39. Brokerage commission and to whom payable (Cl. 38)		
40. Nos. of additional clauses covering special provisions, if agreed				

It is mutually agreed that this Contract shall be performed subject to the conditions in the Charter consisting of Part I and Part II.

Signature (Owners)	Signature (Charterers)

Printed and sold by Fr. G. Knudtzon Ltd., 55 Toldbodgade, DK-1253 Copenhagen K
by authority of WORLD FOOD PROGRAMME, ROME

PART II
'Worldfood' Charter Party

1. Vessel

(a) The Owners shall

before and at the beginning of the loaded voyage exercise due diligence to make the Vessel seaworthy and in every way fit for the voyage, with a full complement of Master, officers and crew for a vessel of her type, tonnage and flag;

ensure that the Vessel and her Master and crew will comply with all safety and health regulations and other statutory rules or regulations and internationally recognised requirements necessary to secure safe and unhindered loading of the cargo, performance of the voyage and discharge of the cargo;

ensure that during the currency of this Charter the Vessel's hull and machinery insurance is fully maintained;

ensure that during the currency of this Charter the Vessel is fully insured in respect of damage to or loss of cargo by the Protection and Indemnity Class of the P.&I. Club stated in Box 23;

have the responsibilities and immunities of the Hague-Visby or Hague Rules, as applicable, as incorporated in Clause 29 of this Charter Party.

(b) The Vessel shall

be classed Lloyd's 100 A1 or equivalent as stated in Box 10. The Owners warrant to maintain that class during the currency of this Charter Party.

2. Voyage

(a) The Vessel shall with all reasonable despatch proceed to the loading port(s) or place(s) stated in Box 24 or so near thereto as she may safely get and lie always safe and afloat, and there load the cargo stated in Box 26, and being so loaded the Vessel shall with all reasonable despatch proceed to the discharging port(s) or place(s) stated in Box 25 or so near thereto as she may safely get and lie always safe and afloat and there deliver the cargo.

If the Charterers have the right to order the Vessel to load and/or discharge at one or more ports out of several ports named or within a specific range, the Charterers shall declare the actual port or ports of loading and/or discharge within the number of days stated in Boxes 24 and 25, respectively.

Unless loading and/or discharging ports are named in this Charter Party, the responsibility for providing safe ports of loading and/or discharging lies with the Charterers.

(b) *Rotation of Ports*

Unless otherwise agreed, loading and/or discharging at two or more ports shall be effected in geographical rotation.

3. Cargo

(a) Unless otherwise stated in Box 26, this Charter Party is for a full and complete cargo as described in Box 26.

(b) The Charterers warrant that the cargo referred to in Box 26 is nondangerous for carriage according to applicable safety regulations including IMO Code(s).

(c) *Part Cargo.* - If agreed and stated in Box 26 that this Charter Party is for a part cargo, the Owners guarantee that any additional cargo shall be non-hazardous and non-injurious to the cargo carried under this Charter Party. Such additional cargo shall be stowed in separate compartments and shall not affect the rate of loading and discharging of the cargo under this Charter Party as stipulated in Boxes 32 and 33, respectively.

The Owners shall pay totally or proportionally the costs of lightening, if any, at the port(s) of discharge incurred due to loading of completion cargo.

(d) Unless otherwise stated in Box 26, all quantities shall be expressed in tons of 1,000 kilograms.

4. Laydays Date and Present Position

(a) Laydays shall not commence before 07.00 on the date stated in Box 27. However, notice of readiness may be given before that date and notice time shall run forthwith,

(b) Present position of the Vessel as per Box 28.

5. Cancelling

(a) The Charterers shall have the option of cancelling the Charter Party if the Vessel has not tendered notice of readiness to load on or before 17.00 hours on the cancelling date stated in Box 29.

(b) Should the Owners anticipate with reasonable certainty that in spite of all reasonable efforts the Vessel will not be ready to load by the cancelling date they shall notify the Charterers thereof without delay, stating the probable date of Vessel's readiness to load. Upon receipt of such notification the Charterers will have the option either to cancel or to postpone the cancellation date. If the Charterers do not within 4 running days of receipt of the Owners' notification declare their option to cancel the Charter Party the fourth running day (or the next working day following that fourth day) after the new date of readiness indicated in the Owners' notification shall be regarded as a new cancelling date and shall be substituted for the date stipulated in Box 29. If the Vessel has not tendered notice of readiness on or before 17.00 hours on the new cancelling date the Charterers shall have the option of cancelling the Charter Party.

6. Advance Notices (Loading)

(a) The Owners or the Master shall give to the Charterers and their Representatives at the loading port as indicated in Box 30 the following notices of E.T.A. (Expected Time of Arrival) at first or sole loading port:

(i) approximate E.T.A. at time of fixture;

(ii) 10 days approximate E.T.A.;

(iii) 5 days approximate E.T.A.;

(iv) 24 hours definite notice of E.T.A.

(b) The Master shall telegraph 'WORLDFOOD' ROME the Vessel's position every 72 hours en route to loading port, and if transiting the Suez Canal and/or the Panama Canal, the Master shall notify the Charterers hereof, stating time of entering and leaving the Canal(s).

7. Advance Notices (Discharging)

(a) The Owners or the Master shall give to the Charterers and to the party(ies) indicated in Box 31 the following notices of E.T.A. (Expected Time of Arrival) at first or sole discharging port:

(i) Upon sailing from loading port (or if more than one loading port from final port of loading) approximate E.T.A., also stating quantity of cargo loaded and estimated arrival draft;

(ii) 10 days approximate E.T.A.;

(iii) 72 hours approximate E.T.A.;

(iv) 24 hours definite notice of E.T.A.

(b) The Master shall telegraph 'WORLDFOOD' ROME the Vessel's position every 72 hours en route to discharge port, and if transitting the Suez Canal and/or the Panama Canal, the Master shall notify the Charterers hereof, stating time of entering and leaving the Canal(s).

8. Notice of Readiness (Loading and Discharging)

(a) At each port of loading and discharging notice of readiness shall be given by the Master to the Charterers or their agents when the Vessel is in the loading or discharging berth and has obtained customs' clearance and free pratique and is in all respects ready to load and discharge.

(b) At loading port before tendering notice of readiness, the Owners and the Master shall ensure that all holds of the Vessel are clean, dry and free from smell and in all respects suitable to receive the cargo to the Shippers'/ Charterers' satisfaction.

(c) If a loading/discharging berth is not designated or if such designated berth is not available upon the Vessel's arrival at or off the port, notice of readiness may be given upon arrival at the customary waiting place at or off the port, whether cleared at Customs or not and whether in free pratique or not.

However, if upon the Vessel's arrival at or off the port she is prevented from proceeding to the loading/discharging berth by her inefficiency, weather, tidal conditions, strikes of tugs or pilots or mandatory regulations, notice of readiness may be given only when such hindrance(s) has (have) ceased.

(d) Notice of readiness to load or discharge shall be tendered between the hours of 09.00 to 17.00 on ordinary working days, Sundays (or their local equivalents) excepted and between the hours of 09.00 to 12.00 on Saturdays (or their local equivalents).

9. Laytime Counting (Loading and Discharging)

(a) At first or sole loading and discharging port laytime for loading and discharging shall commence at 07.00 hours on the next working day following tendering of notice of readiness in accordance with Clause 8(d).

(b) In the case of second or subsequent port(s) of loading and discharging, laytime shall count upon the Master's tendering of notice of readiness, whether in berth or not, provided the notice of readiness is tendered in accordance with Clause 8(d); otherwise the laytime shall commence to count at 07.00 hours on the next working day.

(c) If the notice of readiness has been tendered while the Vessel is at or off the port, in accordance with Clause 8(c), the laytime shall commence to count and shall count as if the Vessel were in berth.

(d) Actual time used for shifting to the loading/discharging berth or to a waiting berth in port shall not count as laytime unless the Vessel is already on demurrage.

(e) If after berthing the Vessel is found not to be ready in all respects to load/ discharge, the actual time lost until the Vessel is in fact ready to load/ discharge (including customs clearance and free pratique, if applicable) shall not count as laytime or as time on demurrage.

(f) Time lost as a result of inefficiency or any other cause, including strike by officers and crew, attributable to the Vessel, her Master, her crew or the Owners which affects the working of the Vessel shall not count as laytime or as time on demurrage.

(g) In the event that the Vessel is waiting for loading or discharging berth and notice of readiness has been tendered according to Clause 9(c), no laytime is to be deducted during such period for reasons of weather unless the vessel occupying the loading or discharging berth in question is actually prevented from working due to weather conditions in which case time so lost is not to count unless the Vessel is already on demurrage.

(h) *Excepted Periods.* - Time from 12.00 hours on Saturday (or in countries where no regular stevedoring work is carried out on Saturday or only performed at overtime rates of pay, from expiration of the regular straight time period on Friday) and from

17.00 hours on the day preceding a national or local holiday until 07.00 hours on Monday or next working day following a holiday not to count unless used, in which case half of such time actually used shall count as laytime.

In countries where Friday is the recognised weekly day of rest, time from 12.00 hours on Thursday until 07.00 hours on Saturday not to count unless used, in which case half of such time actually used shall count as laytime.

(i) Laytime between ports of loading and discharging to be non-reversible.

If the Vessel has to load or discharge at two or more ports, the multiple operation is to be regarded as a single one for the purpose of laytime computation.

10. Loading and Discharging

(a) *Bulk Cargo.* - If loading bulk cargo, the cargo shall be loaded and spout trimmed by the Charterers at their expense but under the supervision of the Master at the rate stated in Box 32 per working day of 24 consecutive hours, weather permitting (subject to excepted periods according to Clause 9).

Other than Bulk Cargo. - If loading other than bulk cargo, the cargo shall be loaded and stowed by the Charterers at their expense but under the supervision of the Master at the rate stated in Box 32 per working day of 24 consecutive hours, weather permitting (subject to excepted periods according to Clause 9).

(b) The cargo shall be discharged by the Receivers at their expense but under the supervision of the Master at the rate stated in Box 33 per working day of 24 consecutive hours, weather permitting (subject to excepted periods according to Clause 9).

(c) At each loading and discharging port stevedores shall be appointed and paid by the Shippers/Receivers.

(d) Cargo Handling - During loading and discharging operations, the Master shall supervise the work performed by the stevedores and shall instruct them properly in regard to handling, loading, stowage and discharging of the cargo.

Should the stevedores refuse to follow his instructions, the Master shall protest to them in writing and shall advise the Charterers immediately thereof.

11. Demurrage/Despatch Money

(a) *Demurrage* in loading and discharging shall be paid by the Charterers at the rate as stated in Box 34 per running day or pro rata.

(b) *Despatch money* at half the demurrage rate shall be paid by the Owners on laytime saved in loading and/or discharging.

(c) Demurrage and Despatch accounts shall be settled when finalising accounts as per Clause 23.

12. Shifting and Warping

(a) *Shifting* - The Charterers shall have the option of ordering the Vessel to load and/or discharge at a second safe berth if required. The costs of shifting from first to second berth shall be for the Owners' account. Time used for shifting shall count as laytime unless shining is performed during excepted periods according to Clause 9.

(b) *Warping* - The Vessel shall be warped alongside the loading/discharging appliances, as reasonably required, at the Owners' risk and expense, but time to count unless warping is performed during excepted periods according to Clause 9.

Overtime expenses for the Vessel's officers and crew and costs for bunkers consumed shall be for the Owners' account.

(c) *Seaworthy Trim* - For shifting between berths and ports, the Vessel shall be left in a seaworthy trim in accordance with the Master's instructions.

13. Dunnage and Cargo Battens

(a) *Dunnage* - The Owners shall provide, lay and erect all dunnage material (including paper, plastic etc.) required for the proper stowage and protection of the cargo.

(b) *Cargo Battens* - The Vessel to have cargo battens fitted, if required.

14. Separation

(a) The Charterers shall have the right to ship parcels of different qualities and/or for different receivers in separate holds within the Vessel's natural segregation and suitable for her trim provided that such parcels can be loaded, carried and discharged in accordance with the Vessel's seaworthiness.

* (b) *For Owners' account* - The Owners shall provide, lay and erect all material required for the proper separation and protection of the cargo at their expense.

* (c) *For Charterers' account* - The Charterers shall provide, lay and erect all material required by the Master for the proper separation of various consignments at their expense, the Owners allowing the use of all separation material available on board. The separation shall be done under Master's supervision.

The separation material paid for by the Charterers remains their property and shall be disposed of upon discharge in accordance with their instructions. In the absence of proper instructions from the Charterers, the Master shall have the liberty to dispose of the separation material. The Owners shall not be responsible for possible damage to, or proved loss of, the separation material supplied by the Charterers.

* *Indicate alternative agreed in Box 35.*

15. Opening and Closing of Hatches

Opening and closing of hatches at loading and discharging ports shall be performed by the Vessel's crew at the Owners' expense. Such operations shall be performed outside of stevedore working hours at all times except when action is necessary for the protection of cargo or it is specifically required that hatches be opened or closed during stevedore working hours. If use of the Vessel's crew is not permitted by local authorities or local union's regulations, shore labour (stevedores) shall be provided and paid for by the Charterers.

The Master has the responsibility of taking action for closing of hatches in the event of inclement weather or the presence of substances harmful to the cargo during loading and discharge.

16. Vessel's Cargo Gear

(a) *Cargo handling gear* - The Owners shall always give free use, throughout the duration of loading and discharge, of all Vessel's cargo handling gear and of sufficient motive power to operate all cargo handling gear simultaneously. The Owners also to make available all slings as on board.

(b) *Breakdowns* - All such equipment to be in good working order up to tested capacity and with valid certificates. Unless caused by negligence of the Charterers' stevedores, time lost by breakdown of Vessel's cargo handling gear - pro rata the total number of cranes/winches required at that time for loading/discharging cargo under this Charter - shall not count as laytime or as time on demurrage, and cost of labour standing-by as a result to be for the Owners' account.

(c) *Cranemen/winchmen* - The Owners shall provide free of charge cranemen/winchmen from crew unless the crew's employment conditions or local union or port regulations prohibit this, in which latter event shore labourers shall be provided and paid for by the Charterers.

Shore cranemen/winchmen shall always work under supervision of the Master.

This Clause shall not apply it Vessel is gearless and stated as such in Box 6.

17. Light

Whenever required, the Owners shall provide free of charge, throughout the duration of loading/discharge, light (as on board) for work on and under deck.

18. Grab Discharge

The Vessel to be suitable for grab discharge and no cargo to be loaded into spaces inaccessible to grabs, namely, deeptanks, bunker spaces, wings and ends of 'tween-decks. However, the Master has liberty of loading into such places for the purpose of stability of the Vessel, and any expense over and above the costs of normal loading, spout trimming and grab discharge to be for the Owners' account. Extra time used for loading and/or discharging into and/or from such places not to count as laytime.

19. Bulk Carrier and Wing Spaces, Securing etc.

If the Vessel is described as a self-trimming bulk-carrier in Box 6 the following provisions shall apply:

The cargo may be loaded into wing spaces if the cargo can bleed into centre holds. The Owners warrant that Vessel is approved by their own classification society or an organisation acceptable thereto for the carriage of bulk grain under the applicable SOLAS regulations. The Owners further warrant that approved information relating to dispensation from trimming ends of filled holds will be on board the Vessel on arrival at the loading port. Any trimming over spout-trimming shall be for the Owners' expense and time so used shall not count as laytime. Any bagging, strapping or securing required to be supplied and paid for by the Owners and time so used shall not count as laytime. Bleeding of bags, if any, at discharge port shall be at the Owners' time, risk and expense.

20. Stevedore Damage

Any damage to the Vessel caused by stevedores is for the account of Shippers at loading ports and for the account of Receivers at discharge ports.

If the Vessel is damaged by the stevedores at the loading and discharge ports, they and the Shippers and Receivers, respectively, shall be notified In writing of such damage at the end of the shift during which the damage is observed, otherwise latest upon completion of loading and discharging respectively. The failure of the Master to give notice of damage as herein provided shall be deemed a waiver of the Owners' right to claim reimbursement for any damage so sustained from the Shippers, Receivers or the Charterers insofar as the latter may have any liability in respect of such damage.

21. Overtime

(a) *Expenses* - All overtime expenses at loading and discharging port(s) shall be for account of the party ordering same.

If overtime is ordered by port authorities or the party (not being the Charterers, Shippers or Receivers) controlling the loading and/or discharging terminal or facility, all overtime expenses are to be paid by Shippers/Receivers or Charterers. Overtime expenses for Vessel's officers and crew shall always be for Owners' account.

(b) *Time Counting* - If overtime be worked during excepted periods ordered by Owners the actual time used shall count. If overtime be worked during excepted periods ordered by the Charterers the actual time used shall not count.

22. Tally

(a) The Cargo Receipt shall be conclusive evidence of quantity of cargo loaded.

(b) If the cargo consists of bags, bales, cases and/or drums, the Vessel shall be responsible for number of packages shipped and the provisions of sub-clause (a) also to apply.

(c) At each loading and discharging port, the Charterers shall appoint recognised tallymen to act jointly on behalf of the Owners and the Charterers. Such joint tally shall be binding upon both parties provided that such tally is kept during the loading and the discharge and all costs shall be for the Charterers' account.

(d) Notwithstanding the foregoing provisions, if the Vessel is loading at Canadian ports and/or relevant ports in the United States of America, the following provisions shall apply:

at each loading port the Owners and the Charterers shall accept the standard terminal procedures for control/checking and tally of cargo at the Charterers' expense. At each discharging port the Charterers shall appoint tallymen to act jointly on behalf of the Owners and the Charterers and all costs shall be for the Charterers' account. Such tally shall be binding upon the Owners and the Charterers provided such tally is kept during the loading and the discharge.

23. Freight Payment

(a) The freight at the rate indicated in Box 36 shall be calculated on the gross intaken weigh/quantity stated in the Cargo Receipt.

(b) 90 (ninety) per cent. of the freight is due and payable by the Charterers within 5 (five) working days after release of signed Cargo Receipt.

(c) Should the Vessel remain on demurrage at loading or discharging ports for a period in excess of 14 days, the Charterers shall pay to the Owners demurrage every 14 days.

(d) The balance of freight with any adjustment for demurrage, despatch money, dead freight and/or any other sums payable to the Owners under this Charter Party and any non-negotiable Cargo Receipt issued hereunder shall be paid promptly by the Charterers upon receipt of the Owners' Invoice in duplicate giving details of freight due, despatch/demurrage incurred at loading and discharging ports and supported by all the following documents in duplicate:

(i) Statement of Facts signed by Master and Charterers' agents both ends;

(ii) Laytime statements (time sheets);

(iii) Receipted commission invoices from all brokers mentioned in the Charter Party;

(iv) A comprehensive Stowage Plan showing gross cargo quantities loaded hold by hold;

(v) Surveyor's report on draft and cubic survey in respect of any dead freight claim which shall also be supported by a voucher approved by the Master and the Charterers/Shippers' representatives at loading port.

(e) The Charterers may deduct from any balance payable under (d) above a sufficient amount as security for duly particularised claims against the Owners for loss of or damage to cargo which shall have been established on discharge, but only insofar as the P&I Club stated in Box 23 shall have failed to provide a Letter of Undertaking to meet any proper liability of the Owners for such claims within 48 hours of a request from the Charterers for such Club Letter of Undertaking, which request shall also particularise the alleged claims as above and shall indicate the total amount of the security required.

(f) The freight and other sums due to the Owners shall be paid in the currency and In the manner stated in Box 37.

24. Dues, Taxes and Charges

(a) *On the Vessel* - The Owners shall pay all dues, duties, taxes and other charges customarily levied on the Vessel, howsoever the amount thereof may be assessed.

(b) *On the cargo* - The Charterers shall pay all dues, duties, taxes and charges levied on the cargo at the port of loading/discharging, howsoever the amount thereof may be assessed.

(c) *On the freight* - Taxes levied on the freight shall be paid by the Owners.

(d) *P.D.R. Yemen* - Notwithstanding the foregoing provisions, if the Vessel is discharging at port(s) in the P.D.R. Yemen, the following provisions shall apply:

'Any and all inward freight commission charged by the National Shipping Co. is to be for the Receivers' account, the Owners only paying the current agency fee for charter vessels.'

(e) *Somalia* - Notwithstanding the foregoing provisions, if the Vessel is discharging at port(s) in Somalia the following provisions shall apply:

'Cargo under this Charter Party exempted by Government Decree XGSW/ 166/5/80 dated 15 November 1980 from current 4% inward freight commission due to Somali Shipping Agency, and which has not been collected from the Shippers by the Carrier. The Owners only paying the current agency fee for charter vessels.'

Cargo Receipts under this Charter shall be claused as follows:

'Consignment exempted by Government Decree XGSW/166/5/80 dated 15 November 1980 from current 4% inward freight commission due to Somali Shipping Agency, and which has not been collected from the Shippers by the Carrier.'

(f) *Ethiopia* - Notwithstanding the foregoing provisions, if the Vessel is discharging at port(s) in Ethiopia the following provisions shall apply:

'Cargo under this Charter Party exempted from supervision and coordination fee charged by MTSC to vessels for inward cargoes to Ethiopia currently at rate of U.S. $1.50 per MT. The Owners only paying current agency fee for charter vessels.'

25. Extra Insurance

Any extra insurance on cargo owing to Vessel's age, class, flag or ownership shall be for the Owners' account and may be deducted from the freight. The Charterers shall furnish evidence of payment supporting any such deduction. Unless a maximum amount has been agreed, such extra insurance shall not exceed the lowest extra premium which would be charged for the Vessel and voyage in the London insurance market.

26. Lien

The Owners shall have a lien on the cargo for freight. The Charterers shall remain responsible for freight, dead- freight and demurrage incurred at port(s) of loading and/or discharge.

27. Liberty

The Vessel shall have liberty to sail with or without pilots, to tow or go to the assistance of vessels in distress, to call at any port or place for oil fuel supplies, and to deviate for the purpose of saving life or property, or for any other reasonable purpose whatsoever.

28. United Nations Emergency Clause

The Charterers have the right in case of an emergency situation arising to change the Vessel's destination, subject only to the Owners' consent, which shall not be unreasonably withheld. In this event, the Owners and the Charterers shall agree on any necessary adjustment in freight rates in consequence of the change of destination. Failing such agreement, the new rate shall be determined by a shipbroker appointed, at the request of either party, by the Institute of Chartered Shipbrokers, London, acting as valuer and not as arbitrator.

29. Exception Clause

(a) The provisions of the International Brussels Convention 1924 as amended by the Protocol signed at Brussels on February 23rd 1968 (the 'Hague-Visby Rules') are to apply to this Charter Party and to any nonnegotiable cargo receipt issued hereunder in those circumstances in which the Hague-Visby Rules would apply compulsorily if a Bill of Lading had been issued.

However in circumstances in which the Hague-Visby Rules are not applicable, it is agreed that the provisions of the International Brussels Convention 1924 (the 'Hague Rules') shall apply to this Charter Party and to any Cargo Receipt issued hereunder.

(b) *Period of responsibility*- The Owners shall not be liable for loss of or damage to the cargo, howsoever arising, prior to loading into and after discharge from the Vessel.

(c) *Deck cargo and live animals* - If shipment of deck cargo and/or live animals agreed, same to be carried at Charterers' risk.

(d) Neither the Owners nor the Charterers shall, except as otherwise provided in this Charter Party, be responsible for any loss, damage, delay or failure in performance hereunder arising or resulting from Act of God; Act of War; seizure under legal process; quarantine restrictions; strikes; boycotts; lockouts; riots; civil commotions and arrest or restraint of Princes, Rulers or people.

30. Cargo Receipt

(a) No bills of lading will be issued for shipments under this Charter Party.

(b)The Owners agree to issue a non-negotiable Cargo Receipt as per the 'Worldfoodreceipt' Cargo Receipt Form attached hereto incorporating all terms, conditions, liberties, clauses and exceptions of this Charter Party. In the event of a conflict of conditions between the Cargo Receipt and this Charter Party, the provisions of this Charter Party shall prevail to the extent of such conflict but no further.

31. P. & I. Charter Party Pollution Clause

The Owners by production of a Certificate of Insurance or otherwise shall satisfy the requirements of:

(a) Section 311 (p) of the United States Federal Water Pollution Control Act, as amended through 1978 (Title 33 U.S. Code, Section 1321(p)), and

(b) Article VII of the International Convention on Civil Liability for Oil Pollution Damage, 1969, as far as applicable.

Save as aforesaid Owners shall not be required by Charterers to establish or maintain financial security or responsibility in respect of oil or other pollution damage to enable the Vessel lawfully to enter, remain in or leave any port, place, territorial or contiguous waters of any country, state or territory in performance of this Charter Party.

32. Both-to-Blame Collision Clause

If the liability for any collision in which the Vessel is involved while performing this Charter Party falls to be determined in accordance with the laws of the United States of America, the following clause shall apply:

'If the Vessel comes into collision with another vessel as a result of the negligence of the other vessel and any act, neglect or default of the Master, mariner, pilot or the servants of the Owners in the navigation or in the management of the Vessel, the owners of the cargo carried hereunder will indemnify the Owners against all loss or liability to the other or non-carrying vessel or her Owners in so far as such loss or liability represents loss of, or damage to, or any claim whatsoever of the owners of the said cargo, paid or payable by the other or non-carrying vessel or her Owners to the owners of said cargo and set-off, recouped or recovered by the other or non-carrying vessel or her Owners as part of their claim against the carrying vessel or Owners.

The foregoing provisions shall also apply where the owners, operators or those in charge of any vessel or vessels or objects other than, or in addition to, the colliding vessels or objects are at fault in respect of a collision or contact.'

33. General Average and New Jason Clause

General Average shall be adjusted and settled at the place indicated in Box 38 according to the York/Antwerp Rules, 1974, or any modification thereof but if, notwithstanding the provisions specified in Box 38, the adjustment is made in accordance with the law and practice of the United States of America, the following clause shall apply:

'In the event of accident, danger, damage or disaster before or after the commencement of the voyage, resulting from any cause whatsoever, whether due to negligence or not, for which, or for the consequence of which, Owners are not responsible, by statute, contract or otherwise, the goods, shippers, consignees or owners of the goods shall contribute with Owners in general average to the payment of any sacrifices, losses or expenses of a general average nature that may be made or incurred and shall pay salvage and special charges incurred in respect of the goods. If a salving Vessel is owned or operated by Owners, salvage shall be paid for as fully as if the said salving Vessel or vessels belonged to strangers. Such deposit as Owners, or their agents, may deem sufficient to cover the estimated contribution of the goods and any salvage and special charges thereon shall, if required, be made by the goods, shippers, consignees or owners of the goods to Owners before delivery'.

34. Strike

(a) *Responsibility* - Neither the Charterers nor the Owners shall be responsible for the consequences of strike or lock-out preventing or delaying the fulfilment of any obligation under this Contract.

(b) *Loading Port* - In the event of strike or lock-out affecting the loading of the cargo, or any part of it, when the Vessel is ready to proceed from her last port or at any time during the voyage to the port or ports of loading or after her arrival there, the Owners may ask the Charterers to declare that they agree to count the laytime as if there were no such hindrance. Unless the Charterers have given such declaration in writing (by telegram, if necessary) within 24 hours, the Owners shall have the option of cancelling this Charter. If part cargo has already been loaded, the Vessel must carry it to the port of discharge (freight payable on loaded quantity only) having liberty to complete with other cargo on the way for Owners' own account.

(c) *Expected strike* - In the event of strike or lock-out which can reasonably be expected - before the loading has commenced - to affect the discharge of cargo, the Owners are at liberty to cancel this Charter unless the Charterers declare (within 24 hours of receipt of Owners' notification of intended cancellation) that they agree to count the laytime at port of discharge as if there were no such hindrance, without prejudice to the Consignees' right of ordering the Vessel to a substitute port of discharge in accordance with sub-clause (d). Time for loading does not count in the said 24 hours.

(d) *Discharging port* - In the event of strike or lock-out affecting the discharging of the cargo on or after Vessel's arrival at or off the port of discharge, the Consignees shall have the option of keeping the Vessel waiting until such strike or lock-out is at an end against paying half demurrage after expiration of the time provided for discharging, or of ordering the Vessel to a safe port where she can safely discharge without risk of being detained by strike or lock-out. Such orders to be given within 48 hours after the Owners have given notice to the Consignees of Vessel's readiness to discharge or of the Owners' request for orders. All conditions of this Charter and of the Cargo Receipt issued hereunder shall apply to the delivery of the cargo at such substitute port, and the Owners shall receive the same freight as if the cargo had been discharged at the original port of destination, except that if the distance to the substitute port exceeds 100 nautical miles, the freight on the cargo delivered at the substitute port to be increased in proportion.

(e) *Notification* - The party who first learns about the occurrence of strike or lock-out shall immediately notify thereof the other party.

35. Ice

Loading Port

(a) *Before Vessel's arrival* - If the Vessel cannot reach the loading port by reason of ice when she is ready to proceed from her last port, or at any time during the voyage, or on her arrival, or if frost sets in after her arrival, the Master - for fear of the Vessel being frozen in - is at liberty to leave without cargo; in such cases this Charter shall be null and void.

(b) *During loading* - If during loading the Master, for fear of Vessel being frozen in, deems it advisable to leave, he has liberty to do so with what cargo he has on board and to proceed to any other port with option of completing cargo for Owners' own account to any port or ports including the port of discharge. Any part cargo thus loaded under this Charter to be forwarded to destination at Vessel's expense against payment of the freight at the rate agreed in Box 36, on quantity delivered (in proportion if lump sum), all other conditions as per Charter.

(c) *Loading at more than one port* - In case of more than one loading port, and if one or more of the ports are closed by ice, the Master or Owners to be at liberty either to load the part cargo at the open port and fill up elsewhere for the Owners' own account as under sub-clause (b) or to declare the Charter null and void unless the Charterers agree to load full cargo at the open port.

Voyage and Discharging Port

(d) *Before Vessel's arrival* - Should ice prevent the Vessel from reaching the port of discharge, the Consignees shall have the option of keeping the Vessel waiting until the re-opening of navigation and paying demurrage, or of ordering the Vessel to a safe and immediately accessible port where she can safely discharge without risk of detention by ice. Such orders to be given within 48 hours after the Owners or Master have given notice to the Charterers of impossibility of reaching port of destination.

(e) *During discharging* - If during discharging the Master, for fear of Vessel being frozen in, deems it advisable to leave he has liberty to do so with what cargo he has on board and to proceed to the nearest safe and accessible port. Such port to be nominated by Charterers/Consignees as soon as possible, but not later than 24 running hours, Sundays and holidays excluded, of receipt of Owners' request for nomination of a substitute discharging port, failing which the Master will himself choose such port.

(f) *Discharging at substitute port* - On delivery of the cargo at such port, all conditions of this Charter Party and of the Cargo Receipt shall apply and the Owners shall receive the same freight as if the Vessel had discharged at the original port of destination except that if the distance to the substitute port exceeds 100 nautical miles, the freight on the cargo delivered at that port to be increased in proportion.

36. War Risks

(a) In these clauses 'War Risks' shall include any blockade or any action which is announced as a blockade by any Government or by any belligerent or by any organized body, sabotage, piracy, and any actual or threatened war, hostilities, warlike operations, civil war, civil commotion, or revolution.

(b) If at any time before the Vessel commences loading, it appears that performance of the contract will subject the Vessel or her Master and crew or her cargo to war risks at any stage of the adventure, the Owners shall be entitled by letter or telegram despatched to the Charterers, to cancel this Charter.

(c) The Master shall not be required to load cargo or to continue loading or to proceed on or to sign Cargo Receipt(s) for any adventure on which or any port at which it appears that the Vessel, her Master and crew or her cargo will be subjected to war risks. In the event of the exercise by the Master of his right under this Clause after part or full cargo has been loaded, the Master shall be at liberty either to discharge such cargo at the loading port or to proceed therewith. In the latter case the Vessel shall have liberty to carry other cargo for Owners' benefit and accordingly to proceed to and load or discharge such other cargo at any other port or ports whatsoever, backwards or forwards, although in a contrary direction to or out of or beyond the ordinary route. In the event of the Master electing to proceed with part cargo under this Clause freight shall in any case be payable on the quantity delivered.

(d) If at the time the Master elects to proceed with part or full cargo under Clause (c), or after the Vessel has led the loading port, or the last of the loading ports, if more than one, it appears that further performance of the contract will subject the Vessel, her Master and crew or her cargo, to war risks, the cargo shall be discharged, or if the discharge has been commenced shall be completed, at any safe port in vicinity of the port of discharge as may be ordered by the Charterers. If no such orders shall be received from the Charterers within 48 hours after the Owners have despatched a request by telegram to the Charterers for the nomination of a substitute discharging port, the Owners shall be at liberty to discharge the cargo at any safe port which they may, in their discretion, decide on and such discharge shall be deemed to be due fulfilment of the contract of affreightment. In the event of cargo being discharged at any such other port, the Owners shall be entitled to freight as if the discharge had been effected at the port or ports named in the Cargo Receipt(s) or to which the Vessel may have been ordered pursuant thereto.

(e) (i) The Vessel shall have liberty to comply with any directions or recommendations as to loading, departure, arrival, routes, ports of call stoppages, destination, zones, waters, discharge, delivery or in any other wise whatsoever (including any direction or recommendation not to go to the port of destination or to delay proceeding thereto or to proceed to some other port) given by any Government or by any belligerent or by any organized body engaged in civil war, hostilities or warlike operations or by any person or body acting or purporting to act as or with the authority of any Government or belligerent or of any such organized body or by any committee or person having under the terms of the war risks insurance on the Vessel, the right to give any such directions or recommendations. If, by reason of or in compliance with any such direction or recommendation, anything is done or is not done, such shall not be deemed a deviation.

(ii) If, by reason of or in compliance with any such directions or recommendations, the Vessel does not proceed to the port or ports named in the Cargo Receipt(s) or to which she may have been ordered pursuant thereto, the Vessel may proceed to any port as directed or recommended or to any safe port which the Owners in their discretion may decide on and there discharge the cargo. Such discharge shall be deemed to be due fulfilment of the contract of affreightment and the Owners shall be entitled to freight as if discharge had been effected at the port or ports named in the Cargo Receipt(s) or to which the Vessel may have been ordered pursuant thereto.

(f) All extra expenses (including insurance costs) involved in discharging cargo at the loading port or in reaching or discharging the cargo at any port as provided in Clauses (d) and (e) (ii) hereof shall be paid by the Charterers and/or cargo owners, and the

Owners shell have a lien on the cargo for all moneys due under these Clauses.

37. Agency

Vessel shall be addressed to the Owners' agents at port(s) or place(s) of loading and discharging, unless otherwise agreed.

38. Brokerage

A brokerage commission at the rate stated in Box 39 on the freight and dead-freight earned is due to the party(ies) mentioned in Box 39.

In case of non-execution at least 1/3 of the brokerage on the estimated amount of freight and dead-freight to be paid by the Owners to the party(ies) mentioned in Box 39 as indemnity for the latter's expenses and work. In case of more voyages the amount of indemnity to be mutually agreed.

39. Law and Arbitration

This Charter Party and any Cargo Receipt issued hereunder shall be governed by English law and any dispute arising out of this Charter Party or any Cargo Receipt issued hereunder shall be referred to arbitration in London in accordance with the provisions of the Arbitration Acts 1950 1979 and any statutory amendment or re-enactment from time to time in force. One arbitrator to be nominated by the Owners and the other by the Charterers and in case the arbitrators shall not agree then to the decision of an umpire to be appointed by the two arbitrators nominated by the parties, the award of the arbitrators or the umpire to be final and binding upon both parties. If one party fails to appoint an arbitrator for fourteen clear days after the other party, having appointed his arbitrator, has served the party making default with notice to make the appointment, the party who has appointed an arbitrator may appoint that arbitrator to act as sole arbitrator in the reference and his award shall be binding on both parties as if he had been appointed by consent.

Any claim must be made in writing and claimant's arbitrator appointed within twelve months of final discharge and where this provision is not complied with the claim shall be deemed to be waived and absolutely barred.

40. Title to Cargo Clause

It is mutually accepted and agreed that this Contract is made between the Vessel's Owners as specified in PART I of this Charter Party (Box 3) and World Food Programme as Charterers and that the latter have full rights to claim and receive substantial and not merely nominal damages for any damage to and/or loss of cargo carried under this Charter Party and/or under any non-negotiable Cargo Receipt(s) issued pursuant to this Charter Party and/or any claim arising out of this Charter Party and/or any nonnegotiable Cargo Receipt(s) issued pursuant to this Charter Party.

4 Time Charterparties

Adopted by
The Documentary Committee of the Chamber
of Shipping of the United Kingdom
and the Documentary Committee of The Japan Shipping Exchange, Inc.

Issued 6/3 1909
Amended 13/3 1911
Amended 6/3 1912
Amended 18/6 1920
Amended 1/3 1939
Amended 1/5 1950
Amended 1/7 1974

Copyright, published by The Baltic
and International Maritime
Conference, Copenhagen

1. Shipbroker	**THE BALTIC AND INTERNATIONAL MARITIME CONFERENCE** UNIFORM TIME- CHARTER (Box Layout 1974) CODE NAME "BALTIME 1939" PART I
	2. Place and date
3. Owners/Place of business	4. Charterers/Place of business
5. Vessel's name	6. GRT/NRT
7. Class	8. Indicated horse power
9. Total tons d.w. (abt.) on Board of Trade summer freeboard	10. Cubic feet grain/bale capacity
11. Permanent bunkers (abt.)	
12. Speed capability in knots (abt.) on a consumption in tons (abt.) of	
13. Present position	
14. Period of hire (Cl. 1)	15. Port of delivery (Cl. 1)
	16. Time of delivery (Cl. 1)
17. (a) Trade limits (Cl.2) (b) Cargo exclusions specially agreed	
18. Bunkers on re-delivery (state min. and max. quantity) (Cl. 5)	
19. Charter hire (Cl. 6)	20. Hire payment (state currency, method and place of payment also beneficiary and bank account) (Cl. 6)
21. Place or range of re-delivery (Cl. 7)	22. War (only to be filled in if Section (C) agreed) Cl. 21)
23. Cancelling date (Cl. 22)	24. Place of arbitration (only to be filled in if place other than London agreed (Cl. 23)
25. Brokerage commission and to whom payable (Cl. 25)	
	26. Numbers of additional clauses covering special provisions, if agreed

It is mutually agreed that this Contract shall be performed subject to the conditions contained in this Charter which shall include Part I as well as Part II. In the event of a conflict of conditions, the provisions of Part I shall prevail over those of Part II to the extent of such conflict.

Signature (Owners)	Signature (Charterers)

Printed and sold by Fr. G. Knudtzon Ltd., 55 Toldbodgade, Copenhagen K
by authority of The Baltic and International Maritime Conference, Copenhagen.

PART II
"BALTIME 1939" Uniform Time-Charter (Box Layout 1974)

It is agreed between the party mentioned in Box 3 as Owners of the Vessel named in Box 5 of the gross net Register tonnage indicated in Box 6, classed as stated in Box 7 and of indicated horse power as stated in Box 8, carrying about the number of tons deadweight indicated in Box 9 on Board the Trade summer freeboard inclusive of bunkers, stores, provisions and boiler water, having as per builder's plan a cubic-feet grain bale capacity as stated in Box 10, exclusive of permanent bunkers which contain about the number of tons stated in Box 11, and fully loaded capable of steaming about the number of knots indicated in Box 12 in good weather and smooth water on a consumption of about the number of tons best Welsh coal or oil-fuel stated in Box 12, now in position as stated in Box 13 and the party mentioned as Charters in Box 4, as follows:

1. **Period Port of Delivery Time of Delivery**
The Owners let and the Charters hire the Vessel for a period of the number of calendar months indicated in Box 14 from the time (not a Sunday or a legal Holiday unless taken over) the Vessel is delivered and placed at the disposal of the Charterers between 9 a.m. and 6 p.m., or between 9 a.m. and 2 p.m. if on Saturday at the port stated in Box 15 in such available berth where she can safely lie always afloat, as the Charterers may direct, she being in every way fitted for ordinary cargo service.
The Vessel to be delivered at the time indicated in Box 16.

2. **Trade**
The Vessel to be employed in lawful trades for the carriage of lawful merchandise only between good and safe ports or places where she can safely lie always afloat within the limits stated in Box 17.
No live stock nor injurious, inflammable or dangerous goods (such as acids, explosives, calcium carbide, ferro silicon, naphtha motor spirit, tar, or any of their products) to be shipped.

3. **Owners to Provide**
The Owners to provide and pay for all provisions and wages, for insurance of the Vessel, for all deck and engine-room stores and maintain her in a thoroughly efficient state in hull and machinery during service.
The Owners to provide one winchman per hatch. If further winchmen are required or if the stevedores refuse or are not permitted to work with the Crew, the Charterers to provide and pay qualified shore-winchmen.

4. **Charterers to Provide**
The Charterers to provide and pay for all coals including galley coal, oil-fuel, water for boilers, port charges, pilotages (whether compulsory or not) canal steersmen, boatage, lights, tug-assistance, consular charges (except those pertaining to the Master, Officers and Crew), canal, dock and other dues and charges, including any foreign general municipality or state taxes, also all dock, harbour and tonnage dues at the ports of delivery and re-delivery (unless incurred through cargo carried before delivery or after re-delivery) agencies, commissions also to arrange and pay for loading, trimming, stowing (including dunnage and shifting boards excepting any already on board), unloading, weighing, tallying and delivery of cargoes, surveys on hatches, meals supplied to officials and men in their service and all other charges and expenses whatsoever including detention and expenses through quarantine (including cost of fumigation and disinfection).
All ropes, slings and special runners actually used for loading and discharging and any special gear, including special ropes, hawsers and chains required by the custom of the port for mooring to be for the Charterers' account. The Vessel to be fitted with winches, derricks, wheels and ordinary runners capable of handling lifts up to 2 tons.

5. **Bunkers**
The Charters at port of delivery and the Owners at port of re-delivery to take over and pay for all coal or oil-fuel remaining in the Vessel's bunkers at current price at the respective ports.

The Vessel to be re-delivered with not less than the number of tongs and not exceeding the number of tons of coal or oil-fuel in the Vessel's bunkers stated in Box 18.

6. **Hire**
The Charterers to pay as hire the rate stated in Box 19 per 30 days, commencing in accordance with Clause 1 until her re-delivery to the Owners.
Payment
Payment of hire to be made in cash, in the currency stated in Box 20, without discount, every 30 days in advance and in the manner prescribed in Box 20.
In default of payment the Owners to have the right of withdrawing the Vessel from the service of the Charterers, without noting any protest and without interference by any court or any other formality whatsoever and without prejudice to any claim the Owners may otherwise have on the Charterers under the Charter.

7. **Re-delivery**
The Vessel to be re-delivered on the expiration of the Charter in the same good order as when delivered to the Charterers (fair wear and tear excepted) at an ice-free port in the Charterers' option at the place or within the range stated in Box 21 between 9 a.m. and 6 p.m. and 9 a.m. and 2 p.m. on Saturday, but the day of re-delivery shall not be a Sunday or legal Holiday.
Notice
The Charterers to give the Owners not less than ten days' notice at which port and on about which day the Vessel shall be re-delivered.
Should the Vessel be ordered on a voyage by which the Charter period will be exceeded the Charterers to have the use of the Vessel to enable them to complete the voyage provided it could allow re-delivery about the time fixed for the termination of the Charter, but for any time exceeding the termination date the Charterers to pay the market rate if higher than the rate stipulated herein.

8. **Cargo Space**
The whole reach and burthen of the Vessel, including lawful deck-capacity to be at Charterers' disposal, reserving proper and sufficient space for the Vessel's Master, Officers, Crew, tackle, apparel, furniture, provisions and stores.

9. **Master**
The Master to prosecute all voyages with the utmost despatch and to render customary assistance with the Vessel's Crew. The Master to be under the orders of the Charterers as regards employment, agency or other arrangements. The Charterers to indemnify the Owners against all consequences or liabilities arising from the Master, Officers or Agents signing Bills of Lading or other documents or otherwise complying with such orders as well as from any irregularity in the Vessel's papers or for overcarrying goods. The Owners not to be responsible for shortage, mixture marks nor for number of pieces or packages, nor for damage to or claims on cargo caused by bad stowage or otherwise.
If the Charterers have reason to be dissatisfied with the conduct of the Master, Officers or Engineers, the Owners on receiving particulars of the complaint promptly to investigate the matter and, if necessary and practicable, to make a change in the appointments.

10. **Directions and Logs**
The Charters to furnish the Master with all instructions and sailing directions and the Master and Engineer to keep full and correct logs accessible to the Charterers or their Agents.

11. **Suspension of Hire etc.**
(A) In the event of drydocking or other necessary measures to maintain the efficiency of the vessel, deficiency of men or Owners stores, breakdown of machinery, damage to hull or other accident either hindering or preventing the working of the Vessel and continuing for more than twentyfour consecutive hours, no hire to be paid in respect of any time lost thereby during the period in which the Vessel is unable to perform the service imme-

diately required. Any hire paid in advance to be adjusted accordingly.
(B) In the event of the Vessel being driven into port or to anchorage through stress of weather, trading to shallow harbours or to rivers or ports with bars or suffering an accident to her cargo, any detention of the Vessel and or expenses resulting from such detention to be for the Charterers' account even if such detention and or expenses, or the cause by reason of which either is incurred be due to or be contributed to by the negligence of the Owners' servants.

12. **Cleaning Boilers**
Cleaning of boilers whenever possible to be done during service, but if impossible the Charterers to give the Owners necessary time for cleaning. Should the Vessel be detained beyond 48 hours hire to cease until again ready.

13. **Responsibility and Exemption**
The Owners only to be responsible for delay in delivery of the Vessel or for delay during the currency of the Charter and for loss or damage to goods onboard, if such delay or loss has been caused by want of due diligence on the part of the Owners or their Manager in making the Vessel seaworthy and fitted for the voyage or any other personal act or omission or default of the Owners or their Manager. The Owners not to be responsible in any other case nor for damage or delay whatsoever and howsoever caused even if caused by the neglect or default of their servants.
The Owners not to be liable for loss or damage arising or resulting from strikes, lockouts or stoppage or restraint of labour (including the Master, Officers or Crew) whether partial or general.
The Charterers to be responsible for loss or damage caused to the Vessel or to the Owners by goods being loaded contrary to the terms of the Charter or by improper or careless bunkering or loading, stowing or discharging of goods or any other improper or negligent act on their part or that of their servants.

14. **Advances**
The Charters or their Agents to advance to the Master, if required, necessary funds for ordinary disbursements for the Vessel's account at any port charging only interest at 6 per cent p. a. such advances to be deducted from hire.

15. **Excluded Ports**
The Vessel not to be ordered to nor bound to enter a) any place where fever or epidemics are prevalent or to which the Master, Officers and Crew by law are not bound to follow the Vessel.
Ice
b) any ice-bound place or any places where lights, lightships, marks and buoys are or are likely to be withdrawn by reason of ice on the Vessel's arrival or where there is risk that ordinarily the Vessel will not be able on account of ice to reach the place or to get out after having completed loading or discharging. The Vessel not to be obliged to force ice. If on account of ice the Master considers it dangerous to remain at the loading or discharging place for fear of the Vessel being frozen in and or damaged, he has liberty to sail to a convenient open place and await the Charterers' fresh instructions.
Unforeseen detention through any of above causes to be for the Charterers' account.

16. **Loss of Vessel**
Should the Vessel be lost or missing, hire to cease from the date when she was lost. If the date of loss cannot be ascertained, half hire to be paid from the date the Vessel was last reports until the calculated date of arrival at the destination. Any hire paid in advance to be adjusted accordingly.

17. **Overtime**
The Vessel to work day and night if required. The Charterers to refund the Owners their outlays for all overtime paid to Officers and Crew according to the hours and rates stated in the Vessel's articles.

18. **Lien**
The Owners to have a lien upon all cargoes and sub-freights belonging to the Time-Charterers and any Bill of Lading freight for all claims under

this Charter, and the Charterers to have a lien on the Vessel for all moneys paid in advance and not earned.

19. Salvage

All salvage and assistance to other vessels to be for the Owners' and the Charterers' equal benefit after deducting the Master's and Crew's proportion and all legal and other expenses including hire paid under the charter for time lost in the salvage, also repairs of damage and coal or oil-fuel consumed. The Charterers to be bound by all measures taken by the Owners in order to secure payment of salvage and to fix the amount.

20. Sublet

The Charterers to have the option of subletting the Vessel giving due notice to the Owners, but the original Charterers always to remain responsible to the Owners for due performance of the Charter.

21. War

(A) The Vessel unless the consent of the Owners be first obtained not to be ordered nor continue to any place or on any voyage nor be used on any service which will bring her within a zone which is dangerous as the result of any actual or threatened act of war, war hostilities, warlike operations, acts of piracy or of hostility or malicious damage against this or any other vessel or its cargo by any person, body or State whatsoever, revolution, civil war, civil commotion or the operation of international law, nor be exposed in any way to any risks or penalties whatsoever consequent upon the imposition of Sanctions, nor carry any goods that may in any way expose her to any risks of seizure, capture, penalties or any other interference or any kind whatsoever by the belligerent or fighting powers or parties or by any Government or Ruler.

(B) Should the Vessel approach or be brought or ordered within such zone, or be exposed in any way to the said risks: (1) the Owners to be enti-

tled from time to time to insure their interests in the Vessel and or hire against any of the risks likely to be involved thereby on such terms as they shall think fit, the Charterers to make a refund to the Owners of the premium on demand and (2) notwithstanding the terms of Clause 11 hire to be paid for all time lost including any lost owing to loss of or injury to the Master, Officers or Crew or to the action of the Crew in refusing to proceed to such zone or to be exposed to such risks.

(C) In the event of the wages of the Master, Officers and or Crew or the cost of provisions and or stores for deck and or engine room and or insurance premiums being increased by reason of or during the existence or any of the matters mentioned in section (A), the amount of any increase to be added to the hire and paid by the Charterers on production of the Owners' account therefor, such account being rendered monthly.

(D) The Vessel to have liberty to comply with any orders or directions as to departure, arrival, routes, ports of call, stoppages, destination, delivery or in any other wise whatsoever given by the Government or the nation under whose flag the Vessel sails or any other Government or any person or body acting or purporting to act with the authority of such Government or by any committee or person having under the terms of the war risks insurance on the Vessel the right to give any such orders or directions.

(E) In the event of the nation under whose flag the Vessel sails becoming involved in war, hostilities, warlike operations, revolution or civil commotion, both the Owners and the Charterers may cancel the Charter and unless otherwise agreed the Vessel to be re-delivered to the Owners at the port of destination or, if prevented through the provisions of section (A) from reaching or entering it, then at a near open and safe port at the Owners' option, after discharge of any cargo on board.

(F) If in compliance with the provisions of this clause anything is done or is not done such not to

be deemed a deviation.

Section (C) is optional and should be considered deleted unless agreed according to Box 22.

22. Cancelling

Should the Vessel not be delivered by the date indicated in Box 23 the Charterers to have the option of cancelling.

If the Vessel cannot be delivered by the cancelling date, the Charterers if required to declare within 48 hours after receiving notice thereof whether they cancel or will take delivery of the Vessel.

23. Arbitration

Any dispute arising under the Charter to be referred to arbitration in London (or such other place as may be agreed according to Box 24), one Arbitrator to be nominated by the Owners and the other by the Charterers, and in case the Arbitrators shall not agree then to the decision of an Umpire to be appointed by them, the award of the Arbitrators or the Umpire to be final and binding upon both parties.

24. General Average

General Average to be settled according to York Antwerp Rules 1974. Hire not to contribute to General Average.

25. Commission

The Owners to pay a commission at the rate stated in Box 25 to the party mentioned in Box 25 on any hire paid under the Charter, but in no case less than is necessary to cover the actual expenses of the Brokers and a reasonable fee for their work. If the full hire is not paid owing to breach of Charter by either of the parties the party liable therefor to indemnify the Brokers against their loss of commission.

Should the parties agree to cancel the Charter, the Owners to indemnify the Brokers against any loss of commission but in such case the commission not to exceed the brokerage on one year's hire.

Code word for this Charter Party
"SHELLTIME 4"

Issued December 1984

Time Charter Party
LONDON, 19

IT IS THIS DAY AGREED between

of   (hereinafter referred to as "Owners", being owners of the
good   vessel called

(hereinafter referred to as "the vessel") described as per Clause 1 hereof and

of   (hereinafter referred to as "Charterers"):

Description and
Condition of
Vessel

1. At the date of delivery of the vessel under this charter
   (a) she shall be classed;
   (b) she shall be in every way fit to carry crude petroleum and/or its products;
   (c) she shall be tight, staunch, strong, in good order and condition, and in every way fit for the
service, with her machinery, boilers, hull and other equipment (including but not limited to hull stress calcula-
tor and radar) in a good and efficient state;
   (d) her tanks, valves and pipelines shall be oil-tight;
   (e) she shall be in every way fitted for burning .

   at sea –   fueloil with a maximum viscosity of   Centistokes at 50 degrees
               Centigrade/any commercial grade of fueloil ("ACGFO") for main propulsion,
               marine diesel oil/ACGFO for auxiliaries
   in port –   marine diesel oil/ACGFO for auxiliaries;

   (f) she shall comply with the regulations in force so as to enable her to pass through the Suez and
Panama Canals by day and night without delay;
   (g) she shall have on board all certificates, documents and equipment required from time to time
by any applicable law to enable her to perform the charter service without delay;
   (h) she shall comply with the description in Form B appended hereto, provided however that if
there is any conflict between the provisions of Form B and any other provision, including this Clause 1, of this
charter such other provision shall govern.

Shipboard
Personnel and
their Duties

2. (a) At the date of delivery of the vessel under this charter
   (i) she shall have a full and efficient complement of master, officers and crew for a vessel of
her tonnage, who shall in any event be not less than the number required by the laws of the flag state and who
shall be trained to operate the vessel and her equipment competently and safely;
   (ii) all shipboard personnel shall hold valid certificates of competence in accordance with
the requirements of the law of the flag state;
   (iii) all shipboard personnel shall be trained in accordance with the relevant provisions of the
International Convention on Standards of Training, Certification and Watchkeeping for Seafarers, 1978;
   (iv) there shall be on board sufficient personnel with a good working knowledge of the
English language to enable cargo operations at loading and discharging places to be carried out efficiently and
safely and to enable communications between the vessel and those loading the vessel or accepting discharge
therefrom to be carried out quickly and efficiently.
   (b) Owners guarantee that throughout the charter service the master shall with the vessel's officers and crew, unless otherwise ordered by Charterers,
   (i) prosecute all voyages with the utmost despatch;
   (ii) render all customary assistance; and
   (iii) load and discharge cargo as rapidly as possible when required by Charterers or their
agents to do so, by night or by day, but always in accordance with the laws of the place of loading or discharging (as the case may be) and in each case in accordance with any applicable laws of the flag state.

Duty to
Maintain

3. (i) Throughout the charter service Owners shall, whenever the passage of time, wear and tear or
any event (whether or not coming within Clause 27 hereof) requires steps to be taken to maintain or restore
the conditions stipulated in Clauses 1 and 2(a), exercise due diligence so to maintain or restore the vessel.
   (ii) If at any time whilst the vessel is on hire under this charter the vessel fails to comply with the
requirement of Clauses 1, 2(a) or 10 then hire shall be reduced to the extent necessary to indemnify Charterers
for such failure. If and to the extent that such failure affects the time taken by the vessel to perform any services under this charter, hire shall be reduced by an amount equal to the value, calculated at the rate of hire, of
the time so lost.
   Any reduction of hire under this sub-Clause (ii) shall be without prejudice to any other remedy available to Charterers, but where such reduction of hire is in respect of time lost, such time shall be excluded from any calculation under Clause 24.
   (iii) If Owners are in breach of their obligation under Clause 3(i) Charterers may so notify Owners
in writing; and if, after the expiry of 30 days following the receipt by Owners of any such notice, Owners have
failed to demonstrate to Charterers' reasonable satisfaction the exercise of due diligene as required in Clause
3(i), the vessel shall be off-hire, and no further hire payments shall be due, until Owners have so demonstrated
that they are exercising such due diligence.

Appendix I

Furthermore, at any time while the vessel is off-hire under this Clause 3 Charterers have the option to terminate this charter by giving notice in writing with effect from the date on which such notice of termination is received by Owners or from any later date stated in such notice. This sub-Clause (iii) is without prejudice to any rights of Charterers or obligations of Owners under this charter or otherwise (including without limitation Charterers' rights under Clause 21 hereof).

Period Trading Limits

4. Owners agree to let and Charterers agree to hire the vessel for a period of commencing from the time and date of delivery of the vessel, for the purpose of carrying all lawful merchandise (subject always to Clause 28) including in particular

in any part of the world, as Charterers shall direct, subject to the limits of the current British Institute Warranties and any subsequent amendments thereof. Notwithstanding the foregoing, but subject to Clause 35,. Charterers may order the vessel to ice-bound waters or to any part of the world outside such limits provided that Owners consent thereto (such consent not to be unreasonably withheld) and that Charterers pay for any insurance premium required by the vessel's underwriters as a consequence of such order.

Charterers shall use due diligence to ensure that the vessel is only employed between and at safe places (which expression when used in this charter shall include ports, berths, wharves, docks, anchorages, submarine lines, alongside vessels or lighters, and other locations including locations at sea) where she can safely lie always afloat. Notwithstanding anything contained in this or any other clause of this charter, Charterers do not warrant the safety of any place to which they order the vessel and shall be under no liability in respect thereof except for loss or damage caused by their failure to exercise due diligence as aforesaid. Subject as above, the vessel shall be loaded and discharged at any places as Charterers may direct, provided that Charterers shall exercise due diligence to ensure that any ship-to-ship transfer operations shall conform to standards not less than those set out in the latest published edition of the ICS/OCIMF Ship-to-Ship Transfer Guide.

The vessel shall be delivered by Owners at a port in

at Owners' option and redelivered to Owners at a port in

at Charterers' option.

Laydays/ Cancelling

5. The vessel shall not be delivered to Charterers before   and Charterers shall have the option of cancelling this charter if the vessel is not ready and at their disposal on or before

Owners to Provide

6. Owners undertake to provide and to pay for all provisions, wages, and shipping and discharging fees and all other expenses of the master, officers and crew; also, except as provided in Clauses 4 and 34 hereof, for all insurance on the vessel, for all deck, cabin and engine-room stores, and for water; for all drydocking, overhaul, maintenance and repairs to the vessel; and for all fumigation expenses and de-rat certificates. Owners' obligations under this Clause 6 extend to all liabilities for customs or import duties arising at any time during the performance of this charter in relation to the personal effects of the master, officers and crew, and in relation to the stores, provisions and other matters aforesaid which Owners are to provide and pay for and Owners shall refund to Charterers any sums Charterers or their agents may have paid or been compelled to pay in respect of any such liability. Any amounts allowable in general average for wages and provisions and stores shall be credited to Charterers insofar as such amounts are in respect of a period when the vessel is on-hire.

Charterers to Provide

7. Charterers shall provide and pay for all fuel (except fuel used for domestic services), towage and pilotage and shall pay agency fees, port charges, commissions, expenses of loading and unloading cargoes, canal dues and all charges other than those payable by Owners in accordance with Clause 6 hereof, provided that all charges for the said items shall be for Owners' account when such items are consumed, employed or incurred for Owners' purposes or while the vessel is off-hire (unless such items reasonably relate to any service given or distance made good and taken into account under Clause 21 or 22); and provided further that any fuel used in connection with a general average sacrifice or expenditure shall be paid for by Owners.

Rate of Hire

8. Subject as herein provided, Charterers shall pay for the use and hire of the vessel at the rate of   per day, and pro rata for any part of a day, from the time and date of her delivery (local time) until the time and date of her redelivery (local time) to Owners.

Payment of Hire

9. Subject to Clause 3(iii), payment of hire shall be made in immediately available funds to:

Account

in   per calendar month in advance, less:

(i) any hire paid which Charterers reasonably estimate to relate to off-hire periods, and

(ii) any amounts disbursed on Owners' behalf, any advances and commission thereon, and charges which are for Owners' account pursuant to any provision hereof, and

(iii) any amounts due or reasonably estimated to become due to Charterers under Clause 3(ii) or 24 hereof,

any such adjustments to be made at the due date for the next monthly payment after the facts have been ascertained. Charterers shall not be responsible for any delay or error by Owners' bank in crediting Owners' account provided that Charterers have made proper and timely payment.

In default of such proper and timely payment,

(a)   Owners shall notify Charterers of such default and Charterers shall within seven days of receipt of such notice pay to Owners the amount due including interest, failing which Owners may withdraw the vessel from the service of Charterers without prejudice to any other rights Owners may have under this charter or otherwise; and

(b)   Interest on any amount due but not paid on the due date shall accrue from the day after that date up to and including the day when payment is made, at a rate per annum which shall be 1% above the U.S. Prime Interest Rate as published by the Chase Manhattan Bank in New York at 12.00 New York time on the due date, or, if no such interest rate is published on that day, the interest rate published on the next preceding day on which such a rate was so published, computed on the basis of a 360 day year of twelve 30-day months, compounded semi-annually.

Space Available to Charterers	10. The whole reach, burthen and decks of the vessel and any passenger accommodation (including Owners' suite) shall be at Charterers' disposal, reserving only proper and sufficient space for the vessel's master, officers, crew, tackle, apparel, furniture, provisions and stores, provided that the weight of stores on board shall not, unless specially agreed, exceed tonnes at any time during the charter period.
Overtime	11. Overtime pay of the master, officers and crew in accordance with ship's articles shall be for Charterers' account when incurred, as a result of complying with the request of Charterers or their agents, for loading, discharging, heating of cargo, bunkering or tank cleaning.
Instructions and Logs	12. Charterers shall from time to time give the master all requisite instructions and sailing directions and he shall keep a full and correct log of the voyage or voyages, which Charterers or their agents may inspect as required. The master shall when required furnish Charterers or their agents with a true copy of such log and with properly completed loading and discharging port sheets and voyage reports for each voyage and other returns as Charterers may require. Charterers shall be entitled to take copies at Owners' expenses of any such documents which are not provided by the master.
Bills of Lading	13. (a) The master (although appointed by the Owners) shall be under the orders and direction of the Charterers as regards employment of the vessel, agency and other arrangements, and shall sign bills of lading as Charterers or their agents may direct (subject always to Clauses 35(a) and 40) without prejudice to this charter. Charterers hereby indemnify Owners against all consequences or liabilities that may arise

(i)   from signing bills of lading in accordance with the directions of Charterers or their agents, to the extent that the terms of such bills of lading fail to conform to the requirements of this charter, or (except as provided in Clause 13(b)) from the master otherwise complying with Charterers' or their agents' orders;

(ii)   from any irregularities in papers supplied by Charterers or their agents.

(b)   Notwithstanding the foregoing, Owners shall not be obliged to comply with any orders from Charterers to discharge all or part of the cargo

(i)   at any place other than that shown on the bill of lading and/or

(ii)   without presentation of an original bill of lading

unless they have received from Charterers both written confirmation of such orders and an indemnity in a form acceptable to Owners.

Conduct of Vessel's Personnel	14. If Charterers complain of the conduct of the master or any of the officers or crew, Owners shall immediately investigate the complaint. If the complaint proves to be well founded, Owners shall, without delay, make a change in the appointments and Owners shall in any event communicate the result of their investigations to Charterers as soon as possible.
Bunkers at Delivery and Redelivery	15. Charterers shall accept and pay for all bunkers on board at the time of delivery, and Owners shall on redelivery (whether it occurs at the end of the charter period or on the earlier termination of this charter) accept and pay for all bunkers remaining on board, at the then-current market prices at the port of delivery or redelivery, as the case may be, or if such prices are not available payment shall be at the then-current market prices at the nearest port at which such prices are available; provided that if delivery or redelivery does not take place in a port payment shall be at the price paid at the vessel's last port of bunkering before delivery or redelivery, as the case may be. Owners shall give Charterers the use and benefit of any fuel contracts they may have in force from time to time, if so required by Charterers, provided suppliers agree.
Stevedores, Pilots, Tugs	16. Stevedores when required shall be employed and paid by Charterers, but this shall not relieve Owners from responsibility at all times for proper stowage, which must be controlled by the master who shall keep a strict account of all cargo loaded and discharged. Owners hereby indemnify Charterers, their servants and agents against all losses, claims, responsibilities and liabilities arising in any way whatsoever from the employment of pilots, tugboats or stevedores, who although employed by Charterers shall be deemed to be the servants of and in the service of Owners and under their instructions (even if such pilots, tugboat personnel or stevedores are in fact the servants of Charterers, their agents or any affiliated company); provided, however, that

(i)   the foregoing indemnity shall not exceed the amount to which Owners would have been entitled to limit their liability if they had themselves employed such pilots, tugboats or stevedores, and

(ii)   Charterers shall be liable for any damage to the vessel caused by or arising out of the use of stevedores, fair wear and tear excepted, to the extent that Owners are unable by the exercise of due diligence to obtain redress therefor from stevedores.

Appendix I

Supernumeraries   17.   Charterers may send representatives in the vessel's available accommodation upon any voyage made under this charter, Owners finding provisions and all requisites as supplied to officers, except liquors. Charterers paying at the rate of   per day for each representative while on board the vessel.

Sub-letting   18.   Charterers may sub-let the vessel, but shall always remain responsible to Owners for due fulfilment of this charter.

Final Voyage   19.   If when a payment of hire is due hereunder Charterers reasonably expect to redeliver the vessel before the next payment of hire would fall due, the hire to be paid shall be assessed on Charterers' reasonable estimate of the time necessary to complete Charterers' programme up to redelivery, and from which estimate Charterers may deduct amounts due or reasonably expected to become due for

     (i)   disbursements on Owners' behalf or charges for Owners' account pursuant to any provision hereof, and

     (ii)   bunkers on board at redelivery pursuant to Clause 15.

Promptly after redelivery any overpayment shall be refunded by Owners or any underpayment made good by Charterers.

If at the time this charter would otherwise terminate in accordance with Clause 4 the vessel is on a ballast voyage to a port of redelivery or is upon a laden voyage, Charterers shall continue to have the use of the vessel at the same rate and conditions as stand herein for as long as necessary to complete such ballast voyage, or to complete such laden voyage and return to a port of redelivery as provided by this charter, as the case may be.

Loss of Vessel   20.   Should the vessel be lost, this charter shall terminate and hire shall cease at noon on the day of her loss; should the vessel be a constructive total loss, this charter shall terminate and hire shall cease at noon on the day on which the vessel's underwriters agree that the vessel is a constructive total loss; should the vessel be missing, this charter shall terminate and hire shall cease at noon on the day on which she was last heard of. Any hire paid in advance and not earned shall be returned to Charterers and Owners shall reimburse Charterers for the value of the estimated quantity of bunkers on board at the time of termination, at the price paid by Charterers at the last bunkering port.

Off-hire   21.   (a)   On each and every occasion that there is loss of time (whether by way of interruption in the vessel's service or, from reduction in the vessel's performance, or in any other manner)

     (i)   due to deficiency of personnel or stores; repairs; gas-freeing for repairs; time in and waiting to enter dry dock for repairs; breakdown (whether partial or total) of machinery, boilers or other parts of the vessel or her equipment (including without limitation tank coatings); overhaul, maintenance or survey; collision, stranding, accident or damage to the vessel; or any other similar cause preventing the efficient working of the vessel; and such loss continues for more than three consecutive hours (if resulting from interruption in the vessel's service) or cumulates to more than three hours (if resulting from partial loss of service); or

     (ii)   due to industrial action, refusal to sail, breach of orders or neglect of duty on the part of the master, officers or crew; or

     (iii)   for the purpose of obtaining medical advice or treatment for or landing any sick or injured person (other than a Charterers' representative carried under Clause 17 hereof) or for the purpose of landing the body of any person (other than a Charterers' representative), and such loss continues for more than three consecutive hours; or

     (iv)   due to any delay in quarantine arising from the master, officers or crew having had communication with the shore at any infected area without the written consent or instructions of Charterers or their agents, or to any detention by customs or other authorities caused by smuggling or other infraction of local law on the part of the master, officers or crew; or

     (v)   due to detention of the vessel by authorities at home or abroad attributable to legal action against or breach of regulations by the vessel, the vessel's owners, or Owners (unless brought about by the act or neglect of Charterers); then

without prejudice to Charterers' rights under Clause 3 or to any other rights of Charterers hereunder or otherwise the vessel shall be off-hire from the commencement of such loss of time until she is again ready and in an efficient state to resume her service from a position not less favourable to Charterers than that at which such loss of time commenced; provided, however, that any service given or distance made good by the vessel whilst off-hire shall be taken into account in assessing the amount to be deducted from hire.

(b)   If the vessel fails to proceed at any guaranteed speed pursuant to Clause 24, and such failure arises wholly or partly from any of the causes set out in Clause 21(a) above, then the period for which the vessel shall be off-hire under this Clause 21 shall be the difference between

     (i)   the time the vessel would have required to perform the relevant service at such guaranteed speed, and

     (ii)   the time actually taken to perform such service (including any loss of time arising from interruption in the performance of such service).

For the avoidance of doubt, all time included under (ii) above shall be excluded from any computation under Clause 24.

(c)   Further and without prejudice to the foregoing, in the event of the vessel deviating (which expression includes without limitation putting back, or putting into any port other than that to which she is bound under the instructions of Charterers) for any cause or purpose mentioned in Clause 21(a), the vessel shall be off-hire from the commencement of such deviation until the time when she is again ready and in an efficient state to resume her service from a position not less favourable to Charterers than that at which the deviation commenced, provided, however, that any service given or distance made good by the vessel whilst so off-hire shall be taken into account in assessing the amount to be deducted from hire. If the vessel, for any cause or purpose mentioned in Clause 21(a), puts into any port other than the port to which she is bound on the instructions of Charterers, the port charges, pilotage and other expenses at such port shall be borne by Owners. Should the vessel be driven into any port or anchorage by stress of weather hire shall continue to be due and payable during any time lost thereby.

(d)　If the vessel's flag state becomes engaged in hostilities, and Charterers in consequence of such hostilities find it commercially impracticable to employ the vessel and have given Owners written notice thereof then from the date of receipt by Owners of such notice until the termination of such commercial impracticability the vessel shall be off-hire and Owners shall have the right to employ the vessel on their own account.

(e)　Time during which the vessel is off-hire under this charter shall count as part of the charter period.

Periodical Drydocking

22.　(a)　Owners have the right and obligation to drydock the vessel at regular intervals of

On each occasion Owners shall propose to Charterers a date on which they wish to drydock the vessel, not less than　　　　　　　before such date; and Charterers shall offer a port for such periodical drydocking and shall take all reasonable steps to make the vessel available as near to such date as practicable.

Owners shall put the vessel in drydock at their expense as soon as practicable after Charterers place the vessel at Owners' disposal clear of cargo other than tank washings and residues. Owners shall be responsible for and pay for the disposal into reception facilities of such tank washings and residues and shall have the right to retain any monies received therefor, without prejudice to any claim for loss of cargo under any bill of lading or this charter.

(b)　If a periodical drydocking is carried out in the port offered by Charterers (which must have suitable accommodation for the purpose and reception facilities for tank washings and residues), the vessel shall be off-hire from the time she arrives at such port until drydocking is completed and she is in every way ready to resume Charterers' service and is at the position at which she went off-hire or a position no less favourable to Charterers, whichever she first attains. However,

(i)　provided that Owners exercise due diligence in gas-freeing, any time lost in gas-freeing to the standard required for entry into drydock for cleaning and painting the hull shall not count as off-hire, whether lost on passage to the drydocking port or after arrival there (notwithstanding Clause 21) and

(ii)　any additional time lost in further gas-freeing to meet the standard required for hot work or entry in cargo tanks shall count as off-hire, whether lost on passage to the drydocking port or after arrival there.

Any time which, but for sub-Clause (i) above, would be off-hire, shall not be included in any calculation under Clause 24.

The expenses of gas-freeing, including without limitation the cost of bunkers, shall be for Owners' account.

(c)　If Owners require the vessel, instead of proceeding to the offered port, to carry out periodical drydocking at a special port selected by them, the vessel shall be off-hire from the time when she is released to proceed to the special port until she next presents for loading in accordance with Charterers' instructions, provided, however, that Charterers shall credit Owners with the time which would have been taken on passage at the service speed had the vessel not proceeded to drydock. All fuel consumed shall be paid for by Owners but Charterers shall credit Owners with the value of the fuel which would have been used on such notional passage calculated at the guaranteed daily consumption for the service speed, and shall further credit Owners with any benefit they may gain in purchasing bunkers at the special port.

(d)　Charterers shall, insofar as cleaning for periodical drydocking may have reduced the amount of tank-cleaning necessary to meet Charterers' requirements, credit Owners with the value of any bunkers which Charterers calculate to have been saved thereby, whether the vessel drydocks at an offered or a special port.

Ship Inspection

23.　Charterers shall have the right at any time during the charter period to make such inspection of the vessel as they may consider necessary. This right may be exercised as often and at such intervals as Charterers in their absolute discretion may determine and whether the vessel is in port or on passage, Owners affording all necessary co-operation and accommodation on board provided, however,

(i)　that neither the exercise nor the non-exercise, nor anything done or not done in the exercise or non-exercise, by Charterers of such right shall in any way reduce the master's or Owners' authority over, or responsibility to Charterers or third parties for, the vessel and every aspect of her operation, nor increase Charterers' responsibilities to Owners or third parties for the same; and

(ii)　that Charterers shall not be liable for any act, neglect or default by themselves, their servants or agents in the exercise or non-exercise of the aforesaid right.

Detailed Description and Performance

24.　(a)　Owners guarantee that the speed and consumption of the vessel shall be as follows:

Average speed in knots	Maximum average bunker consumption	
	main propulsion fuel oil/diesel oil	auxiliaries fuel oil/diesel oil
Laden	tonnes	tonnes
Ballast		

The foregoing bunker consumptions are for all purposes except cargo heating and tank cleaning and shall be pro-rated between the speeds shown.

The service speed of the vessel is   knots laden and   knots in ballast and in the absence of Charterers' orders to the contrary the vessel shall proceed at the service speed. However if more than one laden and one ballast speed are shown in the table above Charterers shall have the right to order the vessel to steam at any speed within the range set out in the table (the "ordered speed").

If the vessel is ordered to proceed at any speed other than the highest speed shown in the table and the average speed actually attained by the vessel during the currency of such order exceeds such ordered speed plus 0.5 knots (the "maximum recognised speed"), then for the purpose of calculating any increase or decrease of hire under this Clause 24 the maximum recognised speed shall be used in place of the average speed actually attained.

For the purposes of this charter the "guaranteed speed" at any time shall be the then-current ordered speed or the service speed, as the case may be.

The average speeds and bunker consumptions shall for the purposes of this Clause 24 be calculated by reference to the observed distance from pilot station to pilot station on all sea passages during each period stipulated in Clause 24 (c), but excluding any time during which the vessel is (or but for Clause 22(b)(i) would be) off-hire and also excluding "Adverse Weather Periods", being (i) any periods during which reduction of speed is necessary for safety in congested waters or in poor visibility (ii) any days, noon to noon, when winds exceed force 8 on the Beaufort Scale for more than 12 hours.

(b)   If during any year from the date on which the vessel enters service (anniversary to anniversary) the vessel falls below or exceeds the performance guaranteed in Clause 24(a) then if such shortfall or excess results

(i)   from a reduction or an increase in the average speed of the vessel, compared to the speed guaranteed in Clause 24(a), then an amount equal to the value at the hire rate of the time so lost or gained, as the case may be, shall be deducted from or added to the hire paid;

(ii)   from an increase or a decrease in the total bunkers consumed, compared to the total bunkers which would have been consumed had the vessel performed as guaranteed in Clause 24(a), an amount equivalent to the value of the additional bunkers consumed or the bunkers saved, as the case may be, based on the average price paid by Charterers for the vessel's bunkers in such period, shall be deducted from or added to the hire paid.

The addition to or deduction from hire so calculated for laden and ballast mileage respectively shall be adjusted to take into account the mileage steamed in each such condition during Adverse Weather Periods, by dividing such addition or deduction by the number of miles over which the performance has been calculated and multiplying by the same number of miles plus the miles steamed during the Adverse Weather Periods, in order to establish the total addition to or deduction from hire to be made for such period.

Reduction of hire under the foregoing sub-Clause (b) shall be without prejudice to any other remedy available to Charterers.

(c)   Calculations under this Clause 24 shall be made for the yearly periods terminating on each successive anniversary of the date on which the vessel enters service, and for the period between the last such anniversary and the date of termination of this charter if less than a year. Claims in respect of reduction of hire arising under this Clause during the final year or part year of the charter period shall in the first instance be settled in accordance with Charterers' estimate made two months before the end of the charter period. Any necessary adjustment after this charter terminates shall be made by payment by Owners to Charterers or by Charterers to Owners as the case may require.

Payments in respect of increase of hire arising under this Clause shall be made promptly after receipt by Charterers of all the information necessary to calculate such increase.

Salvage

25.   Subject to the provisions of Clause 21 hereof, all loss of time and all expenses (excluding any damage to or loss of the vessel or tortious liabilities to third parties) incurred in saving or attempting to save life or in successful or unsuccessful attempts at salvage shall be borne equally by Owners and Charterers provided that Charterers shall not be liable to contribute towards any salvage payable by Owners arising in any way out of services rendered under this Clause 25.

All salvage and all proceeds from derelicts shall be divided equally between Owners and Charterers, after deducting the master's, officers' and crew's share.

Lien

26.   Owners shall have a lien upon all cargoes and all freights, sub-freights and demurrage for any amounts due under this charter; and Charterers shall have a lien on the vessel for all monies paid in advance and not earned, and for all claims for damages arising from any breach by Owners of this charter.

Exceptions

27.   (a)   The vessel, her master and Owners shall not, unless otherwise in this charter expressly provided, be liable for any loss or damage or delay or failure arising or resulting from any act, neglect or default of the master, pilots, mariners or other servants of Owners in the navigation or management of the vessel; fire, unless caused by the actual fault or privity of Owners; collision or stranding; dangers and accidents of the sea; explosion, bursting of boilers, breakage of shafts or any latent defect in hull, equipment or machinery; provided, however, that Clauses 1, 2, 3 and 24 hereof shall be unaffected by the foregoing. Further, neither the vessel, her master or Owners, nor Charterers shall, unless otherwise in this charter expressly provided, be liable for any loss or damage, or delay or failure in performance hereunder arising or resulting from act of God, act of war, seizure under legal process, quarantine restrictions, strikes, lock-outs, riots, restraints of labour, civil commotions or arrest or restraint of princes, rulers or people.

(b)   The vessel shall have liberty to sail with or without pilots, to tow or go to the assistance of vessels in distress and to deviate for the purpose of saving life or property.

(c)   Clause 27(a) shall not apply to or affect any liability of Owners or the vessel or any other relevant person in respect of

(i)   loss or damage caused to any berth, jetty, dock, dolphin, buoy, mooring line, pipe or crane or other works or equipment whatsoever at or near any place to which the vessel may proceed under this charter, whether or not such works or equipment belong to Charterers, or

(ii)   any claim (whether brought by Charterers or any other person) arising out of any loss of or damage to or in connection with cargo. All such claims shall be subject to the Hague-Visby Rules or the Hague Rules, as the case may be, which ought pursuant to Clause 38 hereof to have been incorporated in the relevant bill of lading (whether or not such Rules were so incorporated) or, if no such bill of lading is issued, to the Hague-Visby Rules.

(d)   In particular and without limitation, the foregoing subsections (a) and (b) of this Clause shall not apply to or in any way affect any provision in this charter relating to off-hire or to reduction of hire.

Injurious Cargoes

28.   No acids, explosives or cargoes injurious to the vessel shall be shipped and without prejudice to the foregoing any damage to the vessel caused by the shipment of any such cargo, and the time taken to repair such damage, shall be for Charterers' account. No voyage shall be undertaken, nor any goods or cargoes loaded, that would expose the vessel to capture or seizure by rulers or governments.

Grade of Bunkers

29.   Charterers shall supply marine diesel oil/fuel oil with a maximum viscosity of   Centistokes at 50 degrees Centigrade/ACGFO for main propulsion and diesel oil/ACGFO for the auxiliaries. If Owners, require the vessel to be supplied with more expensive bunkers they shall be liable for the extra cost thereof.

Charterers warrant that all bunkers provided by them in accordance herewith shall be of a quality complying with the International Marine Bunker Supply Terms and Conditions of Shell International Trading Company and with its specification for marine fuels as amended from time to time.

Disbursements

30.   Should the master require advances for ordinary disbursements at any port, Charterers or their agents shall make such advances to him, in consideration of which Owners shall pay a commission of two and a half per cent, and all such advances and commission shall be deducted from hire.

Laying-up

31.   Charterers shall have the option, after consultation with Owners, of requiring Owners to lay up the vessel at a safe place nominated by Charterers, in which case the hire provided for under this charter shall be adjusted to reflect any net increases in expenditure reasonably incurred or any net saving which should reasonably be made by Owners as a result of such lay-up. Charterers may exercise the said option any number of times during the charter period.

Requisition

32.   Should the vessel be requisitioned by any government, de facto or de jure, during the period of this charter, the vessel shall be off-hire during the period of such requisition, and any hire paid by such government in respect of such requisition period shall be for Owners' account. Any such requisition period shall count as part of the charter period.

Outbreak of War

33.   If war or hostilities break out between any two or more of the following countries: U.S.A., U.S.S.R., P.R.C., U.K., Netherlands - both Owners and Charterers shall have the right to cancel this charter.

Additional War Expenses

34.   If the vessel is ordered to trade in areas where there is war (de facto or de jure) or threat of war, Charterers shall reimburse Owners for any additional insurance premia, crew bonuses and other expenses which are reasonably incurred by Owners as a consequence of such orders, provided that Charterers are given notice of such expenses as soon as practicable and in any event before such expenses are incurred, and provided further that Owners obtain from their insurers a waiver of any subrogated rights against Charterers in respect of any claims by Owners under their war risk insurance arising out of compliance with such orders.

War Risks

35.   (a)   The master shall not be required or bound to sign bills of lading for any place which in his or Owners' reasonable opinion is dangerous or impossible for the vessel to enter or reach owing to any blockade, war, hostilities, warlike operations, civil war, civil commotions or revolutions.

(b)   If in the reasonable opinion of the master or Owners it becomes, for any of the reasons set out in Clause 35(a) or by the operation of international law, dangerous, impossible or prohibited for the vessel to reach or enter, or to load or discharge cargo at any place to which the vessel has been ordered pursuant to this charter (a "place of peril"), then Charterers or their agents shall be immediately notified by telex or radio messages, and Charterers shall thereupon have the right to order the cargo, or such part of it as may be affected, to be loaded or discharged, as the case may be, at any other place within the trading limits of this charter (provided such other place is not itself a place of peril). If any place of discharge is or becomes a place of peril, and no orders have been received from Charterers or their agents within 48 hours after dispatch of such messages, then Owners shall be at liberty to discharge the cargo or such part of it as may be affected at any place which they or the master may in their or his discretion select within the trading limits of this charter and such discharge shall be deemed to be due fulfilment of Owners' obligations under this charter so far as cargo so discharged is concerned.

(c)   The vessel shall have liberty to comply with any directions or recommendations as to departure, arrival, routes, ports of call, stoppages, destinations, zones, waters, delivery or in any other wise whatsoever given by the government of the state under whose flag the vessel sails or any other government or local authority or by any person or body acting or purporting to act as or with the authority of any such government or local authority including any de facto government or local authority or by any person or body acting or purporting to act as or with the authority of any such government or local authority or by any committee or person having under the terms of the war risks insurance on the vessel the right to give any such directions or recommendations. If by reason of or in compliance with any such directions or recommendations anything is done or is not done, such shall not be deemed a deviation.

If by reason of or in compliance with any such direction or recommendation the vessel does not proceed to any place of discharge to which she has been ordered pursuant to this charter, the vessel may proceed to any place which the master or Owners in his or their discretion select and there discharge the cargo or such part of it as may be affected. Such discharge shall be deemed to be due fulfilment of Owners' obligations under this charter so far as cargo so discharged is concerned.

Charterers shall procure that all bills of lading issued under this charter shall contain the Chamber of Shipping War Risks Clause 1952.

Both to Blame Collision Clause

36. If the liability for any collision in which the vessel is involved while performing this charter falls to be determined in accordance with the laws of the United States of America, the following provision shall apply:

"If the ship comes into collision with another ship as a result of the negligence of the other ship and any act, neglect or default of the master, mariner, pilot or the servants of the carrier in the navigation or in the management of the ship, the owners of the cargo carried hereunder will indemnify the carrier against all loss, or liability to the other or non-carrying ship or her owners in so far as such loss or liability represents loss of, or damage to, or any claim whatsoever of the owners of the said cargo, paid or payable by the other or non-carrying ship or her owners to the owners of the said cargo and set off, recouped or recovered by the other or non-carrying ship or her owners as part of their claim against the carrying ship or carrier."

"The foregoing provisions shall also apply where the owners, operators or those in charge of any ship or ships or objects other than, or in addition to, the colliding ships or objects are at fault in respect of a collision or contact."

Charterers shall procure that all bills of lading issued under this charter shall contain a provision in the foregoing terms to be applicable where the liability for any collision in which the vessel is involved falls to be determined in accordance with the laws of the United States of America.

New Jason Clause

37. General average contributions shall be payable according to the York/Antwerp Rules, 1974, and shall be adjusted in London in accordance with English law and practice but should adjustment be made in accordance with the law and practice of the United States of America, the following provision shall apply:

"In the event of accident, danger, damage or disaster before or after the commencement of the voyage, resulting from any cause whatsoever, whether due to negligence or not, for which, or for the consequence of which, the carrier is not responsible by statute, contract or otherwise, the cargo, shippers, consignees or owners of the cargo shall contribute with the carrier in general average to the payment of any sacrifices, losses or expenses of a general average nature that may be made or incurred and shall pay salvage and special charges incurred in respect of the cargo."

"If a salving ship is owned or operated by the carrier, salvage shall be paid for as fully as if the said salving ship or ships belonged to strangers. Such deposit as the carrier or his agents may deem sufficient to cover the estimated contribution of the cargo and any salvage and special charges thereon shall, if required, be made by the cargo, shippers, consignees or owners of the cargo to the carrier before delivery."

Charterers shall procure that all bills of lading issued under this charter shall contain a provision in the foregoing terms, to be applicable where adjustment of general average is made in accordance with the laws and practice of the United States of America.

Clause Paramount

38. Charterers shall procure that all bills of lading issued pursuant to this charter shall contain the following clause:

"(1) Subject to sub-clause (2) hereof, this bill of lading shall be governed by, and have effect subject to, the rules contained in the International Convention for the Unification of Certain rules relating to Bills of Lading signed at Brussels on 25th August 1924 (hereafter the "Hague Rules") as amended by the Protocol signed at Brussels on 23rd February 1968 (hereafter the "Hague-Visby Rules"). Nothing contained herein shall be deemed to be either a surrender by the carrier of any of his rights or immunities or any increase of any of his responsibilities or liabilities under the Hague-Visby Rules."

"(2) If there is governing legislation which applies the Hague Rules compulsorily to this bill of lading, to the exclusion of the Hague-Visby Rules, then this bill of lading shall have effect subject to the Hague Rules. Nothing herein contained shall be deemed to be either a surrender by the carrier of any of his rights or immunities or an increase of any of his responsibilities or liabilities under the Hague Rules."

"(3) If any term of this bill of lading is repugnant to the Hague-Visby Rules, or Hague rules if applicable, such term shall be void to that extent but no further."

"(4) Nothing in this bill of lading shall be construed as in any way restricting, excluding or waiving the right of any relevant party or person to limit his liability under any available legislation and/or law."

TOVALOP

39. Owners warrant that the vessel is:
(i)   a tanker in TOVALOP and
(ii) properly entered in   P & I Club

and will so remain during the currency of this charter.

When an escape or discharge of Oil occurs from the vessel and causes or threatens to cause Pollution Damage, or when there is the threat of an escape or discharge of Oil (i.e. a grave and imminent danger of the escape or discharge of Oil which, if it occurred, would create a serious danger of Pollution Damage, whether or not an escape or discharge in fact subsequently occurs), then Charterers may, at their option, upon notice to Owners or master, undertake such measures as are reasonably necessary to prevent or minimise such Pollution Damage or to remove the Threat, unless Owners promptly undertake the same. Charterers shall keep Owners advised of the nature and result of any such measures taken by them and, if time permits, the nature of the measures intended to be taken by them. Any of the aforementioned measures taken by Charterers shall be deemed taken on Owners' authority as Owners' agent, and shall be at Owners' expense except to the extent that:

(1)   any such escape or discharge or Threat was caused or contributed to by Charterers, or

(2)   by reason of the exceptions set out in Article III, paragraph 2, of the 1969 International Convention on Civil Liability for Oil Pollution Damage, Owners are or, had the said Convention applied to such escape or discharge or to the Threat, would have been exempt from liability for the same, or

(3)   the cost of such measures together with all other liabilities, costs and expenses of Owners arising out of or in connection with such escape or discharge or Threat exceeds one hundred and sixty United States Dollars (US $160) per ton of the vessel's Tonnage or sixteen million eight hundred thousand United States Dollars (US $16,800,000), whichever is the lesser, save and insofar as Owners shall be entitled to recover such excess under either the 1971 International Convention on the Establishment of an International Fund for Compensation for Oil Pollution Damage or under CRISTAL:

PROVIDED ALWAYS that if Owners in their absolute discretion consider said measures should be discontinued, Owners shall so notify Charterers and thereafter Charterers shall have no right to continue said measures under the provisions of this Clause 39 and all further liability to Charterers under this Clause 39 shall thereupon cease.

The above provisions are not in derogation of such other rights as Charterers or Owners may have under this charter or may otherwise have or acquire by law or any International Convention or TOVALOP.

The term "TOVALOP" means the Tanker Owners' Voluntary Agreement Concerning Liability for Oil Pollution dated 7th January 1969, as amended from time to time, and the term "CRISTAL" means the Contract Regarding an Interim Supplement to Tanker Liability for Oil Pollution dated 14th January 1971, as amended from time to time. The terms "Oil", "Pollution Damage", and "Tonnage" shall for the purposes of this Clause 39 have the meanings ascribed to them in TOVALOP.

Export Restrictions

40.   The master shall not be required or bound to sign bills of lading for the carriage of cargo to any place to which export of such cargo is prohibited under the laws, rules or regulations of the country in which the cargo was produced and/or shipped.

Charterers shall procure that all bills of lading issued under this charter shall contain the following clause:

"If any laws rules or regulations applied by the government of the country in which the cargo was produced and/or shipped, or any relevant agency thereof, impose a prohibition on export of the cargo to the place of discharge designated in or ordered under this bill of lading, carriers shall be entitled to require cargo owners forthwith to nominate an alternative discharge place for the discharge of the cargo, or such part of it as may be affected, which alternative place shall not be subject to the prohibition, and carriers shall be entitled to accept orders from the cargo owners to proceed to and discharge at such alternative place. If cargo owners fail to nominate an alternative place within 72 hours after they or their agents have received from carriers notice of such prohibition, carriers shall be at liberty to discharge the cargo or such part of it as may be affected by the prohibition at any safe place on which they or the master may in their or his absolute discretion decide and which is not subject to the prohibition, and such discharge shall constitute due performance of the contract contained in this bill of lading so far as the cargo so discharged is concerned".

The foregoing provision shall apply mutatis mutandis to this charter, the references to a bill of lading being deemed to be references to this charter.

Law and Litigation

41.   (a)   This charter shall be construed and the relations between the parties determined in accordance with the laws of England.

(b)   Any dispute arising under this charter shall be decided by the English Courts to whose jurisdiction the parties hereby agree.

(c)   Notwithstanding the foregoing, but without prejudice to any party's right to arrest or maintain the arrest of any maritime property, either party may, by giving written notice of election to the other party, elect to have any such dispute referred to the arbitration of a single arbitrator in London in accordance with the provisions of the Arbitration Act 1950, or any statutory modification or re-enactment thereof for the time being in force.

(i)   A party shall lose its right to make such an election only if:

(a)   it receives from the other party a written notice of dispute which –

(1)   states expressly that a dispute has arisen out of this charter;

(2)   specifies the nature of the dispute; and

(3)   refers expressly to this clause 41(c)

and

(b)   it fails to give notice of election to have the dispute referred to arbitration not later than 30 days from the date of receipt of such notice of dispute.

(ii)   The parties hereby agree that either party may –

(a)   appeal to the High Court on any question of law arising out of an award;

(b)   apply to the High Court for an order that the arbitrator state the reasons for his award;

(c)   give notice to the arbitrator that a reasoned award is required; and

(d)   apply to the High Court to determine any question of law arising in the course of the reference.

(d)   It shall be a condition precedent to the right of any party to a stay of any legal proceedings in which maritime property has been, or may be, arrested in connection with a dispute under this charter, that that party furnishes to the other party security to which that other party would have been entitled in such legal proceedings in the absence of a stay.

Construction

42.   The side headings have been included in this charter for convenience of reference and shall in no way affect the construction hereof.

SHELLTIME 4. STANDARD CHARTER PARTY AMENDMENTS

1. AMENDMENTS TO STANDARD TEXT

Lines 6 and 25 After 'charter' add 'and throughout the charter period'

Clause 3 after line 59 add

'Owners shall advise charterers immediately, in writing, should the vessel fail an inspection by, but not limited to, a governmental and/or port state authority, and/or terminal and/or major charterer of similar tonnage. Owners shall simultaneously advise charterers of their proposed course of action to remedy the defects which have caused the failure of such inspection.

If, in charterers reasonably held view, failure of such inspection prevents normal commercial operations charterers have the option to place the vessel offhire from the date and time that she fails such inspection until the date and time that the vessel passes a reinspection by the same organisation, which shall be in a position no less favourable to charterers than that at which she went offhire.'

Clause 11 Delete.

Clause 15 Delete. Substitute the following

'Charterers shall accept and pay for all bunkers at the time of delivery and owners shall on redelivery (whether it occurs at the end of the charter period or on the earlier termination of this charter) accept and pay for all bunkers remaining on board at the price actually paid, on a first in first out basis. Such prices are to be supported by paid invoices.

Vessel to be delivered to and redelivered from the charter period with a minimum quantity of bunkers on board sufficient to reach the nearest main bunkering port.

Notwithstanding anything contained in this charter party all bunkers on board the vessel shall, throughout the duration of this charter, remain the property of the charterer and can only be purchased on the terms specified in the charter party at the end of the charter period or on the earlier termination of the charter, whichever occurs first.'

Clause 17 line 182 Insert 'USD15'.

Clause 21 line 256 Add 'Any periods of offhire earned under clause 21 and 22 may be added to the charter period in charterers option.'

Clause 22 delete. Substitute 'vessel shall be drydocked in an emergency only'.

Clause 24 Vessel performance to be guaranteed up to and including Beaufort 8 on a penalty only basis. Clause to be suitably amended.

Clause 27 Delete lines 380-384 inclusive. Substitute

'ii) any claim (whether brought by charterers or any other person) arising out of any loss of or damage to or in connection with the cargo. Any such claim shall be subject to the Hague-Visby Rules or the Hague Rules or the Hamburg Rules as the case may be, which ought pursuant to Clause 38 hereof to have been incorporated in the relevant Bill of Lading (whether or not such Rules were so incorporated), or if no such Bill of Lading is issued to the Hague-Visby Rules unless the Hamburg Rules compulsorily apply in which case to the Hamburg Rules.'

Clause 29 line 396. After 'marine fuels' insert ' in accordance with ISO standards RMH35'.

Clause 33 Delete reference to 'USSR' substitute the following 'the countries or republics having been part of the former USSR (except that declaration of war solely between any two or more of the countries or republics having been part of the former USSR shall be exempted).'

Clause 37 line 462, after '1974' add 'and as amended in 1990 and 1994'.

Clause 38 Delete entire clause (lines 478-493 inclusive). Substitute

'Charterers shall procure that all Bills of Lading issued pursuant to this charter shall contain the following clause:

'(1) Subject to sub-clause (2) or (3) hereof, this Bill of Lading shall be governed by and have the effect subject to the rules contained in the International Convention for the Unification of Certain Rules relating to Bills of Lading signed at Brussels on 25th August 1924 (hereafter the 'Hague Rules') as amended by the Protocol signed at Brussels on 23rd February 1968 (hereafter the 'Hague-Visby Rules'). Nothing contained herein shall be deemed to be either a surrender by the carrier of any of his rights or immunities or any increase of any of his responsibilities or liabilities under the Hague-Visby Rules.'

'(2) If there is governing legislation which applies the Hague Rules compulsorily to this Bill of Lading, to the exclusion of the Hague-Visby Rules, then this Bill of Lading shall have effect subject to the Hague Rules. Nothing herein contained shall be deemed to be either a surrender by the carrier of any of his rights or immunities or an increase of any of his responsibilities or liabilities under the Hague Rules.'

'(3) If there is governing legislation which applies the United Nations Convention on the Carriage of Goods by Sea 1978 (hereafter the 'Hamburg Rules') compulsorily to this Bill of Lading to the exclusion of the Hague-Visby Rules, then this Bill of Lading shall have effect subject to the Hamburg Rules. Nothing herein contained shall be deemed to be either a surrender by the carrier of any of his rights or immunities or an increase of any of his responsibilities or liabilities under the Hamburg Rules.'

'(4) If any term of this Bill of Lading is repugnant to the Hague-Visby Rules, or Hague Rules or Hamburg Rules, if applicable, such term shall be void to that extent but no further.'

'(5) Nothing in this Bill of Lading shall be construed as in any way restricting, excluding or waiving the right of any relevant party or person to limit his liability under any available legislation and/or law.'

Clause 39 Delete.

5 Bills of Lading

Bill of Lading for Combined Transport shipment or Port to Port shipment

| Shipper | B/L No.: |
| | Reference: |

P&O Nedlloyd

Consignee or Order (for U.S. Trade only: Not Negotiable unless consigned 'To Order')

| Notify Party/Address (It is agreed that no responsibility shall attach to the Carrier or his Agents for failure to notify (see clause 20 on reverse)) | Place of Receipt (Applicable only when this document is used as a Combined Transport Bill of Lading) |

| Vessel and Voy. No. | Place of Delivery (Applicable only when this document is used as a Combined Transport Bill of Lading) |

| Port of Loading | Port of Discharge | |

Undermentioned particulars as declared by Shipper, but not acknowledged by the Carrier (see clause 11)

Marks and Nos; Container Nos;	Number and kind of Packages; Description of Goods	Gross Weight (kg)	Measurement (cbm)

| * Total No. of Containers/Packages received by the Carrier | Movement | Freight payable at |

EXCESS VALUATION: REFER TO CLAUSE 7 (3) ON REVERSE SIDE (U.S. TRADE ONLY).

Received by the Carrier from the Shipper in apparent good order and condition (unless otherwise noted herein) the total number or quantity of Containers or other packages or units indicated in the box above entitled "*Total No. of Containers/Packages received by the Carrier" for Carriage subject to all the terms and conditions hereof (INCLUDING THE TERMS AND CONDITIONS ON THE REVERSE HEREOF AND THE TERMS AND CONDITIONS OF THE CARRIER'S APPLICABLE TARIFF) from the Place of Receipt or the Port of Loading, whichever is applicable, to the Port of Discharge or the Place of Delivery, whichever is applicable. If the Carrier so requires, before he arranges delivery of the Goods one original Bill of Lading, duly endorsed, must be surrendered by the Merchant to the Carrier at the Port of Discharge or at some other location acceptable to the Carrier. In accepting this Bill of Lading the Merchant expressly accepts and agrees to all its terms and conditions whether printed, stamped or written, or otherwise incorporated, notwithstanding the non-signing of this Bill of Lading by the Merchant.

| Number of Original Bills of Lading | Place and Date of Issue | IN WITNESS of the contract herein contained the number of originals stated opposite has been issued, one of which being accomplished the other(s) to be void |

018070

CANCELLED SPECIMEN COPY

2/DRS B/L2 5/97 (S)

TERMS AND CONDITIONS

(Enlarged print available from the Carrier or his agents.)

1. DEFINITIONS

In this Bill of Lading the word:—

"Carrier" means the party named in the Signature box on the face hereof.

"Merchant" includes any Person who at any time has been or becomes the Shipper, Holder, Consignee, Receiver of the Goods, any Person who owns or is entitled to the possession of the Goods or of this Bill of Lading and any Person acting on behalf of any such Person.

"Holder" means any Person for the time being in possession of or entitled to the possession of this Bill of Lading.

"Person" includes an individual, group, company or other entity.

"Sub-Contractor" includes (but is not limited to) owners and operators of vessels (other than the Carrier), stevedores, terminal and groupage operators, road and rail transport operators and any independent contractor employed by the Carrier in performance of the Carriage and any sub-sub-contractors thereof.

"indemnify" includes defend, indemnify and hold harmless whether or not the obligation to indemnify arises out of negligent or non-negligent acts or omissions of the Carrier, his servant, agents or Sub-Contractor.

"Goods" means the whole or any part of the cargo received from the Shipper and includes the packing and any equipment or Container not supplied by or on behalf of the Carrier.

"Container" includes any container, trailer, transportable tank, flat or pallet, or any similar article used to consolidate goods and any ancillary equipment.

"Carriage" means the whole or any part of the operations and services undertaken by the Carrier in respect of the Goods covered by this Bill of Lading.

"Port of Loading" means any port at which the Goods are loaded on board any vessel (which may be either a feeder vessel or an ocean vessel) and is not necessarily the vessel named overleaf) for Carriage under this Bill of Lading.

"Port of Discharge" means any port at which the Goods are discharged from any vessel (which may be either a feeder vessel or an ocean vessel and is not necessarily the vessel named overleaf) after Carriage under this Bill of Lading.

"Vessel" means any waterborne craft used in the Carriage under this Bill of Lading which may be a feeder vessel or an ocean vessel.

"Combined Transport" arises if the Place of Receipt and/or the Place of Delivery are indicated on the face hereof in the relevant spaces.

"Port to Port" arises if the Carriage is not Combined Transport.

"Shipped on Board" relates only to the Container into which the Goods are stuffed/loaded.

"Freight" includes all charges payable to the Carrier in accordance with the applicable Tariff and this Bill of Lading.

"Hague Rules" means the provisions of the International Convention for the Unification of Certain Rules relating to Bills of Lading signed at Brussels on 25th August, 1924 and includes the amendments by the Protocol signed at Brussels on 23rd February, 1968, but only if such amendments are compulsorily applicable to this Bill of Lading. (It is expressly provided that nothing in this Bill of Lading shall be construed as contractually applying said Rules as amended by said Protocol).

2. CARRIER'S TARIFF

The terms and conditions of the Carrier's applicable Tariff are incorporated herein. Particular attention is drawn to the terms and conditions therein relating to container and vehicle demurrage. Copies of the relevant provisions of the applicable Tariff are obtainable from the Carrier or his agents upon request. In the case of inconsistency between this Bill of Lading and the applicable Tariff, this Bill of Lading shall prevail.

3. WARRANTY

The Merchant warrants that in agreeing to the terms and conditions hereof he is, or has the authority of the Person owning or entitled to the possession of the Goods and this Bill of Lading.

4. SUB-CONTRACTING AND INDEMNITY

(1) The Carrier shall be entitled to sub-contract the Carriage on any terms whatsoever.

[Remaining body text continues in multiple dense columns — numbered clauses 4 through 28 covering Sub-Contracting and Indemnity, Carrier's Responsibility, Carriage Affected by Condition of Goods, Description of Goods, Shipper's and Merchant's Responsibility, Sundry Liability Provisions, Shipper-Packed Containers, Inspection of Goods, Freight and Charges, Lien, Live Animals, Methods and Routes of Carriage, Matters Affecting Performance, Notification and Delivery, FCL Multiple Bills of Lading, General Average and Salvage, Limitation of Liability, Variation of the Contract, Law and Jurisdiction, Validity, Dangerous Goods, US Clause Paramount, and related provisions.]

Code Name: "MULTIDOC 95"

Consignor	MT Doc. No.

Reference No.

Negotiable

MULTIMODAL TRANSPORT BILL OF LADING

Issued by The Baltic and International Maritime Council (BIMCO), subject to the UNCTAD/ICC Rules for Multimodal Transport Documents (ICC Publication No. 481).

Issued 1995

Consigned to order of

Notify party/address

Place of receipt	
Ocean Vessel	Port of loading
Port of discharge	Place of delivery
Marks and Nos.	Quantity and description of goods	Gross weight, kg, Measurement, m³

Particulars above declared by Consignor

Freight and charges

RECEIVED the goods in apparent good order and condition and, as far as ascertained by reasonable means of checking, as specified above unless otherwise stated.

The MTO, in accordance with and to the extent of the provisions contained in this MT Bill of Lading, and with liberty to sub-contract, undertakes to perform and/or in his own name to procure performance of the multimodal transport and the delivery of the goods, including all services related thereto, from the place and time of taking the goods in charge to the place and time of delivery and accepts responsibility for such transport and such services.

One of the MT Bills of Lading must be surrendered duly endorsed in exchange for the goods or delivery order.

IN WITNESS whereof MT Bill(s) of Lading has/have been signed in the number indicated below, one of which being accomplished the other(s) to be void.

Consignor's declared value of	Freight payable at	Place and date of issue
subject to payment of above extra charge.	Number of original MT Bills of Lading	Signed for the Multimodal Transport Operator (MTO)

.... as Carrier

Note:
The Merchant's attention is called to the fact that according to Clauses 10 to 12 of this MT Bill of Lading, the liability of the MTO is, in most cases, limited in respect of loss of or damage to the goods.

by ....

As agent(s) only to the MTO

p.t.o.

Printed and sold by Fr. G. Knudtzon Ltd., 55 Toldbodgade, DK-1253 Copenhagen K, Telefax +45 33 93 11 84 by authority of The Baltic and International Maritime Council (BIMCO), Copenhagen

Copyright, published by
The Baltic and International Maritime Council (BIMCO), Copenhagen, 1995

MULTIMODAL TRANSPORT BILL OF LADING

CODE NAME: "MULTIDOC 95"

I. GENERAL PROVISIONS

1. Applicability
The provisions of this Contract shall apply irrespective of whether there is a unimodal or a Multimodal Transport Contract involving one or several modes of transport.

2. Definitions
"Multimodal Transport Contract" means a single Contract for the carriage of Goods by at least two different modes of transport.

"Multimodal Transport Bill of Lading" (MT Bill of Lading) means this document evidencing a Multimodal Transport Contract and which can be replaced by electronic data interchange messages insofar as permitted by applicable law and is issued in a negotiable form.

"Multimodal Transport Operator" (MTO) means the person named on the face hereof who concludes a Multimodal Transport Contract and assumes responsibility for the performance thereof as a Carrier.

"Carrier" means the person who actually performs or undertakes to perform the carriage, or part thereof, whether he is identical with the Multimodal Transport Operator or not.

"Merchant" includes the Shipper, the Receiver, the Consignor, the Consignee, the holder of this MT Bill of Lading and the owner of the Goods.

"Consignor" means the person who concludes the Multimodal Transport Contract with the Multimodal Transport Operator.

"Consignee" means the person entitled to receive the Goods from the Multimodal Transport Operator.

"Taken in charge" means that the Goods have been handed over to and accepted for carriage by the MTO.

"Delivery" means
(i) the handing over of the Goods to the Consignee; or
(ii) the placing of the Goods at the disposal of the Consignee in accordance with the Multimodal Transport Contract or with the law or usage of the particular trade applicable at the place of delivery; or
(iii) the handing over of the Goods to an authority or other third party to whom, pursuant to the law or regulations applicable at the place of delivery, the Goods must be handed over.

"Special Drawing Rights" (SDR) means the unit of account as defined by the International Monetary Fund.

"Goods" means any property including live animals as well as containers, pallets or similar articles of transport or packaging not supplied by the MTO, irrespective of whether such property is to be or is carried on or under deck.

3. MTO's Tariff
The terms of the MTO's applicable tariff at the date of shipment are incorporated herein. Copies of the relevant provisions of the applicable tariff are available from the MTO upon request. In the case of inconsistency between this MT Bill of Lading and the applicable tariff, this MT Bill of Lading shall prevail.

4. Time Bar
The MTO shall, unless otherwise expressly agreed, be discharged of all liability under this MT Bill of Lading unless suit is brought within nine months after:
(i) the Delivery of the Goods; or
(ii) the date when the Goods should have been delivered; or
(iii) the date when, in accordance with sub-clause 10 (e) failure to deliver the Goods would give the Consignee the right to treat the Goods as lost.

5. Law and Jurisdiction
Disputes arising under this MT Bill of Lading shall be determined by the courts and in accordance with the law at the place where the MTO has his principal place of business.

II. PERFORMANCE OF THE CONTRACT

6. Methods and Routes of Transportation
(a) The MTO is entitled to perform the transport in any reasonable manner and by any reasonable means, methods and routes.
(b) In accordance herewith, for instance, in the event of carriage by sea, vessels may sail with or without pilots, undergo repairs, adjust equipment, drydock and tow vessels in all situations.

7. Optional Stowage
(a) Goods may be stowed by the MTO by means of containers, trailers, transportable tanks, flats, pallets, or similar articles of transport used to consolidate Goods.
(b) Containers, trailers, transportable tanks and covered flats, whether stowed by the MTO or received by him in a stowed condition, may be carried on or under deck without notice to the Merchant.

8. Delivery of the Goods to the Consignee
The MTO undertakes to perform or to procure the performance of all acts necessary to ensure Delivery of the Goods:
(i) when the MT Bill of Lading has been issued in a negotiable form "to bearer", to the person surrendering one original of the document; or
(ii) when the MT Bill of Lading has been issued in a negotiable form "to order", to the person surrendering one original of the document duly endorsed; or
(iii) when the MT Bill of Lading has been issued in a negotiable form to a named person, to that person upon proof of his identity and surrender of one original document; if such document has been transferred "to order" or in blank, the provisions of (ii) above apply.

9. Hindrances, etc. Affecting Performance
(a) The MTO shall use reasonable endeavours to complete the transport and to deliver the Goods at the place designated for Delivery.
(b) If at any time the performance of the Contract as evidenced by this MT Bill of Lading is or will be affected by any hindrance, risk, delay, difficulty or disadvantage of whatsoever kind, and if by virtue of sub-clause 9 (a) the MTO has no duty to complete the performance of the Contract, the MTO (whether or not the transport is commenced) may elect to
(i) treat the performance of this Contract as terminated and place the Goods at the Merchant's disposal at any place which the MTO shall deem safe and convenient; or
(ii) deliver the Goods at the place designated for Delivery.
(c) If the Goods are not taken Delivery of by the Merchant within a reasonable time after the MTO has called upon him to take Delivery, the MTO shall be at liberty to put the Goods in safe custody on behalf of the Merchant at the latter's risk and expense.
(d) In any event the MTO shall be entitled to full freight for Goods received for transportation and additional compensation for extra costs resulting from the circumstances referred to above.

III. LIABILITY OF THE MTO

10. Basis of Liability
(a) The responsibility of the MTO for the Goods under this Contract covers the period from the time the MTO has taken the Goods into his charge to the time of their Delivery.
(b) Subject to the defences set forth in Clauses 11 and 12, the MTO shall be liable for loss of or damage to the Goods, as well as for delay in Delivery, if the occurrence which caused the loss, damage or delay in Delivery took place while the Goods were in his charge as defined in sub-clause 10 (a), unless the MTO proves that no fault or neglect of his own, his servants or agents or any other person referred to in sub-clause 10 (c) has caused or contributed to the loss, damage or delay in Delivery. However, the MTO shall only be liable for loss following from delay in Delivery if the Consignor has made a written declaration of interest in timely Delivery which has been accepted in writing by the MTO.
(c) The MTO shall be responsible for the acts and omissions of his servants or agents, when any such servant or agent is acting within the scope of his employment, or of any other person of whose services he makes use for the performance of the Contract, as if such acts and omissions were his own.
(d) Delay in Delivery occurs when the Goods have not been delivered within the time expressly agreed upon or, in the absence of such agreement, within the time which it would be reasonable to require of a diligent MTO, having regard to the circumstances of the case.
(e) If the Goods have not been delivered within ninety (90) consecutive days following the date of Delivery determined according to Clause 10 (d) above, the claimant may, in the absence of evidence to the contrary, treat the Goods as lost.

11. Defences for Carriage by Sea or Inland Waterways
Notwithstanding the provisions of Clause 10 (b), the MTO shall not be responsible for loss, damage or delay in Delivery with respect to Goods carried by sea or inland waterways when such loss, damage or delay during such carriage results from:
(i) act, neglect or default of the master, mariner, pilot or the servants of the Carrier in the navigation or in the management of the vessel;
(ii) fire, unless caused by the actual fault or privity of the Carrier;
(iii) the causes listed in the Hague-Visby Rules article 4.2 (c) to (p);
however, always provided that whenever loss or damage has resulted from unseaworthiness of the vessel, the MTO can prove that due diligence has been exercised to make the vessel seaworthy at the commencement of the voyage.

12. Limitation of Liability
(a) Unless the nature and value of the Goods have been declared by the Consignor before the Goods have been taken in charge by the MTO and inserted in the MT Bill of Lading, the MTO shall in no event be or become liable for any loss of or damage to the Goods in an amount exceeding:
(i) when the Carriage of Goods by Sea Act of the United States of America, 1936 (US COGSA) applies USD 500 per package or customary freight unit; or
(ii) when any other law applies, the equivalent of 666.67 SDR per package or unit or two SDR per kilogramme of gross weight of the Goods lost or damaged, whichever is the higher.
(b) Where a container, pallet, or similar article of transport is loaded with more than one package or unit, the packages or other shipping units enumerated in the MT Bill of Lading as packed in such article of transport are deemed packages or shipping units. Except as aforesaid, such article of transport shall be considered the package or unit.
(c) Notwithstanding the above-mentioned provisions, if the Multimodal Transport does not, according to the Contract, include carriage of Goods by sea or by inland waterways, the liability of the MTO shall be limited to an amount not exceeding 8.33 SDR per kilogramme of gross weight of the Goods lost or damaged.
(d) In any case, when the loss of or damage to the Goods occurred during one particular stage of the Multimodal Transport, in respect of which an applicable international convention or mandatory national law would have provided another limit of liability if a separate contract of carriage had been made for that particular stage of transport, then the limit of the MTO's liability for such loss or damage shall be determined by reference to the provisions of such convention or mandatory national law.
(e) If the MTO is liable in respect of loss following from delay in Delivery, or consequential loss or damage other than loss of or damage to the Goods, the liability of the MTO shall be limited to an amount not exceeding the equivalent of the freight under the Multimodal Transport Contract for the Multimodal Transport.
(f) The aggregate liability of the MTO shall not exceed the limits of liability for total loss of the Goods.
(g) The MTO is not entitled to the benefit of the limitation of liability if it is proved that the loss, damage or delay in Delivery resulted from a personal act or omission of the MTO done with the intent to cause such loss, damage or delay, or recklessly and with knowledge that such loss, damage or delay would probably result.

13. Assessment of Compensation
(a) Assessment of compensation for loss of or damage to the Goods shall be made by reference to the value of such Goods at the place and time they are delivered to the Consignee or at the place and time when, in accordance with the Multimodal Transport Contract, they should have been so delivered.
(b) The value of the Goods shall be determined according to the current commodity exchange price or, if there is no such price, according to the current market price or, if there is no commodity exchange price or current market price, by reference to the normal value of Goods of the same kind and quality.

14. Notice of Loss of or Damage to the Goods
(a) Unless notice of loss of or damage to the Goods, specifying the general nature of such loss or damage, is given in writing by the Consignee to the MTO when the Goods are handed over to the Consignee, such handing over is prima facie evidence of the Delivery by the MTO of the Goods as described in the MT Bill of Lading.
(b) Where the loss or damage is not apparent, the same prima facie effect shall apply if notice in writing is not given within six consecutive days after the day when the Goods were handed over to the Consignee.

15. Defences and Limits for the MTO, Servants, etc.
(a) The provisions of this Contract apply to all claims against the MTO relating to the performance of the Multimodal Transport Contract, whether the claim be founded in contract or in tort.
(b) The Merchant undertakes that no claim shall be made against any servant, agent or other persons whose services the MTO has used in order to perform the Multimodal Transport Contract and if any claim should nevertheless be made, to indemnify the MTO against all consequences thereof.
(c) However, the provisions of this Contract apply whenever claims relating to the performance of the Multimodal Transport Contract are made against any servant, agent or other person whose services the MTO has used in order to perform the Multimodal Transport Contract, whether such claims are founded in contract or in tort. In entering into this Contract, the MTO, to the extent of such provisions, does so not only on his own behalf but also as agent or trustee for such persons. The aggregate liability of the MTO and such persons shall not exceed the limits in Clause 12.

IV. DESCRIPTION OF GOODS

16. MTO's Responsibility
The information in the MT Bill of Lading shall be prima facie evidence of the taking in charge by the MTO of the Goods as described by such information unless a contrary indication, such as "shipper's weight, load and count", "shipper-packed container" or similar expressions, have been made in the printed text or superimposed on the document. Proof to the contrary shall not be admissible when the MT Bill of Lading has been transferred, or the equivalent electronic data interchange message has been transmitted to and acknowledged by the Consignee who in good faith has relied and acted thereon.

17. Consignor's Responsibility
(a) The Consignor shall be deemed to have guaranteed to the MTO the accuracy, at the time the Goods were taken in charge by the MTO, of all particulars relating to the general nature of the Goods, their marks, number, weight, volume and quantity and, if applicable, to the dangerous character of the Goods as furnished by him or on his behalf for insertion in the MT Bill of Lading.
(b) The Consignor shall indemnify the MTO for any loss or expense caused by inaccuracies in or inadequacies of the particulars referred to above.
(c) The right of the MTO to such indemnity shall in no way limit his liability under the Multimodal Transport Contract to any person other than the Consignor.
(d) The Consignor shall remain liable even if the MT Bill of Lading has been transferred by him.

18. Return of Containers
a) Containers, pallets or similar articles of transport supplied by or on behalf of the MTO shall be returned to the MTO in the same order and condition as when handed over to the Merchant, normal wear and tear excepted, with interiors clean and within the time prescribed in the MTO's tariff or elsewhere.
b)(i) The Consignor shall be liable for any loss of, damage to, or delay, including demurrage, of such articles, incurred during the period between handing over to the Consignor and return to the MTO for carriage.
(ii) The Consignor and the Consignee shall be jointly and severally liable for any loss of, damage to, or delay, including demurrage, of such articles, incurred during the period between handing over to the Consignee and return to the MTO.

19. Dangerous Goods
(a) The Consignor shall comply with all internationally recognised requirements and all rules which apply according to national law or by reason of international convention, relating to the carriage of Goods of a dangerous nature, and shall in any event inform the MTO in writing of the exact nature of the danger before Goods of a dangerous nature are taken in charge by the MTO and indicate to him, if need be, the precautions to be taken.
(b) If the Consignor fails to provide such information and the MTO is unaware of the dangerous nature of the Goods and the necessary precautions to be taken and if, at any time, they are deemed to be a hazard to life or property, they may at any place be unloaded, destroyed or rendered harmless, as circumstances may require, without compensation and the Consignor shall be liable for all loss, damage, delay or expenses arising out of their being taken in charge, or their carriage, or of any service incidental thereto.
The burden of proving that the MTO knew the exact nature of the danger constituted by the carriage of the said Goods shall rest upon the person entitled to the Goods.
(c) If any Goods shipped with the knowledge of the MTO as to their dangerous nature shall become a danger to the vessel or cargo, they may in like manner be landed at any place or destroyed or rendered innocuous by the MTO without liability on the part of the MTO except to General Average, if any.

20. Consignor-packed Containers, etc.
(a) If a container has not been filled, packed or stowed by the MTO, the MTO shall not be liable for any loss of or damage to its contents and the Consignor shall indemnify any loss or expense incurred by the MTO if such loss, damage or expense has been caused by:
(i) negligent filling, packing or stowing of the container;
(ii) the contents being unsuitable for carriage in container; or
(iii) the unsuitability or defective condition of the container unless the container has been supplied by the MTO and the unsuitability or defective condition would not have been apparent upon reasonable inspection at or prior to the time when the container was filled, packed or stowed.
(b) The provisions of sub-clause (a) of this Clause also apply with respect to trailers, transportable tanks, flats and pallets which have not been filled, packed or stowed by the MTO.
(c) The MTO does not accept liability for damage due to the unsuitability or defective condition of reefer equipment or trailers supplied by the Merchant.

V. FREIGHT AND LIEN

21. Freight
(a) Freight shall be deemed earned when the Goods have been taken into charge by the MTO and shall be paid in any event.
(b) The Merchant's attention is drawn to the stipulations concerning currency in which the freight and charges are to be paid, rate of exchange, devaluation and other contingencies relative to freight and charges in the relevant tariff conditions. If no such stipulation as to devaluation exists or is applicable the following provision shall apply:

If the currency in which freight and charges are quoted is devalued or revalued between the date of the freight agreement and the date when the freight and charges are paid, then all freight and charges shall be automatically and immediately changed in proportion to the extent of the devaluation or revaluation of the said currency. When the MTO has consented to payment in other currency than the above mentioned currency, then all freight and charges shall – subject to the preceding paragraph – be paid at the highest selling rate of exchange for banker's sight draft current on the day when such freight and charges are paid. If the banks are closed on the day when the freight is paid the rate to be used will be the one in force on the last day the banks were open.

(c) For the purpose of verifying the freight basis, the MTO reserves the right to have the contents of containers, trailers or similar articles of transport inspected in order to ascertain the weight, measurement, value, or nature of the Goods. If on such inspection it is found that the declaration is not correct, it is agreed that a sum equal either to five times the difference between the correct freight and the freight charges or to double the correct freight less the freight charges, whichever sum is the smaller, shall be payable as liquidated damages to the MTO notwithstanding any other sum having been stated on this MT Bill of Lading as the freight payable.
(d) All dues, taxes and charges levied on the Goods and other expenses in connection therewith shall be paid by the Merchant.

22. Lien
The MTO shall have a lien on the Goods for any amount due under this Contract and for the costs of recovering the same, and may enforce such lien in any reasonable manner, including sale or disposal of the Goods.

VI. MISCELLANEOUS PROVISIONS

23. General Average
(a) General Average shall be adjusted at any port or place at the MTO's option, and to be settled according to the York-Antwerp Rules 1994, or any modification thereof, this covering all Goods, whether carried on or under deck. The New Jason Clause as approved by BIMCO to be considered as incorporated herein.
(b) Such security including a cash deposit as the MTO may deem sufficient to cover the estimated contribution of the Goods and any salvage and special charges thereon, shall, if required, be submitted to the MTO prior to Delivery of the Goods.

24. Both-to-Blame Collision Clause
The Both-to-Blame Collision Clause as adopted by BIMCO shall be considered incorporated herein.

25. U.S. Trade
In case the Contract evidenced by this MT Bill of Lading is subject to U.S. COGSA, then the provisions stated in said Act shall govern before loading and after discharge and throughout the entire time the Goods are in the Carrier's custody.

Shipped by	**TANKER BILL OF LADING**	1
. . . .		2
Consignee		3
. . . . or order		4
Motor/steam vessel		5
Name of Master		6
Flag		7
Port of Loading		8
Port of Discharge		9
. . . .		10

QUANTITY AND GRADE AS FURNISHED BY THE SHIPPER — 11

(In case of packages or units the exact number should be stated) — 12

.... 13
.... 14
.... 15
.... 16
.... 17
.... 18
.... 19
.... 20

The stated weights and/or quantities and grades are ~plied by the Shipper and these weights and/or — 21
quantities and grades are unknown to the Master. — 22

CLAUSES/ENDORSEMENTS

	Cargo shipped under deck and loading completed — 23
	on the day . . . . of . . . . — 24
	year . . . . in apparent good order and — 25
	condition and to be delivered (subject to the — 26
	liberties, conditions, exceptions and limitations — 27
	hereinafter contained) in the like order and condition — 28
	at named discharge port or so near thereunto as — 29
	she may safely get and there discharge always — 30
	afloat. Freight shall be earned concurrently with — 31
	delivery and calculated on the gross quantity as — 32
	furnished by Shipper. Clauses 1 to 11 inclusive on — 33
	the reverse of this Bill of Lading are incorporated — 34
	herein and form part of this Bill of Lading. — 35
	In witness whereof the Master of the said vessel has — 36
	signed . . . . original Bills of Lading all of — 37
	this tenor and date one of which being accomplished — 38
	the others to stand void. — 39
	. . . . — 40
	MASTER — 41

Printed By Shell NOVEMBER 1991

1. The vessel shall be at liberty

a) to call at any ports, places or transhipment areas in any order for the purpose of loading, transhipping or discharging cargo (including cargo covered by this Bill of Lading) or taking on board bunkers; or

b) to tranship cargo (including cargo covered by this Bill of Lading) to or from any other vessel or vessels in port or at sea by any means including, without limitations to the generality of the foregoing, by ship-to-ship transfer, submarine pipeline, land pipeline and intermediate storage or any one or more of them; or

c) to tow or be towed, to assist vessels in all positions of distress, to sail without pilots and to deviate for the purpose of saving life or property or for the purpose of embarking or disembarking persons, spares or supplies by helicopter; or

d) to deviate for any other reasonable purpose.

2. If on passage to the nominated port or place of discharging the Master finds that such port or place is inaccessible owing to ice, he shall immediately request Cargo Owners by radio for revised orders and remain outside the area of ice-bound waters. Upon receipt of such request Cargo Owners shall give orders for the vessel to proceed to an alternative ice-free and accessible port or place of discharge where there are facilities for receiving the cargo in bulk.

3. If on or after the vessel's arrival at a nominated port or place of discharge there is a danger of the vessel being frozen in, the Master shall proceed to the nearest safe and ice-free position and at the same time request Cargo Owners by radio for revised orders. Immediately upon receipt of such request Cargo Owners shall give orders for the vessel either to proceed to an alternative ice-free and accessible port or place of discharge where there is no danger of the vessel being frozen in and where there are facilities for receiving the cargo in bulk or to return and discharge at the nominated port or place. If the vessel discharges at the nominated port or place, any risk of physical damage to the vessel by reason of her returning to a port or place in which there is a danger of her being frozen in and any delay should she be detained thereon on account of ice shall be for Cargo Owners' account.

4. (A) The Master shall not be required or bound to sign Bills of Lading for any blockaded port or place or for any port or place which the Master or Owners in his or their discretion consider dangerous or impossible to enter or reach.

(B) (i) If the nominated port or place of discharge be blockaded or

(ii) If owing to any war, hostilities, warlike operation, civil war, civil commotions, revolutions, or the operation of international law (a) entry to any such port or place of discharging or discharging of cargo at any such port or place be considered by the Master or Owners in his or their discretion dangerous or prohibited or (b) it be considered by the Master or Owners in his or their discretion dangerous or impossible or prohibited for the vessel to reach such port or place of discharging,

Cargo owners shall have the right to order the cargo or such part of it as may be affected to be discharged at any other port or place of discharging in the vicinity of the said port or place of discharging (provided such other port or place is not blockaded or that entry thereto or discharging of cargo thereat or reaching the same is not in the Master's or Owners' discretion dangerous or prohibited. If in respect of a port or place of discharging no orders be received from Cargo Owners within 48 hours after they or their agents have received from the Owners a request for the nomination of a substitute port or place, Owners shall then be at liberty to discharge the cargo at any port or place which they or the Master may in their or his discretion decide on and such discharging shall be deemed to be due fulfilment of the contract or contracts of affreightment or of the contract contained in or evidenced by this Bill of Lading so far as cargo so discharged is concerned. In the event of the cargo being discharged at any such other port or place the Owners shall be entitled to freight as if the voyage performed were that originally nominated. All extra expenses involved in reaching and discharging the cargo at any such other port shall be paid by the Cargo Owners and Owners shall have a lien on the cargo for freight and all extra expenses.

(C) The vessel shall have liberty to comply with any directions or recommendations as to departure, arrival, routes, ports of call, stoppages, destinations, zones, waters, delivery or in any otherwise whatsoever given by the government of the nation under whose flag the vessel sails or any other government or local authority including any de facto government or local authority or by any person or body acting or purporting to act as or with the authority of any such government or authority or by any committee or person having under the terms of the war risks insurance on the vessel the right to give any such directions or recommendations. If by reason of or in compliance with any such directions or recommendations, anything is done or is not done such shall be deemed not to be a deviation.

If by reason of or in compliance with any such directions or recommendations the vessel does not proceed to the port or ports, place or places of discharging originally nominated or to which she may have been properly ordered pursuant to the terms of this Bill of Lading, the vessel may proceed to any port or place of discharging which the Master or Owners in his or their discretion may decide on and there discharge the cargo. Such discharging shall be deemed to be due fulfilment of the contract or contracts of affreightment or of the contract contained in or evidenced by this Bill of Lading, and Owners shall be entitled to freight as if discharging had been effected at the port or place of discharging originally nominated. All extra expenses involved in reaching and discharging the cargo at any such other port or place of discharging shall be paid by the Cargo Owners and Owners shall have a lien on the cargo for freight and all extra expenses.

5. General Average shall be payable according to the York/Antwerp rules 1974 as amended 1990 and shall be adjusted in London, but should the adjustment be made in accordance with the law and practice of the United States of America, the following clause shall apply:-

NEW JASON CLAUSE – In the event of accident, danger, damage or disaster before or after the commencement of the voyage, resulting from any cause whatsoever, whether due to negligence or not, for which, or for the consequences of which, the Carrier is not responsible, by statute, contract or otherwise, the cargo, shippers, consignees or owners of the cargo shall contribute with the Carrier in General Average to the payment of any sacrifices, losses or expenses of a General Average nature that may be made or incurred, and shall pay the salvage and special charges incurred in respect of the cargo. If a salving vessel is owned or operated by the Carrier, salvage shall be paid for as fully as if the said salving vessel or vessels belong to strangers. Such deposit as the Carrier or his agent may deem sufficient to cover the estimated contribution of the cargo and any salvage and special charges thereon shall, if required, be made by the cargo, shippers, consignees, or Owners of the cargo to the Carrier before delivery.

6. BOTH TO BLAME CLAUSE – If the liability for any collision in which the vessel is involved while performing this Bill of Lading falls to be determined in accordance with the laws of the United States of America, the following clause shall apply:-

BOTH TO BLAME COLLISION CLAUSE – If the vessel comes into collision with another vessel as a result of the negligence of the other vessel and any act, neglect or default of the Master, mariner, pilot or of the servants of the Carrier in the navigation or in the management of the vessel, the owners of the cargo carried hereunder will indemnify the Carrier against all loss or liability to the other or non-carrying vessel or her owners insofar as such loss or liability represents loss of or damage to or any claim whatsoever of the owners of the said cargo paid or payable by the other or non-carrying vessel or her owners to the owners of the said cargo and set off, recouped or recovered by the other or non-carrying vessel or her owners as part of their claim against the carrying vessel or Carrier. The foregoing provisions shall also apply when the owners, operators or those in charge of any vessel or vessels or objects other than, or in addition to, the colliding vessels or objects are at fault in respect of a collision or contact.

7. CLAUSE PARAMOUNT

(1) Subject to sub-clause (2) or (3) hereof, this Bill of Lading shall be governed by, and have effect subject to, the rules contained in the International Convention for the Unification of Certain Rules relating to Bills of Lading signed at Brussels on 25th August 1924 (hereafter the "Hague Rules") as amended by the Protocol signed at Brussels on 23rd February 1968 (hereafter the "Hague-Visby Rules"). Nothing contained herein shall be deemed to be either a surrender by the carrier of any of his rights or immunities or any increase of any of his responsibilities or liabilities under the Hague-Visby Rules.

(2) If there is governing legislation which applies the Hague Rules compulsorily to this Bill of Lading, to the exclusion of the Hague-Visby Rules, then this Bill of Lading shall have effect subject to the Hague Rules. Nothing herein contained shall be deemed to be either a surrender by the carrier of any of his rights or immunities or an increase of any of his responsibilities or liabilities under the Hague Rules.

(3) If there is governing legislation which applies the United Nations Convention on the Carriage of Goods by Sea 1978 (Hamburg Rules) compulsory to this Bill of Lading to the exclusion of the Hague Visby Rules, then this Bill of Lading shall have effect subject to the Hamburg Rules. Nothing herein contained shall be deemed to be either a surrender by the carrier of any of his rights or immunities or an increase of any of his responsibilities or liabilities under the Hamburg Rules.

(4) If any term of this Bill of Lading is repugnant to the Hague Visby Rules, or Hague Rules, if applicable, such term shall be void to that extent but no further.

(5) Nothing in this Bill of Lading shall be construed as in any way restricting, excluding or waiving the right of any relevant party or person to limit his liability under any available legislation and/or law.

8. EXEMPTIONS AND IMMUNITIES OF ALL SERVANTS AND AGENTS OF THE OWNER

No servant or agent of Owners (including every independent contractor from time to time employed by Owners' shall in any circumstances whatsoever be under any liability whatsoever to the shipper, consignees or owner of the cargo or to any holder of this Bill of Lading for any loss, damage or delay of whatsoever kind arising or resulting directly or indirectly from any act, neglect or default on his part while acting in the course of or in connection with his employment, and, without prejudice to the generality of the foregoing provisions in this Clause, every exemption, limitation, condition and liberty herein contained and every right, exemption from liability, defence and immunity of whatsoever nature applicable to Owners or to which Owners are entitled hereunder shall also be available and shall extend to protect every such servant or agent of Owners acting as aforesaid and the purpose of all the foregoing provisions of this Clause. Owners are or shall be deemed to be acting as agent or trustee on behalf of and for the benefit of all persons who are or might be their servants or agents from time to time (including independent contractors as aforesaid) and all such persons shall to this extent be or be deemed to be parties to the contract contained in or evidenced by this Bill of Lading.

9. In the event of the cargo herein mentioned being lost or damaged Owners in addition to the rights, immunities and limitations of liability herein contained or to which they may otherwise be entitled and without prejudice thereto shall be entitled to such limitation of liability in respect of such loss or damage as may be provided by the law of the country of the vessel's flag in force at the date of issue hereof and for the purposes of any limitation of liability neither this Bill of Lading nor the contract contained in or evidenced hereby shall, notwithstanding anything herein contained, be construed to be or to give rise to a personal contract so as to deprive Owners of such limitation.

10. (A) The contract contained in or evidenced by this Bill of Lading shall, notwithstanding any other term set out or incorporated herein, be construed and the relations between the parties determined in accordance with the law of England.

(B) Any dispute arising out of this Bill of Lading shall be decided by the English Courts to whose jurisdiction the parties hereby agree.

Notwithstanding the foregoing, but without prejudice to any party's right to arrest or maintain the arrest of any maritime property, either party may, by giving written notice of election to the other party, elect to have any such dispute referred to the arbitration of a single arbitrator in London in accordance with the provisions of the Arbitration Act 1950, or any statutory modification or re-enactment thereof for the time being in force.

A party shall lose its right to make such an election only if –

(a) it receives from the other party a written notice of dispute which –

(i) states expressly that a dispute has arisen out of this Bill of Lading;

(ii) specifies the nature of the dispute; and

(iii) refers expressly to this Clause 10 (B).

and

(b) it fails to give notice of election to have the dispute referred to arbitration not later than 30 days from the date of receipt of the notice of dispute.

The parties hereby agree that either party may –

(a) appeal to the High Court on any question of law arising out of an award;

(b) apply to the High Court for an order that the arbitrator state the reasons for his award;

(c) give notice to the arbitrator that a reasoned award is required; and

(d) apply to the High Court to determine any questions of law arising in the course of the reference.

It shall be a condition precedent to the right of any party to a stay of any legal proceedings in which maritime property has been, or may be, arrested in connection with a dispute under this Bill of Lading, that that party furnishes to the other party security to which that other party would have been entitled in such legal proceedings in the absence of a stay.

11. Owners shall have an absolute lien upon the cargo to which this Bill of Lading relates and any documents relating thereto for:

(i) all demurrage, shifting expenses and cargo dues, deviation payments, and general average payable under or in connection with the contract contained in or evidenced by this Bill of Lading or payable in connection with the said cargo, and

(ii) the cost of recovery thereof, including any expenses whatsoever arising from the exercise of the lien.

2nd Impression

42
43
44
45
46
47
48
49
50
51
52
53
54
55
56
57
58
59
60
61
62
63
64
65
66
67
68
69
70
71
72
73
74
75
76
77
78
79
80
81
82
83
84
85
86
87
88
89
90
91
92
93
94
95
96
97
98
99
100
101
102
103
104
105
106
107
108
109
110
111
112
113
114
115
116
117
118
119
120
121
122
123
124
125
126
127
128
129
130
131
132
133
134
135
136
137
138
139
140
141
142
143
144

© C of S 1979/1987

*Applicable only when document used as a through bill of lading

Particulars declared by shipper

Shipper	VAT no.

**COMMON
SHORT FORM
BILL OF LADING**

Shipper's reference

Forwarder's reference

B/L no.

Consignee	VAT no.

Name of carrier

Notify party and address

The contract evidenced by this Short Form Bill of Lading is subject to the exceptions, limitations, conditions and liberties (including those relating to pre-carriage and on-carriage) set out in the Carrier's Standard Conditions applicable to the voyage covered by this Short Form Bill of Lading and operative on its date of issue. If the carriage is one where the provisions of the Hague Rules contained in the International Convention for unification of certain rules relating to Bills of Lading, dated Brussels on 25th August, 1924, as amended by the Protocol signed at Brussels on 23rd February, 1968 (the Hague Visby Rules) are compulsorily applicable under Article X, the said Standard Conditions contain or shall be deemed to contain a Clause giving effect to the Hague Visby Rules. Otherwise, except as provided below, the said Standard Conditions contain or shall be deemed to contain a Clause giving effect to the provisions of the Hague Rules.
The Carrier hereby agrees that to the extent of any inconsistency the said clause shall prevail over the exceptions, limitations, conditions and liberties set out in the said Standard Conditions in respect of any period to which the Hague Rules or the Hague Visby Rules by their terms apply. Unless the Standard Conditions expressly provide otherwise, neither the Hague Rules nor the Hague Visby Rules shall apply to this contract where the goods carried hereunder consist of live animals or cargo which by this contract is stated as being carried on deck and is so carried.
Notwithstanding anything contained in the said Standard Conditions, the term Carrier in this Short Form Bill of Lading shall mean the Carrier named on the front thereof.
A copy of the Carrier's said Standard Conditions applicable hereto may be inspected or will be supplied on request at the office of the Carrier or the Carrier's Principal Agents.

Pre-carriage by*	Place of receipt by pre-carrier*
Vessel	Port of loading
Port of discharge	Place of delivery by on-carrier*

Shipping marks; container number	Number and kind of packages; description of goods	Gross weight	Measurement

Freight details; charges etc.

RECEIVED FOR CARRIAGE as above in apparent good order and condition, unless otherwise stated hereon, the goods described in the above particulars.

IN WITNESS whereof the number of original bills of lading stated below have been signed, all of this tenor and date, one of which being accomplished the others to stand void.

| C of S
CSF
BL
1987 | | |

Ocean freight payable at	Place and date of issue
Number of original Bs/L	Signature for carrier; carrier's principal place of business

SPECIMEN

Authorised and licensed by the Chamber of Shipping ©1979/1987/1992

6 Sea Waybills

Non-Negotiable Waybill for Combined Transport shipment or Port to Port shipment

| Shipper | Waybill No.: |
| | Reference: |

Consignee (If the name above in this space is a Bank, the Bank named is specifically excluded from the list of parties coming within the definition of Merchant in the Carrier's contract of carriage and incurs no liability to the Carrier under said contract unless applying for delivery in its own name.)

P&O Nedlloyd

| Notify Party/Address (It is agreed that no responsibility shall attach to the Carrier or his Agents for failure to notify) | Place of Receipt (Applicable only when this document is used as a Combined Transport Waybill) |

| Vessel and Voy. No. | Place of Delivery (Applicable only when this document is used as a Combined Transport Waybill) |

| Port of Loading | Port of Discharge |

Undermentioned particulars as declared by Shipper, but not acknowledged by the Carrier

| Marks and Nos; Container Nos; | Number and kind of Packages; description of Goods | Gross Weight (kg) | Measurement (cbm) |

SPECIMEN WAYBILL

| * Total No. of Containers/Packages received by the Carrier | Movement | Freight payable at |

Received by the Carrier from the Shipper in apparent good order and condition (unless otherwise noted herein) the total number or quantity of Containers or other packages or units indicated in the box above entitled "Total No. of Containers/Packages received by the Carrier" for Carriage from the Place of Receipt or the Port of Loading, whichever applicable, to the Port of Discharge or the Place of Delivery, whichever applicable, SUBJECT TO THE TERMS OF THE CARRIER'S STANDARD BILL OF LADING TERMS AND CONDITIONS AND TARIFF FOR THE RELEVANT TRADE, WHICH ARE MUTATIS MUTANDIS APPLICABLE TO THIS WAYBILL (copies of which may be obtained from the Carrier or his agent). Except for live animals and Goods which are stated herein to be carried on deck and are so carried, these terms and conditions are warranted by the Carrier in respect of the sea portion of the Carriage to apply the Hague Rules or Hague Visby Rules, whichever would have been applicable if this Waybill were a Bill of Lading. In either case the provisions of Article III Rule 4 of the Hague Visby Rules are deemed to be incorporated herein.
The contract evidenced by this Waybill is deemed to be a contract of carriage as defined in Article 1 (b) of the Hague Rules and Hague Visby Rules. However this Waybill is not a document of title to the Goods. Delivery will be made to the Consignee named, or his authorised agents, on production of proof of identity at the Port of Discharge or the Place of Delivery, whichever applicable. Should the Consignee require delivery to a party and/or premises other than as shown above in the "Consignee" box, then written instructions must be given by the Consignee to the Carrier or his agent. Unless the Shipper expressly waives his right to control the Goods until delivery by means of a clause on the face hereof, such instructions from the Consignee will be subject to any instruction to the contrary by the Shipper:
Unless instructed to the contrary by the Shipper prior to the commencement of Carriage and noted accordingly on the face hereof, the Carrier will, subject to the aforesaid terms and conditions, process cargo claims with the Consignee. Claims settlement, if any, shall be a complete discharge of the Carrier's liability to the Shipper. The Shipper accepts the said standard terms and conditions on his own behalf, on behalf of the Consignee and the Owner of the Goods, and authorises the Consignee to bring suit against the Carrier in his own name but as agent of the Shipper, and warrants that he has authority so to accept and authorise. The Shipper further undertakes that no claim or allegation in respect of the Goods shall be made against the Carrier by any person other than in accordance with the terms and conditions of this Waybill.

| This Waybill is issued subject to the CMI Uniform Rules For Sea Waybills | Place and Date of Issue | IN WITNESS whereof this Waybill is signed. |

P&O Nedlloyd

P&O Nedlloyd Ltd, Beagle House, Braham Street, London E1 8EP   3/DRS W/B2 5/97 (C)

Code Name: "MULTIWAYBILL 95"

Consignor

MT Doc. No.

Reference No.

MULTIMODAL TRANSPORT WAYBILL

Issued by The Baltic and International Maritime Council (BIMCO), subject to the UNCTAD/ICC Rules for Multimodal Transport Documents (ICC Publication No. 481) and to the CMI Uniform Rules for Sea Waybills

Issued 1995

Consignee (not to order)

Notify party/address

Place of receipt

Ocean Vessel   Port of loading

Port of discharge   Place of delivery

Marks and Nos.   Quantity and description of goods   Gross weight, kg, Measurement, m³

Particulars above declared by Consignor

Freight and charges

RECEIVED the goods in apparent good order and condition and, as far as ascertained by reasonable means of checking, as specified above unless otherwise stated.

The MTO, in accordance with and to the extent of the provisions contained in this MT Waybill, and with liberty to sub-contract, undertakes to perform and/or in his own name to procure performance of the multimodal transport and the delivery of the goods, including all services related thereto, from the place and time of taking the goods in charge to the place and time of delivery and accepts responsibility for such transport and such services.

The Consignor shall be entitled to transfer right of control of the cargo to the Consignee, the exercise of such option to be noted on this MT Waybill and to be made no later than the receipt of the cargo by the Carrier.

Consignor's declared value of .....   Freight payable at   Place and date of issue

subject to payment of above extra charge.

Signed for the Multimodal Transport Operator as (MTO)

.... as Carrier

Note:
The Merchant's attention is called to the fact that according to Clauses 10 to 12 of this MT Waybill, the liability of the MTO is, in most cases, limited in respect of loss of or damage to the goods.

by ....

As agent(s) only to the MTO

p.t.o.

NON-NEGOTIABLE SPECIMEN

Printed and sold by Fr. G. Knudtzon Ltd., 55 Toldbodgade, DK-1253 Copenhagen K, Telefax +45 33 93 11 84 by authority of The Baltic and International Maritime Council (BIMCO), Copenhagen

Copyright, published by The Baltic and International Maritime Council (BIMCO), Copenhagen, 1995

MULTIMODAL TRANSPORT WAYBILL

CODE NAME: "MULTIWAYBILL 95"

I. GENERAL PROVISIONS

1. Applicability

The provisions of this Contract shall apply irrespective of whether there is a unimodal or a Multimodal Transport Contract involving one or several modes of transport.

2. Definitions

"Multimodal Transport Contract" means a single Contract for the carriage of Goods by at least two different modes of transport.

"Multimodal Transport Waybill" (MT Waybill) means this document evidencing a Multimodal Transport Contract and which can be replaced by electronic data interchange messages insofar as permitted by applicable law and is issued in a non-negotiable form clearly indicating a named Consignee.

"Multimodal Transport Operator" (MTO) means the person named on the face hereof who concludes a Multimodal Transport Contract and assumes responsibility for the performance thereof as a Carrier.

"Carrier" means the person who actually performs or undertakes to perform the carriage, or part thereof, whether he is identical with the Multimodal Transport Operator or not.

"Merchant" includes the Shipper, the Receiver, the Consignor, the Consignee and the owner of the Goods.

"Consignor" means the person who concludes the Multimodal Transport Contract with the Multimodal Transport Operator.

"Consignee" means the person entitled to receive the Goods from the Multimodal Transport Operator.

"Taken in charge" means that the Goods have been handed over to and accepted for carriage by the MTO.

"Delivery" means
(i) the handing over of the Goods to the Consignee; or
(ii) the placing of the Goods at the disposal of the Consignee in accordance with the Multimodal Transport Contract or with the law or usage of the particular trade applicable at the place of delivery; or
(iii) the handing over of the Goods to an authority or other third party to whom, pursuant to the law or regulations applicable at the place of delivery, the Goods must be handed over.

"Special Drawing Rights" (SDR) means the unit of account as defined by the International Monetary Fund.

"Goods" means any property including live animals as well as containers, pallets or similar articles of transport or packaging not supplied by the MTO, irrespective of whether such property is to be or is carried on or under deck.

3. MTO's Tariff

The terms of the MTO's applicable tariff at the date of shipment are incorporated herein. Copies of the relevant provisions of the applicable tariff are available from the MTO upon request. In the case of inconsistency between this MT Waybill and the applicable tariff, this MT Waybill shall prevail.

4. Time Bar

The MTO shall, unless otherwise expressly agreed, be discharged of all liability under this MT Waybill unless suit is brought within nine months after:
(i) the Delivery of the Goods; or
(ii) the date when the Goods should have been delivered; or
(iii) the date when, in accordance with sub-clause 10 (e) failure to deliver the Goods would give the Consignee the right to treat the Goods as lost.

5. Law and Jurisdiction

Disputes arising under this MT Waybill shall be determined by the courts and in accordance with the law at the place where the MTO has his principal place of business.

II. PERFORMANCE OF THE CONTRACT

6. Methods and Routes of Transportation

(a) The MTO is entitled to perform the transport in any reasonable manner and by any reasonable means, methods and routes.
(b) In accordance herewith, for instance, in the event of carriage by sea, vessels may sail with or without pilots, undergo repairs, adjust equipment, drydock and tow vessels in all situations.

7. Optional Stowage

(a) Goods may be stowed by the MTO by means of containers, trailers, transportable tanks, flats, pallets, or similar articles of transport used to consolidate Goods.
(b) Containers, trailers, transportable tanks and covered flats, whether stowed by the MTO or received by him in a stowed condition, may be carried on or under deck without notice to the Merchant.

8. Delivery of the Goods to the Consignee

The MTO undertakes to perform or to procure the performance of all acts necessary to ensure Delivery of the Goods, upon proof of his identity, to the person named as Consignee in the document or a person as instructed by the Consignor or by a person who has acquired the Consignor's or the Consignee's rights under the Multimodal Transport Contract to give such instructions.

9. Hindrances, etc. Affecting Performance

(a) The MTO shall use reasonable endeavours to complete the transport and to deliver the Goods at the place designated for Delivery.
(b) If at any time the performance of the Contract as evidenced by this MT Waybill is or will be affected by any hindrance, risk, delay, difficulty or disadvantage of whatsoever kind, and if by virtue of sub-clause 9 (a) the MTO has no duty to complete the performance of the Contract, the MTO (whether or not the transport is commenced) may elect to
(i) treat the performance of this Contract as terminated and place the Goods at the Merchant's disposal at any place which the MTO shall deem safe and convenient; or
(ii) deliver the Goods at the place designated for Delivery.
(c) If the Goods are not taken Delivery of by the Merchant within a reasonable time after the MTO has called upon him to take Delivery, the MTO shall be at liberty to put the Goods in safe custody on behalf of the Merchant at the latter's risk and expense.
(d) In any event the MTO shall be entitled to full freight for Goods received for transportation and additional compensation for extra costs resulting from the circumstances referred to above.

III. LIABILITY OF THE MTO

10. Basis of Liability

(a) The responsibility of the MTO for the Goods under this Contract covers the period from the time the MTO has taken the Goods into his charge to the time of their Delivery.
(b) Subject to the defences set forth in Clauses 11 and 12, the MTO shall be liable for loss of or damage to the Goods, as well as for delay in Delivery, if the occurrence which caused the loss, damage or delay in Delivery took place while the Goods were in his charge as defined in sub-clause 10 (a), unless the MTO proves that no fault or neglect of his own, his servants or agents or any other person referred to in sub-clause 10 (c) has caused or contributed to the loss, damage or delay in Delivery. However, the MTO shall only be liable for loss following from delay in Delivery if the Consignor has made a written declaration of interest in timely Delivery which has been accepted in writing by the MTO.
(c) The MTO shall be responsible for the acts and omissions of his servants or agents, when any such servant or agent is acting within the scope of his employment, or of any other person of whose services he makes use for the performance of the Contract, as if such acts and omissions were his own.
(d) Delay in Delivery occurs when the Goods have not been delivered within the time expressly agreed upon or, in the absence of such agreement, within the time which it would be reasonable to require of a diligent MTO, having regard to the circumstances of the case.
(e) If the Goods have not been delivered within ninety (90) consecutive days following the date of Delivery determined according to Clause 10 (d) above, the claimant may, in the absence of evidence to the contrary, treat the Goods as lost.

11. Defences for Carriage by Sea or Inland Waterways

Notwithstanding the provisions of Clause 10 (b), the MTO shall not be responsible for loss, damage or delay in Delivery with respect to Goods carried by sea or inland waterways when such loss, damage or delay during such carriage results from:
(i) act, neglect or default of the master, mariner, pilot or the servants of the Carrier in the navigation or in the management of the vessel;
(ii) fire, unless caused by the actual fault or privity of the Carrier;
(iii) the causes listed in the Hague-Visby Rules article 4.2 (c) to (p);
however, always provided that whenever loss or damage has resulted from unseaworthiness of the vessel, the MTO can prove that due diligence has been exercised to make the vessel seaworthy at the commencement of the voyage.

12. Limitation of Liability

(a) Unless the nature and value of the Goods have been declared by the Consignor before the Goods have been taken in charge by the MTO and inserted in the MT Waybill, the MTO shall in no event be or become liable for any loss of or damage to the Goods in an amount exceeding:
(i) when the Carriage of Goods by Sea Act of the United States of America, 1936 (US COGSA) applies USD 500 per package or customary freight unit; or
(ii) when any other law applies, the equivalent of 666.67 SDR per package or unit or two SDR per kilogramme of gross weight of the Goods lost or damaged, whichever is the higher.
(b) Where a container, pallet, or similar article of transport is loaded with more than one package or unit, the packages or other shipping units enumerated in the MT Waybill as packed in such article of transport are deemed packages or shipping units. Except as aforesaid, such article of transport shall be considered the package or unit.
(c) Notwithstanding the above-mentioned provisions, if the Multimodal Transport does not, according to the Contract, include carriage of Goods by sea or by inland waterways, the liability of the MTO shall be limited to an amount not exceeding 8.33 SDR per kilogramme of gross weight of the Goods lost or damaged.
(d) In any case, when the loss of or damage to the Goods occurred during one particular stage of the Multimodal Transport, in respect of which an applicable international convention or mandatory national law would have provided another limit of liability if a separate contract of carriage had been made for that particular stage of transport, then the limit of the MTO's liability for such loss or damage shall be determined by reference to the provisions of such convention or mandatory national law.
(e) If the MTO is liable in respect of loss following from delay in Delivery, or consequential loss or damage other than loss of or damage to the Goods, the liability of the MTO shall be limited to an amount not exceeding the equivalent of the freight under the Multimodal Transport Contract for the Multimodal Transport.
(f) The aggregate liability of the MTO shall not exceed the limits of liability for total loss of the Goods.
(g) The MTO is not entitled to the benefit of the limitation of liability if it is proved that the loss, damage or delay in Delivery resulted from a personal act or omission of the MTO done with the intent to cause such loss, damage or delay, or recklessly and with knowledge that such loss, damage or delay would probably result.

13. Assessment of Compensation

(a) Assessment of compensation for loss of or damage to the Goods shall be made by reference to the value of such Goods at the place and time they are delivered to the Consignee or at the place and time when, in accordance with the Multimodal Transport Contract, they should have been so delivered.
(b) The value of the Goods shall be determined according to the current commodity exchange price or, if there is no such price, according to the current market price or, if there is no commodity exchange price or current market price, by reference to the normal value of Goods of the same kind and quality.

14. Notice of Loss of or Damage to the Goods

(a) Unless notice of loss of or damage to the Goods, specifying the general nature of such loss or damage, is given in writing by the Consignee to the MTO when the Goods are handed over to the Consignee, such handing over is prima facie evidence of the Delivery by the MTO of the Goods as described in the MT Waybill.
(b) Where the loss or damage is not apparent, the same prima facie effect shall apply if notice in writing is not given within six consecutive days after the day when the Goods were handed over to the Consignee.

15. Defences and Limits for the MTO, Servants, etc.

(a) The provisions of this Contract apply to all claims against the MTO relating to the performance of the Multimodal Transport Contract, whether the claim be founded in contract or in tort.
(b) The Merchant undertakes that no claim shall be made against any servant, agent or other persons whose services the MTO has used in order to perform the Multimodal Transport Contract and if any claim should nevertheless be made, to indemnify the MTO against all consequences thereof.
(c) However, the provisions of this Contract apply whenever claims relating to the performance of the Multimodal Transport Contract are made against any servant, agent or other person whose services the MTO has used in order to perform the Multimodal Transport Contract, whether such claims are founded in contract or in tort. In entering into this Contract, the MTO, to the extent of such provisions, does so not only on his own behalf but also as agent or trustee for such persons. The aggregate liability of the MTO and such persons shall not exceed the limits in Clause 12.

IV. DESCRIPTION OF GOODS

16. MTO's Responsibility

The information in the MT Waybill shall be prima facie evidence of the taking in charge by the MTO of the Goods as described by such information unless a contrary indication, such as "shipper's weight, load and count", "shipper-packed container" or similar expressions, have been made in the printed text or superimposed on the document. As between the Carrier and the Consignee the information in the MT Waybill shall be conclusive evidence of receipt of the Goods as so stated and proof to the contrary shall not be permitted provided always that the Consignee has acted in good faith.

17. Consignor's Responsibility

(a) The Consignor shall be deemed to have guaranteed to the MTO the accuracy, at the time the Goods were taken in charge by the MTO, of all particulars relating to the general nature of the Goods, their marks, number, weight, volume and quantity and, if applicable, to the dangerous character of the Goods as furnished by him or on his behalf for insertion in the MT Waybill.
(b) The Consignor shall indemnify the MTO for any loss or expense caused by inaccuracies in or inadequacies of the particulars referred to above.
(c) The right of the MTO to such indemnity shall in no way limit his liability under the Multimodal Transport Contract to any person other than the Consignor.
(d) The Consignor shall remain liable even if the Goods have been delivered.

18. Return of Containers

a) Containers, pallets or similar articles of transport supplied by or on behalf of the MTO shall be returned to the MTO in the same order and condition as handed over to the Merchant, normal wear and tear excepted, with interiors clean and within the time prescribed in the MTO's tariff or elsewhere.
b)(i) The Consignor shall be liable for any loss of, damage to, or delay, including demurrage, of such articles, incurred during the period between handing over to the Consignor and return to the MTO for carriage.
(ii) The Consignor and the Consignee shall be jointly and severally liable for any loss of, damage to, or delay, including demurrage, of such articles, incurred during the period between handing over to the Consignee and return to the MTO.

19. Dangerous Goods

(a) The Consignor shall comply with all internationally recognised requirements and all rules which apply according to national law or by reason of international convention, relating to the carriage of Goods of a dangerous nature, and shall in any event inform the MTO in writing of the exact nature of the danger before Goods of a dangerous nature are taken in charge by the MTO and indicate to him, if need be, the precautions to be taken.
(b) If the Consignor fails to provide such information and the MTO is unaware of the dangerous nature of the Goods and the necessary precautions to be taken and if, at any time, they are deemed to be a hazard to life or property, they may at any place be unloaded, destroyed or rendered harmless, as circumstances may require, without compensation and the Consignor shall be liable for all loss, damage, delay or expenses arising out of their being taken in charge, or their carriage, or of any service incidental thereto.
The burden of proving that the MTO knew the exact nature of the danger constituted by the carriage of the said Goods shall rest upon the Claimant.
(c) If any Goods shipped with the knowledge of the MTO as to their dangerous nature shall become a danger to the vessel or cargo, they may in like manner be landed at any place or destroyed or rendered innocuous by the MTO without liability on the part of the MTO except to General Average, if any.

20. Consignor-packed Containers, etc.

(a) If a container has not been filled, packed or stowed by the MTO, the MTO shall not be liable for any loss of or damage to its contents and the Consignor shall indemnify any loss or expense incurred by the MTO if such loss, damage or expense has been caused by:
(i) negligent filling, packing or stowing of the container;
(ii) the contents being unsuitable for carriage in container; or
(iii) the unsuitability or defective condition of the container unless the container has been supplied by the MTO and the unsuitability or defective condition would not have been apparent upon reasonable inspection at or prior to the time when the container was filled, packed or stowed.
(b) The provisions of sub-clause (a) of this Clause also apply with respect to trailers, transportable tanks, flats and pallets which have not been filled, packed or stowed by the MTO.
(c) The MTO does not accept liability for damage due to the unsuitability or defective condition of reefer equipment or trailers supplied by the Merchant.

V. FREIGHT AND LIEN

21. Freight

(a) Freight shall be deemed earned when the Goods have been taken into charge by the MTO and shall be paid in any event.
(b) The Merchant's attention is drawn to the stipulations concerning currency in which the freight and charges are to be paid, rate of exchange, devaluation and other contingencies relative to freight and charges in the relevant tariff conditions. If no such stipulation as to devaluation exists or is applicable the following provision shall apply:
If the currency in which freight and charges are quoted is devalued or revalued between the date of the freight agreement and the date when the freight and charges are paid, then all freight and charges shall be automatically and immediately changed in proportion to the extent of the devaluation or revaluation of the said currency. When the MTO has consented to payment in other currency than the above mentioned currency, then all freight and charges shall – subject to the preceding paragraph – be paid at the highest selling rate of exchange for banker's sight draft current on the day when such freight and charges are paid. If the banks are closed on the day when the freight is paid the rate to be used will be the one in force on the last day the banks were open.
(c) For the purpose of verifying the freight basis, the MTO reserves the right to have the contents of containers, trailers or similar articles of transport inspected in order to ascertain the weight, measurement, value, or nature of the Goods. If on such inspection it is found that the declaration is not correct, it is agreed that a sum equal either to five times the difference between the correct freight and the freight charges or to double the correct freight less the freight charges, whichever sum is the smaller, shall be payable as liquidated damages to the MTO notwithstanding any other sum having been stated on this MT Waybill as the freight payable.
(d) All dues, taxes and charges levied on the Goods and other expenses in connection therewith shall be paid by the Merchant.

22. Lien

The MTO shall have a lien on the Goods for any amount due under this Contract and for the costs of recovering the same, and may enforce such lien in any reasonable manner, including sale or disposal of the Goods.

VI. MISCELLANEOUS PROVISIONS

23. General Average

(a) General Average shall be adjusted at any port or place at the MTO's option, and to be settled according to the York-Antwerp Rules 1994, or any modification thereof, this covering all Goods, whether carried on or under deck. The New Jason Clause as approved by BIMCO to be considered as incorporated herein.
(b) Such security including a cash deposit as the MTO may deem sufficient to cover the estimated contribution of the Goods and any salvage and special charges thereon, shall, if required, be submitted to the MTO prior to Delivery of the Goods.

24. Both-to-Blame Collision Clause

The Both-to-Blame Collision Clause as adopted by BIMCO shall be considered incorporated herein.

25. U.S. Trade

In case the Contract evidenced by this MT Waybill is subject to U.S. COGSA, then the provisions stated in said Act shall govern before loading and after discharge and throughout the entire time the Goods are in the Carrier's custody.

© C of S 1979/1987

*Applicable only when document used as a Through Sea Waybill

Particulars declared by shipper

Shipper	VAT no.

NON-NEGOTIABLE SEA WAYBILL

SWB No.

Shipper's reference

Forwarder's reference

Consignee	VAT no.

Name of carrier

Notify Party and Address

The contract evidenced by this Waybill is subject to the exceptions, limitations, conditions and liberties (including those relating to pre-carriage and on-carriage) set out in the Carrier's Standard Conditions of Carriage applicable to the voyage covered by this Waybill and operative on its date of issue: if the carriage is one where had a Bill of Lading been issued the provisions of the Hague Rules contained in the International Convention for unification of certain rules relating to Bills of Lading, dated Brussels, 25th August, 1924, as amended by the Protocol signed at Brussels on the 23rd February, 1968 (the Hague Visby Rules) are compulsorily applicable under Article X, the said Standard Conditions contain or shall be deemed to contain a Clause giving effect to the Hague Visby Rules. Otherwise the said Standard Conditions contain or shall be deemed to contain a Clause giving effect to the provisions of the Hague Rules. In neither case shall the proviso to the first sentence of Article V of the Hague Rules or the Hague Visby Rules apply. The Carrier hereby agrees (i) that to the extent of any inconsistency the said clause shall prevail over the said Standard Conditions in respect of any period to which the Hague Rules or the Hague Visby Rules by their terms apply, and (ii) that for the purpose of the terms of this Contract of Carriage this Waybill falls within the definition of Article 1(b) of the Hague Rules and the Hague Visby Rules.

The shipper accepts the said Standard Conditions on his own behalf and on behalf of the Consignee and the owner of the goods and warrants that he has authority to do so. The consignee by presenting this Waybill and/or requesting delivery of the goods further undertakes all liabilities of the Shipper hereunder, such undertaking being additional and without prejudice to the Shipper's own liability. The benefit of the contract, evidenced by this Waybill shall thereby be transferred to the Consignee or other persons presenting this Waybill.

Notwithstanding anything contained in the said Standard Conditions, the term Carrier in this Waybill shall mean the Carrier named on the front hereof.

A copy of the Carrier's said Standard Conditions applicable hereto may be inspected or will be supplied on request at the office of the Carrier or the Carrier's Principal Agents.

Pre-carriage by*	Place of receipt by pre-carrier*
Vessel	Port of loading
Port of discharge	Place of delivery by on-carrier*

Shipping marks; container number	Number and kind of packages; description of goods	Gross weight	Measurement

Freight details; charges etc.

RECEIVED FOR CARRIAGE as above in apparent good order and condition, unless otherwise stated hereon, the goods described in the above particulars.

C of S
SWB
1987

Ocean freight payable at	Place and date of issue
	Signature for carrier; carrier's principal place of business

Authorised and licensed by the Chamber of Shipping ©1979/1987

THE HAMBURG RULES

Bills of Lading

Report by the secretariat of UNCTAD

[United Nations Conference on Trade and Development, Geneva]

Published by the United Nations, New York, 1971

ECONOMIC ASPECTS

A. Introduction

146. The bill of lading is a commercial document performing a complex set of functions. So far as its commercial aspects are concerned, the question is how these functions are defined, and how effectively they are performed ... [B]y and large, except for certain weaknesses as a receipt, the bill of lading fulfils its function reasonably effectively. This conclusion does not, however, express any opinion concerning the costs imposed on trade by modern practice relating to the bill of lading. In other words, commercial effectiveness and economic efficiency are different things.

147. Clearly, there must be an economic cost. The organization of trade and the related documentation, the making and settling of claims for lost and damaged cargo and all the other activities connected with the facilitation of trade involve costs. Hence, the pertinent question is not whether the bill of lading imposes costs on trade. The answer to that question is clearly that it imposes costs, and even the most perfect commercial instrument which could be devised would impose costs. The pertinent question which has to be asked consists of two parts. First, what is the level of the economic costs imposed in relation to the commercial function performed (that is, the cost effectiveness)? Secondly, on whom do the costs fall? This second question is relevant, whether or not the economic costs are shown to be reasonable in the circumstances.

148. The present chapter is concerned with these two questions and it shows that the bill of lading as at present constituted fails on the grounds of cost effectiveness – that is, the costs imposed are too high in relation to the commercial functions performed – and that the costs fall more heavily on the cargo owner than seems to be justified.

149. Most of the difficulties to be discussed arise when cargo is lost or damaged and the cargo owner lodges a claim with the carrier for compensation. To give a qualitative perspective to the discussion, the UNCTAD secretariat endeavoured to obtain information regarding cargo claims for a recent year. It hoped to be able to show the total value of cargo carried by ocean transport during the particular year and, in relation to this, to show the value of cargo claims made. The figures would then have indicated the magnitude of the losses suffered by cargo owners as a result of loss, damage or delay to cargo. The secretariat hoped to break down the figure of

cargo claims to show what percentage of these was accepted in full by the carriers, what percentage of the claims was settled by compromise and what percentage was rejected.

150. Had this specific data been available, not only would a valuable perspective have been given, but the extent to which claims were rejected would have been a first indication of the impact of the exceptions listed under article 4, paragraph 2, of the Hague Rules, which permit carriers to avoid liability for cargo damage in a large number of circumstances. Similarly, the value of the claims settled by compromise might have provided some indication of the uncertainty inherent in the functioning of the Rules. The data could have been no more than indicative, and certainly no definitive judgement as to whether the economic costs were excessive or not could have been based on the results.

151. Questions were asked of bodies such as the International Chamber of Shipping, and in the questionnaire sent by the secretariat to shipping lines and to insurers in order to obtain the required information. Global figures could not be obtained, since no organization collects the data. Although a good deal of information was obtained regarding the experience of individual insurers, P and I clubs and shipping lines, this did not enable the secretariat to calculate the desired magnitudes. With regard to the settlement of claims, the experience reported by different respondents was so diverse that no meaningful indications could be derived. In some cases, for example, up to three-quarters of the claims made were accepted by the carriers, while in other cases the proportion of claims accepted was as low as 20 per cent.

152. In consequence, a quantitative perspective which would be in any sense useful cannot be given. It must be stressed, however, that the lack of sufficient quantitative information in no way prevents economic judgements from being made. Indeed, even if it had been obtained, the information would have been indicative only, a useful background, but nothing approaching a "proof" of the scale of the problem. In fact, there are many aspects of economic performance in the world which are, by their nature, not quantifiable, and the cost effectiveness of the bill of lading is one of these. This inability to quantify the problem is inherent in the situation, not simply attributable to lack of data.

B. Cost effectiveness of the bill of lading

153. The question of the cost effectiveness of the bill of lading resolves itself primarily into that of where the risk for loss lies and who bears the costs of insuring against that risk. There are other less important points, some of which will be considered briefly.

Overlapping insurance

154. Cargo owners insure those risks ... which they feel obliged to cover either because liability for such risks is not accepted by carriers or because the risks are uncertainly allocated between the parties concerned or, by not being specified, apparently fall on the cargo owner. Ideally, cargo owners should not need to insure against the risk of loss or damage to their goods which is covered by the liabilities falling upon the carrier under the contract of carriage. These risks and liabilities are spelt out in article 3 of the Rules, which provides, inter alia, that, apart from the carrier's obligation to make the ship seaworthy,

he is required, subject to article 4 (which specifies his rights and immunities), to properly and carefully load, handle, stow, carry, keep, care for and discharge the goods carried.

155. It will be seen from the analysis in chapter VI below that the apportionment and definition of risks and liabilities are not at all clearly demarcated in the Rules, and that the position is further complicated by the uncertainties concerning such matters as the burden of proof, and procedure. Thus, it often happens that cargo owners have no alternative but to over-insure, lest they be exposed to the incidence of risk for which carriers might not compensate them, even though carriers may be liable to do so under the Rules.

156. The extent of the insurance cover is a matter of individual preference on the part of the cargo owner. If he purchases the maximum cover – eg an all-risks policy – he will almost certainly be over-insured, since it will include liabilities for which the carrier would ordinarily be responsible. Alternatively, he can insure under a limited form of policy, e.g. against total loss of cargo only, in which case, in the event of less-than-total loss, he would be under-insured, in that this less-than-total loss is not covered. Insurance policies are not usually issued for individual risks. The assured generally enters into a 'package deal', and among the risks covered by the premium paid by the cargo owner will be included those for which his contract of carriage places the liability on the carrier. Thus, the additional insurance by the cargo owner includes insurance against risks for which the carriers are already responsible. In this way, insurance policies overlap, since both carrier and cargo owner are insuring against the same risks.

157. It might be useful to illustrate how ambiguity in the definition of risks can lead to overlapping insurance. One can take as an example the risk of perils of the sea, in respect of which the carrier is immune from liability under his contract of carriage and against which the cargo owner can insure. Overlapping insurance can arise in this way: the immunities can be construed, in one sense, '... as a list of possible causes for loss of or damage to cargo for which the carrier cannot be blamed. As such, the catalogue has of course no legal significance – there are obviously a number of other causes which might be relied upon by a carrier to exculpate himself'. This means that until a cargo owner accepts a statement by the carrier that a peril of the sea caused the loss, and that the loss is therefore unrecompensable, or it is so decided by arbitration or litigation, the words of the immunity clause have no operative legal force of their own but are of uncertain effect. Accordingly, the cargo owner has to continue insuring against 'perils of the sea', even though there may be circumstances in which the carrier would be liable to him for loss caused by perils of the sea.

158. It was precisely this type of uncertainty in the working of the law which was in the mind of Sir Norman Hill, the principal spokesman for British shipowners in many international conferences, when he said '... those doubts and uncertainties have for 50 years burdened overseas commerce with the cost of double insurance in respect of many of the risks incident to the voyage'. Although these statements were made before the Hague Rules came into general operation, the position is not markedly different today.

159. If cargo owners could be certain of being covered against some risks by the carrier under the contract of carriage, and if they could be assured that they could recover the full value of their claims, they would have no need to go outside their terms of carriage and pay premiums to cargo insurers to cover the same risks. Under existing laws and practices, this does not seem to be possible. They must, therefore, pay unnecessary premium for so long as the uncertainty remains.

Shifting the risk as a measure of economic effectiveness

160. Overlapping insurance arises because of uncertainty as to where the risk for loss or damage lies. Such uncertainty is inevitable when the division of the risks between the carrier and the cargo owner is not clear, as is the case under the Hague Rules. The uncertainty can be reduced by clearly demarcating the respective risks of the parties concerned, but since even in that situation argument could arise about the physical circumstances of the loss, uncertainty can be eliminated only by shifting all of the risks on to either the carrier or the cargo owner. Thus to determine whether the present economic costs are or are not excessive, one has to compare the present level of costs with what that level would be if all risks were clearly moved on to either the carrier or the cargo owner.

161. For the sake of argument, the problem of overlapping insurance will be assumed to be non-existent. It will be assumed that through insurance by the carrier and the cargo owner all risks are exactly covered, no more, no less. If this were the position, then there is no reason to believe that a redistribution of risks would necessarily lead to any increase in the over-all cost of insurance. What would happen if, for example, risks were redistributed so that the carrier bore more, is that freight rates quoted to include insurance in a CIF sales contract would rise, but their rise would be exactly matched by a fall in the insurance costs borne by the cargo owner. Similarly, if all the risks were shifted towards the cargo owner, freight rates, where they include insurance, should fall, while the cargo owner's insurance costs would rise. There are three circumstances in which it appears that this might not happen.

162. The first circumstance is where there was a marked difference in the costs of the insurance bought by the carrier and that bought by the cargo owner. In this case, if more risks were attributed to the party for whom the insurance was the more expensive, then total costs would rise. However, it is more logical that risks should be shifted towards the carrier than that they should be shifted towards the cargo owner. Generally, the carrier rather than the cargo owner will have the benefit of lower insurance costs because he operates on a larger scale. Therefore, the likelihood of a rise in costs in this circumstance is remote. An advantage of shifting the risk to the cargo owner is that he may have a clearer idea of the value of the cargo than the shipowner and may thus more easily avoid any costs of over-insurance which might be incurred if the carrier arranged all the insurance.

163. The second circumstance is that in which a shift of the risks might lead to more insurance being bought than was previously the case. It was assumed above that all risks were exactly covered by insurance. In fact, the cargo owner may at present undertake no more insurance than that which is implied in the

CIF contract. In this case, if the carrier takes on more liabilities, he will insure against them, and the insurance element in the freight rate will rise correspondingly. The cargo owner will thus be paying more than before, because his goods will be covered by additional insurance, which presumably he would prefer to do without, this preference being inferred from the fact that he did not formerly take out such additional insurance. However, he is only in this position so long as he is forced to accept a CIF contract and unable to find a C and F contract. If any redistribution of the risks was associated with a provision to the effect that no cargo owner should be forced to accept a CIF contract if it stipulated more insurance than he wished to buy, then no extra cost would arise. Even if extra costs were involved, it must be emphasized that this extra cost would arise not because the cost of the same amount of insurance had risen but because more insurance was being bought.

164. The third circumstance in which costs might rise would occur if P and I clubs took a very pessimistic view of the volume of claims to be met and increased contributions from their members very sharply to cover a larger volume of claims. The shipping lines would then increase their freight rates to cover the extra P and I insurance. At the end of the year, when the P and I clubs found that they had overprovided, the shipping lines would not necessarily reduce their freight rates and certainly would not return to shippers the excess insurance costs which they had charged to them. This chain of events is probably a fairly unlikely one. It implies that all P and I clubs extract from their members at the beginning of a period enough money to cover all the claims that may arise during the period. If, in practice, they receive a contribution from their members at the beginning of the period and then ask for supplementary contributions as experience during the period is gained and the exact volume of losses is known, then the course of events outlined above does not occur. Further, there is not in fact any additional economic cost, since the extra cost to the cargo owner (i.e. the higher freight rate) is exactly matched by an extra gain to the carrier. There will have been a changed incidence of cost, but no change in costs.

165. Thus, it can be seen that action to shift all risks towards the carrier would not increase the overall costs of exactly covering these risks. Clearly, therefore, the economic cost of the present regime is excessive, the excess being exactly indicated by the extent of overlapping insurance which arises because of uncertainty.

Delay in settlement

166. One economic cost arises from delay in the settlement of claims. If there is no uncertainty as to who bears the risks, then, when once the fact of loss or damage has been proved, there is no reason why cargo claims should not be settled immediately. In the situation of uncertainty, however, the settlement of claims is frequently very protracted. For example, one shipping line reported to the UNCTAD secretariat that by the end of 1969 over one-third of the claims made in 1968 had not been dealt with. There is a clear economic cost here, only partly offset by the savings in interest cost on the part of the carrier, who enjoys the use of funds belonging to the cargo owner during the period until settlement is made.

Arbitration and litigation

167. There are two aspects to this question. Owing to complexities and uncertainties, more claims go to arbitration or result in litigation than if the procedures were more clear-cut. Arbitration and litigation manifestly impose costs, including the indirect or unpaid element of the time which carriers and cargo owners spend in preparing for and attending proceedings. The cost of travelling to attend arbitration and litigation proceedings is also high. Carriers usually stipulate in their bills of lading where such proceedings will occur, which in practice usually means that it is the cargo owner who has to travel to attend the proceedings. For the present, however, the concern is only with the fact of the cost of travelling and attendance, which is the same whichever party bears it.

C. The incidence of the costs

168. There can be no dispute concerning the incidence of the costs of overlapping insurance. It is the cargo owner who must take and pay for the extra insurance (or stand the loss of his goods if he does not). He cannot shift the incidence on to the carrier and hence he has to bear this burden. It is also clear that the economic burden of delays in settlement falls entirely on the cargo owner; indeed it is to the carrier's advantage to delay settlement. Also, where carriers determine the venue of arbitration, the costs of attending fall more heavily on the cargo owner than on the carrier.

Unit limitation of liability

169. Even where carriers accept full responsibility for loss or damage to cargo and settle a claim, it is subject to the unit limitation of liability. The cargo owner receives the limited sum from the carrier; the carrier is reimbursed to a similar extent by his P and I club, less the applicable deductible. The only case in which the cargo owner does not lose is that where he has himself insured the cargo.

170. How important is this question of limitation of liability? One major shipping line informed the UNCTAD secretariat that, had there not been any per package limitation, then in 1965, for an unstated proportion of the claims paid, the amount paid out would have risen from £1.25 million to around £6 million. On the other hand, one respondent with nearly 3,000 claims for 1968 stated that the unit limitation applied to only 12 of these. These two pieces of evidence are clearly contradictory. Other evidence obtained by the secretariat was not sufficiently conclusive to enable the contradiction to be resolved. Thus, there is no way of knowing definitely whether unit limitation is a major or a minor problem.

171. Whatever the dimension of the problem, its incidence falls on the cargo owner, not on the carrier. If the problem is small, it could be removed without difficulty or hardship to carriers. If the problem is serious, then the need to deal with it is the greater as the incidence is not shared but falls entirely on the cargo owner.

D. The position of developing countries

172. It has been shown that the bill of lading fails the test of cost effectiveness. It has also been shown that the incidence of the costs of the present regime lies

heavily on the cargo owner, and this is true wherever the cargo owner is situated. It remains to be seen whether these factors have any special and undue impact on the developing countries.

173. Where there is an inequitable incidence of costs, no international transfer of income occurs in cases where both parties are in the same country. Where, however, the parties are in different countries, the inequitable incidence of costs leads to a real income transfer between the two countries. Since the developing countries are more important as cargo owners than as carriers, the present system is unfavourable to them and gives rise to a real income transfer from poor countries to rich ones. It needs to be noted that there is exactly the same real income transfer from non-shipowning developed countries.

174. Payments for exports are usually made against production of clean bills of lading after shipment, and any cargo claims are raised against the carrier at destination by importers. It is importers who are affected by the present position. With respect to the exports of developing countries, so long as the importers are in developed countries any loss falls on them. Thus, in so far as their exports are concerned, the present legal position regarding bills of lading appears to have relatively little direct economic impact on exports from developing countries.

175. The value of cargo claims arising on imports into developing countries represents the value of the goods lost or damaged, i.e. monetary loss, plus the loss of the use of the goods until replaced. The effect of the loss of the use of the goods exceeds in most cases the effect of a similar loss affecting developed countries. Inventory holdings in developing countries are usually minimal because of shortage of working capital, while many countries are distant from their sources of supply, with the consequence that the time taken to replace lost or damaged goods represents a serious practical and economic problem for them. Except in the simplest cases, compensation from carriers and insurers usually takes considerable time. The re-ordering of the goods, the cost and problems of securing additional foreign exchange before the claim for loss is settled, the transit time of the goods re-ordered, all add up to additional economic waste and considerable hardship. As an indicator of real loss, the bare monetary figure of cargo claims is inadequate, and the additional indirect adverse economic impact must not be overlooked.

E. Conclusion

176. The conclusions of this discussion can be stated in the form of four simple propositions:

(a) The bill of lading as at present constituted fails the test of cost effectiveness;

(b) The incidence of the costs involved is mainly on the cargo owners and only to a limited extent on the carriers;

(c) There is a real income transfer from countries which are more important as cargo owners than as carriers to those which are important as carriers;

(d) The developing countries as a group are among the losers in the real income transfer.

THE UNITED NATIONS CONVENTION ON THE CARRIAGE OF GOODS BY SEA 1978

Preamble

THE STATES PARTIES TO THIS CONVENTION, HAVING RECOGNIZED the desirability of determining by agreement certain rules relating to the carriage of goods by sea,

HAVE DECIDED to conclude a Convention for this purpose and have thereto agreed as follows:

PART 1. GENERAL PROVISIONS

Article 1. Definitions

In this Convention:

1. 'Carrier' means any person by whom or in whose name a contract of carriage of goods by sea has been concluded with a shipper.

2. 'Actual carrier' means any person to whom the performance of the carriage of the goods, or of part of the carriage, has been entrusted by the carrier, and includes any other person to whom such performance has been entrusted.

3. 'Shipper' means any person by whom or in whose name or on whose behalf a contract of carriage of goods by sea has been concluded with a carrier, or any person by whom or in whose name or on whose behalf the goods are actually delivered to the carrier in relation to the contract of carriage by sea.

4. 'Consignee' means the person entitled to take delivery of the goods.

5. 'Goods' includes live animals; where the goods are consolidated in a container, pallet or similar article of transport or where they are packed, 'goods' includes such article of transport or packaging if supplied by the shipper.

6. 'Contract of carriage by sea' means any contract whereby the carrier undertakes against payment of freight to carry goods by sea from one port to another; however, a contract which involves carriage by sea and also carriage by some other means is deemed to be a contract of carriage by sea for the purposes of this Convention only in so far as it relates to the carriage by sea.

7. 'Bill of lading' means a document which evidences a contract of carriage by sea and the taking over or loading of the goods by the carrier, and by which the carrier undertakes to deliver the goods against surrender of the document. A provision in the document that the goods are to be delivered to the order of a named person, or to order, or to bearer, constitutes such an undertaking.

8. 'Writing' includes, *inter alia*, telegram and telex.

Article 2. Scope of application

1. The provisions of this Convention are applicable to all contracts of carriage by sea between two different States, if:

(a) the port of loading as provided for in the contract of carriage by sea is located in a Contracting State, or

(b) the port of discharge as provided for in the contract of carriage by sea is located in a Contracting State, or

(c) one of the optional ports of discharge provided for in the contract of carriage by sea is the actual port of discharge and such port is located in a Contracting State, or

(d) the bill of lading or other document evidencing the contract of carriage by sea is issued in a Contracting State, or

(e) the bill of lading or other document evidencing the contract of carriage by sea provides that the provisions of this Convention or the legislation of any State giving effect to them are to govern the contract.

2. The provisions of this Convention are applicable without regard to the nationality of the ship, the carrier, the actual carrier, the shipper, the consignee or any other interested person.

3. The provisions of this Convention are not applicable to charterparties. However, where a bill of lading is issued pursuant to a charter-party, the provisions of the Convention apply to such a bill of lading if it governs the relation between the carrier and the holder of the bill of lading, not being the charterer.

4. If a contract provides for future carriage of goods in a series of shipments during an agreed period, the provisions of this Convention apply to each shipment. However, where a shipment is made under a charter-party, the provisions of para. 3 of this Article apply.

Article 3. Interpretation of the Convention

In the interpretation and application of the provisions of this Convention regard shall be had to its international character and to the need to promote uniformity.

PART II. LIABILITY OF THE CARRIER

Article 4. Period of responsibility

1. The responsibility of the carrier for the goods under this Convention covers the period during which the carrier is in charge of the goods at the port of loading, during the carriage and at the port of discharge.

2. For the purpose of para 1 of this Article, the carrier is deemed to be in charge of the goods

(a) from the time he has taken over the goods from:

  (i) the shipper, or a person acting on his behalf; or

  (ii) an authority or other third party to whom, pursuant to law or regulations applicable at the port of loading, the goods must be handed over for shipment;

(b) until the time he has delivered the goods:

  (i) by handing over the goods to the consignee; or

  (ii) in cases where the consignee does not receive the goods from the carrier, by placing them at the disposal of the consignee in accordance with the contract or with the law or with the usage of the particular trade, applicable at the port of discharge; or

(iii) by handing over the goods to an authority or other third party to whom, pursuant to law or regulations applicable at the port of discharge, the goods must be handed over.

3. In paras 1 and 2 of this Article, reference to the carrier or to the consignee means, in addition to the carrier or the consignee, the servants or agents, respectively of the carrier or the consignee.

Article 5. Basis of liability

1. The carrier is liable for loss resulting from loss of or damage to the goods, as well as from delay in delivery, if the occurrence which caused the loss, damage or delay took place while the goods were in his charge as defined in art 4, unless the carrier proves that he, his servants or agents took all measures that could reasonably be required to avoid the occurrence and its consequences.

2. Delay in delivery occurs when the goods have not been delivered at the port of discharge provided for in the contract of carriage by sea within the time expressly agreed upon or, in the absence of such agreement, within the time which it would be reasonable to require of a diligent carrier, having regard to the circumstances of the case.

3. The person entitled to make a claim for the loss of goods may treat the goods as lost if they have not been delivered as required by art 4 within 60 consecutive days following the expiry of the time for delivery according to para 2 of this Article.

4. (a) The carrier is liable:

(i) for loss of or damage to the goods or delay in delivery caused by fire, if the claimant proves that the fire arose from fault or neglect on the part of the carrier, his servants or agents;

(ii) for such loss, damage or delay in delivery which is proved by the claimant to have resulted from the fault or neglect of the carrier, his servants or agents, in taking all measures that could reasonably be required to put out the fire and avoid or mitigate its consequences.

(b) In case of fire on board the ship affecting the goods, if the claimant or the carrier so desires, a survey in accordance with shipping practices must be held into the cause and circumstances of the fire, and a copy of the surveyor's report shall be made available on demand to the carrier and the claimant.

5. With respect to live animals, the carrier is not liable for loss, damage or delay in delivery resulting from any special risks inherent in that kind of carriage. If the carrier proves that he has complied with any special instructions given to him by the shipper respecting the animals and that, in the circumstances of the case, the loss, damage or delay in delivery could be attributed to such risks, it is presumed that the loss, damage or delay in delivery was so caused, unless there is proof that all or a part of the loss, damage or delay in delivery resulted from fault or neglect on the part of the carrier, his servants or agents.

6. The carrier is not liable, except in general average, where loss, damage or delay in delivery resulted from measures to save life or from reasonable measures to save property at sea.

7. Where fault or neglect on the part of the carrier, his servants or agents combines with another cause to produce loss, damage or delay in delivery the carrier is liable only to the extent that the loss, damage or delay in delivery is attributable to such fault or neglect, provided that the carrier proves the amount of the loss, damage or delay in delivery not attributable thereto.

Article 6. Limits of liability

1. (a) The liability of the carrier for loss resulting from loss of or damage to goods according to the provisions of art 5 is limited to an amount equivalent to 835 units of account per package or other shipping unit or 2.5 units of account per kilogramme of gross weight of the goods lost or damaged, whichever is the higher.

(b) The liability of the carrier for delay in delivery according to the provisions of art 5 is limited to an amount equivalent to two and a half times the freight payable for the goods delayed, but not exceeding the total freight payable under the contract of carriage of goods by sea.

(c) In no case shall the aggregate liability of the carrier, under both sub-paras (a) and (b) of this paragraph, exceed the limitation which would be established under subpara (a) of this paragraph for total loss of the goods with respect to which such liability was incurred.

2. For the purpose of calculating which amount is the higher in accordance with para 1(a) of this Article the following rules apply:

(a) Where a container, pallet or similar article of transport is used to consolidate goods, the package or other shipping units enumerated in the bill of lading, if issued, or otherwise in any other document evidencing the contract of carriage by sea, as packed in such article of transport are deemed packages or shipping units. Except as aforesaid the goods in such article of transport are deemed one shipping unit.

(b) In cases where the article of transport itself has been lost or damaged, that article of transport, if not owned or otherwise supplied by the carrier, is considered one separate shipping unit.

3. Unit of account means the unit of account mentioned in art 26.

4. By agreement between the carrier and the shipper, limits of liability exceeding those provided for in para 1 may be fixed.

Article 7. Application to non-contractual claims

1. The defences and limits of liability provided for in this Convention apply in any action against the carrier in respect of loss or damage to the goods covered by the contract of carriage by sea, as well as of delay in delivery whether the action is founded in contract, in tort or otherwise.

2. If such an action is brought against a servant or agent of the carrier, such servant or agent, if he proves that he acted within the scope of his employment, is entitled to avail himself of the defences and limits of liability which the carrier is entitled to invoke under this Convention.

3. Except as provided in art 8, the aggregate of the amounts recoverable from the carrier and from any persons referred to in para 2 of this Article shall not exceed the limits of liability provided for in this Convention.

Article 8. Loss of right to limit responsibility

1. The carrier is not entitled to the benefit of the limitation of liability provided for in art 6 if it is proved that the loss, damage or delay in delivery resulted from an act or omission of the carrier done with the intent to cause such loss, damage or delay, or recklessly and with knowledge that such loss, damage or delay would probably result.

2. Notwithstanding the provisions of para 2 of art 7, a servant or agent of the carrier is not entitled to the benefit of the limitation of liability provided for in art 6 if it is proved that the loss, damage or delay in delivery resulted from an act or omission of such servant or agent, done with the intent to cause such loss, damage or delay, or recklessly and with knowledge that such loss, damage or delay would probably result.

Article 9. Deck cargo

1. The carrier is entitled to carry the goods on deck only if such carriage is in accordance with an agreement with the shipper or with the usage trade or is required by statutory rules or regulations.

2. If the carrier and the shipper have agreed that the goods shall or may be carried on deck, the carrier must insert in the bill of lading or other document evidencing the contract of carriage by sea a statement to that effect. In the absence of such a statement the carrier has the burden of proving that an agreement for carriage on deck has been entered into; however, the carrier is not entitled to invoke such an agreement against a third party, including a consignee, who has acquired the bill of lading in good faith.

3. Where the goods have been carried on deck contrary to the provisions of para 1 of this Article or where the carrier may not under para 2 of this Article invoke an agreement for carriage on deck, the carrier, notwithstanding the provisions of para 1 of art 5, is liable for loss of or damage to the goods, as well as for delay in delivery, resulting solely from the carriage on deck, and the extent of his liability is to be determined in accordance with the provisions of art 6 or art 8 of this Convention as the case may be.

4. Carriage of goods on deck contrary to express agreement for carriage under deck is deemed to be an act or omission of the carrier within the meaning of art 8.

Article 10. Liability of the carrier and actual carrier

1. Where the performance of the carriage or part thereof has been entrusted to an actual carrier, whether or not in pursuance of a liberty under the contract of carriage by sea to do so, the carrier nevertheless remains responsible for the entire carriage according to the provisions of this Convention. The carrier is responsible, in relation to the carriage performed by the actual carrier, for the acts and omissions of the actual carrier and of his servants and agents acting within the scope of their employment.

2. All the provisions of this Convention governing the responsibility of the carrier also apply to the responsibility of the actual carrier for the carriage performed by him. The provisions of paras 2 and 3 of art 7 and of para 2 of art 8 apply if an action is brought against a servant or agent of the actual carrier.

3. Any special agreement under which the carrier assumes obligations not imposed by this Convention or waives rights conferred by this Convention affects the actual carrier only if agreed to by him expressly and in writing. Whether or not the actual carrier has so agreed, the carrier nevertheless remains bound by the obligations or waivers resulting from such special agreement.

4. Where and to the extent that both the carrier and the actual carrier are liable, their liability is joint and several.

5. The aggregate of the amounts recoverable from the carrier, the actual carrier and their servants and agents shall not exceed the limits of liability provided for in this Convention.

6. Nothing in this Article shall prejudice any right of recourse as between the carrier and the actual carrier.

Article 11. Through carriage

1. Notwithstanding the provisions of para 1 of art 10, where a contract of carriage by sea provides explicitly that a specified part of the carriage covered by the said contract is to be performed by a named person other than the carrier, the contract may also provide that the carrier is not liable for loss, damage or delay in delivery caused by an occurrence which takes place while the goods are in the charge of the actual carrier during such part of the carriage. Nevertheless, any stipulation limiting or excluding such liability is without effect if no judicial proceedings can be instituted against the actual carrier in a court competent under paras 1 or 2 of art 21. The burden of proving that any loss, damage or delay in delivery has been caused by such an occurrence rests upon the carrier.

2. The actual carrier is responsible in accordance with the provisions of para 2 of art 10 for loss, damage or delay in delivery caused by an occurrence which takes place while the goods are in his charge.

PART III. LIABILITY OF THE SHIPPER

Article 12. General rule

The shipper is not liable for loss sustained by the carrier or the actual carrier, or for damage sustained by the ship, unless such loss or damage was caused by the fault or neglect of the shipper, his servants or agents. Nor is any servant or agent of the shipper liable for such loss or damage unless the loss or damage was caused by fault or neglect on his part.

Article 13. Special rules on dangerous goods

1. The shipper must mark or label in a suitable manner dangerous goods as dangerous.

2. Where the shipper hands over dangerous goods to the carrier or an actual carrier, as the case may be, the shipper must inform him of the dangerous

character of the goods and, if necessary, of the precautions to be taken. If the shipper fails to do so and such carrier or actual carrier does not otherwise have knowledge of their dangerous character:

(a) the shipper is liable to the carrier and any actual carrier for the loss resulting from the shipment of such goods, and

(b) the goods may at any time be unloaded, destroyed or rendered innocuous, as the circumstances may require, without payment of compensation.

3. The provisions of para 2 of this Article may not be invoked by any person if during the carriage he has taken the goods in his charge with knowledge of their dangerous character.

4. If, in cases where the provisions of para 2, sub-para (b), of this Article do not apply or may not be invoked, dangerous goods become an actual danger to life or property, they may be unloaded, destroyed or rendered innocuous, as the circumstances may require, without payment of compensation except where there is an obligation to contribute in general average or where the carrier is liable in accordance with the provisions of art 5.

PART IV. TRANSPORT DOCUMENTS

Article 14. Issue of bill of lading

1. When the carrier or the actual carrier takes the goods in his charge, the carrier must, on demand of the shipper, issue to the shipper a bill of lading.

2. The bill of lading may be signed by a person having authority from the carrier. A bill of lading signed by the master of the ship carrying the goods is deemed to have been signed on behalf of the carrier.

3. The signature on the bill of lading may be in handwriting, printed in facsimile, perforated, stamped, in symbols, or made by any other mechanical or electronic means, if not inconsistent with the law of the country where the bill of lading is issued.

Article 15. Contents of bill of lading

1. The bill of lading must include, *inter alia*, the following particulars:

(a) the general nature of the goods, the leading marks necessary for identification of the goods, an express statement, if applicable, as to the dangerous character of the goods, the number of packages or pieces, and the weight of the goods or their quantity otherwise expressed, all such particulars as furnished by the shipper;

(b) the apparent condition of the goods;

(c) the name and principal place of business of the carrier;

(d) the name of the shipper;

(e) the consignee if named by the shipper;

(f) the port of loading under the contract of carriage by sea and the date on which the goods were taken over by the carrier at the port of loading;

(g) the port of discharge under the contract of carriage by sea;

(h) the number of originals of the bill of lading, if more than one;

(i) the place of issuance of the bill of lading;

(j) the signature of the carrier or a person acting on his behalf;

(k) the freight to the extent payable by the consignee or other indication that freight is payable by him;

(l) the statement referred to in para 3 of art 23;

(m) the statement, if applicable, that the goods shall or may be carried on deck;

(n) the date or the period of delivery of the goods at the port of discharge if expressly agreed upon between the parties; and

(o) any increased limit or limits of liability where agreed in accordance with para 4 of art 6.

2. After the goods have been loaded on board, if the shipper so demands, the carrier must issue to the shipper a 'shipped' bill of lading which, in addition to the particulars required under para 1 of this Article, must state that the goods are on board a named ship or ships, and the date or dates of loading. If the carrier has previously issued to the shipper a bill of lading or other document of title with respect to any of such goods, on request of the carrier, the shipper must surrender such document in exchange for a 'shipped' bill of lading. The carrier may amend any previously issued document in order to meet the shipper's demand for a 'shipped' bill of lading if, as amended, such document includes all the information required to be contained in a 'shipped' bill of lading.

3. The absence in the bill of lading of one or more particulars referred to in this Article does not affect the legal character of the document as a bill of lading provided that it nevertheless meets the requirements set out in para 7 of Article 1.

Article 16. Bills of lading: reservations and evidentiary effect

1. If the bill of lading contains particulars concerning the general nature, leading marks, number of packages or pieces, weight or quantity of the goods which the carrier or other person issuing the bill of lading on his behalf knows or has reasonable grounds to suspect do not accurately represent the goods actually taken over or, where a 'shipped' bill of lading is issued, loaded, or if he had no reasonable means of checking such particulars, the carrier or such other person must insert in the bill of lading a reservation specifying these inaccuracies, grounds of suspicion or the absence of reasonable means of checking.

2. If the carrier or other person issuing the bill of lading on his behalf fails to note on the bill of lading the apparent condition of the goods, he is deemed to have noted on the bill of lading that the goods were in apparent good condition.

3. Except for particulars in respect of which and to the extent to which a reservation permitted under para 1 of this Article has been entered:

(a) the bill of lading is prima facie evidence of the taking over or, where a 'shipped' bill of lading is issued, loading, by the carrier of the goods as described in the bill of lading; and

(b) proof to the contrary by the carrier is not admissible if the bill of lading has been transferred to a third party, including a consignee, who in good faith has acted in reliance on the description of the goods therein.

4. A bill of lading which does not, as provided in para 1, sub-para (k) of art 15, set forth the freight or otherwise indicate that freight is payable by the consignee or does not set forth demurrage incurred at the port of loading payable by the consignee, is *prima facie* evidence that no freight or such demurrage is payable by him. However, proof to the contrary by the carrier is not admissible when the bill of lading has been transferred to a third party, including a consignee, who in good faith has acted in reliance on the absence in the bill of lading of any such indication.

Article 17. Guarantees by the shipper

1. The shipper is deemed to have guaranteed to the carrier the accuracy of particulars relating to the general nature of the goods, their marks, number, weight and quantity as furnished by him for insertion in the bill of lading. The shipper must indemnify the carrier against the loss resulting from inaccuracies in such particulars. The shipper remains liable even if the bill of lading has been transferred by him. The right of the carrier to such indemnity in no way limits his liability under the contract of carriage by sea to any person other than the shipper.

2. Any letter of guarantee or agreement by which the shipper undertakes to indemnify the carrier against loss resulting from the issuance of the bill of lading by the carrier, or by a person acting on his behalf, without entering a reservation relating to particulars furnished by the shipper for insertion in the bill of lading, or to the apparent condition of the goods, is void and of no effect as against any third party, including a consignee, to whom the bill of lading has been transferred.

3. Such letter of guarantee or agreement is valid as against the shipper unless the carrier or the person acting on his behalf, by omitting the reservation referred to in para 2 of this Article, intends to defraud a third party, including a consignee, who acts in reliance on the description of the goods in the bill of lading. In the latter case, if the reservation omitted relates to particulars furnished by the shipper for insertion in the bill of lading, the carrier has no right of indemnity from the shipper pursuant to para 1 of this Article.

4. In the case of intended fraud referred to in para 3 of this Article the carrier is liable, without the benefit of the limitation of liability provided for in this Convention, for the loss incurred by a third party, including a consignee, because he has acted in reliance on the description of the goods in the bill of lading.

Article 18. Documents other than bills of lading

Where a carrier issues a document other than a bill of lading to evidence the receipt of the goods to be carried, such a document is prima facie evidence of the conclusion of the contract of carriage by sea and the taking over by the carrier of the goods as therein described.

PART V. CLAIMS AND ACTIONS

Article 19. Notice of loss, damage or delay

1. Unless notice of loss or damage, specifying the general nature of such loss or damage, is given in writing by the consignee to the carrier not later than the working day after the day when the goods were handed over to the consignee, such handing over is prima facie evidence of the delivery by the carrier of the goods as described in the document of transport or, if no such document has been issued, in good condition.

2. Where the loss or damage is not apparent, the provisions of para 1 of this Article apply correspondingly if notice in writing is not given within 15 consecutive days after the day when the goods were handed over to the consignee.

3. If the state of the goods at the time they were handed over to the consignee has been the subject of a joint survey or inspection by the parties, notice in writing need not be given of loss or damage ascertained during such survey or inspection.

4. In the case of any actual or apprehended loss or damage the carrier and the consignee must give all reasonable facilities to each other for inspecting and tallying the goods.

5. No compensation shall be payable for loss resulting from delay in delivery unless a notice has been given in writing to the carrier within 60 consecutive days after the day when the goods were handed over to the consignee.

6. If the goods have been delivered by an actual carrier, any notice given under this Article to him shall have the same effect as if it had been given to the carrier, and any notice given to the carrier shall have effect as if given to such actual carrier.

7. Unless notice of loss or damage, specifying the general nature of the loss or damage, is given in writing by the carrier or actual carrier to the shipper not later than 90 consecutive days after the occurrence of such loss or damage or after the delivery of the goods in accordance with para 2 of art 4, whichever is later, the failure to give such notice is prima facie evidence that the carrier or the actual carrier has sustained no loss or damage due to the fault or neglect of the shipper, his servants or agents.

8. For the purpose of this Article, notice given to a person acting on the carrier's or the actual carrier's behalf, including the master or the officer in charge of the ship, or to a person acting on the shipper's behalf is deemed to have been given to the carrier, to the actual carrier or to the shipper, respectively.

Article 20. Limitation of actions

1. Any action relating to carriage of goods under this Convention is time barred if judicial or arbitral proceedings have not been instituted within a period of two years.

2. The limitation period commences on the day on which the carrier has delivered the goods or part thereof or, in cases where no goods have been delivered, on the last day on which the goods should have been delivered.

3. The day on which the limitation period commences is not included in the period.

4. The person against whom a claim is made may at any time during the running of the limitation period extend that period by a declaration in writing to the claimant. This period may be further extended by another declaration or declarations.

5. An action for indemnity by a person held liable may be instituted even after the expiration of the limitation period provided for in the preceding paragraphs if instituted within the time allowed by the law of the State where proceedings are instituted. However, the time allowed shall not be less than 90 days commencing from the day when the person instituting such action for indemnity has settled the claim or has been served with process in the action against himself.

Article 21. Jurisdiction

1. In judicial proceedings relating to carriage of goods under this Convention the plaintiff, at his option, may institute an action in a court which, according to the law of the State where the court is situated, is competent and within the jurisdiction of which is situated one of the following places:

(a) the principal place of business or, in the absence thereof, the habitual residence of the defendant; or

(b) the place where the contract was made provided that the defendant has there a place of business, branch or agency through which the contract was made; or

(c) the port of loading or the port of discharge; or

(d) any additional place designated for that purpose in the contract of carriage by sea.

2. (a) Notwithstanding the preceding provisions of this Article, an action may be instituted in the courts of any port or place in a Contracting State at which the carrying vessel or any other vessel of the same ownership may have been arrested in accordance with applicable rules of the law of that State and of international law. However, in such a case, at the petition of the defendant, the claimant must remove the action, at his choice, to one of the jurisdictions referred to in para 1 of this Article for the determination of the claim, but before such removal the defendant must furnish security sufficient to ensure payment of any judgment that may subsequently be awarded to the claimant in the action.

(b) All questions relating to the sufficiency or otherwise of the security shall be determined by the court of the port or place of the arrest.

3. No judicial proceedings relating to carriage of goods under this Convention may be instituted in a place not specified in paras 1 or 2 of this Article. The provisions of this paragraph do not constitute an obstacle to the jurisdiction of the Contracting States for provisional or protective measures.

4. (a) Where an action has been instituted in a court competent under paras 1 or 2 of this Article or where judgment has been delivered by such a court, no new action may be started between the same parties on the same grounds unless the judgment of the court before which the first action was instituted is not enforceable in the country in which the new proceedings are instituted;

(b) for the purpose of this Article the institution of measures with a view to obtaining enforcement of a judgment is not to be considered as the starting of a new action;

(c) for the purpose of this Article, the removal of an action to a different court within the same country, or to a court in another country, in accordance with para 2(a) of this Article, is not to be considered as the starting of a new action.

5. Notwithstanding the provisions of the preceding paragraphs, an agreement made by the parties, after a claim under the contract of carriage by sea has arisen, which designates the place where the claimant may institute an action, is effective.

Article 22. Arbitration

1. Subject to the provisions of this Article, parties may provide by agreement evidenced in writing that any dispute that may arise relating to carriage of goods under this Convention shall be referred to arbitration.

2. Where a charterparty contains a provision that disputes arising thereunder shall be referred to arbitration and a bill of lading issued pursuant to the charterparty does not contain a special annotation providing that such provision shall be binding upon the holder of the bill of lading, the carrier may not invoke such provision as against a holder having acquired the bill of lading in good faith.

3. The arbitration proceedings shall, at the option of the claimant, be instituted at one of the following places:

(a) a place in a State within whose territory is situated:

    (i) the principal place of business of the defendant or, in the absence thereof, the habitual residence of the defendant; or

    (ii) the place where the contract was made, provided that the defendant has there a place of business, branch or agency through which the contract was made; or

    (iii) the port of loading or the port of discharge; or

(b) any place designated for that purpose in the arbitration clause or agreement.

4. The arbitrator or arbitration tribunal shall apply the rules of this Convention.

5. The provisions of paras 3 and 4 of this Article are deemed to be part of every arbitration clause or agreement, and any term of such clause or agreement which is inconsistent therewith is null and void.

6. Nothing in this Article affects the validity of an agreement relating to arbitration made by the parties after the claim under the contract of carriage by sea has arisen.

PART VI. SUPPLEMENTARY PROVISIONS

Article 23. Contractual stipulations

1. Any stipulation in a contract of carriage by sea, in a bill of lading, or in any other document evidencing the contract of carriage by sea is null and void to the extent that it derogates, directly or indirectly, from the provisions of this Convention. The nullity of such a stipulation does not affect the validity of the other provisions of the contract or document of which it forms a part. A clause assigning benefit of insurance of the goods in favour of the carrier, or any similar clause, is null and void.

2. Notwithstanding the provisions of para 1 of this Article, a carrier may increase his responsibilities and obligation under this Convention.

3. Where a bill of lading or any other document evidencing the contract of carriage by sea is issued, it must contain a statement that the carriage is subject to the provisions of this Convention which nullify any stipulation derogating therefrom to the detriment of the shipper or the consignee.

4. Where the claimant in respect of the goods has incurred loss as a result of a stipulation which is null and void by virtue of the present Article, or as a result of the omission of the statement referred to in para 3 of this Article, the carrier must pay compensation to the extent required in order to give the claimant compensation in accordance with the provisions of this Convention for any loss of or damage to the goods as well as for delay in delivery. The carrier must, in addition, pay compensation for costs incurred by the claimant for the purpose of exercising his right, provided that costs incurred in the action where the foregoing provision is invoked are to be determined in accordance with the law of the State where proceedings are instituted.

Article 24. General average

1. Nothing in this Convention shall prevent the application of provisions in the contract of carriage by sea or national law regarding the adjustment of general average.

2. With the exception of art 20, the provisions of this Convention relating to the liability of the carrier for loss of or damage to the goods also determine whether the consignee may refuse contribution in general average and the liability of the carrier to indemnify the consignee in respect of any such contribution made or any salvage paid.

Article 25. Other conventions

1. This Convention does not modify the rights or duties of the carrier, the actual carrier and their servants and agents, provided for in international conventions or national law relating to the limitation of liability of owners of seagoing ships.

2. The provisions of arts 21 and 22 of this Convention do not prevent the application of the mandatory provisions of any other multi-lateral convention

already in force at the date of this Convention relating to matters dealt with in the said Articles, provided that the dispute arises exclusively between parties having their principal place of business in States members of such other convention. However, this paragraph does not affect the application of para 4 of art 22 of this Convention.

3. No liability shall arise under the provisions of this Convention for damage caused by a nuclear incident if the operator of a nuclear installation is liable for such damage: (a) under either the Paris Convention of 29 July 1960, on Third Party Liability in the Field of Nuclear Energy as amended by the Additional Protocol of 28 January 1964, or the Vienna Convention of 21 May 1963, on Civil Liability for Nuclear Damage, or (b) by virtue of national law governing the liability for such damage, provided that such law is in all respects as favourable to persons who may suffer damage as either the Paris or Vienna Conventions.

4. No liability shall arise under the provisions of this Convention for any loss of or damage to or delay in delivery of luggage for which the carrier is responsible under any international convention or national law relating to the carriage of passengers and their luggage by sea.

5. Nothing contained in this Convention prevents a Contracting State from applying any other international convention which is already in force at the date of this Convention and which applies mandatorily to contracts of carriage of goods primarily by a mode of transport other than transport by sea. This provision also applies to any subsequent revision or amendment of such international convention.

Article 26. Unit of account

1. The unit of account referred to in art 6 of this Convention is the Special Drawing Right as defined by the International Monetary Fund. The amounts mentioned in art 6 are to be converted into the national currency of a State according to the value of such currency at the date of judgment or the date agreed upon by the parties. The value of a national currency, in terms of the Special Drawing Right, of a Contracting State which is a member of the International Monetary Fund is to be calculated in accordance with the method of valuation applied by the International Monetary Fund in effect at the date in question for its operations and transactions. The value of a national currency in terms of the Special Drawing Right of a Contracting State which is not a member of the International Monetary Fund is to be calculated in a manner determined by that State.

2. Nevertheless, those States which are not members of the International Monetary Fund and whose law does not permit the application of the provisions of para 1 of this Article may, at the time of signature, or at the time of ratification, acceptance, approval or accession or at any time thereafter, declare that the limits of liability provided for in this Convention to be applied in their territories shall be fixed as: 12,500 monetary units per package or other shipping unit or 37.5 monetary units per kilogramme of gross weight of the goods.

3. The monetary unit referred to in para 2 of this Article corresponds to sixty-five and a half milligrammes of gold of millesimal fineness nine hundred. The conversion of the amounts referred to in para 2 into the national currency is to be made according to the law of the State concerned.

4. The calculation mentioned in the last sentence of para 1 and the conversion mentioned in para 3 of this Article is to be made in such a manner as to express in the national currency of the Contracting State as far as possible the same real value for the amounts in art 6 as is expressed there in units of account. Contracting States must communicate to the depositary the manner of calculation pursuant to para 1 of this Article, or the result of the conversion mentioned in para 3 of this Article, as the case may be, at the time of signature or when depositing their instruments of ratification, acceptance, approval or accession, or when availing themselves of the option provided for in para 2 of this Article and whenever there is a change in the manner of such calculation or in the result of such conversion.

Note

The Hamburg Rules were Annex 1 to the Final Act of the UN Conference on the Carriage of Goods by Sea 1978. The following was also annexed as Annex II@

'Common Understanding Adopted by the United Nations Conference on the Carriage of Goods by Sea. It is the common understanding that the liability of the carrier under this Convention is based on the principle of presumed fault or neglect. This means that, as a rule, the burden of proof rests on the carrier but, with respect to certain cases, the provisions of the Convention modify this rule.'

References

Sweeney, JC (1975) 7 *JMLC* 69, 327, 487, 615; (1977) 8 *JMLC* 167

Mankabady, S (ed), *The Hamburg Rules, 1978*, Sijthoff, Leyden-Boston

Tetley, W [1979] *LMCLQ* 1

Pixa, RR (1979) 19 *Virginia Journal of Int Law* 433

Symposium on the Unification of International Trade Law: Hamburg Rules (Basnayake, S, Hellawell, R, Selvig, E, Ramberg, J, Sweeney, J) (1979) *Am Jo of Comp Law* 353–440

O'Hare, CW (1980) 29 *ICLQ* 219

Yancey, BW (1983) 57 *Tulane L Rev* 1238

Kindred, HM (1983) 7 *Dalhousie LJ* 620

UNCTAD, 'The Economic and Commercial Implications of the Entry into Force of the Hamburg Rules', 1991

Honnold, JO (1993) 24 *JMLC* 75

Luddeke, C and Johnson, A, *The Hamburg Rules*, 2nd edn, 1995, London: Lloyd's of London Press

Force, R (1996) 70 *Tulane L Rev* 2051

Act of God

An accident due to natural causes, directly and exclusively without human intervention which could not have been prevented by taking reasonable care.

Arrest

Detention of vessel under judicial process.

ASBA

Association of Shipbrokers and Agents (USA).

Average (General or Particular)

See introduction to Chapter 17, 'General Average'.

Bare boat charter

See 'Demise charter', below.

Barratry

A wrongful act wilfully committed by master or crew without the privity of the shipowner.

Bill of lading

A receipt for goods issued under or pursuant to a contract of affreightment (as to which see below) which constitutes transferable evidence of title and may also contain evidence of the terms of the contract.

BIMCO

Baltic and International Maritime Council.

Booking note

A confirmation (which may be contractually binding) of the availability of space on a vessel, usually a liner.

Box

A container.

Breakbulk cargo

General liner cargo; cargo which is not uniform in size or weight; cargo not packed for rapid mechanical handling; cargo which is not containerised.

Bunkers

Originally used to refer to the compartments on a ship in which fuel is stored. Now used to refer to the fuel itself, and hence 'bunkering' for refuelling.

Carrier

A natural or juridical person who contracts to carry goods by sea. Not necessarily a shipowner; may be a charterer or subcharterer (see 'Disponent Owner', below) or indeed anyone who is in a position to procure the necessary tonnage to carry out the promised contractual service. Shipping or forwarding agents who enter into contracts of affreightment with shippers not as agents but as principals (eg by undertaking to carry a full container load (FCL) or a less than full container load (LCL) from door-to-door) are sometimes referred to as 'Non Vessel Owning Carriers' (NVOC's).

Chartering brokers

Shipbrokers acting on behalf of charterers.

Charterparty

A contract either to let a ship on hire (see 'Demise Charter', below) or to provide the services of the whole or part of a ship either for an agreed time (see 'Time Charter', below) or for an agreed voyage (Voyage Charter).

Clause Paramount

See 'Paramount Clause' (below).

Class

The condition of a vessel as determined by one of the world's classification societies, eg Lloyd's Register of Shipping: see further the section in Singh & Colinvaux, *Shipowners*, 1967, London: Stevens, p 163; Lux, J, *Classification Societies*, 1993, London: Lloyd's of London Press; Cane, PF [1994] *LMCLQ* 173.

Clean bill of lading

One which bears no superimposed clause or notation which declares a defective condition of goods or packing. (Contrast a 'foul' or 'claused' bill of lading.)

CMI

Comité Maritime International: a representative body of national maritime law associations, with permanent headquarters in Antwerp, whose main object is the unification of maritime laws. See further the section by Cyril Miller in Singh & Colinvaux, *Shipowners*, 1967, London: Stevens, p 154; see also Frank, L (1926) 42 *LQR* 25; Scott and Miller [1947] *ILQ* 482; Gold, Edgar, *Maritime Transport*, 1981, Lexington Books, p 126; Berlingieri, F (1983) 57 *Tulane LR* 1260.

COGSA

Carriage of Goods by Sea Act.

Combined transport

Carriage under a contract to carry by at least two different means or modes of transport (hence 'multi-modal transport'), eg road/rail/sea/inland waterway/air. Sometimes used (as in the International Chamber of Commerce Uniform Rules for a Combined Transport Document) to refer specifically to a contract in which one carrier contracts as principal for all stages of a multi-modal journey and not just as principal for one leg of the journey and as agent to arrange the remainder. 'Through Transport' is sometimes used to distinguish the last type of contract.

Contract of affreightment

Generic term which covers all contracts for the carriage of goods by sea. Also used in a more limited sense when it means a contract, which may not relate to a particular vessel, by which a carrier undertakes during a specific period to carry an agreed (usually large) quantity of goods between defined locations.

Dead freight

Damages payable to a carrier for failure to comply with a contractual duty to load a cargo of agreed quantity.

Deadweight tonnage

See 'Tonnage', below.

Demise charter

A contract for the hire of a ship. One by virtue of which exclusive possession of the vessel passes from the owner to the charterer. Under such a charter the charterer takes responsibility for the operation of the vessel and in consequence will have to man and equip the vessel, hence the expression 'bare boat charter'.

Demise clause

A clause in a contract of affreightment which states that if the vessel is not owned or demise chartered by the party issuing the bill of lading, then the contract is to take effect as a contract with the owner or demise charterer.

Demurrage

Liquidated damages payable if a vessel is delayed in loading or discharging beyond an agreed time.

Despatch

Money which a shipowner has agreed to pay to a charterer who takes less than an agreed time for loading/discharging.

Deviation

In the context of a contract for the carriage of goods by sea, geographical deviation is unjustified voluntary departure from the vessel's contractual route.

Disponent (ship)owner

A charterer who subcharters.

Dunnage

Material used to ensure ventilation of cargo and to prevent cargo from moving or from suffering damage from contact with the vessel itself or from other cargo.

FONASBA

Federation of National Associations of Shipbrokers and Agents.

Forwarding agent

Employed by cargo interests. Duties vary but may include: identifying a liner service with a vessel sailing from a convenient port on a suitable date; reserving space on the vessel; arranging for goods to be packed in a container; arranging for goods to be delivered to or collected by the sea carrier; preparation of documentation including dealing with Customs; collecting bill of lading when issued by carrier. See generally, Hill DG [1975] *LMCLQ* 27, 137, 303.

Freight

Remuneration payable to carrier under a contract of affreightment for the carriage and delivery of goods. See further Chapter 12 'Freight' and there compare Advance Freight, Lump Sum Freight, Pro Rata Freight, and Back Freight.

General ship

At one time, an expression used to refer to a vessel operated by a common carrier (as to which see Chapter 2). May also refer to vessel carrying the goods of a number of shippers on the terms of bills of lading.

Laytime

Period of time in which it is agreed that a ship will be loaded/discharged.

Lighter

A craft which is not self-propelled; a dumb barge.

Liner agent

Agent employed by a shipping line as general agent in a particular port. Duties vary but may include advertising the dates on which the line's vessels will sail; supervising loading or discharge; preparing and issuing bills of lading; collecting freight.

Liner conference

A group of ship operators in a trade who, amongst other things, may use a common tariff and who often also operate a rationalised sailing schedule.

Liner service

A regular service between fixed ports.

Marine/Ocean bill of lading

Terminology used in UCP to refer to a bill of lading issued in respect of carriage only from port-to-port and not, eg from door-to-door.

Orlop deck

Lowest deck.

Owner's brokers

Shipbrokers acting on behalf of shipowners.

P and I Clubs

Protection and Indemnity Associations formed to provide mutual insurance cover, principally for shipowners, against third party liability not covered by usual forms of hull or cargo policies.

Paramount clause

A clause used to incorporate the Hague or Hague-Visby Rules in a bill of lading. See further, Selvig, E (1961) 10 *Am J Comp L* 205.

Port agent

Shipowner's agent in a particular port. See further, Albert Morris [1982] 2 *LMCLQ* 218.

Received for shipment bill of lading

A bill of lading acknowledging receipt of the goods but not that they have been loaded on board ship.

Ship types

Bulk Carriers (dry): vessels built to carry dry bulk cargoes such as grain, ore, coal, cement, fertiliser, scrap, woodchips or logs.

Cellular Container Ships: vessels designed to carry containers stowed in permanent frames ('cells') into which containers must be lifted, hence 'lift on/lift off' and 'lo/lo'.

Combi Carrier: a vessel designed to carry both containers and roll-on, roll-off traffic ['Ro Ro'] or break-bulk cargo.

Lakes Trader: vessel equipped to standard required in the St Lawrence Seaway.

LNG/LPG Carriers: vessels intended to carry liquified natural or other gas.

OBO: a vessel built to carry either liquid or dry bulk cargo such as, eg ore/bulk/oil.

Panamax bulker: bulk carrier built to the maximum dimensions which allow it to pass through the Panama Canal.

Reefer: refrigerated vessel.

Tanker: vessel designed to carry liquids in bulk.

Tweendecker: traditional design with one intermediate deck and suitable for the carriage of bagged commodities such as rice, sugar, cement or of bulk cargoes.

ULCC: ultra large (in excess of 350,000 deadweight tons) crude (petroleum) carrier.

VLCC: very large (between 200,000 and 350,000 deadweight tons) crude carrier.

Shipped bill of lading

A bill of lading acknowledging that the goods to which it relates are on board a named ship.

Stripping

Unpacking a container.

Stuffing

Packing a container.

'Subject stem'

An expression used to qualify an agreement to load under a charter by making the obligation subject to the agreement of suppliers to make cargo available at the relevant time.

Sweat damage

Damage caused to cargo by condensation.

Tank top

Plating on the upper side of a ship's double bottom when the latter is subdivided to form tanks for the storage of, eg fuel/water/water ballast.

TEU

'Twenty-foot Equivalent Unit'. Standard unit of measurement of size of containers; eg one 40ft container = 2 TEU.

Time charter

A charterparty by which the shipowner undertakes that during a defined period his vessel and crew will be put at the disposal of the charterer for agreed purposes.

Tonnage

Deadweight tonnage: a measure of the lifting capacity of a ship. Deadweight cargo capacity is the deadweight capacity available to lift cargo: the total deadweight tonnage less the tonnage which is used for fuel, stores, crew and fresh water. The cubic capacity of a vessel may be stated either as 'grain capacity' when what is in question is the space available for free flowing bulk cargoes, or as 'bale capacity' in the case of cargo shipped in, eg, bales or boxes and not in bulk.

Displacement tonnage: the weight of a ship and everything aboard.

Gross tonnage: a measure of the size of a registered ship based on the cubic capacity of enclosed spaces on the ship.

Net tonnage: gross tonnage less non-revenue earning spaces.

Tons. Short tons: 2,000 lbs. Long tons: 2,240 lbs.

Metric tonnes: 1000 kg (2205 lbs).

Measurement tons: a unit of 40 cubic feet traditionally used as a basis on which to calculate freight charges in breakbulk liner shipping. (Compare measurement tonne = one cubic metre = 35.33 cubic feet.) An agreement to pay freight on 'tons weight or measurement' gives the carrier the right to calculate freight on the basis most favourable to him.

Tramp shipping

Vessels not trading on a fixed schedule but rather subject to the availability of cargo.

UNCTAD

United Nations Conference on Trade and Development.

UNCITRAL

United Nations Commission on International Trade Law.

WORLDSCALE

An index designed to express the current charter value of a particular oil carrier irrespective of route or position.

INDEX